# Developing a Cosmic Ideology based on Holy Scripture

OTHER BOOKS BY DANIEL H. SHUBIN:

A History of Russian Christianity in 4 volumes:
1. From the Earliest Years through Tsar Ivan IV
2. The Patriarchal Era through Tsar Peter the Great: 1586 to 1725
3. The Synodal Era and the Sectarians: 1725 to 1894
4. The Orthodox Church of the 20$^{th}$ Century: 1894 to 1990

Leo Tolstoy and the Kingdom of God within You
Daniel and Alla Andreev
Skovoroda: The World Tried to Catch Me but Could Not
Helena Roerich: Living Ethics and the Teaching for a New Epoch
Concordia Antarova: Her Theatrical Life, her Theosophic Life
Tsiolkovski: The Cosmic Scientist and his Cosmic Philosophy
Russia's Wisdom
Tsars, Pseudo-Tsars and Russia's Era of Upheavals
Monastery Prisons
The Gospel of the Prince of Peace
Porfiri Ivanov: Russia's Naturalist Healer
Alexander Dobrolubov: Russia's Mystic Pilgrim
New Rosicrucians of Early Soviet Russia
Abel: the Russian Monk and Seer
The Tolstoyan Movement (The Tolstovtzi)
Final Months of Leo Tolstoy
History of the Early Dukhabors
Rose of the World – Daniel Andreev (Tr.)
I Must Tell – Maria Rolnikaite (Tr.)
Menace Eastern Light, the Man in the Grey Suit – Jung Stilling (Tr.)
Rose Flames: The Covenant of the Holy Spirit - Volokhvyanskaya (Tr.)
The Third Testament – Anna Schmidt (Tr.)
War and Peace – Leo Tolstoy (Tr.)
Gospels in Brief – Leo Tolstoy (Tr.)

# Developing a Cosmic Ideology based on Holy Scripture

Daniel H. Shubin

RESOURCE *Publications* • Eugene, Oregon

## IN MEMORIAM:

Joseph Daniel Shubin

September 23, 1977 – June 29, 2022

Thank you God for the 44 years of his corporeal existence

DEVELOPING A COSMIC IDEOLOGY BASED ON HOLY SCRIPTURE

Copyright © 2024 Daniel H. Shubin. All rights reserved. Except for brief quotations in critical publications or reviews, no part of this book may be reproduced in any manner without prior written permission from the publisher. Write: Permissions, Wipf and Stock Publishers, 199 W. 8th Ave., Suite 3, Eugene, OR 97401.

Resource Publications
An Imprint of Wipf and Stock Publishers
199 W. 8th Ave., Suite 3
Eugene, OR 97401

www.wipfandstock.com

PAPERBACK ISBN: 979-8-3852-1927-8
HARDCOVER ISBN: 979-8-3852-1928-5
EBOOK ISBN: 979-8-3852-1929-2

Cover photograph: first page of an ancient copy of the Gospel of Mark

# Table of Contents

Prologue     7

### Part One:
### The Book on God's Lap
1. Excerpts from the Book on God's Lap     9

### Part Two:
### Attributes of Heaven and Earth
1. The Attributes of Heaven     82
2. The Attributes of Earth     119
3. The Earthly Life     165
4. The Judgment and Restoration     190

### Part Three
### Kingdoms and Covenants
1. The Covenants     210
2. The Kingdoms     267
3. The Salvation of God     289

### Part Four
### The Ministry and Message of Jesus and the Apostles
1. The Career of Jesus the Anointed     320
2. The Message of Jesus and the Apostles     363
3. The Israel of God     401
4. Christianity's Deviation from Scriptural Concepts     431
5. Christianity as a New Religion     446
6. Jesus the Essene or the Nazoraen (another perspective of his life)     488

### Part Five
### Heavenly Relationships: Some Articles on Biblical Topics
1. Covenant Lights     511
2. Saga of John the Baptizer     516
3. Luke: Evangelist and Physician     533

| | | |
|---|---|---|
| 4. | Can you let your Conscience be your Guide? | 544 |
| 5. | The Great Concession | 548 |
| 6. | Privilege to Live | 551 |
| 7. | About the Human | 555 |

## PART SIX
### THE GOSPEL OF THE PRINCE OF PEACE

| | | |
|---|---|---|
| 1. | Historical Background of Christian Pacifism | 576 |
| 2. | The Gospel of the Prince of Peace | 586 |
| 3. | The First Three Centuries | 602 |
| 4. | Development of Militarist Christendom | 621 |
| 5. | Brief History of Christian Pacifism | 637 |
| 6. | The Contemporary Christian Pacifist | 651 |

## Prologue

The purpose of this compilation of dissertations is to provide the author's interpretive theology of Sacred Scripture. I call it developing a cosmic ideology because it is all encompassing dealing with the topics of the realm of spirit and the realm of matter. The topics covered under the realm of spirit include the LORD (*Yahweh*) God and the invisible world of heaven; the realm of matter is the material created universe, including humanity, the earth, and all creation, its purpose and future. This volume will answer the question as to why there is something instead of nothing, and why there is creation, time, life and infinity and all evolving from the concept that God is love.

Along with this a sketch on the career of Jesus son of God the Anointed (*Christ*) is provided, beginning with his birth in heaven and through his incarnation and life on earth, and concluding with his present role and work in heaven. This volume includes sections dealing with the deviation of historical and contemporary Christianity from the original concepts as defined by Sacred Scripture and as codified in this treatise.

I also discuss the topics of kingdoms and covenants, defined and accomplished throughout the history of the people of Israel, both old and new, as recorded in the Holy Bible.

Parallel with the above are the sections dealing with the message of Jesus the Anointed – the Christ or Messiah – and the New Covenant and the spiritual Kingdom that he initiated. This section includes the message of John the Baptizer and the Apostles in their historical context. The beliefs and practices of the new Messianic communities established by the apostles are also explained in their historical context. A discussion on the last days of old Israel and the termination of the old covenant is especially covered. One chapter on the premise of Jesus being a Essene Nazoraen is also included.

The interpretations of the various subjects covered are the result of 50 years of Bible study and Bible teaching by the author, with a parallel study of both secular and religious history. This author considers the conclusions drawn over the years to be valuable for other students of the Bible and Christian church history.

It is especially the gospels and letters of Paul apostle that are misinterpreted more than any other section in Scripture. The gospels in temporary sermons are not read in the historical context of Judea of the

First century under Roman military occupation. Paul apostle has been rewritten by scholars, no longer understood in terms as defined by the Hebrew OT and Jewish sages, but according to Hellenic philosophy.

From my own experiences, I have seen nothing more sad or pathetic than individuals whose lives were vain or futile. Without the knowledge of God and our Savior, a substitution is made in lieu of this knowledge with something else that is conceived by our own minds. What the human mind has conceived outside of obedience to the Holy Scriptures only engenders its own injury or even destruction. This injury resulting from a lack of obedience to the will of God manifests itself in the form of discord and a lack of harmony, from the lowest social level of a individual, and every possible sin and wickedness that is conceivable in the human mind. It appears in the basic social system of the stable society, plagued with crime among its citizens. Even on a national level and international, war and the resulting devastation, often causing famines, widespread disease and plague, and massive suffering of millions of the innocent masses.

The salvation attained through Jesus the Anointed – Christ or Messiah – is prosperous and successful living in accord with the moral code and divine instruction. The author hopes that every person reading this volume will seriously consider its concepts and incorporate them into his and her life for *Yahweh* God to bless them.

(I have used the more etymologically correct *Yahweh* instead of the modern *Jehovah* or the appellation LORD in my volume as the name of supreme Deity, as well as Anointed in lieu of Christ.)

The final section is a treatise on Christian pacifism. It will provide an insight into the message preached by Jesus of Nazareth, the Son of God; that the essence of the gospel is the deliverance of humanity from its perpetual self-destructive trend of warfare. This book will also unveil how his message of peaceful coexistence and toleration was transformed into a message of militarism, and how the Apostolic community was transformed into an ecclesiastical political institution. Evidence will also be provided to the reader to testify that the only proper manner for a Christian to conduct himself in the matter of war and military service is to refuse.

Daniel H. Shubin
March 2, 2024

# PART ONE

## EXCERPTS FROM THE BOOK ON GOD'S LAP

### INTRODUCTION

Early in my life I realized that I had no control over my life, that I was guided by some unseen force for some purpose unknowable to me at the time, and which purpose I will never totally understand in this life. I gaze at the skies and contemplate on the immensity of the celestial spatial regions and attempt to grasp my significance in all of this. It did not make me feel more insignificant, but had the opposite affect on me.

My existence could not be futile because I am a complex conscious entity. I did not evolve arbitrary or aimlessly or accidentally or redundantly. I have a conscious individuality and this is my soul, my identity, and I am the only one of myself that will ever be in the entire universe. There will never be another me in all of history even over billions of years of the existence of the corporeal universe.

I had to evolved from someplace and that someplace was the supreme divine entity that we call God, and He materializes as this thing that I will call the Love-force, the engine that drives the universe forward in one direction and that direction is the materialization of the concept of love. What I call God does not reside in the realm in which I reside, but in the realm of spirit. It is somewhere else. I cannot define where this somewhere else is, except that it is also right here and we are in it, and it envelops us, and it is the realm of spirit. The permanent and real world is the realm of spirit; our world is artificial, meaning, created and corporeal.

This part will answer the question as to why there is something instead of nothing, and why there is creation, time, life and infinity and all evolving from the concept that God is love.

To converse with someone about this is next to impossible because all we know is the corporeal. What we know is with what we can identify, and it is the corporeal world of our puny existence of a few years relative to the billions of the existential universe and the infinity into the past and future of the spirit universe. So most people cannot identify with anything beyond the 5 senses: what we can feel and hear and taste and smell and touch.

The revelation I received was of the existence of this realm of spirit, and the principal overwhelming statement prevailing there is: GOD IS LOVE.

Yes, God is love. All that exists is the product of this statement, meaning, love is the display of God, the supreme deity.

Sometimes it may not seem or appear to be this way with the amount of suffering, failure, disaster, difficulty we face in life. Not to mention is the hate, prejudice, malice, hurt, harm, injury, war, genocide, insult, violence and coercion that seems to have overwhelmed societies and civilizations all through history as far back as we know. The key is that no matter how bad some people acted, the world got back on track to continue with goodness, kindness, consideration, empathy, humanitarianism and altruism and philanthropy.

If love was not the principal driving and controlling force in our world, it would have destroyed itself a long time ago, or soon after its creation. But this did not happen. Love always got the world back on track. People's individual drives toward destruction did not destroy humanity or the world. Love always got it restored and intervened to continue.

This is because there is a goal in the long run. Just as there is a purpose for the Supreme Deity, or Love-force, to originally create the corporeal universe out of its own essence, its own spirit substance, so there is a purpose in the long run, or in the consummation. God has an ultimate purpose for creating this universe as we know it, and He has an ultimate purpose for creating each and every one of us as conscious entities.

# I

There exists another realm separate from the realm in which we reside. This realm is apart and dissociated from ours, where humanity resides. This other realm is another world of another nature and another constitution than the one created humanity is affixed to. This other world or realm consists of spirit. It is not a material or corporeal world made of matter, as our world of the created material universe. It is a world composed of another substance – spirit – which is immaterial, meaning not of matter. It is not distant because it envelops the same space as the material creation, but in a different frame.

This realm of spirit is alien from the capability of a human to relate or identify. The human in their present state is not designed to reside in or interact with the realm of spirit, because the human is material. The real world is not the created universe of sight and sound and touch and human experience in which we reside. It is the realm of spirit that is the real world. It is permanent, immortal and consistent. Our material world is plastic; the divine realm is genuine and concrete. There exists an invisible gulf of chasm between the material realm and divine realm, but not a chasm that is material, which can be seen or felt, but a division of 2 incompatible and alien time-substance-energy systems. This material world is transitory and ever under development, but is a witness to the real world

We cannot readily identify with spirit because we are material, corporeal, temporary and encased in time and space. All with what we as humans can identify needs to be perceivable to our 5 senses: touch, taste, sound, sight and smell. If it is not corporeal our senses do not perceive it and so we do not recognize its existence and so as a result we do not acknowledge it. This does not mean it does not exist, as many conclude as a result. On the contrary the perfection of the existential corporeal creation testifies to the absolute need and requirement of such a spirit-realm to operate and administer the corporeal world. This is the only proper premise to conclude. It cannot be otherwise. Thought, for example, is something that is ethereal, intangible, immaterial, but it still exists, as it is generated by our brain. Memory can also be placed in the same category. We cannot touch it, but it resides somewhere inside of us. It consists of spirit.

The spirit-realm resides outside the time and space of the material universe. Time or space does not exist in the spirit-realm, as there is no need for it since the spirit-realm transcends them. Time is unknown in the spirit-realm as there is no way to measure it anyway. It's space cannot be measured either, as it is everywhere and right here. The fact of an existence of a spirit-realm is likewise next to impossible for the typical corporeal human to fathom. The spirit-realm is a parallel universe but of a different nature. The spirit-realm is sometimes called heaven.

This is hard to fathom no doubt, and what is more difficult to fathom or acknowledge is that this spirit-realm does not have a creator.

The spirit-realm just always existed because…

## II

The most difficult of all concepts to accept is that of an ultimate or supreme deity: that there exists somewhere else, somewhere out there, an Entity of some sort that is not us, that is not of this world, that is not material or corporeal; that consists of that something of which we do not consist, and which is the pinnacle or consummation of existence, meaning that there is nothing that transcends it; that there is nothing higher, greater, larger, more powerful or omnipotent, or knowledgeable or capable or wiser, or anything possible, than It is; that there is nothing that can exist longer than It, as It has existed from time infinite without end into the past and that it possesses the capacity to exist and will exist infinitely into the future without end; that It is unassailable, indestructible, unfathomable, invisible and inalterable; that it is infinitely omnipotent; and that It has no origin. This ultimate deity I will call God, as the typical appellation utilized to refer to a supreme entity transcending our world and us. Such a God created – or is the originator of – first, the entire spirit-realm and second, the entire material universe beginning with the first atom and all atoms in the corporeal universe and all time and space involved.

God is spirit, meaning, He consists of a substance that is not matter; He is not composed of atoms, but is spirit. He resides in the spirit-realm, which is invisible to us and in a region that is outside of time and space, being infinite and timeless.

God the Love-force and supreme deity reside in this spirit-realm and saturate and permeate it.

It is difficult to fathom the existence of spirit itself much less an Entity that is composed of spirit and who resides in this spirit-realm. It is alien to us; it is distant, transcendent and metaphysical; it transcends all material creation. Spirit has an effect and impacts on us, although invisible. Spirit permeates the world and environs of our existence; it is right here, all around us and envelops us, but it is a different realm than the one in which we reside; it is the real world in which the corporeal resides but alien to us as it is a different substance.

## III

The most profound single statement in the entirety of the Holy Bible was made by Apostle John in his First Letter:

## GOD IS LOVE

Of course a superficial perusal of these words would engender agreement that Yes, God is love. If a person displays love then he is displaying God in his action. The opposite likewise being true, that if a person displays harm or injury then he is not displaying God. However this statement means more than just this. I understand it in the following manner: what we consider to be that supreme being or absolute deity or omnipotence or force or creator – God – is the materialization of the concept of love. It is something that transcends a personal entity: God is a divine spirit-force that is the materialization of the concept of love.

From a more metaphysical perspective, love is the supreme deity, love-force or engine that drives the universe, both the corporeal and the spirit realms. Something needs to design and create all of it, drive all of it, control all of it, administer all of it, and provide purpose and goal to all of it as a reason in order to accomplish all of this, and so this something is love materialized as a divine force.

Just the concept of a supreme entity residing in this spirit-realm is difficult enough to accept, much less acknowledging that this entity called God maintains this omnipotence and capacity to create the entirety of the spirit and corporeal universes and operate and administrate it. The spirit-realm has existed infinitely into the past without a beginning and will exist infinitely into the future without an end, and it resides outside of time and space. God, or love materialized as a divine force, resides in and envelops and permeates this spirit-realm. God is the ultimate and omnipotent deity beginningless and endless without a creator – as also being the creator of all that resides in the spirit-realm. He always existed, and while in this capacity of omnipotent and supreme entity He expresses Himself as love because He is love. It – the Love-force – likewise has no origin; it just always was, since It is supreme deity.

In summary:

Supreme deity is a divine force that is the spirit materialization of the concept of love. It is impersonal, as it cannot conduct itself in any other manner, as it is inherent to proceed this way. This spirit-engine is super-intelligent, all-encompassing and permeating the spirit universe, and it has conceived and designed and created the corporeal universe and operates it from the realm of the spirit with a purpose for every entity and object. It drives all material existence with a beneficial goal and it cannot do otherwise. It just can't, because it is the materialization of the concept of love, and so cannot do otherwise. Sorry. It automatically drives itself forward propelled by its own spirit-force and in the direction of its infinite goal and purpose of the materialization of love. Its energy or drive is infinite and inexhaustible; it will proceed endlessly into the future without depletion of any energy. It also has the ability to create additional force or energy at its discretion in order to create more matter as needed for more creation.

Supreme deity has no origin; it always was. It existed from infinitely into the past without a beginning and will exist infinitely into the future without an end. It operates each atom and pervades to the furthermost reaches of the universe, which is expanding for the creation of more material creation, and supreme deity is not love unless it is creating objects of its love with an eternal purpose.

## IV

So we have postulated the existence of the spirit-realm: infinite into the past and future without end in either direction and encompassing and permeating a vast region beyond the conceivable existential universe, distant from us yet here right now, and it is a different realm yet simultaneous and parallel and coexistent with ours, although outside of time and space as we know it. We have also confirmed the existence of God as residing in this spirit-realm: omnipotent, creative, the driving force of both universes. It is so difficult for us to grasp that such power and force and omnipotence to create does exist; the capacity to design and create first the sprit-realm and all that resides in the spirit-realm universe, and then beginning from the atom to a completely independently-functioning galaxy and billions of such galaxies. The power of such a supreme entity is beyond comprehension and especially since He has existed infinitely into the past without a beginning. God was always. It has to be this way.

God is likewise infinitely intelligent. This attribute causes overwhelming awe in us as it is so difficult for us to grasp that such intelligence to create does exist; an intelligence to design and create, beginning from the atom to a completely functioning galaxy and billions of galaxies. The intelligence of such a supreme entity is beyond comprehension and especially since It has existed infinitely into the past without a beginning.

Between the existence and power and intelligence of such a supreme entity it is easy for a corporeal human such as ourselves with a pea-brain to deny its existence, since how can it contain the immensity and omnipotence that is required in order to do everything that It is supposed to do? How can it be infinite into the past and future without a beginning or end? How can it encompass and permeate the entirety of both the spirit and materials realms? This is unfathomable to the limited corporeal human mind and so leads to the denial of such a supreme Entity or at least avoiding discussing or acknowledging or thinking about Its existence. As a result corporeal humanity turns to items that it can understand and with which it can identify and feel with the 5 basic tangible senses of touch, smell, sight, hear and taste, and concentrates on it over the few meager years of this corporeal existence, a few drops in the ocean of years.

From another perspective, spirit is not vacuum. Spirit is substance but of another nature than the corporeal; it is ethereal. Vacuum is the absence of any substance, such as in outer space, where no atoms exist. There is no vacuum in the spirit-realm as spirit pervades and saturates the entirety of the infinite region.

## V

Two interpretations to the essential perspective of God will be discussed in the subsequent chapters. The first is the superior and the second is the inferior and which is the generally accepted concept of God.

The first is God being the materialization of the concept of love, meaning, God being a divine force, an engine where love is the fuel that propels it, an impersonal force that thinks, initiates, creates, drives, administers and operates the entirety of both the spirit and corporeal universes while implementing Its purpose of love for the infinite. It possesses a goal of a terminal consummation of the purpose of love in every thought, intent, motion and action. It is like a computer that is programmed to do something and does what it has been programmed to do period, without feelings or sensations or guilt or happiness or emotions or second thoughts; it is immutable, unchangeable and inflexible. It is programmed to accomplish love in the long run and cannot do otherwise since this is its inherent nature. It operates independent of any external influence or affects or impacts. It just does and there is nothing you can do to change it. I will refer to this perspective of God as the Love-force to distinguish it from the personal God. This is the superior concept of God.

The second interpretation is a personal God in the traditional sense: a supreme deity who possesses anthropomorphic characteristics to make Him identifiable to His human creation. Since God created the human – male and female – in His image and likeness, then God possesses the same attributes and traits of His human creation. This understanding is the inferior, where God is a kind of superman. From another perspective, the human created God in our image, but a male one, to make him palatable and comprehensible, and with whom we can identify.

At some point in time that we would consider infinitely into the past a notion or idea for a corporeal universe initiated in God, meaning, in this impersonal supreme deity identified as Love-force. Love necessitates creation of objects to which to display love. This had to be as is impossible for God as a Love-force to conduct Himself otherwise or proceed in any other manner except to have the welfare of His creation in mind and in the end in all that He does, because God – this Love-force – is the manifestation or materialization of the concept of love. So the ultimate goal of any conscious entity that the Love-force creates needs to be a benevolent one of good purpose and worth having exerted all this effort to design, create and progress its life over its span and which is infinitely into the future.

It is especially difficult to relate to the reader the state of affairs at this earliest of history, not only because of its complexity, containing so many facets of simultaneous events, but the capacity of such a divine Entity, the Love-force, to accomplish it all. Once we can accept the Love-force as having existed from time infinite into the past without beginning and will into the infinite future without end, and with all the attributes of power and intelligence mentioned above, then the next steps are relative easy as they become the product of such an Entity.

## VI

This Love-force is impersonal. It has no emotion and operates in a completely neutral manner and without any interference by anything else, although none else exists that can anyway. It does solely what it has to do, its own volition, and it will always be good in the long run because it is the result of its nature of being this Love-force. It needs not to confer with anything else or get advice or approval for its intents or actions, or anything else pertaining to any of its creation or anything derived from It, as It is the supreme in all matters.

This Love-force transcends emotions or feelings. The Love-force cannot allow emotions or feelings interfere with the execution of its will. Emotion and feeling are what this Love-force created and installed into humanity for the corporeal life, and how this effects human emotions and feelings will be further discussed. For Love-force to ask advice of a created entity such as an Angel or human would indicate that It is not self-contained, flawless, perfect and independent. Love-force in this respect is a massive spirit-engine propelled by the drive to create objects of Its love that this Love-force must display, or else it would not be love materialized.

One important aspect of the love-force is that it generates itself as the need for it to accomplish its purpose. Somehow the love-force can create or generate more of itself out of itself or out of spirit or out of Supreme Deity, since this is the purpose of Its existence and so must always have love-force to continue its work. No doubt the reader will find this difficult to fathom as to how something has the capacity to generate more of itself when the needs arises and especially since the need has existed infinitely into the past and will infinitely into the future as whatever demand is required.

So this Love-force needs to start creating, as love cannot exist unless there is an object of its love. So the Love-force is a divine drive forward that cannot remain stationary or immobile and is definitely not inert. So if this Love-force exists it has no choice except to display its love to some object. If no object exists then this Love-force has to create an object to which to display its love. It has no other choice. So at the initial beginning – meaning the beginning of when this Love-force started to initiate its purpose of displaying love – only this Love-force existed in the vacuum of the spirit-realm, and nothing else. Not finding an object of its love, due to its nature it initiated the start of creation to create objects of its love.

First is the notion or idea, then the plan to execute it, then its schedule and finally its execution. But the execution is not solely its immediate materialization or fabrication, but its predetermined destiny and progress infinitely into the future. The entirety of universal progress from the moment of inception and infinitely into the future was planned and scheduled at this time and before time was even created. This is a massive network of $10^{40}$ years[1] applying to each individual galaxy all interconnected like links on a chain and interwoven in every direction like a fabric in 3 dimensions plus the dimension of time. Nothing arbitrary or independent can occur because it will have an affect on the next link in the network in all 4 dimensions. Nothing can occur arbitrarily or independent of the Love-force plan for that event or movement or reaction. Every motion is based on the ultimate plan and intent of the Love-force, otherwise ruin will occur with the downstream effects or they will veer off to another route different from that of the Love-force.

Self-conscious objects need to exist just as long as It exists, which is infinite without an end, and toward an ultimate and consummate purpose that will prove Itself as being this embodiment of love, as the creation, especially conscious humanity, will display the love bestowed on it. Self-conscious entities are humanity as opposed to the balance of the conscious animal kingdom, while the unconscious are the balance of the plant and mineral kingdoms.

This is the reason there is something instead of nothing – the drive of love. If supreme deity existed with all the attributes noted It would be stationary or stagnant or inert if there was nothing to motivate it into action. But because the concept of love is inherently part of the supreme deity, this drives the force into creativity. Love as an essential trait of the supreme deity, and which always has been, is the drive forward for it to be creative, to create objects of love. It has to create. This is the reason there is something instead of nothing. There is no other way.

The animal, plant and mineral creations are perfect items of creation, but are incidental as they are utilized on a temporary basis in order to accomplish God's will for self-conscious creation – humanity.

## VII

The single most impressive and outstanding achievement in all history is the creation of matter out of spirit. Yes, the manufacture of matter out of spirit: two completely alien substances of two different realms. Yes, spirit becoming matter. How? Anybody's guess, but God, this Love-force, has

---

[1] This is the time span of the present material galaxy as defined by Konstantine Tsiolkovski, Russian astro-physicist, and is cyclic with repetition of creation and collapse of subsequent galaxies each lasting this long.

the capacity to create matter. This was necessary in order to generate an object of Its love in a realm that was not spirit, and creating at the same time a new realm that consisted of matter, time and space; a new corporeal universe apart from the spirit-realm where time and space and matter do not exist. The new corporeal universe would be under Its administration and subjection. The corporeal human, possessing a self-consciousness of its existence would be the pinnacle of the new material creation. This was the route this Love-force decided to take.

So God took some of His spirit-substance and created matter out of it. The new substance matter began with Helium, the one nucleus proton and one electron, although 99.94% of the area of the atom is vacant. Although the atom is mostly space and the electron is mostly energy, God assigned gravity to the proton nucleus, as likewise to the neutron nucleus component. So each atom automatically maintains a small amount of gravitational pull. The size and mass of the electron is negligible in relationship to the size and mass of the nucleus, and it consists of energy driven by the Love-force.

The electron rotates or revolves on an orbit around the nucleus at a velocity of 60 miles/second, or faster or slower, depending on whose calculations you use. Some scientists postulate the velocity of the electron between 1% and 50% of the velocity of light (186,000 miles/second). All values are still immensely fast relative to the size of the atom. The orbit is not on one plane, but equally moving in 3 dimensions spherically to provide what would appear as a spherical cover or shell for the atom.

This type of orbit and velocity of the electron covering the atom makes it appear – if we could actually see it – like a tennis ball or billiard ball. The revolution of the electron is so fast in a spherical orbit that it gives the impression of the atom having a solid shell. So matter is actually empty space with a shell of an energy-filled electron rotating or revolving around the nucleus in a spherical route.

God designed the orbit, mass and size, velocity and energy of the electron so it just continues to spin without every stopping or losing velocity or losing energy or deviating from its orbit. It is divine spirit that propels the electron, otherwise there is no reason as to why it would operate in this manner independent of all else without end in sight: perfect orbit, mass, velocity and energy level, all never ending. All the same can be applied to the subsequent atoms to the largest of them all with their increase of number of protons and neutrons and electrons. It is apparent that God added neutrons to the atom's nucleus solely to increase its mass, as otherwise the neutral object serves no other purpose. So did God create matter – the basic building block of all material creation – using the substance of His spirit.

Simultaneously with the creation of the atom and atoms of various quantity of protons, neutrons and electrons is the creation of their ability to join together by sharing electrons in common or united orbits thereby creating a molecule or a larger mass. God assigning characteristics to each molecule allows substances to be created, thereby increasing the available variety or diversity of substances or compounds by which to assemble the corporeal universe.

Simultaneous is the creation of the 3 states of matter: gas, liquid and solid, thereby expanding by three-fold the quantity of compounds. Of course intermediate states also exist, such as foam (gas-liquid or gas-solid) and gelatin (liquid-solid). This increases the diversity and quantity of compounds that now can be formed, naturally or artificially.

## VIII

Simultaneously with the atom as matter space was created, a new existential realm and dimension unknown up to that time. The atom cannot exist in the spirit-realm because it is matter and so with the creation of matter God saw the necessity of creating a new environment or the realm of space in which the atom could reside. Although most of material space is vacant and most of outer space is a vacuum of empty space, nevertheless it is still part of the material world as it allows a region where the material world can reside. Without space as we know it matter could not exist, so God created space so matter would have a place to reside. Space was originally created to be infinite, and large enough to occupy whatever the amount of matter is created. In addition to this, material space is continually being created with the expansion of the universe in order to make room for new matter being created.

Two additional items need to be noted that are just as important for the function of the material universe but are not material, yet without which the corporeal universe cannot exist. These are time and light.

Time was first and foremost created as matter or space cannot exist outside of it. The corporeal universe needs time as the atom operates in time with the spherical orbital movement of the electron around the nucleus. Time is an integral and inherent part of the new material realm and defines its progress. Time does not exist in the spirit-realm, as everything there is timeless, meaning everything is the immediate present no matter how far into the past or future you may travel. God views the $10^{40}$ years of the present time span of the present galaxy as a person looks at a map, and so applicable to all the other galaxies of the material universe. God sees everything from beginning to its consummation in the future as though viewing a chronological chart of events. All of it is right in front of Him, and who designed, implemented and administered all of it right there. So did God plan all of material eternity like drawing a chart containing each and every event and then executing it.

Light was created immediately simultaneous to time, as time is defined by the speed of light, which is 186,000 miles/second. Nothing can travel faster than the speed of light, because time will come to a stop reaching this velocity. Time is the same everywhere in the universe; it never changes as it is defined by the speed of light, and which also never changes: so one second is the time it takes light to travel 186,000 miles. Scientists have been able to speed particles near that velocity, except that the mass of the object increases the closer to the speed of light it gets, and so the mass attains this immovable size at that velocity anyway.

With light the material universe is visible to the corporeal eye. There is no need for light in the spirit-realm as all is spirit and all is visible to the Love-force; light is only necessary for the material universe for our perception. A living entity is able to perceive the material universe only if light is present to illuminate it.

A secondary facet of light creation is that its production is due to combustion. Light does not just occur out of nowhere, suddenly appearing out of a vacuum. Light is one direct product of combustion; the other product being heat.

## IX

Temperature was also created simultaneous with matter and each compound having its unique and special character at any temperature with its corresponding temperatures for its change of states: vaporization, condensation, solidification, or sublimation. Temperature also has its limits, but primarily at the lower end of the scale. Absolute zero is the temperature at which molecular creativity ceases to function. Just as it is impossible to reach the speed of light, so it is impossible to reach absolute zero. The upper end of the temperature scale would be where all matter pulverizes, only comparable to the surface of the sun, for example, or atomic fission, the destruction of the atom to produce heat and light.

Lesser attributes such as elasticity, hardness, malleability, brittleness and transparency, were also assigned to each compound at this time, at the creation of each.

Color, an attribute first of light, was created at the same time as light. In reality there is no need for light to divide into a spectrum of colors, as everything could just as well exist in black and white and all the other shades of grey in between. God did this in order to bring beauty into the corporeal universe, the result of God being a Love-force.

Combustion then becomes another simultaneous and parallel creation with light, as without fire there is no light. Fire or combustion with the ability of some compounds to ignite and burn, emitting heat and light, are both so necessary for the corporeal universe to exist and for live creation to survive and prosper. Contradistinctive to some compounds ability to ignite and burn is the creation of compounds that cannot burn and some of which are used to extinguish a flame. Phosphorous was created as a means of ignition by way of a slight amount of friction applied to it, so a fire can be started. (Interesting that phosphorous is also necessary for the brain to function.)

As mentioned above God created certain compounds that can have this chemical reaction or reduction in order to produce light and heat. Somewhere along the line God installed energy into each compound, meaning each compound has a certain amount of caloric value. Should this compound ignite and combust, or should this compound be placed in a chemical reaction to draw available heat from it, then this amount is available. This can occur though a chemical reaction or combustion. This means that God initially took some of his spirit-nature and converted it into energy and installed this energy into each compound, and to some varying degree that He felt would be proper for that compound's use. This is different than the energy of an electron, but is inherent in the molecular structure of the compound, that when ignition occurs the breakdown of the compound into simpler compounds releases heat – energy – and light.

The sun of our solar system and the suns of other solar systems are in a process of combustion, emitting light and heat. The process being either atomic fission or atomic fusion, an immense amount of heat and light is emitted, and our sun is an average size, and its capacity has been so far 14 billion years, and at least that much remaining. This allows us to conclude the amount of energy that creator God installed in the atom, that whether to destroy the atom, or cause 2 atoms to fuse together into one atom, the amount of heat and light that is generated. So did God take his spirit-essence and convert it into energy and then install this energy into the atom, and that can only be released through the processes of atomic fission or fusion. Another unfathomable miracle: taking spirit and converting it into energy and installing this energy into an atom to make it available later through combustion.

All of the above being the initial building blocks of the corporeal universe.

### X

An atom is energy and mass. The mass portion is understandable with protons and neutrons. The energy is contained in the electron and its orbit around the nucleus. But what causes the electron to continue to rotate without stopping? If it rotated around the nucleus in the same manner as a planet rotates around its sun and with only the kinetic energy applied to it to keep it in orbit continually without resistance as it floats in a vacuum, this would be understandable, but such is not the case because the electron has an electrical charge and is energy, and the energy does not exhaust. So spirit is converted into energy that is installed in the electron to keep its electrical charge and keep it rotating around the nucleus. It is spirit that serves as the energy force of the electron, pushing it along.

The electron also has a brain, otherwise it would not know what to do in chemical reactions or in the formation of molecules. The atom's brain is also spirit that is wired by God to perform in a certain manner in the presence of other atoms and in the creation of molecules and of course atomic fusion and fission. If an atom did not have a brain that was programmed for it to operate in this manner it would not know what to do. It cannot be otherwise.

About this time gravitational pull was organized out of the individual gravity of the many atoms forming molecules and larger substances. Gravity is the most powerful force in the universe. God created each atom to maintain some gravitational force. It may not be much in an individual atom, but as atoms amass the force increases. With gravity what is astounding is that this force or pull can extend billions of miles should the mass of the object be large enough. Gravity's use and effect is complex and I will later explain its several necessary functions in a logical and simple manner.

## XI

An enigma still unresolved satisfactorily by scientists is how light can transmit heat through a vacuum. Until relatively recently the intelligent population felt a substance existed in the spatial regions that could transmit heat in the same way as molecules transmit sound. Sound is transmitted through the medium – whether air or liquid or solid – with one molecule striking another until it reaches the audio system of the listener, or dissipates into the medium if the listener is too far away. This proposition made sense and so it was applied to the question of how heat was transmitted from the sun through a vacuum, and in this case the medium was aether.

Otherwise how can light, which is a wave, transmit heat through a vacuum, which is emptiness? Technically it should not. What made the question more difficult is that light-carrying heat will warm surfaces that have the ability to absorb light, while the light is reflecting off surfaces that do not have the ability to absorb light, or where the light passes through a substance that is transparent and so does not heat the object.

Of course, due to imperfections in the manufacture of items that are white, or items that do not totally reflect, or items not totally transparent, some of the item is heated. But when the light reflects from such items it will heat the next item it encounters that can absorb heat. White or light colored surfaces tend to reflect light and so absorb little heat, and so with glass and mirrors that reflect light, and so they absorb little heat. A lot of sunshine falls on Antarctica but because the snow and ice are so white, the light is reflected back into the atmosphere and so do not heat them sufficiently so they melt. With the low density of air, the molecules being so spare, the light barely heats the air and just passes through it.

The possibility of the existence of aether is still a valid question until a reasonable resolution is provided by scientists as to how light can transmit heat through a vacuum.

## XII

The subsequent metaphysical question is the origin of all this energy. From where did it come? Is there an origin to energy and all the energy in the universe and which was necessary in order to design and create the universe and for it to operate indefinitely into the future? If God is infinite into the past and future without beginning and end, this means He always possessed energy as spirit – the energy to produce the material universe and where energy can be released. The corporeal human can only stand in awe at the amount of energy God or the Love-force possesses into order to accomplish all of this, and how He can install this amount of energy into atoms and molecules and compounds. Of course all is this is beyond our ability to comprehend, or even start to comprehend, not just the amount of energy, but that it always was and always will be either as matter or as energy, and since the Love-force is an infinite size of mass in the spirit-realm, more matter can be created if so necessary out of spirit and whenever it is needed.

It only takes a few pounds of refined Uranium to produce the amount of energy that is released in an atomic reaction or bomb, as a example of the amount of energy that the Supreme deity as a spirit does possess in order to create the material universe. And as mentioned earlier, the Supreme deity has the capacity to self-create more matter and energy as needed for his existential purpose.

The travel of light through space allows the fire that produces light to illuminate the bodies it encounters. Again, the amount of energy released in these atomic reactions on suns – or stars – for the light to travel billions of years to reach Earth as sparkles in the night sky is overwhelming.

So matter, time, light, energy and space in the material realm were all instantaneously and simultaneously created along with minor attributes such as gravity, the electro-magnetic field, color, temperature, states of matter and combustion. Once this was accomplished God began assembling the material universe. This is the Big Bang as pertaining to the first galaxy that Love-force created. Without all of these created items available ahead of time the corporeal universe as we know it could not function. Of course the entire infinite sequence of events was also defined by God right to the smallest link of the interconnecting network of all events of history right to the micro-second of the entirety of billions of billions of years, or $10^{40}$ years of our galactic history, so all events could progress in an orderly manner to accomplish the volition of God or the Love-force. It cannot be otherwise.

An example is a sweater made of several strands of yarn in a 3-dimensional pattern that is interwoven with all the other yarn. All it takes is one thread to be cut and then the entire sweater unravels. So it is with history, if any one event occurs on its own volition then it disrupts the entire sequence of evens to the end of eternity, just as the sweater unraveling. So God predestined or scheduled each microsecond of time for all to flow in an orderly manner and solely to accomplish the volition and purpose of the Love-force, and nothing can be allowed to interfere. It cannot be otherwise.

## XIII

An entire galaxy needs to be designed right to the atom before its creation can begin. One reason is due to the gravitational force the central mass – the Black Hole – needs to maintain in order to keep all the planetary bodies in its respective solar or planetary system in their proper orbit at its specified distance from the central mass, and the distance of their orbits designed so they do not interfere with the gravitational pull of any other planetary body or system. So the central mass – the Black Hole – is first created as needed for its gravitational pull.

Once the central mass is created next are the individual suns in their mass, orbit and distance from the central mass. The mass of the individual suns and their rotation on their axis is designed, as mentioned above, to emit constant heat and light, as well as possess the gravitational pull to keep all their respective planetary bodies in proper orbit. The composition of the individual suns are determined at this time with material that is combustible, meaning, through atomic reaction, to provided sufficient heat and light over the course of its operation to all the planetary bodies of its respective solar system. The design at this time would also include the orbit, velocity and mass of each major planetary body. Incidental objects, such as asteroids and comets are included in the design. Once the sun is designed it is created and placed in motion around the central mass and ignited.

Next is the design of the individual planets, as many as God wants in whatever size and mass and orbit and velocity He wants, for orderly celestial operation. The planets of solid structure are not so affected by the heat emitted by the sun reaching them, while planets whose composition are some solidified or liquefied gas are further away from the sun in low temperature regions, meaning where little of the sun's heat can reach them, and so the planet can maintain its solidified gas or liquid composition without it evaporating. The velocity and orbit of each planet is based on its mass and distance from its sun. No doubt each has its eternal purpose that God has designed for it. Moons are subsequent secondary heavenly bodies whose actual purpose (apart from the Earth's moon) is still debatable, and especially for example why the planet Jupiter needs 95 moons, each of them a certain size and at a distance away from each other so their gravitational pull does not interfere with their orbits.

Small items such as asteroids that just float about do not rotate on an axis as the absorption of light is minor and the heat has little effect on them with the small surface area exposed to outer space. Asteroids however are also in an orbit around the sun relative to their mass and distance, otherwise they would collapse into the sun.

As mentioned above, God designs the speed of rotation of the planetary body on its axis to keep surface temperature close to uniform or within limits so one side does not get any hotter than necessary and so curb damage due to excessive heat from the sun, or damage due to excessive cold when not sufficiently exposed to the sun, all based on the composition of the planet and its size.

So is the galaxy created, adding one planetary system after another until the quantity that God wants for it is complete. Time to accomplish this, one sun after another, is no doubt in the $10^{40}$ years as we know it for the Milky Way galaxy, or using the value of 14 billion years applying to solely our solar system. Using the Milky Way galaxy as an example, it has a diameter of 100,000 to 200,000 light-years; it contains from 100 to 400 billion stars or suns, and with at least that many planets, and moons in addition; the galaxy moves at 400 miles/second into the spatial expanse, about 70 light-years per year. (The observable corporeal universe has a span of about 50 billion light-years and contains about 2 trillion galaxies.)

Once in orbit each sun needs to be ignited and over the entire surface. Of course, each sun is composed of a material that once ignited it will provide both sufficient light and sufficient heat for its respective planetary system as a constant rate determined earlier. The mass of each sun is designed to operate, once ignited, for the designed lifetime of the planetary system, of which ours is functioning now for over 14 billion years (the proposed age of our solar system) and with no indication of any terminal point. Some scientists claim that our sun still has the capacity to burn another 8 billions years until it reduces its capacity to sustain atomic reactions to where it can no longer provide light and heat and gravitational pull to operate our planetary system. By that time, life on Earth would have served its purpose and then God will initiate its next stage, whatever that is, as with the other planets and bodies of our planetary system. The universe can be recycled as necessary with creation and demise of suns and galaxies and the recycle or new creation of heat.

Since God, the supreme deity, is an infinite and inexhaustible and unstoppable Love-force it cannot be otherwise. As an inherent Love-force it can only proceed in one direction and that is the direction of its nature – forward, which means creativity and the administration of creation infinitely into the future. As long as God exists so will His creation.

Once the creation of the first galaxy was completed, put into motion, and operating independently with the central mass holding all floating objects in orbits, suns ignited and emitting heat and light to all their respective planetary bodies, then time had arrived for the creation of another galaxy in the universe. Existing galaxies are moving further into outer space and to a distance where the next galaxy will not be affected by the gravitational pull of the others, and each operates independently of any other. So the Love-force creates galaxies and with infinite space in which to locate them and more space can always be created. There is no limit to available space for galaxies as space is infinite and the expansion is available.

## XIV

Science readily admits that the present corporeal universe had an acknowledged beginning. Science cannot define or determine its origin, meaning its condition prior to a beginning, nor will it attempt to do so, as this means the possible admissions of creation by design or by an intermediate sovereign deity. Science will admit a beginning at about 14 billion years ago. How is this date determined? By observing the expansion of the universe through the velocity of galaxies – it speed of expansion – and then working backward to determine when the universe exited the starting gate. But this is not the age of the entire universe, but only the age of our Milky Way galaxy as scientists formulate. In reality this is an artificial number since it does not include intervals in time for divine creation.

The age of our material galaxy is actually closer to $10^{40}$ years, meaning, 1 with 40 zeros after it. This age of our Milky Way galaxy was calculated by the Russian astrophysicist Konstantin Tsiolkovski. This was the Big Bang. Yes, our galaxy begin its formation or start some $10^{40}$ years ago, and will continue into the future for at least this many more years before contracting and collapsing and starting all over again. The scenario of universal repetition is cyclic according to Tsiolkovski.

The age of the entire material or existential universe is beyond calculation into the past, since who knows when the first galaxy had its origination, and by now it would be so far away beyond our ability to notice its existence. The universe needed to expand to allow more galaxies to be created, and then each needs to be created and put into operation, so we can allow some $10^{40}$ years using Tsiolkovski's time for our galaxy to apply to each of the billions of other galaxies. So the universe is very old, beyond our capacity to understand how old, and of course, the existence of God, being infinite into the past, would place Him even further back. (In discussion I will use these figures for consistency sake, as no one really knows under such circumstances the point in time any galaxy or planetary system started.)

## XV

According to the "Big Bang" theory, some 14 billion years ago all the matter in our universe was attracted to each other due to gravitational pull of one toward another. This caused one large single mass of all the matter in the universe to be created. Due to the size and density of this mass its own gravitational pull caused it to start to shrink, and the process of shrinking due to its own gravitational pull on itself generated heat. Eventually the increase in heat due to shrinkage caused the mass to explode into many fiery balls all ignited by the explosion, each spinning and burning and so caused the creation of the corporeal universe. But this premise is not feasible due to the many other variables involved to be set in perfect formation.

This supposition cannot be applied to the creation of the entire universe as each galaxy is a creation independent of any other; yet it can be applied in a certain manner – to be further explained – to specifically individual galaxies, and to the Milky Way as I surmise it, $10^{40}$ years being the age of our Milky Way galaxy. The reason for this is first, as noted above, the universe is expanding and galaxies are moving away from one another at a steady velocity further into the spatial expanse, and each galaxy is far enough from any other galaxy at a distance so the gravitation pull of each will not have an effect on any other; second is that each galaxy has its own center around which all the solar systems of that galaxy revolve, this Black Hole or central mass.

So a long while ago the initial galaxy was created or formed, whichever galaxy it was, and galaxies since then have been created and set in motion deliberately moving away from one another to so allow apace for new galaxies to be created and at a distance so their respectful gravities do not interfere with one another.

The Milky Way galaxy "Big Bang" occurred $10^{40}$ years ago. The central orb – called a Black Hole – is a mass of immense size with sufficient gravitational pull to keep everything in the Milky Way galaxy in constant orbit around itself. This central mass cannot be seen as it is not aflame or emanating light, but it exists at some cryogenic temperature matching the heat-deficient outer space and which also keeps it compact. Due to this blackness, with no light emitted on its own and no light imposed on it from any burning mass, such as a nearby star or sun due its distance from the illuminating body, it cannot be seen as it blends it with the darkness of outer space.

## XVI

According to Albert Einstein, gravity is the most powerful force in the universe. God created each atom to maintain some gravitational force. It may not be much in an individual atom, but as atoms amass the force increases. With gravity what is astounding is that this force or pull can extend billions of miles should the mass of the object be large enough. Gravity's use and effect is complex and I hope to explain its several necessary functions in a logical and simple manner.

First is for the planetary body to have the ability to keep items secured to its surface. Without the gravitational pull of the planetary body nothing would remain secured to its surface and including the contents of the body. Everything would just float everywhere and float away or bump into each other. We would not the able to properly swallow and the entire contents of the body to its core would be loose and disperse into outer space. If God did not create gravity, even if he created a round planetary body, it would disperse into outer space as it is the pull of the center on the solid crust that keeps the body in its original spherical form and together in one mass. The very center of any planetary body has no gravity, and the gravity increases relative to the distance from the core. This is why a solid crust is necessary: to keep the liquid core from floating away. A planetary body's core is most likely liquid to keep flexibility in the center due to the pressure of the outer layers. Lava is an indication of the composition of the core as pressure from the outer layers on the central liquid core and the resulting heat cause it to expand, causing some lava to force its way to the surface.

The same use of gravity as described above would apply to the atmosphere of any planetary body, since if gravity did not exist then the atmosphere would dissipate into outer space. Using Earth as an example, $CO_2$ – carbon dioxide – is a heavy gas as well as having an ability to retain heat more than the other gases that compose most of Earth's atmosphere: $N_2$ at 78% (MW: 14), and $O_2$ at 18% (MW: 16), while $CO_2$ is about 2% (MW: 22). As a result $CO_2$ tends to lay closer to the surface of Earth, and so make it available to plants, since plants metabolize $CO_2$ and utilize the heat available in its molecule.

Just as metabolism in a cell, where mitochondria uses oxygen to provide life to the cell and utilize nutrients, so is photosynthesis in a plant, and which chemical process was created simultaneously with the plant cell. A plant reduces carbon dioxide – $CO_2$ – to us the carbon as energy, since plants are organic, and then in the process emit the oxygen – $O_2$ – into the atmosphere for organisms to use in metabolism. This is a cycle of organisms emitting $CO_2$ after utilizing the $O_2$, and then the plants utilizing the $CO_2$ and emitting $O_2$, while the carbon transfer to organisms as food from the plants and the soil. God created this exchange simultaneously with both plants and organisms for them to grow and survive. It could not be otherwise.

## XVII

The stable orbit of a planetary body around the sun or around another planetary body is a complex combination of mass-distance-velocity of each of the items that are installed in exactly a perfect arrangement for perfect operation ahead of time and simultaneously by God. This also incorporates as mentioned above the velocity of rotation of each body relative to its diameter and distance to keep temperature stable over the course of its rotation. God has set the complex combination of mass-distance-velocity of each system in perfect proportion at the moment He designed the planetary bodies of each solar system. The proportions need to be perfect; if any of the 3 changes in either direction then there is a problem. It could not be otherwise.

If we can in this scenario visualize the gravitational pull of some larger planetary body as a rubber band. The larger planetary body has a specific gravitational pull relative to its mass; it will exert a specific amount of gravitation pull and relative to the distance and velocity of the smaller planetary body. The smaller planetary body needs to have these 3 criteria of mass-distance-velocity to remain in a perfect orbit around the larger planetary body.

I will use Earth and its sun as an example, as God designed this orbit to have these perfect relative proportions. The gravitational pull of the sun is like a rubber band in perfect stretch. If the Earth's mass increases, or if its velocity increases, or if its distance increases any then it will overcome the pull of the sun and fly away. If the Earth's mass decreases, or if its velocity decreases, or if its mass decreases any, then it will be drawn toward the sun and crash into it. All of these criteria of the Earth of mass-distance-velocity relative to mass of the sun are in perfect proportions. Velocity of the smaller planetary body once installed will not change as it soars in a vacuum with no resistance, and mass is fixed and distance is fixed, all done simultaneously relative to the mass of the larger planetary body. Once installed and operating it cannot change and will not change, as no external forces are available to cause it to change, meaning that it travels in a vacuum without friction to impede it or interfere with its motion. So it was God the creator who put the smaller planetary body into motion relative to its mass and distance, and so it will remain infinitely into the future. This is creation by design as 4 proportional elements are involved for perfect operation, and this likewise pertains to any such orbital system in the corporeal universe, and there are billions of them.

The same concept can be applied to any other planetary system in the universe, pertaining to the sun or star, planets, moons and asteroids, and of course the solar system revolving around a Black Hole center of the galaxy, while the galaxies are moving further into outer space and kept at a distance where there respective gravitational pulls do not affect each other. So with the individual planetary orbits, or lunar orbits, that are far enough away from each other that they do not interfere with each other, or else they will pull toward each other and crash into each other. All of this was designed prior to the creation.

Of course all it takes is one planetary body of just about any size to change any of the criteria of mass-distance-velocity planetary motion to cause it to either fly away into outer space or for it to collapse into a larger planetary body, starting a change reaction affecting one planetary body after another as orbits change due to impact or some other deviation causing havoc in the galaxy, and then subsequent galaxies. But this will never occur because the universe was created perfect.

God put everything into perfect order and alignment all at one moment in time. Understandable with distance and mass, but velocity needs to be set at one moment due to its travel through a vacuum. Along with this is the location of all masses in orbit not to cause disruption or interference with the orbits of another or else havoc will ensue.

The anomaly is the comet that seems to just wander from one solar system to another within the galaxy and yet never crash into some planetary body. It always flies toward some sun and the whips around it and back into outer space. I feel this anomaly is God's toy playing or fooling with the universe to install something in it that makes it even harder for the typical human to find some non-divine reason for its existence, when only divine planning can resolve the dilemma of the comet.

The mass of Earth and the size and mass of the moon are also designed in proper proportions one to another to function properly. The unanswerable question is how was the rotation of the moon around Earth installed to be exactly at the same rate of the rotation of the moon around its own axis. Another dilemma science cannot answer based on evolution. The idea of a Big Bang developing planetary systems cannot occur due to 4 simultaneous criteria of the smaller planetary body's mass-distance-velocity relative to the mass of the larger planetary body around which it will orbit. Velocity is the most important to install as it must be perfect.

## XVIII

The creation with which we have so far dealt has been one of lifeless matter. There is a distinct difference between creation that is life and lifeless, meaning, animate and inanimate, and the essential defining trait in differentiating the two is that life can reproduce itself while lifeless cannot. God is a life-providing spirit due to His inherent nature of being life, and the material creation so far consisting of matter does not contain any of God's life-providing spirit or life-force; it is solely matter. Life first contains God's spirit, part of Him, meaning, life possesses some of the life-force that constitutes God, and so life-force creates. It has to create because God is a creator. Is has to be this way.

Lifeless matter cannot create or reproduce because it does not possess the life-force; all it does is exist and follow the predetermined course of existence due to external forces. It cannot move on its own, and so the Second Law of Thermodynamics. But life-matter can move on its own without external force because some of God's spirit, or life-force or divine energy, is installed into it at the moment of its creation simultaneously with the capacity for reproduction, which is a life-force in itself.

For life-matter to exist God created another category of compounds that can maintain and contain life and these are proteins. Parallel with proteins are the compounds necessary to sustain life, such as enzymes, nutrients, vitamins, calories and food in general, and the ability to convert all of this into a manner that it can sustain life and continue the process of life.

Life cannot exist unless it has the capacity to reproduce; this is why life and reproduction were created simultaneously. (This is the flaw in any theory of organic evolution: to have life and reproduction of exactly the same organism simultaneously evolve on its own is impossible, as too many variables are involved.)

When God created a plant, He also created the capacity for the plant to reproduce exactly the same plant through a seed. So the plant and seed were created simultaneously. This is asexual reproduction. When God created an animal, from the smallest bacteria or amoeba to the largest elephant and whale, He likewise simultaneously created their capacity to reproduce exactly another of the same species. It cannot be otherwise.

The next miraculous invention of reproductive capacity, and even more miraculous than asexual reproduction, is sexual reproduction: that 2 items from 2 animals of the same species of different genders need to be united to create another of the same. (This is the death stake in the heart of the theory of evolution.) For sexual reproduction to occur, 5 items needed to be created and must occur simultaneously: life, male and female gender, and the capacity for male and female to join together to reproduce. So God created all 5 items for every living entity having sexual reproduction simultaneously: male, female, life and coitus of the 2. So not to oversimplify sexual reproduction, the testicular organs of the male were created to provide sperm and the organs of the female were created to provide egg for fertilization and a region of gestation, the uterus, all simultaneously for sexual reproduction. Every variable was simultaneously and parallel created in 2 genders of male and female. It cannot be otherwise.

Marriage was created as a form of imitation of the Love-force in the procreation of humans. (This is also the only acceptable relationship between the genders as it is the only manner that reproduction can occur. Any other form of physical sexual activity – homosexual or deviant LGBT – is an abomination to the Love-force, since it is a distortion or aberration of the manner that the Love-force designed for reproduction.)

Only 2 relationships are permitted between the genders and that is either celibacy or marital monogamy. All else is classified as immorality. (Sex change cannot occur in reality, as gender is determined by X and Y chromosomes at conception. Any sex change is only superficial with organs, but the chromosomes still remain the same and cannot be changed.)

Some fruit trees and corn for example also require a type of sexual reproduction with fertilization for fruit to produce. All of this is not only purpose by design of a supreme entity, but requiring a simultaneous creation of all facets in the plants for reproduction.

Subsequent to the above miracles of sexual reproduction is the capacity to create either male or female genders at the point of conception, with each having the necessary organs to create the unique gender, and likewise in about equal quantity of each for humans. Something likewise that had to be created simultaneous and parallel with the reproductive systems of each sexual organism.

## XIX

Emotions are a category that pertain to the human and not to any other living entity. Only the human can experience sorrow and gladness, hate and love, malice and compassion, regret and joy, apathy and empathy, depression and exuberance, suffering and pleasure, hurt and appreciation, and offense and gratitude. This includes the ability to enjoy beauty, nature, excitement and thrill, goals for the future and purpose of life, contentment with possessions, good feelings about health and also concern with the welfare of others. Such do not exist in the animal or plant or mineral kingdoms, but are indigenous to humans. Emotions or pain are part of the human psyche.

The Love-force however is without emotion as it is impersonal.

Somehow the facet of the Love-force assigned to create emotion in a human being had a difficult task to accomplish as spirit does not contain or possess this trait of emotion. It had to be created as a new product, something never having existed in eternity past. The means to accomplish this was to take existing animal-level product and list all the emotions a human would need, and somehow miraculously create and install it, and then the Love-force to transfer itself into the animal entity to experience the same emotion, until it achieved its intent. The Love-force would create, for example, sadness, and install it into the entity, and then migrate into the entity to experience the emotion. Then decide if this was sufficient and operating property or functioning to achieve its purpose, or decide to modify or improve, and of course, its ability to interact with other emotions. So with every emotion that a person can possible experience or feel.

Such an effort would have been time-consuming and pain-staking over the course of the work and tedious to perfect the emotional capacity of the human, creating and installing the emotion, migrating into the entity to experience it, and then continue the process of all the emotions, both negative and positive for the human to experience.

This would especially pertain to coitus with the number of sexual energies involved and the glands involved and the various physiological parts of both male and female involved to operate simultaneously and in cohesion, and creating the pleasure of orgasm and ejaculation. This drive installed as something to promote breeding in marriage or pleasure between the genders, and lasting to old age. So the Love-force creates this drive and installs it in the entity and then enters the entity to experience the drive and all the facets of coitus and its conclusions, and then exits after it functions properly. So then the package of emotions and sexual drive and its parts is subsequently installed into each human at the moment of its conception. It has to be this way. There is no other.

## XX

God or the Love-force did not initially create corporeal life-matter to live indefinitely. God created it to be temporary in order to be cyclic, for the opportunity for more to be born or generated and live, to have an opportunity at life, then pass away and let additional have an opportunity at life. It is especially this way with corporeal humanity, as many as God destined to be created will have an opportunity at corporeal life and then pass away, and so allow another in their place to have the same opportunity, and so generation after generation.

Earth possesses only so large of a surface and can only handle so many inhabitants at the same time and only produce so much food on the land surface available, and this would pose a problem should all the people who were born live indefinitely. If the accounts of Genesis are correct with Adam living 930 years, and Methuselah 969 years and all the others having a similar longevity, Earth could have reached its point of population saturation, and then God decided to decrease the human lifespan to compensate.

God created corporeal human life for an infinitesimal fraction of what it could be, but this gives the opportunity for a start in life, and so the reason for Earth. Human life begins on Earth and then migrates after death. (This will be further discussed.) Earth is the starting point for the indefinite future and so the reason for the route of childhood, adolescence, adulthood, maturity, and then old age: a basic exposure and introduction to life.

Researchers have estimated the total quantity of humans born in historic times – meaning over the past 6,000 years or so – to be about 100 billion. This is quite a quantity if they were all to live on Earth all at the same time, and so the reason for the creation of an entire galaxy consisting of billions of planetary systems with no doubt each one have sufficient number of planets that can sustain life or at least one in each. Of course, God can create any kind of life-form He wants to be able to live and thrive in any environment that He wants as He is unlimited in His potential in creativity. In addition are many more billions of galaxies, as well as more being created as the universe expands. So plenty of planets to sustain life should be available.

Death of the body is expected for every created life-force or organism; it is not a secret or should be a surprise. It has happened and will happen to everyone; no organism is exempt. If this is the case and the Love-force creates conscious entities – humans – on a regular and consistent basis and galaxies are likewise created on a regular and consistent basis then the purpose of new planets similar to Earth are for the souls to migrate there and materialize and continue life. This is not a far-fetched idea or fantasy but very objective in the light of circumstance as described with the creation of conscious entities.

A human is too complex of an organism with self-consciousness to just live once and then be discarded, and especially because of his possession of self-consciousness. Animals are conscious due to their nature as living organisms, yet they do not possess self-consciousness: they do not know they exist, very plainly stated. They possess no past or future or grasp why they exist. They do not maintain an invisible soul or self-identity. An animal soul is its instinct; the human soul is its identity. So a human is too complex of a creation and with self-consciousness to just discard after a few miniscule years in a corporeal existence. God the Love-force created each human for infinite or eternal existence and the justification of this premise is that the human possesses self-consciousness.

An animal is born with instinct. The extent of the soul of an animal is its instinct. This is the invisible and inherent knowledge with which every animal is born. No animal is born without a complete education to guide it from birth to death. From the moment of birth, all knowledge and ability that the animal needs to survive, mate and reproduce, rear its young, build or find shelter, defend itself from the elements and enemies is inherent. Instinct is congenital. This instinct resides in every creature, from amoebae to elephant to zebra, from the smallest single cell organism to the most complex of massive land and sea creature. Not one needs a day of education, nor needs to recognize one letter of an alphabet. If means of communication exists between those of the same species, it is naturally contained in their nature.

An animal also has an ability beyond that of a human to naturally adapt to environment. With its natural clothing as insulation, it can easier withstand changes in climate, temperature and endure exposure to the elements.

## XXI

So the corporeal life is a preparation for the future life, an elementary school to adapt to life in order to advance in life once reconstituted or resurrected elsewhere after the event we call death. Life becomes a test as to how we treat people under circumstances. Since the Love-force created us some love-force remains in us, plus the premise that we will live postmortem in some or another state.

At the same time the drive for survival was also installed into the nature of a corporeal human. If this drive for survival did not exist we would be less than animals or like an amoeba: just wallowing until we die doing the least amount of anything. This drive for survival is part of the instinct nature of an animal but only to the extent of minimum survival. As mentioned earlier an animal has all the education it needs at birth with instinct to survive, but no capacity for advancement. Animals live, survive, die and that is it. They will defend themselves to the extent they can based on the capabilities provided them, such as wild animals, or venomous snakes or spiders, or will flee if threatened as with domestic animals and birds. Their reaction is however they are initially programmed to react to the situation. With humans it is the choice of 3: self-defense using violence; flight to escape the situation; or non-resistance, meaning, to do nothing and accept whatever happens. Humans have a choice that can be made at each scenario when threatened, while animals react based on instinct already programmed into them.

One facet of the corporeal human that separates us from animals is the drive for advancement. Animals are educationally stationary or stagnant; they are not taught. They can be trained, but training is not education. Only humans can be educated and because it is part of our self-consciousness; it is part of the love-force residing within us to advance. We cannot do otherwise, we have to advance, to learn, to plan ahead, to think of the future, because of the love-force that resides within us.

## XXII

Sometimes I wonder if the creation of species is the Love-force's hobby. Maybe that the creation of what seems be an innumerable quantity of species of plant and animals and in between organisms is nothing more than God's hobby to fill our Earth with creatures, to make it picturesque with color and activity and something to cover bare ground so it does not appear like a moonscape.

Of course nothing that God does is in vain, meaning, without definite purpose, as every animate and non-animate matter has its purpose somewhere in course of the existence of our planetary system, now some 14 billions of age so far with about another 8 billions years ahead until the sun is no longer able to serve its purpose. Each organism is too complex of a design and created object that God would exert so much time into the design of every cell for metabolism, its location in the ecological environment, time of its birth and time of its demise. No matter if this is an amoeba or gnat or worm or some moss or slime, God exerted the effort for its design and creation and so its purpose over the billions of years of Earth's existence, and maybe longer in some other region. It has to be this way, as nothing God does is a waste of time, or to squander time, or to kill time; everything has a reason and purpose.

Since God is a Love-force then beauty is at the forefront of all of creation, and so color was created of the three major red-blue-yellow colors and hues in between and of course black and white and the immeasurable number of shades in between. In reality, there is nothing wrong with seeing everything in black and white and shades in between, but God created color to beautify. God designed the human mind to appreciate colorful beauty and as an indication of God's love of beauty and for color as beauty in the corporeal life. So we implement this in the arts using paints and pigments and architecture.

Life-force produces protein as a byproduct and so necessary as part of nourishment for a human's diet. The decay of plants and animals at their demise as organic matter in the ground provides nutrients to the soil and which in turn enrich the soil. Where this does not occur there the soil is depleted and it no longer has the capacity to produce quality. The waste byproduct of life-force organisms also adds protein to the soil. So did God create a cycle for the continual enrichment of soil to produce proper nourishment for his life-force creatures.

Science uses the terms organic and inorganic to separate life-matter from non-life-matter (animate from inanimate) respectfully, but the intent is the same.

An incidental part of life-force creation is the vertically bilateral mirror-image design of animals. The left and right are a reflection of each other and exactly identical. This likewise was simultaneously created at the point of the creation of that particular species of animal. Very few animals do not have this design, like the sand bass fish for example, and because its present design with the eyes on one side of the head allows the sand bass to lie flat on the ocean's bottom and blend with the sand with both eyes open and watching. So did God deliberately create the sand bass fish in this manner, while 99.94% of the balance of animals are vertically, bilateral mirror images. The reason is practicality for the function of the organism.

Interesting the animals that are the prey have their eyes on the sides of the head, so they are see better peripherally, while animals that are the predator have their eyes in the front in order to attack better. So did God create animals for their purpose: some are prey and so designed, while others are predator and so designed.

## XXIII

At the same time God planned the creation of organisms He also included the design and subsequent creation of pathogens, harmful bacteria, viruses, poisons, venom, hallucinogens, addictive chemicals such as nicotine, narcotics, alcohol, and other compounds that can harm or destroy life-matter. Poisonous spiders, malaria mosquitoes, bubonic plague fleas and Lyme disease ticks, rabid dogs, venomous snakes, and scorpions were likewise planned and created alongside the balance of animals. Other diseases affecting humans, such as infections, cancer, tuberculosis, tonsillitis, appendicitis, and leukemia, and minor nuisances such as headaches, tooth decay, and myopia and hyperopia, need to also be included in the same batch. These can be divided into the categories of life-matter: pathogens; lifeless-matter: chemicals; and DNA structure. Of course all of the above were designed and created alongside or maybe subsequent to other life-matter and lifeless-matter.

But how can we justify their design and creation by a God considered to be a Love-force, whose only direction is the materialization of Love. A complex question to answer: Why did not God as a love-force create a world without the capacity of harm or causing suffering? It would have been much easier for God to create a world without all the above items and causes and effects as they took additional time and effort to create and implement in the world and in the organisms that they affect.[2] The human for example had to be created such to be able to succumb to the effects of all the above. Nicotine is just a chemical, but God created the human with the capacity of addiction to nicotine; more work on His part to have had to do, when not to do it would have been much easier. Hallucinogens and other mind-disorienting drugs likewise. From a rational perspective a world without harmful effects is easier and better and would best reflect the attitude of a Love-force ultimate deity-creator. But such was not the case so an investigation is necessary to discover why this facet of creation exists.

The same would apply to chemicals that can kill a person. The formulation of which has the ability to remove or deactivate the life-force residing in a person, whether on the nerve system or brain. God also provided humans with the capacity to design and manufacture weapons to terminate a person's life, whether another's or their own. An enigma but not without a purpose.

Non-tangible items separate from the corporeal should also be mentioned here as they are directly part of the human psyche, and these are emotions. Somehow they are generated by the human mind as a reaction to events and of course it is God who designed and created the human psyche to generate emotions. The better emotions, such as love, friendship, compassion, devotion, enjoyment, empathy and sympathy, are understandable for a God that is a love-force to create and install for purpose in a human. Then we have the harmful emotions that tend to do damage when there is no reason for it: hate, prejudice, anger, malice, cruelty, vengeance and meanness, as well as many others. Again we have destructive emotions that God as a Love-force designed and created and installed, although they seem to be antithetic to God as a Love-force. In the same vein as above, it would have been easier for God not to create

---

[2] Regarding myself, I have coronary arterial heart disease with 3 stints installed, and also bradycardia. I have a sister who died of leukemia and a brother who died of liver cirrhosis due to alcohol abuse. My mother died of a degenerative bone disease, and my father of esophageal cancer. Our son died of covid-related pneumonia and a pulmonary embolism.

such malevolent feelings than to do so and deal with the repercussions and effects. Of course there is a reason to be determined.

## XXIV

Every life-organism has a brain. Atoms and lifeless or inanimate compounds also have a brain but theirs solely operates in a mechanical manner since the life-force does not reside in them and it is part of their molecular structure and proceeds no further.

The life-organism is complex because it involves reproduction, respiration, metabolism or photosynthesis, and an infinite number of related processes to keep the organism alive for the time allotted it by the life-force. There is also a distinct difference between the plant life-force and the animal life-force and the human life-force. The difference between plant and animal can be simply explained by the plant metabolizing carbon dioxide, and the animal metabolizing oxygen. In addition a plant is consumed by the animal. A third reason is the manner of reproduction, and primarily pertaining to the higher animals of sexual reproduction. These should be sufficient criteria for the distinction between plant and animal for the purpose of this treatise and also apparent to the observer of life-organism to separate them into these categories.

As mentioned above each cell has brain, it has to, or else it can't function as something needs to control and operate the cell, like the hypochondria for example. It cannot operate without a brain telling it what to do, and wherever it is located.

A plant – as a total and independently functioning living form – also has a brain, but where it is, is anybody's guess. It likewise has to have one, otherwise what controls the entire plant's operation? What tells the seed to sprout and when? To grow upwards and the roots to grow downwards, even if planted on an incline? To create roots and enough to secure the plant; trunk and one large enough to hold up the branches; branches that are located such that the plant is balanced in every direction; and seeds, leaves, bark, and fruit; and not to mention the coloration of the plant? And the ability for the plants with its internal vessels to draw nutrients from the root and to the outermost leaves of the plant, and sometimes several hundred feet into the air, and without a pressurized circulatory system? What to do as seasons and whether patterns change? Yes, it needs a brain.

Even moss that seems to be a hybrid between plant and animal needs a brain.

Maybe the invisible life-force is a plant's brain? Maybe it is this invisible, intangible force attached or assigned to each plant to regulate its function over the course of the life span allotted to it by the life-force. This seems to be the most reasonable: an invisible, intangible life-force is assigned to each seed as a brain to regulate growth, cellular activity, cell division, photosynthesis, change $CO_2$ into C and $O_2$, and add color and odor to make the plant attractive. When the life-force brain tells the plant to die, then it disintegrates into the elements and the life-force brain returns to its original life-force to be recycled into another seed.

With simple animals – a term I will use to refer to bacteria, virus, amoeba, plankton, squid, jellyfish and snails, and similar organisms that do not have a brain as a specific organ – they function much as plants do with a life-force brain that penetrates the organism. It controls metabolism, cell division as a means of reproduction, and growth. As with plants, the life-force brain is programmed by the life-force for all that the simple animal needs to do over the course of its life and when it is to die and decompose. With the demise of the organism the life-force brain returns to the life-force that created it originally.

## XXV

The brain in the higher animals is a distinct and identifiable organ of the body located in the cranium. The brain-spirit – which I will term the intangible complex force that operates the brain – is likewise programmed for the operation of the animal from birth to death by the Life-force. The brain itself is a mass of tissue much like any other organ of the animal body, except it is designed and formed for the specific purpose of memory retention, operation of the heart and other organs, thought, speech, sight, audio, taste, emotion, synthesis of information, and growth. Essentially the brain tells the balance of the body what to do via a complex nerve system. The issue of the brain's operation is complex to be able to dictate in this manner and even more so for the human.

The brain is tissue, yet the life-force has programmed this mass of tissue to do what other organs do not do and cannot do, as those noted above. Something miraculous for a mass of corporeal tissue permeated with the life-force that has the capacity to generate intangible or incorporeal items like thought, emotion, contemplation, analysis, conclusion, memory, and synthesize information, in addition to controlling all functions of the body. That a mass of tissue can do all of this is another miracle of creation, as it dictates to every cell in the body what to do at every moment. The nervous system transmits commands from the brain to the sensory points, causing for example the heart to pulse and lungs to respire. But not all cells are connected to the nervous system, so it is this intangible and incorporeal life-force that connects everything together to communicate. The body is saturated with life-spirit that keeps the body alive, meaning, respiring. When the life-spirit leaves the body it stops respiring and thereby dies.

Love leading to marriage is another enigma that somehow has been programmed into a person's brain that does not exist in animals. Why love? Why affection or fondness? Why do something special for your spouse or offspring or family member or associate that is not really needed or required? Why does any of the above emotions exist when the only necessary function is attraction between the genders of all animals for breading for proliferation of the species and that is all. It really does not need to exist, but God the Love-force created love and affection between the human genders. As with all the emotions, He designed this and installed it into a human during development and then transferred Himself into the human to experience it and then improved and then back and forth until it was perfected. Love provides purpose in a person's life with the life-long dedication toward the welfare of another, and for a person to feel that there is another entity that has a lifelong concern for their welfare. So did God create love and affection and fondness. It had to be.

## XXVI

One very important process the brain controls is ageing. The brain is programmed to control the growth of the body from birth to death and so controls the ageing process. The Love-force defined your existence at some point in time long before the Earth was placed into operation in order to fit you in someplace and designed the Earth for your presence and residency, as one more animate organism among all the others to be born, live and die. The body does not need to age; it is only because the Love-force programmed the brain in this manner that your body does what it does. As mentioned above, Adam lived 930 years, Noah 950 years,

Methuselah 969 years; so if these numbers are correct, the brain can adjust the metabolism of the human to slow the ageing process should it be programmed to do so. The brain tells every cell in the body what to do at what time to do it, so when you feel you are getting old, it is because the brain is telling the body to do this. If you have liver spots on your skin, or wrinkles on your face, or your stomach or buttocks are sagging, or your libido is weak, or your hair and beard is turning grey, or you are losing your eyesight and need glasses, or you cannot remember as well, or your reflexes are not as fast as in the past, it is because your brain is telling the body to do this as time progresses because the life-force programmed your brain to do this, and there is nothing you can do about it. Eventually the brain will tell the body to closed its vital functions and respiration and you will die. The brain has an invisible clock programmed into it from the start during the embryonic stage to know when to age the body and how. For you to be healthy and active and beautiful at age 19, and not so much at age 59. It is the brain's clock to dictate when change in the body should occur: as the clock ticks away so does the body.

One proof is some diseases where the body does not age, and it is sometimes called Syndrome X. I have friend whose daughter is age 35, but she looks like she is 14 and still has mental growth like a child who is 12. Her brain is programmed such that it is telling the body not to age very fast. Another friend of mine had a son who aged within 2 years and then died; her condition was known as progeria. This is evidence that ageing is the result of how the life-force programmed the brain prior to birth, and the body does what the brain tells it to, and nothing you can do about it. This is also evidence that if the life-force wants you can live forever and without ageing.

Of course this is not a reason to abuse your body with alcohol, narcotics, tobacco, promiscuity leading to venereal disease, or other self-imposed harmful items, as divine *karma* will somehow, somewhere and at some time intervene to impress upon you how wrong it was to ruin your body created by God specifically so you could experience corporeal conscious life. Then you will realize how wrong it was for you to have done this to your body.

The life-force drives the human to want to live, just as the Supreme deity is eternally alive, so this facet of His character is also instilled into the human. Humans in general want to thrive in life, to succeed, to be financially stable, to enjoy all that life has to offer them and most take advantage of this, as it is the spark of the Love-force residing in a person that generates this feeling. Although suicides do occur, in general it is a rare event relative to the number of humans alive and it takes tremendous efforts for the drive to self-terminate life to defeat the drive to remain alive. This is why most suicides fail as it was not the intention of the individual to carry this to its terminal point. This is the Love-force in action to keep the person alive to the maximum extent possible (although the brain was also wired to end this person's corporeal life at this time in this manner. More on this later.)

## XXVII

The corporeal human maintains self-consciousness;[3] animals and plants do not. Animals live moment to moment; humans possess a past and a future and plan ahead appropriately. This Love-force essence residing in a human is identity or soul, meaning, soul is your identity. Animals have no identity; they are all alike. Each human is unique. Not in all the universe and not in all history will there ever be another you, because you are individually designed and personally created by none other than God Himself, the Love-force, and God assigned you an identify – your soul – and which you will possess and maintain for all time infinitely into the future and you will never lose it. Soul is in the state of a thought-form: invisible and intangible, but composed of spirit-substance. This is why the soul is immortal; it will never be erased from history, although it can be unconscious if God so wills it during intermediate stages, still it will also indelibly remain in God's memory.

If we can imagine or visualize a warehouse in the heavens with many racks and shelves, and boxes on the shelves, and in each box are souls that were personally handcrafted by God out of His Love-force and programmed for existence, and they are there stored in an unconscious state until use.

When a child is born God takes a soul out of a box, one that He determines to be appropriate for the couple, taking into consideration race, nationality, location and time in history. He determines its gender and installs it into the child at the moment of its first breath. At that moment the child becomes an independent, living, self-conscious entity. It is an animated soul, an identity; a corporeal human with a life-force residing in

---

[3] "I think, therefore I am." Rene Descartes

it. The child's brain takes over from the mother's brain that controlled it during gestation via the umbilical cord.

Upon death of the vital organs or brain function, and termination of respiration of the corporeal human, its soul is transferred back into the box in this unconscious state until the next stage arrives for its conscious existence. While in this box it can experience the bodiless intermediate stage.

During the intermediate stage, God can return the memory of all its conduct and activity to the soul or identity, including thoughts, intentions, emotions, biases and prejudices – all of the incorporeal facts of the human experience on Earth – now in a thought-form, if He wants. All of this incorporeal baggage is attached to the soul, or at least residing in God's memory and never to be forgotten as long as God exist. It remains part of the soul or part of God's memory until God eradicates or erases it, since it is a thought-form.

After the demise of the body and the exit of the soul from the body the life-force also exits and returns to its source life-force. The soul now resides outside the realm of time and space as we know it, meaning that it has no concept of time or space traversed, and so a little time or a lot, and a little space or a lot, can transpire until consciousness is again applied to the soul via the life-force to animate it. Although still in the state of a spirit-substance it is possible for the soul to maintain self-consciousness should God allow it. This is necessary to impose divine *karma* and for the person to experience the pain and suffering he imposed on others, should this be the case, or the joy and happiness imposed on others, should that be the case.

Since the soul is outside the realm of time and space once beyond demise of the body, it can at least travel through space at the velocity of light as an incorporeal entity. The specific time assigned for retribution via divine *karma* can occur whenever God decides. Perhaps I can compare the state of the soul during this conscious intermediate stage of divine *karma* as like a person secured to a bed to the point he is stationary, totally incapable of motion, paralyzed and without ability to move or even gesture, as though in a dream-state, or alive buried in a grave, as he is in this incorporeal state, and without any physical senses, except he does have the capacity to recollect and sense pain and distress. So maybe the pain will be similar to an electric shock or coronary thrombosis or kidney stone blockage of the urinary track, but somehow God will implement the means to this person to feel all the pain and suffering he imposed on another or others if he did not repent and make restitution and amends, or acting as though with impunity, negligence or irresponsibility, or deliberate malice, as mentioned above.

## XXVIII

Somehow and should this be the case this person in this isolated and lonely, static position will be able to visualize and feel the pain and anguish that others suffered due to his bad conduct and actions, and to the point that he will feel as though in the depths of a lake of fire. He will recollect and experience what he did to others and their consequences. God will disclose to him, instill in his mind, all that he wanted to forget or did not care about or wanted to escape, and there will be no way to escape or avoid as he will be confined in this immobile and motionless state with no choice but to face what he did and answer for what he did when these actions and words are brought to his attention. This will continue until the total experience concludes. It cannot be otherwise.

In contradistinction, and should this be the case, those who did right in their life will be comforted during this intermediate state with the long-term benefits of their good and appropriate conduct during their corporeal life when they will experience and visualize all of the joy and benevolence that their benefactors received. This will likewise continued until the total experience concluded. It cannot be otherwise.

Just as the culprits will reside in a state of pain and anguish as a result of their bad conduct, so at the opposite side of the pendulum will the kind enjoy calm and satisfaction as a result of their good conduct. At the same time the victims will receive their due comfort and consolation as a result of their innocent suffering, and as a result of suffering for what was right, during the course of their corporeal life. Once this intermediate stage concludes then they proceed to the next stage in their divine development.

Those suffering for their bad conduct, after their determined sentence is completed and they have learned their lesson and reformed themselves, will also join the above group and migrate to the next stage. There is no endless retribution for bad conduct as fundamental Christians believe and preach, otherwise nothing is accomplished with endless pain as it only displays a masochistic supreme deity. The purpose of feeling the anguish and pain they imposed on others is justice first and discipline second. If the sentence was without an end then this is an indication that the Love-force was not able, or did not want, to achieve its goal of reform and restoration of the culprit. To cremate disobedient souls in a hell fire to terminate their existence would testify to the failure of the Love-force in its eternal purpose of the eternal beneficial goal of the self-conscious human.

The Love-force is divine and so will be able to accomplish anything with overwhelming love. Once these 2 facets are completed they may proceed to the next stage of restoration. So is the plan and intent of the Love-force. (This doctrine is known as universal reconciliation in Christian theology.) Love must conquer all, it has no choice but to do this; no other alternative is available. So the Love-force will route the disobedient soul through this course for it to recognize its error and especially after experiencing the pain it imposed on others through its bad conduct. So eventually love will conquer and the person now reformed will have a new or at least better perspective on life and others and himself. The Love-force has its purpose and that is a purpose for each of its creation and especially conscious humanity. It cannot be otherwise.

## XXIX

Life is a test. It is a test of our inner attitude toward others and toward ourselves. Our inner attitude is displayed in our outer attitude toward others and ourselves. We either pass the test or fail the test with each action of ourselves toward another or each encounter of ours with another. If kindness is displayed toward us by another, they pass the test, and this is under any circumstance or any scenario or any place. If kindness is not displayed toward us then they fail the test, and of course regardless of circumstances. If kindness is displayed then they pass the test. Excuses for not showing kindness are not acceptable. No excuses exist. Another person not being part of our race or culture, religion or conviction, political affiliation, economic status (higher or lower), or location of residence, intelligence or educational level (higher or lower), and many other such superficial criteria, or any other bias or prejudice against another, are insufficient reason for not displaying kindness.

Either love is a natural part of a person's inner composition or it is not. If a person displays kindness not due to sincerity, but out of some ulterior motive, then the benefit of kindness is not attributed to him, but rather the hypocrisy of such a display. If kindness is displayed due to the other being a member of family, some close business or social associate, when the act of kindness would be to your advantage – and this being the reason for the display of kindness – this only displays the insincerity and hypocrisy of your inner person, as the motive is not love or the benefit of the other at the sacrifice of yourself, but ambition in the long run, so it is not attributed to your benefit, but to your detriment.

What happens to you is not important. What is important is what you do to the other person. Since evaluation of a person's intent is based on conduct or behavior, this refers to what you do to the other. If you are maltreated, abused, harmed, hurt, injured, insulted, embarrassed, and the like, you need to tolerate and endure it without reaction or repercussion. How the other person treated you is how that person's brain is wired or programmed. This is his intent and volition. Your situation is to endure and tolerate, even to your injury and death without displaying vengeance or force in return. That person has failed the test. You have passed the test and with great success.

An example to be provided is Jesus, first when he was arrested. Jesus did not stop or reprimand Judas Iscariot when he approached him and said, "Greetings," and kissed him. Jesus told him to continue what his intent was, although Jesus knew well what was going to occur to him; second when the soldiers approached Jesus to arrest him, Peter took his knife and struck a servant on the side of the head attempting to kill him, but only succeeded in cutting off an ear. Apparently the servant saw the knife coming and turned his head. The ear fell on the ground. Instead of Jesus approving of Peter's action he rebuked him and then healed the servant by reattaching the ear. Peter failed the test by using violence; the servant failed the test by using violence. Jesus passed the test by displaying kindness to the servant who came to arrest him by reattaching his ear and not resisting arrest.

Another example is when the Sanhedrin tried Jesus, he did not defend himself. He passed the test since in defending himself he would only cause more hate embedded in the members and they were going to accomplish their intent regardless of what Jesus had to say in defense. For Jesus to do anything would have been futile and make matters worse.

It was the same when he stood in the presence of both Herod and Pontius Pilate. All of them failed the test; Jesus passed the test. Why? Because as he said, "My kingdom is not of this world. If my kingdom was of this world, my servants would fight." So the division between the members of the kingdom of this world and the Kingdom of God. The members of the kingdom of this world will utilize violence and force to protect it and themselves; the members of the kingdom of God will not as theirs is incorporeal and part of the spirit-realm.

Our life is this test as to what resides inside us and how we display this. If love resides inside us then only kindness will be displayed regardless of what harm or hurt in imposed on us, and so we always pass the test, but the other person fails.

The person who displays kindness does this as a result of love that inherently resides in him; he cannot conduct himself in any other manner. This is his nature and the person can solely display his nature. If a person displays kindness with the expectation of receiving kindness or favor in the future, then such a person does not retain love within himself, since true love does not seek something in return. True love is displayed solely for the benefit of the other party. If a display of kindness is made for some selfish or ambitious purpose, this is not love but business. "True love does not seek its own." Such a person does not have true love residing in him and so will always fail the test. The person whose natural self is true love will always pass the test as his intent is the benefit of the other party and not himself.

So what is important is not you as you will eventually conclude your corporeal existence sooner or later, but that love residing in you as part of your inherent nature, that you displayed kindness at all occasions under any all circumstances and scenarios no matter how much they were to your disadvantage. This is the ultimate proof or testimony of true love residing in a person as part of their inherent nature, that kindness is displayed even if to their disadvantage, to their detriment, as for example, during persecution for belief in God, or for standing for what is right, for reprimanding hypocrisy, for conducting yourself morally, and for refusing immoral or inappropriate behavior even under pressure from others. Kindness is displayed even if it be to death, meaning no hate or spite displayed to the murderers.

## XXX

The question of suffering and death is as old as conscious human existence and any resolution to this question or dilemma is as good as any other, meaning that there are as many opinions as there are conscious entities and they are all equally valid. The lesson of the Book of Job is to accept it, endure it, tolerate it, and that is all. Don't question why. Don't waste your time trying to find the reason for it, because the question transcends the corporeal world in which we reside, so you won't fine a resolution. If you ask God the Love-force, as did Job, you will receive a rebuke in response: "It is none of your business, and who do you think you are to even ask such a question, much less expect an answer. Since when does a piece of dirt of limited lifespan have the right to require of God an answer to the question of your suffering?"[4]

God does not have to answer us because He is God; He does not answer to anyone, or else He would not be God, the ultimate supreme deity. He condescends to no one and does not have to. It is us as corporeal conscious entities who need to submit to His authority and accept whatever occurs in life as being the volition of the supreme deity or His divine will, and not complain or question. It cannot be otherwise.

(Such an approach can be fatalistic, as it can cause a person to become lethargic or irresponsible if a person felt his destiny is subject to acts of nature, and so he does the least in life, or just enough to survive. Such a fatalistic approach also causes a person to be cold and callous toward others.)

Another approach or perspective to the question is contradistinctive to the above and this focuses not so much on the person suffering, but on others as to how they react to the suffering person, or his illness, or catastrophe due to some element of nature, or what we call acts of God: weather initiated events over which we have no control.

From this other perspective it is not your personal suffering that matters, but how others treat you or deal with you as a result of your suffering. It likewise applies to you should your health and condition be good as too how you treat others who suffer, or how you are deal with the situation of the innocent suffering of others. This will be further discussed as life being a test.

I am not referring to suffering due to self-imposed tragedy, such as the effects of alcohol, narcotics, nicotine, hallucinogens, venereal disease as the result of promiscuity, botched abortions resulting from illicit sexual relations; likewise psychological issues due to dishonesty, adultery or infidelity; bad business practices, or just being mean to others; or the result of a crime or criminal act such as murder, battery, mayhem, arson and such

---

[4] Job 40:1

that lands a person in jail or some high security penitentiary or even capital punishment. These people got exactly what they deserved and so need to accept the consequences of their actions. The reason for suffering for all the above conduct and activity is due to your personal choice to conduct yourself in this manner and you deserve the retribution as justice: the consequences of your bad decision. The reason for such suffering is apparent and it is self-imposed and so expected and understandable. So no further explanation is necessary in such situations of self-imposed suffering.

## XXXI

As mentioned above life is a test of our attitude toward others. The person who maintains the Love-force as part of their nature has a tendency for more toleration of offences; no reaction or repercussion or vendetta or vengeance for battery or insult or harm or hurt imposed; no grudge carried into the future; while instead trying to use reconciliation, humility, contriteness, and not blaming or finding fault with the other; and in general, disregarding or at least ignoring the incident that was to his disadvantage.

The reasons of course are 2. First is that the person maintains the Love-force in him; he cannot conduct himself otherwise. The second is because the person believes life is a test and that life is forever. So does he conduct himself in this manner, even to death, not fearing death, since he will have passed the test and life continues post-mortem. Suffering and deprivation is temporal and will eventually end, while life is infinite.

If this person was to strike back, return the hurt or harm imposed (eye for an eye and tooth for a tooth), then he fails the test. So it is not worth it for the person who believes life is infinite to waste his time with a violent reaction, vendetta, retribution, faultfinding, or carrying a grudge. Violence will never resolve a problem first, and second, you may just get injured yourself attempting to prove yourself right by using might (thinking might is right), and this will be to your discredit or disadvantage in the long run. If you believe in a just God, in divine *karma*, then put the matter behind you and suffer the loss and God will rectify the matter one way or another and eventually, and so you will pass the test. There is no such thing as impunity because what comes around goes around, no one can walk away from harm imposed and pretend it never happened. If you do something wrong and do not exert the effort to rectify the situation, somewhere, somehow it will return to haunt you and you will feel the other person's pain and distress.

In addition, if you extend assistance to solve the other's personal problem for conducting himself to start in this hateful or spiteful manner you pass the test. By not helping the other person you may be allowing him to continue his same conduct.

The victim may indicate his displeasure if the offence did not constitute a serious enough crime to involve police authority or the judicial system, and hope this will initiate some effort on the part of the culprit to resolve the matter, make restitution, reconcile, apologize ask for forgiveness, or at least admit guilt or wrong in the matter. If none of this occurs then the victim must ignore the situation and offence and go on his way, and so he passes the test while the culprit has failed the test.

Of course the person imposing the hurt or harm or injury or death fails the test from the start by allowing his emotions to go out of control and so conducting himself in such an offensive manner. Such conduct is not just if corporeally applied, but also includes emotional or mental damage, or business damage, or manipulation to take advantage of someone, or to put someone else at risk rather than yourself, or avoiding responsibility, or blaming failure or bad conduct on another; or passing some venereal disease to a participant in a sexual act; or impregnating a girl and then abandoning her or convincing her to get an abortion; I think the reader can understand what it is I am trying to say.

## XXXII

A person's soul or identity was created by the Love-force before the creation of the world and stored until time comes along for the soul's incarnation. It also simultaneously created every person's DNA for that person to be different than any other person and unique in himself. This is so each person maintains individualism. This equally applies in every respect to the female as much as to the male (although the male pronoun is used here). He is a unique individuality with his own talents, traits, tastes, likes and dislikes, character, ability, educational capacity, and all else that makes you – you, and not any other person in the universe. These are incorporeal facets of a person's individualism. Simultaneous and coexistent are a person's physical traits: height, weight, hair, eyes, and complexion. The Love-force also created the races, for each to be distinct from others and thereby provide a superficial identity with their particular race. This consists likewise of skin pigmentation and facial and other physical features. Each race is designed and created by the Love-force and without any superiority of one over another, as this would be antithetical to the display of love: all are equal creations of the one God. Everything is in the genes that God designs and creates for each person, so no one is superior to another in any respect; it is just how God created you.

Gender is also determined by the Love-force when DNA is designed, as the number of X or Y chromosomes. So since God the creator determines the number of chromosomes and X and Y, so the male is not superior to the female, they are equally God's creation. Any male who maltreats a female considering her a lower level creature will suffer heavily as a result of divine *karma*. Likewise all females need to be treated equally, and since their attributes are determined by DNA as God designed it. So to treat one female better than another because she is more attractive or more talented than the other is wrong. It is all in the DNA as God designed all females and so all should be treated the same without preference of one over the other due to superficial attributes. This is again a test.

Females also need to treat each other the same regardless of some having better attributes than the other, as it is all in the DNA as God created it. The same applies to males.

Such attributes of both the incorporeal and corporeal become a person's individuality that form his identity as different than any other. This physical identity distinguishes each of us from every other person in the world, and allows us recognition or recognizability, as 2 faces are never identical, not even in identical twins. There is always a manner of distinguishing each person. This also allows us to feel that we are a display of God's love having created us special into what we are, and that we are not just another assembly-line product, cookie-cutter pattern of a human. That we are individual provides us self-worth knowing that the creator God spent the time and effort to create us and for our eternal plan of existence. It cannot be otherwise.

It is quite futile or shallow for a person to feel that God spent all this time and effort into creating him and materializing him in existence for just a few meager years of corporeal life on Earth. Such thinking is extremely shallow. To believe in the evolution of humanity ignores the uniqueness of the DNA of each person as a individuality. If the DNA of every human was identical then the supposition could be make of a natural evolution, but this is not the case. That each person's DNA – and we are talking about many billions over history – is different testifies to the need of a creator supreme deity. It cannot be otherwise.

God can recreate DNA after a person's demise when the opportunity arises for this person to again materialize.

## XXXIII

What we call mental or physical retardation or handicap is the result of God wiring or designing that person's brain in a manner that this is the result. A person is not retarded or handicapped because he wants to be, or because a demon is residing in him that needs to be cast out, or because his parents sinned, or because someone cast a voodoo spell on him or stuck pins in a doll representing him. It is solely the manner that creator God designed and formed the brain that defines a person's mental and physical traits. Dyslexia or some learning disability is due to how God designed the brain and it is a test.[5] He needs assistance to be a success in life. Will they whose brains cause them to be successful in life deride and discredit him? Or take advantage of him because he cannot make the right decisions? Or discard him as being a drain or parasite on society? Or will they use their God-given resources to help a dyslexic person? To better train him to be useful in society? Feeling sorry for him that God did not create him the way that God created them.

So this is a test of those whose brain is better designed by God than theirs. Will they display kindness to those whose brain was not designed by God to be as perfect to the extent theirs was? No person cannot ever claim himself or place himself superior to another in any respect, or demeanor another, or discredit another for inabilities or bad decisions, when it is not they personally, but it is God who designed their brain in this manner.

Any person of superior intelligence or capability faces the test and he will deal with divine *karma* sometime later if he refuses to assist someone mentally retarded or physically handicapped. It has to be this way.

---

[5] I can say this because of having a son who has dyslexia and he can barely read or write, or hold a job as a result. But this is how God created him. So I use him as an example.

Since DNA is a corporeal item, attitude toward God does not need to be different in any person. This is something that arises from the life-force in a person. The person considered retarded or handicapped will be returned to a normal condition in the post-mortem stage, as any corporeal deficiencies will be rectified and restored to perfection. Physical or mental deficiencies are temporal and only pertain to the present corporeal life and as a test for those who have none or are in a better physical and mental state.

In the same manner a person who has more talent should not be honored above a person who has less talent, because it is not the person himself, but the manner that God designed the DNA. The same would pertain to women who have better physical attributes or attractiveness causing them to be more appealing to the male. They cannot be considered above other women, who are not so appealing or attractive, because this is inherent in their DNA and they were so designed. All males and females need to be treated equally in terms of physical attributes, because the physical is superficial and based on DNA.

In the same vein, a male or female endowed with more talent or education must not take advantage of what they have to use it to their benefit, but use it to the benefit of those who do not possess what God has provided them.

(Gender change is only superficial, as male and female is determined by the X and Y chromosomes, and this cannot be changed. Change of gender is an aberration and insult to God who determined your gender at conception.)

## XXXIV

Conscience installed in each corporeal human is a basic element of life-force to impress on an individual that what he did to another was improper. A person can heed the effects of conscience on his psyche or not. Conscience can be seared or emaciated so it has no effect on a person. So you have for example Germans who operated gas chambers killing innumerable innocent men, women and elderly and children, and other who operated the crematoriums, then others who removed gold from teeth, as well as those who went through their clothing to salvage any valuables, all of whom went home after a hard day's work at the extermination camp and to have dinner with the family, and read the newspapers or go for some recreation that evening with friends, and think nothing of what they did that day. They have a good night's sleep and are ready the next day back at work. So people with a seared conscience. Or a jet fighter pilot who watches soldiers load 500 lb bombs to the fuselage of his jet, and then he takes off and drops the bombs from 20,000 feet on not knowing what and returning to the airfield with other pilots and not worrying about what damage or injury or death their mission may have caused. In their case they refuse to acknowledge the existence of a conscience. After their mission they drink coffee as they exchange stories with other soldiers and their superiors pat them on the back for a job well done. Such persons have no empathy, they care less about anybody else except those who would do them benefit: no remorse for what the bombs did when they hit the ground, whether a German or Russian or American or British aviator and regardless upon what country it fell. They did the job their superior ordered them to do: they followed orders. Such men are callous and insensitive to the plight or suffering of others. Of course they failed the test, and due to divine *karma* they will experience the same pain as did those upon whom their bombs fell and impacted.

Should the culprit heed his conscience or the victim's indication of his displeasure at the offence and make effort toward restitution and restoring the situation to its previous form, or at least an apology, the culprit has passed the test and the wrong has been made right to reasonable extent possible. Even an apology has effectiveness if no means remain to rectify the wrong.

For society to curb crime they must first have Love-force residing in them in order to be able to do what is necessary in education, social programs, school activities, church worship services, sports, and moral training, for crime to never occur, or should it occur, to reform the criminal. They pass the test. If nothing is done beyond incarceration, they fail the test. Society and government have the responsibility to provide a safe environment for all residents by having a crime-free society, then it passes the test. If crime continues it fails the test.

The threat of divine *karma* is installed by the life-force to motivate a person toward kindness, or rectifying a wrong, or at least admitting a wrong committed and apologizing. The consequences of divine *karma* are very appropriate and fair justice: it is the culprit experiencing the pain he imposed or caused the victim. Divine *karma* is easy to understand:

retribution. It cannot be otherwise. "Eye for an eye and tooth for a tooth, pain for pain and wound for wound," except that it is divinely arranged and executed without the need for human intervention or imposition. It will happen at some designated time and place, and to the extent necessary for the culprit to feel the pain and anguish and distress he imposed on his victim, and without him being able to do anything about it. He will be trapped between a rock and hard spot with no route of escape or means to avoid what he will and must accept. It cannot be otherwise if God is just, and He is. God has no other choice except to proceed in this manner, it is His inherent nature as a love-force.

## XXXV

Love does not allow injustice, meaning the culprit to have impunity while allowing the victim to innocently suffer. Justice to the victim will only occur if *karma* is divinely imposed. Although the victim may probably never know, it will nevertheless be arranged and executed at some time and some place after sufficient time has passed to allow the culprit ample opportunity to repent and make amends and restitution. *Karma* is imposed if this is not accomplished within the time allotted by God divine. The victim of course has proceeded further with his life putting the event behind him, but God has not forgotten. God's memory is as long as He is and which is infinite. The execution of divine *karma* could be in this lifetime or distant into the future or a million years from now, but at some time and some place this retribution or judgment will occur. It cannot be otherwise. The culprit will feel whatever impropriety he imposed on another; all the consequences of the culprit's actions – physical, verbal or emotional – he will feel it.

The offence or crime does not need to solely be some physical impact, but also any item classified as a crime: perjury, insult, felony, violation, infringement on the rights of others, immorality, or pretty much anything considered wrongdoing. Theft can be applied to some intangible item, such as credit, just as much as to a tangible item. Someone provides false testimony under oath; dishonest business transaction; theft; selling narcotics; injury inflicted in war or violence; and with so many other injurious scenarios, the culprit will feel the pain and anguish his victims felt. It may even feel like burning in a lake of fire forever and ever.

A person selling narcotics will feel the pain suffered by the one who bought it and had his life ruined; the sufferings of the pregnant girl abandoned and what occurs to the child or her abortion somehow will be appropriately imposed; the drunk driver causing death and damage will likewise feel what he caused others; the effects of napalm on innocent villagers will be passed to the pilot and other airmen and the manufacturers of the product who made good money and now lead good lives at the expense of the sufferings of others. I feel the following culprits will be in the depths of the lake of fire: those in the business of designing, manufacturing and selling guns, bombs, missiles, military aircraft and tanks, atomic weapons, cluster bombs, napalm, grenades, mustard gas and other toxic gases, Sarin and Zyklon-B and other lethal gasses, narcotics and hallucinogens, cigarettes, liquor, and those designing and building and operating the gas chambers and crematoriums.

In addition are those involved in pornography. Whether an actor or actress, meaning a participant in the film, or in the filming, production, distribution, and sales of pornography, sexually deviant entertainment, or exploitation of women in any manner for sexual gratification. All of them will likewise face the results of their actions that cause the decrease of morality in society and the pain suffered by those having watched such entertainment.

It is not as if all these people did not know exactly what they were doing, or did not know exactly for what their products were to be used, or what their effects would be. Yes, they did know and they did proceed willingly, and then got a paycheck for doing this as money was to be made with the manufacture and sales of these products to kill and injure people. The more comfortable these people lived as a result of their products the worse their suffering at the depths of the lake of fire, or as it will seem to them as they experience the effects of their business and manufacture.

A few more to add to the list are those who participate in violent protest and confrontation, riots, rebellions, mutiny, revolutions, and of course war in general. None of this is necessary. There was no need for a Civil War in the USA, 1861-1864. Let the Confederacy create its own country and the 2 learn to live in peaceful coexistence. Instead 635,000 men died, and all Americans. If we cannot learn to live in peaceful coexistence then destruction and mayhem will be the product. Easy to understand: war is the judgment of God upon nations that cannot learn to live in peaceful coexistence. The killing continues until people get tired of killing and then it stops, and now time to have to rebuilt the nations and societies and bury all the dead, and those surviving of each nation considered those who died as heroes of their respective nation. The hero is the soldier who killed more of the enemy, and this applies to each side.

The lesson never seems to be learned as the subsequent generation will forget the previous, not to mention how the media tends to romanticize war: how great these men were who died in battle, except that their superiors on both sides of the front did not send them into battle to die, but to kill as many of the enemy they possible could without themselves dying in the process. If they die in the process they are hailed as heroes but they are still dead and war will continue. So sad. Yet the attitude of their superiors and leaders is that soldiers are expendable; there are more available to become cannon fodder. These superiors will likewise incur divine *karma* as they relive the horror of war that those whom they sent into battle did and those who suffered at their hands, especially the many innocent men and women and children and elderly as casualties and collateral damage of war.

These are just a few examples, but the list is endless. I think the reader knows by now how divine *karma* or just retribution operates, and needs to operate for justice to be implemented by a just God. Now a just God is not a vengeful supreme entity, but with purpose in mind (as mentioned above), and so the sentence will last until He determines that the purpose is accomplished; no more, no less. God will place this sentence on his calendar. Since life is infinite there is plenty of time to execute this, and since the universe is essentially infinite, not to mention the intermediate post-mortem stage, there are plenty of places to do this. One the sentence on the person ends the culprit will have learned his lesson and be reformed and will no longer conduct himself in a bad manner. The divine *karma* will have served its purpose.

## XXXVI

Yes, God the Love-force did create toxins in chemicals and venoms in animals simultaneously with the species. Of course how the animal can manufacture a chemical that will not enter its own blood stream is another miracle of creation. So an organ with impervious lining manufactures the venom until it is injected into the victim. The mosquito or black widow do not sting you out of spite or malice or for some premeditated reason. It is part of their instinct as a defense mechanism for survival. Because the insect has no conscience or feelings, it cannot feel guilty for what it did, but continues on its way not thinking about it at all. Or a rattlesnake or some other venomous snake bites you due to the reaction of self-defense if threatened and thinks nothing of it and should you die.

Two facets of justification of the Love-force for creating such insects and animals with the poison to kill and hurt exist or the creation of harmful bacteria and virus. One is the reaction of other people. What will they do if they notice you are envenomed? Help or abandon? What will they do if you are diagnosed with some illness or disease and especially some incurable or crippling disease? Will they help you or not? If they help they pass the test; if they don't they fail. So kindness is displayed in the implementation of medical science to find cures for diseases such as polio, smallpox, measles, tetanus, cancer, tuberculosis, and malaria and others, as well as the construction and operation of hospitals and medical facilities. These people pass the test as it displays kindness residing in them, a concern for the welfare of others.

The other facet deals with the person who is the victim of some poisonous snake or insect or disease: The question arises as to why he is innocently suffering from this sting or bacteria. He did nothing to the insect, but the insect thinks he did and so reacted by pumping some venom into him, and you suffer and perhaps even die. "Why would a God who is the Love-force allow this?" is the question that ultimately arises. "What did I do to deserve this? Why did God right from the start not create venom or toxins?" Such questions penetrate the mind of the victim as he suffers. Cancers that naturally arise become a moral dilemma to the person as he decays, and after this he engenders a spite toward the creator God, that he is unjustly suffering, and so the dilemma with our friend Job of Uz.

The person who has a sense of immortality, knowing his life is infinite, will deal patiently, knowing there is a divine purpose involved somehow, and to build his ability to endure worst suffering or pain in the future. He will endure the deprivation of health patiently and so pass the test. The person who develops spite and anger toward God fails the test, and this will spill over in his treatment of other people who are not suffering as he is. So disease is a test of both the person infected and the one healthy.

Yes, God has a purpose for creating toxins and venoms and installing them into the defense mechanisms of some animals. If a person should die as a result, then during the intermediate stage God will disclose to him the reason for all this occurring, and that God never abandoned him in any case. This likewise pertains to diseases and harmful bacteria.

## XXXVII

Every person has an impulse of survival that resides in their body of flesh. This is that special spirit of animation enlivening the human that drives it to live, as mentioned above. This spirit is impelled to reside in the body as long as possible. This drive of this special spirit to remain in the body results in the immaterial attribute of fear when threatened. This has a side effect of a survival tendency for the human: to run from danger, to defend themselves from harm, to seek assistance when in difficult circumstances, to eat when hungry, and many other reactions for survival.

Pain is common to all creation. Physical pain first. This would include the effects of hunger, that is, the pain internally a human feels when gastric juices fill the cavity of the stomach and begin to irritate the lining. Pain is also produced from disease, an internal or external injury, or failure or malfunction of a vital organ. Pain is the result of the transmission of impulses by the nerves from the area affected and to the brain, to inform the soul that the body is in danger or in the process of injury or threat of damage. This will motivate a reaction for personal survival or escape. God created a nerve system in humans far exceeding that of any other creature. The human is far more sensitive and aware of changes and threats to their well-being than any other creature. Since the human body does not have natural clothing, the skin is more sensitive to heat, cold and injury.

Psychological and emotional pain follows the same vein. It is an impression upon the soul of immediate danger or the threat of danger. It impresses upon the person the loss of security or happiness. This occurs with the death or illness of a close friend or relative. Emotion allows a person to be empathetic. It allows them to identity with the struggles and losses and difficulties of another. With an injury upon the soul, such as betrayal or violation of personal trust, the emotional pain is a warning against future involvement of unstable or unsure relationships, and a command for greater concern for a person's own long term survival.

Fear is the basis of the impulse to survive. Animals and humans both have a fear-facet part of their nature. God created this facet of fear as part of the body's reflexes for survival. Fear warns the person of a threat to their life in order to make provisions to react in a survival mode: attack, defend, flee or reconcile. Fear is a good response because its concern is the safety and survival of the person. It will restrain a person from inflicting harm upon themselves. Fear of the possible harmful consequences of drug abuse, promiscuity, suicide, deprivation, carelessness or negligence, motivates a person to live safely and conservatively.

Anger results from fear and demand for survival. Anger is the response of the body to the threat of survival. Anger is that emotion created by God for the human in order for them to want to banish from existence or society or the vicinity anything that poses as a threat to survival.

Anger is good if it is controlled and not allowed to affect someone unnecessarily or unintentionally. Latent anger is what generates laws penalizing criminals, establishes a judicial system and tribunals. Latent anger is the basis for developing an organized and trained police force. All of this because of the spirit wanting the body to survive. The anger is directly at those within the society that pose a threat to the safety of the residents. Violent anger is anger without control by the soul and leads to development of the evil impulse. This impulse drives a person into an offensive attack against threats to their safety and survival. This causes havoc and ruin for the person themselves and their victims. These people fail the test as they allow the carnal instinct to control their emotions and body, instead of reason and calm. The evil impulse evolves from the desire for survival with the conscious subdued. This is just how it is and needs to be controlled to curb harm in response.

## XXXVIII

It is so difficult for a person to deliberately take the life of another, as this is all we know of life, and to deprive another person of their life is depriving that person of all they have, and nothing else remains for that person if he is deprived of his life, once it is gone. So we have this conscious as mentioned earlier to impress on us that we have done the worst to another living human entity that could possible be done in taking away his life from him as this event can never be reversed. Material objects can be replaced; offences can be reconciled; injuries can be medically treated for the most part; but the deprivation of the corporeal life of another cannot be reinstituted. No way. Not at all. Impossible. Once gone it is gone. And it is only you to blame if deliberately imposing this on the other or the consequence of some irresponsible conduct, whether driving under the influence of some intoxicant, selling a narcotic that can kill, or war, or poisoning, or not avoiding an accident you could have, or expression of anger in violence or vengeance, or a fatal event that is foreseeable but you did it anyway. To transmit some incurable disease you know you have is likewise killing.

As far as war is concerned, this is why military training is required, so a person will not feel bad for killing. Military training is a manner of subduing or suppressing guilt feelings ahead of time with simulated killing training of use of firearms, so they will not interfere when the situation arises on the battlefield that the soldier needs to aim at another human with a lethal weapon and pull the trigger and deprive that person of his life, plus all the repercussions that death will have on his family, knowing that someone deprived their loved one of their corporeal life. The emotional reaction cannot be totally suppressed as eventually it resurrects in the form of some syndrome – PTSD – and affects the person later, sometimes to the point of suicide. This is part of the divine *karma* imposed on the killer, and more so in the future until the sentence is completed and the person realizes any violence or killing is not a display of love or kindness. In the future advancement of the person he will realize the importance of not getting angry at another, or not following orders of their superiors to kill, but rather refuse to be part of war, military service, riot, protest, revolution, or harm and injury and violence.

## XXXIX

Why is death so difficult to grasp for the average person? Because it is the termination of life as we know it. All we know is our corporeal life. Anything beyond this life is an enigma, something distant from our corporeal realm with which we cannot identify; it is indefinable, intangible, unsearchable and unknowable. Is also inescapable. The present corporeal life we can identify with, but we cannot identify with anything outside the corporeal realm, even the spirit-realm as mentioned above. The Love-force has installed in us this emotional attachment to the corporeal life, both our own and that of others. This is why when we notice another deceased it is as though part of our life also deceases. Due to our identification with the other, that part of ourselves has also deceased, and that eventually this may and of course will occur to us.

Bereavement is a process each person who loses a loved one needs to traverse. The closer the person was to you the greater the sadness and bereavement. The comfort can be located in two regions: first is that the person did have the opportunity to a corporeal self-conscious life gifted to him by God the Love-force, and second, a post-mortem life should the person believe in this.

Death is a process of transition from the corporeal to the incorporeal and a next stage of the infinity of a person's existence. Few though have this approach, only those who have been enlightened to the existence of the spirit-realm and within whom the Love-force resides. For them death is a transition. Corporeal life is the beginning and must proceed into the indefinite future. Having this attitude such a person does not involve himself in the events mentioned above where harm and damage is imposed on others, as it is antithetic to the conviction of life being a display of love and kindness.

Defense of the present corporeal life is most prevalent among those who cannot identify with the concept of life being infinite. As a result when threatened with the terminate of the only life the know – the present corporeal – they utilize whatever means are available to somehow preserve it or maintain what little is left or prolong it, at whatever cost, or even at the cost of the other, knowing that eventually they will succumb to death themselves sooner or later. But every minute sometimes counts if this life is all you have.

I can understand reasonable means like medical care, but I cannot justify it if it is at the expense or sacrifice of another, that you feel your life is more important than theirs.

## XL

What occurs in the next stage of the soul's development is a series of guesses and surmises on my part, but the purpose and goal still follow the initial course implemented by the Love-force and the soul will blend into it eventually for the indefinite future. The universe is a large place and getting larger and not in vain, but for a good purpose to provide residencies for Earth's past population and its increasing population generation after generation over the course of many billions of years into the future consisting of billions of more souls, as many as the Love-force created and stored in heaven's warehouses. This much I feel I can state as a reliable premise. But the soul needs to be taught and trained in order to continue the work of the Love-force, so maybe a few billion years is what it takes in our measurement of time in the spirit-realm, as this is the amount of time it takes to create a new galaxy and prepare it for habitation and so the soul will somehow blend back into the corporeal realm of time and space elsewhere and continue the work of the Love-force. This event can be called resurrection or reincarnation. Either term can here apply and it means a return to life in some corporeal capacity somewhere.

Perhaps the soul will blend into the Love-force and become part of it in the creation of galaxies to be used in the intermediate stages of development to divinity. There is a lot of work to be done over the course of infinity. We will find out when we get there.

The basic premise up to now upon which the entirety of the soul's journey is concerned is free volition. The self-conscious entity, realizing its own existence and relative to the balance of the universe, as well of his planetary body, society and family, concludes and grasps the fact that he can do as he wants. Whatever he wants to do he decides and proposes to do; he can do whatever he wants, what pleases him, and for the worst does whatever it is that is on his mind. This pertains to conduct that is both good and bad. Noticing that once attaining the age of maturity, or gaining this feeling of individual independence, that he no longer needs to be subject to the authority of parents and obedient to their wants and demands, and noticing that there is nothing that is forcing him to make one choice over another, concludes that he possesses a free volition, so he can do as he wants.

Of course conduct is also limited to not harming anyone or infringing on the rights of another, and obeying the law of the land in which this person is residing, and taking into consideration the norms and customs of his nationality and culture and the age in which he is residing. For the most part the choice is his own to decide and so proceed. Responsibility for one's actions is included in the choices of a responsible individual, and vice versa. This compels us to make the proper decisions in life, those to the benefit of ourselves, family and society.

Free volition is a natural trait of the self-conscious entity, the corporeal human, or is it otherwise?

## XLI

In reality, individual free choice – volition or free will – does not exist and it cannot exist. As mentioned above any decision independent of the predetermined route of the Love-force will cause a series of deviations in the future leading to chaos. Only if one scenario follows another in perfect order and sequence can the course be achieved.

There is no such thing as an accident. Every event is the product of a series of previous events and incidents and all of which have been predetermined to occur at a certain time and certain place to cause this event or incident as the subsequent. And that event is designed to cause the next even in conjunction with other events all occurring simultaneously. Nothing is arbitrary, accidental, unintended or independent. The dominoes are already set in a specific manner and they will fall as oriented once the first one is pushed. It has to be this way.

The Love-force is the sole entity that possesses volition and even then due to its nature it can only display love in the long-term purpose and goal. It cannot function in a harmful or detrimental manner, as this is opposite to its nature, and it is possible for the Love-force to operate opposite to its nature. The volition of the Love-force is fixed as far as its predetermined course is concerned, but from that point it uses its volition to accomplish its long term purpose.

Every motion of each atom has been planned prior to the beginning of time and space for that particular galaxy, or programmed in a manner of action, by the Love-force and which put everything into motion and execution of its supreme volition for the purpose that extends into infinity. The Love-force accomplishes all of this and there is not one atom or entity that can do anything of its own independent will other that it has been programmed to do or controlled by the Love-force. Everything that has motion is a robot doing what it is supposed to do and when and where as determined by the Love-force. It cannot be any other way. This is why whatever happens is meant to be, although you have the impression is it your decision or control. You are a robot although you think you are not.

This leads us to face another great miracle of creation by the supreme deity and that is the creation of an entity that is self-conscious – the human – having the impression it contains or possesses free will or volition to conduct itself independently based on the decision of its own choice, when it does not. Yes, another great miracle of creation: a robot thinking it does what it wants to do, whenever and wherever it wants, and not thinking or realizing it is actually a robot with not one shred of independent volition of any motion. This is what you are: a robot doing what you were programmed to do all the time of your corporeal existence under the impression this is the entirety of your free choice of action. So has the self-conscious entity been programmed to think about itself. Your brain was programmed from the moment you are born to the moment you expire, and your post-mortem life infinitely thereafter, for you to do what you did, are doing, and will do. Yes, this is how it is. And this pertains to every creation from amoeba to elephant to zebra.

This is definitely an unfathomable concept to have to accept or grasp, that the supreme Deity created an entity with the impression it is master of its destiny or possessor of volition when this is not at all the case. Every motion or thought is long determined for the balance of your life and eternal into the future. You are a robot doing what you were programmed to do at you birth although under the impression and thinking everything was due to your individual free choices. Sorry, but yes, this is how it is. The good part is that because it is all controlled by the Love-force the eventual intent is good and beneficial for you. Trust that it is.

## XLII

It is overwhelming, just overwhelming, to grasp this concept. Every motion, scene, event, scenario, action, incident and movement is all part of the eternal plan and control of the Love-force for the entire universe over the course of infinity, and especially the self-conscious human entity. Also included is every thought, notion, idea, decision, desire, intent, and all that pops out of our head. Such unfathomable of a concept to grasp if we can grasp it, or we can just refuse to grasp, because such an immense concept put into action by the Love-force of this other realm that is spirit and not matter is beyond our capacity to grasp.

It is hard enough to accept what I have previously described as us operating under the guise of free volition, much less now have to advance to accept something that transcends the premise of free volition to the premise that all is programmed by the Love-force and what we do is ordained for us to do while we are under the impression it was always our free volition. This overwhelms the corporeal human psyche, that all of these spirit-entities are making these decisions for us at every microsecond while we progress through time thinking nothing of it. Yes, every microsecond of our life is programmed into our brain, from birth to death and through the intermediate stages and further into infinity, and into all other brains to operate in unison all together.

For some this revelation is wonderful, that God has a role in guiding their life and they have no doubt that God will do the right thing with their life and all they need to do is get in step with it: connect with the architect of the universe. And this is fine as long as the person is willing to do exactly that: sacrifice his personal likes and goals and intents, decipher what the architect of the universe intends for him and follow that course. In reality and for the most part the person will do the opposite and have the goals and intent of the architect of the universe conform with his, so to make life as easy as possible and without much intensity or concentration.

For others it descends into fatalism and so blame God all along and do as little as possible to survive and nothing toward advancement, and your life is nothing more than a ball in a pinball machine. You get pushed into life and chock a few points and some thrills and movement, and then the game ends. Yes, for them life is a game to last for a while and then the game is over and you feel nothing remains in the future for you. How pathetic an attitude.

Yet they ignore the possibility of a purpose for the Love-force to have already programmed them for their corporeal life and the purpose of Love-force to lead them through his particular course.

Once in the intermediate stage the revelations are disclosed to you of God's eternal plan for you and you will willingly and voluntarily subject yourself to them due to the immense amount of kindness that will be displayed to you by the Love-force, although you will have the impression you are conforming to the will of the Love-force as a result of your own volition. However you are still a robot under the impression you are making independent choices. Sorry, but this is how it is for each self-conscious entity created. Like it or not and there is nothing you can do about it because the Love-force will permeate you with kindness and you will appropriately react and to the effects of divine love thinking you are doing this voluntarily when actually it is part of the plan determined for you by the Love-force.

This is why everything that happens is meant to happen, and it could not be otherwise. And this is not so bad, but actually better.

## XLIII

There is still no reason not to do the right think in life, meaning, what is virtuous, honest, beneficial, kind, considerate, and all of the other cardinal virtues of which we hear about, and act with integrity and rectitude. If a person believes in their infinity, that the supreme deity God created him, that the Love-force has planned every facet, scene, event and motion of his life, he will not be afraid to always do what is right; never afraid of any person and never fearing any situation, or that something will get the better of him. Although this should and will occur over the course of a person's life, it is only superficial as nothing can interfere or alter the course of life that the Love-force has planned for him even if it means suffering or death for doing what is right. To do what is correct and proper and virtuous is also part of the nature in whom the Love-force resides. They pass the test.

There is no reason for a person to ever turn to harm, hurt, injury, dishonesty, theft or cheat or prejudice or bias or hate, or any of the seven cardinal sins, if the person believes the Love-force resides in him and will conduct him through life somehow or other. This is also a test for others whether they will help such a person who is in need so he will not have to turn to criminal activity to survive. If they help they pass the test. If they don't they fail.

The final topic to discuss in this category is similar. No reason exists that can justify a person depriving himself of his own life: suicide. No reason is sufficient for a person to kill himself. Tough occasions will arise, but a person needs to believe the Love-force that created him did so for good purpose and this purpose for his corporeal life is thwarted and interrupted should the person terminate his life. A person needs to believe that the Love-force will eventually rectify the situation, as all distresses and depressions and anxieties are temporal. A person who refuses self-imposed death passes the test. At the same time, another who recognizes suicidal tendencies has the obligation to help this person, so both pass the test, otherwise both will fail.

There is likewise no reason to turn to intoxicants or narcotics as a means of escape from the difficulties of life. There is no event, no calamity or catastrophe that a person cannot survive if he believes that the Love-force is handling both his present and his future. He needs to know that all will be fine. Intoxicants and hallucinogens distort a person's ability to think and rationalize clearly and objectively; they interfere with his ability to properly deal with reality, so he is no longer in a position to make proper decisions pertaining to his future on a rational basis and so will made the wrong decisions. By avoiding mind-altering chemicals a person allows the Love-force to control his life and which is always for the better.

Perseverance is the answer.

For someone to help a person who develops a chemical dependence on alcohol or a narcotic – including tobacco – or a psychological addiction to gambling, or a behavioral addiction to sexual excess such as pornography or purchasing sexual services – is a display of love. If one person notices another disintegrating physically, morally or emotionally, as a result of addiction or preoccupation with harmful activities, and does nothing, he fails the test. Of course, divine *karma* will occur in the form of himself becoming addicted and others refusing to help him, or someone in his family, while he disintegrates and so understands how is feels not to be helped when help is available. It cannot be otherwise. Yes, each of us is our brother's keeper.

## XLIV

Creation of society and government is a materialization of the Love-force with a group of cooperative individuals to make the best of corporeal life possible, the best that the Love-force will make available. The concept of self-government is based on the display of respect and consideration to each other on an organized basis, with the divinely-attributed talents and capabilities of each member utilizing them on a cooperative basis. So good government consists of a successful civilization consisting of successful economy, culture, education, medical care, and welfare for population, and especially the young and old and underprivileged. Every nation and legislation needs to maintain the display of life or the welfare of society in mind over the long term, always thinking in terms of the future.

If there is one obstacle or barricade to a successful society it is selfishness. This inhibits the contributions of excess funds to help the ill, widows and orphans, educational facilities, medical and social services. Just because a person is born with an innate capacity – part of his DNA as designed by the Love-force – to become more successful in business and so acquires obscene amounts of wealth it is not a sufficient reason to solely increase his standard of living, and his family's, and not share with those not born with the same business savvy or the better DNA design. Society must advance together to succeed as love displayed by those who have a congenital ability to succeed in financial matters to invest their wealth not in themselves or immediate family, but to help those advance who were not born with the same abilities. Love is displayed when the wealthy use their wealth to help the underprivileged, handicapped, widowed and orphaned, uneducated, and those caught in bad circumstances. Love is displayed when all have equal access to services such as education and medical care.

Excess wealth is any amount beyond the basics of shelter, food and amenities for a decent life.

## XLV

Somehow the soul will again materialize corporeally at some future time and place. With the vast size of the universe and time being infinite the soul could travel for millions or billions of years over the immeasurable light-years of the spatial expanse to some new residence and there materialize or reincarnate or resurrect, to use popular terms. This will occur to the soul independent of time and space. The soul is incorporeal during the intermediate post-mortem stage, and when the soul again materializes and again regains its senses it will not have sensed the amount of time and space traversed. It has to be this way for the Love-force to continue its purpose for this soul and each soul.

What will happen here is anybody's guess, except be assured the Love-force only travels in one direction forward with the sole purpose of the display of love, and which will also become an inherent part of each soul. The soul of each corporeal human will then and eventually proceed on its own after having traversed perhaps millions of years of experience in another galaxy in another time-frame, and this will allow the soul to evolve or develop into a Love-force of its own. The process will be more than voluntary once exposed to such a extensive amount of experience and permeated by the Love-force of the future so the soul wants to sacrifice itself to the betterment of all other souls behind it that are on the same course of transcendence and advancement. The souls permeated with love to the extent that love is the new nature of the soul – willingly and voluntarily – will likewise have only one direction to proceed with one same goal and this cannot be otherwise. You will merge into the arteries of the Love-force as it flows forward.

After the consummation of the training and corporeal education of the soul it will shed its shroud and advance to the stage of a thought-form or spirit-entity. You become part of the Love-force that will now be a driving force or engine of the corporeal universe on its creation and control of administration with the new additional souls materializing into existence. Eventually your soul – meaning you the reader – will evolve as a thought-form love-force spirit-entity part of the engine of the universe and part of creator God outside of time and space. So difficult to grasp such a concept, but the love permeating us, overwhelming us, will initiate this motivation in us to set our personal ambitions aside to sacrifice ourselves to this purpose and goal. Yes, we eventually will advance to be outside time and space becoming an incorporeal spirit-entity, thought-form, love-force, as part of universal love development of newly created souls and galaxies.

Of course, millions of millions of years of time is available to attain to this goal and purpose and subsequently to accomplish the work of the future. Any other purpose is shallow, myopic and fatalistic.

## XLVI

Somewhere along the line once the Love-force becomes the nature of our soul will we no longer be robots. Once we have reached that plateau where we work as a team with the Love-force and blend and merge into it will we be liberated from the capacity of a robot now doing the volition of the Love-force, thinking it is our voluntary decision to actually being a genuine entity having a mind of our own and volition of our own, except this will only occur after perhaps millions of years of training and exposure in the arena of the Love-force. Now our soul blends and merges into It so we ourselves understand it so well that we proceed on the same route forward of the display of love. It has become us. So the work entails effort in the incorporeal universe for the purpose of the corporeal universe.

Every moment of effort in the advanced stages will be personal satisfaction of achievements that are to a greater purpose than ourselves and this drive of the Love-force in us will want us to do more and without and end in sight and so no end will be provided so we can continue without an end with the continued creation of time and space. It is the joy of the materialization of sacrifice to an achievement of purpose beyond ourselves and the gratification of joy and fulfillment from the effort and which becomes fuel for the fire to continue. Each achievement for the benefit of souls in the creation becomes the fuel for the engine to continue forever.

It cannot be otherwise or else our life is an empty object, or God's toy for his temporary vain fun, or a joke that God is playing on us, to create us and set us free on Earth to our own misery and eventual demise and no more after that, and then we vanish serving no purpose. So it has to be an infinite purpose and goal, or none at all. It can only be one or the other, and so it is the one directed toward infinity of time and purpose to our happiness and benefit.

So hard to grasp and more now than at the onset of this book that this Love-force is the engine driving both the incorporeal and corporeal creations of the universe. The supreme deity God is this Love-force: the materialization of the concept of Love and outside of time and space, and the entire corporeal and incorporeal universes are the object of the Love-force as love cannot exist without an object to which to display love, and the greater the love the greater the number of objects that need to exist to which to display this much love. The magnitude of the universe that astronomy presents to us is the magnitude of the invisible ethereal Love-force, and the energy and capacity to accomplish this has existed from time infinite into the past and will infinitely into the future without end and without exhaustion. Love needs to materialize and so it does in this manner: it cannot do otherwise. It has to as an impersonal Love-force.

Love grows with the creation of new entities – self-conscious souls – and so the need for the expansion of the universe. I cannot think or perceive of any other scenario.

The understanding that many have of a personal God residing in heaven is adequate for them. The reality is far greater.

## XLVII

From another perspective I feel that if you, the reader, could calm and relax and meditate on your life over the years, if you could contemplate on all the events you remember that had an impact on your life, I feel you will realize that you had little free volition in the decisions that you made, meaning, that most of them were due to circumstances.

Let's view this objectively. If you reflect on your life you will realize that we have little or no free volition to speak of. Not one of us selected the day for us to be born, or where to be born, or when to be born, or to whom to be born, meaning, we did not select our parents or our culture or era or economic status or our family, or the religion of our family. We had zero choice regarding the manner we were raised or education, or nourished, or amount of exercise or exposure to the world around us. This was decided by others. We had no choice on our environment, early friendships, influences, mentoring or social activities. All of this was provided us by others. By the time we gained an independent cognizance of the world around us and our situation we were in our mid-teens and so only continued to do what we were trained and taught to do as a result of our upbringing, the result of our education and associations, the effects and influence of society on us, as well as advertising and political propaganda, so our choices were for the most part pre-determined. What we did is what was expected of us, or what we expected of ourselves based on the circumstances of our environment.

Even as time progressed, reflecting on the events of our life, they were choices that were not so much independent, but based on circumstances we found ourselves in, and so the choices we made were based on these circumstances and not independent. So it is with marriage, and our own family, and the cycle repeats itself.

In reality, everything we did was because it was supposed to happen this way; we did not have any other choice. Perhaps at the time we felt it was an independent decision based on our individual volition, but in later years, contemplating on the various events, we realize that we just fell in line with the progress of history, and it was because of events prior to us that caused us to make the decisions we did make.

I bring this up, and after reflections on my own life – and I am 72 years of age right now – and I realize that all that happened to me was suppose to happen; that all of my decisions were due to events preceding me and so I had no choice except to make these decisions and due to these circumstances over which I had no control. So it is with everyone else, and it cannot be any other way. So there is no such thing as free choice or an independent volition, otherwise all will descend into chaos, with each person doing whatever it is he or she wants to do, and what a mess.

For life to have been as orderly as it was had to be planned and implemented by the divine Love-force. Our life was orderly, although with its share of difficulties and tragedies, but it was all in an orderly manner. So free choice or volition never existed in our life, but it was the Love-force that routed our life through all of these circumstances and events and accidents and incidents, and which started a long, long time ago, because every event has an affect and impact on the next and subsequent events.

## XLVIII

Happiness is something that is self-generating, meaning, that the source of happiness is inexhaustible, infinite, ever available, obtainable and never-failing. The source of happiness is the love-force and there is an infinite amount of it and will always be and it will never be depleted or exhausted.

One important aspect of the Love-force is that it generates itself as the need for it to accomplish its purpose increases; somehow the Love-force can create or generate more of itself out of itself, since this is its purpose of existence and so must always have Love-force to continue its work. No doubt the reader will find this difficult to fathom as to how something has the capacity to generate more of itself when the needs arises and especially since the need has existed infinitely into the past and will infinitely into the future as whatever demand is required.

One of the laws of thermodynamics is that nature abhors a vacuum. If a vacuum exists then effort is automatically generated to attempt to fill it with matter. It is the same way with happiness on Earth. If there is a void or vacuum of happiness then the Love-force will generate some to fill the void of its existence, as much as needed. This is the reason why after any tragedy or disaster matters somehow tend to return to a state of normalcy or the state prior to the tragedy or disaster. If a lack of happiness exists the Love-force automatically starts to generate it to fill the lack of it.

People will in time recover from war, natural disaster, disease, famine, or some unexpected catastrophe, although difficultly, but it always occurs. It has to. Wars for example cause massive destruction and loss of life. What happens is that eventually people get tired of killing and destroying, or when the amount killed or property destroyed reaches a stalemate, the war ends. Then reconstruction begins and the civilizations are rebuilt and restored and societies return to the state in which they were prior to the start of the war. This is cyclic since time began.

Happiness is lacking during war and as a result the Love-force starts creating some and permeating the warring factions with it and which causes the war to eventually end. More happiness is interjected into the various societies involved in war until the void is filled and the society is returned to the state in which it was prior to war. The same can be applied to just above any other disaster that occurs. Everything eventually returns to its original state.

The same can be applied to the loss of a loved one: a parent loses a child, for example. Eventually the parents recover from the loss and continue their life. This is because the death has caused a lack of happiness in the grieving family members and so the love-force intervenes and fills the void by generating some happiness and installing into the void. Otherwise there would never be any recovery from pain due to loss of loved ones.

It has to be this way, otherwise a war will end until not one person remains, or societies will never rebuild, or ill and diseased people will never get well, or once a disaster strikes an individual or region it will never get rebuilt. The love-force due to its nature must create happiness and interject it whenever a lack of it or void exists in order to restore, and this happiness is self-generated by the love-force as part of its inherent nature. It has to be this way, it cannot be otherwise.

## XLIX

In the light of all provided in this treatise from the beginning we should be on our hands and knees day and night in humility and sincerity thanking God with all our heart and mind and strength for displaying this love toward us by creating us and providing us conscious existence, having the ability to lead our life in the manner we want although it is actually the Love-force that is leading and guiding and maneuvering and controlling our life in the direction It wants and which is to our benefit in the long run, and so all that happens is meant to be and for the purpose dictated by the Love-force as it is all God's display of love toward us, whether we feel this way or not during our corporeal existence.

We need to prostrate ourselves flat on the floor and abandon ourselves to God's will, for the Love-force to take charge of our life and control it totally. We need to let God take total control of our life without reservations. We need to let God take control of our thoughts, mind, attitude, intentions, plans, goals and our purpose of life. God needs to be our life and so will be when we allow the Love-force to operate through us, that our entire essence is the display of love. We cannot do otherwise. We cannot conduct ourselves other than to thank God day and night for His kindness, generosity, benevolence and concern for our welfare; to thank God for all He did and does and will do for us.

In some respects this is a dichotomy difficult to fathom, knowing that He created us to be objects of His love and which He could not have done otherwise because this is His nature, and so our life is under His control anyway and will be into the future without end. Amen and amen.

So why do we pray? We hope that a power that is beyond ours and that resides in the heavens will do what we as weak and deficient creatures are incapable of doing ourselves with a problem that is beyond our ability to resolve. Yet, if whatever happens is meant to be, why pray? Because it brings us closer to the Love-force or whatever it is that we recognize as God. It comforts us that we have the ability to approach a power that is greater than ours and which resides in some region that is not corporeal but heavenly.

We should never turn against our God should our prayers not be answered or should the worse occur rather than the better. The reason is that the Love-force already has control of the situation, and regardless of our attitude the result is already determined. Whatever should the result be it is always in our best interests because our evaluation or conclusion is myopic, while the Love-force thinks in terms of the indefinite future. This is more important than the near future.

L

All my life I visualized supreme deity as a superman, and which is typical of historic Christianity and most religions. Then revelations brought me to the cognizance of all of what I related above. In addition, I also concluded the following:

Not comprehending the infinity of the Supreme deity or concept of the divine Love-force is the reason Christian-denomination churches remain shallow with their Christmas Jesus and 3 wise men and Santa Claus and Christmas tree next to the manger; and their Easter Sunday with rabbits and colored egg hunts; and Jesus still hanging on that stake[6] and he never

---

[6] This is the correct translation of the Greek word *stauros*; it is mistranslated in the NT as cross throughout.

seems to go anywhere, although he is a spirit in heaven. This is the extent of their penetration into divine mysteries, or the secrets of the kingdom of God. They can't grasp this concept.

They cannot understand the concept of a spirit-entity that is supreme deity, and so they devolve into corporeal projections thinking this is the reality. They create God after the image of our corporeal self and environment and what we want in terms of religion. Very few have transcended the superficial level of ecumenical Christendom, just a handful penetrate into the realm of Spirit. Like a pyramid with big base of size of ecumenical Christianity, but the closer to heaven the narrower or smaller the group that ascends.

From another perspective, I conclude that most people see no need for accepting, or even acknowledging, the concept of a Supreme deity of the type I described above, or his universal plan for all humanity, I guess about 99.94% of the population. They are content with things just the way they are, or else make do with the best they can, or how circumstances dictate, but all of it is corporeal. They just have no need for something spirit and incorporeal as it does nothing for them that is tangible, and distracts attention from the important matter of life, like success and happiness and entertainment and recreation and sports and travel and do what you want to do with your life, because once you are gone you are gone, and none have been presented any or sufficient evidence that there is something else out there. Jesus' resurrection is nice but you cannot take it seriously, which attitude resides in the back of their mind. And to fly into the sky? Be real.

As a result history continues as it has since day one, not allowing belief in an invisible supreme deity to interfere with their personal life or the reality of temporal existence. We few are rare and dispersed and they can't see us anywhere as they can't lift their heads to even notice higher levels of spirit transcendence. Eventually all will be rectified in the future as this is the goal of the Love-force for each creation of a self-conscious entity.

# PART TWO:

## THE ATTRIBUTES OF HEAVEN AND EARTH

### 1. THE ATTRIBUTES OF HEAVEN

The purpose of this dissertation is to provide the author's interpretive theology of Sacred Scripture known as the Holy Bible. I deal with the topics of the realm of spirit and the realm of matter. The topics covered under the realm of spirit include *Yahweh* God and the invisible world of heaven; the realm of matter is the material created universe, including humanity, the earth, and all creation, its purpose and future. Along with this is provided a sketch on the career of Jesus son of God, beginning with his birth of his Father in heaven and through his incarnation and life on earth, and concluding with his present role and work in heaven. This volume concludes with a section dealing with the deviation of historical and contemporary Christianity from the original concepts as defined by Sacred Scripture and as codified in this treatise. I am convicted of the truth of all interpretations provided to the reader, that they are in accord with the inspired word of *Yahweh* God as revealed in His Holy Bible.

    The interpretations of the various subjects covered are the result of 50 years of Bible study and Bible teaching by the author, with a parallel study of both secular and religious history. I consider the conclusions drawn over the years to be valuable for other students of the Bible and Christian church history.

    I consider this an interpretive theology because of the manner that the various topics are discussed. It is more of a narrative form. To appreciate my approach regarding this interpretive theology the entirety of the volume must be read before drawing final conclusions on its worthiness or accuracy. The reason is due to the situation that all the topics covered are interwoven with each other. The volume is like a painted landscape scene. To paint such a portrait, a beginning is made on the canvas and continues on until completed. Likewise the viewer begins at a point and inspects the painting from one side to another and top to bottom. So with compiling this interpretive theology: The discussion begins at one point discussed and then is followed by related points. The topics are interwoven to the point that the fabric cannot be cut into distinct sections without a disruption. A conclusion drawn in one section may be continued in discussion in another section until all is canvassed.

This volume is not intended to repeat the contents of other volumes on theology, many of which are excellent, thorough and far more informative and exhaustive. My intent is to present his own convictions regarding *Yahweh* God and His material and immaterial creation, its contents, purpose and involvement with ourselves. I have excluded from his concepts any influence or intervention from sources outside Scripture. For this reason many of the conclusions drawn and concepts provided may seem alien or flawed by the reader whose background stems from historical and contemporary schools of Christianity.

The theme of sola-Scriptura or back to the Bible had been preached by many. Yet to uproot and discard generations of doctrines alien to Scripture is near impossible, especially since much of this has been considered Orthodox for centuries. First required is an intensive and non-biased study of Scripture and developing concepts and doctrines based on the study. A second or parallel important study is that of history, the same eras when the inspired word was spoken or written. This forces the student to understand the inspired word in its historical context. The primary necessity of this approach is to be able to understand the message in the same manner as the listeners of the inspired prophet or apostle. The correct understanding of Scripture is in its historical context.

It is especially the gospels and letters of Paul apostle that are misinterpreted more than any other section in Scripture. The gospels in temporary sermons are not read in the historical context of Judea of the First century under Roman military occupation. Paul apostle has been rewritten by scholars, no longer understood in terms as defined by the Hebrew OT and Jewish sages, but according to Hellenic philosophy.

The final section of this volume is brief and provides a detailed and accurate study on the incorporation of alien concepts and doctrines into Christian assemblies as history progressed from the apostolic assemblies of the mid $2^{nd}$ century and through the beginning of the $5^{th}$ century. This section utilizes primarily the writings of the apologists, ante-Nicene, and Nicene Fathers, up to the Council of Chalcedon. Parallel with this historical perspective is the attitude of anti-Semitism in the same period.

The importance of the inclusion of anti-Semitism is for the reader to realize its effect on the attitude of the apologists and early church Fathers. It was the heavy influence of Greek philosophy combined with anti-Semitism that provided the impetus for the creeds, theology and Christology of the early Ecumenical Councils, which then became the bedrock of historical Christianity and established Christian doctrines for future generations of Church theologians and reformers.

The epilogue is the author's thoughts of accepting the concepts of Scripture as defined in this volume, and its advantage to the person and the community.

## THE REALM OF SPIRIT

There exists another world than the world we reside in. This world is apart and dissociated from the world in which created humanity resides. This other world is another realm of another nature and another constitution than the one created humanity is affixed. This other world or realm is the realm of spirit. It is not a material world made of matter, as is the world of the created material universe. It is a world composed of another substance which is immaterial, meaning not of matter. It is not distant because it envelops the same space as the material creation, but in a different frame.

This realm of spirit is alien from the capability of a human to experience, except in part with the baptism of the Holy Spirit. Even this experience is so infinitesimal it is only a witness to its existence. The human is designed by *Yahweh* God with senses to experience and interact with the physical world of their environment. The human in their present state is not designed to reside in or interact with the realm of spirit, because the human is material. The real world is not the created universe of sight and sound and touch and human experience. It is the realm of spirit which is the real world. It is permanent, immortal and consistent. Our material world is plastic; the divine realm is genuine and concrete. There exists an invisible gulf of chasm between the material realm and divine realm, but not a chasm that is material that can be seen or felt, but a division of 2 incompatible and alien time-substance-energy systems. This material world is transitory and ever under development, but is a witness to the real world

## HEAVEN

The Bible refers to this realm of spirit as heaven. One difficulty in Bible interpretation is that one word exists in Hebrew for both sky and heaven. The reason is obvious: God resides "out there" somewhere. It is a matter of semantics whether the Hebrew *shamayin* should refer to sky or outer space, or refer to heaven as the unseen divine realm. In the KJV OT (Old Testament), *shamayin* is rendered 398 times as heaven, and 21 times as air. In the Greek, the equivalent word is *ouranos*. The KJV NT (New Testament) renders this word 10 times as air, 5 times as sky, and 268 times as heaven. More contemporary versions of the bible utilize the renderings of air and sky more frequently due to the context of the passages:

> Birds are in the sky not heaven. Jer 4:25. Matt 8:20.
> Stars are in outer space, not heaven. Gen 26:4. Matt 2:2, 24:29.

The relationship between the realms is defined by David Psalmist:

> As for the heavens the heavens belong to *Yahweh*. But the earth He gave to humans. Ps 115:16.

This heaven or divine realm of spirit is the residence of *Yahweh* God and the spirit entities. They are the messengers and sons of *Yahweh* God.

The concepts of a material and bodily existence do not exist in heaven: death, decay, sickness, hate, anger, or any other characteristic of human nature or the created world humanity resides in. All the emotion, conscience or experience of a human does not and can not exist in heaven, because all of this evolves from a material creation. The attributes of the material realm reside with the created universe, and because they are material, are alien and inapplicable to the nature and environment of the realm of spirit, heaven.

Time as we know it does not exist in heaven. All is infinite.

The goal and purpose of heaven is the generation of the material realm and its active progress through time and indefinitely into the future. This realm of spirit is administration and execution of every movement or thought in our material realm. Heaven is power and knowledge and organization on behalf of the material universe. It is this unseen and divine realm that defines and generates the infinite progress of this world: second by second on every parcel of ground on every planet and body in the universe.

The evidence of heaven or the administration of the divine realm over the material universe is found in life. There exists a distinction between what is considered alive and what is considered dead. There is an unseen essence that resides in the creature when it is alive, which does not when it is dead. This is the spirit of animation gifted to every living and breathing creature at the time of its birth. Whether it be a human or an animal that is killed or dies from natural causes, during the process of dying some invisible substance exists the live creature.

This is the evidence of the divine realm. Life evolves from it and is dependent on it.

## THE HUMAN EXPERIENCE OF HEAVEN

For a human to enter and view the divine realm, heaven, the person must be divinely altered in nature. This is not a physical or psychological alternation, but one of entering into a state of ability to identify and communicate with this realm. John apostle defined it in this manner:

> I was in the spirit on the Lord's day. Rev 1:10.
> At once I was in the spirit. Rev 4:2.
> And he carried me away in the Spirit into the wilderness. Rev 17:3.

The Spirit of *Yahweh* God enveloped John apostle to allow him to observe revelations of the divine realm, but only in allegories and hyperbolas. John apostle could not personally enter the divine realm, because he is material, but he was able to grasp its contents through revelation in visions. Paul apostle defined this realm of spirit as the Third Heaven. 2 Cor 12:2. This can be interpreted as follows: The First heaven is the sky; the Second heaven is outer space. The Third would then be beyond it, but not in a material sense, and would pertain to heaven, the realm of spirit. Not having a more accurate manner of defining such an environment, Paul apostle followed the tradition of his rabbis as describing it as if beyond the limits of the physical universe. Much like John apostle he experienced this divine realm in or out of the body, meaning, in the body but in the Spirit transmitting him into this divine realm of heaven.

Isaiah prophet likewise was "in the Spirit" with his vision of *Yahweh* God upon His throne. Is 6:1. The same with Daniel prophet with his similar vision. Dan 7:9-14. Ezekiel wrote the following:

> The Spirit lifted me up and took me away. Eze 3:14.
> And the Spirit lifted me up between heaven and earth, and brought me in the visions of God to Jerusalem. Eze 8:3.

These visions are all allegories used to convey understandably to the human mind the activities of heaven. Since heaven is spirit, there are no material thrones or Seraphim with wings, neither is *Yahweh* God actually as described. This is the manner that *Yahweh* God has selected to portray the objects and entities and activity of His divine realm to obedient created humanity.

## *EL* AND *ELOHIM*

The Hebrew has 2 words that refer to deity and divinity: *El* and *Elohim*. The latter is the plural form of the former, but is used often in a singular tense. This is comparably to the use of English words group or assembly. *Elohim* encompasses the pantheon of the divine realm. *El* is specific. For example,

> "*Yahweh*, the *Elohim* of your fathers, the *El* of Abraham, the *El* of Isaac, and the *El* of Jacob." Ex 3:15.

The molten calf was spoken of by Aaron in this manner:

> "This is your *elohim*, Israel, who brought you out of Egypt." Ex 32:3.

The calf represented the pantheon of deity in the divine realm. The Aramaic form of *El* is *Eloah* and is primarily found in the book of Daniel.

## YAHWEH GOD AS SPIRIT

*Yahweh* God is a definite entity with self-consciousness and identity. He has a specific residence in the divine realm. It is much like any individual in the material realm having a residence, or the central government of a nation located in the capital city. *Yahweh* God also has contact and omniscience of all that occurs in His universe, in both the divine and material realms. The spirit that pervades the divine realm relates to *Yahweh* God all that transpires, His spirit omnipresent. As an entity *Yahweh* God resides in this divine realm, heaven. Paul described it as follows:

> Who alone has immortality and dwells in unapproachable light, whom no man has ever seen or can see. 1 Tim 6:16.
> Where can I flee from Your Spirit? Or where can I flee from you presence? If I ascend to heaven, You are there. If make by bed in *Sheol*, You are there. Ps 139:7-8.

No matter where an individual may travel or hide, the spirit of this divine realm is present. Jesus spoke of *Yahweh* God in this manner,

> "God is spirit." John 4:26.

The substance of the composition of *Yahweh* God is that of spirit: invisible, ethereal, immaterial, but very tangible. The entities of heaven and including *Yahweh* God Himself have no figure or form, because they are spirit. Material entities require figure and form as part of the material existence. *Yahweh* God and the entities of heaven are likewise genderless. There is no need for a division of genders in the divine realm. The male and female were created by *Yahweh* God as part of human existence for marriage, social needs and procreation. None of this applies in heaven. *Yahweh* God does not need gender, a figure, or hands, arms, legs, feet or a torso; because He is spirit. The Scriptures do regularly attribute to *Yahweh* God human traits and characteristics. This is done by the inspired authors to portray *Yahweh* God in a manner that can be easily understood by humans. This includes the visions of Him sitting on a throne or soaring through the sky.

## THE NATURE OF YAHWEH GOD

The nature of *Yahweh* God is sacrifice, an eternally living entity dedicated to an eternal purpose on behalf of His creation, which purpose is conceived, initiated and accomplished on His own. *Yahweh* God is not a dead sacrifice, like those of voluntary martyrdom, or those perishing in persecution or inquisition or combat. The nature of *Yahweh* God is that of an eternal living sacrifice. His dedication in heaven is a selfless entity, meaning, void of personal ambition or gain. His eternal effort is in the best interest of His creation. It is the constant and total administration of innumerable spirit entities for the daily and long term progress and history of the material realm and especially created humanity.

If we could make *Yahweh* God on His throne comparable to a person in some equivalent business capacity, He would be Chief Executive Officer and Chief Operations Officer. He would be working around the clock planning births and deaths, lives and interactions; people of stature and people less significant; events in countries and the progress of history with the most miniscule of detail, periods of war and distress and havoc, and periods of peace and harmony and success; famines and abundance; calm and storm; plague and health. The life of every person equally important since His personal involvement places him and her in history, all accomplished according to the counsel of His own will. He indefatigably administrating all the messengers and sons of God in heaven to execute His counsel for the progress of billions of years of activity in the created universe. From the movement of the atom to the generation of a galaxy; from the sperm entering the ovum to the dictates of the despot to the slave who both evolve from the same; from the child playing to the adult massacring; from the physician saving to the military conscript devastating; from the activities of a typical mundane day to the interweave of international affairs over a millennium; all of this executed in an incomparable order, well orchestrated by the supreme deity. All creation and history attests to His dedication and administration on behalf of His creation.

The nature of *Yahweh* God is love. There is no deviation from this nature of His. He is immutable in this nature of His. But for love to be genuine there must exists objects of love and subsequently a benefit to be provided to the objects of His love. To manifest His nature the creation is brought into existence, and especially conscious existence.

> Ever since the creation of the world His invisible nature, namely, His eternal power and deity, has been clearly perceived in the things that have been made. Rom 1:20.

This ability to reproduce is a part of that image and likeness of *Yahweh* God upon all living creatures, and especially created humanity. Every organism that reproduces has the ability to produce hundreds or thousands of the same species. *Yahweh* God uses natural organisms, both plants and animal, to reflect His nature as an eternal creator, since with the ability to reproduce all species of every living organisms can live forever.

## *YAHWEH* – SOLE DEITY

From its initial words Scripture indicates the existence of a sole supreme or only deity. This supreme deity is a living entity and is genderless, but for sake of convenience the male pronoun is used to refer to *Yahweh* as "He" or "Him". The supreme deity has a name to identify Himself, a name consisting of 4 Hebrew letters, transliterated into English as YHWH, commonly pronounced as *Yahweh* or *Yaveh*. This is His personal name and a name to identify Him as opposed to any other entity. The name YHWH is used about 6,600 times in OT Scripture. Because the inter-Testamental books (Apocrypha) and NT are in Greek, the name is not found, although in some manuscripts the name in Hebrew is inserted into the Greek text. The Greek *Kyrios*, Lord, as the equivalent to the Hebrew *Adonai*, is rendered as a translation of the Hebrew YHWH in 137 places in the NT. For example: Matt 1:20-24. Luke 1:67. Acts 2:20-39. This conclusion is based on the usage of the Greek *Kyrios* compared to its equivalent use in the Hebrew OT. Luke 1:67, as the equivalent of Ps 72:18, could just as easily be rendered as "Blessed be *Yahweh* – the deity of Israel."

> "I have sworn to *Yahweh*, the supreme Deity (El), Sovereign of heaven and earth," said Abraham in Gen 14:22.

The important point made clear to the ancient saints was that *Yahweh* God was the sole deity existing in the universe, and that all other so-called "gods" were the fabrication of people's imagination and superstition. Only *Yahweh* God is self-sufficient and self-propagating. All else that exists in the universe, both in the material realm and spiritual realm, acquired its existence from *Yahweh* God and is dependant on Him for its continuation.

That *Yahweh* God is sole deity is regularly indicated in Scripture, both OT and NT. The one passage most referenced is also the one passage of variant interpretation between the Jewish sages and the patristic fathers of the early church. Deut 6:4. My rendering is the following:

> Listen Israel, *Yahweh* our Deity is sole deity. Deut 6:4.

Other translations support this rendering.

> Hear O Israel, *Yahweh* is our God – *Yahweh* alone. (Rotherhams).
> Hear O Israel, *Yahweh* is our God, *Yahweh* alone. (American Revised 1901. margin)
> Hear O Israel, The LORD is our God, the LORD alone. (Tanakh, the Jewish Bible)

That this is the intended reading is attested to by several other texts dealing with the same topic in the OT and NT: There is only one deity and that is *Yahweh* Elohim.

> To you it was shown that you might know that *Yahweh* is God (Elohim = deity): there is no other besides Him. Deut 4:35.
> So now O *Yahweh* our God, I beseech You, save us from his hand, that all the kingdoms of the earth may know that You *Yahweh* are alone God. 2 King 19:19 and 15.
> Let them know that You alone, whose name is *Yahweh*, are Supreme over all the earth. Ps 83:18.
> How can you believe who receive glory from one another and do not seek the glory that comes from the only God? John 5:44.
> You believe there is one God, you do well. Jam 2:19.
> One God and Father of us all, who is above all and through all and in all. Eph 4:6.

The point made by *Yahweh* God in Deut 6:4 is that He is sole deity, and that no other deity exists. This passage does not deal with the "oneness" of God. The intent of the word "one" in this verse is that of "only one" or "sole." The idea of having to state the concept of supreme deity as a "oneness" is purposeless. For this reason the command was given:

> Do not have any gods besides Me. Ex 20:3.

Plainly, there is no other deity beside *Yahweh* God to be recognized. Although Scripture does refer to the deities of other nations as gods. Josh 10:16. Ps 77:13. This was utilized by the inspired authors to convey to their readers that *Yahweh* God and the deity of Israel was superior to anything or anyone else that others may venerate or obey.

## THE NAME OF GOD

That *Yahweh* God allows Himself to be called by His personal name is indicative of His desire to be close to created humanity, in order that they could identify with a creator who is close to His creation. This was in contradistinction to the alien pseudo-deities who were distant and isolated from the people who claimed their reverence. The concept of a name attached to the entity who is supreme deity banishes the concept of a "god" who is nebulous or undefined, such as Plato's supreme one, or the Christian triune godhead, or as the personification of a philosophical concept or element of nature. To refer to *Yahweh* only in terms of "God" causes Him to be distant and vague. "God" is an office or position, like president or prime minister. The judges and men of high authority in Israel are labeled gods, in Hebrew *elohim*. Ps 82:1-8. The judges of ancient Israel are also referred to as god. Ex 21:6, 22:8. Moses is also called god. Ex 7:1. This was because of his authority to stand in the presence of Pharaoh to speak on behalf of *Yahweh* God. To always refer to the ruler of our nation as president is fine as long as only the office or position is dealt with in a business or official manner, but there is no identification of the president as a person or individual. An individual cannot know the president on a personal basis if he is always referred to as president and not by his name. Only if the president has a name and individuals refer to him by this name can he be known personally and become a friend, and then can a relationship develop. A relationship cannot develop with a nebulous or vague or distant office, but only with someone that can be identified with on a personal basis.

The correct reference to our supreme creator should be *Yahweh* Elohim or *Yahweh* Deity, much like referring to the original supreme ruler of America as President Washington. This phrase is the correct manner that *Yahweh* God wants to be referred to and so is used in Scripture. The Hebrew *adonai*, translated as LORD is not the name of the supreme deity. It is His capacity and is equivalent to the English master. Referring to

*Yahweh* God solely as *Adonai* has the same evasive impact as using "God," it does not convey the ability to identify with the supreme deity as does the use of His personal name. The term *Yahweh Elohim* is used about 540 times in Scripture, and is commonly translated as LORD God.

The terms "name of God," or "the name of the Lord," or a variant forms, is utilized in Scripture at lest 110 times. Ex 15:3. Ps 83:8. Ex 6:3. Translators of popular and contemporary versions have failed to identify the supreme deity correctly by changing His identity: He no longer has a personal name, but only a title. This obliteration of His name and subsequent use of a title deliberately locates the supreme deity at a distance and defines Him as vague and nebulous. This intent is the direct purpose of the translators, and in order to easily be able to divide or redefined Him as a triune godhead. Translators replacing His personal identity with some cognitive title deprive Him of a personal identity. This is especially noticeable in the Greek Septuagint, where the name *Yahweh* is rendered as *Kyrios*, Lord, the equivalent of the Hebrew *Adonai*.

In OT eras, individuals publicly "Announced the name *Yahweh*." This is the proper rendering of "Call on the name of the Lord". Gen 4:26. Abraham called on the name *Yahweh*. Gen 12:8. David likewise. Ps 116:4. Others proclaimed the name *Yahweh*. Deut 32:3. David wanted to build a house for the name *Yahweh*. 1 King 5:3. The enigma of Bible translation lies in the conflict of calling upon the name of someone and then replacing that name with a title.

Some literal Bible translations render YHWH as *Jehovah* (Young's Literal, American Revised of 1901); or as *Yahweh* (Rotherham's Emphasized Bible and the New Jerusalem Bible).

## ANTHROPOMORPHISM AND ANTHROPOPATHISM

The included description of *Yahweh* God scattered throughout Scripture often attributes to Him the characteristics of created humanity, as well as the better attributes of creatures. Even though *Yahweh* God is a spirit without form or gender, such descriptions are provided by inspired authors of Scripture. The 2 terms of the title of this section deal with the application of physical characteristics and non-physical characteristics of a person to a non-material entity. The purpose of inspired authors is easy enough to understand: For the individual to be able to identify with a superior entity residing in another realm in terms of themselves. This identification of characteristics between a spirit entity and human would bring the deity close to his created humanity.

> Ex 6:6. Num 11:23. *Yahweh* God is described as having an outstretched and strong arm.
> Ex 9:9. *Yahweh* God has a hand. 1 Sam 12:15. Ps 75:8.
> Gen 6:8. *Yahweh* God has eyes to see goodness in certain individuals. Ps 34:15.
> 1 King 16:25. *Yahweh* God has eyes to see evil in certain individuals.
> Ps 5:21. *Yahweh* God sees all that occurs in the life of His created humanity.
> Lev 24:12. *Yahweh* God has a mind with which to think. Rom 11:34. 1 Cor 2:16.
> Ex 4:14. *Yahweh* God becomes angry from violation of His law by His people. Josh 7:1. Jer 4:8.
> Jer 50:15, 28. *Yahweh* God takes vengeance against the wicked. Jer 51:11.
> Pr 3:11-12. *Yahweh* God disciplines His children in the same manner as a legitimate and loving parent. Heb 12:5-7. Deut 8:5.
> Ex 19:4. *Yahweh* God carried the people of Israel on the wings of an eagle in their exodus from Egypt.

These are just a few isolated examples of attributing physical and emotional human traits to the supreme deity *Yahweh* God in order for created humanity to be able to identity with Him and so feel close to Him.

There are 2 apparitions of *Yahweh* God in Scripture that are difficult but explainable. Both of these occurred in His appearance to Moses. The first is in Ex 24:9-11. The covenant between *Yahweh* God and Israel is instituted in verses 6-7. Then the elders ascend mount Horeb with Moses to personally meet with the entity with whom they concluded this covenant. In this passage elders of Israel ate and drank in the presence of the God of Israel. This was a covenant meal with both parties present. To the general public *Yahweh* God revealed Himself in the thunder, lightning, smoke, trumpet and earthquake as the indication of His presence and majesty. But to a private few, He manifested Himself in some type of semi-material or ghost-like figure. Since *Yahweh* God is spirit, this appearance was made in a manner the balance of elders could perceive His personal presence. *Yahweh* God as a spirit migrated from the realm of spirit, heaven, and manifested Himself in this perceivable form, to be recorded for future generations. All would know with Whom their fathers concluded the covenant at Horeb.

The second apparition is that of Ex 33:17-23. In this apparition similar to the one above *Yahweh* God appeared in a semi-material form, just enough for Moses to acknowledge the immediate presence of *Yahweh* God. He hid behind a rock on the side of a cliff while Moses walked by, seeing His person but not actually seeing His face. Moses could not have seen His face anyway. *Yahweh* God being a spirit has no face. A face is human for earthly identity and identification. This is why *Yahweh* God told Moses he could not see His face. What would Moses see? *Yahweh* God transcends earthly identify or identification. He cannot have an earthly face.

## SPIRIT OF *YAHWEH* GOD

The one word Spirit is used in the English language to describe a myriad of functional entities and energies in heaven and on earth. *Yahweh* God is spirit, and He possesses a spirit that is omnipresent. The messengers are spirit. There is a spirit that causes life in the material realm, a spirit of animation. Even the mind or mental capacity of a human is termed spirit in Scripture. The New Testament repeated speaks of Holy Spirit. This use of a single word to apply to many areas and facets likewise causes difficulty in definition. Throughout this treatise the variations and types of spirit will be individually discussed.

Holy Spirit is that living and active spirit from *Yahweh* God which is the transition and connection between heaven and believing humanity. It is part of His consecrated nature and divine energy that emanates from His person to enliven with a divine impulse those believing in Him. Holy Spirit is that animating power of the living *Yahweh* God that migrates from *Yahweh* God in His divine realm of spirit and into the body of believing humanity in the created universe. Holy Spirit is not the spirit of animation residing in all living creation: this is an enlivening of the body. Holy Spirit transcends the human spirit of animation and witnesses to the realm of spirit and testifies to the nature of *Yahweh* God. Holy Spirit is the presence in a believing human of an attribute of *Yahweh* God.

The euphemisms of Holy Spirit are many in Scripture and all pertain to the same: Spirit of *Yahweh* (i.e. spirit of the LORD) or Spirit of holiness, in the OT; Spirit of God and Spirit of Jesus the Anointed, or plainly Spirit of Messiah, in the NT. Holy Spirit is the presence of the living God in our world. *Yahweh* God has always had a presence in the material world in the human body of believers, and it is through this Spirit which emanates out of Him that His presence is felt and provided for created humanity.

By revelation Holy Spirit inspires. It is the message of *Yahweh* God to prophets and those capable of receiving revelation from Him, including apostles and others noted in Scripture. The living essence of *Yahweh* God migrates into our material realm and fills the body of believers. This is the Holy Spirit of Scripture. This has occurred regularly beginning with the progenitors Adam and Eve and in every generation to the present. Not all are noted in Scripture, only a few such as the schools of prophets of Elisha's era or the apostolic community. Holy Spirit emanates out of *Yahweh* God and materializes in the baptism of Spirit. It becomes encouragement, strength, and comfort for His people.

Holy Spirit is not a distinct entity or independent from *Yahweh* God in respect, and is not a facet or portion of Him; neither is it a separate person comprising an indivisible part of Him. Holy Spirit is His living essence that appears in created humanity and resides in believers, whenever and wherever *Yahweh* God decides. Like *Yahweh* God Himself, Holy Spirit is genderless. It has no attributes of its own, because it emanates from *Yahweh* God as His essence. The attributes noted in Scripture pertaining to Holy Spirit are a reflection of the attributes of *Yahweh* God Himself, since it is through His Holy Spirit that He reveals Himself to His believers. Holy Spirit has no form, personality, mind, thoughts or character of its own, other than that of *Yahweh* God. Properly Holy Spirit should be referred to as "It" in Scripture rather than "He," since Holy Spirit is not a distinct creature or entity with gender, but an invisible arm of the nature of *Yahweh* God.

Holy Spirit is to be experienced by being "in the Spirit" as were the prophets and apostles and believers of Bible times. The error in defining Holy Spirit as a person of a triune Deity by theologians, philosophers and scholars results from the lack or deprivation of the baptism of Spirit. A person immersed into Holy Spirit experiences the living essence of *Yahweh* God Himself, the pledge of our inheritance, the power of our resurrection from death, a revelation and witness of heaven the origin of Holy Spirit. A lack of this experience results in an incorrect interpretation.

These have an inability to compare spiritual items with spiritual. Holy Spirit baptism is the experience of the true believer in *Yahweh* God and His Son Jesus leading to a proper knowledge of deity and the realm of spirit and the interaction between these two arenas.

## *YAHWEH* GOD AS SOLE SOURCE

If there is an attitude that is noticeable in the saints from the age it is the acknowledgement that *Yahweh* God is sole source. He is the source and responsible party of all that occurs on earth, whether natural elements, birth, death, and the various tragedies and blessings that surface in a person's life. There was no room in the life of the ancient saints for supernatural mythological entities that were identified with the elements or disease or death or blessing. There was no devil or satan as a genuine spirit entity that tempted individuals and led them to criminal activity.

Hannah the mother of Samuel likewise concluded the same in 1 Sam 2:6-7, and so did Eliphaz the friend of Job in Job 5:18. *Yahweh* God Himself claimed responsibility for the congenital handicaps of a person. Ex 4:11. *Yahweh* God adamantly states the he is the source of all success, as well as the source of vengeance and penalty against the criminal. Deut 32:39. Is 45:7. Amos 3:6.

The saints in ancient times acknowledged that *Yahweh* God was the source of both success and failure, blessing and curse, benefit and tragedy. But He was not to be blamed or charged with injustice. As the supreme deity all His effort on earth occurred according to the council of His own will. Eph 1:11. His judgments are just and proper. Rev 15:3. Ps 145:17. *Yahweh* God was never the one to be charged with some injustice as a result of what occurred on earth. Some did charge *Yahweh* God with injustice, as Job did in Job 12:13-25, but to no avail.

A parallel event is noted in 1 Kings 22:5-23. This lying spirit in the mouths of some 400 prophets of *Yahweh* God only confirmed the attitude that both kings already had in order for them to face their penalty. They were beyond the point of any repentance. Ahab was to die to answer with his own life the life of Naboth, for whose death he and his wife Jezebel were responsible. 1 King 21:17-19. Jezebel died in a hideous manner sometime later. Both of their premature deaths fulfilled the prophecy of Elijah.

*Yahweh* God was the source of the just penalty of these individuals and many more and solely because of the crimes they willingly committed against Israel. Likewise *Yahweh* God is the source of all blessing and benefit on earth unto those obedient and faithful to Him.

## SONS OF GOD

There are 2 classes or sorts of creation or entities within the realm of spirit. The first are the sons of God; the second are the Messengers. Both are spirit: formless, genderless, immaterial and ethereal since they are entities of heaven. The proper translation of *malak* in the Hebrew, and *aggelos* in the Greek, is messenger. (At some later date the Greek word *aggelos* was transliterated into the English Angel in Bible translations at the discretion of the translators. Rotherham in his Emphasized Bible correctly and throughout renders these terms as messenger.) The difference between the 2 classes are primarily in generation, and the secondary reason is that of purpose. One is a product of *Yahweh* God, the other is a creation. *Yahweh* God is Father of the sons of God, while He is creator of Messengers.

The difference in generation of the 2 classes has a material comparison. A married couple through sexual union can produce a child just like themselves: of the same nature - flesh, same features – human, and same form. The same married couple can also take some pre-existing material and build some operable equipment, work of art, structure, etc. Both classes are creations of the married couple, but the former is derived of the identical substance and nature of the couple and evolves from the womb of the mother, while the latter is manufactured or assembled.

The sons of God are similar to the former class. Although genderless and not a product of a union, they have nevertheless evolved or emanated directly out of *Yahweh* God. They have the same nature as their Father *Yahweh* God and are made of the same substance. The concept is difficult to grasp because the human mind cannot visualize a spirit entity who is a genderless parent give birth or cause another spirit entity to emanate. In this case the parent is *Yahweh* God, and the offspring he engenders and produces are His sons, although in reality they are genderless. These have the ability of independent thought and action as part of the nature of their Father inherited by them. They are in the fullness of the image and likeness of their parent *Yahweh* God. This concept also applies to Emmanuel, who is Jesus, son of *Yahweh* God.

Who among the sons of God is like *Yahweh*? Ps 89:5.

Sons of God are also mentioned in Job 1:6, 2:1, and 38:7, as residing in heaven and having access to *Yahweh* God their Father.

## MESSENGERS AND ANGELS

The latter class are the Messengers or Angels. *Yahweh* God created them as entities out of His pre-existent spirit. Although they are spirit beings, they would be considered manufactured entities and then programmed to automatically fulfill the will and counsel of *Yahweh* God. They have no ability to think or act independently of *Yahweh* God their Creator. They are created as needed to fulfill the assigned task and then retired. They are referred to as spirits.

Who makes His messengers spirits, and His servants flames of fire. Heb 1:8 quote from Ps 104:4.

A few examples of spirits manifesting as messengers follow:

Gen 16:7-14. In this passage a pregnant Hagar flees from her mistress and Sarah. In the desert Hagar meets with a messenger of *Yahweh*. The messenger is a materialization of a spirit entity in the appearance of a human, and conveys a personal message of *Yahweh* God to Hagar, for her to return to Sarah. He also relays to her the promise of a large progeny.

Gen 18:1-33. The portrayal here is 3 messengers meeting with Abraham and Sarah. They have the appearance of humans. Gen 18:22. The chapter and meeting is divided in to 2 parts: First is the promise of a son to the aged couple; the second is the destruction of Sodom. A point to be noticed here is that the messengers of *Yahweh* possess His name. Gen 18:1 reads, "*Yahweh* appeared to [Abraham]." These entities from heaven, composed of the spirit of *Yahweh* God, speak in the first person. After 2 of the messengers depart for Sodom in verse 22, the third speaks in the first person, "And *Yahweh* said." Gen 18:26. These messengers speak on behalf of the Supreme Deity. This phenomenon is mentioned in the following passage.

Behold I send my messenger before you, to guard you on the way and to bring you to the place which I have prepared. Give heed to him and hearken to his voice, do not rebel against him, for he will not pardon your violation; for My name is in him. Ex 23:20-21.

This is the same situation as with the messenger with Abraham; the name of *Yahweh* God was in him, meaning that he could speak in the first person as *Yahweh* God because he spoke as His regent or representative. The messenger was the means by which *Yahweh* God personally conveyed His word and instruction unto the people. The messenger was the earthly mouthpiece of *Yahweh* God.

Ex 3:1-16. This is the famous burning bush passage where the messenger of *Yahweh* (angel of the LORD) appears to Moses. So he is called in verse 2. Later in the passage the entity identifies himself as the God of the patriarchs, *Yahweh*: verses 6-7. Now it is *Yahweh* God speaking to Moses. As in the above occurrence, the messenger is a spirit entity who is the mouthpiece of *Yahweh* God materializing in the presence of Moses to convey a personal message.

In another respect the messenger of *Yahweh* is much like the Spirit of truth which is to be sent by Jesus and which proceeds from *Yahweh* God. John 15:26.

When the Spirit of truth comes, he will guide you unto all the truth; for he will not speak on his own authority, but whatever he hears he will speak and he will declare to you the things that are to come. John 16:13.

The pronoun is masculine as so translated as "he," although the Spirit is genderless as are the messengers genderless. The Holy Spirit can be equated with the messenger of *Yahweh* speaking through the person of a prophet. He can likewise speak in the first person as *Yahweh* God, since the Spirit of truth is utilizing this person as Its mouthpiece.

## RELATED MESSENGERS

Other manifestations of heavenly messengers are mentioned in Scripture. The heavenly Messengers are ministering Spirit-entities who appear in some apparition or form to assist the believers in times of crises or need.

Appearing in the form of a human, they were the materialization of a spirit entity as the mouthpiece of *Yahweh* God, to convey a message in the first person, having His name in them.

> Gen 28:12. Jacob's dream of the ladder reaching to heaven with messengers ascending and descending on it. Jacob refers to this incident later in his life in Gen 48:5.
> Gen 32:24-30. Such was the man who wrestled with Jacob during the night.
> Josh 5:13-15. The commander of the army of *Yahweh* who appeared to Joshua.
> Judg 13:1-21. The messenger who promised the birth of Samson to his parents.
> Luke 1:11-20. Gabriel and his message to Zechariah.
> Luke 1:26-37. Gabriel and his message to Mary of Nazareth.
> Acts 12:6-11. A divine messenger appears to Peter apostle in prison. He opens the prison and city gates for Peter and leads him to safety.
> Acts 27:23-24. A messenger appeared to Paul apostle during the night and informed him that they would be delivered from ship wreak.
> Heb 13:2. There were occasions when *Yahweh* God sent a messenger as a test of the hospitality of those who claimed to be believers.
> Rev 19:9-10. An angel appeared to John apostle with words for John to write. John wanted to worship the messenger but he would not allow John, telling John that he was likewise a fellow servant of God.
> Rev 22:8-9. John apostle a second time attempts to worship the messenger revealing to him these secrets of God, but was not permitted.
> Dan 3:25,28. When Nebuchadnezzar looked into the fiery furnace to see what he thought were the charred remains of the 3 young men of Israel, he saw them alive along with another entity he described as "like a son of the gods." This entity was later defined by Nebuchadnezzar as being the Messenger (angel) of the God of the 3 Israelite young men.[7] To protect and assure His believers under duress and persecution, *Yahweh* God sent a messenger from heaven and who materialized in a form visible to the 3 young men and to the King of Babylon. Apparently the Messenger had some supernatural form or distinguishing characteristic for Nebuchadnezzar to identity him as "a

---

[7] There is no evidence to state that this was Jesus, as some commentators claim.

son of the gods." (This is in contradistinction to the form seen in the vision of Dan 7:13, which is described as a son of humanity, or human.)

There are several passages in Scripture where the Hebrew *malak* refers to humans.

2 Chron 36:15-16, Obo 1:1. The prophets as messengers of *Yahweh* God.
Eccl 5:6. A human messenger.
Is 42:19. Israel as the messenger.
Hag 1:13. Haggai is messenger of *Yahweh* God.
Mal 2:7. Priest is messenger of *Yahweh* God.
Mal 3:1. Matt 11:10. John the Baptizer is the messenger.

Interesting to note that the word *malak* is used in both Gen 32:1 and 3; but translators have rendered it as angels in verse 1, while messengers in verse 3. It is just as easy to understand the *malak* in verse 1 to be earthly Messengers sent by *Yahweh* God. It is by interpretation whether to apply *malak* to a heavenly Messenger or earthly one.

The Bible book of Malachi may not be actually someone with that name, but the meaning of the word being Messenger as the title.

## EMANATION OF THE SON OF YAHWEH GOD

*Yahweh* God has a son, and his name is Emmanuel.

Immanuel or Jesus is not unlike the spirit entities termed sons of God; however he is distinct from the messengers or the ministering spirits. He is a new entity evolving or emanating out of His Father. The comparison is with physical childbirth, the child inheriting the identical nature of the parents. Jesus is homo-ousian with his father *Yahweh* God, meaning of the same substance or essence - spirit.

There are 2 passages to note regarding this. One is the Messianic Psalm 2, also utilized by Paul apostle. The second is the Septuagint and Aramaic reading of another Messianic Psalm.

He (*Yahweh*) said to me, "You are My son, today I have begotten you. Ps 2:7. Acts 13:33.

Out of the womb before the morning star I gave you birth. Ps 110:3 (LXX, Vulgate. Syriac).
Arrayed in the beauty of holiness from the womb, I have begotten thee as a child from the ages. Ps 110:10. (Aramaic translation by George Lamsa).

John apostle calls Jesus "the only begotten son." John 1:18. And in the same gospel later Jesus refers to himself as "The only begotten son." The indication here is that Jesus is the only one of the sons of *Yahweh* God who materialized or incarnated as a human.

Never once in Scripture does Jesus refer to himself as *Yahweh* God or as a facet or person part of a triune deity. The term son of God is used 45 times in the NT to refer to Jesus. There is throughout the NT a vein of expression that Jesus the son has a distinct and conscious existence from *Yahweh* God his father. That Jesus was born before other spirit entities is definitely stated.

The beginning of the creation of God. Rev 3:14.
The first born of all creation. Col 1:15.

One verse refers to his appearance on earth:

And again when He brings the first born into the world, he says, "Let all God's messengers worship him." Heb 1:6.

The Gk. *oikoumenos* is used in this verse and not the Gk. *kosmos*. The *oikoumenos* is the inhabited earth or land. This reference in Hebrews is to the birth of Jesus in Bethlehem. At that time heaven's messengers were summoned to worship him. Luke 2:13.

## JESUS SON OF YAHWEH GOD

The proper name for Jesus is actually Joshua, which is the English equivalent of the Hebrew *Yeshua*, and the equivalent of the Greek *Iesus*, or Jesus transliterated into English. *Yeshua* is the name that his parents gave him at birth, after the OT hero. But because the standard is already established for his name as Jesus in the English language, instead of the proper Joshua, I will continue to use it here. It was also a very popular name in Israel, such as Jesus son of Sirach, the Jewish sage, and Bar-Jesus, a Jewish false-prophet of Cyprus. Act 13:6.

Emmanuel is actually the proper name for Jesus son of God, as he is God with us, in accord with the prophetic words of Is 7:14. This would be applicable for his personal name for all ages. The name Jesus was primarily for his earthly career to save his people, the nation Israel, from the consequences of their sins. Matt 1:21,25.

His popular designation is Jesus the Christ, *Christus* in Greek, which means Anointed, or Messiah transliterated from the Hebrew *Yeshua ha Mashiah*. This may be difficult for the reader from this point on, as I will use the actual meaning or translation into English of the Greek word Anointed, which is Christ. The reason is that Christ was created by the translators of the NT from Greek into English rather than using it correct translation, which is Anointed. The same for the use of the Hebrew word *ha-Mashiah*, transliterated as Messiah instead of properly translating the word as Anointed, and so it is translated in the entirety of the OT, except in 2 passages in the Book of Daniel. 9:25-26, and Messiah in the NT: John 1:41, 4:25.

(This is the reason why in the balance of this book the words Messiah and Christ will be rendered as Anointed, (except in quotations by the Apologists or Ecclesiastical Fathers) as this is the proper translated of this Hebrew and Greek word. This will be awkward to the reader, but sorry this is true and correct to the original and actual meaning of these words in their original language.)

In light of the description above of the birth of the sons of God, Jesus was the first to be born of all his brethren. Rom 8:29. Because he was the first-born he had a special or greater portion, if this be possible, of the image and likeness of his Father. When the term only-begotten is used by Jesus referring to himself, John 3:16, this applies to his birth on earth. He was the only son of *Yahweh* God to be incarnated as a human. Jesus also possessed the fullness of the divinity of his Father. Col 2:9. The fact that *Yahweh* God is his Father is clear.

> We always thank God, the Father of our *Adonai*, Jesus the Anointed, when we pray for you. Col 1:3.

John apostle's words as follows are important here:

No one has ever seen God. The only son, who is in the bosom of the Father, he has made him known. John 1:17.

To simplify, Jesus has a divine nature because he is of the same nature and substance as his Father as also the other sons of God.

## JESUS SUBJECT TO A SUPERIOR DEITY

Because *Yahweh* God is Supreme Deity all that exists in the created realms, both heaven and earth, is subject to him. All His creation renders to Him honor and praise and loyalty.

> Worthy are You, our Lord and God, to receive glory and honor and power, for You created all and by Your will they exist and were created. Rev 4:11.

The sons of *Yahweh* God likewise are under subjection to Him, not only as to a Father but also as Supreme Deity. Emmanuel, or Jesus, is likewise subject to *Yahweh* God as Deity. This is mentioned several times in Scripture by both Paul apostle and Peter apostle, and by Jesus himself.

> That together you may with one voice glorify the God and Father of our Lord Jesus the Anointed. Rom 15:6.
> Blessed be the God and Father of our Lord Jesus the Anointed, the Father of mercies and God of all comfort. 2 Cor 1:3.
> The God and Father of the Lord Jesus, he who is blessed forever, knows that I do not lie. 2 Cor 11:31.
> Blessed be the God and Father of our Lord Jesus the Anointed. Eph 1:4.
> That the God of our Lord Jesus the Anointed, the Father of glory. Eph 1:17.
> Blessed be the God and Father of our Lord Jesus the Anointed. 1 Pet 1:3.
> "I am ascending to my Father and your Father, to my God and your God," said Jesus to Mary Magdalene. John 20:17.

Jesus does have a god to whom he is subject and whom he must venerate. The above passages by Paul and Peter apostles were composed after the ascension of Jesus to heaven. The personal stature of Jesus in heaven is described in the following.

> He is the radiance of His glory and the exact impress of His nature (hypostasis). Heb 1:3.

Jesus is an image of the glory of His Father and maintains this resemblance. He possesses the hypostasis of *Yahweh* God, His very substance and nature. Yet Jesus is still subservient to his Father both in heaven and on earth today and always.

## THE RELATIONSHIP BETWEEN FATHER AND SON

The relationship between the Father *Yahweh* God and His son Jesus is clearly defined in many passages of Scripture, which will be here discussed. The noticeable relationship between the 2 is that one is superior and the other is inferior. The superior *Yahweh* God is the entity who gives birth, delegates, sends, bestows, commands, teaches, sets the example, consecrates, resurrects, is self-sufficient, and who is Supreme Deity. The inferior in the relationship is Jesus His son. He is born; he is delegated to; he receives, accepts, is commanded, is taught, is consecrated, needs a example to emulate, is resurrected from death, is dependant on *Yahweh* God His Father for his existence, and is subject to Deity above himself. The relationship between the 2 indicates a subjection of one unto the other; an obedience of one to the other. The one born was dependant on the one giving birth for existence; the one sent is subject to the sender; the one delegated to is subject to the one who delegates; the one who receives or accepts receives and accepts because he originally lacks these items; the one commanded is under authority, and must fulfill the command and without excuse or debate; the one who is taught needs teaching because of a lack of original education, and needs an example because of original incapability of correct conduct and action; and etc. Of course, this or any relationship can only occur between 2 independent and distinct entities.

A few of the passages dealing with this relationship are as follows:

Matt 24:36. Mark 13:32. The son does not know the time of the end, neither do the messengers (Angels). Only the Father knows.

John 3:16-17. *Yahweh* God gave His son to the world and sent His son into the world to deliver it.

John 3:35. *Yahweh* God gave all things to His son.

John 5:19. *Yahweh* God set the example of action for His son.

John 5:22. *Yahweh* God has delegated trial and sentence or reward to His son in order the honor attributed to *Yahweh* God as judge and executor would likewise be attributed to His son. Part of his education would have been for Jesus to learn to become a just judge.

John 5:26. *Yahweh* God is self-sufficient for His own existence. The son was granted this capability of being self-sufficient by His Father. Earlier the son was dependant on His Father for his permanence, but then received this capability of being self-sufficient from His Father. John 6:57.

John 5:30, 6:38. The son has his own will independent of his Father. The son however has abandoned his own will in favor of fulfilling the will of his Father. All that Jesus did was a fulfillment of his Father's intent and desire. His own was set aside in favor of his Father's. Matt 26:39.

John 6:46. The son viewed his Father in the realm of spirit, heaven. The son saw the characteristics and activities of his Father. Because Jesus saw the fullness of his Father he can disclose and proclaim his Father to the people.

John 6:57, 7:28. It is *Yahweh* God who sent His son. The decision to enter the physical world was not the decision of the son, but the decision of the Father.

John 7:16, 12:49-50. Jesus taught what was given to him by his Father; he did not teach what he derived on his own.

John 8:29. The efforts of Jesus were to accomplish that which would be pleasing to his Father.

John 10:36. It was *Yahweh* God who consecrated His son, anointed him with the Holy Spirit for him to possess the sanctification necessary to fulfill his ministry.

John 10:38. *Yahweh* God in Jesus and Jesus in *Yahweh* God indicates a harmony and agreement of attitude that pervaded both father and son. Each had identical thinking and intent and conclusion as the others. For this reason Jesus could act as agent on behalf of *Yahweh* God.

John 14:28. Jesus acknowledges the superiority of His Father *Yahweh* God, and the inferiority of himself in the relationship, and acknowledges his subjection to his Father.

John 17:17. *Yahweh* God is supreme deity even to His son Jesus. The son must also revere and pay homage to *Yahweh* God, not only as father but also as deity.

Acts 2:24, 31, 3:15. The son was resurrected from death by His Father. Also Eph 1:20.

Acts 5:31. It was *Yahweh* God who exalted His son making him leader and savior after his resurrection from death and ascension to heaven.

1 Cor 1:30. God made Jesus our wisdom, rectitude, sanctification and redemption.

1 Cor 15:24. The time will come at the consummation when Jesus will complete his delegated work and deliver the kingdom to his Father. The kingdom at this time will have attained the perfection and fullness desired of *Yahweh* God.

1 Cor 15:28. At the consummation the subjection of the son Jesus and all perfected creation will reach its pinnacle.

2 Cor 5:18-19. God was in Jesus reconciling the world to Himself.

2 Cor 5:21. God made Jesus to be sin (sacrifice), who knew no sin.

Phil 2:9-11. *Yahweh* God exalted his Son Jesus after accomplishing on earth the task delegated to him. He gave him a name to which all should subject themselves and to which all must give homage. Confessing that Jesus is Master is to the credit of *Yahweh* God his Father.

Col 1:15, Heb 1:3. Jesus is the image of his Father. The image is not the same as the original. An image is another item that is a replica. Jesus was not the same entity as his Father. He was a reflection of all that the Father consists of. Note also 2 Cor 4:4.

Col 1:19, 2:9. The fullness of *Yahweh* God resided in Jesus.

Heb 1:4. With the ascension of Jesus to heaven he became superior to the messengers, now having acquired his superior rank.

Heb 3:2. *Yahweh* God appointed Jesus to fulfill certain responsibilities, and he was faithful to Him in this appointment.

Heb 9:24. Jesus appeared before his Father as the sacrifice for the sins of the people. *Yahweh* God accepted Jesus as the sacrifice for sin.

1 John 5:18. Jesus was born of God.

Rev 1:18. Jesus died. He had the capability of dying. Now with his exaltation, he is alive for evermore, no longer subject to termination of his life.

Rev 2:21. Earlier Jesus was not sitting on the throne with *Yahweh* God his Father. Now with his victory, his Father has granted him to sit alongside Him on His throne. Also Eph 1:20.

The capacity of Jesus mentioned in most of these passages refers to his residence in heaven, in the realm of spirit prior to his incarnation. A few deal with the years of his life on earth after his $30^{th}$ birthday when he began his ministry. In heaven it was his Father *Yahweh* God who instructed him, delegated to him, sent him, commanded him, taught him, and set the example for him. The relationship defined in Scripture is such: Jesus was inferior to and subject to the authority of His Father *Yahweh* God. Realizing this and being an independent entity distinct from his Father, Jesus accepted the command and delegated responsibility. To fulfill the command He had to abandon his own will and intentions in favor of his Father's will and intentions for him. Jesus subjected himself to the authority of his Father and disclosed this to Jews and his apostles during his ministry.

The same interpretation can be applied to the resurrection of Jesus from death. Jesus did not resurrect himself. Although as son of *Yahweh* God he could have arranged it. John 10:18. However he did not utilize his power in this situation. Again he relieved himself of his divine authority in order to die the death of all men. Jesus depended on his Father to resurrect him. Had *Yahweh* God decided not to resurrect him (only for argument sake), Jesus would have remained in this state of termination of life.

John 6:27. The seal on a document in ancient times was equivalent to the present day use of a corporate seal on a contract or the stamp of a professional engineer on a drawing. The stamp authenticates and validates the document or drawings and give it an authority of its own, to be guaranteed by the corporate officers or by the professional engineer. So it is with Jesus. *Yahweh* God has placed His personal corporate stamp upon him giving him an authority of his own guaranteed by his Father.

## ACCUSATION OF THE PHARISEES

Statements of Jesus during his ministry indicate an equality with his Father. These must be interpreted together with the passages above and not separate from them.

Jesus called *Yahweh* God his father. He did not call himself God or call himself the Father or supreme deity or a facet of an indivisibly divided divinity. John 5:17-18. When Jews heard this statement the equality with *Yahweh* God was that of authority. Jesus claimed to have the same authority as *Yahweh* God because he was Messiah, the anointed of *Yahweh* God and thereby rightful heir and agent. The topic in John 5:18 dealt with Sabbath observance, not theology. As far as the Pharisees were concerned, Jesus worked on the day of rest. He justified his work on that day because of it being an act of charity or philanthropy, and *Yahweh* God would have conducted Himself likewise. This was a violation of the 4$^{th}$ commandment according to Pharisees, but which Jesus felt was permissible. Pharisees felt this reinterpretation of Sabbath observance belonged only to *Yahweh* God, who instituted the day and commandment. A person who took the authority to alter or modify it claimed equal authority with *Yahweh* God who originally instituted it. For this reason Pharisees concluded and accused Jesus of placing himself on an equal level of authority as *Yahweh* God.

The accusation of Jews mentioned in John 10:33, that Jesus made himself "God" must be understood in the context of the conversation. Jesus in his ministry had the same authority as did *Yahweh* God, speaking on His behalf as His agent, since he was the Anointed. This was the rebuke of Jesus to the Pharisees, quoting Ps 82:1,6. David refers to judges in authority as gods, and the same would apply to the Anointed.

The facts of the relationship should be accepted as written and in the context of the conversations between the Anointed and Pharisees. The unity of the person of Jesus in the realm of spirit and in the incarnation is not a mystery, but is clearly defined by Scripture. The passages quoted witness to this subordination of Jesus unto His Father as the result of their relationship between them, that of father and son. The unity between the 2 provided the Anointed the capability to act as agent on behalf of His Father. This was the argument of Pharisees against him. The discussions were not of a theological basis dealing with persons of a multi-faceted indivisible deity, but with the right of the Anointed to speak and act as agent of *Yahweh* God.

## UNITY OF FATHER AND SON

The cohesive unity and harmony between *Yahweh* God and Jesus is described as a unity.

I am my father are one. John 10:30.

This short statement does not deal with a unity of persons into an indivisible entity, but is a continuation of the passage beginning at John 10:25. Jesus spoke with the Pharisees regarding his right and privilege to act as agent on behalf of *Yahweh* God because he is the Anointed. The thinking, that is, attitude of both father and son was identical on every matter. This Jesus stated in the words,

"The father is in me and I am in the father." John 10:38.

A physical correlation to this is community law of a married couple. (In California either spouse has legal right to make legal decisions on behalf of both of them, and the other spouse is obligated to follow suit without question. This is similar to joint bank accounts, where both have equal access to deposit, withdraw, and decide on allocation of funds. Either spouse can make a legally binding contract on behalf of both of them. The wife can speak on behalf of her husband and the husband can do likewise because they are legally married.) The Bible considers a legally married couple one person. Gen 2:24. Even though they are 2 distinct and separate entities, the Bible refers to them as one person. This is not because of the physical union, but due to a psychological and intellectual union and harmony that develops as a result of the marriage. A husband and wife should know each other well enough that one can act as agent for another and the other trusting the decision without doubt.

In a spiritual sense the same concept can apply to a father and son. The example provided by the Jewish sages is the following:

Though his father die, yet he is as though not dead: for he has left one behind him who is like himself. Sirach 30:4.

In this passage of Jewish wisdom, this son inherited all the non-material qualities of his father, that when the father passed away the son continued in his footsteps, having identical attitude, intent, and intellect as did the father. The Pharisees were no doubt familiar with the passage and so were able to make the connection very easy when Jesus stated he was son of *Yahweh* God.

This harmony is further mentioned in the following passages.

Holy father, keep them in your name that You have given me, that they may be one even as we are one. John 17:11.

That they may be one even as you Father are in me and I am in You, that they also may be in us, so that the world may believe that You have sent me. The glory which You have given me I have given to them that they may be one even as we are one. I in them and You in me that they may become perfectly one, so that the world may know that You have sent me and have loved them even as You have loved me. John 17:21-23.

This is a psychological and intellectual harmony and cohesion between the apostles and *Yahweh* God their father, learning about the Father from Jesus to such an extent that a familiarity forms. They know the Father so well that they can speak on His behalf. The apostles knowing *Yahweh* God so well as the type of son mentioned above would be a witness of Jesus as sent by *Yahweh* God. This spiritual union is the unity or "one" that is described in this prayer.

Paul apostle attained this unity or "one" with the Anointed Jesus where he said:

But we have the mind of the Anointed. 1 Cor 2:16.

He felt that a person can draw so close to Jesus, know him so well, possess his Spirit, that a person can think in the same manner that Jesus would think.

## SON OF MAN

A lack of Hebrew and Aramaic scholarship affects the proper understanding of many words and phrases of Scripture. This is especially true pertaining to the gospel. As mentioned earlier, Jesus and his disciples spoke Aramaic in general conversation, and especially Jesus with the crowds and individuals that sought his advise. In the synagogue and temple Jesus would have spoken Hebrew. The gospels as we know them are actually a translation from the Aramaic and Hebrew and into Greek. To properly understand the message and teaching of Jesus the original Aramaic is required. The term "son of man" will be discussed at this time.

> *Bar-Nasha* is an Aramaic word derived from *bar* which means son and *nasha* man. *Bar-Nasha* means son of man. This term is also used to mean mankind, humanity, a man, human being, an ordinary man. When an Oriental declines honors and homage, he says, I do not deserve this honor, I am nothing, I am just a man, a plain working man. (George M. Lamsa, Gospel Light)

The Aramaic *Bar-nasha* used in general conversation means this person or this human. The equivalent term in Hebrew is *ben adam*. It is used to refer to Ezekiel prophet. Eze 2:1, 4:1. The Aramaic term *bar nasha* is used in Dan 7:13 to indicate that the entity seen by Daniel prophet in his vision appeared as a human, in contrast to the beast previously seen and *Yahweh* God sitting on His throne. The equivalent terms in Hebrew and Aramaic for son of man are used 107 times total in the OT, and in every occasion is the equivalent of the English "human being." Both Balaam diviner and David king used the equivalent Hebrew term:

> God is not a man (Heb. *nos*) that He should lie or a son of man (Heb. *ben adam*) that He should repent. Num 23:19.
> What is man that You are mindful of him, and the son of man that You consider him. Heb 2:6 quote from Ps 8:4.

In both these passages the term son of man is used in poetic form to refer to humans.

Since the historical used of *bar nasha* in Scripture is that of human being, the conclusion to be drawn is that Jesus used this term to refer to himself without the use of the word "I". A comparison of gospel texts indicate that Jesus used the term son of man to be understood as referring to himself.

> Who do men say that the son of man is? Matt 16:13.
> Who do people say that I am? Luke 8:18.

Since both passages are translations from the Aramaic and into Greek, Matthew rendered his literally, while Luke in translating into Greek was more direct with the intent of Jesus. It is obvious that this use of the term son of man in the Aramaic world of Jesus was a polite manner of referring to oneself without the specific term "I".

## JOHN 1:1-18

My concept of the interpretation of John 1:1-18, must be understood in terms of the typical audience of the era, how a typical Jew living dispersed in the Roman Empire after the Jewish War would understand it. *Logos* must not be assigned meanings determined by the Greek philosophers or the Hellenistic Jewish philosopher Philo. The reader of the NT must remember that the gospel writers were Jews with a Jewish cultural background, heritage, and an education based on the wisdom of their sages and Rabbis. John apostle was self educated from attending synagogue services over the years. He definitely had some contact with the priests and Rabbis of Jerusalem since he was known by the high priest Caiaphas. John 18:15.

*Logos* has 24 different rendering in the KJV NT. Primarily word, but also: speech, saying, account, matter, rumor, and utterance. The Greek word *logos* is primarily a translation of the Hebrew *dabar*, and occasionally *emer*. The OT utilizes the phrase "Word of the LORD " (*dabar* YHWH) 241 times, and this is predominantly translated in the LXX as *"logos adonai."* *Dabar* is also rendered in the Hebrew as commandment, referring to the 10 Commandments, in Ex 34:28, Deut 4:13, 10:4.

The correct understanding then of the *logos* of John 1 is: The divine instruction of *Yahweh* God communicated to His people Israel through the prophets. The error of Christian commentators is applying a meaning to *logos* based on Greek philosophy and the Jewish Philo. Based on the context of John apostle's gospel, Jesus' purpose was to reveal his Father to the people of Israel, meaning to educate the people in the divine instruction and moral code. This was the word of John 1:1. The proper rendering of the initial passage of John's gospel is as follows:

> Originally was the word, and the word was toward God, and the word was God. The same was originally with God. John 1:1-2. (Based on Rotherham's Emphasized Bible and Knock's Concordant Literal).

The word "originally" can also be rendered "from time immemorial." This refers to the original divine instruction and moral code introduced into the world with the progenitors Adam and Eve. "In the beginning" of human residence, or at the "original" habitation of the newly created earth, did *Yahweh* God educate the initial residents regarding Himself. *Yahweh* God revealed Himself in terms of a moral code and then transmitted to Adam and Eve His divine instruction for their life. The word was directed "toward God." This phrase, the Greek *pros tos theos*, has a correct rendering of "toward God," and not "with God." A study of the use of the Greek *"pros"* will prove its use as a direction: unto (338 times), toward (10 times), to (176 times), in the KJV Bible.

The "all things" of John 1:3 must correlate with life and light. I contend that the "all things" John refers to is the system of divine religion beginning with the sacrificial offering of the sons of Adam and Eve, Cain and Abel. The true religious system of all ages from the fall was instituted by *Yahweh* God as light, meaning divine enlightenment, and life, meaning long term prosperity, joy and longevity on earth. The darkness of John 1:5, refers to false religion, superstition and ignorance of the moral code and divine instruction.

## JESUS AS THE WORD OF GOD

The ministry of Jesus essentially began with his immersion into the water of the Jordan River by John the Baptizer. I contend the entirety of divine instruction was embodied in Jesus of Nazareth.

> And the word became flesh and resided among us. And we gazed upon his glory, a glory as an only-begotten from his Father, full of favor and truth. John 1:14.

When the Holy Spirit descended and settled upon Jesus, it entered his body and filled his soul with the entirety of the dictates, commands, moral code and instruction of *Yahweh* God. Jesus was the true enlightenment bringing to the people of Israel the correct and reliable knowledge of *Yahweh* God his Father and divine instruction for the salvation of their life. Paul apostle correlates the incarnation of the word or divine instruction in Jesus as follows:

In whom are hid all the treasures of wisdom and knowledge. Col 2:3.

The world of John 1:10, is not the entire world, it is the world of John apostle, referring to the Jewish world of Palestine and the dispersion. This Jewish world was created by the promises of *Yahweh* God, by His word ages ago, and which Jewish world refused the message of the embodiment of the same word. To try and apply this section of Scripture to some metaphysical and esoteric *logos* of Plato and Philo and other philosophers departs from the intent of John apostle. He was trying to explain to readers that *Yahweh* God embodied the entirety of His divine instruction and moral code into His son appearing as a human having the name Jesus of Nazareth. Having total possession of the instruction of *Yahweh* God, he expounded it authoritatively and was able to legislate and introduce interpretation of this word to the people. This is why the Pharisees accused Jesus of claiming he was God. John 5:18. Only *Yahweh* God had the authority to legislate new dictates and laws and instruction. For Jesus of Nazareth to do this was blasphemous; he was usurping authority that only belonged to *Yahweh* God. By introducing new interpretations of the law given to Israel by Moses, and abrogating the sacrificial system, priesthood and temple services of this law, Jesus placed himself on the same level of the divine entity who instituted all of this. Jesus was able to do this, and because he was delegated so and was the incarnation of this word.

## *YESHUA* ADONAI

When the Jews of the civilized world gathered in Jerusalem to celebrate Pentecost, on this particular holiday many of them heard the sermon of Peter apostle. As Jews awaiting their Anointed – the Messiah, some of them already accepting Jesus of Nazareth as the Anointed, and others still undecided, they listened intently to the words of Peter.

> For David did not ascend into heaven, but he himself says, "The Lord said to my Lord (*Yahweh* said to my *Adonai*), Sit at my right side until I make your enemies a stool for your feet." Let all the house of Israel therefore know for sure that God has made him our Lord and Christ (*Adonai* and the Anointed), this Jesus whom you crucified. Acts 2:34-35.

The resurrection of Jesus from death and his ascension to heaven was the verification that *Yahweh* their God made Jesus of Nazareth *Adonai* and the Anointed. The Greek *kyrios* used here in the Greek Acts is the equivalent of the Hebrew *Adonai*, both meaning lord or master. The sermon of Peter apostle would have been in Hebrew, or at least in Aramaic with the quotations from Scripture in Hebrew. Peter actually used the words *Adonai* and Messiah in his sermon. The use of the word *Adonai* pertaining to Jesus in based on the Messianic Psalm.

> *Yahweh* says to my *Adonai*, "Sit at my right side until I make your enemies your footstool." Ps 110:1.

The typical Jew listening to Peter apostle that day understood exactly what he meant. The enemies were those who conspired against Jesus and executed him. The victory was his resurrection from death. Jesus of Nazareth was the lord (*Adonai*) to whom David submitted. The balance of the Psalm dealt with the Anointed attaining the priesthood of Melchizedek and ascending the throne of authority over the kingdoms of the world. Jesus of Nazareth was the *Adonai* and the Anointed of Ps 110.

The term repeatedly used in the NT, Lord Jesus Christ, in Hebrew is *Adonai Yeshua ha-Meshiah*. Whenever this term was mentioned, or the reduced form of Lord Jesus or even just Lord, the reference was to Jesus of Nazareth as person spoken of in Ps 110:1. This is how the typical Jew understood these words when spoken by a Jewish Christian. This was the intended meaning conveyed by the apostles when using this term in their letters.

One item in addition to realize is that the typical Greek reader, when he read the appellation "christ," he interpreted this as meaning "anointed," as this was its proper meaning. So the typical Greek reader read Jesus Christ as Jesus the Anointed, which is correct, and so with the Apostle Paul. The use of the term "Christ in you," used by Paul, actually means, the Anointing in you. This is correctly rendered in the following passage:

> But the anointing (*christos*) which you received from him...
> 1 John 2:27

Because the NT was written in Greek, a translation from the Hebrew and Aramaic, all such terms were translated into their equivalent Greek. *Adonai* became *Kyrios* and Messiah (meaning the Anointed) became Christ, and *Yeshua* became Jesus. In Greek, Acts 2:34 reads, "*Kyrios* says to my *kyrios*," which is hardly intelligible. Likewise Matt 22:43. Because the word *Kyrios* was also the translation of YHWH in the OT Greek translation, the apostles to avoid confusion in their NT letters always referred to *Yahweh* God as God or Father.

> Yet for us there is one God, the Father, from whom are all things and for whom we exist, and one Lord, Jesus the Anointed (Hebrew: *Adonai Yeshua* Messiah), through whom are all things and through whom we exist. 1 Cor 8:6.
> Grace, mercy and peace from God the Father and the Anointed Jesus our *Adonai*. 2 Tim 1:2.

The apostles utilized this method of writing in order to distinguish *Yahweh* God from His Son, whom He exalted to be lord and anointed savior unto His people Israel.

## 2. THE ATTRIBUTES OF EARTH

### TIME

The concept of time is well defined in Scripture and the chronology of the ages can be understood by correlating time as we know it in the universe with Scripture.

> Before all time, now and for ever. Jude 25

This verse refers to the existence of *Yahweh* God from before the beginning of time and into the infinite future.

Time as we know it surfaced some 15 to 20 billion years ago coincident with the material creation. The derivation of this date or event is discussed in more detail in the section on creation. Prior to the material creation time as we know it did not exist. The reason is because there was no need of time since there was no material creation. There is no indication that the material universe will ever terminate its existence. When a person views the stars in the night sky, what is actually seen is the light that was emitted anywhere from several hours earlier, several years earlier, or several million years earlier. It is old light that is actually seen and not the object itself.

*Yahweh* God Himself transcends time. He is beyond and outside the frame and constraints of time. Within the realm of spirit, heaven, there is no concept or existence of the progress of time as we know it. Time as it exists on earth and in the material universe has progressed billions of light years of existence, but having no relative comparison with the realm of spirit. The creation of time was coincidental with the creation of the material universe. It was a necessity for the regular and further development of galaxies, solar systems and living organisms. It is time that allows the development of life to progress on earth. It was *Yahweh* God who created time as we know it. The 2 words in Scripture pertaining to time are the following: Hebrew *olam* and Greek equivalent *aeon*. They are both translated as age, some interval of time of either definite or indefinite length.

> But in these last days He has spoken to us by a Son, whom He appointed the heir of all things, through whom also He created the ages. Heb 1:2.

Similar uses of the Greek *aeon* is also found in the letters of Paul apostle.

> The plan of the mystery hidden from the ages in God who created all things. Eph 3:9.
> This was according to the purpose of the ages that He has realized in the Anointed Jesus our Lord. Eph 3:11.

These passages deal with the mystery of how the gentiles would be admitted into the covenant. This was a secret hidden from people from its conception from ancient times.

There is no word in Hebrew that means eternal or forever or of infinite time duration. This applies to time both infinitely into the future as well as into the past. The Jews understood history in terms of successive internals or periods of time, each one an *olam*. All length of time is described in Hebrew OT using *olam* or its Greek cognate *aeon* in the NT. Bible translators have taken the liberty to render these 2 words into as many meanings as they consider adequate to complement their particular inclinations. It is possible by interpretation to prove that infinity is implied in various passages, but this is not the literal rendering. A few examples will be provided. (World was used for *aeon* by the translators of the KJV Bible, but has been corrected to age in more contemporary and literal versions.)

> Gen 17:7. The covenant with Abraham lasted for the *olam*, it was effective for a long duration and then was terminated.
> Ex 12:24. Putting blood on the lintel and door posts was not for ever, but for the age. It was only observed until the advent of Jesus.
> Ps 90:1-2. Literally rendered, "From the age and unto the age, You are *Elohim*." By interpretation this passage states that *Yahweh* God is deity from the beginning of time and to the end of time.
> Philemon 15. Actually meaning: For the age. Since neither Philemon nor Onesimus would live forever the indication is for some long and undefined duration. Onesimus would be the property of Philemon as a slave until the finally dies, which would terminate the age.

The Greek adjective *aionious* or *aeonion*, is derived from the noun *aeon*, and follows the same semantics. It refers to something of age-long duration. This adjective describes the noun as existing for some long and undefined length of time into the distant future. Whether it is infinite is based on interpretation, and not always so.

Literal translations of the Bible render *olam* and *aeon* as age or eon, and render *aeonian* as age-long or transliterated as eonian. These Bibles are the *Concordant Version* of A.E. Knoch; the *Emphasized Bible* of J.B. Rotherham; and the *Emphatic Diaglott* of B. Wilson.

## CREATION

In order to have creation there must be material in order to sustain creation. The material creation is composed of matter. The source of matter of the present material universe is *Yahweh* God Himself. *Yahweh* God took some of the substance existing within the realm of spirit – spirit - and made something new out of it – matter. Creation could not have been *ex nihilo* – out of nothing. A vacuum is a void, it is an absence of matter. There is nothing in a void or vacuum from which to create.

> By faith we understand that the ages were formed by the word of God, so that what is seen was made out of that which is unseen. Heb 11:3.

The point to be made by the writer of Hebrews is that the unseen is spirit, and what is seen is the material universe. The creation was made out of pre-existent invisible spirit of *Yahweh* God. He as master builder and architect has the capability to transform one type of material into another type, in this case, spirit into matter. Some 40 billion years ago according to time as we know it, *Yahweh* God took some of that spirit that pervades and composes the realm of heaven and transformed it into matter. Scientists have designated this phenomenon as the "big bang." But why it would even occur has not yet been defined by the same scientists, or the origin of the material that composed the big bang, or the state of the universe prior to the big bang.

Evolution is impossible because nothing can ascend on its own power. The $2^{nd}$ law of thermodynamics witnesses to the existence of an infinitely scientific divine genius with infinite power to generate a universe.

The Jewish sages viewed it in this manner;:

> And I (Ezra) said, O Lord, You spoke from the beginning of creation, even the First day, and said: "Let heaven and earth be made." And Your word was perfect work. 2 Esd 6:38.
> He who lives for ever created all things in general. Sirach 18:1.

With the event known as the big bang time as we know it began. At that moment the clock of the material universe starting ticking.

## GENESIS ONE

I contend that Moses in writing Gen 1, was concerned with the process of development of the surface of the earth for habitation by living organisms, from the smallest and to the largest. A restoration from its previous condition. Moses was not concerned with the universe in general; this is covered in other passages in Scriptures. *Yahweh* God inspired Moses to record the analytical manner that the earth was restored, prepared as a residence for the human, the pinnacle of the creation of organisms. The phrase, "In the beginning," refers to the beginning of the restoration of the earth for habitation and history. Gen 1:1. The first verse of the Bible could just as easily be translated in this manner:

> In the beginning God created the sky and land. Gen 1:1.

This is also the concept provided by Jewish sages in 2 Esd 6:38-59.

> All this I (Ezra) have spoken before You Lord, because You made the world for our sake. 2 Esd 6:55.

Even though the earth itself is billions of years old, up to 40 billion years, the age of our galaxy, it was about 6,000 years ago that *Yahweh* God began its restoration for habitation. No doubt the surface of the earth at that time resembled that of the moon or Mars. Ancient, potmarked with craters, lacking an atmosphere, lacking vegetation, and devoid of any living organism. "Creating the heavens and the earth," can be interpreted as installing first an atmosphere and sky, and a stratosphere, the essential equivalent of firmament. Then *Yahweh* God proceeded to restore the surface of the earth for plant growth, provide rivers, lakes, depressions for oceans and seas, mountains and valleys, deserts and jungles, and all else required to beautify it. Continents, mountains and oceans all arranged in a manner to provide certain areas as prime inhabitable property for human, but also every parcel capable of habitation by the creature designed for that parcel by *Yahweh* God.

This treatise will not deal with the specifics of the 6 days of creation or development, except for a few comments. I have the conviction that all said in Gen 1 and 2 is the truth of *Yahweh* God regarding the restoration of the earth for the residence of humanity, plants and animals. This would include locating the earth in this solar system and the orbit at present, along with the sun, moon and balance of planets, moons and asteroids and comets. All in a delicate balance so as to support and develop life on earth and to beautify the universe. The installment of the sun and earth in its orbits with the moon would be the work of the $4^{th}$ day. This is described in Gen 1:14-17.

The days of the first week of creation may well have been of length greater than 24 hours. Since the installment of the sun as timekeeper for the solar day and year not occurring until the $4^{th}$ day, these first 4 days may well have been millions of years long. This would have been time plenty as we know it for *Yahweh* God to develop the earth for residence and to create the species and fill the earth with them.

## ORIGIN OF SPECIES

The origin of animal species begins on the $5^{th}$ day and concludes on the $6^{th}$ day with humans. *Yahweh* God personally and with the assistance or means of His spirit entities and sons of God designed each of the species on an individual basis. The heavenly entities determined which category each would be located in mammal, fish, bird, reptile or amphibian, or a lesser organism. They decided their size, appearance, diet, life-span, method of reproduction, development from embryonic stage to adult state, and etc. The word "kind" used in Gen 1:21, 24,-25, could well be replaced with the word "species". This is the meaning of the Hebrew word *min*, used in these verses. This is the intent of the author: *Yahweh* God is the designer and developer of the species. Each of the species was an important part of the ecological cycle and environmental balance of the earth. This was factored into their creation by *Yahweh* God: to provide an animal population from the equator to the poles; from the depths of the oceans to fresh water, to every climate and environment on earth. The species were gifted an ability to adapt to a certain amount minor changes in climate and environment. This adaptation capability allows species to survive and continue to flourish generation after generation regardless of the effects or changes of nature and the elements. New species are not created. Since the conclusion of the 6$^{th}$ day of creation week, no new species of an animal capable of reproduction has appeared. (The mule is not considered a species since it cannot reproduce; the nectarine is a hybrid.) The progenitor of every species was instilled with a spirit of animation, which guarantees the species life and reproduction. Whether the smallest of amoebae or the large of whales, *Yahweh* God instills with spirit this mass of formed and designed soil to match the particular species and the creature is alive, perspiring, converting food into energy, and independent, active, and with the ability to reproduce.

Like humans, the animal and plant population were created from soil. The sons of God using their power gathered the soil together and formed each specie into its designated shape and with the ability to reproduce. The original male and female of the species of each animal created on the 5$^{th}$ and 6$^{th}$ day, and plants on the 3$^{rd}$ day, were created with the ability to reproduce.

This is the primary flaw in the theory of evolution, making it improbable. When did reproduction begin and how did it begin? With an evolutionary process the first creature would have originally acquired the ability to reproduce, whether sexually or asexually. But if the original organism reproduced asexually, then why did the organism decide to all of a sudden generate a male and female for the next generation each with the necessary paraphernalia necessary to complement the other for sexual reproduction? There is no reason why. Natural evolution of any sort is impossible, because an organism on its own cannot develop an ability to reproduce, and especially within its short and terminal life span. The only manner of acquiring an ability to reproduce at the origination of life is by supernatural and original acquisition, and with the division of the genders each gender having an ability to complement the other. The first generation of all species had this ability to reproduce: sexually in the higher animals, and asexually with the lower organisms. All of this was designed and installed by *Yahweh* God for the eternal regular population of the earth.

## DINOSAURS AND CAVE MEN

The one enigma baffling paleontologists and geologists are dinosaurs. Creatures large and small of which today only fossils remain. The dinosaurs and all other creatures identified as pre-historic were likewise created on the 5th and 6th days of creation week. They served a purpose during the early earth, that period of time up to the flood of Noah. At that time *Yahweh* God determined that their purpose was at an end and so they were not included in the number that entered the ark. All the dinosaurs and such pre-historic creatures perished in the flood.

That some of the behemoth mammoths froze in the arctic regions in solid blocks of ice is indicative of the sudden change of temperature and climate at the beginning of the flood of Noah. The balance of dinosaurs drowned and slowly decayed in the water. Their bones were covered by silt and soil, only to be rediscovered by paleontologists when the earth rose above the waters. This is the best conclusion that I can draw correlating Scripture with geological and paleontological discoveries.

Some scholars have focused on the indefinite length of days 5 through 7 of creation week, perhaps millions of years long, to justify the existence of dinosaurs during pre-historic times. But this is just conjecture. The idea of cave men supposedly living tens of thousands of years into the past is also ludicrous. These people lived during the era between creation and the flood, and were probably no different than some of the aboriginal and native tribes dwelling presently in remote areas of central Africa, Australia, Indonesia and the Amazon. The so-called bones of such people supposedly dating back to such eras is likewise ludicrous. Entire skeletons have never been uncovered of any missing link or of pre-historic people. Bones cannot endure intact the length of time advocated by such researches. Eventually they decay into dust when exposed to the elements. Many of these so-called discoveries have been exposed as frauds, scientists so desperate to make a name for themselves.

The fool says in his heart. "There is no God." Ps 14:1.

## THE DAYS

The use of a creation week in Gen 1 and 2 was utilized by Moses to establish a pattern for the life of created humanity. *Yahweh* God in reality does not need 6 days to create and a day to rest. *Yahweh* God needs no rest: He is indefatigable. In this passage Moses deliberately divided the development of the earth and its occupation into 7 periods as an example for created humanity. A divinely inspired pattern was developed in this passage for future generations.

A division between the days had also to be established. *Yahweh* God decided that sundown meant the conclusion of the day. Later Jewish sages became more concerned about the time that the old day concluded. Their concern was due to the fact that work was proscribed on Sabbaths. For this reason the precise moment was necessary so that work would cease before the new day, if it was a Sabbath, would begin. The conclusion of the Jewish sages was the appearance of 3 stars in the sky; this determined sunset and the end of the old day and beginning of the next.

The most important matter for observance of every day is the statement repeated several times.

And *Yahweh* God saw that it was good. Gen 1:12,18,25,31.

All that *Yahweh* God created at this time was "good". This He expressed after a surveillance of His creation efforts that day. Whether be the weather cycle, ecological cycle, the species and nature of plants and animals, or the texture and condition of the surface of the earth, it was "good."

## IMMORTAL CREATION

Whether the original creation was designed for true immortality or designed to regular replenishment is not clearly defined in Scripture. There appears to be evidence and witness to equally tip the scale in each direction. I lean in the direction that created humanity was designed to be regularly replaced, but not until a short interval of a state of immortality. This would allow many to have the opportunity to live, prosper and continually populate the earth, after an example of perfection is provided. This concept will be discussed. Paul apostle implies a deliberate change from immortality to mortality in order to increase the population for others to share in the blessings of *Yahweh* God.

> For God has consigned all people to disobedience that he may have mercy upon all. Rom 11:33.

The concept of original immortality is the general course of interpretation of most Bible students and teachers and Jewish sages.

The original creation, according to the Jewish sages, was designed and established to be permanent: without decay due to age, without termination:

> For God made not death: neither has He pleasure in the death of the living. For He created all things that they might have their being; and the generations of the world were healthful; and there is no poison of destruction in them, nor the dominion of death upon the earth. Wisdom 1:12-13.

> For God created man to be immortal, and made him to be an image of His own eternity. Wisdom 2:23.

Apparently all creation would live to maturity and reproduce and increase their individual species on the earth. Somehow the natural growth of the species would curtail at some point of maturity and so remain there eternally and without end. The same would apply with created humanity. Somehow the world would be able to occupy comfortably all the increase of species over the progress of millions of years. But these are only conjectures. We will probably never know exactly the intentions of *Yahweh* God in the settlement of the earth for long-term existence and increase of population, and how this would be accomplished on a finite land mass such as the earth.

How long of a period transpired between the initial Sabbath and entrance of the snake into the garden is only a conjecture. I would have the impression that about 100 or 200 years had transpired. The progress during this interim can only be defined by those passages that foretell life and the condition of the earth after the restoration. If the earth is to revert back to original creation at some defined point in the future, then we can conclude that these same passages can likewise apply to the original creation.

# THE PINNACLE OF *YAHWEH* GOD's CREATION

The human, both male and female, is the pinnacle of *Yahweh* God's creative process. All was complete on earth for their introduction into it toward evening of the 6$^{th}$ day of creation week. It is because of the human that the earth was restored for residence by *Yahweh* God, and in turn, the human would glorify God for His goodness and life. *Yahweh* God would be glorified more in the human than any other specie of plant and animal life, because the human possessed the image and likeness of the *Elohim*, the Godhead-deity. No other creation can claim this blessing or title, only the human, and the human can claim it throughout their life, only if they do not disclaim or reject it. The balance of species are original, each one was created based on its own species. Gen 1:21, 24. That the human is the pinnacle of the creation of *Yahweh* God is clearly expressed.

> What is a person that You are mindful of him, and the human that You care for him? Yet You have made him a little less than gods, but crowned him with honor and glory. Ps 8:4-5.

This passage is repeated in Heb 2:6-7, except that the word gods (Heb. *elohim*) is replaced by the Greek *aggelos* (messenger or commonly angels).

No other creature has the characteristics or attributes of the human that so much reflect and retain the same characteristics and attributes of *Yahweh* God who created them. The concern of the creator for the human is beyond the ability of the human to comprehend. They are the pinnacle of His creative abilities and each one contains a personal imprint of the hands of the creator Himself.

That all humanity evolves from the progenitors Adam and Eve is based on the statement that "Eve is the mother of every one living." Gen 3:20.

## THE HUMAN

The composition of the human is very clearly explained and in detail by Scripture. Soil constitutes the material human body. According to Scripture, all living creation is constituted from soil.

> You are dust, and to dust you return. Gen 3:19
>
> For He knows our frame; he remembers that we are dust. Ps 103:14.
>
> Remember that You have made me of clay, and You will turn me to dust again. Did You not pour me out like milk, and curdle me like cheese? You clothed me with skin and flesh, and knit me together with bones and sinews. You have granted me life and steadfast love; and Your care has preserved my spirit. Job 10:9-12
>
> May the God of peace sanctify you wholly; and may your spirit and soul and body be kept sound and blameless at the coming of our Lord Jesus the Anointed. 1 Thess 5:23.

Paul apostle's brief note on the 3 parts that constitute a living human is the bedrock of understanding: spirit, soul and body. A person is soil formed into a human form possessing a spirit of animation and an identity, called soul. The constitution of man is soil and at the termination of life returns back to the soil he and she was originally created of. The question as to whether conscious existence exists after the termination of life will be discussed after investigating the constitution of humans.

Moses by divine inspiration describes the creation of original humanity.

> Then *Yahweh* God formed the human from dust from the ground, and breathed into his nostrils the breath of life; and the human became a living soul. Gen 2:7.
>
> And all humans are from the ground, and Adam was created of earth. Sirach 33:10.

Job martyr in his grief describes his own origination in similar terms:

> The spirit of God has made me, and the breath of the Almighty gives me life. Behold I am toward God as you are; I too was formed from a piece of clay. Job 33:4,6.

If we could imagine *Yahweh* God as the great artist or sculptor in the garden of Eden, the home which He prepared for the pinnacle of His creation. He takes some of the soil and clay and with His hands molds a figure of a person, an adult male, and I would suppose a young adult in the prime of his life. But the figure of clay and soil is lifeless: no motion, no sensation, no consciousness, like a mannequin or wax figure. But *Yahweh*

God is pleased in what He has formed. *Yahweh* God then blows upon the figure and breathes into his nostrils. I would think it be similar to resuscitation of a drowning victim. The breath exits *Yahweh* God through His lips and enters the human figure. The figure begins to breathe on its own, breathe the air of the atmosphere, its heart begins to pump, the blood is flowing to all parts of the body and the brain begins its deliberations. The cold and morbid clay figure is now warm, reaching normal body temperature. His eyes open and he looks around him. This breathe of *Yahweh* God is the spirit of animation possessed by all living creatures. Paul apostle states that God is the source of all life. 1 Tim 6:13.

Adam is now a conscious entity, he is a living soul. Adam has conscious existence, distinct from the lifeless mannequin he was earlier. *Yahweh* God created a special spirit of animation with the creation of living entities, whether human or animal, as distinct from that of plants. When a body possesses this spirit of animation, it is alive. When this spirit vacates the body, it is dead. This passage with the creation of the original human defines his constituency: body, soul, spirit. When *Yahweh* God decided to terminate conscious existence He removed His spirit of animation from Adam and Adam returned back to the original components of his composition. Adam then was no longer a living soul. Adam's state was now the same as it was prior to his creation.

Only by way of biological reproduction is life created. But life is not actually created in procreation. Life is transmitted by the animated creature or organism through sexual or asexual reproduction to the new creature or organism. This is the method ordained by *Yahweh* God for the reproduction of life. This unseen energy force of life is spirit of animation from the realm of spirit, from heaven, which is sent and infused as required to give life, and subsequently removed when the termination of life is decreed.

## BODY

The body is soil reconstituted into skin, tissue, organs, bone, blood and muscle and fat and nerves. The brain is the same, and cannot exist on its own. The heart pumps blood and nothing more. Surgeries are performed regularly and these have no effect on identity or personality or individualism. Transplants, organs moved from a donor to a recipient, even a heart, blood transfusions, occur regularly. But never does the character or identity of the person change or alter as a result of the foreign organ relocated into a new body.

The body also renovates itself in cell reproduction. The parts of the body that do not renovate themselves are the muscles, nerves and bone. The cells of the balance of the body reproduce and then die, replaced by new cells that reproduce from old cells. In reality a person is not the same body they were gifted with at birth, at least 90% of it. Every 7 years or so about 90% of the cells in the body are exchanged for new cells.

The purpose of the above short treatise on the body is to indicate that the body is not the origin or location of any emotion, sensation, motivation or character. All of this evolves from the ethereal and invisible object: soul.

The fact that the heart is used as the source of love or affection is only in a poetic sense. The heart only pumps blood and has no emotion to display. In reality, not the heart nor the kidneys have any ability to display emotions, because they are strictly organs of the body. The use of kidneys is in Ps 16:7, Rev 2:23, and other passages, though translated as reins. The kidneys only cleanse blood and have no fortitude of their own. It is poetic license to assign emotion to certain organs of the body.

## SOUL

Adam has an identity and this identity is his soul. The living Adam is soul. The same identity will never again in history arise or exist on earth. A person is a soul. To exist and be a conscious entity, that is, to be a living soul, it must possess a body assigned to it and spirit of animation to make that body a living body, a functional body. You are a soul and this soul is your identity as a distinct conscious entity. This soul is you.

The soul is everything that a person consists of in life. Not only identity, but what a person likes and dislikes, prefers and objects, what is satisfying and what is unsatisfying. Soul is individualism and personality and character. Soul is what makes you unique, special and different from every other on earth, present, past and future. Soul is you as a self-conscious entity, realizing that you are you, alive, breathing, functioning, and having a future. Soul places you in a frame of time, place and relation to the balance of the universe. Soul is the personal realization of self-conscious existence.

Soul is invisible; it is non-existent as a defined entity or object when absence from a functional and living body. Soul is immaterial and ethereal, but real and concrete in the realm of spirit. The identity of a deceased individual does not vanish nor is forever terminated. It continues in the memory of *Yahweh* God on a list in the annals of heaven, but no more than this.

The soul contains emotions and sensations that the person possesses. Soul is what makes a person happy on one occasion and sorrowful on another. Soul is the personal experience that gives a person purpose and goal to live long, or self-negation or fatalism that results in suicide. Soul is the character of the person; soul causes anger and patience and forgiveness. Soul is high or low self-esteem, having or not having self-confidence. The molding of the soul becomes the drive to philanthropy, self-sacrifice and edification, or becomes the motivation to crime and violence. Soul is the love that the person possesses and the hate. A person is whatever our soul makes it, molds it, and directs it.

You have conscious existence only as long as the body that Yahweh God gives you is capable of functioning. All of its organs and especially the vital organs must be in good operating condition. Once the body is no longer capable of functioning, the spirit of animation vacates it and the soul is no longer conscious. In the state of death, the soul is reduced to an identity that is stored in the massive vaults of the memory of *Yahweh* God awaiting the final judgment of the great white throne.

## PEOPLE AS SOULS

In general Scripture refers to living individuals as souls. The soul is not viewed as a separate facet divisible from the body, that a concern for the soul is anything other than concern for the entire person. Souls mean entities, and the total life of the individual is reflected in identifying a person as a soul. The Hebrew word for soul is *nephesh*; while in Greek it is *psyche*.

> Gen 12:5. Abraham acquired people (souls) in Haran.
> Gen 46:26. Forty-six individuals (souls) belonging to Jacob entered Egypt.
> Gen 37:21. Ruben did not want his brothers to take Joseph's life (soul).

Matt 6:25. Food is for the soul and clothing is for the body.

Acts 2:41. About 3,000 individuals (souls) were added to the Apostolic community.

Heb 13:17. Leaders of the assembly are concerned for the welfare of the entire person (soul).

1 Pet 1:9. The result of faith is the salvation of the total person (soul) in all facets of their life.

Matt 10:28. They can kill the body but not the soul. (Here the soul is used figuratively to symbolize the beliefs or convictions of a person.)

Rev 12:11. They loved not their soul (life) even unto death, meaning they were willing to die for their faith as martyrs.

Acts 2:27. When David died he was buried. He did not ascend to heaven. In this Messianic passage, the person of Jesus of Nazareth did not remain long in the sepulcher.

## SPIRIT OF ANIMATION

Once born and breathing the child is now a living soul with its own identity. If a living child dies its identity vanishes, since the child has not lived long enough to accept or realize conscious existence.

The spirit of animation that enters a new born and allows it to breathe on its own is the spirit of *Yahweh* God breathed into the child. Now indwelling in the child it impels it to live. Children want to live. Children want to play, learn, discover, exercise. Often they refuse to go to sleep, because they want to experience life. This spirit is an inherent impulse that drives the body to live. It keeps the rhythm of the heart steady – that message from the brain to the muscles of the heart, to drive the heart to pump blood. This spirit drives the muscles of the chest to flex the lungs, to draw air and expel air. This spirit causes every organ and tissue of the body to function and in unison with the body as a whole to provide the opportunity for life.

This spirit of animation drives the body to live even to old age. This spirit will not leave the body unless it absolutely has to, because *Yahweh* God assigns it to that body for the length of its natural life. It will reside there until some occurrence that weakens or damages the body to the point no strength remains to retain this divinely assigned life-spirit. The spirit only leaves the body when the body disintegrates or fails so it can no longer function. Some bacteria infects the body and disrupts the function of some organ, until that organ fails. The heart or brain arteries or veins are blocked to prevent movement of blood: that part of the heart or brain fails due to lack of oxygen. In an accident, blood is lost from bleeding, or some other damage to tissue occurs, to the point that the body is irreparable and no longer operational, and then the spirit departs. Old age slowly causes the body to weaken, much like a piece of steel slowly rusting until the load can no longer be supported or wood in water slowly rotting. Likewise the body in old age: when no more strength remains in it to retain the powerful special spirit of animation bequeathed to that person at their birth, the spirit departs.

Even the simplest of living organisms, such as a plant or single cell organism, has a definite distinction between the states of life and death. A laboratory cannot infuse this invisible force energy into some material object and cause it to live. Never has a laboratory been able to achieve animation of an inanimate object. It is impossible. It has never been accomplished because there is no control over the spirit of animation by a person. The spirit that causes animation is a product of and is indigenous to heaven. Science has not likewise been able to create reproduction, and any attempt at animation has been solely for the specific experiment.

Healing of destroyed or severed tissue, or healing from sickness, is the work of the same special spirit of animation in the body, to drive the body to live. *Yahweh* God has installed in the body the ability for this spirit to heal minor damage and infections. Within these limits the body can recover. When a person cuts himself, it is the spirit that drives the cells and tissue to repair the damage. Likewise with surgery, the physician assists the divine ability for damage repair using that knowledge of medicine and surgery gifted by *Yahweh* God.

> Honor a physician with the honor due unto him for the uses that you may have of him, for the Lord has created him. For of the Most High comes healing and he shall receive honor of the king. The skill of the physician shall life up his head and in the sight of great men he shall be in admiration. The Lord created medicines out of the earth and he that is wise will not reject them. Sirach 38:1-4.

But no human has a guarantee from *Yahweh* God regarding the body or soul that they receive. Maladies and physical defects abound in every created person. It is not the right attitude of the human to complain to

*Yahweh* God or feel sorry for ones own self because the body they receive is not perfect in every respect. A complaint because the body they receive may have a flaw, a congenital birth defect, or some inherited trait that the person finds objectionable, is ingratitude to the creator.

> *Yahweh* said to [Moses], "Who has made man's mouth? Who makes him dumb, or deaf, or seeing, or blind? Is it not I, *Yahweh*?" Ex 4:11.

Every person must thank *Yahweh* God for the opportunity of conscious existence that *Yahweh* God has gifted them. Every human must make the most of the life that *Yahweh* God has given them as a result of His love. Whether the life be long or short, in whatever age in history or location on earth; whichever family they are born in, financial status, religion or race, whatever the circumstances a person is placed in by *Yahweh* God, they must always bless *Yahweh* God by thanking Him for the opportunity to live, to have a conscious existence. Gratitude is always offered to *Yahweh* God for His effort in the creation of ourselves. Such individuals He will bless in their life.

## IMAGE OF YAHWEH GOD

The image and likeness of *Yahweh* God will be defined and then compared with animals who have not this feature. This image and likeness is not a physical attribute. *Yahweh* God, the sons of *Yahweh* God, messengers, and the heavenly hosts are incorporeal. The character of *Yahweh* God is the basic constituency of the image and likeness of Himself, also inherent in spirit entities. Both this image and likeness of *Yahweh* God is unseen, invisible, and an attribute that materializes in attitude and conduct. All of this applies to both genders equally, and without exception.

To the image of *Yahweh* God I will assign the moral nature of *Yahweh* God and the related psychological attributes of His character. To the likeness of *Yahweh* God, I will assign the creativity of *Yahweh* God, the mental faculties. Through these 2 qualities *Yahweh* God could look from heaven and see Himself in the human.

An image is a replica of the original. Although a replica is not the original, by viewing its appearance it resembles the original: it has superficial qualities of the original. I feel it is appropriate to attribute the moral nature of *Yahweh* God as his image upon the human, both male and female. The moral nature upon earth is a sense of right and wrong; acceptable conduct and unacceptable; what is beneficial and what is injurious; what is edifying and what is detrimental. The moral nature of the human reflects the moral nature of *Yahweh* God. It is because of the moral nature that humanity issues laws and statutes. For all humanity to live in harmony and mutual benefit is this gift impressed on the nature of every human at their birth. Because of this moral nature humans gather together in common causes for long term and mutual benefit. Governments are formed, judicial systems are instituted, and hospitals for the ill. All of this to initiate life, liberty and pursuit of happiness.

The justice of *Yahweh* God is evident in the human as the demand for justice on earth. A penalty is imposed upon the violator of the life, property or possessions of another. Just as *Yahweh* God is a god who imposes retribution upon every criminal to the extent of their violation of His divine instruction, so does government installed by humans impose a penalty upon the criminal for their crime against another or against society. For every individual to take responsibility for their actions, laws are legislated as penalties.

When the human reverts to animal behavior, then they lose the image and likeness of *Yahweh* God. It is replaced by that nature of animals. They act by instinct, instead of by knowledge and reason; they fight for survival, instead of live in cooperation and peaceful coexistence. Amoral conduct, and especially sexual deviation, is the loss of the image of *Yahweh* God.

## THE HUMAN AS A FREE MORAL AGENT

A parallel notion with the human possessing the moral nature of *Yahweh* God as His image upon them is the fact that the human is a free moral agent, possessing volition. A human has the choice of moral conduct. An individual chooses their conduct or mode of behavior or physical expression or life style. A human has the capacity to make a choice and decision in regard to their words, deeds and attitudes. Free choice of conduct is an inherent part of the constituency of the human and this is also the image of *Yahweh* God. Just as no entity can force *Yahweh* God to so anything without it already in accord with the determined counsel of his will, so with humans. Nobody forces you to do anything against your will without your agreement and submission. Our volition is given to us free and uncontrolled to do with as we please.

In simple terms, nobody forces you to do some thing. Every motion, movement, word, act, attitude is the result of the voluntary choice of the individual or resulting from this choice. What occurs is the result of a person's volition, directly or indirectly. No choice in *Yahweh* God's view is involuntary or the result of coercion. Every choice is the result of a premeditated decision, the personal volition of a free moral agent.

The devil is not the source of sin or crime. The devil does not force an individual to do anything that is against that person's will to do. The devil in Scripture is the personification of temptation. Matt 4:3. Temptation leads people to violate the law of *Yahweh* God, or injure others or themselves, but the final choice lies upon the individual who succumbs to temptation. One choice is to sin and voluntarily succumb to the influence of temptation. The other choice is to resist – and this also is a free choice – and the devil will flee from you. Jam 4:7.

As a free moral agent blame cannot be placed on another for any decision or choice made. Although the benefit of possessing the image of *Yahweh* God is that of reflecting His moral nature, as well as having a free volition in choice, the disadvantage is that an individual must assume total responsibility for every action. Blame cannot be placed on *Yahweh* God or anyone else or anything else for what may occur in a person's life. *Yahweh* God transcends blame or accusation.

## CONSCIENCE

Conscience is that agent in a human installed by *Yahweh* God as part of His image. This deals with the moral facet of *Yahweh* God imparted to created humanity. The conscience serves to impress upon the human conduct that may be harmful or inappropriate. With no other education or formal training in conduct or the law of *Yahweh* God the conscience can guide an individual to proper conduct by impressing a feeling of guilt whenever behavior is wrong. To listen to ones conscience is acceptable only with no knowledge of the moral code or standards legislated by *Yahweh* God regarding that particular matter. This way no individual can claim an excuse for harm or injury or a crime committed. This is the basic, most fundamental purpose of *Yahweh* God gifting created humanity a personal conscience: for no person to be able to circumvent responsibility for a violation.

> All who have sinned without the law will perish without the law, and all who have sinned under the law will be judged by the law. Rom 2:12.

This was the manner selected by *Yahweh* God in order for His created human to feel guilt and remorse for injury or harm or a crime committed. If it were not for conscience, there would be no drive for repentance, for confession. If there were no conscience, a person would never sense that anything wrong was committed should they commit a crime.

In one respect, conscience is a type of human instinct. But unlike animals that will not face an inquiry, the human will face an inquiry into actions. If no other standard is available for determining proper or acceptable behavior, then conscience becomes the standard. This becomes the law of *Yahweh* God or the moral code by which an individual will be judged. This explanation was provided by Paul apostle to Romans, a superstitious people without a moral law for their nation. The standard *Yahweh* God will use to judge them as pagans or barbarians will be their conscience.

> When gentiles who have not the law do by nature what the law requires, they are a law to themselves, even though they do not have the law. They show that what the law requires is written on their hears, while their conscience also bears witness and their conflicting thoughts either accuse or excuse them – on that day when according to my gospel God judges the secrets of men by the Anointed Jesus. Rom 2:14-16.

Conscience is only beneficial when an individual allows it to do the work assigned to it by *Yahweh* God: guilt. By training the conscience to keep us aware of offenses, it is possible to become very sensitive to the circumstances of others. A person can early sense if an action or mode of conduct is not beneficial to the other party. Empathy will then increase.

Just as a person can train their conscience to be sensitive to the needs of others, the conscience can also be made insensitive. By rejecting the feelings of guilt and acting otherwise, by continuing in injury and crime, the work of the conscience can be smothered or annulled. Paul apostle wrote of this:

Through the pretensions of liars whose consciences are seared.
1 Tim 4:2.

To sear is to scorch or emaciate with intense heat, as with a hot iron or branding iron. Such individuals by training have mortified the conscience. There is no more sense of guilt whenever harm or injury or crime is committed. Such people have no conscience. They cannot sense emotion arising from the intended or unintended suffering of another. It does not bother them to afflict injury or even to murder. Since they have no moral standard and no conscience remaining they are judged as though dead in their sins. Eph 2:1-3. When Paul apostle wrote about individuals who will be judged without the law, he was referring to these. Since they have no moral standard and no sense of guilt the strictest and severest penalty will be imposed upon them.

In one respect empathy is a derivative of conscience. It allows a person to understand the feelings of another by directing or imposing the same circumstance upon themselves.

## HUMANS AND ANIMALS

The human varies most in size as opposed to the other species of animals. In general, a species of animals are all about the same size, weight, and length, and variations are minor. But with the human, the size varies from the short to tall, thin to robust, small frame to large.

*Yahweh* God deliberately created the human to have such a variety in size and shape in both male and female in order for each person to be unique; to realize that in both physical and immaterial qualities he and she are unique from every other person on earth. There is no other person on earth that looks just like you. Every individual has a unique appearance, combined with color of eyes and hair. The extent and type of facial hair on the male adds to his uniqueness that there is no other person like himself in all the world. In this manner every person realizes that their creation was a personal work of *Yahweh* God, and not some assembly line stereotype. A persons' unique physical features adds to their personal identity.

The human body is designed to wear clothes. It is susceptible to illness from exposure to cold and is frail in its defense against heat and sunlight. Clothes beautify the human. (So-called nudist camps or beaches are few and far between, often temporal like a novelty for a family or individual.)

Clothing is the norm for humans, and I am convinced that the more clothing a person wears, the more beautiful they look. Clothes cover the body to make the human body beautiful, and so *Yahweh* God gave humans the talent, both to male and female, to make clothes for the body. In reality, the human figure is unsightly. With only a few exceptions, none of us would be able to stand the sight of others without clothing. The genitalia likewise of both male and female is unsightly, and is definitely designed to be covered and hidden from public view. *Yahweh* God created the human in such a fashion that they would use their talent to beautify the human body through proper attire.

Children at an early age must be protected from the elements and taken well care of by parents. This type of care does not exist among animals. Children must be dressed, fed, and protected until such an age they can handle such matters on their own. There is no evidence of immaturity in adult animals or mental illness.

Humans have a sense of appreciation for beauty. We decorate homes, plant gardens, and treasure natural wonders and resources. Humans enjoy parks and forests and beaches, the snow and the desert, and can glean a picturesque beauty in all of them. Likewise the opposite is present. Humans dislike and are repulsed by tastelessness, vulgarity, crudeness, including that of sexual perversion and pornography. Animals have no sense of beauty or appreciation.

In the same vein humans have an inclination toward friendship and orderly conduct. This is also reflected in our manners. Courtesy, amicability, cooperation, are traits of humans, not animals. All of these evolving from the image of *Yahweh* God upon the human; not existing in animals.

The human is the only creature that has a sense of shame. The human sense of shame does not allow them to function as an animal. Only the human must attend to toilet needs in private. Only humans have instituted rules in regard to decency. Only humans must wear clothes to protect their body from the elements and to beautify their body. The human alone was created without natural clothing, and so must make and wear clothes. The segregation of the sexes in sleeping, bathing and natural function exist only among humans, and such rules are made by the community. The only exception is that of a married couple.

Animals have no moral nature and no conscience. There is no concept of right or wrong for an animal; no code of conduct defining what is acceptable and what is not. Animals exist for purposes of survival based on their instinct. An animal cannot sense guilt or feel blame for some injurious action. An animal has no conscience to impress guilt on it for some injurious act. Animals react based on their instinct. They are born, grow and beautify the earth, fulfill their purpose in the ecosystem and environment; they reproduce and subsequently die. Their death is due to some inherent reason part of their nature, or else are killed for food, either by humans or by some other animal. They attack only to defend themselves when threatened or for food. They have no remorse for attacking their prey. If an animal kills a human while defending itself, or kills a defenseless human for food, the animal is not guilty of murder. An animal does not sense a wrong in depriving a person of their life. Animals have no basis for a moral nature. They live in the open and do not think twice about it and have an automatic ability to adapt to the environment and protect themselves from the elements and source food. They wear only the natural clothing that *Yahweh* God has naturally provided them and with no separation of the genders. An animal then has no sense of shame or embarrassment. It is not part of their nature to sense shame or embarrassment, only the human does. It is an animal that can give birth, deliver its young, without assistance of any type.

## LIKENESS OF YAHWEH GOD

The likeness of *Yahweh* Elohim I will define as the creative ability of the human, and their related mental and educational development. This likewise is an invisible and inherent part of the nature of both male and female. The human is like *Yahweh* God because of their ability of being an innovator, a creator of original design and mechanisms, art and architecture, a developer of ideas and concepts, a discoverer and researcher, a traveler to the outermost ends and areas of the Earth to view what is there to find.

Parallel with this is the fact that the human needs an education. Without training and schooling by the previous generation a human is incapable of achieving or accomplishing anything, much less survive. A child must be taught from an early age to care for itself. A child must be taught to dress, read and write, be taught arithmetic and science, taught what to eat, what to drink, and to stay away from strangers. None of this is naturally acquired. For a human to survive the elements a compete education is required. A child must also be taught conduct, morals and ethics, and must be trained to behave in a certain manner acceptable and beneficial to the society and culture they are part of. Children are naturally inquisitive. The questions of why and how come, a desire to expand in knowledge and satisfy the void of ignorance. It is only the human with this mind of requiring and demanding education, and advancing in knowledge and its application. The human with its ability to learn and to create what is new or different is the likeness of *Yahweh* God upon them.

Some individuals can acquire more knowledge than others, achieve greater scholastic goals, progress in technology, culture and business. Even among the genders the female is actually more capable of advancing in knowledge than the male. The ability for some to advance scholastically further than others persists on an individual basis, for every individual to be distinct from every other. It is not based on race, culture, nationality or ethnic background. Provided that education is available, along with a proper domestic and social environment, progress in scholastics is achievable for every person, regardless of race, culture, nationality or ethnic background.

The likeness of *Yahweh* God is original creativity, inasmuch as *Yahweh* God is a creator. He mentally developed the original concept of a material universe and its materialization and progress for the infinite future. *Yahweh* God took some of His own nature as a creator and gifted it to created humanity. When a person receives an education and puts to use this education in some facet of their society, *Yahweh* God can view a reflection of Himself in that person. This likeness of *Yahweh* God in original creativity extends to many areas and not just construction. It can be applied to the arts and literature, history and geography, liberal arts and philosophy, and science and engineering. All of these fields utilize individuals possessing the likeness of *Yahweh* God upon themselves, who have proceeded to develop it and practice it.

Just as becoming amoral causes a person to lose the image of *Yahweh* God, so does the person who destroys and devastates the efforts of previous generations and who suppresses educational advancement lose the likeness of *Yahweh* God. War, the most effective manner of destruction of peoples, cultures and civilizations, is indicative of a lack of the likeness of *Yahweh* God. These individuals, like the amoral, do not even behave as animals behave which follow their divine instinct. Both the amoral and devastators of advancement are sub-human, depriving themselves and rejecting the image and likeness of *Yahweh* God which they were gifted with at their birth.

*Yahweh* God will bless those who utilize to a beneficial purpose the gifts of His image and likeness upon them, which will proceed generations into the future.

## MEMORY

A miraculous capability of the human and to a minor extent animals is memory. *Yahweh* God has created the human with the ability to retain images, information, experiences and thoughts. Not just a short term retention, but over decades of life. As the human develops the memory follows, the earliest retention for most is beginning at age 5 or 6. Maximum capacity of retention and adsorption is at about age 20. The information is retained for use at lest to age 60, although absorption begins to decline in early 50's. Passing away at an old age was preferred because the faculties of memory would decrease along with the weakening of the body. Due to this degradation of the faculties the person is hardly or not at all aware of their own existence, environment or condition of health. Passing away in old age is painless and in comfort, like falling asleep.

Memory is a facet of the image of *Yahweh* God gifted to humans. It could not have developed on its own. Without memory a human could not survive on earth. Animals live in the present. Humans have a memory to be able to grasp the past and to develop a future. Humans have a memory to transmit information acquired to future generations.

## THE TREES OF EDEN

At some point in time during the early Earth, during the life of the progenitors Adam and Eve, a massive transformation occurred on earth effecting the life and progress of the entire population, civilizations, and plant and animal life for the ages to come. This upheaval is commonly termed the fall. In the passages that describe the conflict that resulted in this tragedy, part are allegorical and the balance is literal. Within the entire scope of events a vein of spiritual instruction exists applicable to and reiterated in every generation since the progenitors.

Jewish tradition indicates that Moses prophet and leader composed the book of Genesis during their sojourn in the deserts of Sinai during those 40 years. Moses saw during these years the many who suffered and died, perhaps a million, perhaps 2 million. Their camp was a small city in transit through deserts of Arabia. Moses watched how people succumbed to temptation and shortly thereafter died, a premature and eventual death. Every situation was a repeat of the first: temptation and succumbing to the temptation. Each one felt that their own decision was superior to the dictate of *Yahweh* God. "I won't die," were words Moses heard year after year, time and time again.

Two trees are mentioned in Gen 2:9. These can be understood allegorically. The fruit of the tree of life is the instruction of *Yahweh* God. If a person lives according to this divine instruction, the revealed will of *Yahweh* God, according to his word and law, that person will be blessed and live long upon the earth.

The tree of knowledge of good and evil symbolizes rebellion against *Yahweh* God. The tree is an allegory for independence from divine and inspired instruction. A person that denies the inspired will of *Yahweh* God as authoritative and binding, and decides instead to follow his own inclinations, eats the fruit of this tree. When a person determines for himself what is good and what is evil, independent of *Yahweh* God, he and she eat of the fruit of this tree. Pr 14:12, 16:25. To depend on a persons own inclinations instead of *Yahweh* God's will only cause error in a persons life. Due to the human's lack of instruction and lack of education in all matters and a lack of restraint of lust and control of emotions and attitudes, the result is self-imposed ruin, injury, devastation and premature death.

For this reason *Yahweh* God informed the original couple that when they eat of the fruit of the tree prohibited by *Yahweh* God, they will begin to die the death. Although most translations render Gen 2:17, as "This day you shall die." The literal and more correct rendering is, "You shall begin to die the death." This is exactly what occurs, the very day a person decides to abandon the divine instruction they begin to morally degenerate. This is how James apostle describes it as follows:

> But each person is tempted when he is lured and enticed by his own lust. Then lust when it has conceived gives birth to sin; and sin when it is fully developed produces death. Jam 1:14-15.

This is eating of the fruit of the tree of knowledge of good and evil.

There is no doubt in my mind that *Yahweh* God gave the progenitors a complete education upon creation and settlement in Eden. This consisted in the instruction of his inspired moral law, and all else required for corporeal prosperity. Adam and Eve received all that was required of *Yahweh* God to lead a benevolent and productive and gratifying life on earth, and especially one acceptable to *Yahweh* God their creator.

## THE VIOLATION OF ADAM AND EVE

Adam and Eve were created as free moral agents with an uncontrolled volition and a capacity to choose according to their own personal desire and without coercion. I contend that temptation existed from the beginning in the garden of Eden, because the snake, which represents temptation, was also in the garden. As long as Adam and Eve resisted temptation all went well for them.

The most debated questions of the ages surfaces here without clear or simple resolution. Were the progenitors Adam and Eve originally created with the natural capacity or impulse to sin? And, Why was the temptation even permitted if *Yahweh* God foreknew their act of disobedience? The pros and cons of both these questions have consumed pages and volumes of treatises over the millennia. So as not to bore the reader, I will present my theory only in brief.

The tree of life is an allegory. It symbolizes the eternity and immortality of the garden of Eden. As long as access existed to this tree it provided the residents and environment indefinite and blessed existence. None of the decay or evils or difficulties of the later post-fall era existed at this time. The purpose of Moses in this passage was to convey to the reader that because of one disobedience sin entered the world and because of one sinner all sinned. Rom 5:12,18. This is an encapsulation: Moses presenting to his people and future generations the results of disobedience and succumbing to temptation. Results that they themselves are effected by and so future generations to the restoration, and without exception. The results of the disobedience did not only effect the violators Adam and Eve, but all of future posterity. Since they are the original progenitors of all future humanity, and since the curse effected their substance and constitution, their nature as a whole, their offspring would also carry on the traits and nature of the parents. This can be compared to an original congenital defect or mutation in the genes that is transmitted generation to generation without any type of correction possible. Pseudo-Ezra in his book reflects the attitude of the Jewish sages of the era:

> O Adam, what have you done? For though it was you that sinned, you are not alone fallen, but all of us descended from you. 2 Esd 7:46.

If both Adam and Eve knew the extensive effect of their disobedience on future generations, they would not have disobeyed the command of *Yahweh* God. I contend equal responsibility for both Adam and Eve, of the opinion that Moses wanted both every male and female to realize a responsibility in their own life for their actions: that one could not shift the blame onto the other. This is apparent in both their attempts to avoid responsibility. Their near-sightedness is no different than that of any other person of any other generation. The same pathetic and general attitude seems to pervade every generation: little care is taken on the impact of our decisions on children or grandchildren or future posterity. Sometimes I wonder whether the complaint of pseudo-Ezra is actually a vented attack or a deep seated spite toward Adam for ruining life for the balance of his posterity. But this is just conjecture.

## THE CURSE UPON THE SERPENT

The curse does not refer specifically to the snake as an animal, since there was no physical alteration of its body. As it was created on the $5^{th}$ day, so does it exist today. The curse applies to the reputation of the snake as compared to other animals.

> Cursed are you above all cattle and above all wild animals. Gen 3:14.

None of the balance of animals has a reputation like the snake This is the most malicious of all animal identities that can be applied to a human. To call a person a snake refers to him as being sly, underhanded, crafty, treacherous, a person who will poison with his venom even the most unsuspecting victim, and then slither away seeking some new victim without remorse. A person can be identified with other animals, such as the pig, dog, donkey, weasel or turkey, but there is nothing more inconsiderate and offensive and damaging than identifying a person with the snake. This allegorical use of "snake in the grass" places this creature at ground level, or cursed beyond that of all other creatures. The ancient snake is also a dragon. Rev 12:9. In this vision John apostle identifies the snake with the dragon with 7 heads and 10 horns, because of the amount of damage that it can cause. But the dragon is still an allegory, and refers to an institution of such character.

The snake still represents temptation, it can cause damage and ruin and injury to individuals and families and societies to the extend of a dragon. The person succumbing to temptation can cause ruin and injury to themselves and others comparable to a dragon. The snake is called slanderer and adversary, the root meanings of devil and satan. Rev 12:9. This is the evil impulse in sinful man that opposes the goodness of *Yahweh* God and opposes the saints of *Yahweh* God.

The animosity or enmity between the snake and the woman is allegorical and symbolizes the attempt by false-religion to corrupt true religion. Gen 3:15. All throughout Scripture inroads are made by superstition, idolatry and paganism into the true worship of *Yahweh* God.

The posterity of the snake are the Pharisees. John 8:44. The relationship between the snake and Eve is solely one of spiritual seduction. There is no evidence whatsoever to justify a physical relationship. Paul apostle mentions that the relationship between the snake and Eve was that of tempter and victim. 2 Cor 11:3. The entire scenario must be understood in the terms that Moses intended for the people of Israel during their sojourn in the deserts and for the future generations of Israelites. Every person is a Adam in his own right and every woman is an Eve with the ability to withstand temptation or succumb to it.

The conflict of Gen 3:15, between the posterity of the snake and the posterity of the woman, surfaced during the ministry of Jesus. The Pharisees bit at the heel of Jesus by having him executed, but Jesus crushed the head of the snake by resurrecting from the dead.

> Then the God of peace will soon crush satan (the adversary) under your feet. Rom 16:20. Heb 2:14.

The words of *Yahweh* God to the snake fulfilled in the above manner.

## THE CURSE UPON EVE

The curse upon the female is noted in Gen 3:16, and consists primarily in 2 items. First is pain during childbirth. In order to understand properly this statement, Eve had to have delivered at least 1 or preferable more children without pain of labor. No doubt after the delivery of Seth, Eve was definitely repentant of her disobedience, but nothing could be done at this time.

The second item is the reduction of the status of a female. Up to this time the female was equal to the male in every respect. This was discussed earlier. But now and due to this disobedience Eve was relegated to a lesser status and now subject to the male. This can be best understood using examples. First, women want to get married. Although not the absolute rule, but in general this is definitely the natural attitude. Women are raised from a early age to expect marriage and develop an attitude of desiring marriage within a certain time frame. Often it doesn't especially matter to whom, as long as the male appears decent, treats her well, and will make the commitment. Women have married almost total strangers, men they hardly knew, men they even disliked or objected, and only for the sake of the state of matrimony. Many marry for no other reason except not to be alone or be branded as a spinster or undesirable. A lack of marriage partner can make a woman feel as if they are less of a woman for not having a husband. For this reason the "woman's desire is for her husband and he will rule over her." Gen 3:16.

## THE CURSE UPON ADAM AND CREATION

The specific reason for Adam's disobedience is noted in Gen 3:17: he failed to fulfill the role of leadership and courage that was divinely assigned to the male. Instead of taking personal responsibility for his choice he decided to evade accepting blame. I do not consider it important that it was the wife that the husband allowed to dictate to him how to conduct himself. The important facet is that the husband allowed another person to dictate his thinking and to control his actions and manipulate him.

The entire nature of the earth was changed with the verdict of *Yahweh* God upon Adam and his male descendents.

"Cursed is the ground because of you, in toil you shall eat of it all the days of your life. Thorns and thistles it shall being forth to you and you shall eat the plants of the field. In the sweat of your face you shall eat bread." Gen 3:17-19.

The moment that *Yahweh* God recited these words the ground became temporal and all that evolved from it became temporal, and every evil and failure existing upon earth materialized. Everything that can possibly ruin and interfere with the success, prosperity and health of a person entered history when *Yahweh* God cursed the ground. Prior to this time the ground and soil was blessed of *Yahweh* God. The soil was eternal and all that evolved from it was eternal, ageless, permanent. This pertained to all living organisms, plants and animals, and the entire structure and composition of the earth. Now all of the original nature of creation changed.

The variant weather patterns existing on earth were initiated on earth at this time: violent weather or dry spells or deluges. Likewise the rise of the various plant diseases and fungi that can destroy crops, and insects such as locusts and flies and gnats and mosquitoes appeared on earth subsequent to these words of *Yahweh* God.

The tragedies of nature or Acts of God: the hurricane, tornado, monsoon, flood, drought or famine, intense heat or extreme cold – all entered the world this day. The human is very weak and fragile compared with the forces of nature. The human is no match. Under these conditions the human must live and must adapt his life to survive the elements. As long as the human subjects himself to the authority of *Yahweh* God by submitting himself to the authority of divine instruction, all will go well with him in spite of these upheavals of nature. Moses mentions this Ps 90:9-10. So much of the time that *Yahweh* God allots a person to life is absorbed by failure and difficulty in life until he finally passes away. Very little time is actually available for some happiness, prosperity and personal achievement. Living under difficult circumstances until the human passes away was the result of *Yahweh* God's curse of the ground.

All possible failure entered the world this day. Labor is no more a pleasure, but now a difficulty, a chore, with regular futility and failure in work accomplished. Beginning at this time men began to face failure in the effort they exert. They are injured and exhausted in their work and face the elements with uncertainty, worry and finally desperation. This verse is the reason for the far reaching incident of the collapse of economies and banks and businesses; the loss of fortunes on bad deals and losses on debts.

Since the ground was cursed of *Yahweh* God and underwent a massive change in structure from eternal to temporal, so now all creation that would evolve from the earth would also be temporal. All humanity, every individual, will reach a point in life that the body will no longer be able to sustain life, and life will terminate. This likewise pertains to all plant life and all organic matter that evolves from the soil, all will eventually decay and decompose and return to the constituents of soil. This cycle has continued for many millennia and will continue so until the restoration.

## EXILE FROM EDEN

The banishment from Eden culminates the sentence of *Yahweh* God on Adam and Eve. The prior perfect and ideal environment now became history. All that remained of Eden was memories. Regret now dominated the mind of the progenitors as they gathered their belongings and migrated to some other area to live. I contend that the banishment from Eden is an allegory created by Moses under to symbolize loss and deprivation of the perfect environment for humanity. In reality the permanent exile from the perfection of environment occurred when nature changed its state from eternal to temporal. Once they awoke to a new temporal world that next morning they were outside the borders of Eden the garden of *Yahweh* God, never to enter again. It did not take long for the results of their disobedience to affect them and for them to fully realize the consequences of their actions. That they no longer resided in Eden became more and more apparent as time passed and when the first weeds sprouted in the cultivated fields overnight; when the progenitors were first stung by a mosquito and were subsequently inflected with malaria: fever, chills, sleeplessness, sweat; when Adam caught a cold and laid in bed with his runny nose, sore throat, headache and fever; when Adam caught dysentery from drinking unboiled water; when Adam worked hard in the fields and only physically exhausted himself and watched his crops ruined by heavy rain or drought or devoured by locusts or destroyed by frost; when Eve endured the pain of labor during the delivery of Seth; when Eve suffered a miscarriage; when Even found herself mistreated by Adam for failing in his domestic and marital expectations of her; when Eve felt insecure day after day worrying over Adam; when Eve drifted into depression from the stress of raising children; when their bodies began to change as they grew older, became weak and more susceptible to injury and the elements; and when they finally passed away.

No more will there be access to again eat of the tree of life until the restoration. It is this sin – disobedience – that separates a human from *Yahweh* God. The promise to again gain the access to this tree to again restore immortality abides in the victory over sin through Jesus. 1 Cor 15:55. Rev 2:7. To this victor, that is to this person, both male and female, who gains the victory over sin, to him and her is access allowed to again eat of the fruit of this tree and to live forever. All this to occur in the restoration.

## DEATH AND DYING

All organisms, whether plant or animal or human, whether amoebae or bacteria or fungi, have their origin from the soil. The original constituents and source of all organic matter is the soil.

"From the earth (soil) you were taken." Gen 3:17, said *Yahweh* God.

The essence that determines if these organic entities are "alive" is their possession of the spirit of life or animation, the breath that *Yahweh* God personally breathes into them. Once the spirit is removed, then the organism returns to its original state: it decays and decomposes into soil. All creatures have a limited life span, though some shorter and other longer. The creation is designed such by *Yahweh* God to reproduce and then terminate existence. The newly-born organisms will grow and at maturity subsequently reproduce and repeat the same cycle. This life span is predetermined for all creatures. The human follows the same pattern as all other organisms in this cycle.

Solomon describes the similarity of demise of both human and animal in identical terms.

> For the fate of the sons of men and the fate of animals is the same; as one dies, so dies the other. They all have the same breath, and man has no advantage over the animals; for all is vanity. For all go to the same place; all are from the dust and all turn to dust again. Eccl 3:19-20.

The final chapter of Ecclesiastics describes in poetic and symbolic language the final moment of a person's conscious existence and his passage into oblivion and demise. Eccl 12:5-7. The silver cord is symbolic of the dictate of *Yahweh* God regarding length of life bestowed upon a person.

As a person grows older the faculties slowly erode and response is deterred. Death still seems distant for many in this condition, because the reality of it is also at a distance, and again due to erosion of the faculties. Under such conditions of frailty of body and mind a person passes away without notice of what is occurring, painlessly, The spirit of animation slowly migrates out of the body while respiration decreases and ceases. The most painful or shocking termination would be that of a serious accident, or suicide by impact, such as jumping off a bridge into icy water or concrete, or electrocution. In this situation the spirit is wrenched out of the body like a car at high speed impacts a block wall. The body reverts into neural convulsions, a shock and pain so excruciating that the person loses consciousness and lapses into lifelessness in moments. Execution by guillotine may sever the head from the torso, but the body would continue alive for a few moments until the spirit departs. The eyes in the severed head may even see the area from the basket with the other heads, while the heart continues to pump blood out the arteries in the neck. This also seems to be a reason why the ancient saints wanted a death in old age, so they would not have to suffer a painful death in younger years with their faculties in excellent condition.

There is a distinct difference in the state of the body in the seconds before death and the seconds after death. The migration of the spirit out of the body could last from a few seconds in a person with a fatal illness or old age or failure of vital organs, or immediate with a person terminating life in some violent manner like execution. The individual loses identity at this point, meaning that the soul lapses into oblivion, not having a functioning body to reside in. The fact that certain body functions may continue for some short period, such as hair or fingernail growth, these body functions would be compared to a plant broken at the stem: withering, yet still growing until all the cells die on a individual basis. The Jewish sages likewise taught the termination of life at death. This was the accepted teaching of Scripture during the era of Jesus.

> From the dead, as from one who does not exist, thanksgiving has ceased. Sirach 17:28.

Job awaited his own demise as a means of relief from his pain and anguish. He describes the state he was to transfer to in Job 3:17-19.

Death as Job described it is a state of withdrawal from the effects of pain and emotion. With the neural system inactive and not functional, there is no pain, and there cannot be pain in the body any longer. Pain can only exist if there is an active and functional nervous system to convey to the brain such sensations. Death terminates the functions of the nervous system. In the interim state the soul or identity has no means of sensing pain since it is a immaterial and ethereal object. The spirit of animation cannot experience pain either since it is spirit.

## DEAD SOULS

That the soul dies was understood typically throughout the Bible, and this phrase was used on a regular basis. The most popular passage is that of Ezekiel prophet.

> The soul that sins shall die. Eze 18:4, 20.

In this passage the soul refers to the person as an identity. Death as a result of the violation of the law of *Yahweh* God was the termination of life. Corpses are likewise referred to as dead souls (*nephesh*) in the original Hebrew of the following passages..

> You shall not make marks in your flesh for a dead soul. Lev 19:28.
> Unto no souls of the dead shall [the priest] approach. Lev 21:11.
> [The Nazarite] shall not approach a dead soul all the days of his separation unto *Yahweh*. Num 6:6.
> Every person that touches a dead soul, a person who has died... Num 19:11,13.
> If any one is unclean by touching a dead soul... Hag 2:13.

One passage worth investigating is in Revelation:

I saw under the altar the souls of those who had been slain for the word of God and for the witness they had borne. Rev 6:9.

This pile of corpses in front of the altar are those mentioned by Jesus in Matt 23:29-35 and John 16:2. These passages refer to all those who died for the word of *Yahweh* God and their testimony. Rev 1:9. Because the corpses are piled in front of the altar indicates that they were a sacrifice unto *Yahweh* God, unwilling to compromise or deny true deity or true faith in *Yahweh* God. These were the lambs led to the slaughter. Rom 8:36. The voice emanating from these corpses is their wait for vengeance, and can be compared to the voice of the blood of Abel that cried from the ground seeking vengeance. Gen 4:10. These were told that the vengeance of *Yahweh* God on their behalf was in the future, and that more persecution was yet to come. When the point arrives that *Yahweh* God can no longer tolerate the death of His saints at the hands of sinners, then He will intervene and execute His sentence upon them.

This passage along with the balance of the book of Revelation is interpreted allegorically, and does not serve as any indication of conscious existence during the interim.

## THE INTERIM STATE

Several passages in the NT are often interpreted such to lay claim to conscious existence during the interim state, to indicate evidence of consciousness. If this is so they would contradict the earlier passages noted above, also from Scripture. The excuse or justification for this is termed progressive revelation, meaning that not the entirety of knowledge in all areas was revealed at one time, but subsequent as time progressed. I agree with this concept and it definitely applies to some important topics and concepts, such as the resurrection, priesthood, covenants, arrival of Jesus, and many others. But new revelation must not contradict previous revelation, but should further explain the concept. New revelation must be able to be interpreted in light of previous revelation, not contradicted. In this situation of dealing with the interim state the same approach must be taken. Any new revelation regarding the interim state located in the gospels and letters of the Apostles must not contradict any previous divine revelation.

The interim state is adequately described:

> But the dead know nothing, and they have no more reward; but the memory of them is lost. Eccl 9:5.
> For there is no work or thought or knowledge or wisdom in Sheol, where you go. Eccl 9:10.
> When his breath departs he returns to his earth; on that very day his thoughts perish. Ps 146:6
> For then I would have laid down and been quiet; I would sleep; then I would be at rest. There the wicked cease from troubling, and there the weary are at rest, there the prisoners are at ease together; they hear not the voice of the taskmaster. Job 3:13, 17-18.

There is no indication or witness at all in the Hebrew or Greek Scriptures regarding any conscious existence of a person during the interim state. This is because the specific revelation of *Yahweh* God clearly teaches in both OT and NT that every human is in a state of unconscious oblivion or inert activity during this period. In essence the human reverts back to his state prior to their conception. All that remains of the human is his identity and conduct recorded in annals in heaven inscribed in the memory of *Yahweh* God. As the Scriptures teach, the spirit returns to *Yahweh* God and the body returns to the earth. The soul or identity has no conscious existence at this time and so does not travel or return anywhere. The reason for this was noted earlier, that conscious existence for a human is possible only with a living body, and depends on a body in a healthy condition. I contend that the state of the dead, or the interim state, has not changed since the demise of the first human, Abel, to our time and will remain the same until the restoration. The concept of conscious existence in the interim was unknown to the people of *Yahweh* God in OT and NT eras. A few passages will be investigated.

Luke 16:19-31. The parable of Dives and Lazarus. This passage is definitely a parable. As indicated in another passage, Jesus said nothing without the use of a parable, and this specific narrative is at the conclusion of 9 parables in Luke 14-16, and is followed by more parables. Even taking serious consideration of the narrative, the rich man is buried but angels transport Lazarus. If one is buried and the other is carried to some distant area, how can they see and talk and hear one another, and especially with a gulf between them? And what about the billions of others that have died? Are they also in the same circumstances? Should not Dives also have been transported by angels or demons to hell fire? Dives suggesting to Lazarus that he deliver a message to living people, the family of Dives, sounds most improbable. Dives would have asked this only if this was possible. Likewise, Dives asking Abraham for water can hardly be realistic. What value is water in hell fire? Material water is useless in the realm of the interim, because it is not a material realm. Any attempt to utilize this passage as a reality of conscious existence in the interim is absurd. It does however have many benefits if interpreted as a parable.

Luke 23:43. The words of Jesus to the thief on the stake. The word paradise is a loan from Persian meaning garden. In this passage, Jesus tells the thief that both of them will be buried that day in a local garden. This will be discussed later in more detail.

Phil 1:21-24. Paul apostle wrote to the Philippians while imprisoned at Caesarea. There under the guard of Roman soldiers he sat in a prison cell for about 2 years. The poor conditions of existence, exposure to the elements, made life seem hopeless and futile for Paul apostle. I contend that Paul apostle felt he reached that point in life that his ministry had ended: he would sit in prison until he died. He could not be released on his own cognizance, and so was at the mercy of the Roman procurator and the Jewish elders for any possible chance of release. For this reason he states that he is perplexed whether to continue to live or just plain die while imprisoned. By dying he is freed from the misery and suffering of confinement, both physical and psychological. By dying he will await and eventually greet Jesus at the resurrection, and his gain here is release from the torment of prison incarceration. But he realized that his death would be a savage blow to the faith of many. For this reason he would prefer to persevere to remain alive in prison.

The only other section that some utilize to attempt to prove conscious existence during the interim is the book of Revelation. This book is one of countless symbolism and allegory from beginning to end. There is no more a lake of fire than a beast with 7 heads and 10 horns, or the number 666 engraved on hands and foreheads or people waving palm branches standing in front of the throne of *Yahweh* God. I find it shallow that any passage in this book would be interpreted and applied literally.

## NEAR-DEATH EXPERIENCES

So-called near death experiences or death experiences can likewise be explained. During sleep, for example, the brain continues to function, but in a reduced state, and a person can dream. These dreams are imaginations generated from an uncontrolled brain, because the body is asleep. The brain likewise generates uncontrolled imaginations or hallucinations, images, during these seconds of the spirit of animation migrating out of the body. If the body can be made functional again, by some stimulation of the heart, the spirit of animation returns and the body again lives. If the body cannot be made functional, damaged beyond repair or brain-dead, or having some other failure of the heart or vital organs, then once the spirit departs nothing can be done to revive or resuscitate the body. But if the body is functional and an immediate stimulation is performed, it may revive with the return of the spirit. During this short interval of perhaps seconds or minutes, the brain generates uncontrolled images. These are still retained in the memory even after recovery from the near-death state and the patient can still remember these images. The fact that many experience the same type of experience, or brain generated imagination, it is because the brain at this time generates the same type of image or hallucination.

After investigating volumes of recorded incidences of this type, I do not see any evidence of post-death conscious existence beyond a few minutes while the brain decays and generates hallucinations.

I remember the personal experience of my mother passing away at the age of 62, after a prolonged illness of some 5 years. During this period I watched the slow decay of her body. She lapsed into a coma about 2 days before her death. It was in her sleep or coma that she passed away during the night. I held my mother by the hand at the mortuary, and she was lifeless, dead. Once the spirit of animation vacated her body during that night she became lifeless. Her soul or identity was now history on earth, now nothing more than a record in heavenly annals, that such a person lived at this time, place, with a record of her activities during her career of 62 years. We buried her 2 days later.

This event particularly assisted me in compiling his concept of the interim state. Even after years of Bible study the conclusion kept slipping away because of the heavy influence of Protestant and Catholic notions of heaven and hell, paradise and purgatory. With the passage of such a close member of the family, and personal involvement in the funeral, the truth of Scripture became evident. I was able to reject the incorrect notions of Protestant and Catholic Christianity, and fully grasp and accept the concept as related in Scripture.

## SLEEP AS A EUPHEMISM FOR DEATH

Jesus, during his ministry on earth, referred to the state of the deceased as sleep, and also Paul apostle referred to the deceased as those asleep in the Lord.

> "Our friend Lazarus has fallen asleep and I go to wake him from sleep." John 11:11.
> Most of whom are still alive though some have fallen asleep. 1 Cor 15:6.
> Then those also who have fallen asleep... 1 Cor 15:18.
> But we would not have you ignorant brethren, concerning those fallen asleep. 1 Thess 4:13.

Gospel writer Matthew refers to those long dead saints of the ages who resurrected with Jesus as asleep. Matt 27:51. John apostle also inferred this when he recorded the words of the messenger,

> "Blessed are the dead who die in the Lord,... they rest from their labors." Rev 14:13.

In this selection of NT passages, death is compared to the state of an individual when they are asleep.

When a person falls asleep and in a sound sleep, he is oblivious to all that occurs around him, and is even unaware of his own existence. A person goes to bed in the evening knowing this and fully convinced that they will awake in the morning. So it is with the saints of *Yahweh* God. These fall asleep knowing that they will be awakened in the future.

Sometime in the distant future and unknown to all, at the restoration they will be awakened from oblivion.

## LAZARUS

I wondered what Lazarus would have said if asked to describe his 4 days of death. First, there was no doubt that he was dead. When the stone was rolled away from the tomb the people nearby smelled the stench of his decomposing body. John 11:39. What would he have said to his audience? Would he have described these 4 days as floating about on clouds with wings and a harp in his hand? Or perhaps in a fiery pit with bright red demons bouncing about with pointed tails and horns holding pitchforks? Or perhaps relaxing in some luxurious environment of a garden with every imaginable pleasure available? I contend that the reply of Lazarus to his inquisitive friends would have been something in the following manner:

"I was very ill and the pain in my body increased. The pain and discomfort and burning in my head and inside my body increased. It reached a point I could no longer tolerate. My spirit wanted to leave but my body kept enduring, my heart kept pumping and the pain increased. Once I reached that plateau of total inability to endure the pain I felt this massive relief. My heart slowed down and within a few heartbeats ceased to function. Something evacuated my body and abandoned me. I don't know what it was, but as it migrated out I began to lapse into a sleep, a quiet undisturbed state and became oblivious to all sensation and emotion. I became cold and very cold. The next moment I lapsed into total unconsciousness and mental inactivity. My memory stops there. I cannot say how long I remained in this condition. Time came to a standstill."

A comparable parallel for individuals lapsing into death who are not under massive pain or accidental death could be that of the effects of general anesthesia prior to a hospital surgery, or the effect of sodium pentothal prior to oral surgery. After surgery and the effects of the anesthesia wear off, the patient remembers nothing and has felt no pain during the surgery.

If a person can undergo massive surgeries, and feel and sense and remember nothing during this period under anesthesia, how much less would consciousness exist when all the organs and nervous system of the body cease to function? And it is only in an active and functional body that sensation can exist. Lazarus would have continued the story of his resurrection as follows:

"All of a sudden I heard a voice. 'Lazarus come forth.' With these words I began to slowly regain consciousness. Some ethereal substance was emerging into my lifeless limbs and my heart began beating. I was very cold at first but then after a minute my body warmed up. I opened my eyes. I realized I was awake. For a few minutes I laid still, wondering what it was that had occurred to me. It took a while before I came to the complete realization that I had regained total consciousness and I was my old self again, alive as I was earlier. It was a shock at first but then I adjusted. I looked about the room and it was dark. I realized that I was in a tomb of some sort; I did see some light at one end, which I surmised to be an entrance. The slab I was laying on was cold and seemed to draw the new warmth I acquired out of my body. I had to get up. It was difficult getting up because I was wrapped up tight in graveclothes. Once I was up I walked toward the light and out into broad daylight."

So did the death and resurrection of Lazarus occur.

## SAUL AND THE NECROMANCER OF ENDOR

The final point to be considered in this section is that of Saul and necromancer of Endor. 1 Sam 28. The narrative is a description of the attempt by the desperate Saul to acquire council from Samuel prophet. He was desperate for divine advice to try and salvage what remained of his kingdom and gain a victory over Philistines. This medium or necromancer definitely had these demonic capabilities to wake the dead and conjure them up to communicate with them on earth. There was no doubt in anybody's mind at this session that this personage was Samuel, and so what they saw was an apparition of the man. The medium best describes him as a god coming out of the earth. The use of the term god is in contradistinction to the term son of man, which is used to refer to someone appearing in the figure of a human. What the necromancer saw was a ghost-like figure without a definite human shape, but yet had features sufficient to be recognizable. This identity of Samuel, his soul, was roused from its inactivity in the realm of the immaterial world, enlivened from its unconscious sleep, as Samuel himself states, "Why have you disturbed me by bringing me up?" 1 Sam 28:15. Samuel was in some unconscious state, and this necromancer had the capability to retrieve his identity, his soul, from its residence and cause it to surface in their presence.

At the conclusion of their conversation Samuel says, "Tomorrow you and your sons shall be with me." 1 Sam 18:19. These words mean exactly what they say. Wherever Samuel was abiding prior to this session, and to where he is now returning, so also Saul and Jonathan and Abinadab and Matchishum will arrive there after their demise on the battlefield. This place cannot refer to heaven or hell, but to the grave in general, and their identity or soul to be transported to a state of inactivity for the indefinite future.

## DEATH AS A PRISON

Death is a prison. It is as if the person is locked in a secured dungeon, lifeless, dark, cold and forgotten. *Yahweh* God asked Job martyr about the residence of the dead in words similar.

Have the gates of death been revealed to you? Job 38:17.

Once an individual is confined to this eternal incarceration, not he nor any other person can release him. The fetters, chains, gate and lock are beyond the strength of the powerless victim.

The true Christian has the keys of the kingdom of heaven. Matt 16:19. In reality though, the keys are in the hands of Jesus. Rev 1:18. This means he has the capability to permit escape from this prison. He has the necessary means of removing the chains and fetters, unlocking the lock on the gates, and opening the gates and freeing the prisoners from the prison of the grave.

That death is a prison and not a paradise or purgatory is also attested to by Peter in his statement about the spirits in prison. 1 Pet 3:19. Exactly how Jesus preached to the remains of those disobedient to the preaching of Noah and who died in the flood is not apparent. I surmise that all the dead of the ages were made aware of His crucifixion and subsequent resurrection during these 3 days and 3 nights, including those who perished in the flood. The reason the balance of the dead are not mentioned by Peter apostle is that the conclusion intended was baptism in 1 Pet 3:22, which flood was an allegorical antecedent. It was from these spirits in the death-prison the Jesus selected those to resurrect along with him, all those obedient to *Yahweh* God throughout the ages. This was discussed earlier.

## ANIMALS

Animals differ from humans in the areas mentioned in several areas above. The most important single point of distinction is that an animal does not have an identity as does a human. An animal is a body and a spirit of animation. It has no individual identity, nor does it possess self-consciousness. An animal only exists due to its generation as offspring.

Like the human though, the initial animals created on the $5^{th}$ and $6^{th}$ days of creation week were created complete, male and female, and with the ability to reproduce. Each was an original design, a species. Every animal is also composed of spirit, soul and body. But there are important differences.

An animal does not have the type of soul as a human does. The extent of the soul in an animal is to contain the divinely gifted instinct. This is the use of the term soul when referring to animals. Rev 8:8, 16:3. The instinct possessed by the animal is not part of its flesh or its spirit. The animal likewise begins to exist as an independent entity at its birth; at this point divine instinct for that particular species is installed. But there is no personal identity with the animal. It does not know that it exists.

An animal is not a free moral agent. It has no ability to decide right or wrong, it cannot answer to someone else for its conduct. Its conduct and reaction and activity is long previously determined and programmed into it through the instinct for that species. It reacts as the instinct causes it to react: flee or defend itself from danger; eat when it is hungry; shelter itself from the elements; and procreate during the season intended for it to continue the species.

An animal has no conscience. It cannot sense guilt. Neither can it sense joy or personal fulfillment or gratification. An animal cannot hate, love, despise, pretend, have sympathy, or take vengeance. It is programmed to react in a certain manner and without personal reflection or emotion and without consideration of right or wrong. An animal has no sense of time, not past, not future, only the immediate. It has no grasp of temporality or eternity. It no doubt knows when it is dying, and struggles to live. This spirit of animation that drives the animal to live is the same spirit in the human. Both drive the animal to survive, to heal its wounds, and reproduce.

When the animal dies its soul vanishes into the ethereal realm; its instinct has completed its purpose and so terminates its existence. Like the human, the animal dies when the spirit of animation vacates the body. This is the explanation of Solomon.

> For the fate of the sons of men and the fate of beasts is the same: as one dies so dies the other. They all have the same breath; for all is vanity. All go to one place; all are from the dust and all turn to dust. Who knows whether the spirit of man goes upward and the spirit of the beast goes down to the earth. Eccl 3:19-21

The point made by Solomon is that the manner of death is common for both animals and humans. When the spirit vacates the body the identity ceases, and the body begins its composition. The difference to be noted though with the human is also brought out by Solomon in the concluding verses of his portrayal of life. Eccl 11:9, and 12:13-14. The human will face a judgment; the animal will not. This is because the human soul is a self-conscious identity, while the animal is not. With death, the identity of the animal terminates and vanishes as if it never existed. It must occur in this manner, otherwise clean animals could not be used for food.

An animal is born with instinct. The extent of the soul of an animal is its instinct. This is the invisible and inherent knowledge that every animal is born with. No animal is born without a complete education to guide it from birth to death. From the moment of birth, all knowledge and ability that the animal needs to survive, mate and reproduce, rear its young, build or find shelter, defend itself from the elements and enemies is inherent. Instinct is congenital. This instinct resides in every creature, from amoebae to elephant to zebra, from the smallest single cell organism to the most complex of massive land and sea creature. Not one needs a day of education, nor needs to recognize one letter of an alphabet. If means of communication exists between those of the same species, it is naturally contained in their nature.

An animal also has an ability beyond that of a human to naturally adapt to environment. With its natural clothing as an insulation, it can easier withstand changes in climate, temperature and endure exposure to the elements.

## PLANTS

Plants have a spirit, but one specially created by *Yahweh* God for the various species. This spirit causes the seed to germinate or spore to grow into a new plant, likewise with the ability to reproduce. As long as the environment is suitable the species will continue forever. Even with a change in climate, seeds can last several years in the ground before geminating. This spirit of plants causes cell division and growth. Like animals and humans, the plant spirit will remain in the plant as long as the body of the plant is capable of retaining life. If the plant is deprived of water and nutrients, or exposed to extreme climate, or is damaged to the point that the plant can no longer sustain life, this spirit departs and the plant returns to soil.

Like living organisms created during creation week, *Yahweh* God created the plant species. Each species was created on an original basis. With the original creation, every plant was gifted with the ability to reproduce. The original tree, fruit, bush or vine, was created by *Yahweh* God with the ability to reproduce itself.

## 3. THE EARTHLY LIFE

### PURPOSE OF CREATION

There are 2 primary reasons for the development of the earth and its population. Some of this has been noted earlier.

1. *Yahweh* God is a creator by nature. This is the result of His nature of love. For *Yahweh* God to love is to create. *Yahweh* God manifests His love by creating an inhabitable world, by beautifying it with natural features. He beautified the earth by populating it with animals of various design and purpose.

2. The creation magnifies *Yahweh* God. All of existence serves to glorify its creator. It is much like a painting, a magnificent work of art, that discloses to every viewer the talent of the artist, the sculpture that advertises the ability of the sculptor. Like a work of art, a textbook in mathematics, a piece of literature well-written, or a volume of research, all attest to the talent and ability of their authors, and so does creation with *Yahweh* God.

Likewise all of the exact creation nature, plants and animals, the terrain of the earth, its balance of weather, and all involved to continue its infinite existence, all attest to the wisdom, strength and purpose of the supreme creator *Yahweh* God. It glorifies and magnifies its creator.

> The heavens announce the glory of God; and the firmament proclaims His craftsmanship. Ps 18:1.

In bestowing names upon the progenitors of created humanity, *Yahweh* God selected the most appropriate that he could find: earth or soil (*adam*) and life (*eva*). Since all life evolved from the earth, and Eve was the mother of all living, Adam and Eve are the single progenitors of all created humanity. There is no evidence to testify of other parallel human creation or evolution. Adam and Eve were created as adults based on the command to marry and begin procreation.

Some of the early life patterns of Adam and Eve can be only ascertained from the changes and curses that were pronounced by *Yahweh* God after the fall. Based on the change brought about by *Yahweh* God, we can determine in general theory of what the original pattern of life consisted in the garden of Eden. This pattern of life which reverted to difficulty is not defined in every aspect, but at least in the areas of labor, childbirth, attitude of a married couple, and termination of life. Each of these will be discussed in this section.

The difficulties of life that entered the world are not a total deprivation of happiness during our temporary earthly life, nor a lack of a reason to work for success. I view this as signs of *Yahweh* God's sovereignty over the elements and his creation, and to impress upon man his necessity of subjection to *Yahweh* God as the wise and omnipotent. The human can easily inflate their ego and substantially, and become haughty and rude due to success. Often it doesn't take much success for a person to think of himself more highly than they should. An individual becomes very self-reliant noticing that personal and financial prosperity is the result of his efforts. Pride destroys the life of the individual and those whom they influence and those who surround them. To help reduce pride and haughtiness and self-reliance *Yahweh* God utilizes the elements so subdue the human, to impress upon the human that he is relatively powerless compared to the omnipotent strength of *Yahweh* God as manifested in the elements of nature. All of the disastrous effects of nature are implemented by *Yahweh* God to impress upon the human the necessity of accepting the sovereignty of *Yahweh* God over our life and the earth.

## LABOR

For Adam work in Eden was a pleasure. The modern person seems to enjoin a good work-out at a health club or at some exercise, at a spa, participating in some sport. All of these exercises exert effort, burn calories, cause sweat, and use and develop muscles. They also tire an individual to the point they need rest, and so sleep well that night.

This would be an adequate manner to describe work in the garden of Eden. Here both male and female enjoyed the exertion of effort. It is a self-satisfying and gratifying pleasure to wake in the morning, fulfill the obligations of the day, and retire in the evening, to be able to look at a person's own constructive effort of that day and be able to say just as

*Yahweh* God did, "This is good." Gen 1:12,18,25,31. Every challenge would be successful. Failure would be unknown. For many individuals a hobby is gratifying and mentally constructive for those not physically equipped or gifted. Perhaps the desk job in Eden could be compared to the effort exerted mentally in a hobby. At the conclusion of the day a similar type of sense of accomplishment can also be felt. But all of this ended with the words,

"Cursed is the earth as a result of you." Gen 3:17.

From this point on work was no longer a pleasure, but a necessity, a drudgery, a demanding effort that would exhaust man and woman both. Failure materialized at this moment of time. An exhaustion and pressure that would drive a person to despair as he fought against the elements to earn a living, this applying to every occupation. There are hazards and dangers no matter what type of physical work is performed, and just as many psychological pressures can apply to a non-physical occupation. Work causes injury and accidents, mistakes and errors. Non-physical occupations have their share of mental stress, boredom, fatigue and strain, the diseases that result from worry and anxiety. Failure is costly and psychologically and physically devastating.

The early life of Adam and Eve and no doubt their sons and daughters was occupied with farming and raising cattle, an agrarian society. They achieved a personal fulfillment from their occupation, always a success.

## MARRIAGE AND CHILDBIRTH

The concept of marriage was divinely instituted with the creation of the first couple, which *Yahweh* God wedded in Eden. As all that *Yahweh* God does is for the benefit of His creation, and especially for created humanity, this concept of marriage is the pinnacle of a social state for humans.

The reasons for the division of the genders and the reunification of them in marriage are social, procreative, purpose, and trust. With 2 genders each having assigned traits, as well as distinguishable shape and appearance, the opposites can interest themselves in the opposite sex. Men with men are no variety, and women with women are no variety. But a male with a female serves as a variety and the motivation to learn and acquaint themselves with the opposite gender. Social interest is more attractive when a person is with someone different than yourself but of the same species.

Most children up to adolescence prefer the company of the same gender. Beginning with adolescence the natural impulse in any person is toward heterosexuality. The period of adolescence is a transfer of this social preference to the opposite gender. Much of this is chemical and physical, with the development of the reproductive organs in both male and female. Chemicals are generated by the body of each gender during adolescence as a result of the divinely-created drive for sexual union. The attention of each gender is directed toward the opposite because of the variety in shape and appearance and because of the purpose the other is created.

Before the sentence of *Yahweh* God upon the female, childbirth was a pleasure. With the pain of labor and delivery we would include the nuisance of the menstrual cycle, which likewise had no reason to exist in the early life. Childbirth was painless and a pleasant if not an ecstatic experience. Just as *Yahweh* God would attain a personal joy at the creation of new life, so the female at this time would have felt a pleasure at delivery.

The conclusion brought to light at this point is that Adam and Eve were engaged in marital relations shortly after their settlement in Eden. Since the faculties for engaging in marital relations were part of male and female anatomy for conception and procreation, *Yahweh* God no doubt united the 2 in a holy matrimony during the week following creation. They then would have immediately began fulfillment of the divine command,

"Be productive and increase and fill the earth." Gen 1:28.

*Yahweh* God created sexual relations and for reasons both of matrimonial pleasure and procreation, and promoted it within their legitimate matrimony. Marital relations are a blessing of *Yahweh* God for His created humanity.

I contend that offspring of Adam and Eve were conceived and delivered prior to the temptation by the snake. This consisted of at least 2 sons and as many daughters. If it were otherwise Eve would have no reason to regret the sentence of *Yahweh* God upon her. She would not be able to understand the curse she brought upon all the future generations of women as a result of her disobedience.

Both Adam and Eve were created as complete individuals in a psychological sense. They lacked nothing: high self esteem, self respect, emotional stability, excellent mental health, without any character flaws or psychotic maladies. This changed with the words,

"Yet your desire shall be for your husband and he shall rule over you." Gen 3:16.

With these words a portion of that personal stability and psychological independence was removed from the female. Now she would need a husband in order to feel "fulfilled." Most women, if not all, want to get married, have a home, have a family. In Eden each gender and especially the female was complete in itself. Neither party lacked emotionally, physically or psychologically, either in marriage or out of marriage. Each had high self esteem and respect and mental stability and balance.

## GENDERS

The genders were created by *Yahweh* God for the success of humanity during their corporeal career. One gender is not superior over the other: both have the image and likeness of *Yahweh* God. Gen 5:1. Each gender has distinguishing traits and features as a physical divine image, as a separation of the genders, and each has an assigned role and responsibility for their life on earth defined by *Yahweh* God. The female is called the weaker sex by Peter apostle. 1 Pet 3:7. This applies to physical weakness, and not moral or psychological, in which the female is often the stronger. The female also requires the support of the male, her husband, to fulfill her role as assistant, mother and parent.

Each of the genders is created with attributes for their specific purpose. The male is designed primarily for physical labor. His physique demands short hair. 1 Cor 12:14. This is the general tradition among males of the civilized societies: the hair of the male above the ears. The beard is also part of the physical image of the male. The patriarchs wore a beard. Scripture specifically refers to the beard of Aaron, Ps 133:2. Ezekiel, Eze 5:1. David, 1 Sam 21:13. Ezra, Ezra 9:3. And to the beard of the servants of David, 2 Sam 10:4-5. *Yahweh* God forbid the Israelite men from turning their beards into a fashion by trimming, Lev 19:27.

Clement of Alexandria wrote about 200 AD, regarding the hair and beard for the believers of that era:

> The hair of the head [of the male], that it may not grow so long as to come down and interfere with the eyes,... But the hair on the chin is not to be disturbed, as it gives no trouble, and lends to the face dignity and paternal terror.[8]
> But God wished women to be smooth, and rejoice in their locks alone growing spontaneously, as a horse in his mane; but has adorned man like the lions with a beard, and endowed him, as an attribute of manhood, with shaggy breasts, a sign this of strength and rule.[9]
> For it is not lawful to pluck out the beard, man's natural and noble ornament.[10]

The female is likewise endowed with attributes for her role and responsibility as an assistant to the male and for child bearing and child raising. 1 Tim 2:15. The hair on the female is to be longer than the male's. 1 Cor 12:15.

This separation of the sexes also pertains to attire. The man to have an attire commensurate with his masculine nature, and distinguished from the that of the female, in accord with their culture. The female likewise. A confusion of the genders in attributes and attire is antithesis to the intent of *Yahweh* God in the creation of the genders and their assigned role and responsibility. Modern fashions should not incline the believer, both male and female, from accepting the image bestowed upon them by the creator *Yahweh* God.

The division of the sexes and the mechanism of reproduction is the greatest enigma in evolutionary theory. Why are there 2 genders? And why are marital relations between these 2 genders required for procreation? Since one organism capable of reproduction is the prerequisite for any future evolutionary progression, when and how did this single reproductive organism decide to reproduce itself this time into 2 genders: Each unable to reproduce itself individually, but each one with half the capability and

---

[8] *Ante-Nicene Fathers*, vol, 2. Page. 286.
[9] Ibid. vol 2. Page 275.
[10] Ibid. vol 2. Page 277.

means for the 2 to unite for reproduction, and then reproduce one or the other of the genders?

This is the unresolveable enigma of evolutionary theory, that all of this should occur in only one generation, on its own without outside premeditated planning or design. No organism can develop this on its own. The only resolution is that *Yahweh* God, the supreme creator, deliberately created the genders as part of His original creation, with their ability to reproduce one just like themselves.

Reproduction exists likewise in plants. When *Yahweh* God created plants, He likewise created them with the natural ability to reproduce: seeds. Gen 1:11-12. Every plant that *Yahweh* God planted in the earth, every one had an original capability to reproduce an identical product, which likewise contained this reproductive capability. This is a miracle of eternal life in a sense, that every species of plant and animal can live into the infinite future.

## DOMINION OVER THE EARTH

These words in Gen 1:27-28 indicate the ability of man to have the control over all that is on Earth, and not the opposite. In Eden he could dominate and tame all living creatures on Earth. The life of the garden of Eden was in harmony with nature, reconciliation with all animals. There no animosity existed between human and animal, and between animals. That every animal was brought to Adam by *Yahweh* God is indicative of the human's dominion over the animal kingdom. The human was at the head, and not subservient in any manner. The nature that presently exists in animals did not exist at that time. Animals did not kill to eat, or fight to defend their habitation or residence, or fight for survival, or fight for mates, or fight to be head of a herd. There was no need for animals to have defense mechanisms or the anatomy for self-defense or self-preservation. No venom in snakes, spiders, wasps or bees.

The dominion would have also pertained to weather and the elements. Although the human would not have direct control over weather and the elements, the concept of dominion would have applied likewise. A harmony prevailed between the human and the environment in every facet. Storms, earthquakes, typhoons, hurricanes, monsoons, floods, famines, or uncomfortable climate, did not exist.

Disease is the result of bacteria and pathogens, and since none of this existed in Eden no illness existed at that time. Such bacteria and disease causing cells were not in a pathological condition. No plagues, no water contamination, no epidemics. The human was in perfect health and in harmony with their environment.

All of this changed with the curse upon the earth in Gen 3:17.

## DEATH

The attitude of the Jewish sages was quoted earlier. The human, along with the plant and animal kingdoms did not face decay and death as time progressed. The constitution of living creation was such that the organism could live indefinitely. It was because of the eternal spirit of *Yahweh* God in His creation that restrained deterioration due to age, illness, injury, or stress.

> For the spirit of the Lord fills the world. Wisdom 1:7.
> For Your incorruptible spirit is in all things. Wisdom 12:1.

It is because death was absent in Eden and the early life before the fall that causes me to conclude that this era of environmental, physical and moral perfection was designed to be temporal. This interim of perfection was intended not as a permanent state for creation and created humanity, but to serve as the intention of *Yahweh* God for the restoration at the conclusion of the ages. This original installation lasting perhaps 100 or 200 years to allow humanity at that time to experience the perfection of *Yahweh* God for His creation was sufficient for the record for future generations. The later generations would have this to look forward to in the resurrection and restoration. This was the intent of *Yahweh* God: to first establish the world of environmental and moral perfection, and then intervene in order to alter it to a condition of temporality and decay, but not without His blessing. With the condition of temporality, humans regularly have the opportunity to enjoin the blessings of life and view the flaws and failures of the present life and environment. The purpose is still to populate the earth and to be productive in life, for more to have the opportunity to live, and hope and perhaps attain the perfect world in the restoration. At the present rate of population growth, and with the incidences of disease, war and disasters of the elements of nature, the present world will never overpopulate. Under present conditions many have the opportunity to live and have the opportunity to enter the future perfect world.

## *YAHWEH* GOD AND HISTORY

*Yahweh* God views time over the progress of billions of years the way a person views a map or a portrait painting or a piece of scenery. As a person views these printed and drawn items from left to right and top to bottom, noticing the lines and figures and colors, so in the same manner does *Yahweh* God view the history and progress of billions of years. He views time from beginning to end, from one end of the universe to the other, and the meticulous and precise movements and activities occurring.

The progress of time of billions of years did not evolve on its own independently and self-sufficiently. Nothing material or spiritual can evolve on its own, and especially the events of such a long duration of time in millions of galaxies. Just as a mapmaker designed and printed a map, and just as an artist conceived of and painted a portrait or scenery, so did *Yahweh* God develop and implement the progress of history from its beginning and infinitely into the future.

> Who performed this and accomplished this, calling the generations from the beginning? I, *Yahweh*, the first, and with the last, I am he. Is 41:4.

> Declaring the end from the beginning, and from ancient times, events not yet occurring. Is 46:10.

The orderly progress of events in the universe is the evidence of a master architect and constructor.

The method of indicating uninterruption for the indefinite future is by way of a negative. Never and none is used in this general context for some situation that will continue long indefinitely.

> Where their worms do not die, and where the fire does not cease.
> Mark 9:48

> For their worn will not die and their fire will not be quenched, and they will become a revulsion to all flesh. Is 66:24.

In the above examples the negative is used to indicate that the punishment will continue without termination. The reference is to the Jerusalem city dump, where the caretakers would place sulfur on the trash to keep the flames alive until all the trash was consumed and only ashes were left. Likewise any organic matter bred worms, and so worms were always to be found in the city dump in the carcasses of dead animals and in decaying organic matter. But eventually the dump came to its termination. The "never" was only applicable as long as the dump was operating.

> Never since the world began has it been heard that any one opened the eyes of a man born blind. John 9:32.

Throughout Scripture the terms forever and ever is used, primarily in the NT. Literally the term is for ages of ages, or, for the eons of eons. The term appears especially in Revelations.

> Rev 19:10. The smoke from the fire consuming the worshippers of the beast and its image ascended for the ages of ages.
> Rev 19:3. The smoke from the fire consuming the prostitute church ascends for ages of ages.
> Rev 20:10. The torment of the devil thrown into the lake of fire and brimstone is to last for ages of ages.
> Rev 21:5. The reign of the saints in the holy new Jerusalem is for ages of ages.

These passages can be interpreted as follows: The smoke will continue until the victims and pseudo-church and devil are consumed and only ashes remain. The memory will be retained without end. Likewise the reign of the saints will continue indefinitely.

## ETERNAL LIFE

The concept of life eternal is not the same in the age of the OT and NT as it is understood today. At the present time and beginning with the apologists of the latter $2^{nd}$ century, when the term eternal life (*zoe aionious*) is read it is understood as life in the millennial and eternal kingdom evolving from our resurrection and translation. Life eternal today means life continuous without termination. This would be true only if the word translated as eternal actually meant that. In Greek the word *aionious* is actually the English eonion or age-lasting, referring to a duration of time of long indefinite length.

The words rendered as life eternal from the Greek are *zoe aionious*. The understanding in Greek of this term is life of a long duration. This is the understanding of this term in the NT. Wherever *zoe aionious* is mentioned in the NT by Jesus and the apostles, it is the promise of a long life. This is one of the many promises of *Yahweh* God, that His people will live long, see prosperity and happiness to a ripe old age, and pass away in relative comfort.

> Ex 20:12. The promise for obedience and honor to parents is a long life in the promised land.
> Deut 30:19-20. Loving God and being obedient will bring a long life in the promised land.
> Pr 3:2, 4:10. Observance of the commands of *Yahweh* God will bring a long life and prosperity.

This is in contradiction to living a short life, incurring premature death, which is the curse of *Yahweh* God upon the disobedient.

In Deut 4:26, 30:18, the disobedience will incur an early death as a result of their repulsive life style and sinful conduct.

Life for the *olam* or *eon* was the hope and goal of the believer in *Yahweh* God and follower of the divine instruction and moral law. Life for the *olam* or *eon* is summarized in Ps 128. Abraham was the example living to 175, while Sarah living to 127.

Life for the *olam* or *eon* was to live long, in good health, with prosperity, peace and harmony, with marital and domestic success. This is the Scriptural definition. During the First century AD, the life span was about 40 for both male and female. Along with this was a high infant mortality rate, about 50% to adulthood or child-bearing age. The reasons for such a short life span were poor living and environmental conditions: disease, war, deviate weather patterns, malnutrition, poverty, and exposure to the elements. This the people interpreted as the curse of *Yahweh* God.

When the rich young ruler in Matt 19:16-19, asked Jesus what he should do to inherit life *aionious*, he wanted to know how to conduct himself so he inherits the promise of *Yahweh* God to live long on the land of the promise. This man wanted the promises of Ps 128 to be fulfilled in him. He did not want to suffer as did much of the balance of the population of his era and die prematurely. In reply to his question Jesus quoted half of the 10 commandments dealing with conduct and the one commandment regarding love. If the young man was to conduct himself in this manner he would inherit life *aionious*. These commands comprise a portion of the covenant of *Yahweh* God: to the extent His people would observe and uphold these commandments, to that extent *Yahweh* God would bless His people. This is the proper understanding whenever in Scripture life eternal or everlasting is promised.

The idea of life *aionious* referring to life after death in the resurrection was unknown to the general population. The disciples did not understand Jesus when he would tell them of his resurrection from death. Mark 9:32. Luke 18:33-34. It was not until later in history that the interpretation of *zoe aionious* changed from a long life on earth to the era of the restoration.

## LIFE ON EARTH

In one respect death allows a cycle of life existence on earth to progress generation after generation. This is the opportunity to be born, grow, fulfill a vocation and raise a family, or whatever we have on our mind to do for the years that *Yahweh* God assigns us, until such time that age or some other incident occurs so that our life should terminate. For individuals to purpose their life for accomplishment during the years of capability is a test of *Yahweh* God of His creation. Knowing that all of us do have a definite life span, one that is not eternal, what we do with our life is very important to *Yahweh* God. It determines whether we think highly of *Yahweh* God who gives us the opportunity to life and enjoy life's blessings, or whether we despise existence. If a person views his life in despair, or as vain or futile, this also indicates their regret that *Yahweh* God ever gave them conscious existence. Such an attitude on the part of a human, whether male or female, grieves *Yahweh* God, makes Him sad and causes Him also to regret that he took such an effort to create a world for created humanity, and that He created this specific individual and placed him in this world as the object of His love.

The object of passing away at a ripe old age would create a sense of accomplishment for the individual who lives within the will of *Yahweh* God and according to His will. The accomplishment could be in terms of marriage, family, business, culture, or some vocation of a general or specific benefit to society. The accomplishment could also be of some private or personal nature, but yet still something remaining behind on Earth after that person terminates their life, a legacy of benefit as an indication that *Yahweh* God made the right decision to create this person, that some credit was given to *Yahweh* God as a result of that person's existence through his or her efforts or life style on Earth.

The term used in Scripture for "fear of God," does not evolve from an immediate threat to the live of a person, but one distant into the future. For a person to have a Fear of God means to realize that the person will answer to *Yahweh* God for any wrong committed. The fear is due to a threat of survival, but the materialization of the threat will not occur until sometime in the future. To conduct yourself having a fear of God is to realize that deprivation of life or some penalty may occur if your life is not according to Scripture. The spirit striving for long term residence in the body will drive the person to live according to the law of *Yahweh* God and His moral code. In this manner security is acquired for the long term future.

## LOSING THE IMAGE AND LIKENESS OF YAHWEH GOD

A person is well able to lose the image and likeness of *Yahweh* God with which they are gifted at birth. This occurs when a person suppresses or ignores the natural emotions of fear and conscience; when a person conducts themselves in a barbarian or bestial manner. Since the human is a free moral agent, each decides whether to possess the image and likeness of *Yahweh* God or not. The result of ignoring and suppressing fear and conscience and morals and ethics and knowledge and creativity causes a person to revert to a soulless entity – only spirit and body. The result of a lack of the divine image and likeness is not a reversion to that of an animal, but worse.

Humans outside the divine image and likeness act totally without concern for anybody and anything, the conduct is unconscionable. This results in uncontrollable anger, murder, robbery, violence, war, destruction, and rebellion against authority. Pertaining to the person itself it results in suicide, drug abuse, alcoholism, immorality, homosexuality and other sexual perversions. In the society it surfaces as incest, pornography, domestic violence, child and spousal abuse; and the non-violent damage resulting from intimidation, manipulation, competition. In addition are the many attitudes that are internal and not always obvious: spite, bigotry, prejudice, racism, envy, desire for revenge, malice.

All of this results from the choice of the person to reject the divinely gifted image and likeness of their creator *Yahweh* God. It also proves that once the human as a free moral agent makes such an arbitrary and treacherous decision to ignore fear and conscience and the moral code, the divine image and likeness is removed from them automatically: they deprive themselves of it. The inevitable result is their ruin and the ruin of the society they associate with. The human becomes sub-human.

For this reason Paul apostle wrote to the Messianic community at Ephesus the following.

> And put on the new nature created after the likeness of God in true rectitude and holiness. Eph 4:24.

As a result of living outside the will, covenant and moral code of *Yahweh* God, the residents had long lost the divine image and likeness. By accepting the gospel of the spiritual kingdom and entering the covenant, they were gradually restoring this divine image and likeness. Paul apostle compares it to a person removing old clothes and attiring himself in a new suit. The balance of the chapter, Eph 4:25-32, focuses on the new life and conduct of the people, now having acquired the new nature.

## LIFE IN THE FLESH

To live in the flesh is to discard that facet of the image of *Yahweh* God which is the moral nature. Just as the conscience can be seared so it no longer impresses sympathy or remorse or guilt, so the moral nature can also be suppressed or mortified so a person becomes totally amoral. At this point the survival impulse envelops their entire nature, so an individual's concern is their own temporary existence, their sole survival. This attitude results in conceit, pride, selfishness, self-centeredness. This attitude routes a person's concern inward, seeking only their own favor, and focused solely on the present and immediate circumstances. This survival impulse now reverts to an evil impulse.

Life in the flesh mentioned in Rom 6-8 can be defined as the immediate gratification of the urge and demands of the body without regard for the future, for another person, and without fear of reprisal by

*Yahweh* God, judgment. All of the above description of the amoral excesses of the Roman Empire were on the mind of Paul apostle when he penned his famous passage.

> For I know that nothing good resides within me, that is, in my flesh. I can will what is right, but I cannot do it. Rom 7:18.
> If by the spirit you mortify the deeds of the body you will live. Rom 8:14.

The attitude taken by Paul apostle in the first passage is not the vein of the Jewish sages, but is the attitude of much of the philosophy of Rome and Greece. The early philosophers taught that the body was inherently evil, and to achieve any type of sanctity it was necessary to deprive the body of the luxuries of life. There was no moral code to be adhered to in the early Roman and Greek philosophies. Paul apostle utilized this amoral trend prevalent in the empire to impress upon the Messianic community that the only manner for the populace engaged in such conduct to sever themselves from it was to spiritual execute it. Accepting the baptism of the Holy Spirit would then be for them a spiritual resurrection unto a moral life. Paul apostle used the terms of their own philosophies as a means of describing repentance and conversion and severance from the amoral and corrupt conduct prevailing in the Roman Empire.

## SEXUAL DRIVE

*Yahweh* God created the sexual impulse in both men and women and it is good. If it were not for the impulse and drive for gratification there would be no reproduction. *Yahweh* God has designed both human genders such that the climax of the sexual drive be the manner of conception for the propagation of the human species. A male achieves his personal fulfillment as a male in normal marital relations and coincidentally with the means of formation of a new creature, a child, physically patterned after image and likeness of its parents and spiritually patterned after the image and likeness of *Yahweh* God. The female likewise achieves ultimate fulfillment as a female in normal marital relations with the goal of conception. The two together become one physically during the progress of physical love. Because of the deep psychological impact of such a divinely implemented union, this was to be confined to a legitimately married couple, wedded in holy matrimony, in order that love, the mutual concern for the welfare of each other, would prevail during pregnancy, delivery and parenthood. *Yahweh* God referred to this as good on the evening of the 6$^{th}$ day when He commands the progenitors to "Be productive and populate the earth." Gen 1:28.

For this reason marital relations are to be taken seriously in every culture and community. The culture and couple that follows the dictates of a monogamous marriage within a Scripture based life is promised the blessings of *Yahweh* God, generation after generation.

Any deviation from the above pattern will shorten the life span of either sex and cause both psychological and physical degradation. Homosexuality, lesbianism, sex change, transvestites, and promiscuity are all a departure from the divinely inspired state of proper relationship between the genders.

## LIFE AND SURVIVAL

The human has an impulse to live. The spirit that *Yahweh* God has bequeathed the human impels the body to live. From conception, at which point a new entity begins formation, the spirit of animation acts to generate growth. A fetus is not a distinct entity. From the point of conception and until independent respiration after delivery the offspring has no real conscious existence. It is not a living soul, an independent and unique entity. Not until *Yahweh* God breathes into the child following delivery and the child breathes on its own does it become a living soul. Only then does it acquire an identity as a person.

> Your hands have made me and fashioned me; give me understanding that I may learn Your commandments. Ps 119:73
> For you formed my inward parts. You arranged me together in my mother's womb. Ps 139:13-16.

While in the womb the fetus does possess life: it is alive and in preparation to become an independent human. It is dependent on its mother for survival during this period of formation and development. It is still alive, though not having a personal identify. The premeditated death of a fetus, or its death as a result of a crime, is considered a crime in Scripture, though not to the same extent of the deliberate death of a human. Ex 21:22.

It is not a tissue that can be indiscriminately discarded at the discretion of the mother or a physician. This non-accidental death of a fetus does not carry the same penalty as the premeditated death of a human, but the fine indicates that the fetus is recognized as a living entity. Aborting a fetus is to deprive it of the opportunity to become a human soul. This is the judgment of *Yahweh* God that such a person will have to face: the deliberate deprivation of the opportunity for a person to be born and live. The mother of the aborted fetus, the father, and nurse and doctor, and all who legislate in favor of it, will answer to *Yahweh* God for their inhumane action.

Still-borns or spontaneous abortions, miscarriages, are never assigned an identity since they are not carried to full term or born alive.

## PAIN, FEAR AND ANGER

Every person has an impulse of survival that resides in their body of flesh. This is that special spirit of animation enlivening the human that drives it to live, as mentioned above. This spirit is impelled to reside in the body as long as possible. This drive of this special spirit to remain in the body results in the immaterial attribute of fear when threatened. This has a side effect of a survival tendency for the human: to run from danger, to defend themselves from harm, to seek assistance when in difficult circumstances, to eat when hungry, and many other reactions for survival.

Pain is common to all creation. Physical pain first. This would include the effects of hunger, that is, the pain internally a human feels when gastric juices fill the cavity of the stomach and begin to irritate the lining. Pain is also produced from disease, an internal or external injury, or failure or malfunction of a vital organ. Pain is the result of the transmission of impulses by the nerves from the area affected and to the brain, to inform the soul that the body is in danger or in the process of injury or threat of damage. This will motivate a reaction for personal survival or escape. *Yahweh* God created a nerve system in humans far exceeding that of any other creature. The human is far more sensitive and aware of changes and threats to their well-being than any other creature. Since the human body does not have a natural clothing, the skin is more sensitive to heat, cold and injury.

Psychological and emotional pain follows the same vein. It is an impression upon the soul of immediate danger or the threat of danger. It impresses upon the person the loss of security or happiness. This occurs with the death or illness of a close friend or relative. Emotion allows a person to be empathetic. It allows them to identity with the struggles and losses and difficulties of another. With a injury upon the soul, such as betrayal or violation of personal trust, the emotional pain is a warning against future involvement of unstable or unsure relationships, and a command for greater concern for a person's own long term survival.

Fear is the basis of the impulse to survive. Animals and humans both have a fear facet of their nature. *Yahweh* God created this facet of fear as part of the body's reflexes for survival. Fear warns the person of a threat to their life in order to make provisions to react in a survival mode: attack, defend, flee or reconcile. Fear is a good response because its concern is the safety and survival of the person. It will restrain a person from inflicting harm upon them. Fear of the possible result from drug abuse, promiscuity, suicide, deprivation, carelessness or negligence, motivates a person to live safely and conservatively.

Anger results from fear and demand for survival. Anger is the response of the body to the threat of survival. Anger is that emotion created by *Yahweh* God for the human in order for them to want to banish from existence or society or the vicinity anything that poses as a threat to survival.

A person's anger does not accomplish the virtue of God. Jam 1:20.

Anger is good if it is controlled and not allowed to affect someone unnecessarily or unintentionally. Latent anger is what generates laws penalizing criminals, establishes a judicial system and tribunals. Latent anger is the basis for developing an organized and trained police force. All of this because of the spirit wanting the body to survive. The anger is directed at those within the society that pose a threat to the safety of the residents. Violent anger is anger without control by the soul and leads to development of the evil impulse. This impulse drives a person into an offensive attack against threats to their safety and survival. This causes havoc and ruin for the person themselves and their victims. The evil impulse evolves from the desire for survival with the conscious subdued and the image of *Yahweh* God discarded. A person in this condition becomes the "devil prowling about like a hungry lion seeking whom he can devour. 1 Pet 5:8. The work or *Yahweh* God can only be effectively accomplished in a calm and controlled environment.

## THE PROBLEM OF EVIL

The one controversy plaguing both the simple and intellectual of the ages has been the reason for evil. In this context evil would refer to all the difficulties of life: the obstacles to success, health, wealth and longevity. This question posed a quandary to several authors of the OT.

> Moses: For all our days pass away under Your wrath, our years come to an end like a sigh. Ps 90:7.
> Job: Man that is born of a woman is of few days, and full of trouble. He proceeds like a flower and withers; he flees like a shadow, and continues not. Job 14:1-2.
> Solomon: For all his days are full of pain, and his work is a vexation; even in the night his mind does not rest. This also is vanity and striving after wind. Eccl 2:23.

The entrance of evil and failure into the world occurred at the words of *Yahweh* God to Adam, "Cursed is the ground as a result of you." Gen 3:17. This was discussed earlier. It is easy to place the blame or responsibility of all evil that affects a person on the Supreme Deity the Creator, *Yahweh* God. But this attitude is shallow. The question, "Why does God permit evil?" should never surface on the lips of any person, since then *Yahweh* God becomes the source and initiator of all suffering, difficulty, temptation, evil and failure. According to James apostle, personal evil evolves from the person himself. Jam 1:13-15.

*Yahweh* God transcends evil. What occurs on earth transcends the omnipotent Supreme Deity. The earth progresses in a specific manner and orderly according to the plan of the ages of *Yahweh* God. For a person to complain to *Yahweh* God is like the pot complaining to the potter.

> Why have you made me so? Rom 9:20.

The monologue of Elihu in Job 32-37 attempted to resolve the dilemma of Job. His conclusion was that every human is routed through a certain course of life as determined by *Yahweh* God. Every person should do their best and take advantage of whatever their situation is for their own personal welfare. I agree with the conclusion of Elihu A person should not complain of any situation of failure or any effect of evil or disaster. As a created being, every person should be thankful for the opportunity to life and so deal in the best way possible with every situation that affects him and her.

Job's other 3 "friends" were correct in their summary of the dilemma of evil, except that it did not apply to *Yahweh* God. Most evil and failure people bring upon themselves, Zophar the friend of Job concluded.

> As I have seen, those who plow iniquity and sow trouble reap the same. By the breath of God they perish, and by the blast of his anger they are consumed. Job 4:8-9.
>
> Know then that God exacts of you less than your guilt deserves. Job 11:6.

What more than often occurs to a person is the result of their own error, their own violation, their own ignorance and their pride. Most tragedy of society is the result of the individual members own free volition: they cause the evil to occur. They subsequently have to deal with the inevitable consequences of their decision. This was the conclusion of Zophar: Every person must eventually deal with the consequences of his their decision. This is a good conclusion that applies to much of humanity.

## YAHWEH GOD AND EVIL

The reply of *Yahweh* God to the complaint of Job is recorded in Job 38-42. In one respect it is a continuation of the attitude of Elihu. The balance of the divine rhetoric is *Yahweh* God giving evidence to Job of His imperviousness and transcendence to the complaints of humans.

The elements of disease, weather, chance and fate, all exist to impress upon the human the omnipotence of *Yahweh* God. Parallel with this is the inability and futility of a human attempting to defy the Supreme Deity with a deliberate violation of His divine instruction and moral code. There is no way for a person to oppose predetermined destiny implemented by *Yahweh* God, and a person is even more futile to suppose some complaint or allocation of blame will be of any benefit. All a person can do is best deal with every storm for the outcome to be as little disruptive as possible.

The best of every situation can be handled with a observance of the moral code of *Yahweh* God. Matt 7:24-27. Then a person has their life, their family, their community, built upon a rock, and they will personally endure to the end of their life without abandoning faith in the true and living God.

## THE SATAN

An immortal rebel living in the realm of spirit or in heaven is an impossibility. There is no place for such a concept in divine theology. The fact that *Yahweh* God is the sole source of all existence, as discussed earlier in this treatise, leaves no room for a concept of a spirit adversary. The fact that *Yahweh* God would create such an entity or even permit such a revolt in the heavens against His authority, as popularized in Christian sermons and commentaries, is ludicrous. *Yahweh* God could never proceed with the fulfillment of the counsel of His will if every move had to face an obstacle and adversary that had to be defeated or fought. *Yahweh* God would likewise not have sole authority and possession in the realm of spirit if it had to be shared with another authority whose intent was only to disrupt and interfere with His intents. Bible translators have arbitrarily rendered the Hebrew word *satan* as adversary when referring to a person, or as a transliteration into *satan* to refer to a personal entity, depending on their purpose.

> Generally speaking, Satan does not occupy in Judaism the central place that he takes in Christianity; Satan in Christianity is almost like the God of Evil of the Persians.[11]

The Hebrew *satan* means adversary or enemy. It is used throughout the OT and NT to refer directly to people or as the embodiment of evil. A few examples will indicate this.

> Num 22:22, 32. The word *satan* is first used in the Bible in this passage of Balaam and his donkey. Here it refers to a messenger of heaven who appeared to Balaam as an adversary to hinder his travel to Balak. The heavenly messenger is not a personal *satan*; he appears here as an adversary to Balaam.

---

[11] *The Messianic Idea in Israel*, Joseph Klausner. Pg. 530.

> 1 Sam 24:4. David king would be an adversary (Heb. *satan*) to the Philistines in the battle against Saul.
> 2 Sam 19:22. Abishai, a son of Zeruiah, was an adversary (Heb. *satan*) to David, in his effort to secure stability for his kingdom.
> 1 King 11:14. *Yahweh* God moved Hadad the Edomite to become an adversary (Heb. *satan*) to Solomon. The same word is used also 1 King 11:23,25.
> 1 Chron 21:1 compared with 2 Sam 24:1. *Yahweh* God sent some person as an adversary (Heb. *satan*) to urge David to conduct a census.
> Matt 16:23. Peter apostle could not grasp the necessity of the criminal execution of Jesus. He was called an adversary (Gk. *satana*) to Jesus' purpose by him.
> 2 Cor 12:7. A physical malady was an adversary, *satan*, to Paul apostle, to restrain him from becoming over elated or egocentric as a result of his revelations. This thorn in the flesh may have been his poor eyesight. Gal 4:13,15.

The messenger that had the idea of testing Job to determine the intent of Job's faith and loyalty to *Yahweh* God was called satan or adversary. But Job did not attribute any of the calamities that befell him to the satan or adversary. Job 1:22, 2:10.

The word satan is also used allegorically as the embodiment of evil and temptation, including the corruption of the Roman Empire.

> 1 Tim 1:20. Hymenaeus and Alexander were excommunicated from the Messianic community.
> 1 Tim 5:15. The unmarried young widows began to conduct themselves immorally, not having a legitimate husband in the faith.
> Acts 5:3. Ananias succumbed to temptation to hoard money from the sale of his property.
> Rev 2:13. An great adversary of the purpose of *Yahweh* God resided in the city Pergamum and who had considerable influence and authority.

In all these examples, typical of Scripture, the Hebrew *satan* is used to either refer to a person who served as an adversary to some purpose, some instigator, a malady, and is used to refer to evil or temptation in general.

## THE DEVIL

The actual meaning of the Greek *diabolos* is calumniator or [false] accuser. Much like the word *satan*, it is translated based on the whims of translators, depending whether the passage can incline toward proving a personal devil. In actual usage in the NT, it refers to people who serve as false-accusers and as the embodiment of evil. Just as Jesus referred to Peter as an adversary (Heb. *satana*), he referred to Judas as an accuser (Gr. *diabolos*). Judas in his betrayal of Jesus proved to be a false-accuser.

> 2 Tim 3:3. Men of Christian office should not be false accusers (Gk. *diaboloi*).
> 2 Tim 3:11. Titus 2:3. Wives of deacons and the aged women are not to be slanderers. (Gk. *diabolos*).
> Rev 2:9-10, used conjointly with *satan*. Some false-accusers were present in Smyrna.

In other passages the word *diabolos* is used as the embodiment of evil. The result of succumbing to temptation, committing a crime, involvement in sin, all of this is reflected in the word devil. 1 John 3:3. Heb 2:14.

The actual authority over life, its beginning and through its termination, is the possession of *Yahweh* God. He as creator determines the beginning of a person's life and its termination. Deut 32:39. Matt 10:29. The practice of sin and crime by a person leads to the premature termination of their life. Rom 6:23. This is the devil, the embodiment of the evil impulse in a person. Jesus came to destroy him that had the power of death, the accuser (*diabolos*). By overcoming sin, death is destroyed. Through Jesus a person can gain the victory over sin and temptation and so triumph. 1 Cor 15:55, 57.

> He who practices sin is of the devil, because the devil sinned from the beginning. The reason the son of God appeared was to destroy the works of the devil. 1 John 3:8.

This statement is true and in accord with Rom 6:12. Whoever conducts themselves inappropriately, in sin and crime and vice is a slave to the devil, to the evil impulse evolving from their body. It is not some supernatural spirit of other-world entity that tempts or leads a person into self-destruction, it is the person themselves. Jam 1:14-15.

Rev 12:7 and 9, using both terms, adversary and false-accuser (*satan* and *diabolos*). They signify temptation and the destructiveness of succumbing to temptation. This is equally represented by the figure of a great dragon. With the resurrection of Jesus a person can withstand and endure temptation and not succumb to it.

The passage of Is 14:12-20 does not prove any rebellion in the realm of spirit by some magnificent angel with his subsequent fall and banishment. This passage pertains to the king of Babylon, Nebuchadnezzar. It is also addressed in Dan 4:1-37, in his vision of the tree that toppled over. Because of his success Nebuchadnezzar became proud. *Yahweh* God then defeated his pride and reduced him to a state of an animal to impress upon him the sovereignty of *Yahweh* God. The passage of Exe 28:11-19, follows the same vein here pertaining to the king of Tyre.

There is no evidence in Scripture to indicate existence of some evil force in the realm of spirit.

## DEMONS

The pseudo-gods of mythology and superstition are referred to as devils and demons in Scripture. The idols or material representations of these pseudo-deities are also called devils and demons. This is apparent initially in OT passages.

> Deut 32:7. Ps 106:36-38. Translated as demons, the Heb. *shed*, actually means spoiler or destroyer.
> Ps 96:5. The gods of the gentiles are figments of their imagination.

In the NT the same vein continues with the use of demons and devils referring to the pseudo-deities of mythology and superstition.

> 1 Cor 10:20-21. The adherents of cult mystery religions of Greece and Rome dedicated their feasts and sacrifices to their particular deity. The Christians were to dedicate their supper to *Yahweh* God the sole and supreme deity, and were not to participate in feasts or sacrifices honoring some pseudo-deity or superstition.

1 Tim 4:1. The doctrine of demons are those of the cult mystery religions.

The other use of demons is that of the physically and mentally ill. It was the general consensus of the population of early eras that diseases were the result of demon possession. Today we know that disease is organic in nature, caused by bacteria or virus, neural damage or abnormal fetal development, effects of foreign chemicals on the body, and other similar causes. Mental illness is the result of chemical imbalance or the effects of a damaging social environment. Pain leading to abnormal behavior was discussed above.

> Matt 17:15-18. Jesus cured an epileptic. Matthew describes it in the terms of his day, as Jesus expelling a demon or foreign entity residing in the person. The demon in this situation is the person's neural damage.
> Matt 12:22, Mark 9:17. The people felt that deafness, blindness, dumbness, were caused by a demon residing in the person. The people viewed the healing as though the malady-possessing demon was vacating the body.
> Matt 8:30-31. The 2 demoniacs of Gadara had some loathsome disease that definitely caused them much pain and discomfort, to the point that it affected their personality and their ability to act normally. For this reason they were labeled demoniac. When these men were healed, their disease was transferred into the swine. This disease then affected the swine, causing them pain and anguish. They became disoriented as they ran and so all went off the edge of a cliff and into the sea.

Jesus in casting out demons was removing the foreign substance causing the disease or deformity. All the uses of demons in Scripture can be explained in logical terms. Even though not every healing was discussed the concept of this section would equally apply to them and can be logically explained.

## 4. JUDGMENT AND RESTORATION

### JUDGMENT

There are several passages in Scripture that indicate a serious inquiry in retrospect. This is the judgment of *Yahweh* God: every individual will face the results of their actions and words and will have to reap the results of them. These are the most important of passages that dealing with this unavoidable event. With actions of a beneficial nature the judgment is concluded with a reward. With actions of an injurious nature the judgment is concluded with appropriate discipline or punishment.

> For he will render to very person according to their works. Rom 2:6.
> For we must all appear before the judgment seat of the Anointed, so that each may receive good or evil, according to what they have done in the body. 2 Cor 5:10
> Behold I come quickly and bring my recompense with me to render to every person for what they have done. Rev 22:12.
> And the dead were judged by what was written in the books, by what they had done. Rev 20:12.
> For this Person will come with his messengers in the glory of his Father, and then he will recompense every person for what they have done. Matt 16:27.

All of these passages may or may not refer to the same event. This is not important. The point to be made is that judgment by *Yahweh* God is definite and inevitable. There definitely will be occurrences in our life for *Yahweh* God to intervene with his judgment. This pertains to this life as well as the future. *Yahweh* God may intervene at any time into a person's life to execute His purpose. The judgment of *Yahweh* God extends to all created humanity of all ages, generations, nations, races, and religions. There are no exceptions to the rule of judgment. Once an individual reaches that age where they can distinguish conduct, when they can recognize why certain conduct is acceptable and other conduct is not, then the judgment is instituted. The standards are not imposed in their entirety at one time, but gradually as a person matures and develops the ability to accept responsibility.

The only exceptions to judgment are that of physical retardation and mental impairment. In these situations the individual is physically incapable of distinguishing types of conduct.

With *Yahweh* God the popular modern claim of innocence by reason of insanity has no validity. Mental illness and insanity is a personal choice. That individual is still responsible for their conduct. I contend that the first character trait of Rev 21:8, refers to the so-called mentally ill. Regularly translated as fearful or cowardly, it refers to those that claim excuse from their criminal activities due to some psychological impairment or neurosis or psychotic state. I reject all mental illness as valid reason or excuse not to live and conduct one self as a decent, law-abiding and moral citizen, and they are equally subject to the judgment as any other mature adult.

## SIN AS CRIME

Sin is a word that has lost its original meaning and impact. No longer does the population call some inappropriate activity sinful or that some specific activity was sin. The word itself in the Hebrew means to miss the mark. It is also translated in the negative form in Judg 20:16, where the passage refers to some left-handed men who could sling a stone and not miss the mark. The Hebrew word *chata*, is translated sin about 200 times, and in related ways in the balance of uses. For our modern usage it would be more accurate to replace the word sin with its contemporary equivalent of crime. Sin is crime, because it is missing the mark of fulfillment of the law of *Yahweh* God. When *Yahweh* God judges the people because of their sins, it is because of their crimes. When a person commits a sin he is committing a crime, a violation of the law of *Yahweh* God.

## THE REASON FOR JUDGMENT

Before dealing with the manner that *Yahweh* God will execute judgment, the reason for the necessity of judgment must first be dealt with. In simple terms the reason can be stated: *Yahweh* God must impress upon every individual the need for personal responsibility for actions. The basis for personal responsibility stems from the fact that every individual is a free moral agent. Humans are created with the ability to choose, to decide for themselves their actions, attitudes, opinions and intentions. Volition is a great gift that *Yahweh* God has given to every created human. As a free moral agent every human can act as he or she so chooses. Decisions are made based on the desire or motivation or interest of the individual. This is free will or volition. So in this light *Yahweh* God views all actions as the result of the volition of an individual, meaning, that every act is directly or indirectly the result of a choice by the individual.

Nobody and nothing can force an individual to act in any manner against their will. Somewhere along the line the individual will make the choice to either yield and succumb to some influence, temptation, deception, intimidation, threat or torture, or else will decide to resist. Even with pressure applied the decision to yield is one of the will. The difficulty to force people to act in a manner opposite to their will has annoyed investigators, inquisitors, torturers and persecutors throughout the ages. The will is an immaterial entity, while the flesh is material. The 2 are alien substances, and the impact of pain upon the flesh will not necessarily force the will to comply. In history, individuals have endured the most cruel and inhumane tortures devised rather than submit their will to another. Torture racks, burning at the stake, incarceration, public shame and disgrace, exile, and every possible method devised has been utilized to change some person's mind about a matter or for them to conduct themselves differently. But the human will has been able to withstand all efforts and claims, and can if it so chooses regardless of the consequences.

The choices a person makes depending on personal preference or external influence occurs regularly, day to day, and several times each day if not each hour. What a person decides to do with their life, education, vocation, family, business, religion, is a freedom that is immeasurable. Many of these choices are moral decisions: right or wrong. But it is not without its consequences. Free will is invaluable, but there is a steep price to be paid for it, and that price is personal responsibility. Free will is inseparable from responsibility. This is the basis for the necessity of a judgment. For every harm, injury, or infraction, the crime committed against another, or even self-inflicted injury, there must be personal responsibility for the results. The personal responsibility will surface in either repentance and restitution, or in judgment resulting in an appropriate penalty.

How will judgment be executed? Some how, some where, and at some time, *Yahweh* God will intervene in a manner of His own selection and impress upon that individual their responsibility for the crime and its long term results by way of a penalty and discipline. *Yahweh* God will impose the penalty on the individual by way of some physical punishment, psychological depression, deprivation of freedom, health or status, or even by way of the deprivation of life, execution. In this manner will *Yahweh* God demand an account from individuals for crimes committed, whether against another individual, against themselves, against nature and the environment or against the safety and welfare of society. This judgment can equally apply to crimes committed to a family, city, religion or nation, just as much as to an individual.

A tragedy occurring to an individual is often just some occurrence that resulted on its own: accident, illness, injury or even death, but it seems not and never because of the displeasure of *Yahweh* God. Accidents do occur on a regular basis that have serious results and consequences. But the focus here is that *Yahweh* God definitely intervenes into a person's life and will require an account from that person should it be deliberate. The natural consequences of defying and violating the divine instruction of *Yahweh* God is the sentence and execution of *Yahweh* God. However a person refusing to acknowledge any crime committed, unrepentant sin, *Yahweh* God will impose His penalty. The list of crimes continues: those related to theft, deceit and fraud; those related to violence, abuse, and murder; those related to manipulation, lying and connivance; those related to false-religion, paganism and superstition; and personal secret vices that harm the individual and others. The vices leading to judgment and penalty are innumerable. Upon them all is the swift and prolonged executed sentence of *Yahweh* God and inescapable under the circumstances.

In all these situations, unless a heartfelt repentance and conversion is carried out in due time *Yahweh* God will intervene with His penalty, to force them to accept personal responsibility for crimes committed. On an individual basis each will suffer the identical anguish and pain of their victim. Each will experience the results of the maltreatment or infraction or infringement imposed on the other until such time that the sentence is completed and accomplishes the purpose in discipline and penalty.

## JUDGMENT AND THE CONSCIENCE

One facet of human nature bestowed on His created humanity is the conscious. It acts as a means of indicating guilt in those areas where the revealed divine instruction of *Yahweh* God is either unavailable or not specific to the situation. The role of the conscious applies to those nations where the divine instruction is not available. Paul apostle writes of their judgment in these terms:

> All who have sinned (committed crimes) without the law will also perish without the law, and all who have sinned under the law will be judged by the law... on that day when according to my gospel God judges the secrets of men by the Anointed Jesus. Rom 2:12, 16.
>
> They show that what the law requires is written on their hearts, while the conscience also bears witness and their conflicting thoughts accuse or perhaps excuse them. Rom 2:15.

In these societies where the principles of conduct and behavior are established based on the conscience the judgment of *Yahweh* God is based on the same code. This first pertains to the individual, and second to the society. To what extent an individual may be excused for some conduct considered unacceptable or criminal in the law of *Yahweh* God but considered acceptable in that barbarian or aboriginal society cannot be determined. Every individual must only realize that the judgment of *Yahweh* God is and will be just, and justice will be served in every situation.

To be judged outside the law is an individual committing a crime in defiance to their own conscience. Paul apostle mentions the following characteristic of some:

> "whose consciences are seared with a hot iron." 1 Tim 4:2

Individuals do exist whose consciences have been evacuated of any emotion or sensation. They have no conscience. To commit a crime does not impose on them any remorse or feeling of guilt or feeling of any wrongdoing. There is no identification with the victims of their crime. Such people are judged by *Yahweh* God outside the law because their crime was committed outside the law, with a seared conscience. This is also mentioned in Eze 36:26. Stone is inanimate. The heart of stone has no feeling or sensation. For a person to have feeling and sensation, they must have a heart of flesh. Such a heart will have sympathy, remorse, guilt and generate repentance and conversion.

## THE GREAT WHITE THRONE

The responsibility of the judgment of the living and the dead at the conclusion of the existing age and at the initiation of the age of restoration and eternity rests with Emmanuel, Jesus son of God. This delegation of responsibility is noted in Scripture. The following are the words of Jesus himself, Paul apostle and Peter apostle.

> The Father judges no one but has given all judgment to the son. John 5:22.
> But now [God] commands all people everywhere to repent, because He has fixed a day on which He will judge the world in rectitude by a person whom He has appointed, and of this He has given assurance to all people by raising him from death. Acts 17:30-31.
> And [God] commanded us to preach to people and to testify that [Jesus] is the one ordained by God to be judge of the living and dead. Acts 10:42.

Because of Jesus' life on earth as a human, having experienced all that a human will experience, he becomes the most appropriate candidate for the responsibility of judge.

> And I saw a great white throne and him who sat upon it, and from him presence earth and sky fled and no place was found for them. Rev 20:11.

The pain that the convicted will endure when the penalty is executed upon this will be no less than as if they were in a lake of fire. Rev 20:15, 21:8. This is the Scriptural allegory that is used to describe the pain and anguish, whether physical or psychological, that is to be endured by the convicted in their execution. In this torment the victim will feel the pain and anguish and suffering that was imposed on others as a result of their crime.

I wonder whether the cries at this time and the pain will be due to the personal punishment imposed for the crime or violation, or due to the regret by the convicted for having committed such a crime once they answer for their actions at the white throne. Regret for committing some crime and especially a heinous crime has forced perpetrators to suicide after realizing the intensity of the crime. I wonder whether this is the intent of the books at the judgment of the great white throne. The books are symbolic of the infinite memory of *Yahweh* God, and opening these books symbolizes reminding every person standing before the throne of their activity on earth. And not just the activity but their effects and impact on others into the future. The one reminded of all this with its intense impact on their emotion, and without any defense of their own, stands as if naked. Rev 16:15. So did Adam stand naked before *Yahweh* God after his sin. Gen 3:11. He had lost his clothing of righteousness.

*Yahweh* God summarily executes the sentence upon the unrepentant both in this life and in the life to come. It is executed in this life in order for the violator or criminal to cease their misconduct so as not to harm or damage any more lives, and this will serve as a threat to others. In the future life also will such a judgment manifest itself, so no individual would ever think that they can escape a crime.

> You have blotted out their name for ever and ever… The very memory of them has perished. Ps 9:5-6.
>
> But the wicked perish. The enemies of *Yahweh* are like the glory of the pastures: they vanish, like smoke they vanish away. Ps 37:20.

The second death is just as much a reality as their first death. A person cannot live long in a fire: it devours the body and the bones and only ashes remain. This is the final termination and total annihilation of the individual whose name is not written in the book of life in the possession of the Lamb. The regret or conscious penalty for crimes committed will last but a short time after the verdict is served by the One sitting on the great white throne. Then the spirit will again leave the body never to enliven it again and the body will dissolve into the elements. The soul or identity of the individual vanishes at this time, as if it never existed.

## BOOK OF LIFE

The fact that there is some type of record in the realm of the spirit, heaven, that deals with life and performance on earth should be no surprise. A book in allegorical terms refers to memory. *Yahweh* God has an infinite memory. As mentioned earlier, *Yahweh* God views the progress of billions of years time in the same manner as a person views a map. Viewing the past in this manner it is easy for *Yahweh* God to bring to the attention of any person in any age and in any area his previous conduct. This record of the activity of every person is mentioned in Rev 20:12-13. It is one of those books that were opened so every human could be judged by his conduct in the earthly life. The repentant who enter the city Jerusalem that descends from heaven have their names written in the book of life in the possession of the Lamb.

> But nothing unclean shall enter it;... but only those who are written in the Lamb's book of life. Rev 21:27.

Another book is termed the book of life. This is the record in heaven of those who are to enter the new holy city Jerusalem, there to receive eternal life. They are part of *Yahweh* God's spiritual kingdom, or those who are the spiritual sons and daughters of *Yahweh* God, however that *Yahweh* God should determine that a certain person should enter His city for permanent eternal residence. Those that meet this criteria have their names recorded in this book. And the converse is also true, those who will not enter this city Jerusalem in the restoration are deleted from entry in this book of life.

The initial mention of such a record is in the passage where Moses intercedes for the people of Israel after they defy and deny *Yahweh* God by creating a molten calf. They acknowledged this molten calf as representing the deity which freed them from slavery in Egypt. Out of the concern that Moses has for his people, realizing the type of people they are, Moses tells *Yahweh* God.

> "But now if You will forgive their sin – and if not blot me, I pray of you, out of Your book which You have written." Ex 32:32.

But the reply of *Yahweh* God to Moses is.

> "Whoever has sinned against me, him will I blot out of My book." Ex 32:33.

The result is the removal or erasure of the names of the perpetrators. The fact that they no longer proceeded with the people of Israel, dying at the foot of the mountain Sinai in the period immediately following the incident, is parallel with Rev 21:27: that the spiritually unclean have no share in the city of *Yahweh* God. David Psalm-writer in Ps 69:22-28, beseeches *Yahweh* God to impose His penalty on the criminals and enemies of *Yahweh* God of his era. One of the penalties requested of David is that their name be blotted out of the book of the living. Ps 69:28. Meaning that they have no more share with those alive, but now their fate is with the deceased. This would likewise apply to the future promises of *Yahweh* God to live again as the following passage indicates.

Both Jesus and Daniel prophet mention the deliverance of people whose name is discovered written in a book.

> And at that time your people, every one who is found written in the book, will be rescued. Dan 12:1-2.
> "Rejoice that your names are written in heaven." Luke 10:20.

Again the same record in heaven and the subsequent reward after the deliverance is the resurrection to life. Dan 12:3. Those who names are not discovered in this book will face shame and endless contempt.

I contend that the members of the assembly of the first-born who are enrolled in heaven are those whose names are written in this book of life. This passage in Heb 12:23, has been translated various ways, but in essence it is the membership list of the assembly of the living God.

Paul apostle mentions that the names of his fellow believers are written in the book of life. Phil 4:3.

## THE MEMORY OF *YAHWEH* GOD

The memory of *Yahweh* God is infinite in accord with His capacity of supreme creator. He knows the end from the beginning. Is 46:10. This is because He initiated all history for its fulfillment on earth. It is people who forget because memory is organic, and only to the extent of the capability and development of the human mind. With *Yahweh* God, His memory is infinite.

In order for judgment to be effective the memory of the events first must not be forgotten. It must be kept in detail regarding the time, place and extent of crime as well as the extent of injury to the victims. The judgment will pertain to all perpetrators involved, whether directly or indirectly involved, along with the effect of the crime or violation on others, both directly or indirectly affected. All of this is retained in the memory of *Yahweh* God. A book is used in Scripture allegorically to pertain to the memory of *Yahweh* God.

> In Your book were written every one of them, the days that were formed for me, when as yet there were none of them. Ps 139:16.
> Then those who feared *Yahweh* spoke with one another; *Yahweh* heeded and heard them and a book of remembrance was written in His presence of those who feared *Yahweh* and thought on His name. Mal 3:16.
> And the dead were judged by what was written in the books, by what they had done. Rev 20:12. Dan 7:10.

The second primary ability for the judgment to be effective is the ability of *Yahweh* God to make the perpetrator and violator aware of the crime and sin and its impact on others. The person standing before judgment at the great white throne must have all their faculties restored after resurrection in order to understand the indictment and evidence. Somehow the indictment will be read with the evidence, recorded for centuries or millennia. The indictment will penetrate the soul of the person who must answer for their action.

This ability to make a person fully cognizant of their crime and its effect on others is an important facet for the sentence and execution to be effective and legitimate. This is because of denial. The human has an infinite capacity of denial. This was noticed by psychologists researching the life of perpetrators of atrocities, holocausts, genocides, organized extermination of human lives, and ruthless killers. The ability to deny ever harming another person is deep rooted in the instinct of survival. Denial is prevalent among those who commit the most heinous of crimes, to those who commit the most petty.

The ability of *Yahweh* God is not only to present acts of distant past to the person on trial, but also to open up that person's own memory, their awareness, of the event. *Yahweh* God will cause every person at judgment to remember themselves in detail, their own deed and its effect on others. The judgment becomes self-fulfilling. With no longer any ability to deny what occurred the person is left to face the consequences of their own deed. The impact of realization will cause the defendant, now with no defense, to dissolve into the elements.

## THE REPENTANT AT JUDGMENT

With a sincere repentance and conversion the sins of these people are no longer recorded in the annals of heaven. Their crime, violations, vices and other acts of impropriety have been erased from the memory of *Yahweh* God.

> I, I am He who blots out your transgressions for My own sake, and I will not remember your sins. Is 43:25.
> Repent therefore and return that your sins may be erased, in order that times of refreshing may come from the presence of the Lord. Acts 3:19.

In their place will be recorded activities of virtue, benevolence, philanthropy and kindness. Rather than discredit heard on the day of judgment, a confession of their merits will be announced on behalf of the repentant. They will hear an invitation to enter the eternal kingdom.

> Come, blessed of my Father, inherit the kingdom prepared for you from the foundation of the world. Matt 25:34.

They will enter the new holy city Jerusalem as their new residence, which shall descend out of heaven and onto the restored earth.

## RESTORATION

The conversion or restoration of the earth at the beginning of the distant age yet to arrive is a fact that is heralded throughout the Scriptures from its beginnings. This concept is dealt with throughout the Bible. This is the hope that humanity longs for. Humanity of every generation, locale, gender, race and nationality have sensed a need and the necessity of world restoration. There has not been a time in the life of any individual that he or she has not felt the absolute necessity of a conversion or restoration of this world to a state of perfect environment. Not only feeling or sensing such a need, but knowing as a concrete fact that at some time in distant future there definitely will occur a massive upheaval in the environment, in the constituency and nature of all living creation that will result in a perfect climate, environment, and state of human and animal existence. This new state will be one of both physical and moral perfection. First pertaining to immortality: an environment without disease, injury, weakness, age, or any physical flaws or handicaps. The second pertains to its moral condition: an environment without hate, malice, war, bloodshed, psychological or mental illness, disrespect or even discourtesy. This innate conviction stems from a natural realization inherent in the human constitution that existence cannot continue forever the way the world has and is progressing. Every person views and experiences the flaws and shortcoming in their life and concludes what *Yahweh* God has impressed upon their minds, that it can be better and will be and one day all creation and environment will experience a massive metamorphosis for the better.

> He has also put eternity into a person's mind, yet so they cannot find out what God has done from beginning to end. Eccl 3:11.

Such impulse resides not only in humans but also in animals and other organisms. This is an invisible attribute that forms part of the nature of organisms, a similar realism of decay and flaw combined with a desire to attain that era of perfection.

> Because the creation will be set free from its bondage to decay and obtain the glorious liberty of the children of God. Rom 8:21.

The prophecy for such restoration no doubt stems back to the era just after the fall or initial catastrophe that altered the condition of existence and environment to the present condition, although no record exists. The general passages of restoration are primarily the words of Isaiah prophet and Ezekiel prophet. Later John apostle received such a revelation. Rev 21. When this will occur is not evident, nor is it revealed to us in any passage of Scripture. The concept of time for *Yahweh* God is different than the concept that exists on earth and other areas of the universe.

> But the day of the Lord will come like a thief, and then the heavens will pass away with a loud noise, and the elements will be dissolved with fire, and the earth and the words that are upon it will be burned up. 2 Pet 3:10,12.

The manner for such a violent metamorphosis is described by Peter apostle: A new environment will arise out of the ashes of the old. This concept was held by many Jews of that time, just as Martha replied to Jesus regarding her brother Lazarus.

> I know that he will rise again in the resurrection at the last day. John 11:24.

The devout Jews of the era were aware of a massive upheaval of the imperfect world at its termination for it to be replaced and to initiate the perfect world. Martha was well aware of this.

## THE NEW SETTLEMENT

The new resettlement of the earth can be compared to the situation of Noah after the flood: out of his sole family *Yahweh* God was to populate the new world. With this one family *Yahweh* God was to create a righteous humanity which would fill the earth generation after generation. The same intent applies to the era after the restoration: one family will survive the upheaval of nature and environment. One family will survive the annihilation of the present temporal and flawed creation, an annihilation by fire. The new family to resettle the new world is the family of *Yahweh* God, His sons and daughters who have attained maturity during their earthly career. This family has Jesus as their eldest brother. Rom 8:29. The initial population will consist of his younger brethren whom he has led unto maturity, unto the fullness of his own stature as son of *Yahweh* God. Eph 4:13. This new family will be a new Adam and Eve, new progenitors of a new righteous humanity to continue generation after generation. What Adam and Eve failed to do, their future counterparts will accomplish.

Noah with his wife, sons and daughters-in-law began a new life on earth after the upheaval of the world-wide flood, a land devastated, consisting of mud and swamp, the stench of decayed corpses of millions of souls who drowned in the waters. The surviving residents were to learn from the mistakes of those who perished. Hopefully the future generations would not repeat the same. Yet they overcame all obstacles and began a new civilization. So will the new family of *Yahweh* God enter a world of ashes and charred remains of cities and civilizations and corpses of those sentenced to die. Is 66:16,24.

One passage of Isaiah prophet applies to this era of reconstruction. Is 33:17-24. The remains of hospitals and cemeteries, fortresses and munitions' factories and military bases will remind the new inhabitants of the doomed failure of previous generations who violated the covenant of *Yahweh* God. The ruins of coliseums, skyscrapers, granite government buildings, churches and cathedrals with towering steeples and massive domes will witness to the failure of previous generations to develop a righteous humanity, one based on their own terms and concepts and not those of *Yahweh* God. These remains of the failure of previous eras will be relics of the temporal age, a reminder to the new eternal kingdom. The ruins of cemeteries and mausoleums and tombstones will witness to the sentence of *Yahweh* God upon the sinful nature of the human of earlier ages. The inhabitants of the new eternal world will view the artifacts of previous ages as a museum of ancient history and civilization, to remind them what does occur to created humanity and environment and civilization should they turn against the divine instruction of *Yahweh* God and follow their own inclination.

The eternal kingdom will arise on this earth, the residence that *Yahweh* God prepared for created humanity. The manner of continuous population or procreation during this eternal era is a point not readily defined by Scripture or distinguishable. The reason apparently being, *Yahweh* God retaining such secrets for this future era, not to be divulged to any human of the present age. Jesus made the statement, that in the resurrection, those who accept such a transformed body will in some way match or be identified with the messengers of *Yahweh* God who reside in heaven, the realm of spirit.

> For those who attain the resurrection will not marry or be given in marriage, since they will be like the messengers (*aggellos*) in heaven. Matt 22:30.

Whether this excludes marital relations as the manner of conception, or excludes marriage totally or even childbirth cannot be fully ascertained. The passage is ambiguous for several reasons. One is that the attributes of messengers in heaven that pertain to marriage is not clearly defined. A second is that the translation from Aramaic into Greek may have lost some of the substance of his words. That some interpreters construe this to mean that the resurrected individual will fly about with wings in the clouds wearing a white robe, a halo and strumming a harp deviates from its intended meaning and is not consistent with the balance of Scripture.

One item to be gleaned from this passage is that the carnal facet of marital relations will not be present, since the transformed body will no longer retain this capacity. No doubt in both these situations an attitude between the genders of greater perfection will replace one based on impulse of sexual union and desire for procreation as a means of survival of themselves through their offspring. Likewise the need for marriage and procreation as a personal fulfillment of being male and female will likewise dissipate. Every male and every female will be complete in themselves. The relationship will be a perfect one. (I personally find it difficult to visualize marital relations continuing in the eternal world.) But exactly how this will be perfected is yet undefined and will remain so until those worthy enough to attain the resurrection finally do so.

Any more description beyond this is conjecture. I consider this amount to be sufficient for the reader without hypothesizing on what may or may not occur during this eternal era without Scriptural evidence.

## THE NEW WORLD TO COME

The final witness to the restoration is the baptism of the Holy Spirit. 1 Cor 2:10. This is the evidence of the world to come gifted to every believer. It is through the manifestation of the Spirit of *Yahweh* God in ourselves that the belief in the restoration is permanently etched upon the mind and heart of every member of the spiritual Israel. The Spirit testifies that the sons and daughters of *Yahweh* God will attain the maturity destined for him and her during this eternal era of restoration. This maturity begun on earth in our mortal body will attain a perfection in the immortal body. The intent of *Yahweh* God for the long term purpose of the millions of years into the future is not defined by Scripture. This eternal life is millions of years or even billions of years long according to time as we measure it. Unaging and development unto a perfection while involved in activities that give growth to the kingdom.

The specific activities of this eternal era is not defined in Scripture, neither is the long term purpose. It would not be conjecture though to conclude that some divine intent is reserved as far as ascension further into the maturity that belongs to *Yahweh* God. To attain unto that fullness and stature and maturity of Jesus son of *Yahweh* God is not without purpose.

> Until we all attain to the unity of the faith, and to the knowledge of the son of God, to a mature person, to the measure of the stature that belongs to the fullness of the Anointed. Eph 4:13.

This could possibly be only conjecture that such a route is required for those *Yahweh* God has predestined in order to raise them unto divinity. This would occur not for their own sake, but as fulfillment of greater purpose or responsibility in the future as determined for them by *Yahweh* God.

> Then comes the end when he delivers the kingdom to God the Father after destroying every rule and authority and power.... When all things are subjected to Him, then the son himself will also be subjected to Him who put all things under him, that God may be all in all. 1 Cor 15:24, 28.
> That you may be filled with all the fullness of God. Eph 3:19.

This concept of universal reconciliation is necessary and possible as God does have a purpose for each of his created conscious entities. This has been discussed earlier.

The universe contains millions of fully equipped galaxies. Each galaxy contains millions of stars, each star representative of a solar system like our own. I will only conjecture here that these millions of solar system planets like our own may have to be developed for habitation, and a complete environmental system implemented, and plants and animals created to fill the planet, and then populated with human like ourselves. Could this conjecture possibly be the future of the human residing within the will of *Yahweh* God and His covenant? For him and her to eventually accept the responsibility of further development of other planets will have the purpose to even more glorify and magnify *Yahweh* God for His overabounding love for all creation.

## RESURRECTION

The resurrection or resuscitation of a corpse unto life is less or just as improbable than the generation of new original life from sperm and ovum. If a person can accept original generation proceeding from marital relations of the 2 genders, it is equally possible to accept the reconstitution of a person who was alive at some earlier period. As discussed earlier, the person, the individual, is the soul. This soul is the identity of that person. But for the soul to have consciousness it must have a tangible and healthy body: either male or female. As humans, the tendency is to identify the body as the person, because every person looks different. The body becomes the identity of the person. If this same soul or identity was assigned to a body having a different appearance or shape, we would not accept it. Paul apostle describes it as follows:

> For our residence is in heaven, from which also we eagerly wait for the Savior, the Lord Jesus, who will transform our wasted body to be identical with the body of his glory, by the exertion of the power he has to subject all things to himself. Phil 3:20-21.
>
> If the Spirit of Him who raised Jesus from death resides in you, He who raised the Anointed Jesus from death will give life to your mortal bodies also through His Spirit that resides in you. Rom 8:11.

The initial facet of resurrection is reconstitution. At this assigned time, *Yahweh* God will dictate the order to His Spirits, those that fulfill His activity of creation. They will reassemble a body with similar appearance and form as their previous body. The work will proceed in the same manner as progenitors Adam and Eve were formed. Into this reconstituted body the breathe of the Almighty will again enter and the soul assigned this appearance and form will gain consciousness. Specifically what age or what stature or what semblance of that person of his or her early life will constitute their physical image is yet to be determined. What will change will be the physical nature and moral nature of the individual. Paul apostle used the best terms he possible could in his era to describe the constitution of the new body, a physical nature adapted for immortal existence. 1 Cor 15:35-41.

The 2nd facet of resurrection pertains to the experience of the individual himself in regaining the life departed from him or her for millennia or minutes. The experience of Lazarus in resurrection as expected was discussed earlier in this volume: his lapse into oblivion and subsequent reconstitution and wakening. In addition, I will utilize 2 basic events that a typical human experiences that will convey the closest parallel to regaining consciousness.

Several years I ago had to undergo oral surgery to remove wisdom teeth. The oral surgeon recommended sodium pentothal as the best anesthesia for the surgery. As the sodium pentothal was pumped into my body the physician asked me to begin counting. As I counted I lapsed into a state of total oblivion. How much time passed under anesthesia I could not determine. The next mental acknowledgement was that of waking up, recovering from anesthesia. Even though this appeared to be timeless oblivion without awareness or sensation of pain or even existence, several hours had passed. I remembered and felt absolutely nothing between the time I lapsed under the effect of the anesthesia and when I began to regain consciousness. The pain I would have felt during surgery had I not been under anesthesia I would not have been able to tolerate. I consider this as the same personal experience of death and resurrection. As a person terminates their life they pass unto their eternal sleep, and as a person resurrects they regain their consciousness.

## THE DAY OF THE TRUMPET

Another description utilized in Scripture is the sudden wake due to the sound of a trumpet. In both the ancient and contemporary eras military recruits are wakened in the morning by a trumpet call. A recruit could be fast asleep, in a sound sleep, and suddenly this loud blast of sound penetrates his ears and he suddenly awakens. Likewise the sound of thunder or some other loud noise at night will startle the sound sleeper and quickly waken them. We open our eyes and look about us and wonder what it was that wakened us. It is not unusual for a person very tired in the evening to lay his head on a pillow and fall asleep so soundly that the alarm seems to ring no sooner than when their eyes closed, and it is already morning.

These are the analogies of Scripture.

> Then the 7th angel blew his trumpet, and there were loud voices in heaven saying, "The kingdom of the world has become that of our Lord and of His Anointed, and he shall reign for ever and ever." Rev 11:15.
> For the Lord himself will descend from heaven with a cry of command, with the archangel's call and with the sound of the trumpet of God. 1 Thess 4:16.

In these passages the authors make use of the trumpet sound as a means of summoning people to gather for a special event. Just as the audible sound of a trumpet blasted from Mount Sinai to summon the nation of old Israel to rendezvous *Yahweh* God, so a spiritual trumpet will sound from the heavens to summon the entirety of the people of both the old and new Israel and all the deceased saints from the age to rendezvous the descent of the powers of heaven for the resurrection of the dead, transformation of the living, and restoration of the earth. This trumpet blast will be spiritual, it will be the inspiration or motivation of the Spirit to the living and the loud volume of spiritual sound will waken the sleeping spirits of the deceased saints. This is the final trumpet mentioned in 1 Cor 15:52, or $7^{th}$ trumpet mentioned in Rev 11:15, which will herald the close of the imperfect age and introduce the eternal and perfect age.

The trumpet so familiar to the military and civilians of the Roman Empire was used as an allegory to waken the deceased saints and initiate the restoration. I feel the above examples to be reliable to propose as the personal experience of resurrection.

## EPILOGUE

When Jesus prayed unto his Father at the Passover he said.

> And this is eternal life, that they know You the only true God, and Jesus, whom You have sent. John 17:3.

The manner of attaining a long and prosperous and successful life blessed of *Yahweh* God is by way of a knowledge of Him and His son Emmanuel. They want to be known personally. *Yahweh* God wants us to be close with Him, as close as Moses who spoke with Him face to face. Num 12:7-8. It is through Jesus that we gain a knowledge of his Father. He in his ministry and through his apostles brings the knowledge of his Father to us.

> And no one knows the Father except the son, and any one to whom the son chooses to reveal Him. Matt 11:27.
> His divine power has granted to us all things that pertain to life and godliness, through the knowledge of Him who called us to His own glory and excellence. 2 Pet 1:3.

*Yahweh* God wants us to know Him as heavenly Father as well as we know our earthly Father. Then we can understand His expectations of us, His dictates to us, His love towards us, and His intended future for us, and receive His gifts and blessings.

May *Yahweh* bless you and keep you.
May *Yahweh* make His face to shine upon you and be gracious to you.
May *Yahweh* make His presence among you and give you peace.
Amen.
Num 6:24-26.

# PART THREE

## KINGDOMS AND COVENANTS

### 1. COVENANTS

This part with the topics of kingdoms and covenants, those defined and accomplished throughout the history of the people of Israel, both old and new, as recorded in the Holy Bible. The kingdom and the covenant are the 2 manners that *Yahweh* God related to and is involved with His created humanity, whether individual or community. The manner that people relate to and involve themselves with one another within the spiritual community is likewise in terms of covenant and rule. No era has progressed on earth since creation without a covenant of *Yahweh* God in effect or available for the individual and populous. Both concepts operate simultaneously in Scripture and are interwoven in every era, in every situation and in every locale where humanity lived and especially Israel.

Parallel with the above are the sections dealing with the message of Jesus, and the New Covenant and the spiritual Kingdom that he initiated. This section includes the message of John the Baptizer and the Apostles in their historical context. The beliefs and practices of the new Messianic communities established by the apostles are also explained in their historical context. A discussion on the last days of old Israel and the termination of the old covenant is especially covered.

The final section of this volume is a historical analysis of the departure from Scripture in regards to the topics covered. Utilizing the writings of the post-apostolic church fathers and the subsequent apologists, the gradual departure from the concepts of the new covenant and the spiritual kingdom as defined in this treatise is researched and documented. The reason for this section is to provide the reader with concrete information and factual evidence proving that many of the teachings of historical Christianity are a departure from the original concepts believed, instituted and practiced by the original Messianic communities. This will provide a means for the reader to return to the faith that was once delivered to the saints.

The salvation attained through Jesus is prosperous and successful living in accord with the moral code and divine instruction. I hope that every person reading this volume will seriously consider its concepts and incorporate them into his and her life for *Yahweh* God to bless them.

## THE TRUTH OF YAHWEH GOD

The truth of *Yahweh* God is axiomatic. A person with a desire to live a life of high moral character will automatically and naturally comprehend the truth and value of adhering to the moral code of *Yahweh* God after its study. A person wanting to gain any extent of happiness, prosperity or success in their life will likewise acknowledge that the precepts contained in Holy Scripture, known as the Bible of the OT and NT, will create this route for their attainment. Jesus said the same to his audience in this manner:

> If any person's will is to do His (the Father's) will, he shall know whether the teaching is from God or whether I am speaking on my own authority. John 7:17.

Only a brief perusal of the Bible is required to conclude that this volume is the greatest collection of wisdom applicable for the prolongation and success of human existence ever compiled. Only the Bible, of all holy books every written, defines accurately and reliably the initial beginnings of the universe and the preparation of this world for residence. Only this book accurately details the origin of created humanity and all living creation. Only this book states in unambiguous terms the reason for the creation of humanity and what their future is from conception and to death, for every person on an individual basis. Only this book, and in terms understandable to both educated and uneducated, explains human nature, from love to hate to marriage to war.

Even though the actual moral instruction of Jesus in the gospel is very meager, he is considered the one who determined and implemented the moral code and divine instruction of Sacred Scripture in general. Jesus is the Word of *Yahweh* God. He is the personification of all divine and beneficial instruction, or the incarnation of the law and instruction of

*Yahweh* God. For this reason Jesus is the materialization of all that the Bible represents and teaches.

The letters of James, Peter, John and Jude are the primary sources of the moral code of Jesus, as they knew Jesus personally and listened to him over the 3 or so years of his ministry, as well as listened to him over the 40 days he was with them in the interval after his resurrection and up to his ascension to heaven. They are the most accurate and dependable record of the moral code Jesus delivered to people during his ministry. Paul apostle is a secondary source, since it was his responsibility in his ministry to bring the gospel to the gentiles. These people did not have a moral code to live by, and so Paul apostle provided them with one based on Sacred Scripture and the teachings of the Jewish sages, one that would apply to the Messianic communities.

For this reason assemblies are formed generation after generation from willing and sincere individuals that acknowledge the truth and benefit in the material contained in this book and the role of Jesus. They identify themselves as a Christian organization, meaning that their assembly or religion acknowledges the teachings of this book as valuable to the extent of utilizing it as a basis of morals and ethics for their assembly. The extent to which each assembly adheres to or observes what is dictated in Scripture depends on the individuals or membership of that particular assembly, and there are as many interpretations and applications of the same Bible as there are assemblies.

The same can apply to this person Jesus. He has been recognized as great teacher, healer, prophet, son of *Yahweh* God, incarnation of God's word, and itinerant rabbi. Each "Christian" assembly identifies with this person Jesus in one way or another because there is no greater individual in any respect with which to identify. Some assemblies identify with a saint or heavenly being, but yet they will still claim identification with Jesus as the supreme identity. Every "Christian" assembly acknowledges that there is no other name in heaven or on earth that will benefit them to the extent that believing in Jesus will. The extent to which a person defines Jesus and applies him to their personal, family, social and business life varies person to person, and assembly to assembly. The extent to which a person believes in Jesus and locates him in the hierarchy of divinity depends on the extent of benefit a person feels they will gain from such belief. There are as many interpretations of the entity of Jesus as there are people who recognize his existence. The basic and common denominator is the same, that this person Jesus has something to offer humanity and did so, and that this book the Bible is a benefit for all who will live according to its instruction. *Yahweh* God Himself seeks people whom He can bless and prosper for adhering to the divine instruction. Moses spoke regarding this:

> Therefore you shall keep His statues and His commandments which I command you this day, that it may go well with you, and with your children after you, and that you may prolong your days in the land which *Yahweh* your God gives you for the age. Deut 4:40, 5:29.

If you the reader can conclude that the words of this book will benefit you and I contend the evidence is axiomatic, then put *Yahweh* God to the test! Accept and adhere to and observe the moral code and divine instruction! *Yahweh* God Himself is willing to challenge any person on the reliability of any promise of His.

> Bring the full tithes into the storehouse, that there may be food in my house, and thereby put me to the test, says *Yahweh* of hosts, if I will not open the windows of heaven for you and pour upon you an overflowing blessing. Mal 3:10. 2 Chron 31:10

This deity above all is trustworthy in all that He states. The example made by the author of Hebrews is that promise made to Abraham patriarch when he and his wife were still childless. Heb 6:17-18. There exists 2 irrefutable items that demonstrate the absolute reliability of *Yahweh* God. I propose the Word and Spirit of *Yahweh* God as the 2 irrefutable items. Because *Yahweh* God is from the realm of spirit, heaven, it is through these 2 items that He reaches into our material realm to manifest Himself.

Every word from *Yahweh* God is reliable. This is confirmed in several places in Scripture. John 6:63, 17:17. Josh 23:14. And every action by way of His holy Spirit working in us through the baptism and gifts is reliable. John 5:36. Because these 2 facets of His nature penetrate the invisible barrier between heaven and the material realm and enter into our life, *Yahweh* God will base His reputation on them. These are the 2 witnesses of Rev 11:3. Since *Yahweh* God is immutable as a result of His nature, in terms of morals and purpose, He utilizes His word and Spirit to reveal His reliability to created humanity. In regard to the advantage of believing in *Yahweh* God and His word and spirit, Isaiah prophet spoke the following:

> If you are willing and obedient you shall eat the good of the land; but if you refuse and rebel you shall be devoured by the sword, for the mouth of *Yahweh* has spoken. Is 1:18-20.

The invitation is to a rational person who is at a crossroad of their life. A choice must be made. The invitation is to begin a new life if difficulties or serious problems have occurred in the recent past. However now the individual must give *Yahweh* God the opportunity to heal previous wounds and reestablish the person in a stable and satisfactory life. If other avenues have failed to rectify difficulties in life, the alternative is voluntary subjection to the dictates of Scripture. Only then will there be an improvement in the personal, social and family life of the individual.

## DEVELOPMENT OF A RIGHTEOUS HUMANITY

The fundamental purpose of the institution of both covenant and rule of *Yahweh* God is to create a righteous humanity, an honorable civilization. Although history infinitely records the failed attempts of thousands of ethnic groups and nationalities, this does not make the establishment of a righteous humanity an impossibility. The concept is part of the nature of every created person and which corporate effort materializes into governments. Nonetheless, all have eventually collapsed, for the largest to the smallest, whether of a long duration or that of a few years, but we cannot deny the benefit that each provided during the course of its existence. The concept of the formation of a righteous humanity however is most successful on an individual or community basis.

The failure of any ethnic group or nationality to establish an honorable civilization is due to failure to enter the covenant of *Yahweh* God and observe it. For a righteous humanity to develop and succeed, every member on an individual basis must present themselves in their subjection to the authority of *Yahweh* God, and accept from Him His moral code and divine instruction. Then every person must recite the words recited by previous generations to enter this covenant.

All that *Yahweh* has spoken we will observe and we will be obedient. Ex 19:6, 24:7.

With this concept applied by *Yahweh* God toward His people and their acceptance and willing subjection and obedience, a righteous humanity can be achieved. This entity of His elect persevere generation after generation. Salvation as an individual is acquired by residing in the will of *Yahweh* God as a participant in his covenant.

## CONCEPT OF THE COVENANT

Every person deals with the concept of covenant on a regular basis. It is a contract agreed to by 2 parties with a benefit to be acquired by each party. It is a win-win agreement. Every covenant or contract has terms and conditions that form its basis. If these are agreeable to both parties, and if both parties uphold the terms and conditions, then both parties will benefit. In many circumstances there is a stronger party and a weaker party. In this situation the stronger party is *Yahweh* God, who composes the contract and defines the terms and conditions, while the weaker party, humanity, has the option of either entering into the covenant-contract or declining. With contracts between humans not everything is always equitable, but with *Yahweh* God the benefit is actually in favor of the weaker party.

> Look down from Your holy residence, from heaven, and bless Your people Israel and the land that You have given us, as You did swear to our fathers, a land flowing with milk and honey. Deut 26:15.

The covenant is dissolved only when an incorrigible breach or violation occurs by the individual or community. It will never be arbitrary decision on the part of Yahweh God and never to be breached by *Yahweh* God. It is always the people who commit the violation or breach. The violators will then be liable to and will incur the penalty phase of the contract. The covenants are eternal, and are always available for any and every person to enter into.

> If we have died with him, we shall also live with him; if we endure, we shall also reign with him; if we deny him, he also will deny us; if we

are faithless, he remains faithful for he cannot deny himself. 2 Tim 2:11-13.

*Yahweh* God has designed such a covenant that it is in the best interests of the weaker party to enter into it. This is what He proposes for created humanity, and in our best interests. If a person voluntarily enters into this covenant with *Yahweh* God, He is faithful in every respect to uphold His portion of the terms and conditions and will do extra. *Yahweh* God will never fail on His part, it is the human that fails. As long as the person who enters into the covenant lives according to this moral code, voluntarily and without coercion, *Yahweh* God will fulfill His portion of the contract and bless this person, but when the person male or female violates or fails to uphold their portion, then *Yahweh* God has no choice except to withdraw His blessing, but it will not occur immediately. Time is allowed for repentance, and the withdrawal of favor and blessing is gradual. This gradual withdrawal is to remind the person of his recession or retreat – apostasy – from grace and that the course taken in violation of the covenant will lead to greater withdrawal of grace from that person's life. If this retreat and violation continues then the withdrawal and blessing will continue until the person has abandoned the covenant entirely. At this point the person is outside the will of *Yahweh* God and must fend for themselves. Repentance at any time and the voluntary return of the person to *Yahweh* God allows the person to again enter the covenant to enjoy His grace and blessing as long as they now uphold the moral code of *Yahweh* God.

## YAHWEH GOD AS A MORAL CODE

*Yahweh* God is not a deity whose attention or favor can be gained or who can be appeased by rite and ritual. The essence of *Yahweh* God is that of a moral code. *Yahweh* God is not the sun or moon or lightning or war or fertility, whose blessing and benefit can be acquired by prescribed ritual, and is not a deity whose wrath can be ameliorated by superficial ceremony. This error did appear in Israel on occasion. One occurrence is noticeable in the circumstance with the Israelites bringing the ark of the covenant into battle in 1 Sam 4. They felt that the presence of the ark would be sufficient for them to gain the victory over their enemy, the Philistines. But wrong they were. With their subsequent defeat the ark of the covenant was captured by the enemy. A second example of error is noted in Jer 9:1-4. The Israelites were convinced that they would automatically and unconditionally be defended from the threat of Babylon because of the presence of the temple. Because the temple was constructed by Solomon son of David, filled with the holy Spirit at its consecration, and regularly had the required services performed properly, they felt *Yahweh* God would defend them. But they also were wrong.

This is the distinction with *Yahweh* God as opposed to all other so-called and venerated deities or supernatural heroes or divine entities. *Yahweh* God was to be identified as a moral code. He was worshipped by way of adherence and observance of this moral code. The ritual of the OT was designed to impress sin as repulsive and offensive behavior, and to lead the people to voluntary fulfillment of the moral code. *Yahweh* God was not to be identified with an image or portrait or identified physically with some creature or creation. The pseudo-deities were identified with creatures and creation. Examples such as the molten calf. Ex 32. The calves of Jeroboam. 2 King 12:28. The brass serpent of Num 21:8-9. It became known as Nehushtan and was venerated at a shrine, but was later destroyed by Hezekiah. 2 King 18:4. Any and all of this imagery is an insult to the omnipotence and omnipresence of *Yahweh* God, and an inappropriate portrayal of His majesty and existence as a spirit. Any identification of *Yahweh* God with any creature or creation corrupted the true knowledge of His person. The ban on utilization of images in worship or identification of *Yahweh* God is not only a misrepresentation of Him, but has an impact on the psyche of the worshipper. The prophet of Israel and the Jewish sages described it in this manner:

> What profit is an idol, when its maker has shaped it, an image, a teacher of lies? Hab 2:18.
> Idolatry is the beginning of immorality. Wisdom of Solomon 14:12.

The truth of such statements lie in the fact that a piece of gold or wood or stone has no moral influence on the person of the worshipper. The statute or image has no ability to convict sin or pronounce verdict for a crime and carry out the penalty. It cannot engender guilt or remorse or repentance. The purpose of the statue, according to the promoters and adherents of religions that utilize them, is to serve as a means to assist the worshipper in communication or channel with the deity the statue represents. This is a logical statement except that there is no reverse effect. For this reason Jeremiah prophet spoke his warning in Jer 10:1-5. Since an image or statue has no retributive capability for sin or crime, veneration of images and statues becomes the license for sin and crime. A person can violate a moral code in its entirety and not ever worry about facing judgment. Idolatry breeds crime, social corruption, oppression and sacrilege. Because the sole use of the image or statue is for communication with its representation, it does not promote a moral code. For this reason the covenant code of *Yahweh* God was adamant in its prohibition of the use of images in worship and which would equally pertain to all figures of Scripture or history.

## THE GODS OF THE NATIONS

There exists in Scripture a concept of supreme deity that is distinct and separate from the concept of the pseudo-deities, or gods of the nations or the tribal gods. These pseudo-deities are today known as myths, and their history as mythology. Even in our own era of the late 20$^{th}$ century, such pseudo-deities continue to be venerated in areas where education is lacking: sub-Sahara Africa, south America, the India sub-continent and south-east Asia, those areas known as the Third World. The pseudo-deities resulted from identifying the elements of nature with forces that were invisible in order to resolve the unknown. Why did the sun shine? for example. Not knowing the actual reason, a deity was suggested, Apollos, and who became fact and subsequently worshipped. What existed deep beneath the surface of the ocean? Not knowing exactly what, a deity was suggested, Neptune, who became fact and was subsequently worshipped. Lightning became Thor; the nether regions of the earth was Pluto; wine was Bacchus; war was Mars; Venus was love and fertility; and the list continues on.

The common people identified the elements of nature with these specific pseudo-deities. Especially important was agriculture, because food production was the primary industry of earlier ages. Fertility in agriculture was a prime concern and also had its assigned deities. In the area of Palestine, or Canaan, the primary pseudo-deity was Baal, which is Master or Lord in Aramaic. Hos 2:16. Baal was the male fertility deity recognized and venerated by the local population. His female counterpart was Astarte, who later developed into Asherah and then into Easter. 2 Chron 33:3, Judg

3:7. Marital relations had a strong identification with the pseudo-deities Baal and Astarte, since their worship was to produce fertility in the field and in the home.

Each of the individual cities or regions of Canaan had a Baal cult they recognized as their own. Baal-Peor was the Master or chief male deity of Peor, Hosea 9:10; but who was distinct from Baal-Zebub worshipped by the Philistines. 2 King 1:2. And Baal-Meon, who was the Master or chief male deity of Meon. Num 32:38. Other pseudo-deities are mentioned in Scripture, each of them the supreme deity of that city of region. Chemosh the deity of Moab. Judg 11:24. Molech the deity of Ammon. 1 King 11:7. Marduk the deity of Babylon. Jer 50:2.

The specific distinction between the true supreme deity *Yahweh* God and the Baals and other pseudo-deities was that *Yahweh* God was a moral code, while the others were myths, fables and superstition, with no moral basis to them. There was no moral code that stood as the foundation of worship or identification of the Baals or pseudo-deities. If a person of that era was in need of morality, apart from conscious or inclination of society, they went to a philosopher.

The method and reason for worship and acceptance of some local pseudo-deity can be best understood in the manner some local resident or ruler would approach their deity. In order for the worshipper to acquire some benefit, he would have to gain the attention of the pseudo-deity. The method of gaining attention of the pseudo-deity was to entrust the help of the sacred attendant, a priest, attached to this deity at a temple or edifice dedicated to it. This priest consecrated for the cause of the pseudo-deity at the place especially assigned him then performs with the worshipper certain rites and ceremonies and maneuvers in some prescribed fashion. The worshipper will then give the priest a gift, some money, or will kill some animal. Part of the animal remains with the priest as a gift, while the balance the worshipper takes home to eat. The subsequent feast is in honor of that particular god. The worshipper is assured this entire maneuver will cause the pseudo-deity to grant his request for prosperity, success, victory, a large harvest of crops, increase offspring, or grant a healing.

If the request of the petitioner is not granted, the priest informs him that he has angered the deity or that the gift was insufficient. The petitioner can increase his gift and try again, or he may decide that this particular deity is weak or inattentive to his request, and so then will attempt the same maneuver at the temple of some other deity and hope that this other one will be appeased with the worship and gift and grant their request. The flaw in this concept is that no moral code exists, which is the real basis for failure or success. Isaiah prophet best describes the futility in the following passage.

> All who make idols are nothing, and the things they delight in do not profit; their witnesses neither see nor know, that they may be put to shame. They know not, nor do they discern; for He has shut their eyes, so that they cannot see, and their minds, so that they cannot understand. Is 44:9, 18.

Scripture abounds with several examples of such conduct. The most prominent is that of the contest of Elijah prophet and the 450 prophets of Baal and 400 prophets of Asherah. 1 King 18:20-39. Here the 950 representatives of the chief male and female deities of Canaanite religion performed a circus of maneuvers to gain the attention of their god: they cried aloud, limped, and cut themselves until they were blood soaked. This is typical of ancient rites to attempt to gain attention and appease the deities. Also worth considering is king Ahaziah who sent his wife to inquire of Baal-Zebub, a local Canaanite deity. 2 Kings 1:2-16. King Ahaziah was no doubt slowly dying from internal bleeding or some other internal disease of vital organs, and wondered whether he would recovered from his accident. The wife was intercepted by a messenger of Elijah prophet, who reprimanded them for their lack of faith in the true supreme deity, *Yahweh* God. King Ahaziah eventually died from the effects of his accident.

Child sacrifice by fire to Molech is also mentioned several times. Lev 18:21. 2 Chron 28:3. With the king of Moab realizing his oncoming defeat the ruler sacrificed his son at the city wall. 2 King 3:26-27. Such a sacrifice of the most valuable possession of a father was sure to gain the attention of the gods and appease them, acquiring supernatural assistance. In reality, the hideous act of the ruler was so repulsive to Israelites that they retreated from the city at this point.

The pagan and idolatrous religions of this era consisted of gross immorality in public festivals. The groves were the Asherah, areas where trees were carved into the form of the male phallus and the female figure with exaggerated features. They were called Asherah poles: Judg 6:25. The ensuing orgy of the participants, adherents of the religion of Baal and

Asherah, were to symbolize the same union of the male and female deities in heaven, the god and goddess of fertility. This antitype was to symbolize agricultural fertility, an abundant yield of produce and harvest for the coming season. Likewise the insemination during the orgies would also produce offspring, to continue the tribe. Such perverted worship of the deity was accompanied by feasting, exotic dancing, drug abuse, consumption of alcoholic beverages, as well as gifts offered to the sacerdotal representative of the deity. Rather than the desired effect, the nation was plagued with venereal disease, alcoholism, drug addiction and overdose, unwanted offspring, and much premature death. Such activity is referred to in Is 65:3-4, 66:17. This ignorance and superstition continued perennially, the succeeding generation repeating the errors of the previous.

## VIOLATION OF COVENANT

The opportunity to live on this earth is a privilege, not a right. It is a privilege allocated by *Yahweh* God and is only valid as long as the residents adhere to the covenant that would be considered applicable to all residents of this planet. I will use the parallel and allegory of a person renting a house or building from the owner. If a person needs a house or building or property for some use and there is a willing owner ready to rent or lease the property, a contract is made up: both agree on the terms and conditions for utilization of the buildings and property, a compensation to be made, and the agreement is signed. As long as the tenants live up to and hold to their part of the contract they are permitted to live there and the owner cannot evict. But if the tenant fails his portion of the agreement, then the owner has the right to evict the tenants. For some minor infraction the owner may and will be tolerant, especially with reparations made and a change in attitude and again adhering to the agreement. But with serious infraction and violation to the point of intolerance, an irremediable and irreparable situation, the owner will proceed to evict the tenants and repossess his property.

So occurred with the population of the earth at the flood. The violation was so massive that *Yahweh* God proceeded with the eviction of the population from off the face of the earth. Gen 6:5-7. By way of the flood did *Yahweh* God evict the tenants off of His property and repossess it. The land was now ready for new tenants. This basic scenario is repeated several times throughout Scripture in varying degrees. It applies to the exile of the residents of the northern Kingdom Israel, *Yahweh* God utilized the armies of Assyria to evict the residents from the northern partial of the promised land. Hos 8:1. Likewise with the residents of the southern Kingdom Judea, *Yahweh* God utilized the armies of Babylon to evict the residents from the southern partial of the promised land. Some 70 years later with a renewal of heart and repentant attitude a remnant was allowed to again inhabit the property of *Yahweh* God. The same scenario again occurred during the Jewish War of 66-70 AD. *Yahweh* God could no longer tolerate the wickedness of the Jewish population and so sent the armies of Rome to devastate Judea, and siege Jerusalem and subsequently destroy the city. The residents of Judea were taken to Rome as slaves and captives, and the balance of the Judean population were dispersed throughout the middle east. The occupants of the property of *Yahweh* God were again evicted, this time for almost 1900 years.

The same applies to the restoration as noted. 2 Pet 3:10-11. During the era at the close of the age and prior to the restoration of the earth, wickedness will again increase throughout the earth, to the extent as during the era of Noah or even worse. The violation of the covenant so serious that *Yahweh* God will use a devastation by fire to evict the residents of this earth and repossess it. The earth will be cleansed by this fire and will be made ready for its new tenants, the people of *Yahweh* God for the eternal Kingdom.

## THE COVENANT ERAS

I contend that salvation from sin, the knowledge of *Yahweh* God, the divine instruction for a life pleasing to *Yahweh* God, and the keys to the kingdom, that is, the knowledge and means of attaining the resurrection and inheriting eternal life, was present on earth from the creation and available to whoever desired it. The periods or eras stemming from the beginning of time and to the final era of the kingdom are designated as dispensations, (but not in the contemporary Darbian or Scoldfield sense as I will describe). On a regular basis *Yahweh* God would renew his covenant established with created humanity, and this would become a new covenant for the next dispensation, and with other minor covenants established in between.

The basic moral law has remained the same. It has not changed. One of the examples of this moral law from the beginning is that of marriage, under the 7th commandment: Do not be immoral. When the Pharisees approached Jesus with the question regarding when divorce should be granted or allowed, he made the statement, "From the beginning it was not so." Matt 19:8. He meant that divorce was permitted at some later date as an accommodation to the people for their barbarian nature. This statement of his also provides the precedent for an original moral code established at the beginning that does not change, meaning consistency throughout the ages. The exception is not the rule. The rule was established by *Yahweh* God at creation; exceptions appeared on an occasional basis as the demand surfaced, and which was only permitted to accommodate the barbarian or uncultured nature of the populous and only for some interval.

## THE INITIAL COVENANT ERA

This first covenant era could be defined as that era of undetermined length from the conclusion of creation week to the fall of Adam and Eve. They lived in this paradise of Eden under this canopy of the shelter of *Yahweh* God. I contend that Cain and Abel and perhaps some daughters as wives for them were born during this interval. A covenant was in force at this time that *Yahweh* God instituted with Adam and Eve on the first day after the Sabbath rest at the conclusion of creation week. The covenant was symbolized by the tree of life. As long as Adam and Eve were obedient to the divine instruction they spiritually partook of the fruit of this tree and lived, but disobedience to the divine instruction by succumbing to temptation violated the covenant. This divine instruction was the moral code established at the beginning and applicable for all humanity throughout all the ages. I contend that it was later codified as the 10 commandments. That a covenant did exist can be verified by the passage of Hosea 6:7.

Some of the early life patterns of Adam and Eve can be only ascertained from the changes and curses that were pronounced by *Yahweh* God after the fall. We earlier determined in general theory what the original pattern of life consisted of in the garden of Eden, but not in every aspect, but at least by the following few: Labor; childbirth; marriage; termination of life.

For Adam work was originally a pleasure. Here both male and female enjoined the exertion of effort as a self-satisfying and gratifying pleasure to wake in the morning, fulfill the obligations of the day, and retire in the evening. To be able to look at a person's own constructive effort of that day and be able to say just as *Yahweh* God did, "This is good." Every challenge would be successful. Failure and injury was unknown. The early life of Adam and Eve and no doubt their sons and daughters was occupied with farming and raising cattle, and agrarian society. They achieved a personal fulfillment from their occupation, always a success.

## LIFE IN PARADISE

The words in Gen 1:27-28 indicate the ability of man to have the superior control over all that is on earth, and not the opposite. In Eden he was able to dominate and tame all living creatures on earth. Life in the garden of Eden was in harmony with nature and all animals, no animosity existing between human and animal, and between animals. That every animal was brought to Adam by *Yahweh* God is indicative of the human's dominion over the animal kingdom. The human was at the head, and not subservient in any manner. The nature that presently exists with animals did not exist at that time. Animals did not kill to eat, or fight to defend their habitation or residence, for fight for survival, or fight for mates, or fight to be head of a heard. There was no need for animals to have defense mechanisms or the anatomy for self-defense or self-preservation. No venom in snakes, spiders, wasps or bees. The dominion would have also pertained to weather and the elements. Although the human would not have direct control over weather and the elements, the concept of dominion would have applied likewise. A harmony prevailed between the human and the environment in every facet. Storms, earthquakes, typhoons, hurricanes, monsoons, floods, famines, or uncomfortable climate, did not exist. Since disease is the result of bacteria and pathogens no illness existed in Eden. No plagues, no contamination, no epidemics. The human was in perfect health and in harmony with their environment.

> For the spirit of the Lord fills the world. Wisdom 1:7.
> For Your incorruptible spirit is in all things. Wisdom 12:1.

The human along with the plant and animal kingdoms did not face decay and death as time progressed in the environment of the original creation. The constitution of living creation was such that the organism could live indefinitely. It was the eternal spirit of *Yahweh* God in His creation that restrained deterioration due to age. So felt the Jewish sages.

## SECOND COVENANT ERA

The second covenant era is that period beginning with the expulsion of Adam and his family from Eden and up to the flood during the career of Noah. The verdict of *Yahweh* God upon Adam and his male descendents was the following as a result of their violation of the covenant:

> Cursed is the ground because of you, in toil you shall eat of it all the days of your life;. Thorns and thistles it shall being forth to you and you shall eat the plants of the field. In the sweat of your face you shall eat bread. Gen 3:17-19.

From this point on work was no longer a pleasure, but a necessity, a drudgery, a demanding effort that would exhaust man and woman both. An exhaustion and pressure that would drive a person to despair as he fought against the elements to earn a living, this applying to every occupation. Labor pain during childbirth also was imposed on the female at this time, as dictated by *Yahweh* God. Gen 3:16.

*Yahweh* God instituted at this time a systematic religion for the descendents of Adam and Eve. This defined religion was above and in addition to the initial moral code. The religion consisted in ceremony and ritual which have divine significance, and were to impress upon the individual their distance from *Yahweh* God and bring that person into His covenant and will. Their distance from *Yahweh* God was apparent now with paradise lost, and the barbaric mind of the people of the era required ritual as an analogy in the requirements of *Yahweh* God.

The fact that sacrifice was acceptable to *Yahweh* God as part of the proper form of worship was repulsive to the early population. Cain no doubt felt that a better sacrifice to *Yahweh* God would be one where there was no need for a life to be taken, where there was no necessity of having to select some innocent animal, cut its neck by force with a knife and watch it die. Although Cain would have his reasons for a substitute sacrifice, and no doubt very good reasons, it is not what *Yahweh* God required of them. By way of killing an innocent animal, an animal fit for human consumption according to the law of *Yahweh* God, He impressed upon the worshipper the extent disobedience was hideous and heinous. After the animal was roasted or barbecued the family of the worshipper would eat the animal in a common meal, this would indirectly give strength and nourishment to the partakers of the sacrifice.

During the era of Noah, Gen 6, the males of the community of *Yahweh* God were attracted by females outside the community, females having no moral character. This is the basis for understanding the passage Gen 6:1-2. This invasion attacked the moral fiber of the community of *Yahweh* God causing immorality and disintegration of the family and the commitment to marriage by the males. Eventually this would have a detrimental effect on the marriageable age women of the community of *Yahweh* God. The attitude of the elders of the community was such that the physical attraction of the beauty of a female had to be overlooked by the male in favor of a long-term marriage commitment, otherwise the lust of the flesh takes precedent and erodes the moral fiber. This moral disintegration occurred at the conclusion of the 2nd covenant era and was proceeded by a massive betrayal of *Yahweh* God, loss of divine virtue, violation of His moral code, and subsequent would-wide violence.

The phrase, "For all flesh corrupted this way upon the earth," Gen 6:12, can be defined in terms of Rom 1:26-27. The Hebrew word *shachth* is primarily translated as destroy (70 out of 91 uses in the OT), while here in Gen 6:11-12, it is rendered as corrupted. The intent of the passage is to indicate moral decline and obscenity during the era prior to the flood. It is apparent according to the record of Scripture that the entire world had lost its sense of decency and become incorrigible. By discarding the moral law in favor of their own, they abandoned the tree of life and ate from the tree of the knowledge of good and evil. They turned their back on *Yahweh* God. This attitude of theirs pierced the heart of *Yahweh* God to the point that He regretted their existence. Gen 6:6. In most respects however their annihilation was deserved. They brought their own demise upon themselves. These individuals of the antediluvian world had to take personal responsibility for their actions and so they answered to *Yahweh* God with their own life.

The only family that upheld the moral code of *Yahweh* God was Noah's, and so they continued in covenant with *Yahweh* God. Noah adhered to the terms and conditions of this spiritual contract, and *Yahweh* God granted him deliverance from the flood. This salvation manifested itself in the command of *Yahweh* God to Noah to build the ark. This ark during its 100-year construction schedule was a witness to the people that if they repent, then there would be refuge for them in the ark. If no repentance was carried out with a conversion, they would answer for their crimes against *Yahweh* God and others with their own life.

## THE THIRD COVENANT ERA

The 3rd covenant era began with the institution of a new covenant with Noah and continued among the gentiles until Jesus. Noah followed the manner of sacrifice he was taught by his forefathers with his offering of clean animals. The fact that *Yahweh* God commanded 7 pair each of clean animals as opposed to 1 pair of the balance to be included in the ark is obviously for breeding to provide food supply for the surviving family and their immediate descendents. Gen 7:2.

The moral code that was introduced initially to Adam and Eve would have been reiterated at this time. Now as a sign of *Yahweh* God's faithfulness a rainbow appeared. Gen 9:8-17. Again *Yahweh* God would be faithful to fulfill His portion of the contract to the extent Noah and his descendants would be obedient to the covenant.

Jewish sages felt that the moral code presented to Noah could offer divine approval to an individual not a descendent of Abraham. They taught that the covenant of Noah continued effective for gentiles throughout the ages even with the implementation of the covenants with Abraham and with Israel. Just because *Yahweh* God selected Abraham and his descendents of the promise and then Israel does not mean that all gentiles were discarded and had no access to salvation. By righteous conduct gentiles could attain the blessing and grace of *Yahweh* God. Jewish sages defined the moral code of Noah as applicable to the gentiles in 7 commandments.[12]

1. The practice of equity.
2. Prohibition of blasphemy of the name of God, *Yahweh*.
3. Prohibition of idolatry.
4. Prohibition of immorality.
5. Prohibition of bloodshed (i.e. murder).
6. Prohibition of robbery.
7. Consumption of an animal that is strangled (i.e. blood.)

---

[12] *Talmud*. Sanhedrin 5ba.

In many respects such a moral code is applicable to every generation. It is to the benefit of every individual that he and she live a moral and ethical life style that is reflected in all areas of education, business, family, and government to build a strong society. This was the intent of *Yahweh* God as if starting anew with Noah to create a righteous society and the rainbow was evidence of the promise. The rainbow symbolized the beauty of this covenant with *Yahweh* God. Just as the light rain falling against the shining sun creates this reflection of light, so *Yahweh* God would shine upon the people and shower them with His grace and blessing.

It is worth noting that 5 of these commandments are included in the 10 commandments, and the other 2 are in other areas of the law given to Israel. The final one about animals that are strangled is identical to Acts 15:20, 29.

## DEPARTURE FROM THE COVENANT OF NOAH

An acceptable form of worship was to be prescribed by *Yahweh* God and not one derived from the elements or environment. The evolution of false-religion began soon after as individuals disobeyed the moral code and true religion and began idolatry – the use of statutes or images in worship. The population subsequent to Noah began to identify the forces of nature with contrived pseudo-deities and which were then transferred to some physical representation. Others equated the stars or planets with the deities and felt that the location of these stellar objects had a direct effect on the forces of nature as well as their personal life. Ignorance and fear pervaded the populous and promoted these pseudo-religions and pseudo-deities. Once the populous accepted it as true and real it encompassed their life and developed into a complete religion with a pantheon of gods or pseudo-gods; priests defended the existence of such entities, the materialization of their superstition and ignorance; priests also extracted gifts and sacrifices and offerings from the people; priests exacted favors from rulers and the wealthy, patrons who would subsidize the construction of massive temples and other monuments to venerate and magnify the cult that surrounded that particular favorite god or goddess. The new cultic priests would identify political, personal or environmental upheavals or conditions with the displeasure of their particular god.

The city Babylon became a promoter of this type of religion with much influence in the neighboring regions. A great leader of the era was Nimrod. The narrative describes him as follows.

Nimrod was a great hunter in the presence of *Yahweh*. Gen 10:9.

The use of the word hunter by the author of Genesis refers to Nimrod as an aggressive military commander seeking conquest. It did not embarrass Nimrod to gather an army and defeat local cities to become a hero and establish Babylon as his capital. His wife was named *Semiramis* and she became in subsequent years a deified queen, worshipped under many names in religions influenced by Babylon, including the Queen of Heaven. Jer 44:17-25. *Tammuz* was the son of *Semiramis*. Eze 8:14.

Nimrod apparently was an ambitious megalomaniac individual gathering disenchanted men and boys seeking glory in victory, to become heroes in the defeat of the other villages and cities to build themselves a kingdom to the credit of their leader and venerated hero. But of what real advantage is there in this type of conquest? To build a kingdom with one person at the principal seat of power entails the deaths of many innocent villagers and residents of the countryside. It entails building a military, an army of men along with the industrial complex required to furnish the military complex clothes, weapons, food, supplies, and training and education. All of this at the expense and sacrifice of residents.

Why not just leave the villages alone?

This combination of the development of pagan religion and the increase of power in the hands of a few military leaders with the balance of the population under despotic subjection was prevalent throughout the inhabited world at this time. The rise of early world powers in the orient, India, Middle East and North Africa date from this era. The rise of certain cities as centers of finance and commerce is also noticeable in these same areas, the witness of ruins of ancient civilizations indicate advancement in architecture, engineering and construction. The monuments of ages past are often thought of as evidence of advancement in these areas, yet the reader must remember several key issues pertaining to the years prior to Abraham and onwards for many centuries. Mechanical means of construction did not exist at this time, not until very recent in relative terms. The manual labor involved in the construction of such edifices and monuments were in the tens of thousands and hundreds of thousands of unskilled and semi-skilled workers. These slaves were conscripted by the religious and secular authorities of their era to construct such monuments to their immortality. Because of this fear of insecurity that their names would be forgotten these religious and secular leaders attempted to gain immortality through feats and conquests, and construction of cities and monuments.

This departure from the covenant that *Yahweh* God concluded with their progenitor Noah moved Him to establish another covenant with an individual who did not have the same type of ideals of the balance of the leaders of religion, government and commerce. Again the world had corrupted itself, but now in terms of paganism, megalomania, finance, military might and conquest. With such an agenda for the secular hierarchy no consideration for the masses of underprivileged would exist. Just because *Yahweh* God found it necessary to establish another covenant at this time by way of Abraham does not mean that the entire world was corrupt and violated the covenant of Noah. The concept of Acts 10:34-35 would have still prevailed among the sincere few.

## FOURTH COVENANT ERA

The 4th covenant era begins with the covenant concluded with Abraham, which purpose was to create a righteous society that would be an example to the balance of the nations. This would be a new nation, one heretofore unknown. This was not an abrogation of the existing covenant of Noah, but one newly created for the long-term purpose of an established nation. The covenant of Noah would still continue on an individual basis among the gentiles who would adhere to the 7 commands.

*Yahweh* God found in Abraham an individual who had an agrarian base, a successful business, well-respected by everybody, with a high morality and integrity; no doubt part of the covenant of Noah. To the extent that Abraham upheld the terms and conditions of the covenant, to this extent *Yahweh* God showered His grace and blessing upon him. Not having a child in earlier years was a test of faith of Abraham, since the people of the era viewed immortality as the future generation to proceed from them, all of this a monument testifying to their earlier existence. According to the record in Gen 11:27-32, Abram appears to be the real head of household, or perhaps the head of the business, owner of the family company, the one making the decisions on behalf of the family. Moving out of Ur they settled in Haran.

Shortly after the death of Terah father of Abram, the portion of the family obedient to the command of *Yahweh* God to migrate left Haran for Canaan. There and in the near-by areas the family of Abram and his descendents resided until their migration to Egypt.

The idea of circumcision as having some allegorical or symbolic meaning is not new. It was practiced by Egyptians and others of the middle east long before Abraham, but now it became the sign of the covenant instituted with Abraham. Gen 17:10. Every male adult would grow and mature aware that his parents had committed him to this covenant, that he should fulfill the obligations of the covenant that was represented by the circumcision. For the male child, this identification was with the forefathers blessed of *Yahweh* God, not just with anybody; and the command was by God Almighty, *El Shadai*, who is *Yahweh* God, the supreme and only genuine deity. Removal of foreskin was removal of secular life from an individual. Just as *Yahweh* God blessed Abraham abundantly and his household for adhering to the covenant, even while uncircumcised, so the same *Yahweh* God will abundantly bless every male who does wear the sign of covenant to the extent he adheres to the covenant. This applies not only to that male as an individual but also his descendents to follow him, whom *Yahweh* God will also bless likewise.

Circumcision indeed is of value if you obey the law. Rom 2:25.

The female had direct access to the promises, through her father who would be a circumcised male of the posterity of one of the 12 sons of Jacob, her mother likewise a daughter of the same, and she marrying likewise a male of the same status as her father.

The point is that every male could become an Abraham, and every female could become a Sarah. Their immortality could be gained through their children and descendents. So it was on an individual basis, yet following the same moral code and divine instruction as with Noah and the same pattern of public worship of *Yahweh* God through the prescribed sacrifices and offerings. The original Abraham and Sarah were not supernatural or superhuman. They were people like any other, except that they adhered to the commands of *Yahweh* God, His instruction. This covenant with Abraham has the greater impact of the creation of an entire distinct nation, and that at some time in the future this covenant would be renewed or reiterated with the new nation of Israel as an entity itself.

## ABRAHAM AND HIS RELIGION

Exactly how humanity "began to call upon the name of *Yahweh*," is unclear. Gen 4:26. This is a Hebrew idiom referring to organized religion. Young's Literal Bible renders this verse as, "Then a beginning was made in preaching the name of *Yahweh*." Some type of organized form of worship was instituted at this time: song, prayer, sermon, along with prescribed ritual to remind the people of unacceptable conduct and violation of the law of *Yahweh* God, including animal sacrifice.

This attitude separated the family of Abraham from the balance of families in Ur of Chaldea. The others continued in their superstition, myths, veneration of images, the identification of the natural elements with contrived deities, the sacrifice to gain attention and appease the non-existent deities, the maneuvers, theatrics and performances of worship, and indulgence, as dictated by the priests who represented these so-called gods. The manner that Abraham venerated *Yahweh* God is stated in the following words of *Yahweh* God to his son Isaac.

> Because Abraham obeyed My voice and kept My charge, My commandments, My statues and My laws. Gen 26:5.

The answer to Abraham's derivation of his religion is the moral code and divine instruction transmitted orally generation after generation. The attempted sacrifice of his son by Abraham in Gen 15:9-11, was no doubt an indication of an imperfection in totally understanding the concept of *Yahweh* God as a moral code. Abraham felt a sacrifice had to be made similar to the adherents of others religions, a sacrifice of appeasement. To bring his son as a sacrifice was no doubt intended to appease *Yahweh* God for some sin of capital magnitude. This indicates that there was still influence of the paganism on Abraham regarding the purpose of sacrifice. Nevertheless, Abraham was sincere in his efforts, following only what it is that *Yahweh* God dictated to him without question. It was true faith, or perhaps better said, blind faith.

Abraham made his request that *Yahweh* God not destroy Sodom for the sake of 10 righteous individuals. *Yahweh* God had respect for Abraham because Abraham had gained this merit by adherence to the moral code. Gen 26:5, 18:19. For this reason *Yahweh* God was willing to grant the petition of Abraham. Merit is gained by faith and faith is indicated by a life in accord with the moral code. A person such as Moses could intervene on behalf of the disobedient Israel at Mount Horeb. Ex 32:11-14. Men such as Daniel and Noah along with Moses had the merit to be able to intervene on behalf of others, and *Yahweh* God would consider their petitions and grant them.

## THE HEBREWS

This 4th covenant era continued only with the descendents of the 12 sons until the initiation of another covenant with the entire nation of Israel. The balance of the gentile world could find salvation to the extent they adhered to the covenant of Noah that continued in effect among the gentiles. With the 430 year interval between Jacob entering Egypt and settling there, a total of 70 persons, the moral code and divine instruction was transmitted orally generation to generation.

The descendents of the 12 tribes in Egypt are named Hebrews. They are identified with this appellation as descendents of Eber the great-grandson of Shem, no doubt a very influential patriarch of his era. According to the genealogical table of Gen 11, Eber outlived Abraham by 64 years. Apparently Eber was so respected and influential in his family that his posterity were named after him as a tribe of their own, that is, the tribe of the Hebrews. These may well be the Habiru of 18th century BC Egypt, and the 15th century BC invaders of Palestine, as recorded by archeologists. Abraham and his descendents were identified with Eber; the wives of the patriarchs beginning shortly after were probably of the same tribe of Eber. If Abraham and Sarah were so concerned about Isaac marrying a local pagan Canaanite, and Isaac and Rebecca were so concerned about marrying the same, Jacob no doubt would have felt exactly the same and preferred or even required his 12 sons to marry Hebrew virgins. No wonder Jacob was so distraught with his daughter Dinah becoming involved with Shechem son of Hamor the Hivite. Gen 34. The idea of only marrying within the nation of Israel and not with the gentiles as commanded by Moses was not an original idea. It was inherited by the Israelites from their forefathers, who only wanted their offspring to marry Hebrews, i.e. the descendents of Eber. So very easily the tribal name of Eber, that is, Hebrew or Habiru, was easily attached to the household of Jacob. Since Jacob had many servants, slaves and related workers and employees, inherited from his father and grandfather, the Egyptians and Canaanites also identified them as Hebrews. Gen 39:14. Ex 1:22.

This 4th covenant era lasted about 500 years, from the migration of the family of Terah out of Ur, through their sojourn in Egypt. The purpose of this covenant era was to created a new nation identified as Hebrews, which was to develop in Egypt under the auspices of the Egyptians. Those servants and employees of the 12 sons and Jacob who migrated were also identified with one of the tribes by marriage over the generations. In this manner it was definitely possible to create a nation of 630,000 adult men plus women and children. The total population of the new nation of Israel probably had a census of 3 to 4 million.

## FIFTH COVENANT ERA

At the proper time and after a display of His omnipotent power in public *Yahweh* God led His newly created nation out of Egypt and to Sinai, specifically Mt. Horeb. There another covenant was concluded, now specifically with the nation as a whole. So begins the 5th covenant era, and which continued until its replacement by Jesus the Anointed.

The covenant was concluded with Israel as a nation in Ex 24. As in all contracts that are presented by the greater or superior party, the terms and conditions are read aloud with the benefits to be gained by each party along with the penalty should the contract be violated or abrogated. First *Yahweh* God spoke to the people directly from the mountain reciting the 10 commandment, that is, the passage Ex 20:2-17. Ex 20:22. Even though *Yahweh* God is a spirit he sent His spirit that materialized in the form of sound waves, which are vibrations, resulting in an audible sound, loud spoken words and the sound of a trumpet. The entirety of the new nation surrounding the mountain heard the words comprising the basis of the covenant, this codification of *Yahweh* God's moral law. Subsequently this moral law was supplemented with additional divine instruction as an addenda, Ex 21-23. All of this instruction was read by Moses in Ex 24:3. After hearing the contents of the covenant the people in unison replied aloud,

"All that *Yahweh* has spoken we will do and we will be obedient." Ex 24:7.

This was their voluntary agreement as individuals and as a nation to enter into this covenant with *Yahweh* God.

## OLD COVENANTS' RELIGION

To magnify His nation *Yahweh* God proceeded to create a functional religion that would involve the entire population on a regular basis: daily, weekly, monthly, and annually, and at every septad and semi-centennial. The religion was not designed to appease the anger of a vengeful deity with the offering of blood sacrifice, as among the pagans, but was designed to curb violation of the moral code, to impress on the offerer of the sacrifice the odious and heinous extent of sin and how detrimental it is on a personal basis and on a national basis. The religion was designed to the same extent to disclose to the offerer the love of *Yahweh* God. Through participation in the religious rites the offerer would realize the extent of the love of *Yahweh* God towards him and her, their family, and their nation. The religion was designed to educate the population about *Yahweh* God, His character, His history, His involvement in the life of the people and their nation, and His future for them.

The concept of many theologians that the religion instituted by *Yahweh* God was just another cult alongside the various other deities of the era is without evidence and opposite to the intent of the Bible record. There is a distinct difference between the concepts of the religion of *Yahweh* God and that of the balance of the pseudo-deities. The concept likewise that the god of the OT is a vengeful blood-thirsty god as opposed to the contrite and forgiving god of the NT is also incorrect. The deity of the OT and NT are the one and same deity, *Yahweh* God. His attitude toward obedience is the same throughout the entire Bible toward any and all people of every age and generation: grace, salvation and blessing. His attitude toward disobedience has not changed either and has likewise been consistent: responsibility for one's own actions and an appropriate penalty for the results of disobedience.

The moral code as the basis of the covenants is unambiguously stipulated in Deut 4:13 and Ex 34:27-28. Even though all else attached to the revelation received at Sinai supplementing the moral code could be violated, with a few exceptions, like the Passover, it was not until the 10 commandments were violated that the covenant would be considered abrogated. This is because the installed religion was to direct the people toward observance of the moral code, which was their salvation. The covenant was not violated if the sacrifices were not performed properly, Lev 10:16-24; the covenant was not violated if the priesthood failed in the details of ceremony and in the temple and tabernacle services; the covenant was not violated if the population failed to observe the many sacrifices, offerings, tithes, holidays or food laws. This does not permit or give license to arbitrary fail to observe, or to deliberately evade observance, or defy such laws.

A specific example of the distinction between the moral law and balance of divine instruction are the words of *Yahweh* God to Saul king through Samuel prophet. 1 Sam 15:22-23. Obeying the voice of *Yahweh* God consisted in the annihilation of the enemy, the Amalekites, that is, the nation of the descendents of Amalek, including all their property and possessions. Saul, however, spared Agag their king, 1 Sam 15:9, along with animals with which the soldiers could feast and celebrate their victory with sacrifices unto *Yahweh* God. The first commandment was violated. This commandment dictated prohibition of any other deities, meaning to recognize any as deity whichever it happened to be, other than *Yahweh* God. Agag was spared because Saul recognized him as a ruler anointed or installed by his deity. Saul recognized Agag as his equal, that is, each was installed in office and delegated authority by their respected deities. Indirectly, by sparing the life of Agag, Saul acknowledged the existence and authority of this Amalekite deity.

The idea of sacrifice of clean animals by Saul unto *Yahweh* God as thanksgiving with a subsequent feast was fine and well, but it was not what *Yahweh* God requested of Saul. The phrase "burnt offerings and sacrifices," refers to the ceremonial portion of the law, while obedience refers to the moral code. Adherence to the moral code will absolve indiscriminate failure to observe the ceremonial or religious law, since this is the purpose of such a law. But even the most meticulous observance of religion will not absolve indiscriminate refusal to adhere to the moral code. Then repentance and confession is required with a change in attitude.

## CONCEPT OF THE TORAH

The idea that the law given to the people of Israel at Sinai was to enslave them in the fetters and shackles of redundant ritual and ceremony is opposite to the reality of the situation. This *Torah* was freedom to the people who would live by it. The divine instruction was liberty.

> Keep them and do them; for that will be your wisdom and your intelligence in the sight of the people, who, when they hear all these statues will say, "Surely this great nation is a wise and intelligent people." For what great nation is there that has a god so near to it as *Yahweh* our God is to us. Deut 4:6-7.
>
> There he (*Yahweh*) made for them a statute and an ordinance and there he tested them, saying, If you will diligently listen to the voice of *Yahweh* your God, and do what is right in His eyes, and heed His commandments and keep all his statutes, I will put none of the diseases upon you which I put upon the Egyptians. For I am *Yahweh*, your healer. Ex 15:25b-26.

When a person or family or tribe or community lived by the *Torah* this was liberation from sin, ignorance, disease, self-imposed suffering, conflict, oppression and premature death. It was liberation from personal insecurity, mental disease and psychological disorders. It was liberation from crime and delinquency, domestic violence and abuse, and all the possible vices that plague humanity. Adherence to the divine instruction was salvation from sin. It was eternal life. It was their resurrection from death. It was their entrance into the Kingdom of God. They lived in this manner because they believed *Yahweh* God, they believed what He said to them, that this was for their benefit. They believed His promises to them. Deut 28:1-14. The righteous lived according to the divine instruction because of their trust and faith in *Yahweh* God. Salvation from sin was attained in observance of the divine instruction because of their faith in the true and living *Yahweh* God. Eph 2:8-9.

The divine instruction implementing the priesthood, tabernacle and temple, and sacrifices and offerings was their religion and was good and beneficial for the era, and because of the barbarity and ignorance of the people. This religion of the OT was fine for the era until such time that another covenant was to be concluded or implemented with the people.

The more enlightened or spiritually minded of the sages were aware of this.

The effort of *Yahweh* God with the newly created nation of Israel was to create a righteous society. Righteous in terms of rectitude or virtue. This was now attainable with the precepts and government enacted and decreed by the sovereign lord of the nation *Yahweh* God and delegated to His servants and ministers: priests, elders, judges, prophets and kings. *Yahweh* God delegated His authority to these people on a regular basis to transmit the instruction of *Yahweh* God to the people. Deut 33:10. 2 Chron 17:9. They were to forewarn the population ahead of time if the tendency appeared to stray from the proper course of life intended for them. Judg 2:1-4. Eze 33. They were to pronounce a guilty verdict on them for violations against the moral code and the sentence they must receive, the penalty. Jer 27:6. They were to complement the people on behalf of *Yahweh* God who wishes to bless His nation. Num 6:22-27. This is why Moses said,

> Nor is it with you only that I made this sworn covenant, but with him who is not here with us this day, as well as with him who stands here with us this day before *Yahweh* our God. Deut 29:14-15. Deut 4:31.
> *Yahweh, Yahweh*, a God merciful and gracious, slow to anger and abounding in steadfast love and faith, keeping steadfast love for thousands, forgiving crime and violation and trespass. Ex 34:6-7.

*Yahweh* God is different from the balance of deities because He can be trusted. Any other deity could not be relied on to reciprocate because they are non-existent.

To the extent that the people of Israel observed the moral code and the supplementary codes of conduct, ceremony, holidays and food, to the same extent *Yahweh* God fulfilled His portion of the covenant and gave benefit to the people in terms of marital and domestic harmony, community success, security of life and general prosperity. The converse was likewise true to the same extent: a person conducting himself contrary would be left to deal with the results of their disobedience and face the penalty.

## CORRUPTION OF THE TORAH BY HISTORIC CHRISTIANITY

The concept that OT *Torah* was a burden and enslavement to rite and ritual did not exist during the ages from its inauguration to the time that the Hasidim surfaced. These were the predecessors of the Sadducees and Pharisees. 1 Macc 2:42, 7:14. Their contribution in their zeal was the oral law, later to be codified as the *Mishna*. Because of the supplements of the oral law, now equated in authority with the *Torah* by the new Hasidim and their ecclesiastical descendents, the *Torah* became a burden and chore to observe. This new generation of Jewish religious elders enforced a stringent and meticulous observance of both the written law and the oral law, forgetting that the purpose of the moral code was to cease and terminate sin or crime. This new legislation and enforcement of new traditions became a new religion, one that was no longer faith in *Yahweh* God, but observance of a religion whose purpose was to separate the Jews from the balance of the nations and create a superficial appearance of piety among those who supported and observed the new religious traditions. They became a nation of pseudo-converts. With the creation of a new religion, the new generation of devotees and supplicants viewed themselves as drawing closer to *Yahweh* God, while others fell behind. These new pietists or spiritual sycophants felt themselves obtaining the favor of *Yahweh* God, while others fell into disfavor. They felt *Yahweh* God turning His attention toward them; while turning away from others.

According to Jewish sages of early eras, at the same time that Moses codified the written law known as the *Torah*, he also orally transmitted certain other rules and traditions to the elders of Israel. These were passed on generation to generation to the era of the Hasidim, and to their spiritual descendents the Pharisees and Sadducees. They then instituted these rules and traditions and likewise enforced them. In reality, rules and traditions that comprised the oral law only began shortly after the success of the Maccabees in their victory over the Romans, 162 BC. At this time zealous elders wanting to resurrect and reestablish the religion of Judaism implemented these newly contrived rules and traditions. The primary underlying purpose was to create a wall or hedge to separate themselves from the influence of Hellenism: Greek life, philosophy, and activities. These new rules and traditions would make Jews distinct from other nationalities and religions, and so they did. This purpose of separation was a benevolent idea, and had a precedence in much of the Torah, but it caused another unforeseen consequence within the Jewish nation itself. It created a superficial piety among those that did fulfill the new generation of traditions, and which only created division within Judaism itself. In reality, this oral law also placed such a burden on the common people that they were unable to fulfill them all. Especially affected were the lower income categories and underprivileged, who were unable to either learn them or meticulously observe them. This was the heavy burden that was laid upon men's shoulders. Matt 23:4.

## THE FAILURES AND RENEWALS OF COVENANTS

The land of Canaan originally was the land of the nations of Canaan. As the population decreased and the population of the Philistines increased the same land was identified as Philistia or later Palestine. With the entrance of Israel into the land it was identified with the name of their own nation. The promises to Abraham and Sarah were definitely fulfilled, since they did increase in population to a quantity or census only comparable to the number of stars in the sky or grains of sand on the seashore. Deut 1:10, 10:22. Heb 11:12. Their possession of the land however was only to the extent they upheld the covenant. Deut 28:1.

This same covenant was renewed once the Promised Land was subdued and subjected to Israel. The elders and population gathered at Shechem to listen to the concluding address of Joshua. Josh 24. After his sermon he admonished the people to serve only *Yahweh* God and not any other deity. In the same vein as the assembly at Sinai, they replied, "Therefore we also will serve *Yahweh*, for He is our deity." Josh 24:18, 24. In response to this and as divine approval, Joshua made a covenant with the people that day, and made statutes and ordinances for them at Shechem, which he wrote in a book. Josh 24:25-26. This was not a new covenant but a renewal of the existing covenant with *Yahweh* God.

Over the years the same covenant was renewed whenever the people and leadership felt the necessity to do so. After realizing their departure from the covenant and repentance was carried out, a renewal was performed in sincerity. Such was the situation during the era of the Judges. Judg 3:9, 8:33-34. The individual mentioned as a *malachi* in Judg 2:1, a messenger, was no doubt a prophet or seer recognized by the people, whose name has long passed into oblivion. His admonishment and appeal to repent and again adhere to the covenant was taken into consideration, and the mention that the "people lifted up their voices and wept," and their subsequent sacrifice, is indicative of a renewal of the covenant. Judg 2:4-5. This same scenario of defeat and restoration occurred on a regular basis over the 400 years of the era of the judges. The violation of the moral code caused the moral fiber to disintegrate and undermine the stability of their society, and subsequently made the nation susceptible to defeat and conquest by local alien nations whose military might exceeded theirs.

The strength of Israel was moral might, protection from its enemies by *Yahweh* God as part of the covenant blessing. Deut 28:7. But the might of alien nations was their military force and ability to conquer and subject the weaker tribes and nations as vassals. This was the lesson to be learned by Israel, that defense and protection from conquest and harm by enemies was dependent on their morality. Moral character in itself was not a defense from some marauding band, their defense was *Yahweh* God. Ex 23:22, 27-28. Their high moral character was indicative of their obedience to Him, and so He would fulfill His promise and defend them from military invasion and conquest. Exactly how this would be accomplished was at His discretion. As examples I provide the following:

The first method was by a leader to arise, such as the judges. They would gather an army of volunteers, and divine assistance promoted their military success and the invaders or aliens were routed from the land. This was Gideon and Samson and Jephthah and Ehud and Barak, or David's victories over the Philistines.

A second method was by miraculous intervention. Such examples would be the Syrian army at Dotham, when they were struck blind by Elisha prophet. 2 King 6:17-23. The 185,000 Assyrians who died one night outside of Jerusalem. 2 King 19:35. The rumor reported to Sennacherib during his siege of Jerusalem. Is 37:7.

A third method, and which is most in accord with the character of *Yahweh* God, was that Israel would be such a beneficial influence on its neighboring nations that they would be eager to live in mutual harmony. These surrounding nations would be themselves blessed because of a peace accord with Israel and realize that Israel is a blessing to them. Only a vestige of a real example is available in Scripture, which is the relationship between Solomon and Hiram of Lebanon. 1 King 5:1. Also the marriage alliance between Solomon and Pharaoh of Egypt. 1 King 3:1. The friendship of Solomon and queen of Sheba. 1 King 10:1-13. *Yahweh*

God's promise to defend His people was regularly fulfilled when they adhered to the covenant He concluded with them.

After the era of the judges concluding with Eli prophet was the short era of Samuel prophet. It was the betrayal of the family of Eli that led to the annulment of the sacerdotal covenant of *Yahweh* God with Eli and his family as high-priests. So severe was the desecration of the covenant that *Yahweh* God said,

> And tell him that I am about to punish his house for ever, for the iniquity that he knew, because his sons became vile, and he did not restrain them. Therefore I swear to the house of Eli that the iniquity of Eli's house shall not be expiated by sacrifice or offering for ever. 1 Sam 3:13-14.

That the promise of *Yahweh* God is conditional on the other party's fulfillment of their obligation is noted in 1 Sam 2:30. Due to the betrayal of the divine obligation assigned to the high priesthood, the promise of *Yahweh* God that the posterity of Eli patriarch should be priests forever was annulled. The complete rejection of the family of Eli from the priesthood was fulfilled some years later. 1 King 2:27.

## LATER COVENANTS

*Yahweh* God also concluded covenants with several kings, but all of them were conditional to the extent that these kings would adhere to the covenant. The first of these was David. 2 Sam 7:12-16. The family of David was to have indefinite possession of the throne until such time that *Yahweh* God should conclude His purpose. Deut 17:14-20. This was specifically dictated to Solomon when *Yahweh* God appeared to him in a dream. The possession of the throne was conditional. 1 King 9:4-9. Nevertheless *Yahweh* God permitted the continuation of the lineage of David as a result of His grace. As with Abijah for example. 1 King 15:4. And Jehoram. 2 Chron 21:7. The 6 year reign of Athaliah daughter of Ahab king of Israel and granddaughter of Omri, was a disruption in the possession of the throne. 2 King 11:3.

This possession of the throne lasted until the termination of the covenant with the southern kingdom Judah, with their expulsion from the land. The male line of David continued though these 70 years and reappears in one of the leaders and governor of the new province, Zerubbabel son of Shealthiel, a great-grandson of Jehoiakim the final legitimate king of Judah. Even though he was a descendent of David king, his responsibility appears to have been involved with the migration and resettlement back into the land of Palestine, and to continue the family line unto the advent of the Anointed son of David. Matt 1:12. Luke 3:27.

Modern scholars and evangelical teachers emphasize this covenant with David. 1 Sam 7:12-16. But it is very similar to covenants made with subsequent rulers of the kingdom, such as Jeroboam, 1 King 11:37-38. *Yahweh* God through Abijah prophet concluded this covenant with Jeroboam, and the promise of a royal house to him is identical with the promise to David, in the words,

"I will be with you and will build you a sure house as I built for David, and I will give Israel to you." 1 King 11:38.

It could have lasted millennia, but was soon annulled with the disobedience of Nadab son of Jeroboam. 1 King 15:27-29.

Asa, great-grandson of Solomon, gathered the entire population of Judah during his reign at the admonishment of Azariah prophet. All of them together as a nation brought sacrifices and entered into covenant with *Yahweh* God. 2 Chron 15:12. During the reign of Josiah son of Amon, king of Judah, the king and citizens renewed the covenant. 2 King 23:3. Likewise with Jehoiada and the people of his era. 2 Chron 23:16. And with Hezekiah. 2 Chron 29:10. None of these were a new covenant, but a renewal of that covenant concluded with Israel through Moses.

During the reign of Manasseh idolatry and violence and crime was rampant in Judea. 2 King 21:2,6,16. The violation and betrayal of the covenant was irreparable and irremediable, but the penalty was postponed about 50 years. This period was purposed by *Yahweh* God so as to create a remnant of the faithful in Israel. The era of spiritual and religious renewal and enthusiasm during the reign of Josiah motivated many to return to a study and practice of Scripture – *Torah*, and become more involved with the temple services. This deep and intense involvement with the religion for layman and elder consisted in the renewal of covenant. 2 King 23:3. Josiah again instituted temple service, and enforced the covenant by destroying temples and idols dedicated to pagan deities. The pagan priests and other officers were deposed. 2 King 23:4-14. The celebration of the holiday Passover was again practiced. 2 Chron 35. All of this left a lasting impression on the young fervent generation, those who would in a decade or so be taken captive to Babylon. These same young and zealous individuals passed on to the succeeding generation in Babylon all that they learned, practiced and experienced in Jerusalem under Josiah king. It was the subsequent generation that was to return back to Jerusalem under Sheshbazzar. They had to be prepared to reinstate the religion in Judea. Ezra was a grandson of Hilkiah priest, who was active in the reforms and covenant renewal of Josiah. Ezra 7:1, 2 Chron 34:14. He no doubt learned from his grandfather the moral law and religion and divine instruction of Israel to prepare him for reestablishing the religion in Judea with the returning exiles.

## TERMINATION OF THE COVENANT WITH ISRAEL AND JUDAH

Due to an intolerable violation of covenant by the people of the northern kingdom Israel, *Yahweh* God utilized the army of Assyria to evict the population and repossess the land. Hos 8:1. The northern kingdom also was not without a remnant. Those individuals who were led captive to Assyria were settled in the various lands of the middle east. 2 King 17:6. All the kings of Israel were considered wicked in the account of 2 Kings in the 80 years prior to the captivity. Not since Jehoash was there a righteous god-fearing king in the northern Kingdom, but during these years *Yahweh* God did have His remnant, a small and scattered group who continued the true faith and worship of *Yahweh* God. These people are spoken of in Is 10:20-22. They were to return from the captivity of the northern 10 tribes to Judea in the future. Nehemiah and those mentioned in the books of Esther and Tobit were part of this remnant. Jewish sages wrote of Tobit that he would travel to Jerusalem to celebrate the festivals of *Yahweh* God, while the balance of the family served the calves of Jeroboam. Tobit 1:5-8.

The surviving remnant mentioned in 2 King 19:30-31 refers to those remaining in Jerusalem after the invasion of the armies of Assyria under Sennacherib. Most of Palestine and its cities were devastated, and only Jerusalem and a few others remained. The religion was restored by Hezekiah after the invaders returned to Assyria. This restoration of the religion consisted in temple restoration. 2 Chron 29. The celebration of Passover. 2 Chron 30. Services then began in the temple according to the instructions of Moses. The remnant surviving the devastation of Sennacherib working close with Hezekiah accomplished the renewal of covenant and religion. 2 Chron 31.

I contend that the latter third of the Book of Isaiah prophet, chapters 40-66, often referred to as deutero-Isaiah, are still the original work of the same Isaiah of the balance of the book. The variation in style and subject is due to its composition in the years following the devastation of the land by Assyria, and the effort of the nation during its restoration under Hezekiah.

The decision of *Yahweh* God to impose on the nation of Judah the penalty for abandoning the covenant was not abrogated even with the religious revival and renewal with Josiah king. Eliakim son of Josiah was made a puppet king by Pharaoh Neco and so began the last years of the southern kingdom. There were 3 invasions of Palestine by the armies of Babylon: 577, 580, and the culmination in 586 BC. This final invasion completed the conquest of Jerusalem and the balance of Palestine. This period of siege and conquest by the armies of Babylon is called the time of Jacob's trouble, or, the time of the distress of Jacob. Jer 30:7. I contend that the chapter Jer 30 pertains to this specific era, and the return of the exiles to Palestine is prophesied in Jer 31:1-14.

*Yahweh* God utilized the army of Babylon as his method of eviction of the population from the land of the promise and His repossession of it. It was during the siege of Jerusalem by Babylon that Jeremiah spoke the prophetic words regarding a new covenant to be concluded some time in the future. Jer 31:31-34, 50:4-5. The existing covenant was still in effect on an individual basis among those who adhered to the moral code. The nation as a whole violated the covenant, which caused its abrogation, losing the land, designated as their inheritance. Those individuals who obeyed the voice of *Yahweh* God spoken through Jeremiah prophet were still blessed in their personal deliverance from the ravage of war.

Although many sincere god-fearing believers were taken captive to Babylon, it was their children and grandchildren that constituted the remnant. The parents were part of the covenant and religious renewal under Josiah and this legacy was passed on to the successive generations in Babylon. Jer 23:3, 31:7.

The promise of *Yahweh* God was such that a remnant would survive the devastation of Judea, survive the trek across the desert to Babylon, endure the 70 years of residence of Babylon, obey the divine summons to return, complete the journey back to Palestine, and there reestablish the nation and religion. All of this is the intent of Jer 31:1-14. The words of Jeremiah prophet were preserved as divinely inspired by the migrants to Babylon, even though he himself migrated to Egypt against his own will and later died there. The more intelligent and inspired of the scribes saw the fulfillment of his words pertaining to Judea and Jerusalem, the siege and exile, and so they preserved his record. With the return to Palestine of the exiles and reestablishment of the nation and religion, more of the words of Jeremiah were fulfilled. Jer 32:36-44.

## RETURN OF THE EXILES

I contend that the section comprising Eze 40-48 was written pertaining to the era following the exile, and not to a distant restoration. Ezekiel was a type of Moses for the $2^{nd}$ migration to the promised land, this time from Babylon to Palestine, and so Ezekiel was inspired to record his revelation from *Yahweh* God for the returning exiles. These passages pertain to the new division of the land, the format and dimensions of the new temple, the priesthood and its officers and services, and the return of the glory of *Yahweh* God to His temple and nation. The spiritual success of the new covenant community is described in Eze 47:12, depicting a river of living water flowing from the temple. The trees and leaves and fruit growing along the river banks represent spiritual food to be provided to the people by the restored religion. Eze 47:12.

Even though much of Ezekiel's prophetic word was not implemented by the remnant, this is not an indication that the prophecy is invalid or inapplicable for the era. In general the restoration of the nation and religion was fulfilled, though not in its perfection as Ezekiel hoped it would.

The historical portions of the OT do not detail the entire progress of Jewish life from the return of the exiles to Judea to the appearance of John son of Zechariah. There are some 84 years between Zerubbabel and Ezra, of which some 80 are unrecorded. After the arrival of Ezra, 13 years passed before the arrival of Nehemiah, and an unknown interlude exists between the 2 visits of Nehemiah. Neh 13:6-7. Between the second term of Nehemiah as governor of Judea and the record of the Maccabees about 250 years transpired, with no Biblical record. The accounts of Josephus Jewish historian are reliable for the period beginning with the Maccabees to the termination of Jewish occupation in 70 AD, but his inclusion of events between Nehemiah and the Maccabees are very meager. The point to be made here is that the fulfillment of every prophetic word of Jeremiah and Ezekiel pertaining to the return of the exiles from Babylon to Judea and the restoration of the kingdom is not recorded in the Bible. This would include also the prophecies of Haggai and Zechariah and other minor prophets whose words also pertain to this era. Because there is no record does not mean a lack of fulfillment. What we can trust as the fulfillment of those prophetic words pertaining to the restoration of Israel in Judea is the witness of the redactors of the OT canon. These scribes and sages rejected the spurious and preserved the genuine. We today must trust the judgment of the scribes and sages, such as Ezra, who acted as redactors in compiling what we today recognize as the OT canon of the 3 major prophets and 12 minor prophets, and Daniel. They witness to us of the fulfillment of the prophetic words of those that pertain to this era of post-exile restoration.

Samuel Sandmel in his book, *The Hebrew Scriptures*, contends that Judea was again devastated in about the year 485 BC. Based on his personal research, he claims that between the end of the of governorship of Zerubbabel and the arrival of Ezra, Judea was devastated by the Edomites and surrounding nations, and that the temple built by Zerubbabel was destroyed. Ps 137:7. Eze 35:5. This was the temple constructed under the directive of Haggai and Zechariah. At the arrival of Ezra there is no temple mentioned, only a house of God, and Jerusalem was in shambles. Another temple was built in the intervening 12 years after the arrival of Ezra and before Nehemiah, according to Sandmel. With the arrival of Nehemiah, the city was not yet rebuilt. He implemented the construction of the city wall and rebuilding of the city.

## RENEWAL OF THE COVENANT

The remnant of faithful worshippers continued generation after generation during the unrecorded years from Nehemiah to the Maccabees, about 420 BC to 175 BC. A type of covenant was again concluded and in effect as witnessed by the restoration of the nation in Judea, rebuilding of the city Jerusalem, and the construction of a new temple. This would have begun with the reading of the *Torah* during the Feast of Tabernacles by Ezra in Neh 8. Again, to the extent the people adhered to the moral law and divine instruction, to the same extent *Yahweh* God would favor and bless His people, as individuals and as a nation. Even though the covenant was abrogated with the destruction of Jerusalem and burning of the Temple of Solomon, it was revived according to the promise of Deut 30:1-10, with their return to Judea. The basis elements of the covenant were always in effect throughout their sojourn in Babylon and with those who dedicated themselves to the reestablishment of the nation and religion in Judea in the following years.

The remnant of covenant Israel then surfaced in recorded history as the family of Mattathias and those that attached themselves to the family, and the Hasidim. 1 Macc 2:42-48. This restoration or renewal of the religion during this era could be considered a renewal of covenant, similar to the era of the judges or the later kings of Judah. It was effective among those Jews that decided to abandon the Greek tradition and philosophy and return to the faith of their fathers. It was because of this national and religious revival that the land was recovered from occupation by Greek military forces. At the head of Greek military occupation and Greek philosophy was Antiochus IV Epiphanes. Under the victories gained by the family of Judas Maccabee an independent state of Israel was established, and which state prevailed for about 100 years. Although many consider this era to be a golden age of the Jews, it was permeated to the core with political struggle for the leadership over the new nation, personal ambitions among the hierarchy of the priests, and competition between Jewish religious factions for domination.

The most pathetic conclusion to this internal struggle was the loss of the new kingdom of Israel to Rome. It was Pompey Roman general who in 65 BC, conquered Judea and entered Jerusalem as victor and new occupation. Very little bloodshed occurred during this invasion, since the new victor took advantage of the internal political and religious power struggles occurring within Judea. Rather than gather an army to defeat the invading Roman army, Pompey was practically invited into Jerusalem by Jewish elders. Jesus referred to this situation when he said, "A kingdom divided against itself is laid waste." Matt 12:25. The nation was internally divided. They were so busy fighting among themselves they hardly noticed when an alien military commander conquered them and laid the country waste. When Pompey's general and army appeared at the gates of Jerusalem there was no chance for defense.

In earlier years the threat of national and religion dissolution was the barbaric forces of superstition, pagan religion, idolatry, and the military of other nations. Now the loss of the land to the Romans was solely due to pride. The leaders could not admit to their sins of internal conflict and competition vying for power and authority with a lack of concern for the population. In this manner did *Yahweh* God again revoke the covenant of possession of the land. Even though Jews still resided in the land, they were as if captives under alien military guard. *Yahweh* God warned the people of pride in His words of Deut 9, and especially that pride is a departure from the worship of *Yahweh* God. Deut 9:19. The violation of covenant consisted in the leadership concluding that it was by their own effort they acquired dominion over the land of Palestine. This violated the covenant by not giving credit to *Yahweh* God. The population received what they deserved because of internal power struggle: the loss of dominion of their own possession.

Now all of Palestine was under Roman military occupation. This then initiated and fostered Jewish resentment and enmity against Romans and was the basis for several rebellions and insurrections against them. This was the attitude prevalent among the population during the ministry of Jesus, and for which purpose he preached his good news of the Kingdom of God.

## SACRIFICE

The concept of blood sacrifice of an animal is different in the worship of *Yahweh* God than in the worship of pseudo-deities. The purpose of the latter was discussed above. In essence the purpose of *Yahweh* God in instituting blood sacrifice of animal was to impress upon the participant the heinous and repulsive extent of sin in the sight of *Yahweh* God. Even though it had similarities to the pagan rite of sacrifice, the concept was very different. The sacrifice unto *Yahweh* God was not to appease Him or gain His attention, but was to impress upon the participant that death is the consequence of sin or crime. Someone had to die for a capital crime committed against *Yahweh* God, just as the criminal must be executed for a capital crime committed against another individual or society. By grasping the concept of how heinous and repulsive sin was, with the countless sacrifices for sin installed in the worship service, the people would adhere to and comply with the moral code and so put an end, a termination to blood sacrifice. This is how the law was to be interpreted as a schoolmaster. Gal 3:24.

In the book of Leviticus, the types of sacrifice are prescribed in detail. The participant was to lay his hands on the head of the animal, thus symbolically transferring the responsibility for crimes committed from the individual to the animal. In all occasions a clean animal had to be offered. An unclean animal was inherently unacceptable since it could not be consumed as food. What was required in the sacrifice protocol was an innocent victim to impress on the participant that an innocent life will be deprived as a result of the crime of the participant. So therefore if no crime were committed then the sacrificed animal would be spared its life. Only with an adherence to the moral code would no more crime be committed.

The passages in Scripture that proclaim the disfavor or reprimand of *Yahweh* God on the sacrificial system are due to the change in attitude of the participants. This new attitude became the same type of attitude prevailing with the pagans and their sacrifices: rites fulfilled to gain the attention of *Yahweh* God and appease His anger, although their conduct being a departure from the moral code with no repentance in progress. This attitude was reprimanded by Isaiah prophet. Is 1:11-20, 66:3-4. The presentation of sacrifice is here denunciated, but not for the concept of sacrifice itself. The worshipper is admonished to have a proper attitude in passages such as Ps 49:7-15. Micah 6:6-8, and the sacrifices are denunciated with a plea for the worshipper to recognize their intended purpose. The benefit of the rite is inherent in its purpose to curb disobedience, not in the pagan attitude of appeasement of the anger of the deity for disobedience. This was the error of later generations, to reduce *Yahweh* God to a rank and concept identical to the pseudo-deities, another cultic and tribal god.

Due to the people's negligence or lack of serious attitude to such admonishments, in time the rites and customs of the pagan deities were incorporated into the temple services. Ahaz king of Judah, during this reign, installed a replica of a pagan altar in Damascus in the temple in Jerusalem. 2 King 16:10-18. Once the people departed from the correct concept of sacrifice, *Yahweh* God no longer heeded the petitioner's requests on behalf of his people. Jer 7:16. Is 1:15.

## THE TEMPLES

During the ministry of Jesus, the greatest edifice in the world was the temple in Jerusalem. The construction of this temple was begun by Herod the Great in about 19 BC, and completed about 60 AD. But it was not the 2$^{nd}$ temple as defined by evangelical Christianity. The temple of Zerubbabel dedicated in Ezra 6:14-16 about 515 BC, is the 2$^{nd}$ temple. As mentioned earlier, another temple may also have been erected in place of the temple of Zerubbabel in about 485 BC. The family of Judas Maccabees renovated and refurbished this temple after its desecration and devastation by Antiochus IV Epiphanes in 164 BC. Herod the Great began the construction of his temple alongside the existing temple in Jerusalem. When construction was completed in the main hall of the new temple to the point that services could be performed, the old temple was demolished. Construction continued until the new temple and its various porticoes and courts were completed. Herod's temple is actually the 3$^{rd}$ or 4$^{th}$ temple. This temple was destroyed in September, 70 AD by the Roman soldiers under General Titus.

In regard to the temple built by Zerubbabel, the construction was inspired by *Yahweh* God, promoted through His prophets Haggai and Zechariah. The splendor mentioned in Hag 2:9 is definitely a spiritual splendor that was attained during the following centuries. The temple of Solomon only lasted about 350 years. Zerubbabel's temple lasted up to 500 years, or the subsequent temple, (if this temple was destroyed in 485 BC), lasted some 465 years. This temple definitely did acquire spiritual splendor in the years following 165 BC, when worship services again began after its cleansing and dedicated by the family of the Maccabees, and during the reign of the Hasmoneans until the succeeding conquest of the city by Pompey in 65 BC. Herod's temple from beginning of construction to the year it was demolished was only about 90 years.

## CORRUPTION OF THE PRIESTHOOD

With their arrogance and personal ambitions the family of the high priest emeritus Annas and his confederates had domination over the temple and its services for over 50 years, intermittently from 7 AD, to 66 AD. This Annas had 5 sons, a son-in-law and grandson, who each held the office of high priest during the 1$^{st}$ century AD. His son-in-law is the infamous Joseph Caiaphas of the gospels. Annas was appointed high priest by Quirinius governor of Syria, and held the office 7 AD through 15 AD. He was deposed by Valerius Gratus governor. His son-in-law Joseph Caiaphas was appointed by the same governor in 18 AD and held office until 36 AD.

The infamous bazaars of Annas was the business conducted in the courtyard of the temple. All of the vendors operated under the administration of Annas high-priest and his family, along with the money changers or bankers. All of them gave the high priest's family a share of the profit or commission for conducting business on the temple grounds. Jesus no doubt realized this at a very early age, traveling with his father Joseph to Jerusalem every Passover, and later on his own as an observant Jew. With his own eyes he saw the corruption of the priesthood, how all the services and ministry and finances were controlled by one man and his sons and son-in-law. Anybody that would confront them or reprimand their corruption or violation of their sacerdotal obligations was excommunicated. John 18:3. Anybody posing as a threat to the stability of the temple and its services or a threat to the supremacy of the family of Annas was quickly removed. Eze 34:21.

I have no doubt that Annas and his family felt that they were doing *Yahweh* God a favor with their efforts, and especially under the circumstances: Roman occupation. They performed the sacrifices on a daily basis and holidays. But their reliance on this edifice and the worship services was in vain. There is no doubt the population was convinced and also the priests that as long as the services continued in the temple, and at any cost, then they were under the shelter of *Yahweh* God and all would go well with them. This is the same attitude that existed among the people in Judea during the era of the career of Jeremiah. Jer 9:1-4. The words of Sadducees to Pontius Pilate correctly displayed their attitude, "We have no king but Caesar." John 19:15. The Roman government had the ultimate control and final decision in regard to the temple and its operation.

The temple itself was built by Herod the Great, the most ruthless dictator of the Jews of the 1$^{st}$ century BC. This enigma baffles me and has no doubt perplexed scholars and students throughout the ages: Why would Jewish elders permit the ruler Herod to construct an edifice for their divine worship services? He implemented the authority of a foreign power and their military occupation in Judea; he executed more Jews than any other single individual: he caused Jews to live in constant fear of their life; he was not aligned with the religion of the Jews in any way or of their genealogy. The same person who constructed a new temple for the Jews, where they can worship their deity, also had 300 important Jewish figures confined waiting to be executed at the moment news of his death was publicized.

Part of the reason is his aptitude for construction. Herod built many large structures and cities in Judea, all for them for the glory of Rome and its emperor. To Herod a temple was just another edifice, he could not distinguish its services as any more useful or sacred than any other building in his domain. But it was definitely to his credit; one more magnificent building to add to his list of accomplishments. During the years of Herod's reign, 37 BC to 4 BC, he was a despot, and right to the day of his death. I contend that Jewish elders had little or nothing to do with the decision of Herod to construct a new temple in place of the old. But once the decision was made those with political aspirations in the temple services volunteered their services. This new temple in Jerusalem for *Yahweh* God would be what Ephesus was for Artemis, and what Athens was for Olympus, and what Rome and Egypt were for their supreme deities. The senior Jewish elders lost sight of the original purpose for sacrifice, but they were now equated with the identical concept of sacrifice of the temples dedicated to other deities. The high priest of the temple of *Yahweh* God was now on a equal footing with the high priests of the temple of other deities. The culmination of corruption in temple service, I contend, was that of permitting Herod the Great to construct a new temple in lieu of and in place of the existing temple in Jerusalem. The permission and cooperation of the Sadduceen high priest family and Sanhedrin with the Idumaen antagonist of Israel is a political enigma of Jewish history.

The Sadduceen high priestly family saw the advantage of cooperation with Herod in allowing him to build a new temple alongside their existing, and then eventually decommissioning and demolishing the old. There was a political advantage to the Sadducees and Sanhedrin: It was power and control and influence over the balance of world-wide Jewry and status as the cultic representatives of *Yahweh* God. This compromise and alignment with secular authority resulted in spiritual prostitution, the priests of the era now gaining the status as cultic representatives of *Yahweh* God.

An antecedent to this situation would be the altar of Ahaz. 1 King 16:10-16. This king of Judah replicated an altar that he saw in a pagan temple in Damascus and had it installed in Solomon's temple. This new altar was then subsequently used for burnt offerings in lieu of the original God-inspired altar of Solomon. The priest Uriah obeyed the king's requests. There is no indication in the Scriptural account that the high priest objected to this modification. The entire scenario is religiously pathetic: the 2 principal leaders of Judah prostituting the religion with no remorse or sense of error. This of course was repulsive to *Yahweh* God, that His temple be paganized. The visions of Ezekiel as recorded in Eze 8, outline the attitude of *Yahweh* God toward this abomination. In this vision a divine messenger accompanied Ezekiel to the temple in Jerusalem. Ezekiel was brought to Babylon during the first invasion of 575 BC, while the temple was still standing. This vision occurred during the interim until 586 BC, with the final defeat of Jerusalem and destruction of the temple. The "seat of the image of jealously which provokes to jealousy," in Eze 8:3, could well refer to this new pagan altar in use inside the temple. This was one of the many abominations practiced in the temple that eventually led to the complete removal of the Spirit of *Yahweh* God from the temple and its subsequent destruction. The idea of jealousy is derived from the 2$^{nd}$ commandment: the prohibition of images in worship. The jealousy of *Yahweh* God was unleashed with the installation of this new altar in Ahaz's temple, and His wrath was executed on those that permitted its use in worship. Herod's temple followed the same vein of services as occurred in the temple of Ahaz to its destruction.

Beginning with the victory of Pompey over Judea in 63 BC, the jurisdiction over the selection and installation of high priest was held by the governor, or by Herod during his reign. The anger of *Yahweh* God stemming from His jealousy began with the compromise and accommodation of Jewish elders with Herod the Great for the demolition of the earlier temple and construction of this new one. Included in *Yahweh* God's anger would be the massive competition among the elite Sadducees for the high priests' office, and their political negotiations with Herod and the later governors of Judea for this supreme religious position. The Jewish high priest from about 30 BC to 66 AD was pontifix maximus, comparable to the Catholic Pope or Eastern Orthodox Patriarch or the pontifix maximus of any number of pagan cults and religions of the era. This is why the Jewish apostate religion is identified as a prostitute sitting upon a beast in the book of Revelation. The beast is the authority of Rome in Judea.

Because it was Caesar who gave the high priests this office and gave religious freedom to Jews, there was a certain allegiance to Rome and its authorities in Judea that was expected from the population. *Yahweh* God may be in heaven, but it was Caesar who delegated the title and office of high priest to the family of Annas and their confederates. It was a limited religious freedom, and a personal monetary income amounting to millions of *shekels* of gold and silver on a yearly basis.

Annas high priest and his subsequent high priest sons, son-in-law and grandson, were no different than the apostate kings and priests of old Israel. Their services of the 1$^{st}$ century matched the temple services conducted that Jeremiah condemned. Jer 2:8-9, 7:9-10. They matched the temple services that Ezekiel condemned in his prophecies, calling them a prostitute religion. Eze 8:3, 10-11, 15:15-52. The priests and religious leaders of ancient Israel and 1$^{st}$ century Israel alike led Israel into religious apostasy, killed the contemporary messengers of *Yahweh* God, and prostituted themselves with foreign secular authority. This culminated in the same concluding event as with Israel in 720 BC, Judah in 586 BC, Judea in 65 BC: the devastation of Jerusalem in 70 AD.

> This people honors Me with their lips, but their heart is distant from Me. In vain do they worship Me teaching as doctrines the commandments of men. Matt 15:7-9

Under the Sadducees of the 1$^{st}$ century AD, the sole supreme deity *Yahweh* God and true religion was reduced to another deity and another routine religion with its prescribed rites and rituals and priestly representatives. No longer was *Yahweh* God a moral code. The divine religion of Israel became another cult alongside Egypt, Babylon and Rome.

## THE SIXTH AND FINAL COVENANT ERA

The covenant of Noah continued effectively among the gentiles throughout the world while the covenant of Moses of Ex 24 applied to Jews, but in both cases only among those who observed the moral code and the extent of divine instruction that applied to them in their cultural and national environment.

At the beginning of the 1$^{st}$ century AD, within Israel and due to the circumstances of the era, *Yahweh* God determined that the time had arrived for implementation of a new covenant with the Jewish people. The words of Jer 31:31-34, pertain to a new covenant with Israel, descendants of the 12 tribes along with those who converted during the interim. The opportunity for gentiles to enter the new covenant was a result of the promise to Abraham, that all the nations of the earth would be blessed by the seed of Abraham. Gen 12:3, 18:18. This promise fulfilled with the gentiles entering into the new covenant instituted by Jesus and so also becoming heirs of the same promise. Rom 15:8-9.

On Passover evening, when Jesus of Nazareth was celebrating the holiday with his disciples, he took one of the cups of wine on the table and said to them.

> This is my blood of the new covenant, which is poured out for many for the remission of sins. Matt 26:28.

With these words Jesus instituted a new covenant of God with His people Israel and with all who would enter it. This is the covenant now in effect and will be until the restoration and resurrection. The covenant was installed with the death of Jesus. Heb 9:15. And *Yahweh* God ratified it with his resurrection from death. Heb 9:11-12. The author of Hebrews also calls Jesus the surety of a better covenant. Heb 7:22. Jesus is the surety or guarantor or the terms and conditions of the new covenant. He is the one who guarantees the blessing and reward, protection and salvation, assistance and spiritual strength, for the people of his spiritual realm, who subject themselves to his rule over them. He is able to do this because he is alive in heaven and has all authority in heaven and on earth. Matt 28:18.

With the institution of a new covenant, a new priesthood was also instituted. Heb 7:11-12. This is not anything new to the new Israel or those Jews awaiting the Anointed or Messiah. A new priesthood with a descendent of David in the principal capacity was prophesied earlier by Ezekiel prophet. Eze 34:23-24. This chapter is a reprimand by Ezekiel prophet directed toward the elders and priests of old Israel addressed as shepherds, for their failure in fulfilling their obligation toward the people of Israel. A new priesthood would arise in the future, a spiritual one not composed of the descendents of the same corrupt individuals whom Ezekiel reprimanded. The priesthood of the new covenant is the order of Melchizedek, while that of the old covenant was the order of Aaron. Upon his ascension into heaven Jesus has become our high priest forever. Heb 3:14.

## JEW AND GENTILE IN THE NEW COVENANT

Jews are no longer treated by *Yahweh* God as a favored corporate entity any more. Every person is an individual and so is his or her relation to *Yahweh* God. This relation is based on the extent to which a person lives according to the divine instruction that serves as the basis for the new covenant. This is concretely and unambiguously stated by Paul apostle in his words.

> Here there cannot be Greek and Jew, circumcised and uncircumcised, barbarian, Scythian, slave, free man, but the Anointed is all and in all. Col 3:11. Gal 3:28.

To treat the Jewish people of any era since the ministry of Jesus as a favored corporate entity with some remaining status or vestige of favoritism or bias by *Yahweh* God is opposite to the dictates of the NT. The only group that resides in the will and favor of *Yahweh* God are those members of His covenant community, and they are all treated as individuals. Every person born on earth beginning with the era of the earthly ministry of Jesus is born neutral in respect to relations with *Yahweh* God. They have this option: To accept Jesus of Nazareth as son of *Yahweh* God, Savior of the world and the Anointed, to make a commitment of obedience and so enter into the covenant, becoming a member of the Messianic community, or not to. All of this equally applies to every person without preference or prejudice by *Yahweh* God.

Paul apostle wrote that Jews of his era and including himself were the elect of *Yahweh* God because they were beloved of *Yahweh* God for the sake of the forefathers. Rom 11:28. Deut 7:8. Jer 26:45. I contend that this was stated as fact to justify *Yahweh* God's selection of a remnant in the transition from the old covenant to the new covenant. This was the final act of *Yahweh* God in the conclusion of the promises to the forefathers, that a few were predestined as the remnant of the house of Judah and the house of Israel with whom the covenant was concluded. Jer 31:34. In this manner the covenant could be offered to the balance of the Jewish local and worldwide population. The apostles unto the circumcision were part of the remnant predestined by grace. Gal 2:9. The condition of the election of Jews because of the love *Yahweh* God had for their forefathers all terminated with the abolition of the old covenant. No more favoritism.

The commission of the apostles to spread the gospel of the kingdom to the nations allowed all who would accept this gospel to become disciples of the Anointed. Matt 28:19. These of the nations who accepted the gospel, about 2,000 years ago, are blessed through the seed of Abraham who is the Anointed. Gen 12:3. Gal 3:14. The manner by which all the nations would be blessed by the seed of Abraham is the entrance of every person regardless of their genealogy into the new covenant of the Anointed, that same covenant originally instituted for Israel and Judah. The commitment made by a willing person just as others did in early eras to be obedient and fulfill all that spoken and dictated by *Yahweh* God as divine instruction and moral law allows the same blessing to be bestowed on them, just as it was bestowed on Abraham and the nation of Israel. Gal 3:29. The blessings of Deut 28:1-14 and Lev 26:9, would equally apply to that individual and his family and the new covenant community they are a member of. Every male gentile can now become an Abraham in his own right and every female can become a Sarah in her own right through the Anointed the seed of Abraham. All of this possible by entering the covenant and abiding by the moral code of the covenant, the 10 commandments, the divine instruction, and the tradition of the apostles. Two passages in Revelation also pertain to the legacy of the OT to apply to the instruction of the gentiles, and the inclusion of the gentiles in the new spiritual kingdom.

> And the leaves of the tree [of life] are for the healing of the nations. Rev 22:2.
> The nations will walk by its light, and the kings of the earth will bring their splendor into it. The glory and honor of the nations will be brought to it. Rev 21:24,26.

That this is the manner as to how every race, color and nationality would be blessed by the Anointed or Messiah is iterated in several passages. Rom 15:8-9. Gal 4:28. Eph 2:19. To be Jesus', meaning to belong to the Anointed or adhere to all that the Anointed represents, means to also be a spiritual descendent of Abraham. A gentile when born from above is spiritually reborn into the nation of the new Israel, which is the Messianic new covenant community. The gentile is now by rebirth a spiritual Israelite. He is not a physical Israelite because the physical is no longer applicable, not even to a Jew anymore. Thus the gentile that joins the new covenant, becoming part of the Messianic community, is now a spiritual Israelite, while the physical Jew who rejects the covenant and Jesus is now outside the will and grace of *Yahweh* God.

## THE GENTILES AND THE COVENANTS

Over half of the NT deals with the gentiles and the new covenant. The word gentile is a transliteration of the Latin *gentilis*, meaning pagan. Its use properly in the OT and NT was to refer to the nations other than Israel. This primarily consists of the book of Acts and the letters of Paul apostle. How the gentiles were to enter the covenant was the enigma of the ages for Jewish sages. The entrance or blessing of the gentiles stems from the promise to Abraham.

> By you shall all the families of the earth be blessed. Gen 12:3. Acts 3:25.
> Abraham shall become a great and mighty nation and all the nations of the earth shall be blessed by him. Gen 18:18.
> And by your seed shall all the nations of the earth be blessed. Gen 22:18.

How the seed or posterity of Abraham would be a blessing to all the nations of the earth no doubt perplexed every reader of the *Torah* since the era of Moses to Jesus. In one respect, Israel was the seed of Abraham by which the nations would be blessed. Isaiah prophet notes this.

> I have kept you and given you as a covenant to the people, to establish the land, to apportion the desolate heritages. Is 49:8.
> I am *Yahweh*. I have called you in righteousness, I have taken you by the hand and kept you; I have given you as a covenant to the people, a light to the nations. Is 42:6.

Israel had the additional responsibility of being the channel by which blessing would be bestowed upon and gifted to other nations. But what would this blessing consist of? Peter apostle defined it to those gathered at the temple in this manner.

> God, having raised up His servant, sent him to you first, to bless you in turning every one of you from your wickedness. Acts 3:26.

The moral code which was gifted by *Yahweh* God to Israel was the blessing upon the gentiles. The divine instruction was originally received by Israel, and they in turn were to impress it upon other nations, deliver it to them for their observance. Israel was to be the channel by which *Yahweh* God spoke to the nations. This would consist of transmitting moral law, admonishment of apostasy, reprimand for impropriety, and consolation during duress. Most of the OT prophets have sections of prophecy dealing with the nations outside of Israel. For example: Isaiah 13-23, Jeremiah 46-51, Ezekiel 25-32. In this manner was Israel, the posterity of Abraham, a blessing to the nations. The word of *Yahweh* God was channeled to these nations through the prophets of Israel.

It was Paul apostle who especially was selected to accomplish or bring to fruition the words of *Yahweh* God to Abraham that all the nations would be blessed through his seed. According to Paul apostle, this seed or posterity is the Anointed or Messiah.

> Now the promises were made to Abraham and to his offspring. It does not say, "And to offsprings," referring to many; but, referring to one, "And to your offspring," who is the Anointed. Gal 3:16.

It is through the Anointed that all the nations would be blessed. This was to be accomplished by providing the members of the nations on an individual basis the means of entering the new covenant and spiritual kingdom. Paul apostle taught the good news of the spiritual kingdom to both Jews and non-Jews. It was the rule of *Yahweh* God over them by their subjection to the moral code by which they would attain the blessing of Abraham. From this time forward Jesus is the surety or guarantee of the covenant. To the extent this person of the nations would observe and adhere to the moral code and divine instruction, to that extent would *Yahweh* God bless that person. Jesus would guarantee it as surety. The blessings of Deut 28:1-14, equally apply to the non-Jew under the new covenant.

By being born from above, born of the word and spirit, the non-Jew became a child of *Yahweh* God to the same extent and manner of a physical Jew. The gentile was grafted into the tree of Israel as a spiritual or adopted son and daughter with equal rights to inheritance. As a spiritual member of Israel, Abraham likewise became their father.

> And if you are the Anointed's, then you are Abraham's posterity, heirs according to the promise. Gal 3:29.

The legacy of the OT law, prophets and writings was passed on the new member. The OT became their book, the ancient history became their history, and ancient Israel became their nation. The non-Jew as a member of the new spiritual Israel had equal claim as any other Jew to the OT and all that it contained and represented.

## THE MYSTERY OF MESSIAH (THE ANOINTED)

The subject of the dissertation of Paul apostle in the passage Eph 2:1 – 3:13, deals with the transfer of the gentiles into the new spiritual community of Israel. Through the body of the Anointed, both groups, Jew and non-Jew now have equal status before God. Paul apostle calls the means by which the gentiles were to become members of the new covenant in the fulfillment of the promise to Abraham as the mystery or secret of the Anointed. Earlier generations were not aware of how this was to be accomplished, but it was finally unveiled in the preaching of the gospel of the kingdom to the gentiles through Paul apostle, and their entrance into the new covenant.

> The secret of the Anointed which was not disclosed to the people of other generations, as it has now been revealed to his holy apostles and prophets by the Spirit, that is, how the gentiles are fellow heirs, members of the same body, and partakers of the promise in the Anointed Jesus through the gospel. Eph 3:5-6.
> The plan of the secret of the Anointed hidden from the ages. Eph 3:9.

In time the many other precepts of the divine instruction were to be absorbed by the non-Jewish members of Israel. This is the intent of the statement.

> For from early generations Moses has in every city those who preach him, for he is read every Sabbath in the synagogues. Acts 15:20, 29.

The edicts of this council of elders and apostles in Jerusalem were issued to cover the more important facets of divine instruction, that would be fundamental and primary for the new membership from the nations. These were: 1. Prohibition of idolatry. 2. Prohibition of immorality. 3 and 4. The proper manner of butchering meat for human consumption. The balance of divine instruction regarding the religion of the new covenant community the gentiles would grasp and implement as time progressed, with their regular attendance at synagogue services. Acts 15:21.

## THE PARABLE OF PAUL APOSTLE

The point to be made by Paul apostle in Rom 9-11 can be summarized as follows. The Jew who sees the blessing of *Yahweh* God bestowed upon the non-Jew who accepts Jesus as the Anointed and enters the new covenant and spiritual kingdom will be motivated to leave behind the old covenant and its attributes and also enter the new covenant and spiritual Israel and accept Jesus as the Anointed. The elect have already obtained the new covenant and spiritual kingdom, because they are the remnant. Rom 11:3. All Israel mentioned in Rom 11:26 refers to the entirety of the new spiritual Israel, not the Israel of the old covenant. "All Israel" cannot refer to all the descendents of the 12 tribes, because many have died over 2,000 years of generations and more are still to die. Paul apostle mentions in Rom 9:8, that it is the children of promise that are the true descendents of Jacob, not the children of the flesh. So it is the spiritual seed that inherits the promises. Therefore the "all Israel" of Rom 11:26, is the entirety of Jew and non-Jew that become the new spiritual Israel, dependent not on genealogy but on faith and conduct.

The parable of Paul apostle in Rom 11:17-24 is an accurate description of this process. Israel is portrayed as an olive tree, productive and healthy. The roots can be interpreted as the patriarchs and forefathers; the soil as the divine instruction and moral code. The trunk of the tree is the house of Judah and the house of Israel. With the arrival of Jesus and his institution of a new covenant there occurred a massive modification in the structure of the branches of the tree. It was no longer a physical Israel, but now a spiritual Israel. The branches symbolized individual Jews. Those that rejected the summons to enter the new covenant and spiritual kingdom were pruned off the tree. Later they were piled up and when dry were set afire. Luke 23:31. This occurred at the 2 Jewish Wars. Those that accepted the new covenant and entered the spiritual kingdom remained on the tree. The non-Jewish nations are portrayed as wild olive trees, while the individual members of these various races, nations, and ethnic groups are the branches on these trees. A wild olive tree represents the balance of the nations: little fruit and poor quality, having thorns, all of this indicative of the lack of moral and ethical character and substance of the nations. The roots of these wild olive trees can symbolize their philosophers, the priests of their religions and mythology. Those individuals of the nations who accepted the invitation into the new covenant were cut off their original tree and grafted into the new tree, now part of the original tree of Israel.

These non-Jewish members of the Messianic community were now to realize that Abraham was their spiritual progenitor; that the divine instruction was now the source for their spiritual and moral nourishment; that the wisdom of the prophets and sages was now their virtue and knowledge; and that the Scriptures of the OT was now their Scripture, just as Paul apostle wrote to the Corinthians. 1 Cor 1:30. Jesus and all that was provided to the earlier generations of the nation of Israel was now the source for the standard of morality and ethics for the non-Jews of the Messianic communities.

To understand this parable better it can be combined with the parable of the vineyard of John 15. The fruitless branches of the vine were pruned off, for them to dry and eventually be set afire. The same can be applied to Paul's Olive tree, the descendents of the flesh would be pruned off regularly, while the descendents of the promise would remain to produce fruit. With the entrance of the new covenant, the Jews who did not accept Jesus as the Anointed and enter the new covenant and spiritual kingdom were pruned off, the tree symbolizing the nation; while those that did remained. The non-Jews or gentiles who did accept Jesus as the Anointed and the new covenant were removed from the trees of their gentile national identities and grafted into the tree of new Israel. Jesus himself mentions the invitation and entrance of gentiles into the kingdom with the expulsion of unbelieving Jews in Matt 8:11-12.

What Paul apostle said in Rom 11:18, about the gentile Christians becoming too proud or else they too will be pruned off, has pathetically become prophecy self-fulfilled. Beginning about the middle of the 2nd century, the Messianic community gained a greater membership of non-Jews and gradually the leadership abandoned their Hebrew roots. The non-

Jews or gentiles of the era accepted gladly this severance from their origin and attachment to Israel, and subsequently became inflated with pride with the termination of the city of Jerusalem as a Jewish city at the conclusion of the Second Jewish War, 132-135 AD, and with the balance of Jewry dispersed. This pride of election over the original descendents of Jacob began a slow abandonment of the divine instruction and authority of the OT. Slowly this was replaced with new concepts of religion and worship based on the background of the gentiles. With this attitude the gentile branches were broken off the olive tree of Israel and grafted back into their own original stock of the wild tree.

At any time, any person of the posterity of the 12 sons of Jacob may be removed from the tree of the physical Israel and be grafted into the tree of the spiritual Israel with their acceptance of Jesus as the Anointed and entrance into the new covenant and spiritual Israel. This likewise pertains to any person on non-Jewish stock. This entire spiritual tree is to be productive as a community generation to generation.

## JEWS TODAY

The subsequent question to arise after the events of the $1^{st}$ and $2^{nd}$ centuries with the failed Jewish Wars and the termination of Israel as a nation is the status of the Jew today. This misconception extends to many extremes. One being that of the Jew as Christ-killer. This distorted attitude has engendered the Crusades, Inquisitions, pogroms and holocausts against the posterity of the Jews. Although not affecting every Jew of every generation, it generally affects those who continue to observe and abide by the religion and identity as established by the rabbis of the $2^{nd}$ century onward. The Christ-killer attitude is inculcated into every Christian every Easter season when they hear about the passion of Jesus and the words of the priests and Jewish elders requesting that the responsibility of the death of Jesus be upon them and their children. The Christian interprets this as an unending line of responsibility, affecting every practicing Jew of every generation.

The opposite extreme installs the Jewish nation still with the covenant of *Yahweh* God concluded with Abraham. This faction of Christianity is known as John Darby dispensational, and feels that this ancient covenant is still in effect. The new covenant is yet to be concluded with the Jews at the $2^{nd}$ advent of Jesus. The Jews are still the chosen people of *Yahweh* God according to the concept of dispensationalism. Sometime in the future they teach another temple will be built and animal sacrifices will again be performed by the Jews. This faction teaches that the sacrifices will be performed following the prophesies of Eze 40-46, as they apply these chapters to the future (even though these chapters pertained to the reestablishment of the kingdom in Judea with the return of exiles from Babylon.) Many of the dispensational school await all Israel to be saved.

Since the 1$^{st}$ century about 100 generations have progressed in history and all have died. This pertains to people of every race, creed, color, ethnic background and nationality. The dissolution of Israel in 135 AD terminated any status the national Israel might claim as a "chosen nation." The favored nation status has been transferred through the believing remnant to the new spiritual Israel. Matt 21:43. This new spiritual nation consists of every race, color and nationality who are part of the new covenant of Jesus.

Salvation on an individual basis applies equally to all everywhere. There is no difference between Jew and gentile. Both are viewed in the same manner by *Yahweh* God in heaven. Col 3:11. Peter apostle described it in the following fashion.

> Truly I perceive that God shows no partiality, but in every nation any one who fears him and does what is right is acceptable to him. Acts 10:34-35.

This pertains to Jew and non-Jew alike. Under the covenant of Noah the individual who follows the basic moral code will attain a certain salvation on earth, but this is not the resurrection and eternal life. For this reason I contend, some Jews survive each generation to pass on to the successive generation their traditions, rites and customs. Not because of any national favor with *Yahweh* God, but only under the terms and conditions of the covenant of Noah. These Jews that live according to this principal moral code acquire a benefit and blessing from *Yahweh* God as a result. For such Jews and the others, because they are outside the covenant of Jesus, the blessing and salvation is confined to the earthly sphere, not to the era of restoration and eternal life. All of this equally pertains to non-Jews since the attitude of *Yahweh* God is the same toward all who are outside the new covenant. The establishment of the nation of Israel is not an indication of the end of the world. This is a materialization of several generations of adherence to a moral code within the criteria of the covenant of Noah.

The establishment of Israel as a state is no different than the independence of the USA in 1776, or Mexico in 1821, or the African states at the end of colonialization in the 1960's. All fall under the same classification: The adherence to a moral code inherits earthly benefit and its related blessings. But eventually that generation dies and new people are born to replace them. They likewise have the opportunity to decide their fate: whether to assimilate into an amoral society within the secular world of their residence, or adhere to a moral code. The blessing and benefit will continue with their decision to adhere to the moral code, otherwise it will cease.

## 2. THE KINGDOMS

### THE KINGDOM OF GOD

The concept of the divine kingdom is a fundamental element of the attitude of *Yahweh* God toward created humanity. It is very much interwoven with the concept of the covenant between *Yahweh* God and His people. The basis of the concept of the divine kingdom is that *Yahweh* God is supreme sovereign or potentate over His own creation, and at the same time a benevolent ruler wanting the best for the populous and residents of His realm. *Yahweh* God is not despotic or dictatorial, seeking subjection of His people using threats, coercion, vengeance or oppression, but describes Himself as sovereign in the following terms.

> His kingdom is an everlasting kingdom, and His dominion is from generation to generation. Dan 3:3,34.
> The kingdom of God is within you. Luke 17:21.
> And let the peace of the Anointed rule in Your hearts. Col 3:15.

These are the characteristics of the sovereign and His rule. *Yahweh* God gains the subjection of His people by way of love. It is to their benefit to voluntarily and willingly be obedient to the dictatorial authority of *Yahweh* God, and to their discredit and injury to disobey and disregard the dictates and authority of *Yahweh* God. This divine kingdom is a spiritual kingdom.

The term government can be used on even terms as kingdom. Both words are equivalent having the same connotation. The difference is that the word kingdom is archaic, while government is modern. In modern American English Jesus, John the Baptizer, and Paul apostle would have said, "The government of God is arriving." This is equivalent to the old KJV rendering of, "The kingdom of God is at hand." The use of the word government would be easier for someone of the modern era to identify with instead of the archaic kingdom. In essence, *Yahweh* God is the head of government, which is His administration and jurisdiction over all His own creation. The specific purpose of the phrase Kingdom of God, or its

Aramaic and Hebrew equivalent Kingdom of Heaven, is the rule of *Yahweh* God over His people as a spiritual and political body. The government of *Yahweh* God is a theocracy, *Yahweh* God governs through individuals dedicated to the fulfillment of the divine instruction on Earth.

## THE GOVERNMENT OF THIS WORLD

The earthly kingdom of *Yahweh* God as depicted in the history of early Bible times was established by *Yahweh* God as a means of introducing His spiritual kingdom.

The spiritual or divine kingdom is a reflection of the earthly kingdom and in many respects invisibly inherent in the earthly kingdom. Government of the people, by the people and for the people is a magnificent concept. Any group of people who bind together to establish a government for themselves to reside together in harmony is divinely inspired. Rom 13:2. But it can only succeed if the people abandon their authority in favor of the authority of *Yahweh* God. Otherwise that government will follow the balance of history and eventually collapse. Dan 2:34-35. The concept of self-government for the benefit of the residents and citizens is a divine concept. At the time Paul apostle penned Rom 13, the most ruthless and tyrannical of all rulers of the era reigned in Rome, Nero Caesar. Yet Paul apostle advocated subjection to the government in general for the sake of the common citizens and residents. His complement was for the sake of government itself, not the policies of Nero Caesar. Legitimate civil government consists of people who accept authority delegated to them by the population in some agreeable form or manner. Others acquire authority through force or subterfuge. Any individual working within a government, having some type of authority is yet subject to an even higher authority, the reason being that all authority is the possession and domain of *Yahweh* God. No individual on earth has a naturally acquired possession of authority over others. Authority extends only from *Yahweh* God, and authority extends from people who voluntarily delegate the rule over themselves to others. Every ruler must answer to the body of people that has selected him and invested him with authority, because rule is for the benefit of the people. Likewise every ruler or member of government must answer to *Yahweh* God, because *Yahweh* God is the source of rule and authority.

The legitimate government on earth in any nation is that circle of individuals to whom authority was delegated by the population by some civil and legitimate means agreeable to the population and without strife and discord. The effective government would be that circle of legitimately empowered individuals who dedicate their life to the benefit of the people and to whom the people willingly subject themselves. The best government is when the divine instruction of *Yahweh* God is implemented as the constitution for the nation, and when the population and government willingly and fervently observe it, uphold it and enforce it. The worse government is anarchy or despotism, where divine instruction is void and both the government and people suffer. The result of violation of denial of the divine instruction is civil war, revolution, economic oppression, political corruption, and a high turnover of civil officials.

The goal of good and effective government based on divine instruction and the moral code of *Yahweh* God is to lead individuals to recognize the spiritual kingdom. Although earthly governments have numbered in the thousands over the millennia and throughout the world, most of them of relatively short duration, the spiritual kingdom has always existed and is unaffected by the circuit of coup and revolution and civil war. The spiritual kingdom will prevail regardless of political achievements or military conquests or military defeats, and all because this kingdom is divine and spiritual.

## CONCEPT OF THE SPIRITUAL RULE OF YAHWEH GOD

The concept of the spiritual kingdom follows the same vein as the covenant of *Yahweh* God. For prosperity and successful living, and the ability to deal with every mishap or tragedy, a person must place themselves under a subjection to the authority of *Yahweh* God. This subjection materializes as a voluntary obedience to the code of conduct and divine instruction of the Bible. Then *Yahweh* God will rule over His people as individuals and as a community. King Nebuchadnezzar realized the spiritual rule of *Yahweh* God with his voluntary subjection to the divine instruction after his ordeal of 7 years. He concludes his experience in his own words.

> His kingdom is an eternal kingdom, and His dominion is from generation to generation. Dan 4:3.

> And at the end of the time I, Nebuchadnezzar, lifted my eyes to heaven, and my understanding returned to me; and I blessed the Most High and praised and honored Him who lives forever, for His dominion is an everlasting dominion, and His kingdom is from generation to generation. All the inhabitants of the earth are reputed as nothing; He does according to His will in the army of heaven and among the inhabitants of the earth. No one can restrain His hand or say to Him, "What have You done?" Dan 4:34-35.

The kingdom of *Yahweh* God on earth is an eternal kingdom that can not be defeated and is impossible to destroy, because it is spiritual. An entity or concept that is divine and spiritual can not be defeated or devastated using material weapons or means.

Another key to grasping the concept of the spiritual kingdom are the words of *Yahweh* God to Samuel and to David, who was king himself over Israel.

> For they have not rejected you, but they have rejected Me from being king over them. 1 Sam 8:7.
>
> *Yahweh* reigns, let the nations tremble! He sits enthroned upon the Cherubim; let the earth quake. *Yahweh* is great in Zion, He is exalted over all the nations. Ps 99:1-2.

It is difficult for an individual to willingly and voluntarily place himself under a stringent code of moral conduct. The tendency of any human is not to observe any statute or ordinance not to a person's immediate benefit, but to avoid and circumvent it in any possibly manner. Observance of law infringing on an individual's personal choice and personal freedom is often under duress and reluctance. People are like water, they take the path of least resistance. This is what *Yahweh* God was relating to Samuel prophet. Up to the coronation of Saul the people were expected to willingly and voluntarily observe and enforce the statutes and ordinances of *Yahweh* God on a tribal and community basis. This was the basis of government of the original confederation of 12 tribes. Each tribe would govern itself according to what was dictated them by *Yahweh* God. All in all there was no central government with a federal military or judicial system to police the population and tend to enforcement of these statutes and ordinances.

For a truly successful national kingdom of *Yahweh* God observance is willing and voluntary.

The failure of the people on an individual basis of the observance of the divine law, coupled together with their poor perception of the spiritual kingdom, led them to demand a leader who would cause Israel to be another nation like the other nations. Every nation had an identity: Babylon, Egypt, Assyria, Moab, Ammon, etc. But Israel under the loose tribal confederation had no identity as a nation, but neither was it supposed to have such an identity. There was not to be any competition: their identity was with *Yahweh* God. A cooperative federation of these tribal states and smaller communities are better designed and organized for the success of the population than a large nation with centralized government. *Yahweh* God knew this and so instituted this with the entrance and settlement of Canaan by the 12 tribes. The reason for the citizens' creation of a large nation was that of identity and defense. Israel no longer cared to be unknown or unrecognized among the list of nations. It wanted to be identified and recognized as a full fledged nation with a supreme earthly ruler and capital city and military defense.

## THE KINGDOM OF EARLY ISRAEL

The confederation of tribal states each married within their own tribe, although marriage between the tribes was also permitted. What was prohibited was marriage outside Israel. Deut 7:3-4. Each tribe having customs and traditions of its own would be preserved intact generation after generation and provide an identity for the individual and for the family. In a large nation a person looses their identity: each person is lost in the crowd. Traditions and customs are lost with marriage outside the cultural and ethic enclave. Heritage is unknown in a melting pot society. A person can get lost in a large nation with a nuclear family, while the extended family of a tribe or community bestows on an individual a sense of attachment and relationship. Marriage within the tribe offers compatibility with the greater chance of long term success and prosperity, and increases the stability of the tribe. An extended family is greater support for newlyweds and new families. A harmony prevails within the smaller tribe with its identity and internal moral support then the strife in a larger cultureless environment, while the larger society is defined in terms of national interests. Its holidays, festivals, traditions, legacy, are routed toward national progress and the benefit and advantage of the state. The individual in the secular society is identified with the nation, no longer with the code of conduct of *Yahweh* God.

A smaller tribe can easily develop better relationships with other tribes than can large nations. The initial confederacy of the 12 tribes did not include provisions for a standing army. Only on occasion with the threat of an enemy did the tribes provide recruits. This was on a voluntary basis on demand by the leader selected of *Yahweh* God. Such were the judges: Othniel, Ehud, Gideon, Jephthah and Samson and others. A standing army was not actually required for the 12 tribe confederacy. This was because of the promise of *Yahweh* God for defense and protection. Ex 23:22. The original defeat of the 7 nations of Canaan was prophesied to Abraham some 500 years earlier, and so was fulfilled. Gen 15:16. The victory was not the result of the strength of Israel's military, since they had no military. They had just surfaced after 40 years of desert nomadic and transient life in the deserts of Arabia, and had not developed a regimented army with trained soldiers, along with the weapons required for organized warfare. It was the physical weakness of the nations and cities of Canaan at this particular point in history that allowed their immediate and total collapse and defeat. This is why Israel succeeded in the annihilation of the nations of Canaan.

The fact that a standing army or standby military later existed in Israel was indicative of a lack of faith in the protective capability of *Yahweh* God and a lack of perception of the type of community that *Yahweh* God intended for His people, a spiritual kingdom. The idea is to live a simple, humble and tranquil life coexisting with neighbors of equal or different heritage. The furthest intent of *Yahweh* God for any of the tribes was for them to make a name for themselves. The decision of certain elders and representatives of the people for a supreme political ruler and military commander was also accompanied by the desire to establish a name for themselves. No longer was Israel to follow the concept of the spiritual kingdom, but now the concept of the secular kingdom, another name on the map over some terrain on planet earth whose boundaries cannot be distinguished from the sky. Now willing to fight its enemies, those that threaten the national identity, the name of their nation, they conscript recruits as pawns, expendable souls as soldiers. This is the conflict of the ages between the divine kingdom and the secular kingdom.

## HISTORY OF ISRAEL'S KINGS

Even with the intent of Israel to become like the other nations, *Yahweh* God routed the selection of leaders such that the first proved a massive failure for Israel. They got what they deserved. Saul was the typical king of his era: ruthless and ambitious. He lacked common sense and peripheral vision, and had a might makes right attitude. How many lives of recruits brought into the military by Saul king perished under his naïve leadership believing they were fighting for the cause of Israel? For this reason David son of Jesse was installed by *Yahweh* God, to organize the kingdom so it would have more of a semblance to the spiritual kingdom.

The later kings of both Israel and Judah were in essence not any different than the kings of any of the surrounding nations. The worship of *Yahweh* God and adherence to His covenant had diffused into another national religion, the cult of *Yahweh*, distant from its original divine intentions provided the people at Sinai. The political struggle within the various dynasties of both the northern and southern kingdom was an embarrassment to *Yahweh* God. The years of division and intra-national disputes and war was embarrassing to the attempt of *Yahweh* God to develop an earthly government that would have some semblance to parallel a spiritual kingdom. The rule of governors in the centuries following the return of a remnant from exile in Babylon and later Assyria was more in line with the attempt of *Yahweh* God to develop a righteous humanity. This newly inaugurated community in Judea was more inclined to serve as a means of grasping the concept of the rule of *Yahweh* God over His people.

The kingdom of Israel was small and fragmented during the years under Persian jurisdiction but grew to a large population by the middle of the $3^{rd}$ century BC. But again the vestige of organized confederation collapsed with the reign of Antiochus Epiphanes beginning 175 BC. The collapse of the Jewish state and religion during this era was due to a lack of leadership in providing a strong religion and government for the Jewish population in Judea in order to withstand both Greek military attack and Hellenist philosophic and religious influx. With the decrease of the divine instruction among the Jews of the $3^{rd}$ century, the void of religious affiliation was filled by the pseudo-religions of Greek mythology and philosophy. This was nothing more than a repeat of the era of the judges.

This compelled certain concerned families to bind together in a campaign against the Greeks and Hellenism. Nationalism was the goal of Jewish partisans during the war of independence, 169-164 BC, under the leadership of the family of Judas Maccabees. Their family became known in Jewish history as the Hasmonaens. The war of independence fought by the Hasmonaens does parallel closely the wars against the invading and occupation alien forces during the era of the judges and especially under Saul. The new Philistines became the Greeks. It was their contemporary occupation that became the new enemy to defeat. With the final treaty made with the Greeks by Jonathan son of Mattathias, the land gained independence and autonomy. This reestablishment of government by the new elite and aristocracy of Israel was successful for initiating temple services and the divine religion. This aristocracy was the new religious elite, the Hasidim, the separatists, and their later successors the Pharisees and Sadducees. The image of the spiritual kingdom provided to the general Jewish population under the rule of the Hasmonaens was better than in earlier ages, however the ruling hierarchy eventually succumbed to strife and competition for positions of both secular and religious leadership. Most of the typical Jewish population cared less about the power struggles in high places, no different than our present age or other ages. The general population seeks stability and civil and religious and economic freedom, regardless of whom is in office.

For the typical and sincere Jew with a yearning to live according to the traditions of their forefathers, to fulfill the rite of circumcision on their male offspring, to bring the sacrifice on Passover every year, and to be able to attend synagogue services on the Sabbath, this 100 year period from 164 BC to about 65 BC was the golden age of Jewish religious freedom and independence. Life could not be better. But with the invasion of Judea in 65 BC by Pompey Roman general, this golden age suddenly terminated. Roman occupation of Palestine began and along with it the Roman control of the high priest's position and temple services. For the typical sincere Jew, this uncircumcised gentile controlling their world was unacceptable, and they had to regain their freedom at any cost. Their identity could have been their Hebrew ancestors in Egypt, under oppression with no freedoms, and somehow this yoke of subjection to foreign control had to be removed.

## THE DICHOTOMY BETWEEN THE SECULAR AND SPIRITUAL KINGDOMS

The freedom fighters originated in Galilee, while the religious hierarchy was centered in Jerusalem. This small disenchanted and revolutionary faction in Galilee was in continual conflict and opposition to the religious elite of Jerusalem. For the freedom fighters in Galilee their goal was civil and economic freedom. For the religious elite, their concern was solely the temple services and freedom to express their traditions according to the dictates of Jewish sages of ages past and recent. The religious elite were willing to compromise secular authority with the Romans provided they received religious autonomy. This they did until the freedom fighters gained control of Jerusalem in about 66 AD. The common tie of the 2 groups was the expectation of the Anointed, an individual anointed of *Yahweh* God, who would evacuate the enemy, the Roman occupation, by means of divine force. He would institute a new era of Jewish civil and religious independence. The vision and expectation of the Anointed held by the majority was hardly justified by Scripture, the prophetic word of the OT. The portrayal of him as the son of David, a military victor, was preferred to the suffering servant of Isaiah.

When Jesus of Nazareth began to proclaim his message many misunderstood his concept of the spiritual kingdom, the divine government. The good news of divine government taught by Jesus of Nazareth was not a novel or heretofore unheard of concept. It was the same concept that *Yahweh* God had been impressing on the residents of this world from the beginning, and especially to His people Israel. *Yahweh* God wants to rule over His people through their personal and voluntary subjection to His divine instruction and code of conduct, and so bless them in their life. The blessing of *Yahweh* God with peace, prosperity and happiness would materialize in the personal and community life of the new spiritual Israel, with the rule of *Yahweh* God over their life. Acts 28:23, 31. This divine instruction and moral code, known as *Torah* to the Israelites, was to have authority over people in their life, since *Yahweh* God as a spirit cannot rule from heaven as does a president or prime minister or dictator. The rule was by obedience to the book of the *Torah*.

The concept of the spiritual kingdom preached by John the Baptizer, Jesus, and subsequent apostles was the voluntary rule of *Yahweh* God over the life of the individual and the community. This is not a secular or ecumenical government with a military, administration, bureaucracies, bureaucrats, taxes and head of state. This was a spiritual kingdom that *Yahweh* God would establish and defend based on His promise to do so. The head of state, administrators, bureaucracies and bureaucrats were all led by the authority in heaven, and the only tax was the charity of the members to assist the underprivileged and community services.

## GOSPEL OF THE KINGDOM

The Jews had lost the concept of the spiritual kingdom long before the ministry of Jesus. Now with the victory of Pompey they also lost the secular kingdom. Under the circumstances of the era it was necessary for a new leader to arise in Israel to reintroduce the concept of the spiritual kingdom that would be their salvation. It was the Anointed descendent of David who would ascend the throne of his maternal ancestor and inherit the rule over Israel. Luke 1:32-33. This Anointed materialized in Jesus of Nazareth, the son of *Yahweh* God. He was first to proclaim his good news of the arrival of the divine and spiritual reign of Himself among his own people. This kingdom would then be inaugurated by the apostles; and subsequently be transmitted to all the nations of the inhabited world. All would have an opportunity to enter it.

> The Lord (*Yahweh*) will give him (Jesus) the throne of his father David, and he will reign over the house of Jacob forever; his kingdom will never end. Luke 1:32-33.
> For he has rescued us from the dominion of darkness and brought us into the kingdom of the beloved son. Col 1:13.

The kingdom advertised by both John the Baptizer and Jesus, along with the 70 and the 12, arrived about 7 days after the ascension of Jesus to heaven. This was the festival of Pentecost. The descent of the holy Spirit onto the earth initiated the reign of Jesus over the house of David, as king over Israel. So was fulfilled the words of Gabriel messenger to Mary. Of this spiritual kingdom there is no end. It will continue unto the restoration unimpeded and uninterrupted among all who are citizens of it. Through the baptism of the holy Spirit and its gifts the presence of Jesus is confirmed among his people, the citizens of his kingdom over whom he reigns. Isaiah prophesied of the materialization of this new nation, the spiritual kingdom, to be accomplished in one day. Is 66:8.

The section of Matt 5:3-11 are titled Beatitudes. These 9 statements were to inform those disciples who gathered with Jesus on a mountain in Galilee the benefit and advantage of the gospel which he taught. The materially poor would now possess the spiritual kingdom. Those who mourned due to the sorrows imposed upon them from suffering and difficulty would find comfort once they became part of the spiritual kingdom, with new friends and relatives. The meek and oppressed would eventually re-inherit the land of Palestine, after peaceful coexistence was established with Roman authority. Those who sought virtue, a Scripturally-based moral code, would obtain it once they entered the spiritual kingdom and began a new life in a new community. Those having a charitable disposition, a benevolent and kind nature, would be able to utilize their sincerity in the new spiritual assembly of Israel. Those pure in heart would be able to grasp the love of *Yahweh* God for them. The peacemakers, those who reconcile individuals and groups in conflict or having animosity, are the new children of *Yahweh* God.

Inevitably, these new citizens will be rejected by those who continue to adhere to the archaic covenants and will be labeled as traitors to the religion of their forefathers. This is not to worry them because in earlier eras others likewise suffered at the hands of their countrymen for advocating a spiritual kingdom and promoting the moral code of *Yahweh* God.

## THE SPIRITUAL KINGDOM OF NEW ISRAEL

It was over this spiritual kingdom that the 12 apostles were to have thrones to sit upon, and from which they would rule over the 12 tribes of Israel. Matt 19:28. Luke 22:29-30. No longer physical thrones, but spiritual. Since the prophecy regarding the new covenant originally pertained to the house of Judah and Israel, so the 12 were to rule over and judge the same. The apostles were kings and priests, and their rule was upon the earth. Rev 1:5, 5:6. This authority was bestowed upon them by the anointment of the holy Spirit. In reality it was not the apostles who governed the spiritual kingdom, but it was Jesus who governed through his inspiration of the holy Spirit and by revelation and prophecy.

The responsibility of the apostles could be compared to the role of Moses. Ex 18:15-16. The judges selected by Moses. Ex 18:24-26. Deborah. Judg 4:4-5. Samson. Judg 15:20. Samuel. 1 Sam 7:15-17. The apostles were to inform the people of the divine instruction and decide on matters pertaining to their new life in the Messianic community. Those who subjected themselves to the rule of Jesus through his delegated spiritual kings and judges, the apostles, were blessed for the indefinite future and were subsequently delivered from the impending wrath. 1 Thess 1:10.

The people of the era at one point attempted to make Jesus their king, but it was not in accord with his divine intentions. John 6:14-15. After feeding 5000 men, women and children, they exclaimed their advocacy of Jesus as the fulfillment of prophecy. It was only because he gave them food that they wanted to make him king. These people wanted a social state, a welfare state, where they would have free access to the necessities of life and not have to work for it. For this reason he escaped the crowd.

The entrance into Jerusalem just prior to the final Passover of his ministry was an example provided to the people regarding himself in accord with prophecy. Matt 21:1-11, Zech 9:9. Jesus of Nazareth did not enter with military escort of regiments and accompanied by celebrities or in chariots with slaves at his sides. The rulers of the gentiles, the emperors and sultans and despots would enter into cities with great parade and pomp. Jesus rode on a donkey, in a most humble fashion. The arrival of the King-Anointed into Jerusalem was an important event for the city, fulfilling the prophecy of Zechariah. The purpose of such a humble and modest entry was to impress on the people that it was not his intent to subjugate the people using force. Jesus required a willing and voluntary acknowledgement of himself as supreme autocrat of Israel and the uncoersive and elective subjection of themselves to his authority for the indefinite future. He impressed upon the people that his kingdom was not one consisting of show of power or majesty as was typical of the kings of other nations. His kingdom was spiritual, and could coexist with any other secular kingdom. Likewise, the people were to acknowledge his ability to deliver them from the consequences of their sins. This he accomplished by affirming the moral code of *Yahweh* God. He offered the people forgiveness or expiation of their violations in exchange for repentance and conversion.

## JESUS AND HIS FAMILY

That the family of Jesus understood his claim as all of Messiah, high-priest, and king of Israel, is noticed in their attitude towards him in John 7:2-5. His own family did not accept his claims, and perhaps due to sibling rivalry, or envy, or due to the criticism of others towards Jesus was now affecting the unity of the family. The suggestion that Jesus go to Jerusalem to celebrate the Feast of Tabernacles in public was a chide towards Jesus, and has its basis in an event recorded in 1 Macc 10:18-21. It was during the Feast of Tabernacles that Jonathan son of Mattathias accepted the position of ruler and high-priest over Israel in about 152 BC. For this reason, the brothers chided Jesus, that if he was going to become king and high-priest, why not during this feast, Tabernacles, as did Jonathan, one of the Maccabees, who removed the Greeks and their Hellenic influence from Judea in early centuries. Jesus then reprimanded his brothers, telling them that the time for him to assume these capacities had not yet arrived. John 7:6. He knew their thoughts.

## PREDESTINATION

In order to accomplish His work on earth, *Yahweh* God selects individuals on earth on a regular basis and designates them for His purpose. These are the predestined, who are leaders, prophets, priests, and apostles, the few through whom *Yahweh* God speaks, acts, and leads. Although they were predestined for this responsibility, they will still be judged and rewarded or penalized on an equal basis with the balance of created humanity. Paul apostle wrote that the members of the assembly at Ephesus were predestined for their election. They no doubt had important work to accomplish among the gentiles in regard to the gospel of the kingdom.

> He chose us in him before the foundation of the world, that we should be holy and blameless before him. He predestined us in love to be His sons through Jesus the Anointed, according to the purpose of His will. Eph 1:4-5.

The fact that these were predestined for this special work does not elevate them above the remaining population. Predestination applies only to a select few who are assigned some specific commission, some essential divine purpose to fulfill during their earthly career. They arise only as the need arises, on the occasion when the demand necessitates their intervention and due to the complex religious and political environment which only *Yahweh* God has control over and thorough knowledge of. *Yahweh* God knows whom to select and when and where, a Samson or Jephthah or Samuel or Ezra, for His purpose to be fulfilled under the circumstances. Ps 75:6-7. What is important is not to be a Biblical hero or martyr, but to be obedient to those who have the divine assignment for the salvation of the people. The reward is the same. Jesus described it in the following manner.

> "He who accepts a prophet in the name of a prophet shall receive a prophet's reward." Matt 10:41.

It is not necessary to be a prophet or Biblical hero or predestined for a special purpose to receive a special reward. The equivalent reward is reserved for the obedient.

## EXAMPLES OF PREDESTINATION

Noah was definitely selected by *Yahweh* God to preach repentance to the disobedient world prior to the flood. But several years after the flood, maybe 15 or 20 years, Noah lapsed into depression, and got drunk. After recovering from his hangover and discovering how his youngest son viewed his naked body while passed out on his tent floor, he cursed Canaan his grandson. It is obvious that the effects of the flood destroying the world and *Yahweh* God delivering only Noah and his family was psychologically devastating for Noah in later years. The impact and realization of the consequences of the flood took some time for its effect on Noah: the millions or billions of humans to die by drowning; cities and civilizations destroyed; cultures perishing, never to surface again. The world was a massive devastation of mud and debris and the stench of decay when Noah left the ark and set his feet upon dry ground. For Noah and his family to repopulate and recreate a new civilization on earth posed more of a strain. True, Noah did offer to *Yahweh* God a sacrifice of thanksgiving after their deliverance from the flood, and *Yahweh* God did conclude a new covenant with Noah and his descendents, but several years later, after rebuilding a new life on the ravaged plain beneath Mt. Ararat, the impact of the events took their toll on Noah. A vineyard planted from a stem or seed takes about 7 seasons to become productive, and Ham had by this time a son who was already at least a teenager, at an accountable age. This is when Noah fell into depression.

The intent here is not to discredit Noah or denigrate him as a faithful servant of *Yahweh* God, but is mentioned only to show that Noah was a human like our own self, that his election and predestination did not make him supernatural or superhuman, or elevated above others. There was no excuse for what Noah did, any more than for any other person. The same provisions apply to all Bible heroes where extensive information is noted, enough to develop a biography and distinguish character traits.

Scripture relates Moses, "was very meek, more than all men that were on the face of the earth." Num 12:3. But in earlier years he flew into a rage and killed an Egyptian man. Ex 2:12. Later he displayed this same violent temper when he struck the rock to let water flow, instead of speaking to it. Num 20:10-11. Likewise obvious are his complaints to *Yahweh* God about having the leadership over the people, that it was not his responsibility. Num 11:10-15. For all of this Moses was sternly rebuked by *Yahweh* God and had to answer for all his unacceptable actions.

David king and Psalmist had several failures, all of which made his life difficult and especially in later years. He reached such a pinnacle as warrior, defender and governor that his ego became so inflated he felt he could do no wrong. This is one of the dangers of having absolute power: it corrupts absolutely. As king he felt he could do whatever he so chose, and without having to answer to anyone for it. So it was under these circumstances that he proceeded with his affair with Bathsheba the wife of Uriah the Hittite and arranged for the death of her husband. Even though David did not personally kill Uriah, his death occurring during a siege of an enemy city, David arranged his death. David conspired with the commander of his army to make sure that Uriah would prematurely die in battle. *Yahweh* God still placed the responsibility on David; it was as if David had killed Uriah personally. This is how *Yahweh* God felt, and so David had to answer for Uriah's blood. This penalty materialized in the various difficulties in David's own family: the death of Bathsheba's child through David; the rape of Tamar; the murder of Amnon, the exile of Absalom; the subsequent rebellion of Absalom; and his attempt to gain the kingdom; and finally the murder of Absalom. In later years his reign was plagued with conspiracy and rebellion.

## THE BENEFITS OF PREDESTINATION

The point to be made in the above is that predestination can become a massive detriment if the ego is inflated because of success or honor or because of the realization of this pre-ordained election. Every one of these examples were selected for this divine capacity and gifted with divine capabilities to execute their task. But as the responsibility is greater, so is the judgment for actions if they become a stumbling block or bad example or lead people astray.

Balaam serves as another example. He was initially hired to curse Israel by Balak king of Moab. Num 22:6-7. However *Yahweh* God appeared to him 3 times with a blessing upon Israel. Num 23-24. Also a 4th time did Balaam prophesize regarding Israel and the nations. Num 24:15-24. Balaam was not a prophet in the true sense of the word, but a seer or diviner. The interesting point to be noticed here are Balaam's words,

> "Let me die the death of the righteous, and let my end be like his." Num 23:10.

He wanted to conclude his years as a righteous man, leaving behind a good memory. But later Balaam conspired with elders of Moab, counseling them to introduce their daughters to the young male population of Israel. In this manner the Moabites would be able to corrupt the morals of the Israelites. Because of this conspiracy, he was executed by the Israelite army on their invasion into the promised land. Num 31:8. Because Balaam became a traitor at a later date, he answered for his intrigue with his own life, dying a very unrighteous death.

Jeremiah was selected and predestined by *Yahweh* God as a prophet even before he was born. Jer 1:5. Jeremiah was probably not as intelligent as many personalities in Scripture, but he knew what was right, what was proper conduct, and what was acceptable to *Yahweh* God. In some ways he had a narrow view, but this was necessary for him to keep him focused on his mission: for Judea to repent before total destruction of the nation by the army of Babylon. But there was no personal glory gained by Jeremiah, nor could any be gained. A very meek person, more so than Moses, I feel, because his sole purpose was to accomplish *Yahweh* God's command, so necessary for the era. Jeremiah was the type of person who viewed the reward as the successful accomplishment of the work

Because of his rebuke of their crimes Jeremiah had people seeking to kill him. Jer 11:18-19. In one passage he mentions His children abandoning him. Jer 10:20. But in another passage he is told not to have a wife because of the difficulty of the era. Jer 16:2. Perhaps like Ezekiel, his wife passed away and so the command referred to remarriage. Eze 24:18. The very people whose life he was attempting to deliver wanted to execute him as a traitor, so they took him and confined him at the bottom of an abandon cistern, hopefully to die there, starve to death. Jer 38:4. Jeremiah prophet of *Yahweh* God sat in the mud, abandoned to die by the very individuals whom he hoped would repent so their life would be spared by *Yahweh* God. Jer 38:6. Any person in their right mind would have long abandoned the effort to warn and try to deliver these traitors, and would have concentrated on himself and his own family, and not waste time on anybody else.

Baruch the secretary of Jeremiah did not suffer or perish in the siege and victory of Babylon over Judea as a result of his assistance of Jeremiah. Jer 45:5. Likewise for Ebedmelech the Ethiopian who rescued Jeremiah from the mud at the bottom of an abandoned cistern. Jer 39:17. The earthly reward was far greater for those who obeyed the words of Jeremiah, than for Jeremiah himself.

The few that obeyed Jeremiah were delivered from the destruction. Even after all that Jeremiah prophesied was fulfilled in detail before their very eyes, the remnant requested divine revelation through him a second time. Jer 42:3. After again disclosing to the remnant the will of *Yahweh* God for them, he was again rejected. Eventually Jeremiah was taken to Egypt by rebellious Jews only to die there. Jer 43:7. The earthly reward was far great for those who obeyed the words of Jeremiah.

## NEW TESTAMENT PREDESTINATION

The next example of the predestination of the elect of *Yahweh* God is John son of Zachariah, commonly known as John the Baptizer. Prophesied by the messenger Gabriel to his father while he was burning incense in the temple, John was to fulfill the prophetic words of Malachi: Luke 1:17. Mal 4:5-6. No doubt John accomplished much in Judea in that era working in the spirit and power of Elijah to reconcile families, to turn the hearts of the parents to the children and the hearts of the children to the parents, to establish family harmony. But John was likewise inspired by the same holy Spirit to reprimand Herod Antipas for divorcing his wife, a daughter of king Aretas of Arabia, and marrying Herodias, his niece as well as the divorced wife of his half-brother Herod Phillip. Even though Herod Antipas had a favorable inclination towards John the Baptizer, to listen to his advice and divine instruction, Herod Antipas was still a servant of the Roman government and involved in both family and national politics, and had his worldly ways. Because of this the subsequent result was the execution of John the Baptizer by decapitation. Matt 14:10.

No doubt many felt that John was foolish for getting involved with the intrigues of the Herod family in the first place: corrupt in politics; violent in dealing with Jewish denizens; treachery within their own family. John was doomed the minute he opened his mouth and exposed the illicit and incestuous marriage of Antipas and Herodias. He essentially dictated his own death sentence by voicing divine disapproval of their relationship. Anybody in their sanity and senses would distance themselves from the Herod family in the difficult environment of Judea of the 1st century AD. As indicated in precious examples, there is no glory to be gained, no reward, no name in neon lights, for being a John the Baptizer. He was selected and predestined for this work and fulfilled the commission.

Sometimes I wonder why anybody would want to become a Bible hero; better to be a peon in the eyes of *Yahweh* God and the people and live a Bible-based life and inherit the blessings of *Yahweh* God. Why try to save the religion or nation with the reward so meager relative to the effort? Paul apostle wrote of "the daily pressure upon me of my anxiety for all the churches." 2 Cor 11:28. And how at his first trial before Nero Caesar, "all abandoned me." 2 Tim 4:16. He lists several men who deserted him when difficulties arose: Demas, Cresens, Titus. 2 Tim 4:10. Alexander the coppersmith, "who did me great harm." 2 Tim 4:14. It was only *Yahweh* God who rescued Paul apostle from the jaws of the lion Nero Caesar at his first trial. 2 Tim 4:17. But at his second trial Paul apostle was convicted of some crime, sentenced and executed. What a pathetic conclusion to the apostle's ministry.

Perhaps this is the reason for the statement as pertaining to John the Baptizer, as he would receive his life back in the first resurrection:

And I also saw the souls of those who were beheaded for their testimony to Jesus and for he word of God... Rev 20:4

Paul apostle describes his own dilemma,

"Woe unto me if I do not preach the gospel." 1 Cor 9:16-18.

Paul realized he had this obligation but no reward for it, because it was not of his own free will but the commission assigned him at an early time by *Yahweh* God. His only reward in the work of an apostle was personal, a personal accomplishment on behalf of *Yahweh* God. His actual reward in the future kingdom would be based on his Bible-based life, equal with all other at the judgment seat of the great white throne.

## THE ELECT OF YAHWEH GOD

The assembly of *Yahweh* God existed from the beginning with the first family, and throughout history without interruption. It is and was the will of *Yahweh* God that there always remains on earth an assembly of true believers or true worshippers. The number of these could be many, as with the nation of Israel, as many as the stars in the sky and grains of sand on the sea shore. Or the number could as small as the family of Noah or the family of Abraham. Or relatively small, as the 7,000 who would not bow the knee to Baal. 1 King 19:18. Or the number that returned to Judea after 70 years of residence in Babylon.

The elect are in a sense one rung lower than those predestined, predestination as defined in the examples cited. The elect are those selected by *Yahweh* God generation after generation to continue presence of the assembly of *Yahweh* God and the institution of true and proper worship and obedience of *Yahweh* God. They are a small group and are also called the remnant.

These received the law and traditions from their parents and grandparents, elders and sages, and transmitted it to the next generation. From Adam and Seth the law of *Yahweh* God was transmitted orally to the era of Noah; from Noah to Shem and through the generations to Abraham. Following the genealogy there are many overlaps in the lives of the patriarchs. The following chronology was assembled to grasp the chronology of the patriarchs following the flood. I accept at face value the ages that are in the Hebrew Bible of the descendants of Adam and Noah. This short chronology is based on the flood occurring year 1.

| | |
|---|---|
| Year 1: | The year of the flood. |
| | Noah was 600 years old. He died 350 years after the flood. |
| | Shem was 98 years old. He died 600 years after flood. |
| Arpakshad | Born 2 years after the flood. |
| Shelah | Born 37 years after the flood. |
| Eber | Born 67 years after the flood. Died year 531 after the flood. He outlived Abraham by 64 years |
| Peleg | Born 101 years after the flood. |
| Reu | Born 131 years after the flood. |
| Serug | Born 163 years after the flood. |
| Nahor | Born 193 years after the flood. |
| Terah | Born 222 years after the flood. |
| Abraham | Born 292 years after the flood. He died 467 years after the flood. (Noah died when Abraham was 58 years of age.) |
| Isaac | Born 392 years after the flood. Died 572 years after the flood. |
| Jacob | Born 452 years after the flood. Died 599 years after the flood. (He died the year before Shem died.) |

Note in the table that Shem son of Noah outlived Abraham by 133 years, and Isaac by 28 years. And that Eber, the patriarch and namesake of the Hebrews, outlived Abraham by 64 years. Jacob patriarch was 79 years old when Eber died. This is some evidence that the descendents of Eber were a formidable segment of the population in the area of Mt Ararat during the years of the sojourn of Abraham, Isaac and Jacob in Canaan, and Joseph in Egypt. I contend that the 12 tribes also consisted of other descendents of Eber that entered Egypt with Jacob and years following, that eventually attached themselves or identified themselves with one of the 12 tribes.

Abraham living in Haran may have personally known both Shem and Eber. Haran is a short distance from Ararat, the mountain upon which the ark settled. If Shem and Eber remained in the area of Ararat in the centuries following the flood, then Abraham could have met with him I contend this occurred, and that the law and covenants and anti-deluvian history was transmitted to Abraham and his household by Shem. The son of Noah would have related to patriarch Abraham the history of the world from creation and through the flood and regarding the era following the flood, including the incidents of Noah's curse on his grandson and the Tower of Babel and mix of languages. Shem would have transmitted this record just as he received it from great-grandfather Methuselah and grandfather Lamech, who both died the year of the flood (or perhaps in the flood), and his father Noah. Methuselah was 243 years old, and Lamech was 56 years old, when Adam died. (Noah was born 126 years after Adam died.)

Jacob likewise while living in Haran for 20 years with father-in-law Laban may also have communicated with Shem at least, if not also Eber. He took this history and moral code back to Canaan and then to Egypt to pass on to his grandchildren.

The purpose of this exercise is to provide the reader a basis for the uninterrupted and continuous transmission of divine information from the beginnings in the garden of Eden and through the time of the migration of the 12 tribal patriarchs into Egypt. This same information was then transmitted orally those 430 years until recorded by Moses in the deserts of Sinai as a permanent record for the new nation of Israel. Moses compiled what is known as the *Torah*, the first 5 books of Holy Scripture, during the 40 years in the desert, and concluded Deuteronomy just prior to the entrance of Israel into the promised land. (Some scholars feel Moses also compiled the book of Job during the same interval.)

The reader is well aware of the transmission of this codified law and divine record of history from this point to the future eras by the prophets and sages of Israel. The Jewish tradition focuses on Ezra as the prime individual after Moses to codify the balance of the books. After the 5 books identified as the Torah, the balance are labeled the Prophets and Writings. Ezra compiled all of them into one codex the scribes later titled the *Tanahk*, known to Christians as the Old Testament.

## THE REMNANT

That segment of Israel during the 1st century that accepted Jesus as the Anointed and entered into his new covenant is the remnant. As mentioned earlier, every age has its remnant of Israel selected by *Yahweh* God for true faith and true religion to continue. This remnant is mentioned in Rom 9:27-28, 11:5. Only a fraction of the Jews of 1st century Jewry accepted Jesus as the Anointed and these are the remnant. The 3,000 from the dispersion who accepted through the preaching of Peter apostle and the others on Pentecost would be considered this remnant. Acts 2:41. Also included would be those mentioned in Acts 4:4, increasing the number to 5,000. Other lesser quantities of Jews living throughout the empire that accepted Jesus as the Anointed and entered into the new covenant completed the number or census of the remnant of Israel. These included the few at Antioch, Phoenicia, and Cyprus. Acts 11:19, 26. Thessalonica and Berea. Acts 17:4,12. And others as mentioned in Rom 11:5.

# 3. THE SALVATION OF GOD

## THE SALVATION OF GOD

The salvation of God is deliverance from the evil of our age and the failures of the society that surrounds us and tends to pervade our life; it is the victory over temptation; it is success in those areas of our life that we have control of, a prosperity that is both spiritual and material. A person attains the salvation of God when the plagues that affect society to its ruin are not present in the covenant member's life. The morality and commandments of God lead us to this salvation: a personal, marital, domestic and community success. Those areas that a person does have control over are physical, psychological, domestic and financial. This is all attainable because God promises this to the covenant member.

> If you observe these laws and are diligent to follow them, then *Yahweh* your God will keep His covenant of love with you, as He swore to your forefathers. He will love you and bless you and increase you. Deut 7:12-13.
> I will look upon you with favor and make you productive, and I will keep My covenant with you. I will walk among you and be your God and you will be My people. Lev 26:9, 12.

This does not mean that a person is immune from all the evil that can plague them in their life. The areas a person has no control over are natural: illness and disease, accidents, weather related calamities, and death The covenant member will make the best of any situation they incur and persevere and not allow such disruptions to ruin their life, or family or community.

## FAITH IN JESUS

Faith in Jesus is to realize without a doubt that *Yahweh* God His Father will treat us justly if we accept the rule of Scripture over our life. Faith in

Jesus means that if a person will conduct them self according to the divine instruction and moral law then *Yahweh* God will without doubt fulfill His promises. This is why Jesus is the surety or guarantor or the terms and conditions of the new covenant. Heb 7:22. He is the one who guarantees the blessing and reward, protection and salvation, assistance and spiritual strength, for the people of his spiritual realm, who subject themselves to his rule over them.

To place our hopes upon Jesus, to take our concerns and place them in his hands, is to acknowledge without doubt that all that will occur in our life and situations will be to our overall benefit and to the credit of *Yahweh* God if we persevere in observance of divine instruction and the moral law. 1 Pet 5:7. Ps 37:5. 2 Time 2:11-13. Faith is not religion. Faith in Jesus is not the fulfillment of rites and traditions and protocol. These are good and can direct us to faith as a schoolmaster or guide, as were the OT priesthood and tabernacle/temple services. Faith is knowing that all thing work together for the good for those who love *Yahweh* God and are called according to His purpose. Rom 8:28.

This is the manner faith in Jesus fits into the concept of the covenant. In order to a person to enter into covenant they must first believe Jesus, knowing that he will guarantee that the covenant will be upheld by *Yahweh* God. If the person accepts this as fact then the covenant becomes effective, but only so long as the person believes in Jesus, and belief is indicated by observance of divine instruction. When a person gives up or abandons believing that Jesus will guarantee the fulfillment of covenant, that individual departs from the moral code and divine instruction. This is a lapse in faith or backsliding. Such an individual can always and at any time return to covenant inclusion by again making the decision to observe divine instruction and moral code.

## THE MORAL CODE OF THE COVENANT

The moral code installed with the initial residents in Eden was later codified as the 10 statements or addresses, but popularly referred to as the 10 Commandments. Twice were these commands transmitted to the people of Israel. First at Mt. Sinai. Ex 20: 2-17. And a second time to the next generation at the Jordan River. Deut 6-21. All of the commandments are recognizable in the rules and covenants prior to Moses and in the conduct of the patriarchs. Many authors have written volumes of treatises on the value and application of the 10 commandment. I will only provide a brief sketch of their meaning and observance pertaining to the covenant between *Yahweh* God and the community, and their inclusion in the contemporary life of a member of the Messianic community.

The fact that the 10 commandments are just as valid under the New Covenant as they were under the old is demonstrated by the passage of Matt 19:16-19. When a young ruler asked Jesus regarding his conduct and behavior in order to inherit eternal life, Jesus told him, "Keep the commandments." The young ruler wanted Jesus to further specify which commandments, since no doubt there were many. Jesus then related to him the 5 of the 10 commandments that dealt with personal relationships with others, and also to have the same sincere concern for his associate as he would for himself, love. The ministry Jesus confirmed the code of conduct instituted in earlier ages, and there is no indication of any NT person altering the moral code of the OT. The writings of the NT confirm this in several passages, and which have been mentioned throughout this volume The following statements of Paul apostle especially apply to the validity of the moral code, which he inherited from his teachers in Judaism.

> So the law is holy, and the commands are holy and just and good. Rom 7:12.
> Owe no one anything except to love one another, for he who loves another has fulfilled the law. For the commandments, "You shall not commit adultery," "You shall not murder," "You shall not steal," "You shall not bear false witness," "You shall not covet," and if there is any other commandment, are all summed up in this saying, namely, "You shall love your neighbor as yourself." Love does no harm to a neighbor; therefore love is the fulfillment of the law. Rom 13:8-10

This code of conduct and moral law was to be inherited by the gentiles as part of their entrance into the new covenant. To the extent they upheld this law, to that extent they would be blessed by *Yahweh* God. In retrospect, the blessing would be a materialization of the benefit from implementing this moral code, which is a righteous humanity, an honorable society. The attainment of such a community would be promoted by mutual forgiveness and reconciliation, the work of the holy Spirit in the sanctification of the members, and their personal dedication to the community and work of

*Yahweh* God. The letters of Paul apostle dictate a high moral standard to those members of the Messianic communities, both Jew and gentile.

## NO OTHERS GODS

Every deity represents or identifies with something. *Yahweh* God was to be identified as that deity who was creator of the universe. Neh 9:6. Acts 14:15. None of the other deities could claim this. They were individually identified with the elements of nature, or as fabrications of ignorant and superstitious people. *Yahweh* God was also to be identified as the deity who led the descendents of the patriarchs from enslavement in Egypt to the promised land. He was also to be identified as a moral code. This was the distinction between *Yahweh* God and the gods of the nations, He was the personification of a moral code, while the others were to be appease by gifts and offerings. The departure of people from worship of *Yahweh* God was to abandon the moral code He represented.

All conduct of an individual stems from their concept of right and wrong. This is why Jesus stated that the wrongs a person does evolve from his heart, meaning the inner person. Matt 15:18-19. Right and wrong are determined by a person based on their moral training, or their lack of moral training. For the believer in God, the Christian, the sole criteria for conduct in personal life and society is the morality of *Yahweh* God. This is why Jesus stated:

> I am the way, the truth, and life. No one comes to the Father except through me. John 14:6.

There is only one definition of correct conduct, and it is the one provided by Scripture personified in this verse by Jesus, and there is no correct knowledge of deity, except for that provided us by him and his apostles, since they continued to teach what he taught them. This is why the apostles wrote to the members of Messianic communities for them to increase in the knowledge of God and Jesus, because this correct knowledge is the key to correct conduct. Titus 1:1-2. 2 Pet 1:2. Judgment is based on conduct, and correct conduct can only be practiced with a correct knowledge of deity, and especially what the deity represents. By gaining the knowledge available though Jesus regarding his Father and His morality a person can draw close to the Father, and attain the kingdom. Conduct is not to be defined by psychologist or philosophers, and there is no room in "Christian" theology for ancient or modern philosophy, or pagan intrusions, or political-economic liberation, or existentialism. The study and use of the concepts derived from these teachings are a worship of other gods.

## NO IMAGES

*Yahweh* God was to be recognized as a spirit. He was not to be identified with the elements of nature, or heavenly bodies or represented by any material object or created entity. Moses mentioned to the people at the Jordan River, that their parents recognized *Yahweh* God as a spirit at Mount Horeb. Deut 4:12,15. *Yahweh* God generated sound waves that were perceived by the entire assembly as spoken words emanating from the mountain. This is why those most distant from the mountain heard audible and clear words.

It is an insult and discredit to *Yahweh* God to try to represent Him in some artistic or fabricated figure. This likewise pertains to any Biblical personage and their use in worship.

Worship in spirit and truth is the manner *Yahweh* God must be venerated. John 4:23-24. This means without the use of any pictures or symbols or rites or utensils. Acknowledging *Yahweh* God as an omnipresent and omniscient spirit is the goal of spiritual worship, and that observance of the moral code is the prime manner of indicating veneration toward Him.

The fact that Cherubim were on the ark of the covenant, and that Solomon adorned his temple with pictorials did not invalidate the rule. These were exceptions to the rule due to the barbaric nature of ancient people. For the Messianic community there was no exception to the rule: worship was in spirit and truth.

## HONOR FOR THE NAME YAHWEH

Respect of supreme deity was important to establish *Yahweh* God as ruler over Israel His people. The name of *Yahweh* God was not to be loosely or arbitrarily used, not in profanity, ridicule, humor or frivolous oaths or curses. A name is a person's identity. A reputation gained by a person is attached to him and her the balance of their life. Through slander or liable a person's reputation can be ruined for life. *Yahweh* God likewise has a reputation. Ex 34:10. To properly magnify their supreme deity the people had to hold *Yahweh* God in high regard, and in this manner His reputation would likewise spread to the other nations, as opposed to their fabricated deities.

## THE REST DAY

The Hebrew word for rest is Sabbath.

*Yahweh* God implemented one day every 7 days for the family to relieve themselves from responsibilities and to bond together. A person working daily has their mind obsessed with worry about making a living. The morning, day and evening routine of work, eat, and sleep, and government politics, national economy, competition, quality and business conduct, can and does drive a person away from domestic happiness. For many men and women, their success is their vocation. Over-involvement in earning a living and business will distance a person from their real source of happiness, contentment and satisfaction: their family. For this reason *Yahweh* God instituted for Israel a cessation from work one day every 7, and the command to spend that day entirely with the family. For the family to pray, dine and socialize together for the day is important for marital and domestic success. This creates a close family bond to last thousands of generations. The Sabbath is a blessing to the members of the spiritual Israel, new and old, to be able to rest from obligations and spend the day with family. *Yahweh* God will also provide financially in 6 days of work for cover for the $7^{th}$. Ex 16:29.

Jesus made the statement:

The Sabbath was made for man and not man for the Sabbath. Mark 2:27.

Much controversy has been created over whether the proper day of rest for the Christian should be Saturday or Sunday. I do not want at this point to delve into the issue, but note that one day does need to be set aside as a Sabbath or rest day by each family on a regular routine.

## HONOR OF PARENTS

This is the first commandment with a promise. Eph 6:2-3. Along with parents this equally applies to all those in a family or community higher in rank or order than yourself. Lev 19:32. This attitude engenders a respect for authority, and which must be impressed on individuals from a young age. This respect will then continue on their entire life and be passed to the next generation. The result of a lack of respect for parents and authority is domestic discord and violence, juvenile delinquency and crime, drug abuse, immorality and its consequences. Only with diligent discipline can respect for authority be impressed on both young and old. Pr 13:24, 22:6. The benefit of such training is long term domestic and community success.

The law of *Yahweh* God also had provisions for rebellious and incorrigible young men. This was capital punishment. Deut 21:18-21. In this manner the balance of young men of the community would learn a lesson and develop a respect for parental authority and become good citizens. A similar rule was also legislated for females, but only in the most extreme of circumstances. In this manner did *Yahweh* God impress upon both young men and women respect for both parents and the priesthood. Maltreatment and insult of parents and elders is serious misconduct and was not tolerated by *Yahweh* God.

## DO NOT MURDER

The initial application of this commandment is to curb violence. All disagreements are to be settled using peaceful or amiable means, and animosity was never to erupt into violence. Coercion was unacceptable conduct.

This commandment likewise pertains to the fact that a single individual on an arbitrary basis does not have the right to deprive another of their life. Scripture defines a systematic method of dealing with capital crimes that would result in capital punishment. There was a justice system implemented consisting of witness to a crime, judges to try the case in all fairness, and an investigation to ascertain the validity of both charges and witnesses. Capital punishment is not murder; it is justice.

Whoever sheds the blood of a person, by a person shall their blood be shed. Gen 9:6.

The purpose of capital punishment is to eradicate crime or criminal conduct from the community. Deut 13:11. The members of the community will hesitate to commit a heinous crime if an efficient and strong criminal justice system exists. The members can then live in safety and security. If the criminal justice system is weak, crime will increase. Eccl 8:11.

Only with a respect for the life, property and reputation of others and an organized judicial system can a civilized society succeed.

The issue of war and military service is discussed in the final section of this volume.

## NO IMMORALITY

Every male has a responsibility that reaches into the successive generations. This can only be guaranteed with a stable and honorable matrimony. The institution of marriage at the beginning of settlement in Eden was earlier discussed. For a husband to be satisfied with his wife, and for a wife to respect her husband can not be overstated in Scripture. Pr 5:15, 18. Mal 2:14. Eph 5:33. Marital fidelity is a trait of the Christian husband and wife.

*Yahweh* God created the marital drive in both men and women and it is good. If it were not for the drive there would be no reproduction, all relationships would be platonic. A male achieves personal fulfillment during marital relations and coincidentally with the means of formation of a new creature, a child, physically patterned after image and likeness of its parents and spiritually patterned after the image and likeness of *Yahweh* God. The female likewise achieves personal fulfillment during marital relations with the goal of conception. The two together become one physically during the progress of physical love. Because of the deep psychological impact of such a divinely implemented union, this was to be confined to a legitimately married couple, wedded in holy matrimony, in order that love, the mutual concern for the welfare of each other, would prevail during pregnancy, delivery and parenthood.

For this reason marital relations are to be taken seriously in every culture and community. The culture and couple that follows the dictates of a monogamous marriage within a Scripture based life is promised the blessings of *Yahweh* God, generation after generation.

Any deviation from the above pattern is detrimental to the life span of either sex and causes both psychological and physical degradation. Homosexuality, pedophilia and promiscuity are all a departure from the divinely inspired state of proper relationship between the sexes. Celibacy imposed on individuals by tenets of their religion have done more damage than good in the centuries such religions have existed. Women are deprived of an opportunity to marry and raise a family because of monastic celibacy. The attempt to curb the drive in the male through austerity and religious conviction only causes it to be stored until it finally erupts. Pedophilia, homosexuality, and other promiscuity is well documented among the celibate clergy of these religions. This also adds to the inability of the priest to identify and sympathize with the parishioners of their congregations. The reason for imposition of celibacy by a religious hierarchy is to provide them with the ability to control the lives of those subservient to them.

Nunnery or female religious celibacy is a type of indentured servitude imposed on women by men under the guise of religious service. This servitude deprived women of self esteem in early years, and turned them into slaves. By promoting women at an early age to become nuns and renounce the "ways of the world" they became a cheap form of labor. Their dedicated servitude is utilized by religious hierarchy at schools, hospitals, convents, churches and as cooks and housekeepers for the upper religious clergy at no cost, and inculcated with the impression they are doing God a service. This likewise deprives women of the opportunity to enjoy married life and a family of their own. Men will likewise answer to *Yahweh* God for this imposed slavery of women under the guise of religious obligation.

Marriage is a purpose for life for each of the couple, and produces for each partner a reason to persist for the future, as well as a trust. Without a lifelong mate, a person loses fulfillment in life. Without a concrete and worthwhile goal a selfish life is a futile life. *Yahweh* God is love, and this is only effective if there is an object of His love. Likewise with a person. This nature of *Yahweh* God in a person drives an individual to seek an object for his love, which then becomes the purpose for his life. The purpose of a husband is to make the wife happy, and the purpose of a wife is to make the husband happy. Each receives from the other affection, consideration, support, security, loyalty, trust, all that is invested into the marriage. This applies to every marriage, whether god-believing or pagan, civilized or barbarian, rich or poor, educated or ignorant. Such marriages are life long because of the security and personal fulfillment that each spouse receives in the relationship.

Marriage is also the development and existence of mutual trust. Property is common to both spouses, beginning with finances and possessions. But we must look further for the trust in marriage that *Yahweh* God has inaugurated. It is knowing that there is always somebody that has a sincere concern for your welfare. Each of the spouses can always trust that the other will be there when they are in need. This is genuine security, knowing that there is always someone you can rely on and who has concern for you and will extend help and assistance under any circumstances. They will worry over you when sick, and rejoice with you when you are well; grieve with you in your sorrow, and share your happiness. Only in a marriage is this type of trusting and mutually beneficial relationship to be found.

## DO NOT STEAL

The single most important criteria of an honorable civilization is that of integrity. *Yahweh* God wants his people to trust one another and be honest in every issue, knowing that they will never have to deal with dishonesty in any business deal or personal matter. The members of an honorable society will never be faced with fraud, embezzlement, or scams, or even worry about being short-changed. Only with a mutual trust in business knowing that every contract, negotiation and deal is of the highest integrity will the economy succeed and the financial state of the society increase, and the material prosperity of the members abound. Eph 4:28.

In some countries of the world, a person apprehended appropriating some item not his personal property is punished. A finger or hand is severed, or time is spent in incarceration, or some monetary penalty is imposed. In this manner respect for the property of others is impressed upon them. If that person still continues and still does not learn respect for the property of others, the penalty increases, including exile, until the lesson is learned.

## DO NOT BE A FALSE WITNESS

Many individuals work hard to develop a good reputation. Their name then acquires an identification, one that correlates with their reputation. Character assassination is a crime and will destroy a person's life. Especially damaging is for a person to be innocently accused of a crime, and then put on trial and sentenced to some penalty. Any person discovered accusing an innocent person of a crime was to receive the codified penalty for that crime himself. Deut 19:16-19.

A second facet of the commandment is to lay blame for personal misconduct on another. It is difficult for a person who commits a crime to admit guilt for it. The reasons being self-incrimination and embarrassment. By placing blame for personal misconduct on another, the person is falsely accusing or indicting the other for responsibility. This commandment requires a person to be responsible for their own harmful or corrupt actions, rather than placing blame on another.

I would like to quote the following passages as applicable here:

> Even so the tongue is a little member and boasts great things. See how great a forest a little fire kindles! And the tongue is a fire, a world of iniquity. The tongue is so set among our members that it defiles the whole body, and sets on fire the course of nature; and it is set on fire by hell. For every kind of beast and bird, of reptile and creature of the sea, is tamed and has been tamed by mankind. But no man can tame the tongue. It is an unruly evil, full of deadly poison. With it we bless our God and Father, and with it we curse men, who have been made in the similitude of God. Out of the same mouth proceed blessing and cursing. My brethren, these things ought not to be so. James 3:5-10
>
> Therefore, putting away lying, each one speak truth with his neighbor, for we are members of one another. Let no corrupt communication proceed out of your mouth, but what is good for necessary edification, that it may impart grace to the hearers. Eph 4:24, 29.

Gossip, slander, malign, character assassination, libel, lies, spreading of rumors, false or distorted information, all can cause horrible damage to a person's reputation and often irreparable. As a result every person needs to choose his words or communication wisely not to ruin another person.

## DO NOT ENVY

*Yahweh* God has blessed every person in one manner or another. Every person should be satisfied with the amount of grace and blessing bestowed upon them and the gifts they have received from *Yahweh* God. The purpose of this commandment is to restrain competition and curb excess accumulation of property. Many are driven by a desire for acquisition of goods, houses, property and money, beyond what they would use in their lifetime or several lifetimes.

This is the reason for the treatise of Paul apostle to Timothy beginning with the popular passage,

"For the love of money is the root of all evils." 1 Tim 6:10-19.

This section of Scripture deals with the pitfalls of working to acquire finances beyond that of personal economic stability. Because of an opportunity to gain financial success, a person will lower their standards of morals and ethics, and even commit a crime for financial gain, such as, embezzlement, fraud, petty theft, and robbery.

A person should never view the success of another person with envy, because there is much that occurs in the life of that other person that they are unaware of. Superficially they neighbor appears prosperous flaunting his wealth, but in secret behind closed doors and often tragedy, insecurity and other domestic failure may prevail. For this reason every person should give gratitude to *Yahweh* God for the amount they have been blessed.

## LOVE

The word love, I contend, is the most misused and misapplied of all words in the vocabulary of the world's languages. To resolve this issue, the word will be defined in a simple manner and correlated with Scripture for its application in the Messianic community. Love is a sincere concern for the welfare of another. In general terms this definition is sufficient. Love materializes in kindness, charity, benevolence, honesty, and also justice and securing safety for the community. Any act of injury, insult, discredit or infringement of another is not love. It is crime. Paul apostle described love in this manner.

Love is the fulfilling of the law. Rom 13:10.

When a person conducts himself according to the moral code of *Yahweh* God, it is indicative of love residing in that person. Our associations with and attitudes toward others, our business, home, government, must be conducted according to the moral code to possess love. This likewise pertains to criminal justice. Love for the general population is shown when civil leaders provide a safe and secure environment to live in, and to penalize violations, imprison and rehabilitate convicts and felons. This provides a concern for the suffering and welfare of those violated and injured. Jesus also provided a definition in the following passage.

Let your light shine in the presence of people, so that when they see your benevolence they will give credit to your Father who is in heaven. Matt 5:16.

Love is present when credit is extended to *Yahweh* God in heaven for the actions of individuals toward the benefit of the community and society. Love materializes in the modern society as education, health and medical care, charities for the underprivileged, and assistance for the elderly. Love in every member will promote the development of a righteous humanity and honorable society.

A misuse of the term love is when it is used to justify wrong, or some violation of God's moral code. This is not love, but a wrong in itself.

## BIBLE FAMILIES

A person "leaving his father and mother," means that he severs himself from their responsibility over him, and is now responsible for himself as well as for his wife. Gen 2:24. According to these words parents are responsible for the care of their offspring until they are married. The responsibility of parents is completed with the marriage of their son to a woman of high moral character of their own culture and race, with the cognizance that this is a life long marriage. The adult male now has a responsibility of his own: wife and children. This does not alleviate the honor to be shown parents and elders, as the commandment dictates. Honor and respect is still to be shown. The man leaving the parents and cleaving to his wife is a matter of reassignment of priority and responsibility. The man should never permit his parents to interfere or separate them in their marriage.

For the wife the sign noted is the cover over her head. 1 Cor 11:10. Prior to her marriage she was under the shelter of her parents. They showed her love and affection, comfort, provided her with shelter, subsistence, an education and training for her future life. From the point of marriage, her husband now has the obligation to provide her with love and affection, comfort, shelter and all the necessities of life for happiness into the distant future.

Perusing through Scripture there are many examples of large families. Abraham took Keturah as wife in his later years and had 6 children. Gen 25:1-2. Jacob had 12 sons and a daughter through his 4 wives. Elkanah through his wife Peniniah had sons and daughters. 1 Sam 1:4. And Hannah in her later years had 3 more sons and 2 daughters in addition to Samuel. 1 Sam 2:21. Aaron priest had 5 sons. Ex 6:23. Others with large progeny include Job, Gideon, David, and Josiah. In the NT, Joseph and Mary had 4 sons and 2 daughters subsequent to Jesus. Phillip evangelist had 4 daughters. Jews advocated large families because they interpreted life beyond the grave as themselves alive in their descendents. Annas high priest had at least 5 sons and a daughter.

The parents wanted to be remembered in their children for generations to come. For this reason childlessness was considered a curse. Not to have offspring had such a strong impact on the life of the person or couple, that for many it was as if they had no reason to live, no meaning to life. The tendency in this barbarian era was to place the blame for childlessness on the wife. Such as with Sarah and Rachel. Gen 29:31. Or with Hannah. 1 Sam 1:5. Elizabeth was so overjoyed at finally expecting a child, that she exclaimed:

> So the Lord has done to me in the days when he looked on me, to take away my reproach among men. Luke 1:25.

Apparently in earlier years, men felt that Elizabeth was less of a woman because she was childless, and this was her "reproach among men." (At present, medical investigations indicate that 60% of childlessness in a couple is due to the husband's impotence.) This is the reason a male took another wife, in order that his name not die with him, such as with

Abraham. Gen 16:1-2. The levirate marriage was based on the same premise. The brother of a childless and deceased husband would produce offspring in the name of the brother through his widow. Even though the biological father was the paternal uncle, the child would be considered a son of his deceased father and not a nephew. This way the life of the father would figuratively continue and not terminate. The most severe of the punishments of *Yahweh* God was the extermination of all the descendents of a person. 1 Sam 15:33.

At the same time the Jewish sages also realized that not having children was sometimes a benefit, as it would allow adoption of orphans. This is the hidden meaning of the words of James apostle.

> Pure and undefiled religion before God is to visit orphans and widows and to themselves in their need... James 1:27

In this manner an orphan would be able to acquire a new parent or parents.

The apostle Paul also adopted Timothy whose father, a Greek, seemed to have disappeared and so he was raised by his mother and grandmother. The two of them – Paul and Timothy – were able to fill the void in each of their lives as a result. God had it planned this way. Childless families can also tale this route.

## MALE ABUSE OF THE WEAKER GENDER

The evolution of the abuse of woman in society by man stems from the words of *Yahweh* God to Eve:

> Yet your desire shall be for your husband, and he shall rule over you. Gen 3:16.

*Yahweh* God altered something in the invisible attribute of the female at this time, for her as an individual to no longer be complete psychologically. From the moment these words were spoken, a woman needed a husband in order to feel "fulfilled." The term "rule over" must be defined in terms of someone providing her shelter and protection, long term security, love and affection, and be satisfied with his marriage to her. This can be described in the following and applies in a general sense. Most women want to get married, while most men do not see a pressing demand for matrimony. Most women want to have a husband, wedding ring, a home of their own, children and raise them; most women want to see their sons and daughters marry, and most women want grandchildren. Many women are not particular about whom they should marry, as long as some male of reasonable character asks them. Some women become so desperate for a husband that they will even interfere with the marriage of another and wrestle control from the wife. If not one male then another, as long as that male will rule over them. Most women want their husbands to have control over affairs of the household, finances, business and related matters, although the wife is often just as capable and so does handle the finances. Many women are disenchanted if they cannot find a husband, and feel they are less of a woman. Older women without a husband often feel substandard, undesirable, and loose self-esteem.

The woman who is jilted by a boyfriend or lover, or the wife discovering the infidelity of her husband, is devastated psychological. It is as if the world has collapsed on her and no hope remains. The wounds inflicted by inconsiderate men and husbands leave permanent scars on the weaker sex. Divorce or abandonment by a husband will destroy the morality of the wife, and often causes the woman to go to extremes: affairs with married men, multiply affairs, abortion, suicide, and other social maladies.

Men have unjustifiably taken advantage of this character void in women over the centuries. Men have enslaved women as sex slaves, concubines, mistresses, housekeepers, and forced the most undesirable labor on them. Men historically mistreat women, and take advantage of this psychological as well as physical weakness. Some early cultures would expose female children to the elements for them to die, because male children were considered more important and more valuable for the family. Men deceive women regarding love and impregnate them and abandon them, and then expect women to terminate unwanted pregnancies. Men blame women for every failure of theirs, no different than Adam who blamed Eve. Gen 3:12. Adam and his generations of male progeny are not much for men if they blame their wife and the women. It is the man that should be the head of the household and the courageous gender. In general, men will have much to answer for before *Yahweh* God at the great white throne because of their poor attitude and treatment of women.

When women are described as the weaker sex, it is not only due to physique, but also in regard to the impact that a failed or disrupted relationship can psychologically have on her. 1 Pet 3:7.

The reason deviate sexual conduct is treated so severely in the Bible is because such conduct is a mental or psychological imbalance or deterioration. It is a distortion of values and conduct that is not organic in nature, but psychological. Pornography is a prime cause of deviate sexual behavior as it displays women not as a spouse to be love and cherished with the divine purpose as mentioned above, but as a sex toy or gratification of a man's lust. As a result society that outlaw pornography have higher success rates in marriage and family and children.

Most criminals whose crimes are in categories such as theft or fraud, and certain types of violence can be rehabilitated. For those that commit sexual crimes, there is often no rehabilitation because the root into the nature of a person is grave and incorrigible. Deviate conduct becomes part of a new distorted nature of that person, and which conduct they then consider natural or acceptable. Once the mind is morally depraved by participation in deviate conduct, such as sodomy or bestiality, the penalty specified in the Bible is capital punishment. Lev 20:13, 15.

## DIVORCE

According to Scripture it is with a death of a spouse that marriage is dissolved. Rom 7:2. I Cor 7:39. Divorce is permitted in the Bible, but only due to extreme circumstances. Provisions were provided to permit the dissolution of a marriage, but only to evade a worse evil that could possibly occur from feuding spouses. With a mutually agreeable divorce, violence and further harm would be precluded. Sometimes forcing 2 people to live together would cause more harm. The provision for divorce also allowed a spouse to expel the other for infidelity. This was not mandatory, but could be utilized, and is understandable after psychological devastation of the offended spouse, or with the contraction of a venereal disease.

Divorce was the exception and to be avoided at all costs. Reconciliation was to be provided the couple having difficulty. This was the advantage of marriage within the culture, race and religion, which allowed compatibility in marriage with less opportunity for strife. The extended family of a married couple with their culture, race and religion, would also be of immense benefit to assistance of spouses to secure a marriage for the distant future. The reason Jesus prohibited divorce, was that the partners now living as individuals would easily become immoral. Matt 5:32.

## THE SECULAR KINGDOM AND THE SPIRITUAL KINGDOM

On occasion a choice must be made whether to follow the law of secular and temporal government, business and social dictates, or the divine instruction of *Yahweh* God, if there is a conflict between the 2. The decision lies in loyalty. To which code of ethics or to which supreme deity or to which potentate does the loyalty lie if a conflict or digression should surface. For the citizen of the spiritual kingdom the question of loyalty should be simple, it is toward Jesus, king of Israel. Much like a loyal citizen of some state or dominion, so is the citizen of the kingdom of *Yahweh* God. Pertaining to the secular world, a loyal citizen will not deny allegiance to his country, regardless of inquisition or prosecution by enemies of the state. Even to the extent of deprivation of personal freedom and possession, calumny or death, a loyal citizen will not abdicate their principles or become a traitor.

The secular world is essentially those who represent or acquire authority in arenas of polity, business and finance, military, entertainment, professional sports, and etc. With this authority they enact and legislate principles that are to their own benefit and advantage of their own realm. If such representatives of the secular arenas find it necessary to impose on covenant members conflicting principles, this becomes a trial for the covenant member. Depending on the principle and severity of threats and personal disadvantage to be incurred, the covenant member may decide that the kingdom of *Yahweh* God is not worth defending or worth suffering for. They may feel the kingdom of *Yahweh* God is not worth the allegiance in light of the deprivation or disadvantage imposed, and so their principles will be compromised. Another may lose faith in the promises and shelter of Jesus entirely and apostatize, deny any adherence to Scripture and then voice loyalty to the secular world as defined by their persecutors.

The covenant member will not violate or compromise principles, that is, the divine instruction and moral code. They are fully convinced that whatever should occur is the best for the spiritual kingdom, even if they should incur deprivation of personal freedom and possessions, discredit, or even death. For this reason many over the centuries have endured persecutions. Occasionally the advances from an assailant are withdrawn once they realize that the faith of the individual is solid and genuine.

The defense of true religion is not with the use of force or weapons by the covenant member. The model of Jesus serves as the example. 1 Pet 2:23. The defense is spiritual, it is with the sword of the spirit the word of God, with virtue the gospel of truth, the shield of faith and the helmet of salvation. Not using physical force, but with the armor of *Yahweh* God. Eph 6:13-17. 2 Cor 10:3-4. The enemy is not the individual persecuting the member of the spiritual kingdom. The enemy is the invisible forces of the carnal human nature. For this reason the enemy cannot be defeated with the same type of force or coercion or attack that is being imposed on the member of the spiritual kingdom. In the end the enemy will not win. Even though Jesus was executed, he subsequently resurrected, which was his victory over those who plotted against him, betrayed him and crucified him. Likewise, the persecutors may gain what seems to them a victory over the believer in Jesus, but the real victory will be gained in the future. The victory of the persecutors is temporal and superficial, the victory of the believer in Jesus is eternal and genuine.

## NATURAL GRACE

The grace of *Yahweh* God consists of everything that *Yahweh* God gifts to His created humanity. 1 Cor 4:8-12. All that created humanity possesses is the result of the grace of *Yahweh* God. Love is directly related to grace. Love is more a personal concern or inner emotion. Grace is the specific gift or protection or benefit bestowed on an individual during their life. Grace is the materialization of love.

Because of the weaknesses and flaws of humanity, both physically and psychologically, our inability to control or subdue temper and rage and hate, our subjection to injury, disease, turmoil and subsequent death, humanity is unable to assist itself, to defend itself, or deliver itself from the consequences of its own evil actions. To live in harmony and happiness and to prosper, humanity is dependant on the intervention of *Yahweh* God with His wisdom, strength and capability to help His own creation. If *Yahweh* God did not regularly intervene in the affairs of humanity, the entire population would have long ago destroyed itself. This necessary intervention into the affairs and intentions of people to deliver us from the result and consequences of our own actions is the grace of *Yahweh* God.

> In past generations He allowed all nations to walk in their own ways, yet He did not leave Himself without witness, for He did good and gave you from heaven rain and harvest, satisfying your hearts with food and gladness. Acts 14:16-17.
> He makes the sun rise on [both] evil and good people, and sends rain on [both] wicked and virtuous people. Matt 5:45.

Grace as the materialization of the love of *Yahweh* God can be classified as either natural grace or divine grace. Natural grace is the sunshine upon both the good and evil. Matt 5:45. It applies to creation in general and to created humanity in their entirety. Natural grace is bestowed upon every person born from the progenitors Adam and Eve. Birth, the opportunity to live, is a manifestation of natural grace. Regardless of race, creed, or color; gender, age, physique, or intelligence; whether believing in *Yahweh* God or not believing in god, or believing in a pantheon of gods or superstitions, natural grace applies to every person. It consists of the good fortune to be born, to have conscious existence, to be raised by parents for them to have some joy in their life; to grow and mature and work and live and then eventually die in old age. This is natural grace. It is culture and ingenuity and the wonders of nature. *Yahweh* God contains such an abundance of overwhelming love that there is no end to the creation of objects of His love, whether or not they acknowledge Him or live according to His dictates. The generations continue year after year, century after century and will do so long into the future beyond our ability to comprehend eternity. The spirit of *Yahweh* God renews the face of the earth after devastation by war, hurricanes and monsoons and floods and tornadoes. Ps 104:30. Natural grace is the nature of *Yahweh* God, He cannot conduct Himself otherwise, not in any other manner. His nature is that materialization of love, which is natural grace.

The rejection of natural grace by the individual or by the masses only subjects the individual and the masses to the results of their own disobedience. Such periodic and regular events such as war and crime, persecution, oppression, and related man-made occurrences of suffering are the result of ungrateful attitude by individuals and masses. *Yahweh* God is personally is unaffected by the ravages of disaster and misfortune or the evil and disobedience of people because He is spirit, and there is nothing that can occur that can directly affect Him. Dan 4:35. Is 40:15.

The natural effects of weather and the elements and "acts of God" are imposed by *Yahweh* God on a periodic basis as rain on the just and the unjust. *Yahweh* God instituted this pattern of the effects of nature upon the world to impress upon created humanity His control over His own creation. Natural catastrophes impress upon the mind of every person that if it were not for the abundance of love of *Yahweh* God, His natural grace, no life would every evolve or survive on earth.

## DIVINE GRACE

The purpose of natural grace is to lead people to divine grace. Under natural grace, death is termination of life with no future. Ps 49:14, 90:3, Eccl 3:20. Paul apostle refers to them as having no hope. 1 Thess 4:13. Natural grace applies to the temporal world and its short life span for the masses of population. All such that perish without divine grace perish like animals, as Solomon describes it. Eccl 3:18. Ps 49:12. *Yahweh* God impresses upon every person that their existence evolves from the natural grace of *Yahweh* God. This life is confined to the present age without divine grace. The tragedy and turmoil of the present life is utilized and effected by *Yahweh* God to impress upon created humanity the futility of advancement and excess success of the present life, since it will all terminate. This is the point made by Solomon in Eccl 2. No matter how much he enjoyed the present life, no matter how much he labored to acquire possessions, no matter how much power he achieved, it was all left behind at death, he not ever to know what would occur with his possessions. Prosperity and success are good when utilized for the benefit of others, but when they are taken personally they can deceive the individual. Prosperity and success can give an individual a feeling of superiority or even immortality. Ps 49:5-6. Tragedy and catastrophe is provided by *Yahweh* God upon a person for them not to sense themselves as superior, and not to sense themselves as having total control over every facet of their life. Ps 49:16-19.

To acknowledge divine grace is to be born again or born from above and so see the kingdom of *Yahweh* God. John 3:3. To enter the kingdom a person must be born of the word and the spirit. John 3:6. Divine grace applies to the members of the Messianic community, to the citizens of the kingdom of God. Without *Yahweh* God intervening into the life of this people there would be no sanctification, no mortification of the flesh, no cessation of sin, no return to the image of *Yahweh* God. When Paul apostle wrote, Eph 2:22, he referred to the intervention and concern of *Yahweh* God for His children, sons and daughters. Regardless of what effort or maneuvers an individual may attempt, we cannot on our own acquire divine grace.

## REPENTANCE

Repentance is to admit to a crime or offense committed or an admission of an existing problem or personal vice. Without acknowledgement that a wrong was committed or that a problem exists there will never occur healing. This can be compared to a person who contracts or develops some organic disease or physical malady. If the person denies it they will never seek medical help and so never recover or heal. Since there is no acknowledgement of illness, the disease will progress until it consumes the individual, renders them invalid, and finally premature death is incurred. So it is with morals, ethics and personal conduct. If an individual has a problem, whether it be personal, domestic, financial, there is no opportunity for healing or restoration without an initial acknowledgement. Once the person admits to the crises or deviate conduct or character flaw, then there is opportunity for healing and restoration.

The more serious the disease the more intense the healing process. But it is only to the extent the person wants the healing and restoration. If the physician states that surgery or medicine, or deprivation of certain habits and activities is required, or other activities and therapy must be assumed, then the individual has the option of following the recommendation or not. So it is with sinful nature that requires healing. The person can adhere and observe the dictates of Scripture or not. This is personal choice. Paul apostle describes in this fashion:

> For the wages of crime is death, but the free gift of God is eternal life in the Anointed Jesus our Lord. Rom 6:23.
> Repent therefore and turn again (be converted), that your sins may be blotted out, that times of refreshing may come from the presence of the Lord. Acts 3:19.

The death is premature death in the earthly life, as opposed to a life of blessing and prosperity in accord with Ps 128. The death is also eternal death without opportunity for inheritance of resurrection.

## CONVERSION

Conversion is the decision and implementation of that decision to be healed and to have a person's own life restored: to remove improper conduct from life and change course to an edifying and benevolent morality.

A person sensitive to rejection or easily influenced by opinion or attitude of others who still persists in some improper conduct will discover it difficult to heal and restore themselves, to live life in subjection to and observance of Scripture. An obstacle to conversion lies in the effect that other people opposed to it may have. The repentant person must be strong enough not to allow the adverse opinions or corrupt influence of others to sway them from total restoration.

> If your right eye causes you to sin, pluck it out and throw it away; it is better that you lose one of your members than that your whole body be thrown into Gehenna. And if your right hand causes one of your members to sin, cut it off and throw it away; it is better that you lose one of your members than your whole body go into Gehenna. Matt 5:29-30.
>
> They are surprised that you do not now join them in the same wild immorality, and they abuse you. 1 Pet 4:4.

The inference by Jesus and Peter apostle here is the repentant individual becoming a social cripple. Because the person no longer participates in detrimental or deviate conduct, the balance of old friends and social circle will view the repentant as a social cripple. This is the correlation of missing an eye or limb. But in the view of Scripture, it is better to be considered a social cripple by unbelievers and the corrupt society, because the kingdom of God is still to be entered. Others may be accepted in social arenas of vices and poor conduct, and they are considered whole in the eyes of wicked society, but the kingdom of *Yahweh* God they will never enter. This is the choice an individual caught in this quandary must make: Superficial acceptance by pseudo-friends while denying moral illness leading to ruin and premature death, or seeking and acquiring help for a healing from moral illness, even if the healing requires severance from the closest of social, business or family ties. Even incurring some superficial loss, the advantage of total moral healing is well worth it, since life will continue long on earth and eternally into the future.

> And every one who has left houses or brothers or sisters or father or mother or children or lands, for my name's sake, will receive a hundredfold and inherit eternal life. Matt 19:29.
> Jesus said, "Here are my mother and my brothers. For whoever does the will of my Father in heaven is my brother and sister and mother." Matt 12:50.

These words of Jesus promise a new company of friends, family and associates. He realized how hard it would be for a person to give up previous relationships and associations, as hard as cutting off a limb or plucking out an eye. But it would be necessary in the process of abandoning vice, crime, improper conduct and severance from harmful influences. Moving from an area of temptation to some new environment of a better influence can also be taxing on an individual or family. For this reason Jesus assures the repentant person that he will provide a new family and relationships to develop and new associations from among the new spiritual Israel. These new people would become unto them a new mother, brother and sister. *Yahweh* God will provide a spiritual community for the repentant individual and their family to join. These will be their support and joy and earthly community for the distant future.

## SANCTIFICATION

A part of the work of divine grace, *Yahweh* God sends His holy Spirit for the sanctification of His people, for them to be cleansed of sin and evil and to have their nature modified to that of the nature of *Yahweh* God. This process begins on earth and will continue centuries into the eternal kingdom following our resurrection.

> Be renewed in the spirit of your minds, and put on the new nature created after the likeness of God in true rectitude and holiness. Eph 4:23-24.

Do not be conformed to this age, but be transformed by the renewal of your mind, that you may prove what is the will of God, what is good and acceptable and perfect. Rom 12:2.

If a person cleanses himself, he will be a vessel for noble purposes, made holy, useful to the master and prepared for every good work. 2 Tim 2:21.

Our sanctification is by divine grace. It is the willing and voluntary intervention of *Yahweh* God into the life of His people to draw them unto Himself and mold them into the image that he intends for them. This divine grace fulfills the promises of the patriarchs. An individual on their own cannot cause fulfillment of any promise of blessing of *Yahweh* God. It is solely the discrete choice of *Yahweh* God to do so.

The response to divine grace by the citizen of the kingdom of God is that promise to live according to the precepts of the kingdom. The works that are referred to by James apostle, Jam 2:22-24, pertain to conduct in accord with Scripture. This is also parallel with the words of John apostle. 1 John 2:3,5. This also pertains specifically to conduct, and what is considered proper conduct for members of the Messianic community and spiritual kingdom.

## CIRCUMCISION

No longer is the physical mark of circumcision for the male, or being the daughter and wife of a circumcised male for the female, the indication of membership in the new covenant community. It is now the circumcision of the heart. The spiritual significance of circumcision is fulfilled in both male and female in the new covenant. Gal 5:2,6. Deut 30:10. Jer 4:4. The removal of vices, crime, and other harmful habits from our life is the fulfillment of circumcision. The true member of the new covenant community has the Bible-based life as his outward and pubic display of the spiritual circumcision. The female also by way of a home and family life that is Bible-based indicates her marriage to the Anointed as spiritual husband, he who was the fulfillment of the purpose of circumcision.

(I contend however that circumcision should still be performed on all males by a physician shortly after birth. The concept of circumcision for hygienic reasons is still applicable. The question then arises whether there exists an inherent flaw in the male physique so that circumcision is required. *Yahweh* God definitely created the male in this manner, and specifically with this extraneous skin that must be severed. The reason being primarily hygienic.)

Even though circumcision as an initiation into the covenant was no longer applicable, Paul apostle nevertheless had this operation performed on the young man Timothy. Acts 16:3. It was fine and acceptable for the gentiles not to undergo this procedure, but it was unacceptable for Timothy to remain that way. I am convinced that Paul apostle acted as a type of step-father to Timothy, who apparently had no father to speak of. Timothy's Greek father is nowhere mentioned. Perhaps this inter-religious marriage failed. It is not uncommon for spouses of different religious and cultural and ethnic backgrounds to separate or divorce due to incompatibility. Such may have been the situation with Timothy. In later years Paul apostle adopted Timothy as his son. 1 Tim 1:2. 2 Tim 1:2, 2:1. The pride of a Jewish father of that era and earlier generations was to have his son circumcised according to the command to Abraham, for him to enter into covenant. The same circumstance may also be applied to Timothy. It was a hidden and personal pride of Paul apostle's to have this surgery performed on Timothy by a local rabbi, to have his foster son fully initiated into the covenant community. In this manner was Timothy now recognized by the balance of Jews and Jewish elders as being one of them.

The non-Jew did not need circumcision as the physical sign of the covenant, an indication of their severance from the secular environment and society. The circumcision was spiritual, or the heart. This was witnessed to through the ages and fulfilled in Jesus.

> And *Yahweh* God will circumcise your heart and the heart of your posterity, so that you will love *Yahweh* your God with all your heart and with all your soul, that you may live. Deut 30:6. Jer 32:39.
> In him (the Anointed) also you were circumcised with a circumcision not accomplished with hands, by removing the body of flesh in the circumcision of the Anointed. Col 2:11.

The baptism of the holy Spirit is the new indication of severance from the secular environment and the new sign of entrance into the new covenant.

In the letter to Galatia the attitude of required rite and ritual again surfaced because of influence from the Pharisaic school: that *Yahweh* God must still be appeased and His attention and favor gained through temple maneuvers and ancient customs. At the foremost of these "works" was circumcision. Gal 6:12-15. It is redundant to think that this act, this "mutilation of the flesh," will gain the attention of *Yahweh* God and His favor. This was the error of the circumcision party, it was a reversion to the pagan concept of a god to be appeased by works.

## JUSTIFICATION BY FAITH

Passages such as Is 1:18, 65:3, Ps 32:1-2, refer to confession and repentance, and not to the offering of a sacrifice. The gentile Romans to whom Paul apostle wrote were not familiar with many of these passages of the OT. They were aware of the Jewish sacrificial system with which they could identify animal sacrifices unto their own gods and burning incense to their own emperor, and priests in the temples of their own mystery religions and cults. But the concept of a Savior, whose death was the culmination and goal of all blood sacrifice was foreign to the typical Roman or Greek. Paul apostle explained it to the Greek Corinthians in this manner,

> "But we preach the crucified Anointed: a stumbling block to Jews and foolishness to Greeks." 1 Cor 1:23.

He was right. Jews could not figure out why their Anointed should die as a criminal betrayed by their own elder and rulers. He did not fulfill their preconceived ideas for Jesus. To the Greeks and Romans it was absurd that a religious savoir and son of the Supreme Deity should be executed as a convicted criminal.

To be justified by faith for the Jew and non-Jew meant that it was right in the sight of *Yahweh* God for a person to believe that Jesus was the sacrifice. The reasons for the death of Jesus by crucifixion were discussed in earlier sections. One other can be added. This is the concept that Jesus was the goal or aim of the sacrificial system. John the Baptizer referred to Jesus in these words,

> "Behold the lamb of God who bears the sins of the world." John 1:29.

Paul apostle also refers to Jesus in a similar manner in 1 Cor 5:7. It was not necessary for the members of the new spiritual Israel to offer sacrifices under the new covenant, because the Anointed culminated the sacrificial system with himself. The gentiles now only had to cease or set aside sin in their life believing in the sacrifice of the Anointed on their behalf. In this manner were the gentile members of the new covenant community justified by faith.

In early eras justification was by faith during the fulfillment of a ceremony, meaning that forgiveness occurred when their hands were laid on the head of the sacrifice and the participant recited orally their crimes and failures to the priest in confession. This fulfilled the cover for the sins of the people, but which also contained the rectitude of *Yahweh* God for the era. Rom 4:7. The participant believed that *Yahweh* God in heaven accepted a person's confession and repentance, provided it was accomplished from his heart and sincerely. This was justification by faith in OT eras pertaining to both Jew and non-Jew. Hab 2:4. 1 King 8:46-53.

The non-Jewish member of the new Israel did not need to offer an animal sacrifice. Jesus was the sacrifice for sin. The non-Jewish member was justified by faith in this manner, that if he believed Jesus was the lamb of *Yahweh* God who removes their sin, then it would be fulfilled. The new sacrifice of thanksgiving was the fruit of the lips, praise and gratitude towards *Yahweh* God in public confession. Heb 13:15. Charity became the new tithe unto *Yahweh* God. Heb 13:16. The non-Jewish member of the new Israel did not need a priest to pray or fulfill a rite on their behalf, or stand between them and *Yahweh* God. Jesus became their high-priest. Each of them was also a priest after the order of Melchizedek in their own right and could pray one for the other. The non-Jewish member of the new Israel did not need to attend the temple, because they became the new temple on earth, since the holy Spirit resided in them. The true temple or tabernacle was located in heaven, where Jesus was sacrifice and high priest. In this manner the non-Jews of the spiritual Israel were justified by faith.

## ETERNAL LIFE

In general the disciples did not have a concept of eternal life in terms of life continuing with their resurrection from death. For the typical Jew of the era and previous eras eternal life had 2 meanings: First was the propagation of the family name through their descendents. Second was a long life with prosperity on earth. A person continued to live beyond the grave figuratively in their offspring, and preferably a male. And of course, named after the father or the paternal grandfather. Luke 1:59. This was especially the manner the forefathers and patriarchs understood life eternal or *aionious*. To continue alive in the seed producing the next generation meant to inherit life beyond the grave. Eliphaz reflecting the attitude of his era stated this.

> You shall know that your descendents shall be many, and your offspring as the grass of the land. You shall arrive at your grave in ripe old age, and a shock of grain arrives at the threshing floor in its season. Job 5:25-26.

Resurrection was understood in OT eras as the deliverance of a person from death. This could be a healing from a terminal disease, as with Hezekiah. Is 38. As rhetorically philosophized by Elihu. Job 33:19-30. Or as with the case of Ahaziah king of Israel. 2 King 1:2-4. Or with David king. Ps 116:8.

The Pharisees claimed to believe in life beyond the grave in terms of a future resurrection from the grave at the advent of the Anointed. Their conviction is noted in Act 23:8. But their theology in this matter was very vague and nebulous. The concept was poorly developed among Jews. This conviction was only advocated by a fraction of the overall Jewish population of the world and only in this small circle of the Pharisaic school. In general the Jewish population and Sadducees followed the interpretation mentioned above regarding life beyond the grave and not the Pharisaic notion. For this reason the disciples had a difficult time when Jesus spoke of his rise from death in 3 days. Luke 18:31-34. They could not grasp what it was he was trying to tell them. This idea of a return back alive from death was alien to them. It was not until after the resurrection of Jesus did they finally grasp his words, and only with Jesus at this time removing that mental block. Luke 24:45-46. John 2:22.

## ABUNDANT LIFE ON EARTH

Living long on the earth and prosperously is a fundamental promise of *Yahweh* in the Bible. Pr 3:2. 9:11. Is 65:20. The first commandment with promise was to respect parents and for the reason of being able to live long in the promised land. Ex 20:12. The OT Scripture abounds in promises regarding living in prosperity unto old age as the fulfillment of the favor and blessing of *Yahweh* God upon an individual. Job, Job 5:26. David, Ps 21:4. Solomon, 3:14. All of the patriarchs prior to the flood and including Noah lived about or over 900 years, with the sole exception of Enoch, who only lived 350 years. Abraham lived to 175, while his wife Sarah lived to 127. After the death of Sarah, Abraham remarried to Keturah and had several more children. During the era of David king the lifespan was at 70 years, with many reaching 80 years. Ps 90:10.

During the era of the apostles the mortality rate was high for children. Disease, famine, war, poverty, and other miseries resulting in premature death plagued the life of the population from birth. About 1/3 of the population of the Roman empire were slaves. The Roman Empire of the 1st Century had a 50% mortality rate to adulthood. Very few, a minute fraction, were actually able to live decently to old age and with some prosperity. Jewish sages taught that the Anointed would establish this new prosperity with the new age. When Jesus gave the indigent and destitute crowd of people free bread to eat they were prepared to make this man king. John 6:15. This man they felt would initiate an era of material prosperity, which they were so determined to have. So when Jesus miraculously fed the people, it was a sign to them of the promised Anointed. The miracle creation of the bread to them the entire 5000 of the crowd was indicative of the coming prosperity that would establish for Israel. The people proceeded to make Jesus king in order to usher in this new age of prosperity.

One specific incident will describe this more accurately. A young ruler asked Jesus, "What must I do to inherit life eternal?" Mat 19:16. This man wanted to know what he had to do to live long and prosperously on earth. He no doubt had seen and experienced enough of the disease and poverty and misery of the balance of the population, all of it resulting in premature death, among those whom he lived. This young ruler was probably a mayor or councilman of a town or part of the hierarchy in the government of Herod Antipas or Pontius Pilate. This young ruler wanted to see his son's sons and the prosperity of Jerusalem. Ps 128:5-6. He wanted the final words of the great Psalm of protection and prosperity to be fulfilled upon him.

With long life I will satisfy him and reveal to him My salvation. Ps 91:17.

Jesus answered him, "Follow the commandments." Then Jesus proceeded to recite those commandments of the 10 that deal with personal relationships, along with loving a close associate as one would himself.

The demand of Jesus for this man to sell all that he had and give to the poor, was directed toward equity, that the rich during this era had the responsibility to assist the under-privileged and utilize this wealth for the benefit of the community. The wealthy were to be charitable. 1 Tim 6:18. This has occurred in our era with the establishment of charities, foundations, grants; with money given to schools, museums, libraries, hospitals; with education and medical insurance paid by employers; with pension and retirement plans. This attitude of equity has created a middle class of some 80% of the population of America; with about 10% poverty and 10% rich. All of this benefit is taken for granted here in America but it did not exist in earlier periods. The separation between rich and poor was very distinct. Other countries in the world and earlier periods had a poor population of 80 to 90%, with a 10% middle class and 3 to 5% rich.

To follow Jesus in this passage did not mean for the young man to arbitrarily distribute his wealth and then become a monk or hermit or recluse with no finances at all. Jesus was hoping to increase the standard of living of the poorer classes with the distribution of the wealth of the richer classes in the manner as mentioned above. Paul apostle writes much on this topic in 2 Cor 8 and 9. He concludes his treatise on charity and financial equity with the words, "God loves a cheerful giver." 2 Cor 9:7.

With this type of concern for the underprivileged the only result is economic growth for the entire community. The idea of life *aionious* on earth has been realized in those counties of free enterprise and financial growth, with a massive decrease in infant mortality and a greater portion of the population living into their 80's and 90's. This was the materialization of the dream of the early sages who hoped to pass away in old age.

# PART FOUR

## THE MINISTRY AND MESSAGE OF JESUS AND THE APOSTLES

### 1. LIFE AND CAREER OF JESUS THE ANOINTED

The purpose for Emmanuel the son of *Yahweh* God, or Jesus the Anointed or Messiah-Christ (*Yeshua ha Mashiah* in Hebrew, meaning Joshua the Anointed in proper English translation), to become human is stated in the words of the messenger Gabriel to Joseph of Nazareth engaged to Mary along with the prophecy of Isaiah prophet.

> For he shall save his people from their sins. Matt 1:21
> For unto us a child is born, to us a son is given; and the government shall be upon his shoulders, and his name will be called: Wonderful Counselor, Mighty God, Everlasting Father, Prince of Peace. Of the increase of his government and of peace there will be no end, upon the throne of David and over his kingdom, to establish it, and to uphold it with justice and rectitude. Is 9:6-7.

This primary purpose was his ministry and career as the Anointed, to introduce and establish among his people the Jews the spiritual kingdom and initiate the new covenant, and as a result save the nation from their annihilation. Prior to discussing his ministry as the Anointed there are 2 facets of his personal being as son of *Yahweh* God that impact on the necessity of the incarnation. These are the 2 categories of king and priest. Both of these will be treated separately at first to explain the requirement for this ethereal entity of the realm of spirit to materialize as a human being.

It is an absolute requirement in both these arenas of rule and intercession for Jesus to have appeared as a human, lived as a human, exerted effort in a ministry among his people, be convicted as a criminal and then be executed.

At some point in time, and probably at a time so far into the distant past that time as we know it did not then exist, Jesus in heaven made the decision to vacate his own will in favor of the Father's. At some time, Jesus abandoned his personal wants, desires, ambitions, and intentions, in favor of the divine purpose and counsel of *Yahweh* God his Father. The result of this decision was attaining the fullness of the glory of *Yahweh* God his Father. But this was not without a price. The price to be paid was the intention itself, an immense sacrifice of himself in now fulfilling the counsel and purpose as dictated to him by his Father. Within the activity of *Yahweh* God, there is no room for personal ambition. There is only room for sacrifice.

The ministry of Jesus in heaven and on earth encompasses 2 primary purposes. First, to magnify the Father *Yahweh* God among created humanity. Secondly, to bring created humanity to acknowledge the love of *Yahweh* God towards them, and to inform them regarding their creator.

Upon executing this personal decision, Jesus was designated by his Father to fulfill a ministry on earth on behalf of His people Israel. This ministry on earth was comprised of the above 2 primary purposes but was focused on the nation Israel. Jesus was to magnify the Father in their presence and was to reveal the Father, their God, to them, meaning, to educate the people about *Yahweh* their sole deity. To accomplish this God delegated to Jesus His divine instruction for his earthly career.

## ATTAINING THE RULE

If we could imagine a kingdom in heaven, in this realm of spirit, where sits the King on His throne. He is *Yahweh* God, having the jurisdiction and administration over all the universe. He has the omnipotent authority over all time and eternity, and the despotic dominion over His own creation. However He is a good king and all His creation recognizes Him as such and voluntarily subjects themselves to His authority for their own benefit. And this king has many sons.

If we could imagine a time in heaven that this king is now old. His sons have been learning about rule from the Father all the eons of time from their beginning. They have watched their Father create matter, utilize this new material to create universes and then worlds, and then develop these worlds for habitation and then populate them with creatures of His own design. His sons were with Him, watching and learning all of what creation consisted. All of His decisions He explained to them. His sons observed every move in His administration and jurisdiction pertaining to the creation on earth.

If we could imagine *Yahweh* God as a distinguished elder statesman having reached the pinnacle and conclusion of His career. Silver headed, full white beard, with many eons of wrinkles on His face. He wants His son to inherit the Earth. The heavenly kingdom will always be the Father's. However there is an inheritance for the first-born and the inheritance is the people of *Yahweh* God and the Earth as their residence. *Yahweh* God wants His son to inherit the legacy bequeathed to Him which He has worked hard to develop, and has worked hard to train His son in its rule from heaven. The time had now arrived for the Father to vacate His throne of rule over the earth and allow His son to inherit the throne, the administration and jurisdiction over the earth. There are 2 passages that refer to this:

> Ask of Me and I will make the nations your inheritance, and the ends of the earth your possession. Ps 2:8.
> He will be great and will be called the Son of the Supreme; and *Yahweh* God will give to him the throne of his father David, and he will reign over the house of Jacob for ever; and of his kingdom there will be no end. Luke 1:32-33.

Before the son can actually sit with the Father upon His throne, there are prerequisites. To be a good and capable ruler, the ruler must know the needs of his people. He must be familiar and understand his subjects. He must identify and empathize with the conditions of life of his subjects and how life progresses. The Father required this prerequisite, for His son to experience the life of a typical subject of His realm, from birth to death, in order to inherit the rule.

For the heir this course of personal education and experience as a subject of his own realm would prepare him for efficient and beneficial rule. Only after finishing the course without failure, and not a minute sooner, would the legacy be transferred to him. This the son, Jesus, agreed to do.

## ATTAINING THE INTERCESSION

As high priest intercessor on behalf of his people, the purpose for the incarnation parallels that of the ruler. As priest in heaven, Jesus accepts the prayers of the people and passes them on to the Father for Him to grant their request. But there was no ability for Jesus to directly identify with those on whose behalf he acted as intercessor. He also had to fulfill the life of a human to understand the needs of the people in their prayers and petitions, to fully identify with them. The following passages relate to Jesus as High Priest under the new covenant.

> *Yahweh* has sworn and will not change His mind, "You are a priest for ever after the order of Melchizedek." Ps 110:4. Heb 5:5-6.
> And I will set up over them one Shepherd, My servant David, and he shall feed them; he shall feed them and be their Shepherd. Eze 34:23-31).

The earthly mediators, these priests of Israel, were effective because they were human themselves and understood the difficulties and trials of their own people. The earthly high priest could directly identify with the people he would pray on behalf of since he was human himself. The priest was a husband, father, grandfather, educator, with responsibilities, weaknesses, susceptible to disease, accidents, old age and death. Identifying with his parishioners the earthly priest was effective in his ministry, understanding them and their situations and circumstances. The mediator on behalf of *Yahweh* God's people on earth was compassionate and empathetic.

None of this however applied to the son of *Yahweh* God in heaven.

Jesus in the heavens as mediator lacked this ability to identify with the suffering of His people. Because of his love for his people, he realized that to be perfect in his ministry of heavenly supreme mediator he would have to become one of them, and become one of them in every possible aspect. Though he was son of *Yahweh* God his earthly experience would have to be typical of any and all humans to understand their plight and grasp the reasons for their prayer and petition.

But what could Jesus have lacked in the heavens?

## JESUS IN HEAVEN

We must realize that the entities of the flesh in the material world and the entities of spirit in the heavens are of different constitution, and because of this they are alien one from another. Since the spirit entities have no body of flesh they cannot experience the same things that humans do and cannot even identify with them. The spirit entities, the sons of *Yahweh* God or the Angel-messengers, do not sense or feel what the human senses or feels because they are spirit and not flesh. The spirit-entities cannot understand or identify with pain, illness, deprivation, hunger, thirst, hate, distrust, bigotry, ignorance, loneliness, abuse, or any type of psychological devastation, depression; congenital defects or neurological maladies, because they are spirit and these afflictions stem from the flesh of a material body. Especially alien from the entities of spirit is the prime tragedy of human existence, death, the termination of life, because in heaven there is no death. The spirit entities have not the emotion or conscience that humans possess and cannot identify with them, because emotion and conscience is a trait of the human flesh. A spirit entity cannot show sympathy or empathy, since these proceed from the soul of a human.

None of the above flaws of human constitution or difficulties of earthly life exist in the realm of the spirit, because they are attributes of the flesh in a material realm. A spirit entity cannot identify with human tragedy because it is a spirit and so cannot feel anything that is attributed to the human flesh. The nervous system exists in humans and not in Angel-messengers or the sons of *Yahweh* God. The necessity of incarnation to rectify this deficiency is mentioned by the author of Hebrews.

> Although he was a son, he learned obedience through what he suffered, and being made perfect he became the source of eternal salvation to all who obey him. Heb 5:8-9.

To be an effective mediator who could identify with petitioners, Jesus had to become flesh and experience all that a typical human experiences, from conception and through burial. Only after this experience could he be an efficient mediator and empathize with the people on whose behalf he accepts petitions to present to his father *Yahweh* God.

The betrayal by Judas also constitutes part of this earthly experience. I contend that Jesus did not know specifically which of the apostles would betray him until close to the final Passover. Jesus had to experience betrayal, what it was like to have someone close to you betray you due to envy and get rid of you for money. No doubt this was psychologically devastating for Jesus, who selected Judas Iscariot, trained him to become an apostle, bestowed upon him the power of the spirit, and felt he was trusted by him. In this manner Jesus knew what it was like to have someone deceive you at the end of their career. The same would apply when the other 11 disciples fled from Jesus just when he needed them the most: at his arrest and trial. Matt 26:56. To experience all a regular person experiences, this event had to be included: abandonment when you need someone the most, and they did it to protect their own skin, to not be identified with Jesus and so risk also being arrested.

## METHOD OF INCARNATION OF JESUS

In heaven Jesus – or Immanuel – was a living entity with his own personal identity. In one respect he could be called a soul of the realm of spirit. *Yahweh* God His Father according to the counsel of His own will formulated a plan by which His son could appear as a human and fulfill his obligations, and assigned this plan to him.

> But when the time had fully arrived God sent His son born of a woman, born under the law. Gal 4:4
> The messenger [Gabriel] said to [Mary], "You will conceive in your womb and bear a son, and you will call his name Jesus." And Mary said to the messenger, "How can this be, since I have no husband?" The messenger said to her, "The Holy Spirit will descend upon you, and the power of the Supreme will overshadow you; therefore the child to be born of you will be called Holy, Son of God. Luke 1:31,34-35.

Since Jesus was already an existing entity, but in heaven, a means was required to make him into a human. When the messenger Gabriel entered the home of Mary he kissed her.[13] Mary was at this time engaged to the older gentleman Joseph. When Gabriel kissed Mary, Jesus as a soul was transferred from heaven and through the messenger Gabriel and into Mary. This soul entered an ova of Mary and fertilized it. Now a chaste virgin had

---

[13] Based on Rom 16:16, I Cor 16:20, I Peter 5:14, and others where kiss is used.

conceived of the Holy Spirit. Jesus was no longer in heaven, no longer with his Father or the messengers or sons of *Yahweh* God. He was now an embryo, in process of development into a human. This was the manner that *Yahweh* God selected for His son to become human, by taking a body of flesh through Mary of Nazareth.

Since Jesus had no earthly father, he took his physical attributes from Mary's side of the family. Jesus would have resembled his maternal grandfather and Mary his mother. Since Mary was Jewish, Jesus had the features of a typical Jew of that era, with a Middle Eastern complexion.

> Since therefore the children share in flesh and blood, he himself likewise partook of the same nature… Heb 2:14.
> And the word became flesh and resided among us, full of grace and truth. John 1:14.

The above passages make clear that the body of Jesus was the same body that the balance of created humanity possesses. It was not special, not supernatural, not superhuman. His body was just like yours and mine. It had to be just like yours and mine in order for Jesus to experience being a human just like you and me. He was susceptible to everything that a normal human is susceptible to: failure, disease, mistakes, accidents, temptation, betrayal, and sin. Yes, sin. If Jesus was not susceptible to sin he would not have been human. But he made decisions not to.

## THE KENOSIS

The passage of Paul apostle in Phil 2:6-11 describes accurately the voluntary removal or deprivation of the divinity and glory of heaven which Jesus possessed and his reduction to a body of human flesh.

> Jesus the Anointed, though he was in a form of deity, did not consider equality with God something to be seized. He emptied himself, taking a form of a slave, and became human. Humbling himself as a human he was obedient unto death, death on the stake. Phil 2:5-8.

The divine nature of Jesus remained in heaven. He did not bring it to Earth with him. The only remnant of his divinity was the memory of it. (With his baptism by the Holy Spirit this divinity was returned to him to accomplish his commission, but it was still restrained by the body of flesh.)

## JOSEPH AND MARY OF NAZARETH

According to early Christian tradition, Joseph was an older gentleman never having been married, probably in his late 20' or early 30's. Mary was in her late teens when she became engaged to Joseph. I contend that this was an arranged marriage, very typical for the era and Jewish tradition. The local matchmaker realized it was time for Joseph to marry, and found for him a girl of good reputation from a traditional Jewish family. The parents of both sides made the preliminary arrangements, and set a wedding date perhaps a few months to a year in the future. Joseph would have been very conservative in his religious beliefs and quiet, hard working, but not attracted to the opposite sex. Mary was probably a very domestic type and not very extrovert. They made a good match.

No doubt there was something special about both of them that *Yahweh* God would select them to raise His son on Earth. *Yahweh* God in heaven was not about to just let any couple on earth raise His son, Not at all. The couple had to have certain attributes and characteristics that would be utilized in Jesus' upbringing. The domestic training of Jesus would have to be oriented towards his work in the future, the ministry as the Anointed. The home had to be traditionally Jewish, and the parents would be the type to show love and affection towards their children. The father would be dedicated to the Jewish tradition, honest with a good reputation, and hard working. The father would teach his sons the *Torah* and the Hebrew prophets and the wisdom of their sages. The mother would be faithful and loyal as their tradition required of mothers.

It wasn't just any couple chosen by *Yahweh* God to raise His son on Earth, but the type who would raise him just as *Yahweh* God would want any member of Israel raised on earth: taught to believe in *Yahweh* God and to fear Him; to believe in the covenant established with Israel; to want to continue in the faith of their forefathers and sages; and to await their Anointed. Of course, Joseph and Mary were not superhuman or supernatural. They were a couple whose engagement was arranged, who were planning to marry and be part of their traditional religious community. They could have been anybody with the spiritual and religious convictions to raise children according to the *Torah* and wisdom of their sages.

## JESUS IS BORN

Shortly after the visit of Gabriel to the home of Mary, she left to visit her relative Elizabeth. According to the record Mary was a descendent of David king, of the genealogy of Judah, while Elizabeth was of the genealogy of Levi. Luke 1:5. The age difference between Mary and Elizabeth could have been 40 or 50 years. Elizabeth was elderly and well past child-bearing age, a retired couple. Elizabeth was probably a sister to a grandparent of Mary. Mary visited with her relative about 3 months. Luke 1:56.

When Mary returned to Nazareth it was obvious to the town folk that she was pregnant. No doubt they felt that she had become involved with a person and attempted to run to another part of the country, but now returned. Mary found it hard if not impossible to explain to them her conception of the Holy Spirit. If Mary was weak in character, this rejection by family and community would have devastated her, perhaps even leading to suicide. But she had that special strength to endure the censure. She had no doubt in the words of messenger Gabriel and knew that all would work itself out in order that the will of *Yahweh* God be accomplished.

Joseph wanted to quietly divorce Mary after discovering about her pregnancy, in order not to ruin his reputation or ruin her life any more than necessary. But a messenger appeared to him in a dream and told him:

> "Do not fear to take Mary to be your wife, for her conception is of the Holy Spirit." Matt 1:20.

Shortly after receiving this revelation he married Mary. The people no doubt assumed that either Joseph was engaged in a premarital affair with Mary and married her quickly, or else that he married her to protect her out of his love for her, willing to forgive her of her affair. We can only conjecture at this point. What is definite though is that people were aware of her pregnancy prior to marriage, and which would be brought to the attention of Jesus in later years during his ministry.

We are unaware of the type of wedding ceremony held for Joseph and Mary, but it was definitely not a celebration of the traditional type, like the one attended in later years in Cana by Jesus and his disciples. Under the circumstances the couple probably lived in some quiet part of Nazareth with little social life. This continued for the next 6 or so months.

I have no reason to debate Scripture record regarding the census. Luke no doubt investigated the matter and was a contemporary of that era. Whatever the reason for the journey to Bethlehem, it was required for the Anointed to be born there in accord with the prophetic word. Micah 5:2, Jer 31:15. I am convinced that Joseph and Mary were forbidden to lodge at the hotel that evening because the owner and guests felt that the child she was to deliver was conceived out of wedlock. They were not about to permit an illegitimate child to be born at their hotel. "Some bastard," they thought. "So what if a man was willing to feel sorry for her and marry her. She can have her baby in the barn," they felt, "that's what she deserves. No room in this hotel for people of her repute." This attitude was totally opposite to the hospitality normally shown toward out-of-towners, and especially a young wife ready to deliver. Judg 19:16-21.

Stables of that era were very filthy and open to the elements. The animals causing an unsanitary condition next to the overnight guests; the stable was cold and damp, and full of flies. Under these conditions Mary gave birth to her first child, a son. With no one available to assist Mary, Joseph performed the delivery. The season of the year was probably middle or late fall, coinciding with the holidays of the latter rain, about October. This would be a secondary reason for Bethlehem hotels to be full. Travelers were residing there during the festival season, and just a few miles from Jerusalem. The shepherds outside Bethlehem watched over sheep that would be sold at the temple market place to out-of-towners for sacrifice.

This is the reason the heavenly messengers informed the shepherds that the Anointed would be born that evening in a stable. Luke 2:8-12. The shepherds knew that nobody in their right mind would allow their wife or any other female to deliver a child in such a filthy area. So when the shepherds arrived at the stable they were surprised at a new born with mother and father in such unsanitary conditions.

The next morning Joseph no doubt found a suitable house to rent for his new family and began looking for work as a carpenter.

## THE TEMPLE VISIT

The initial obligation of circumcision was fulfilled 8 days after the birth of Jesus. Either the father Joseph or another qualified individual in the area was called upon to fulfill the rite commanded Abraham patriarch. Gen 17:9-14. Although the child knew nothing of the representation of this mutilation, he had now accepted the sign of the covenant between *Yahweh* God and his people – that of severance from the world and a dedication unto the purpose of *Yahweh* God and life according to His dictates. As noted in Luke 2:21, the child was then given a name according to the desire of the parents. In this case Jesus, as was commanded by Gabriel messenger. Luke 1:21. The name Jesus in Hebrew was Joshua, meaning *Yahweh* is salvation: *Yah-shua*.

The visit of the family of Joseph and Mary to the Jerusalem temple as noted in Like 2:22-24 was to fulfill the obligations imposed upon all women after childbirth as well as a certain obligation on all the firstborn males of the people of Israel, the descendents of the 12 sons of Jacob. The visit to the temple occurred about after 40 days from the birth of Jesus. Since Bethlehem is a short distance from Jerusalem, about 15 miles, it would have been convenient to remain there until after this necessary visit for the fulfillment of these divine rites.

The first of the 2 obligations of the new family in their visit is based on the command of Lev 12:2-8. This was the purification of Mary from her unsanitary condition due to childbirth. According to the dictate, after delivery, 40 days for a boy, 80 days for a girl, the mother was to offer a offering as an atonement for her. Her first 7 days are considered unclean, an unsanitary state, and the following period through the end are considered days of purification. After this period the mother was to bring an offering to again be united to the grace of *Yahweh* God and the community of Israel and likewise be again to physically unite with her husband.

At the temple Mary would have appeared in the area designated as the Women's Court and near the door to the area known as the Men's Court. There the priest took the birds from Mary. Luke 2:24. He would enter the temple and kill them on the alter by tearing off the head from the body with his hands. He then returned to Mary with some of the blood to sprinkle on her. Thus she was cleansed. The offering of the 2 birds, either doves or pigeons, indicate that Joseph and Mary were in the lower income class or even poverty level at this time. This was typical of new families, and especially one relocated such a distance from their home. This first obligation dealt only with Mary. As an observant Jew she also would have fulfilled this with all of her remaining children

The second reason for the temple visit was for the redemption of their firstborn son Jesus. This law of redemption affected legitimate Israelite families only once in their lifetime, shortly after the birth of their firstborn son. This same law also affected the firstborn of cattle, sheep and other domestic animals. Deut 15:19. God endeavored to impress upon the people that He was the origin of all life. The law of redemption was the means of impressing this on them. Since all creation is the property of *Yahweh* God the Creator, He instituted the buy-back or redemption of the firstborn males among humans and unclean animals. Cattle and other clean animals were to be offered to *Yahweh* God as sacrifice.

> Every thing that opens the womb of all flesh whether man or animal, which they offer to *Yahweh*, shall be yours (the Levites); nevertheless the firstborn of man you shall redeem and the firstling of unclean animals you shall redeem. And their redemption price you shall fix at 5 shekels in silver, at a month old you shall redeem them. Num 18:15-16.

In accord with the above and at this convenient time, since Mary was required to appear there anyway, the second obligation was fulfilled. Joseph and Mary entered the Woman's Court of the temple. A priest would appear who would stand as *Yahweh* God's representative in this matter. Joseph would give the child to the priest as a symbolic gesture of offering the child to *Yahweh* God. Then Joseph would give the priest 5 shekels in silver to redeem – buy-back – his son. The priest would then return the child to the father. The priest would take the redemption money and pronounced 2 blessings on the new family:

1. A blessing on the happy event of now having a son. He would continue the family name, and take care of the parents in their old age.
2. A blessing in regard to the redemption, to impress upon the parents that this child is a creation of *Yahweh* God, and their responsibility to raise him accordingly.

The meeting with Simon the righteous and Anna prophetess occurred as Joseph and Mary entered the temple area. Luke 2:25-38.

After the completion of their obligations the family returned to Bethlehem. At this point Joseph and Mary would have consummated their marriage and begin normal marital activity. This is the reason Scripture refers to Jesus as her firstborn, because of other children in the family. Luke 2:7. Matt 13:55-56. Remaining in Bethlehem for some time after, perhaps another year or two, Joseph and Mary would have had an additional child, one that Joseph could truly call his, along with the others to follow. Why the family did not return to Nazareth immediately is not known. Perhaps waiting awhile was best under the circumstances.

## THE MAGI

At some time after settling in a home in Bethlehem, visitors arrived in Jerusalem from some foreign country. Matt 2:1-12. There is no real explanation of who these men were, where they came from and what their long term purpose was in journeying the many miles from "the east" to Bethlehem. It is a poor conjecture that there were 3 of them and that they were from Persia and Zoroastrian. I contend there were about 30 of them or even more including servants: a long caravan and massive retinue that would be worthy of a visit to the future king of Israel. If only 3 this would hardly cause a stir in Jerusalem and even less concern Herod the Great. A number of them with many servants and camels would. They were probably from the Jewish colony in Babylon, and seeking the star mentioned by Balaam.

> I see him but not now; I behold him but not here. A star will arise out of Jacob, and a scepter shall rise out of Israel. Num 24:17.

The greatest of Jewish sages remained in Babylon after the captivity and the city had the greatest population of Jews in the world, far more than Jerusalem. While religious leaders in Judea were broiling over politics, Romans, traditions and temple services, those in Babylon were studiously involved in prophecy pertaining to the Anointed.

The visit to Bethlehem would have been a most unusual sight for the local residents, although their stay was brief. They visited the family in the house they were living in. Matt 2:11. The gifts were definitely useful in the near future for the family. For a carpenter alone in a small village away from his home, and with a new family, the gold was needed. These gifts financed the midnight escape and trip to Egypt. This would help the family reestablish themselves in their new home in that foreign country.

Since the decision of Herod the Great was to put to death all the children 2 years and younger, Jesus was probably from 6 months to 1-1/2 years old. Mary may have even had another child by this time. Of what is known of the population of the environs of Bethlehem, and calculating the number of children in the area 2 years and under, the number put to death by Herod's soldiers was probably about 10 or 20. Not many, but still tragic.

After a temporary sojourn in Egypt of some 2 to 4 years the family returned to Judea and then traveled on to Nazareth their home town. There they settled in a house. By this time the family of Joseph and Mary would have grown to 2 or 3 children in addition to Jesus. With such a family it was easier for them to again be accepted in the circle of relatives and friends, attend synagogue and establish a business.

## JESUS' EXPOSURE

To a typical visitor or traveler through Nazareth Jesus was just another child in town. He looked like the other boys his age, he attended synagogue with his father and the rest of his family every Sabbath. His life as a child was identical with and no different from any other child of the era living in the area. He helped his father in the carpenter shop and at installations at other people's homes. On Sabbath afternoons and summer evenings Jesus walked in the fields near his home and meditated.

The largest city of Galilee and a provincial capital was Sepphoris, about 5 miles to the north. Much of Joseph's work would have been done there. It was a Roman city having an amphitheater, a forum, hot baths, paved roads, and many public building. A large city such as Sepphoris with its population of wealthy Romans and Jewish businessmen would keep an aggressive and talented carpenter steadily busy. Sepphoris was burned down in about 3 AD by Roman troops. The rebuilding of the city would have kept Joseph busy for several years. It would also give Jesus good insight into the lives of the gentiles of Judea and their attitude towards the Jews. Joseph would also have worked in the other cities of

Galilee, including Capernaum, Cana, and Tiberias. There Jesus was likewise exposed to the friction between Romans and Jews. He saw the maltreatment of Jews by Roman soldiers: public beatings, forced servitude, over-taxation. A regular sight was the crucifixion of revolutionary Jews by Roman soldiers. He watched likewise how hard his father worked to run an honest business, and how he was taken advantage of, not paid for work and materials, and treated poorly because of his residence in Nazareth.

He overheard his father talking with townsmen about the events of the day, the political turmoil of Galilee with its occupation by Roman soldiers; revolutionaries in the city of Gishala stirring up the Jewish population to rebel against Roman authority. No doubt he heard of the burning of Sepphoris and the public crucifixion of the Jewish revolutionaries by Roman soldiers. This occurred during the years that Jesus was in Egypt.

Jesus saw the poverty of his people: the leper colonies located distant from populated areas filled with the variously diseased; the helpless blind and deaf and mute; the underprivileged orphans and widows; and the many with no knowledge of the law of *Yahweh* God or the moral code. Visiting Jerusalem with the family during the regular festivals, Jesus became familiar with the Pharisees and their superficial piety, their haughtiness and their contempt toward Galileans. He spoke with Sadducees and their self-ordained religious aristocracy, their rejection of the Jewish Scripture outside the Torah; their compromise with the Roman governors to control the temple and its services; their control of the temple as a business. He saw the bickering and bartering of the money changers and purveyors of animals for sacrifice; how the divine worship of *Yahweh* God had turned into a lucrative business for the aristocratic and religious family of Annas, high priest emeritus. The corruption was so prominent and there was nothing that the common people could do about it. But Jesus also saw the beauty in the services and its value in deliverance of the people from sin. He realized that the divine religion was the embodiment of the gifts of *Yahweh* God to His people, and could be a blessing to Israel if they were to follow in His law and moral code.

By combining his exposures to Greeks, Romans, Galileans, Jews of Jerusalem and their attitudes one to another, he saw in the distant future the devastation of Israel. To save the people from annihilation from the Romans, it would take a special person. It was no doubt the Anointed that Scripture spoke of, that their sages wrote about, and the people awaited, who would deliver the people. All of this Jesus meditated about in his early years in Nazareth.

Jesus would have learned the Aramaic language as the general means of conversation; Hebrew as the language of the synagogue and the *Tanakh* as read; and maybe a little Latin and Greek, due to exposure to the non-Jewish occupiers and residents of the region for business purposes.

## JESUS' CHILDHOOD

What is important is the personal experience of Jesus as a human to understand in all practical aspects what it is to be human. I deny all the accounts of the infancy gospels and the Gnostic gospels. These are pipe dreamers, wanting to create narratives of missing years that did not exist and attribute supernatural power to a child as though a prodigy.

Jesus could not have any noticeable characteristics that would identify him as special or as a prodigy. I feel the opposite would be the real situation. To experience childhood for all children, that is, to know this in every respect, Jesus would have been physically weaker than others his age, and perhaps slower educationally, and succumbing more to illness, but at the same time acute to events and circumstances occurring around him. Jesus had to endure every childhood illness common at the time, including dysentery from bacteria laden well water, malaria from a mosquito in a local swamp, perhaps measles and chicken pox, typical injuries from sports events, accidents at work and home. In addition to this would have been the continual harassment due to the questionable circumstances of his conception.

In every physical aspect, Jesus was no different than any other Jewish child. This would equally apply to his emotional and mental faculties up to adolescence. Although he was son of *Yahweh* God, his cognizance of this was restrained by the body of flesh. In later years of childhood he developed this cognizance slowly, only as his mental faculties developed, just as with any other human. He knew at first he was different than the other boys, but to define it he could not. The reality was disclosed to him from within himself as time progressed in maturity and development of his faculties. The memory of most individuals records events going back to about age 8, or in some age 6. Memory is later still in a greater part of the population in terms of personal identification and cognizance of choice and existence. The same would pertain to Jesus in the body of flesh, it would have been at about age 10 or 12 that he began to realize that he was different from the other children: that Joseph was not really his father, but *Yahweh* God was. This revelation was gradual and as it grew in him he feared a different purpose for his life, different than the dreams and ambitions of his contemporaries. At this time there was nothing that he could do, since he was restrained by his body of flesh. He still had to attend school at the synagogue and services there every Sabbath; he still had to work with his father, and he still was susceptible to and succumbed to sickness and accidents and worry and mistakes and every facet of childhood and adolescent experience.

As the revelation and cognizance increased so did Jesus understanding of his future purpose increase. Sometime into the future, at about the age of 30, he would be commissioned as the Anointed. At that time he would fulfill the embassy, the responsibility assigned him by *Yahweh* God his Father. Then he would die, he concluded. But shortly after his Father would resurrect him from death and he would eventually return to his home in heaven. But as a teenage this was just a dream, an imagination that lurked in his mind or implanted in the recesses of his memory. It was almost as if he could remember back to the life in heaven, but not quite. So it was with Jesus in his teenage years, his true identity still vague and not totally disclosed to him.

## THE FAMILY OF JOSEPH AND MARY

I contend that sublime family strife existed in the home of Joseph and Mary, but not to a point of actual dissociation. Jesus was the first-born of Mary, but their next son, perhaps James mentioned in Matt 13:55, was the first-born of both Joseph and Mary. Perhaps the first-born of both Joseph and Mary felt he should have the preeminence among the siblings, rather then the brother who may not have been the son of their father Joseph. This caused bitter animosity between the 2 older boys.

Mary kept the sayings spoken to her by the divine messenger and prophetic words in her heart. Luke 1:38, 2:51. Mary knew that Jesus was special but not exactly how. The words spoken to her by Gabriel needed to have a fulfillment, but how this would occur was further away in Mary's mind than even in Jesus'. His birth in a stable, their initial years in Bethlehem and the years in Egypt, created a special attachment toward Jesus. It was made stronger by the fact that Mary was in her late teens when Jesus was born, and the age difference was minor. For this reason, I contend that Mary showed favoritism toward Jesus, and the other sons resented this favoritism. No doubt they were aware of the questionable circumstances that surrounded their bother's conception. This bitterness extended also to their mother, "How could she actually believe that Jesus was divine," no doubt they thought. It could be compared to the situation with Jacob and his favoritism towards Joseph, which only created a resentment with his other brothers.

This bitterness of his half-brothers toward him increased with the disclosure of Jesus to the population that he was the awaited Anointed. This is noticeable in John 7:1-9. This bitterness reached such a extremity that the brothers severed all association with him and possibly with Mary their mother also. Finally toward the end of his life Mary was alone with her son at his crucifixion. Jesus told John disciple to take Mary to his home for the remainder of her life. John 19:26-27. Apparently her other children had abandoned her as a result of all that occurred. (I contend that the books of James and Jude in the NT bear the names of apostles James son of Alphaeus and Judas who is also Thaddaeus, and not the brothers of Jesus.)

## JESUS PROGRESSING IN LIFE

By the time Jesus reached his early 20's, he had gained full cognizance of himself as Emmanuel, son of *Yahweh* God. His mental faculties were perfected and disclosure was permitted by *Yahweh* God. This allowed him to remember the entirety of his existence in the realm of the spirit, with the messengers and ministering spirits and the other sons of *Yahweh* God. He remembered the creation of the messengers and how He planned and executed the creation of the material universe. He remembered how all of them in heaven developed the earth for habitation and created the progenitors of the human race. Jesus remembered his purpose as the eternal living sacrifice, to fulfill on Earth life as a human unto death, and the ministry as the Anointed.

But this was all still distant from him. All of this was like the remnants of a dream after waking. He was still restrained by his body of flesh, and still had no power of *Yahweh* God as he had earlier and was again to inherit in the future. He had nothing to disclose himself as special compared to others. He never mentioned one word of any of this to anybody, except perhaps his mother Mary. Who would believe him even if he tried? They would just throw at him the questionable circumstances of his conception. And why Nazareth and not Jerusalem? And why Joseph and Mary, and not the family of Annas or the Hasmonaens? He realized he was human and had to continue and persist in that body of weak flesh until beginning his ministry. But even that was not an end, but another beginning for something greater he had to accomplish, and without failure.

I contend that sometime after the birth of Mary and Joseph's final child Joseph died. It was Joseph who raised Jesus to adulthood from a child. No other person cared for him as much as did Joseph of Nazareth. This now made Jesus of Nazareth the head of the household, perhaps in his early 20's. There is no mention in Scripture of Joseph after their visit to Jerusalem at his age of 12, and John mentions the family moving to Capernaum at the beginning of his ministry as the Anointed. John 2:12. The impact on his family of his disclosure and initiation of his ministry as the Anointed was immense, causing suspicion and spite from neighbors and residents in Nazareth. This required them to relocate. This animosity again surfaces in a later visit to Nazareth. Matt 13:54-58.

Although being son of *Yahweh* God was still impressed on his mind along with his future ministry, the matters at hand were demanding and pressing. After the death of the only father Jesus knew on Earth he took over the obligation of father over his half-brothers and half-sisters still at home. Some of them may have married by this time. Jesus now inherited greater responsibilities: caring for siblings; raising the older children in the tradition of the Jewish sages and religion of Israel; continuing the family carpentry business and teaching it to his younger brothers; sheltering the family from the influence of Hellenism; marrying his sisters to acceptable young men of their own religion and culture; marrying his brothers to girls of their own Jewish community; and helping console his mother in her grief caused by the death of Joseph, her husband of some 20 years. Along with this was the yearly trip to Jerusalem with the entire family to fulfill the Passover sacrifice and festival.

These were the earthly domestic demands on Jesus day to day, year after years, until that point in time when his Father disclosed to him that his purpose and ministry as the Anointed was to begin. Jesus was about 30 years old. Luke 3:23.

## JESUS AND DEATH

Two situations of psychological impact upon Jesus of Nazareth that he had to deal with must be mentioned at this time. The first is the death of father Joseph, or the death of another close relative.

In heaven there is no death. This phenomenon is restricted to the earthly existence. The termination of life is totally alien to the eternal existence of the spirit-entities in heaven. The fact that a corporeal living entity was temporal, that they would cease conscious existence and terminate identity had the greatest psychological impact on Jesus than any other event in his early life. Dealing with the death of his father Joseph was especially devastating because this was the person Jesus grew up accepting as father, and who called Jesus son, who treated him as if he actually was his son. The death of others earlier in his life, such as a grandparent or elder of the synagogue began a disclosure to Jesus regarding death, but Joseph his father would have been the primary. This disclosed to Jesus about the temporality of his own life, his own earthly conscious existence. One day he would also die and be buried in the same manner, and be mourned over by considerate family and friends.

Although Jesus was son of *Yahweh* God, his eternal existence applied only to heaven when he was a residence there as a spirit entity. That state in heaven precluded any termination of life. But in the body of flesh he had inherited the curse of his progenitor Adam, to work for sustenance by the sweat of his brow until death. As a human Jesus was destined to follow the pattern of all humanity possessing the effects of the sin of the progenitors and so terminate conscious existence.

As an observant Jew in the tradition of the patriarchs Joseph would have laid his hands upon the heads of his children to bless them, including Jesus, prior to his death, as did Isaac. Gen 27:27.

Viewing the aged body of Joseph was a immense education for Jesus, seeing what the elements had done to him over the years as he "earned bread by the sweat of his brow," and his sacrifice for his wife and children, and at the same time adhering to the faith of his forefathers trying to enjoy the blessings of *Yahweh* God upon himself and his family. With hospitals and convalescent homes unknown, Jesus and his brothers would have been at the bedside of their father in their family home when he passed away, just as with Jacob patriarch. Gen 49:33. The impact no doubt lingered for several days or weeks, or until the family was again stabilized in their normal regimen, now with Jesus as head of the household. Mary would have advocated this, although Jesus assuming this position may also have lead to strife with his brothers.

## JESUS AND MARRIAGE

The second situation of psychological impact was marriage and his relation to the opposite gender. What would have been the reaction of Jesus as adolescence came along and sexual drive began in him when he came in close proximity to an attractive girl? Since Jesus was a male with the same constituents as any other male, the sexual drive and development in him was the same. No doubt girls flirted with him as he matured, and perhaps eyes of a matchmaker were in motion to find some young lady as a spouse for Jesus. If he did not have the same drive as a normal heterosexual male, Jesus would not have shared in flesh and blood and partook of the sake nature as humanity. Heb 2:14. As a mature adult male he definitely was capable of normal marital relations and fathering a child. His children would have been patterned after his mother's side of the family, just as he was.

But Jesus' marrying is improbable for three reasons.

First was that Jesus himself found it inconceivable that he should marry. Knowing that he was son of *Yahweh* God, the idea of having a marital relationship with a female over the balance of his life was alien to his basic nature. Not alien to his human nature, as mentioned above, but alien to his previous life in heaven as a spirit entity. In that realm, there is no marriage, no sex, no childbirth, no love between husband and wife. These are characteristics and facets of the earthly life for procreation. Jesus transcended physical procreation. The thought of himself, a divine entity embodied in flesh, impregnating a wife was beyond his mental ability to grasp.

Second, marriage would have interfered with his ministry of the Anointed. Knowing that his early life was a preparation for his future work, and that he would be soon commissioned as the Anointed, and his total person would be enveloped in this matter, marriage would only have interfered. He could not keep a wife supported and happy and raise children at the same time he was traveling throughout Israel preaching the gospel of the kingdom. His treason by Judas Iscariot, trial by the Sanhedrin, sentence by the Roman governor, and execution by crucifixion, would have been devastating for his wife and children. It would be better to spare them from this upheaval in their life.

Third, the earthly responsibilities of raising the family of his step-father Joseph after his death was an adequate substitute or proxy family for Jesus. He was close to his mother and had equal domestic and parental responsibilities as any other father. In addition to this was running the business and supporting the family. All of this was an adequate substitution for a family of Jesus' own.

A secondary but minor point to be mentioned is that attitude of other families toward Jesus and his questionable conception. Few families of observant and conservative reputation would have allowed their daughter to marry Jesus. This is a minor point, and it may or may not have surfaced.

## JESUS' ATTITUDE TOWARD WOMEN

*Yahweh* God routed Jesus' life on earth in the family of Joseph and Mary such that he could still experience all aspects of human life even without marriage and having a wife and children. As a result of this, Jesus learned early to treat the female as an equal to the male. His close relationship to his mother and having to raise his sisters developed this in him. He also saw how Greek women were treated in Sepphoris, in households with no morals. No doubt he saw the dilemma of women who condescended to selling themselves to survive, and how poorly they were treated by clients, and the damage it caused in households.

According to the Jewish sages a female was equal to the male in every earthly aspect, and was to be treated likewise. This is the reason he could deal with prostitutes during his ministry, since he viewed them as equal humans, not as objects for the gratification of males. The females were attracted to Jesus for this reason. Luke 8:2-3. They found a man of high religious rank who did not condescend to them or discredit them. He had compassion for them, realizing the difficult straits they were in, how poorly many of them were treated by fathers, husbands, masters and lovers. These women found in Jesus a teacher of divine instruction and moral law who was genuinely interested in their welfare; a person they could trust; a man of integrity without any intention of taking advantage of them. They were willing to support him in his important work. First as a means of gratitude, and second, knowing that he would benefit others and especially other women just as he had benefited them. The incident of the woman of ill repute who washed the feet of Jesus with her hair and tears is a good example of how women felt toward Jesus. Luke 7:36-50. He helped them in their personal life, giving them hope and the opportunity to repent and enter the kingdom of God. In return she showed her love and gratitude with this public act of affection. She knew no other manner of showing gratitude for what Jesus did for her.

Another incident is Mary sister of Lazarus, who poured a fragrant perfume on the body of Jesus at their home. John 12:3-8. In this manner did Mary show public gratitude for what Jesus did for their family in resurrecting brother Lazarus from death.

## JESUS AND SIN

In all the situations of life that Jesus experienced, in the religious, business, and domestic areas, and society and personal associations, he did not sin, meaning, he did not deliberately violate law or commit crime. That Jesus could have sinned is inherent in his state, the body of flesh, this earthly residence of his. He inherited the curse of Adam, and so was liable to every weakness and temptation that can surface in a person, or any that they can succumb to.

It is necessary to define Jesus not as a flawless or perfect person. This is in regard to the general physical weaknesses of the typical body of flesh, as mentioned above dealing with disease, accidents, and etc. Also a mistake or an accident should not be classified as sin. These occur on a regular basis and effect every person in their life. Every person makes mistakes and bad judgment calls, and injures himself and on occasion another. Jesus likewise would have endured this in his regular life. But this is not sin as a crime. No doubt Jesus did make many mistakes while growing up and maturing, whether school or business, in carpentry, or even in the prescribed rituals of the demands of the priests. But these are not sin.

The deliberate violation of the divine instruction and moral law is sin or crime against *Yahweh* God. This Jesus of Nazareth did not do. Not once in his life did he succumb to temptation and deliberately violate another person: Commandments 5 through 10. Never in his life did he violate the dictates of his Father *Yahweh* God: Commandments 1 through 4. In every respect he had a concern for the welfare of others: the commandment to love his associate. In no respect did he advocate another deity or religion, other than *Yahweh* God and the divine religion of Israel: the commandment to love *Yahweh* God. In this respect are the words of Heb 4:15 true. He never sinned insofar as a deliberate or premeditated violation of the divine instruction or moral law, some crime.

The initial indication of the capability for Jesus to violate the law is the temptation in the desert. At the conclusion of a 40 day fast a tempter came to him 3 times. Matt 4:1-11. The tempter would have approached Jesus only if there was the possibility of him succumbing. Jesus had to deal with this to understand what sincere people of *Yahweh* God have to endure when they are faced with temptation, and must prevail over it. Jesus resisted the tempter and he fled from him.

If Jesus could not have sinned, then temptation is senseless. Why should temptation tempt a person to violate some law or dictate if that person is incapable of violation, or has a nature that is alien to infraction or offense. Temptation was provided to Jesus as a regular occurrence specifically to lead him to sin by the tempter. Jesus had to experience the same type of temptation that any other person would deal with, whether it be the opportunity to cheat or defraud in business; or commit some crime; or the opportunity to commit some sexual sin; or some violence or abuse. Jesus was faced with all of it, and could have violated the divine instruction and moral law, but made the decision not to. Scripture witnesses to this.

> For we have not a high priest who is unable to sympathize with our weaknesses, but one who in every respect has been tempted as we are, yet without sinning. Heb 4:15.
> He committed no sin; no guile was found on his lips. 1 Pet 2:22.
> For our sake He made him to be sin [offering] who knew no sin, so that in him we might become the rectitude of God. 2 Cor 5:21.

If Jesus could not have sinned, then his body of flesh was not the same as ours. Jesus overcame sin in the flesh by regularly deciding to adhere to the divine instruction and moral law. This is the reason John the Baptizer initially refused to baptize Jesus in the Jordan River. Matt 3:14-15. John the Baptizer knew his cousin well and knew that Jesus never committed a crime or deliberately violated any law of *Yahweh* God. Jesus had nothing to repent of. Jesus took careful consideration of every situation and adhered to the moral law. He did not allow politics, business demands, pressure from family or peers to interfere with doing what he knew was correct as defined by Scripture. He did not allow opinions or distractions or manipulation by others to sway his emotions or attitudes away from the rectitude of the moral law.

At an early age Jesus trained his senses, his attitudes, to conform to the will of his Father. He set aside his own personal ambitions, opinions, convictions as a human which he developed over the years living in Nazareth of Galilee, all in favor of the Father's. No doubt there was an internal struggle within the person of Jesus. His flesh was demanding and dictating certain attitudes and actions based on the environment and political climate of his era, while his personal identity was instructing him to prepare to his ministry as the Anointed. Jesus knew that he could not be effective as an itinerant Rabbi among the people, as a teacher and prophet, if he had a tainted history, a criminal background or bad reputation. To accomplish his embassy, his mission, he had to have a clean record. He could not put himself in a position for a priest or elder or citizen to question his moral integrity. To successfully accomplish his commission as the Anointed, Jesus had to overcome every temptation and so appear to Israel without the stain of violation of divine instruction and moral code. In this regard Jesus sinned not.

This was likewise an example for all others of the era and future generations. Jesus proved to humanity that a person in the flesh born by the word and spirit can progress through life and not sin, not commit a crime. John apostle mentions this.

> No one born of God commits sin, because God's nature resides in them, and they cannot sin because they are born of God. 1 John 3:9.
> We know that any one born of God does not sin, because He who was born of God preserves him, and the evil one does not touch him. 1 John 5:18.

Because Jesus was able to conduct himself in accord with the divine instruction and commandments of God, others can also, and he was a human just as any other human. This is an important facet of his earthly career, to prove ability for obedience to God.

## BAPTISM OF JESUS OF NAZARETH

Until the day that John the Baptizer immersed Jesus in the water of Jordan river, when the Holy Spirit descended upon Jesus on the shore after he walked out of the river, Jesus had no supernatural power. All he had was the cognizance of this identity and the gradual revelation of his life in heaven until his conception in Mary of Nazareth. Then all was a blank until later years growing in Nazareth as a child when gradual these secrets were disclosed. Isaiah prophet defines the 7 facets of the spirit of *Yahweh* God that were bestowed upon Jesus of Nazareth: wisdom, understanding, counsel, might, knowledge, fear of *Yahweh*, and a delight in the fear of *Yahweh*. Is 11:2-3. He also received the fullness of the deity at this time. Col 2:9. However, the exercise of all these gifts and divinity was restrained by his body of flesh. Matt 13:58.

At the descent of the Spirit several things occurred.

*Yahweh* God anointed Jesus of Nazareth; this was his official commission as the Anointed. It was the assignment of authority by *Yahweh* God to fulfill the prophecies pertaining to the suffering servant, to institute the new covenant, to establish the spiritual kingdom in Israel, and to deliver the nation from their sins and future devastation. This also gave him the authority and ability to select apostles and bestow on them the power of the Spirit, for them to expand his ministry and continue it after his ascension.

He acquired the complete knowledge of his previous existence from the time of his birth of *Yahweh* God, and all that occurred in heaven during the eons. Previously it was vague; like the remnants of a dream after waking.

He acquired a concept of his work for the next 2 or 3 years. He was to teach divine instruction and moral law of his Father *Yahweh* God to the people, to disclose to the people the attributes of his Father for them to know about Him, His attitude and His expectations of His nation. He would also have to reprimand the religious elders of their hypocrisy and failure to uphold their divine obligation. He knew that one whom he would select as a disciple would betray him, but not exactly how, and this would have its psychological devastation on him, to understand betrayal and envy. Included in this earthly experience was rejection by elders, an illegal pseudo-trial, sentence and then execution. He knew he would have to face a death to typify all death to prove his love for created humanity and especially his nation Israel.

He accepted from *Yahweh* God the power of the Holy Spirit to enable him to perform healing, discard demons, return life to the dead, and view the intents and secrets contained in the minds of people. This included an authority over nature, above and beyond that of physical healing.

He acquired the spirit of prophecy. Jesus saw what no other person saw as the result of the course the Jewish leaders and commoners were taking. If they were to continue as they were the nation would be annihilated by the merciless and ruthless Roman army. What occurred with Israel with the invasions and defeat by Assyria, what occurred with Judea with the invasions and defeat by Babylon, and then subsequently with Greece and Rome, was also to occur to that generation and their children. They would then be dispersed as in earlier eras. He was to be another Jeremiah, teaching reconciliation and peaceful coexistence with enemies for their own salvation. Jesus saw all of this in his prophetic vision, and it was added to his list of obligations to fulfill on earth in order to accomplish the commission assigned him and then return home to heaven. Yet he still did not know when the judgment on Israel would occur. Matt 24:36.

The voice from heaven was a public pronouncement from *Yahweh* God regarding the commission of His son as the Anointed.

This is My beloved Son, with whom I am well-pleased. Matt 3:17.

What John the Baptizer saw in the sky that he compared to a dove has perplexed me from the first day I read it. Did he see a dove, or something like a dove? Most probably the spirit of *Yahweh* God materialized as a cloud shaped like a bird, and landed upon the person of Jesus as he stood on the bank of the Jordan. The cloud as a materialization of the spirit of *Yahweh* God on earth is found at the dedication of the tabernacle by Moses. Ex 40:34. And at the dedication of the temple by Solomon. 1 King 8:10.

## DEATH OF JESUS

There is no doubt that the most hideous of situations for Jesus to deal with while in the early years of his earthly career was the expectation of his own death, the termination of his life, ceasing to exist as a conscious entity. Since Jesus was human, a human, he would terminate or conclude life in the same manner as all of humanity beginning with the initial death,

Abel, murdered by his brother Cain. His spirit would leave the body and render the body lifeless. His soul or identity would reside in oblivion until such time that the command of God would reconstitute his body again and spirit return to it. Because Jesus was a human he was dealt with as a human until such time that he would return back to the realm of the spirit, back to heaven. This is why Jesus is indicated in Scripture as dead or having died, and not specifically referring to only the body of Jesus, but to Jesus as a conscious entity. He had no conscious existence these 3 days and nights.

> I died, and behold I am alive for evermore. Rev 1:18.
> The Anointed died for our sins according to Scripture, that he was buried, that he was raised on the third day in accordance with Scripture. 1 Cor 15:3-4.

Jesus' personal fear of death was no doubt greater than his fear of the incarnation, when he had to conclude life in heaven in order to be conceived as a human in the uterus of Mary. The fact that Jesus cried for Lazarus at his death is indicative of Jesus' understanding of the state of Lazarus in the tomb. John 11:35. Jesus' own personal fear of death is noted in his words in the garden of Gethsemane.

> "My Father, if it be possible, let this cup pass from me; nevertheless, not as I will, but as You will. Matt 26:39.

The cup represents suicide. To drink of this cup was an idiom used referring to voluntary and premeditated suicide. The analogy is derived from people drinking some poison to commit suicide. The most infamous of all suicides of the era is that of Socrates, who drank hemlock from a cup. This analogy persisted as an idiom in the Hellenistic world, that to drink of the cup meant suicide by poisoning.

Jesus was at a fork in the road during these final minutes in the garden of Gethsemane, He could avoid or circumvent death of he so chose to. Since he was the son of *Yahweh* God he could have used his authority to command a countless number of heavenly messengers to rescue him at this time and return him to his previous residence in heaven and so be reinstated in some capacity as a son of *Yahweh* God. But to have done this would be to reject the will of the Father for him and to do his own will. He would have become a disappointment to his Father and the sons of *Yahweh* God and ministering spirits in heaven, not completing the course assigned him to complete as a human on earth.

Jesus making the decision to fulfill the will of his Father would result in a premature and hideous death. This decision to allow the soldiers to arrest him and take him to trial was the beginning of the end for Jesus. There was no turning back once the decision was made to proceed with his arrest. This is why his spirit was willing while his flesh was weak. Matt 26:41. His faith in his own resurrection from the state of death had to overcome the fear of enduring termination of life; his flesh sought survival in terms of the near future, the immediate future, which was to escape from Gethsemane and flee. The flesh would be satisfied if he were to flee in the opposite direction away from arrest and shame and execution or flee back into heaven into the safe realm of internal safety and immortality. By prayer and contemplation of the situation and future of himself and others, Jesus was able to overcome the immediate struggle for survival of his flesh and proceed with fulfillment of his purpose. His decision was suicidal. Shortly after this prayer for strength messengers arrived to assist him and assure him in his decision. Matt 26:43.

I contend that the Holy Spirit received by Jesus at the time of his baptism by John the Baptizer at the Jordan River, along with his divinity, left the presence of Jesus' body at some just prior to his arrest at Gethsemane. The Holy Spirit of power had to be removed from the presence of Jesus during his trial and conviction and until the conclusion of his execution in order for Jesus to feel the pain of rejection, betrayal, innocent conviction, public shame and death in the same manner as any other human caught in similar circumstances; to experience this as would any other human not having the power and comfort of the Holy Spirit. If Jesus had special assistance from heaven or special strength and comfort from the Holy Spirit during this final day of his life, then he would not have been like unto his brethren in all things. Heb 2:14. To reach the goal he had to give up the Holy Spirit and his divinity sometime prior to his arrest. The arrival of these messengers to strengthen him was the last of any divine intervention into his career until his resurrection.

## EXECUTION OF JESUS THE ANOINTED

The execution of criminals by Roman soldiery was performed with the victim stark naked. As far as the Roman sentries were concerned the victim was a convicted criminal. He had no rights; he abandoned any civil rights he may have had once his crime was committed. He did not even have need for clothing; his public shame and exposure would contribute to the public display of his criminal nature. The Roman soldiers stationed at the base of the crucifixion stakes upon which hung the convicted criminals gambled for the clothing of the victims. This is the evidence indicating the crucifixion of Jesus stark naked: the soldiers removed his clothing and gambled for them. Matt 27:35.

One item to be noted here is that in this volume the Greek word *stauros* is translated as stake, which is the correct translation, and not cross,[14] although rendered this way in the NT by translators.

The victim hung on a single vertical pole, a stake (*stauros*), not on a cross as usually portrayed. One nail was inserted into both hands below the wrist between the radius and the ulna. The victim hung on this nail. A second nail was inserted through the shins between the tibia and the fibula. This kept the victim's feet secured to the stake and prevented him from jumping off the stake and escaping. The feet were only a foot or two above the ground. The victim would hang in this position in public display until they would finally expire. (Contemporary portrayals of Jesus crucified do not correctly portray his position.) The fact that the women are distant from the place of crucifixion is due to this obscene scenario. At the beginning of the crucifixion they are close enough to speak. John 20:26-27. But later they are described standing and viewing the scene in the distance. Matt 27:55. Apparently once the clothing was removed and the bodies placed in public display the women were forced to stand at a distance.

The final words of Jesus on the stake were these:

"Father into Your hands I commit my spirit." And having said this he breathed his last. Luke 23:46.
When Jesus had received the vinegar, he said, "It is finished." And he bowed his head and gave up the spirit. John 19:30.

---

[14] As noted in Young's Analytical Concordance, and New International Dictionary of New Testament Theology, Volume 1, article on Cross, page 391.

"Father into Your hands I commit my spirit." And having said this he breathed his last. Luke 23:46.
And then Jesus cried with a loud voice and yielded his spirit. Matt 27:50.

The demise of Jesus occurred when the spirit of animation vacated his body, after about 6 hours of torture hanging on this stake in public display. His body was now lifeless, his life terminated. His identity or soul was now stored in some recess of the memory of *Yahweh* God, in the annals of the book of life in heaven.

Jesus was dead for 3 days and 3 nights according to Scripture.

I contend that *Yahweh* God was well pleased that His son was completing the responsibility assigned him in heaven. *Yahweh* God was filled with pleasure knowing that His son did not fail in any respect any item he was required to accomplish during his career. John 18:4. *Yahweh* God in heaven cheered and rooted for his son during his final hours as he hung on the crucifixion stake, just as a contemporary parent would cheer and root for their son in some contest or match. Like the elation of a parent when their son crosses the finish line in a race or wins against the competitor in a match, so was the elation of *Yahweh* God in heaven with the exclamation of His son, "It is finished." John 19:30. Jesus had run the race and finished his course and fought the good fight of faith and won.

> Yet *Yahweh* was pleased to crush him; He has put him to grief; when he makes himself an offering for sin... Is 53:10

Like with most of his career, this final stretch was one that Jesus had to complete on his own. The father could not do this for him any more than a parent completing a race in a stadium for their son. No doubt Jesus felt alone during these final hours, beginning with his arrest in Gethsemane. But he had to accomplish it on his own.

"My God, my God, why have you abandoned me?" Matt 27:48.

During the final moments of life, Jesus felt abandoned by all: his disciples, his relatives, the religious leaders, and especially by *Yahweh* God his Father. However the course had to be completed and entirely on his own. David king felt the same way when he was persecuted by Saul king. Ps

22:1. But *Yahweh* God never did abandon David, and neither did he abandon Jesus. During these finial minutes of the career of His son, *Yahweh* God was viewing with great satisfaction and intensity his son winning the good fight of faith, heroically defeating temptation, accomplishing the eternal redemption of all who would believe in him, and on his own.

> For our sake He made him to be sin who knew no sin, so that in him we might become the rectitude of God. 2 Cor 5:21.

Jesus as mentioned about was impeccable in his earthly career, law observant in all respects. He knew no sin, meaning he never participated in or committed a crime or deliberate violation of the moral law of his Father *Yahweh* God. The sin that *Yahweh* God made him become is noted by Paul apostle.

> The Anointed redeemed us from the curse of the law, having become a curse for us, for it is written, "Cursed be every person who hangs on a tree." Gal 3:13.

Sentenced to execution as criminal and executed as a criminal by the Romans was considered repulsive and so labeled as sin.

## THE POST-MORTEM OF JESUS THE ANOINTED

I contend that Jesus had no conscious existence during these 3 days and 3 nights, in accord with his own words. Rev 1:18. He was in the same state of initial decay as any other human who would die, that state described in the earlier sections on the interim state. Embalming his body in about 100 lbs. of a perfumed cream did retard the initial stages of decay. John 19:39. If Jesus had not resurrected his body eventually would have decayed back into the natural elements of composition of dust and the identity of Jesus would have remained only in the memory of his Father *Yahweh* God. He would await the general resurrection of the dead, just as the balance of created humanity. Such was his state during the 3 days and 3 nights.

Jesus knew that he could have arranged his own resurrection having access to the powers of heaven as a son of *Yahweh* God. But Jesus did not allow himself this option, because to exercise this option would interfere with the fulfillment of the prophetic words regarding the length of time he was to spend in the grave dead. John 2:19, Hosea 6:2. As a human he had to be revived or reinstated to life by the spirit sent from *Yahweh* God.

The discussion with the thief also in crucifixion as recorded in Luke 23:43, has posed a difficult resolution. "This day you shall be with me in the garden," is a better rendering of the statement of Jesus rather than using the Persian word paradise. This word paradise is a loan word from the Farsi language meaning garden. This criminal being executed by crucifixion alongside Jesus had a vain hope thinking that only acknowledgement of guilt will gain him entrance into the kingdom of God. He was definitely guilty of committing some capital crime and so was sentenced to death by a Roman court, and even admitted that his execution was the result of the crime he committed. In their conversation Jesus essentially reprimands him for having this vain hope by telling him that just as he was to die and be buried, so the convicted thief would also die that day and be buried. The use of the word garden, I contend, referred to the cemetery of the both of them. Even in our own era most cemeteries have a garden or park appearance and comfortable environment. Paul apostle uses the word paradise in 2 Cor 12:3, referring to the garden Eden, as seen in a vision.

The Biblical record can easily prove that all the theories that attempt to circumvent the actual death of Jesus due to execution by crucifixion are false. The one Roman soldier that noticed that Jesus had died was not about to be deceived or distracted by the events of the evening. Knowing well that the victim should hang in such a position days before expiring he quickly ascertained that something could possibly be wrong with the condition of the victim, perhaps lapsing into a coma. Criminals sentenced to crucifixion normally do not die in a matter of a few hours. Blood loss is at a very slow pace. As time progresses the muscles slowly tighten and torture the victim. The vital organs slowly fail. Death is the result of long term exhaustion and exposure to the elements after at least 2 days and as long as 4 or 5, depending on the severity of the exposure and health of the individual. The victim's legs were sometimes broken to speed up the process. Blood would fill up the cavity created by the broken bones, and now the body was totally suspended by the nail through the wrists. Since the victim was only a foot or so above ground, it was easy to break the legs. The heart was under massive stress to pump blood to the feet and back again. The upper limbs in their vertical position also made blood circulation difficult.

Not about to allow the body to be removed without positive indication of death the soldier plunged his spear underneath the rib cage of Jesus on his left side, shredding the skin and flesh. The lower ribs of Jesus would have been at about shoulder height of the soldier. He then plunged the spear deep into the heart and punctured it; as the soldier withdrew his spear the contents of the heart spilled out. Coagulated blood and what appeared to be a clear fluid spilled out through the tear in Jesus' limp torso. The clear fluid was most likely blood plasma remaining from the coagulation of the blood, or perhaps lymph fluid in the heart. Another possibility is pleural fluid in the cavity surrounding the lungs, which would have collected the fluid as a result of congestive heart failure. Jesus most probably died of congestive heart failure. The penetration of the spear into the heart of Jesus, and the contents of the heart eliminated and in public display, was total and satisfactory proof to the soldier that Jesus was dead. The soldier then confirmed the death of Jesus of Nazareth to Pilate and permitted the removal of the body for disposal.

The blood and clear fluid spilled out of the heart and flowed down the side of Jesus' left leg and dripped into the ground at the base of the stake off his feet. The blood soaked into the soil and eventually decayed. The disciples standing locally and watching the events totally gave up hope at this point seeing the person they considered and who claimed to be the Anointed of *Yahweh* God now dead. Disciples John and Thomas were 2 of those who witnessed the demise of Jesus of Nazareth.

## THE RESURRECTION OF JESUS THE ANOINTED

After 3 days and 3 nights spirit was sent by *Yahweh* God to reconstitute the body of Jesus, to prepare it and allow it to live again. The spirit entered it and Jesus again became conscious and felt personal consciousness. His body was reconstituted back into its original nature, but yet much is still unknown as to whether it was the type of body that Paul apostle writes about in 1 Cor 15:49, or whether it returned back to exactly the same constitution as just prior to his death.

I am of the opinion that the immediate resurrected body of Jesus was identical to his earlier body in order to prove to the disciples that he was the same person. Although on occasion he used his power for some special effect, this was only for a specific purpose. This would be to enter a locked room where the disciples were hiding in fear of Jews. John 20:19. Or that his 2 traveling companions on the road to Emmaus would not recognize him. Luke 24:31. Or that the disciples who returned to fishing in Lake Galilee also would not recognize him. John 22:12.

When Jesus opened his eyes and regained consciousness, much like a person waking from a deep sleep or from anesthesia, he probably yawned and looked about at the darkness of the sepulcher. He then sat up and took the napkin or cloth wrapped around his head off, and set it off to the side. He then proceeded to unwrap the strips of cloth his body was wrapped in; these he left off to the side in a pile. John 20:5-7. The grave clothes were laying in one part of the sepulcher in a pile with the head cover in another area.

## THE OTHER RESURRECTION

Another resurrection also occurred at this time that is often overlooked by readers, noted as follows:

> And the tombs were opened; and many bodies of the saints who had fallen asleep were raised. And coming out of the tombs after his resurrection they entered the holy city and appeared to many. Matt 27:51-52.

These people are not identified. The writer of Hebrews refers to these resurrected saints as, "the spirits of the righteous made perfect." Heb 12:23. Any attempt to identify them is pure conjecture. In general they are the first fruits who are stated in 1 Cor 15:23. This phrase first fruits refers to the initial ripened produce that was offered to the priests at the location of the tabernacle and temple under the old covenant. The necessity of this resurrection was to prove to the people that he as the Anointed was the fulfillment of Old Covenant prophesies such as Dan 12:2, pertaining to the hope of the Old Covenant saints. These may have been those who attained the salvation of God under the covenants beginning with Adam and Eve. The Anointed, whom they awaited, now led them out of the grave. How they identified themselves to the public with proof of their resurrection, how long of a time they were on earth, and what subsequently occurred is unknown. Earlier attempts have identified them with the 144,000 of Rev

7:3-8, and those redeemed from the earth of Rev 14:1. But this cannot be substantiated.

I contend that all of these eventually ascended into heaven in a manner similar to Jesus. They will return with Jesus to establish his kingdom on earth at the time of the restoration. These will be those whom we will greet on earth or in the clouds. 1 Thess 4:14.

## MARY MAGDALENE AND ASCERTAINING THOMAS

This treatise will not deal with the numerous appearances of Jesus to disciples and friends and their chronology, as this is well detailed by other authors. Only the appearances to Mary Magdalene and disciple Thomas will be discussed.

Shortly after leaving the tomb Jesus was greeted by Mary Magdalene and by another Mary. Mary Magdalene recognized him. John 20:16-17. She was so overjoyed at his presence that she fell down to ground, grabbed him by the feet and held him tight. Jesus then said to her, "Cling not unto me, because I have not yet ascended to my father and your father, to my God and your God." Matt 28:9-10. The ladies then released him and went unto Jerusalem to inform the other disciples.

To call Thomas disciple "doubting Thomas" is a misnomer and also an insult. He should be properly labeled "verifying Thomas" or "ascertaining Thomas". He was no doubt one of the more intelligent and acute of the apostles and was not about to allow some imposter or charlatan pose as the resurrected Anointed. Because of his firm demand for verification his witness is the single most reliable witness in the gospels to the resurrection of Jesus. No doubt Thomas was at Golgotha during the crucifixion and witnessed the soldier thrust his spear under the ribs of Jesus and into his heart. Thomas saw with his own eyes the contents of the heart spill out. Thomas saw the nails in the hands and feet of Jesus as he hung on the stake. Now a week later he was not about to let someone surface claiming to be the same person and so deceive him and others. I wonder whether others who also heard of the statements of Jesus regarding his resurrection from death wanted to gain fame by claiming to be him alive again. Thomas wanted undeniable proof that this person who was now claiming to the other disciples that he was the resurrected Jesus was the same person whom Thomas saw nailed, crucified and pierced. Thomas was no fool.

Then [Jesus] said to Thomas, "Put your finger here and see my hands; and put out your hand and place it in my side…" John 20:27.

This is the reason Jesus offered his hands and feet to Thomas, to verify that he was not a fraud or imposter. Thomas then placed his own finger into the hole that the nails made in the hands of Jesus and in his feet. But this was insufficient evidence. Any person that escaped crucifixion would have such holes. Jesus then told him to place his hand in the ribs, which Thomas also took advantage of, placing his entire hand under the rib cage of Jesus and placing a finger directly into the heart through the hole made by the spear. Thomas was overwhelmed by what he felt. This was the reason for the exclamation of Thomas, "My lord and my god." John 20:28. There was no doubt about it, this was the same and identical person whom Thomas saw die about a week earlier, but now alive and well. The disciple John recorded this event for future generations. This served as evidence for all the disciples and the others in the same room regarding Jesus' resurrection.

According to the Bible record, Jesus proved himself alive after his death by many undeniable proofs. Acts 1:3. I likewise accept their witness that Jesus of Nazareth, who died by crucifixion, resurrected unto life for 40 days and then ascended into heaven to where he was prior to his incarnation.

## THE BODY OF JESUS

For the Jews to better understand the sacrifice of Jesus of Nazareth, referring to the display upon the stake at Golgotha, he is compared to the Passover lamb. This is first mentioned by John the Baptizer to the crowd gathered at the Jordan River.

Behold the lamb of God that removes the sins of the world. John 1:29.

Although the body of Jesus is identical in composition to the body of any other human, the writer of Hebrews utilizes the scene at Golgotha as a means of the Jews understanding Jesus of Nazareth as the sacrifice of all ages, that as the Anointed he is the consummation of the institution of animal sacrifice in the divine religion of Israel.

And by that will we have been sanctified through the offering of the body of Jesus the Anointed once for all. Heb 10:10.

The entire passage of Heb 10:1-18 deals with the Anointed as the consummate sacrifice in a manner that the Jews of the era could understand.

## JESUS RETURNS TO HEAVEN

Shortly after his appearance, Jesus made the statement to Mary Magdalene that he still had not ascended to his Father and God. Matt 28:9-10. No doubt it was after this incident that Jesus ascended to the invisible realm of heaven and appeared before *Yahweh* God his Father. There is no indication how this occurred with Jesus in his body, except that by some supernatural miracle his body temporarily dissolved until his return to the material realm on earth and then he reassumed his bodily nature. In terms of earthly time this would have occurred over the course of the first day of the week, after his appearance to the 2 woman and Peter, but before meeting with Luke and Cleopas on the road to Emmaus. Since the realm of the spirit transcends time, much more could have occurred in heaven.

There are several passages that describe what occurred when Jesus returned to the presence of *Yahweh* God in heaven shortly after his resurrection.

> Behold with the clouds of heaven there came one appearing as a person, and he came up to the Ancient of Days and was presented before Him. And to him was given dominion and glory and kingdom, that all peoples should serve him. His dominion is an eternal dominion which will never pass away, and his kingdom is one that will never be destroyed. Dan 7:13-14.
> Just as I have conquered and sat down with the Father on His throne. Rev 3:21.

For completing to the satisfaction of the Father human life and knowing now the needs of his subjects, he was now capable of assuming the rule over them. *Yahweh* God delegated to His son the reign over the kingdom and the subjection of the people to him. He was seated upon the throne next to his Father.

> God has highly exalted him and bestowed upon him a name that is above every name, that at the name of Jesus every knee will bend, in heaven and on earth and under the earth, and every tongue will confess that Jesus the Anointed is *Adonai* (Lord), to the glory of [*Yahweh*] God the Father. Phil 2:9-11. Also Eph 1:21-22.

Very similar to the above passage pertaining to Jesus' exaltation, but this passage deals with his justification after his discredit. The fact that Jesus would be unjustly persecuted and discredited and finally shamed by the authorities of the era before the general population is recorded in Is 52. Now that Jesus is justified by *Yahweh* God before his enemies they are forced to now accept him for exactly what he claimed himself to be, King of Israel. His enemies are forced to subject themselves and render homage to the same person that they earlier discredited and shamed. This triumph was fulfilled in the resurrection, as an indication to *Yahweh* God's enemies that Jesus is rightful heir to the throne and judge of all peoples.

> For the Anointed has entered, not into a sanctuary constructed, a copy of the real one, but into heaven itself, now to appear in the presence of God on our behalf. Heb 9:24.
> When he made purification for sins, he sat at the right side of the Majesty above. Heb 1:4.

The 3$^{rd}$ purpose of Jesus ascending to heaven at this time is here stated. He brought at this time his own eternal life - symbolized by blood - before *Yahweh* God. In the capacity of both high priest and sacrifice he procured eternal redemption for those who accept him as high priest and his sacrifice on their behalf. On earth it was a human, Jesus of Nazareth, who died, and which event represented a greater event in heaven, Jesus son of *Yahweh* God presenting himself as both eternal priest and living sacrifice on behalf of his people. What occurred on earth to him as a human was a type of what occurred in heaven to him as a spirit entity at his ascension. This can be explained as follows: The physical blood of Jesus flowed down his body, onto the stake and on the ground. There in the ground the physical blood of Jesus eventually decayed and reverted back into the elements of soil, just as with the blood of any other human. The blood of heaven was symbolic of the life of Jesus himself. Just as he dedicated the final years of his life on earth on behalf of his people Israel, so in heaven he dedicates his life likewise for all eternity.

Having watched ticker-tapes parades for heroes and military parades with great honor bestowed upon the victors after some war, I wonders whether such may have occurred in heaven. With the return of the son of *Yahweh* God home after such an ordeal on earth, could the messengers and ministering spirits and sons of *Yahweh* God have lined the access or path to the throne of *Yahweh* God, shouting praises at him while waving and clapping their hands? The scene of Rev 5:11-12, portraying the hosts of heaven giving praise to the Lamb can well be applied here.

After all this victorious festivity was completed in heaven Jesus returned to the earth and reassumed his former body. He showed himself first to the 2 disciples on the road to Emmaus, and then to the others for the balance of 40 days.

## THE ACTIVITY OF JESUS AT PRESENT

With the ascension of Jesus to heaven, he ascended the throne of glory of his Father *Yahweh* God. Rev 3:21. His work as high priest on behalf of the people of the New Covenant began. Heb 4:14. And his work as judge began in preparation for the great day. Acts 17:31.

All in all the progress in the heavens continues now as it did 2,000 or 6,000 years ago. It is the progress on earth that seems to continually change generation after generation. Heaven cannot change, it must be stable to provide a concrete and dependable basis for the millennia and eons of history in the material spheres, the life on earth and the universal creation. For this reason the author of Hebrews states:

> Jesus the Anointed [is] the same yesterday, today and tomorrow. Heb 13:8.

Today Jesus son of *Yahweh* God, the high priest of our profession, stands before *Yahweh* God who sits upon His throne. Here Jesus tells his father, "Have mercy upon these people father, Have mercy upon those who strive to live according to Your will and covenant and moral code. Have mercy upon them for my sake. Send to them strength, grace and the comfort of

Your Holy Spirit. Send it to those who repent and believe in You, who ask in my name. I know what it is like down there. I was one of them."

*Yahweh* God grants his son – the mediator on their behalf – their petition. *Yahweh* God receives the request of His son, is cooperative with the son in granting his request, and proceeds to fulfill it and do all necessary for the petitioners. The Holy Spirit flows from the Father to the believer on earth at the request of His son, the supreme mediator. John 14:26.

*Yahweh* God is willing to be cooperative with the son in fulfilling His requests because of 2 reasons. The initial reason is the concern of the son for his people. The son is an eternally living sacrifice on behalf of his people. The son realizes the needs of his people having experienced the same and knowing their needs. The second reason *Yahweh* God grants the request of His son is because the son was willing to become one of them. The son was willing and did accomplish the dictate of the Father. The son vacated his exalted position in heaven to become a human, and was a human experiencing all typical circumstances that apply to a human, even to a death to typify the death of every person on earth. *Yahweh* God grants the request of His son because the incarnation though death experience proved beyond doubt the sincerity of the son in wanting to help his people.

The most difficult concept for members of Christianity to acknowledge is that Jesus has ascended to heaven and resides as a spirit in the heavens. He is no longer in a manger and no longer hangs on a stake. Stephen noted this in the words of his admonishment to the religious leaders:

> But he full of the Holy Spirit, gazed into heaven and saw the glory of God and Jesus standing at the right hand of God. Acts 7:55.

The vision of John apostle in Rev 1:13-16, provides us with the Jesus of today, or as he has been since the day of his ascension to heaven 40 days after his resurrection. This is the real Jesus allegorically described: aged, strong, authoritative, wearing a garment symbolic of royalty and priestly service. Maturity of the true Christian will only occur when the maturity of Jesus is accepted, when the images of Jesus in a manger or on a cross are finally reduced to their place in past history, and he is acknowledged as attaining the fullness of his Father *Yahweh*.

## JESUS HAS ALREADY RETURNED

Jesus also returned as he promised, although not in the manner the people expected him to and this was fulfilled on the holy day of Pentecost with the 120 gathered.

The apostle Paul writes that the church is the body of Jesus, 1 Cor 12:12, 27. This spiritual body of Jesus was created on this holy day of Pentecost. It was created out of the 120 who were gathered, and when God blew with his Holy Spirit into the assembly they became the living body of Jesus the Anointed on earth. So in this manner did Jesus return to earth, in his spiritual body – the church.

## WHO KILLED JESUS ?

Opinions vary regarding the party or individual responsible for the death of Jesus son of *Yahweh* God. The Scriptures however are very specific about this topic.

> And how our chief priests and rulers delivered him up to be condemned to death, and crucified him. Luke 24:20.
> None of the rulers of this age understood this; for it they had they would not have crucified the Lord of glory. 1 Cor 2:8.
> Men of Israel,... this Jesus,... you crucified and killed by the hands of lawless men. Acts 2:23.

Similar statements are also made by Peter in Acts 2:13, and 4:28.

In the first 2 passages the specific reference is to the governing hierarchy of the priesthood – the Sanhedrin. It was the senior priests and elders having the authority who are specifically designated as taking the active effort in prosecution and demanding the sentence of capital punishment. Then we have the mob that stood before Pontius Pilate and cried,

> "Away with him, away with him. Let him be crucified." John 19:15.
> "Let his blood be upon us and our children." Matt 27:25.

The general population of Israel were in their homes that night celebrating Passover while the trial against Jesus was underway in the Sanhedrin and later in the palace of Herod. They were eating the Passover and could not leave their homes in accord with Ex 12:22. None of the general population was allowed in public that evening. It was however the priests that violated this rule and deliberately in order that the population not know what was occurring. This is the reason the priests would not enter the chambers of Pilate at his palace: they did not want to defile themselves since they still had to eat the Passover with their families that evening. John 18:28. This also indicates that Jesus celebrated the Passover with his disciples at the same time as the balance of Jews in Jerusalem. Jesus and his disciples left Jerusalem earlier that evening in order to allow the priests and soldiers to arrest him and conclude the trial without upsetting the Jerusalem population that special festival evening.

It was not the general population that was directly responsible, but solely the religious hierarchy. For this reason anti-Semitism is a distortion of Scripture. It is not Jews of previous or later generations, or Jews of other areas, or even those of the era who were not aware of the trial and sentence, who are implicated in the death of Jesus. The Jews responsible for the murder of Jesus were strictly those at this trial by the Sanhedrin, those demanding his execution, and those who discredited him during crucifixion. All of them faced judgment for their crime during the siege and destruction of Jerusalem about 40 years later. His blood was upon them and their children. These prophetic words of the Sadducees were fulfilled.

## 2. THE MESSAGE OF JESUS AND THE APOSTLES

### LANGUAGE OF THE GOSPELS

One point long forgotten or avoided by students of the Greek NT is that the primary means of communication of Jesus the Anointed and the 1st century middle-eastern world was the Aramaic language. Aramaic was the daily and domestic and business language of the era beginning about 500 BC and up to shortly after the 2nd Jewish War of 132-135 AD. This was the language of the Jews who lived in Babylon the 70 years, and the language of the exiles who returned from Babylon to Jerusalem under the leaders Zerubbabel and Ezra. Most of the book of Daniel is Aramaic, along with a large section in Ezra, and one verse in Jeremiah. Jer 10:10.

When Jews in Jerusalem gathered at the water gate to listen to Ezra read the Scriptures to them, circa 440 BC, it was necessary to have certain others to help the people understand the meaning of the law. Neh 8:7-8. The returned exiles from Babylon had lost vernacular of the Hebrew language and now were fluent in Aramaic. Ezra read in Hebrew and these other men with Ezra translated what was read into Aramaic for the population to understand.

Hebrew was the synagogue and temple language. It was known by all the priests, scribes and all involved in the religious services. The general Jewish population had some knowledge of Hebrew in order to understand the Law and Prophets and Writings - *Tanahk* - read in the synagogue every Sabbath. But the extent of Hebrew was very narrow, since few schools were available to teach it and the only use of it was related to religious services.

When Jesus of Nazareth spoke and taught the disciples and his audience that gathered about him, it was not in Greek and not in Hebrew that he taught, but in Aramaic. What we read in the Greek NT gospels is not actually what Jesus said. All of it is a translation from Aramaic into Greek. Traditionally, the gospel of Matthew is considered to be originally written in Aramaic, and was subsequently translated into Greek. The Aramaic original is long lost. The gospels of John and Luke appear to have been written originally in Greek, because the vocabulary matches directly with *koine* Greek literature rather than evidence of translation from another language. Luke himself would have acquired his information in Aramaic form from reputable sources after much investigation and translated it himself into Greek for the general population.

One item to note is that it was not the intent of the final Gospel redactors to provide a biography of Jesus or a narrative of his ministry for the Jews. They already knew this. Whoever these final redactors were, and who published the final versions utilizing their source information, their audience were the gentiles, meaning the non-Jewish citizens and residents of the Roman Empire, whose common language was Greek. They took what previous manuscripts were available in Aramaic – so with Matthew, Mark and Luke – and translated into Greek and supplemented them with whatever other stories or narratives they could find. The Gospel of John, most likely, was originally composed in Greek.

Their intent was primarily the ministry of Jesus: his life and teachings between the time of his baptism by John at the Jordan River. and his ascension to heaven after his resurrection from death. The birth and infancy narratives were included only as an introduction or as supplementary information to correlate the fulfillment of OT prophecies about Jesus' conception and birth.

Scholars who researched the chronology of the composition of the 4 Gospels, claim the earliest is the Gospel of Mark, originally composed about 60 AD, 30 years after Jesus death, just before the Jewish War; the next Gospel of Matthew about 80 to 90 AD, and shortly thereafter the Gospel of Luke about 90 to 100 AD, both after the conclusion of the Jewish War. Later the Gospel of John was composed, about 120-130 AD, just before the Bar Kochba Rebellion of 132-135 AD.

The final redacted Gospels were probably circulated about 150 AD to the general public, about 120 years after Jesus' death, but no earlier, and maybe as late as 180 AD, and which is most probable.

The redactors of the final Greek versions were most likely early gentile converts of the Apostle Paul or maybe Timothy or Appolos or Titus or another preaching to the non-Jewish residents of the Roman Empire. Their purpose in composing the narratives of Jesus' teaching and ministry was to convert people to their new Christian religion. The Gospels were not for the Jews, or a refutation of the reason as to why the Jews of the era refused to accept Jesus as God's Anointed or Messiah. They were intended to be a tool for conversion of the gentiles: it was a history of Jesus' ministry, his parables and moral instruction, incidents with people and confrontations, including why the Pharisees did not like him, why the Sadducees wanted to kill him, and how Jesus was betrayed to Pontius Pilate and executed as a political criminal. But then Jesus resurrected from death 3 days later.

The purpose of the Gospels were a tool for the conversion of non-Jews to the new religion of Christianity, and so they solely focused on the era of Jesus' ministry.

With the gospel of Mark, the church historian Eusebius indicates that it was actually Peter apostle who dictated to Mark the ministry of Jesus.[15] I contend that as Peter apostle dictated in Aramaic, Mark mentally translated into Greek and so wrote it. This is the best reason to account for certain variations in the words of Jesus in Greek, which are difficult to understand and especially when translated from Greek into English. One example will be cited, which is the passage.

> "It is easier for a camel to go through the eye of a needle than for a rich man to enter into the kingdom of God." Luke 18:25.

This verse taken at face value makes no sense as an allegory, and there is no door in the walls of Jerusalem called the eye of a needle. This was a later interpolation by Christian preachers to account for the difficulty in interpretation. But in the Aramaic, the word for camel and the word for rope are pronounced identically. The translators of the gospels into Greek from Aramaic incorrectly rendered the Aramaic word rope as camel. George Lamsa in his Aramaic translation renders this passage correctly. "It is easier for a rope to pass through the eye of a needle..." Which rendering is understandable as an allegory. Since Mark is considered the earliest gospel, and which was utilized by both Matthew and Luke, including Mark's translation into Greek of Peter apostles account in the original Aramaic, this same variation appears in all 3 gospels. The blame of incorrect translation could be placed on the gospel-writer Mark.

---

[15] *Ecclesiastical History*, Eusebius, Bk. II, Chap. XV.

# THE JEWISH MESSIANIC HOPE

With the advent of the Anointed, Jews of the era hoped for the return of their land, their repossession it. They looked for the removal of the aliens and their influence and military. These were the Romans who had military occupation of the land, and the government, taxation and cult of their emperor in Judea. In fulfillment of the hopes of influential Jewish sages beginning 65 BC, after the defeat by Pompey, the Anointed would defect the alien military occupation and return control of the land to Israel. The contemporary residents hoped that the Anointed would act just as David did when he defeated the Philistines and expanded the kingdom by military conquest, so would the Anointed son of David likewise defeat the Romans. the Anointed would conscript an army, manufacture weapons and uniforms, and use his divine strategy to gain a supernatural victory over the Romans. Subsequently Jews would reestablish the kingdom and the Messianic age would begin and last forever.

All of these hopes were good intentions, but not what Scripture dictated regarding the work of the Anointed. No doubt Jews hoped to be exalted in the presence of their enemies, and as if turn the tables on them. Instead of being in captivity in their own homeland they would be the victors. The promise of Is 61:5-7 and other similar passages whet the appetite of many a Jew for a supernatural military, political and religious leader to rescue them from enemy occupation and oppression. Applicable to the contemporary history of the era was the drive of enmity and spite of the Jews toward the Roman occupation. This had recently erupted in revolt and insurrection in the northern portion of Judea, the crime of several men in the Galilean cities of Sepphoris and Grishala. Their sin was fostering revolt against the Romans. All of such groups advocating violent overthrow of the Roman military occupation were outlawed by the Roman authority, and as such, were summarily executed after apprehension. The provincial capital Sepphoris was burnt by the Romans in 3 AD to subdue insurrection in Galilee. Thousands were executed in the early years under Herod the Great, and hundreds of thousands in the Jewish Wars of 66-70 AD, and 132-135 AD.

## JESUS' PERFECTION OF THE RELIGION OF ISRAEL

It was never the intent of Jesus to start a new religion. A person only needs to study thoroughly the 4 Gospels to determine this. No where does Jesus make any statement of starting a new religion. His intent was to spiritualize the religion of Israel and this would be his new congregation.

Jesus made this statement in his Sermon on the Mount, and which also can be understood if we append it with a passage from Apostle Paul:

> I have not come to abolish the law or the prophets, but to fulfill. Matt 5:17
> For the Anointed is the goal of the law... Rom 10:4

So what does this mean? Jesus' intent was to perfect the religion of Israel by spiritualizing it: all the rites and ceremonies would terminate and the spiritual significance would materialize.

When Jesus was walking through Samaria he stopped at the well of Jacob, where a woman of the city also was coming to draw water. They started a conversation about water and this sparked an interest in the woman as far as where the proper place of worship is. The Samaritans would worship at a mountain called Gerizim, while the Jews would worship at the temple at Jerusalem. So Jesus response was the following:

> The time is coming when neither on this mountain nor in Jerusalem will you worship the Father... But the time is coming and now is when the true worshippers will worship the Father in Spirit and truth, for such the Father seeks to worship him. God is spirit and those who worship him must worship in Spirit and truth. John 4:21, 23-24

I have compiled the following list in regard to the spiritualization of the religion of Israel which intent was Jesus' to accomplish.

1. What Jesus is saying is that the place does not matter. The objective is to worship God as a spirit, and the person can do this wherever he or she is. Jesus regarding this, "Where 2 or 3 are gathered, I am among them." Matt 18:20. So a person does not have to go to some special place to worship God.

2. The place does not need superficial decoration, such as stained glass windows, depictions of Jesus as a corpse on a cross or as a shepherd, or any of the holy men or women of the ages, or a cross or crucifix. Since God is a spirit, no superficial decoration is needed.
3. Jesus terminated the sacrifices and offering presented in the temple. He was the Passover sacrifice to start. The balance are fulfilled in ourselves, as the Apostle wrote, "Present your bodies as a living sacrifice, holy and acceptable to God, which is your spiritual worship." Rom 12:1.
4. Jesus terminated the Aaron priesthood and replaced it with the spiritual priesthood of Melchizedek. "He has made us to be kings and priests on Earth." Rev 1:6. The Apostle Peter also stated that we are a "Holy Priesthood," 1 Peter 2:5; and a "Royal Priesthood," 1 Peter 2:9. As a result the new Messianic community does not have an ordained priesthood, as any person can pray for another.
5. Genealogy is no longer based on being a member of the posterity of Abraham, but now consists of those who are born again, born of the water and spirit. John 3:3-6.
6. The kingdom is also spiritual. No longer is the physical land of Israel a sacred region, but as the Apostle Paul said, "Your residency is in heaven." Phil 3:20.
7. The battle against enemies is now a spiritual battle, not a physical. The Apostle Paul wrote, "For we are not contending against flesh and blood, but against the principalities, against the power of wickedness in high places, against the world rulers of this present darkness." Eph 6:12. This is why true Christians do not serve in the military or engage in war, as the war is not against a physical enemy, but a spiritual one.

In this manner did Jesus consummate the religion of Israel, to bring it to perfection.

## JESUS AS MESSIAH OR THE ANOINTED OF GOD

Violence in previous generations decimated the population of Israel, devastated the land and brought more tragedy to the nation. The Jews were ill-equipped to defeat a powerful and formidable enemy such as Rome.

The manner proposed by Jesus to deliver the nation from devastation was by reconciling the people as individuals with the Roman occupation. Peaceful coexistence was the sole means of the survival of Israel under Roman occupation.

When Jesus said, "Resist not evil," he was not speaking of the general law of retribution for a crime committed. Matt 5:39. Crime must be resisted and dealt with judicially. In this context the words of not resisting evil are followed by the attitude that the soldiers of Roman occupation had toward the Jews: abusing them in public; illegal appropriation of their property; demands of the Jews for transport, food and other services. Jesus was requiring his fellow Jews to be tolerant of this mistreatment by the Roman soldiers, and not seek retribution or vengeance. Eventually the spiritual kingdom will gain the victory if the Jews place their hope in *Yahweh* God and not their revolutionary leaders.

When Jesus said, "Love your enemies and pray for those who persecute you," he was not referring to any enemy. Matt 5:44. Nowhere in Scripture does it say to hate your enemy. Even when Moses dictates to the people of Israel to annihilate the nations of Canaan he does not utilize the word hate. There was a difference between the necessity of executing the judgment of *Yahweh* God upon the identified enemy in organized warfare in OT times and the judgment upon a criminal, and the attitude of hate. In reality there is no reason to hate anybody. Hate is an emotion; execution of a criminal is judgment. Regularly David king and psalm-writer relates vengeance and retribution on enemies. Ps 41:10. But the explicit statement to hate an enemy is not to be found. This concept of hating an enemy evolved during the era of the Hasmonaens and their struggle for independence from Greek occupation and Hellenic philosophical invasion. 1 Macc 4:18. This attitude again surfaced with the Roman occupation beginning in 65 BC, and which climaxed under the rule of Herod the Great during the final decade of his life. The freedom fighters and many of the Jewish hierarchy taught the people to hate the Romans, and which only caused a greater rift between the residents and the occupation forces. This resulted in the massacre of tens of thousands of Jews during the reign of Herod the Great. Jewish children were engrained with the attitude from childhood that the Roman occupation forces were the enemy and should be hated.

When Jesus told his disciples, "Bless those that curse you and do good to those who hate you," he referring to a change of attitude the Jews must undergo toward the Roman occupation force, if they wanted to avoid total annihilation in the future. Matt 5:44. The victory over the enemy was to be gained by reconciliation. This change of attitude by the Jewish population of Palestine towards the Roman occupation forces would deliver them from their enemies. Luke 1:68-71. The spiritual kingdom would then flourish in the new spiritual Israel coincidental with peaceful coexistence. His would materialize as a spiritual community flourishing within a secular government. Jesus referred to himself as being in the world but not part of it. John 17:14.

Growing up in Nazareth only 3 miles from the political center of Galilee, Sepphoris, and traveling with his father in the carpentry business throughout most of Galilee, Jesus was well familiar with the political unrest of the area. It was in Galilee that violent overthrow was conceived by disenchanted and oppressed Jews seeking independence, and all of this Jesus saw during those years living in Nazareth. He also saw the regiments of Roman troops in rank and file marching down the main roads and highways with their banners, and the armed disciplined soldiers making their presence known to all the residents. As a prophet Jesus saw in the distant future the annihilation of his people if this course of adverse political action against Roman authority persisted. Even as a young man he heard rumors and was propositioned with invitations to join such groups, but he early realized that the Romans were no match for the unorganized Jews. The regimented military force of Rome could easily quell any disturbance or even war. These unorganized Jewish splinter groups with their own unstable leadership and lack of cohesion were no match for the well-trained and disciplined ranks of Roman soldiers, who were instilled by their leadership to savage and ruthless war. Cowardice or desertion by a Roman soldier was treason and grounds for immediate and public execution and disgrace of office. The Jews who advocated independence through violent overthrow had no such discipline or organization on such a large scale.

This was the primary purpose of the appearance of the Anointed Jesus, to deliver Israel from devastation by Rome by inaugurating the spiritual kingdom and forming the Messianic community, the spiritual Israel under the new covenant. Jesus wanted his people to show Romans that there was no intention of violent overthrown, and that the 2 uncommon nationalities could reside in a peaceful coexistence. Jesus wanted Jews to go out of their way to cooperate with Romans to show them they meant them no harm.

The few revolutionaries who sought independence from Rome were to cease and desist with a cognizance that the real kingdom was not to be gained in war and military struggle.

The relative status or relation of the 2 factions was later summarized in the parable noted in Luke 14:31-32. Here Jesus spoke of a king having an army of 10,000 who should first consider whether his military force is enough to defeat another king whose army was 20,000. The wise and intelligent king would send a delegation to conclude a peace treaty rather than risk defeat. With such a peace treaty agreed to by both parties, neither will suffer casualties and property losses. This is to the greatest benefit of the king with the smaller army, who has now secured deliverance of his entire population instead of massive and shameful defeat. This was the intent of this parable to the multitudes. Luke 14:25. Their leaders in Galilee promoting violent overthrow of Roman occupation were the king with the army of 10,000; and the Romans were the army of 20,000. If their countrymen and themselves had any wisdom at all they would seek peaceful coexistence with the Romans. In this manner they would deliver themselves from military defeat and massive devastation.

The purpose of the ministry of Jesus is disclosed in this parable. It was not armed revolt against the Romans to gain independence, but the effort on behalf of the people to them to conclude a peace treaty, peaceful coexistence with the Romans.

Another passage is the following statement Jesus made as he was led to crucifixion:

> And a great multitude of the people followed Him, and women who also mourned and lamented Him. But Jesus, turning to them, said, "Daughters of Jerusalem, do not weep for Me, but weep for yourselves and for your children. For indeed the days are coming in which they will say, 'Blessed *are* the barren, wombs that never bore, and breasts which never nursed!' Then they will begin to say to the mountains, "Fall on us!" and to the hills, "Cover us!" 'For if they do these things in the green wood, what will be done in the dry?" Luke 23:27-30

Jesus was speaking of the time when the Roman armies would surround Jerusalem to siege and destroy it. It would be better of mothers did not have children, as they would suffer and many be killed at the hands of the Roman soldiers.

This seems to be the most difficult point for Christianity to accept, that the primary reason for the ministry of Jesus as the Anointed was to rescue the contemporary and successive generations of Jews from annihilation and the land from devastation by the Roman military. In this manner Jesus was to rescue his people from their crimes.

## JESUS IN THE TEMPLE

*Yahweh* God executed his retribution in ancient times in the middle east through instruments of his will. He does not personally accomplish His vengeance or penalty, because He is spirit. *Yahweh* God utilizes instruments in performing His will: people and armies; natural disasters and weather; disease, and etc. All of these effects are instruments and are utilized in some manner at the proper time and place for the proper and effective result.

*Yahweh* God stated through Jeremiah prophet that He will execute judgment on the southern kingdom Judea for violation of the covenant. Jer 7:14. In reality *Yahweh* God utilized an instrument to do so: the army of Babylon. Jer 5:15-17. Later *Yahweh* God stated that He will execute judgment on Babylon for pride and violation of the law of *Yahweh* God. Jer 51:14,24-25. Then *Yahweh* God states that the armies of Media and Persian will be the instrument by which this penalty will be imposed on Babylon. Jer 51:20-23. In Ex 23:23, *Yahweh* God clearly states that He will blot out or expunge the nations of Canaan out of existence. But in Deut 7:2, Israel is commanded to utterly destroy them. As in the previous cases, *Yahweh* God is executing the judgment sentence on them, but now using the army of Israel as His instrument.

The same applies to statements by Jesus, who was judge and jury and pronounced the guilty verdict on the Sadducees. Matt 23:32-36. This final day of teaching in the temple begins at Matt 21:23. The balance of Matt 21 and chapters 22 and 23 all occur in the temple. Several scenarios occurring one after another: priests and elders and Herodians, Pharisees and Sadducees, all of them taking their turn questioning and attempting to entrap Jesus. On every occasion Jesus was able to answer them without incriminating himself. The crowd of worshippers and disciples watched the confrontations and debates and verbal altercations between them, and listened to his parables of the 2 sons, the wicked tenants, and the marriage feast. The confrontation culminated in the reprimand of hypocrisy of the priests and elders in Matt 23. If we could imagine what occurred at this time, the final minutes of Jesus' presence in the temple, he is telling the people of the hypocrisy and corruption of these religious leaders. The crowd huddles around him and the priests and elders a short distance away. Then he points to them and recites the words:

> That upon you may come all the righteous blood shed on Earth… Truly I say to you, all this will come upon this generation. Matt 23:35-36.

The people are aghast at his words. The priests and elders are astounded at his threat. Never before had someone threatened the elders and priests with the vengeance of *Yahweh* God, that they were guilty of the murder of earlier prophets of God sent to them to preach repentance. Jesus then gathered his small group of disciples and exited the temple. His words meant exactly what he said, that sometime in the near future the family of the high priest Annas, the Sadducees and their associates would answer for the lives of the ancient and contemporary saints with their own life. There was no doubt in anybody's mind: they felt that Jesus himself would fulfill his threat against them.

## THE THREE QUESTIONS OF THE DISCIPLES

Jesus and his retinue of disciples left the court of the temple and proceeded down the steps. Toward the outer edge of the temple grounds the disciples began to complement the beauty and grandeur and massive size of the temple. Jesus replied to their boasts of the massive stones that served as walls,

> "You see all these, do you not? I say to you, there will not be left here one stone upon another that will not be thrown down." Matt 24:2.

Perhaps someone had reiterated the words of Jesus about destroying the temple and rebuilding it in 3 days. This is recorded in John 2:19. The statement of the disciples were to focus the attention of Jesus to his words. This was also accepted by the elders and priests as a direct threat, that he would himself destroy the temple. Those who heard him understood his statement as a direct threat. During the mock trial of Jesus by the Sanhedrin, 2 men said, "This fellow said, 'I am able to destroy the temple of God and to build it in 3 days.'" Matt 26:61. Also as Jesus was suspended from the stake during crucifixion miscreants harassed him saying, "You who would destroy the temple and build it in 3 days, save yourself." Matt 27:40. Mark 15:29. The general audience along with the disciples, elders and priests understood Jesus as saying that he would himself accomplish the dismantle or demolition of the temple.

Leaving the temple grounds Jesus and his retinue left the boundaries of the city and went to a quiet area at the mount of Olives. From the hillside where the teacher sat with his disciples the temple could be clearly seen. The questions posed by the disciples vary slightly in the 3 synoptic gospels. Mark and Luke agree that 2 questions were submitted to Jesus, while Matthew records 3 questions:

> "Tell us when this will be and what will be the sign when these things are all to occur." Mark 13:4. Luke 21:7.
> "Tell us when this will be, and what will be the sign of your arrival, and of the close of the age." Matt 24:3.

Both questions of Mark and Luke and 2 of the 3 questions of Matthew pertain to recent points of discussion: The execution of the elders and priests, and the demolition of the temple. The disciples had just heard the reprimands and conversations and heard the statement of Jesus regarding the demolition of the temple. Now as they sat on the mount of Olives the disciples were interested as to when Jesus was going to fulfill his words, when was all of this to occur. The 3$^{rd}$ question of Matthew pertains to the close of the age of Moses, the old covenant, with the subsequent initiation of the age of the new covenant. There is no reason to doubt that the disciples also understood that this was to occur prior to the demise of that generation, since this statement of Jesus is recorded in all 3 gospel accounts. Matt 23:36. Mark 13:30. Luke 21:32. There is no evidence or justifiable reason to allocate the questions of the disciples to anything other than those points of discussion not over 1 hour earlier, and the 3$^{rd}$ question of the end of the age, which pertained to the fulfillment of 2 of the parables recited that day in the temple: vengeance on the wicked tenants, and the marriage feast for the king's son. Both of these parables to materialize at the conclusion of the age. Matt 24 is not to be isolated from Matt 21-23. The train of thought, or the vein of discussion, continues from Matt 23 and into Matt 24 and then into Matt 25.

One of the reasons for misinterpretation of Matt 24 is the archaic mistranslation of the Greek *aeon* as world. The KJV translation reads, "End of the world." This mistranslation has created a milieu of misconceptions of the intent of this passage. Later translations such as the ASV of 1901, and the Douay-Confraterity, did not correct it. Only with the RSV of 1952 and subsequent versions was the word *aeon* correctly rendered as age. This statement in the NT is responsible for the so-called doctrine of eschatology more that any other single passage, when in actuality there is no end of the world as we know it. This world has existed for millions of years into the past and will continue to do so for millions of years into the future.

The correct rendering of the final question to Jesus by the disciples is, "When will the close of the age occur?" If Jesus be the Anointed, whom he claimed he was and gave people the impression he was, and later he admitted in the presence of the priests and elders that he was, the disciples wanted to know when the present age of Moses, the old covenant, was to conclude, and the new age to begin under himself with the institution of a new covenant and the spiritual kingdom. The return of Jesus to execute the above tasks must be separated from events that are destined to occur at some time distant into the future, such as the restoration of the earth to its original immortal and pristine state, the resurrection from death, and the eternal kingdom.

## FULFILLMENT OF THE 3 QUESTIONS

Regarding the first question on the demolition of the temple, on September 9, 70 AD, a Roman soldier shot a flaming arrow into the temple. This caused the curtains to catch fire. As a result of this, the temple structure burned and within days was rubble. According to traditional sources, while the temple was burning the heat was so intense that it melted the gold that served as the cover on the dome. This gold then flowed like a liquid down the side of the walls of the temples. When the flames cooled the gold remained in the crevices between the stones. To recover the gold, and in order to remove the gold from the crevices, the soldiers dismantled the temple walls stone by stone. When the soldiers finished their task not one stone was atop another.

After the Jewish War of 132-135 AD, with the defeat of Bar Kochba by the Roman military, what was left of the temple was razed and Roman Emperor Hadrian had the balance of the temple foundation dismantled. When Micah said that Jerusalem would be plowed like a field and become a heap of ruins, Micah 3:12, not only was his reference to the area where the temple of Solomon once stood in its grandeur, but also equally pertained to the area where the magnificent temple built by Herod the Great stood. After the army of Hadrian was finished, Zion could "be plowed as a field," and Jerusalem was "a heap of ruins." What is today known as the wailing wall is a testimony to the fulfillment of Jesus' words. The wailing wall is not a wall at all. These stones were laid by Herod's workmen underground as a foundation for the walls of the temple.

The 2nd question asked by the disciples pertained to the priests and elders responsibility for the death of the saints of *Yahweh* God. The Sadducees themselves accepted the responsibility for innocent blood in their statement to Pontius Pilate. Matt 27:25. This was prophecy self-fulfilled. They admitted to Pilate that Jesus was innocent of charges that would demand capital punishment. They definitely knew it when they made such a statement, and so they agreed to be personally responsible and also attached the responsibility to their offspring. It cannot be forgotten though that these words applied specifically to that generation of Jews and not to any other. That generation did answer for the murder of Jesus during the Jewish Wars, and they were the victims of the bloodshed during the siege of Jerusalem, from April to September, 70 AD. Priests and worshippers were massacred on the temple grounds in the thousands as a result of the strife for control of the city. The majority of priests and elders were killed by the feuding factions in the city, killed by their own countrymen in attempts to gain political control of the city. The Roman military executed few priests. There are 2 passages in Revelation that indicate in allegorical form the execution of the guilty Sadducees and priests and destruction of Jerusalem for the death of ancient prophets of Israel.

> As they have shed the blood of your saints and prophets, so you have given them blood to drink as they deserve. Rev 15:6.
> In her was found the blood of prophets and saints and all who have been killed in the land. Rev 18:24.

The phrase from Abel to Zechariah in Matt 23:35, refers to the entire gamut of holy men executed and persecuted in OT times. In the Hebrew Bible the arrangement of books is different than the English, which is based on the Septuagint. The book 2 Chronicles is the final book in the OT Hebrew Bible. The murder of Zechariah priest is mentioned is 2 Chron 24:20-21. In essence Jesus told the elders and priests they would answer with their own life for every holy person killed or persecuted from the first in the Bible to the last. (The addition of the statement "son of Berechiah" appears to be an insertion by a scribe or redactor to refer to Zechariah prophet, the $2^{nd}$ to the final book of the OT Septuagint order of books.)

## THE LAST DAYS

The Jewish sages of the era taught that the Anointed would deliver the people from their enemies and initiate a new realm, the age of the Anointed. That period of time just prior to the materialization of the age of the Anointed, the closing years of the old covenant and old Israel, is referred to in the NT as the "last days." The study of those passages dealing with this follows.

On Pentecost after the ascension of Jesus Peter apostle gave his sermon regarding the descent and baptism of the holy Spirit. He quoted the OT prophecy in Joel 2:22-23, and indicated that the event occurring that day was its fulfillment.

> But this is what was spoken by the prophet Joel, "And in the last days it shall be, God declares, that I will pour out My spirit upon all flesh..." Acts 2:16-17.

This prophecy pertained to the outpour of the holy Spirit at the close of the old age, that period just prior to the beginning of the new age of the Anointed. Peter apostle correlated the "last days" of Joel prophet to the days subsequent to the ministry of Jesus of Nazareth. The outpour of the holy Spirit was the inauguration of the Messianic age. A typical Jew in Jerusalem would apply the words of Peter apostle that day to their own era. Peter apostle testified that Jesus of Nazareth was the promised Anointed. Acts 2:22-24. His resurrection from death was the divine testimony that he was the fulfillment of such prophecies as Ps 16:8-11 and Ps 110:1. Those familiar with the teaching of the Jewish sages and the OT prophecies would correlate Joel's words "last days" to their era, with the immediate materialization of the spiritual kingdom, the age of the Anointed.

The writer of the book of Hebrews follows the same vein as he writes to Messianic Jews of the new spiritual community.

> In many and various ways God spoke of old to our fathers by the prophets; but in these last days he has spoken to us by a son..." Heb 1:1-2

The last days referred to in this introduction to his Messianic treatise are the years of the ministry of Jesus. The writer spoke with the understanding they were living in the years of the termination of the old covenant, old kingdom, old priesthood, old sacrificial system, old temple, old rites, old genealogy, and the old age. All of this to be immediately replaced by a new covenant, new spiritual kingdom, new priesthood, new sacrifice, new temple, new genealogy, consummation of rites, and the new Messianic age, all of which was implemented by Jesus of Nazareth son of *Yahweh* God.

> But as it is, he has appeared once for all at the end of the ages to put away sin by the sacrifice of himself. Heb 9:26.

The ages mentioned in this passage refer to all the covenant eras beginning after the fall of the progenitors Adam and Eve. The first sacrifice for sin, or sin offering, was that of Cain and Abel. Many ages have transpired since the implementation of a sacrificial system with its rites and manner of sacrifice of clean animals. It was at the conclusion of these many ages that the sacrifice of *Yahweh* God appeared to once remove sin by the sacrifice of himself. Ps 40:6-7. After the crucifixion of Jesus, any other sacrifice was ineffective and obsolete.

There was no doubt in the mind of the author of Hebrews that Jesus son of *Yahweh* God appeared to the nation Israel during the final days or conclusion of the age of the old covenant. The temple was still standing and sacrifices were still being performed at the time the author wrote Hebrews. For this reason he wrote:

> And in speaking of a new covenant he treats the first as obsolete. And what is becoming obsolete is ready to vanish away. Heb 8:13.

The disappearance of what had become obsolete and archaic was consummated in the demolition of the temple. With the temple destroyed, the priesthood abolished, and sacrifices terminated, the covenant of Moses lost all effectiveness and was replaced in its totality by the covenant of Jesus. All of this occurred within a few years of the composition of the book to the Hebrews.

One other passage to review is the statement by Paul apostle.

> Now these things occurred to them as a warning, but they were written for our instruction, upon whom the end of the ages has come. 1 Cor 10:12.

The various covenants instituted by *Yahweh* God over the millennia since the initial population of the earth was discussed earlier in this volume. Each one of these periods of covenant effectiveness was an age. Thus the period of the ministry of Jesus is aptly termed the end of the ages. There would be no more ages to follow in earthly living or covenant institution, since the covenant of Jesus is the final one until the restoration and resurrection. The end is also understood as pertaining to the end of the physical nation of Israel as chosen of *Yahweh* God and a manifest cohesive body that *Yahweh* God recognized as His people. This was replaced by the spiritual kingdom of the new Israel.

The indication of when the old age would finally conclude and so initiate the new is explained by Jesus to his disciples in Matt 24 and Luke 21:5-33. Matthew, Mark and Luke record the statement of Jesus saying that his predictions and these events will occur within the time frame of the generation alive at that time. Matt 24:34. The specific time of the consummation of the close of that age is stated by Jesus. It was to occur immediately after the gospel of the spiritual kingdom was heard by all nations.

> And this gospel of the kingdom will be preached in the entire world as a testimony to all nations, and then the end will come. Matt 24:14.
> The gospel that you heard which has been preached to every creature under heaven, and of which I, Paul, became a minister. Col 1:23.

This reference is in line with other words of Jesus.

> For truly I say to you, you will barely pass through all the towns of Israel by the time this person (i.e. himself) arrives. Matt 10:23.

Every Jew living in the inhabited earth would have the opportunity to hear the good news of the spiritual kingdom before the age would close. Every Jew would have the opportunity to be born from above, be born of the word and spirit, and enter into the spiritual kingdom before the termination of the old. Now part of the spiritual kingdom they would be delivered by Jesus from the wrath to cover the entire inhabited world, the Roman Empire. Parallel with this was the upheaval during the Roman Civil War between the death of Nero Caesar in 68 AD and the ascension of Vespacian in 70 AD. The apostles and evangelists will barely have sufficient time to disclose the concept of the spiritual kingdom to the areas inhabited by Jews by the time the initial rebellions against Roman authority would begin in Judea. The purpose of disclosing this concept of the spiritual kingdom was for a testimony or witness unto the Jews of the era, that those who do not accept and enter the spiritual kingdom will perish in the political upheavals and civil wars of the season of temptation. Paul apostle and other apostles and evangelists spread the good news of the spiritual kingdom throughout the Roman Empire and Middle East and then shortly after the age ended.

## WITNESSES TO THE END OF THE OLD COVENANT

There are 2 enigmatic statements made by Jesus in the gospels that have baffled me for several decades, until concluding that Jesus' reference is to events in the immediate future. These 2 passages will be discussed individually.

> Truly I say to you, there are some standing here who will not taste death before they see this person coming in his kingdom. Matt 16:28.

The disciples numbered at least 70 at this time. Not all of them would die before the collapse of Israel as a nation. Some of them would remain alive to participate in the spiritual kingdom of the Messianic age, comprised of every race, color and ethnic origin, and be a witness to the words of Jesus.

In 1 Cor 15:6, Paul apostle mentions that some of the early witnesses had passed away, although many were still alive.

> If it is my will that he (John) remain until I (Jesus) come, what is that to you (Peter)? John 21:22.

Historical chroniclers and early Christian tradition testifies that all of the original 12 apostles, including Paul apostle, died before 66 AD, with the sole exception of John son of Zebedee. After John apostle's release from Patmos he moved to Ephesus to live there and in subsequent years wrote the gospel and 3 letters that bear his name as author. It was the will of Jesus that one of the original 12 survive the close of the age and greet the Messianic age. John apostle was to witness to the consummation of all the words recorded in the 3 synoptic gospels and Paul apostle regarding the events surrounding the close of the age and the return of Jesus to fulfill his words against the corrupt priests and elders.

> This is the disciple who is bearing witness to these matters, and who has written these matters, and we know that his (John's) testimony is true. John 21:24.

John apostle lived his final years as a testimony to the fulfillment of all spoken by Jesus. This is the reason that his gospel does not deal with this topic. Since John wrote after 70 AD, there was no reason to deal with the end of the age. John's focus was on the ministry and the effort of Jesus to convince the people, priests and elders that the was the Anointed, and that his words should be taken seriously. The events of the Jewish War were sufficient witness to the result of their rejection of Jesus as the Anointed. The word that he spoke did judge them on that last day.

## MIGRATION OUT OF JUDEA

The Christian Historian of the 4th century Eusebius records that the Messianic Jews fled Jerusalem prior to the beginning of the Jewish War.

> The whole body however of the church at Jerusalem, having been commanded by a divine revelation, given to men of approved piety

there before the war, removed from the city and dwelt at a certain town beyond the Jordan, called Pella.[16]

The migration to this city on the east side of the Jordan River, a Greek city, was the result of the statement by Jesus in Luke 21:20-21 and Matt 24:15-16. The catastrophe to be delivered from is that noted in Luke 21:20-21 and Matt 24:21. This is the salvation that Jesus taught the Jews of his era. Daniel prophet indicated that the area east of the Jordan and Dead Sea would be untouched by the upheaval of the end of the age, that this area would be a safe haven.

> But these shall be delivered out of his hand: Edom and Moab, and the main portion of Ammon. Dan 11:41.

This event can also be correlated with the flight of the wife clothed with the sun noted in Rev 12:7. The Jewish War lasted 1260 days, or 42 months, or 3-1/2 years, from the time that Vespacian's army entered the north of Judea in the spring of 66 AD to the conquest of Jerusalem in September 70 AD. This era is also referred to as the season of temptation or hour of tribulation, in Rev 3:10. The saints that fled Jerusalem to Pella can be identified with the 144,000 mentioned in Rev 7:3-4. They were allowed to leave prior to the beginning of the great tribulation, the Jewish War. The great multitude described in Rev 7:9-17, are those saints who remained in Judea. Instead of migrating to refuge they remained and endured great tribulation. Rev 7:14.

I contend that those who accepted the concept of the spiritual kingdom and Jesus as the Anointed heeded the warnings and prophecies and fled out of the areas that would be ravaged by war. Those taking refuge in these cities isolated from the "wrath which is to come," received the salvation that Jesus spoke about. Matt 3:7. This likewise applied to others living throughout the Roman Empire, to escape the turmoil of the era. 1 Thess 1:10. The Messianic communities were to look forward to the consummation of the age.

> Now when these things begin to take place, look up and raise your heads because your redemption arrives. Luke 21:28

---

[16] Ecclesiastical History, Bk. 3, chap. 5.

So also when you see these things taking place you know that the kingdom of God is near. Truly I say to you, this generation will not pass away till all has occurred. Heaven and earth will pass away, but my words will not pass away. Luke 21:31-33.

It was in these cities of the Messianic communities of the new spiritual Israel that Jesus returned by way of his baptism of the holy Spirit to consummate his spiritual kingdom. The Messianic communities reigned with the Anointed a 1000 years it seems within their spiritual kingdom in all consolation and joy, while the balance of the Jewish nation and Roman Empire was broiling in war, famine, plague, political conflict, social upheaval, receiving the due consequence for their crimes and unrepentant attitude. This was the manner of the return of Jesus to execute his judgment upon them. 2 Thess 1:7-10.

The hosts of heaven rejoiced at the inauguration of the spiritual kingdom of the Anointed on earth. They proclaimed their joy and the victory in these words:

The kingdom of this world has become that of our Lord and His Anointed and he shall reign for ages of ages. Rev 11:15

To leave Judea and Jerusalem was not an easy matter for many Jews. Only if an individual truly believed that Jesus of Nazareth was the Anointed and that his words would be fulfilled in that generation would they leave. The Messianic community had no more attachment to Jerusalem; like Abraham, they sought the city whose builder and maker is God. Heb 10:10. They likewise were not involved in the politics of Judea or in the Jewish religion, and especially the Pharisaic oral law. Since Jesus was high priest, sacrifice and temple, they had no reason to associate with the temple or any of its services, no reason to attend, and no reason to affiliate with any party or school within Judaism. Since their kingdom was spiritual, they had no reason to fight Romans for possession of the land. Nothing remained for the members of the Messianic community in Jerusalem.

To blaspheme the holy Spirit was to deny Jesus as the Anointed, to deny Jesus as son of *Yahweh* God and to attribute his witness to evil forces or evil intents. Matt 12:31-32. This deprived the accuser of accepting the salvation that their Anointed intended and desired for them. All such that spoke evil of the miracles of Jesus eventually perished along with their families and adherents in the Jewish War. The penalty for blasphemy in that age of the old covenant was their deprivation of the blessings of *Yahweh* God that would result from accepting the message of Jesus. The penalty in the Messianic age to come would be their total deprivation of the spiritual kingdom. The strong impact of the statement that they "will not be forgiven," lies in the fact that their children and grandchildren would also be deprived of the blessings to evolve from the message of Jesus. The grandchildren would suffer in the $2^{nd}$ Jewish War.

The subsequent generations of these blasphemers of his miracle-working holy Spirit would only know Jesus of Nazareth as attempting to destroy their divinely inspired religion, destroying the traditions of their forefathers, another messianic charlatan. The grandchildren of those who discredited Jesus may well have joined the ranks of the pseudo-messiah Semeon bar-Kochba in his abortive and failed attempted to gain Jewish independence in the $2^{nd}$ Jewish War of 132-135 AD. This $2^{nd}$ war against Roman authority was the materialization of the words, "no forgiveness in the age to come."

> I have come in my Father's name and you do not receive me; if another comes in his own name, him you will receive. John 5:43

Jesus came in the name of his Father *Yahweh* God, with the witness of his Father and fulfillment of all spoken by the prophets. Only a fraction of the population of Jewry accepted his message at that time. He was rejected by the hierarchy of the Jewish religion, betrayed by them and brought to the Roman governor for his sentence of execution. In place of Jesus of Nazareth, the surviving Jewish elders and influential men of the following century rallied behind a leader who surfaced in his own name, Semeon bar Kochba. He was recognized and identified as the Anointed by the greatest of rabbis of the era, Rabbi Akiva. He identified bar Kochba as the son of the star of Num 24:17, modifying his name to bar Coziba. This messianic pretender came in his own name and was recognized by the elders of his era. He led that generation of zealots against the Romans only again to be defeated.

## ANNAS

I sometimes wonder whether Annas may have felt he was the Anointed, of if not he, then one of his sons. This is not unusual for individuals in exceptional high offices to feel as if they may be divine or supernatural. This ego-centric attitude no doubt resulted from their accomplishments, the respect they feel they earned, their accumulated wealth, immense knowledge, power they possess, and a large family. Annas no doubt made many compromises and performed many political favors for Quirinius governor of Syria to have the office of high-priest granted to him and to hold it for some 11 years, and subsequently the same was done with Valerius Gratus and Pontius Pilate on behalf of Joseph Caiaphas his son-in-law, for him to hold this office 18 years. For all of his effort on behalf of the temple, as high priest emeritus, a large family in the priesthood, the principle individual in Jewry upholding the divine ancestral religion, having authority and respect throughout the world, he just may have felt himself to be the Anointed.

I wonder what went through the mind of Annas those hours during Passover when Jesus of Nazareth stood before him. John 18:13. Was Annas the imposter or was Jesus? But what of the many years of dedication of Annas? I contend that Annas realized Jesus of Nazareth was the Anointed, but his pride prohibited him from publicly acknowledging it. There is no record of the specific questions or conclusions made by Annas. Obviously under the circumstances he had no choice except to voice that Jesus should be silenced or exiled, or whatever means was necessary for him to no longer exert influence on the population. If Annas was to publicly acknowledge the claim of Jesus as the Anointed, he would watch his entire empire crumble. He would see the fulfillment of every prophetic text and every passage by the sages of previous centuries that dealt with the consummation of the ministry of the Anointed. Annas was so familiar with all these texts he learned as a student and scholar of the Torah and Mishna. Annas knew exactly what the Anointed was to accomplish in his ministry and he saw it in Jesus but could not permit himself to admit it. Annas had too much to loose. The religious empire of the temple and its services, his family and their positions, their income and wealth, and his power and prestige, would all dissolve into the elements and be replaced with a spiritual kingdom and a spiritual religion based on the moral code. This was the sublime failure of the religion of Annas, failure to uphold the moral code, failure to teach it and failure to live up to it. Success was in institutionalized religion and that was the life of Annas: religion and the politics that encompassed religion.

Annas lived until about 60 AD; his age about 80. He died prior to the installation of his 5$^{th}$ son as high-priest, his namesake Annas II. The grandson, Matthias son of Theophilus son of Annas, was the final high priest to be appointed by King Agrippa II, about the year 65, the year prior to the outbreak of war against Rome. He was deposed after the war began and was replaced by a priest elected by the new Jewish officers in charge in Jerusalem.

All in all Annas concluded that the Jewish nation would be better off with himself having religious and political control rather than admitting that this Jesus of questionable birth from Nazareth should ascend as high priest of the new covenant and king of the spiritual Israel. Nevertheless, his entire posterity, his confederates and political associates, and his entire sect of Sadducees, all suffered and died, or were taken captive at the hands of the Roman military. His wealth was plundered by new Jewish leaders from Galilee at the beginning of the Jewish War. His name resides among the Jews as a discredit to their religious history. The Romans, with whom he dealt in many political maneuvers and dealings, now became the enemy. This proud exclamation of theirs 40 years earlier rejecting *Yahweh* God as true king and source of all religious authority only served as evidence against them in their crime of betrayal and invoked a verdict of guilty for the murder of Jesus of Nazareth from the one sitting on the throne in heaven.

This final defeat of the apostate Jewish religion is disclosed in Revelation, Rev 17:16-17. In the end the prostitute religion is destroyed by the Roman beast military. The same beast – Rome – which earlier supported the prostitute – Jerusalem – now turns against it and burns her at the stake. This is reminiscent of the command in Lev 21:9, that the daughter of a priest who becomes a prostitute is to be executed by burning. So did it occur with this daughter of Jerusalem: the temple and all that pertained to it.

## THE MESSAGE OF JOHN THE BAPTIZER

The prophesy of Malachi in his final chapter speaks of the time when *Yahweh* God will send Elijah prophet to the people of Israel before His day of judgment upon them, in order to turn the hearts of the parents to the children, and the hearts of the children to the parents, so that He will not totally destroy them. Mal 4:5-6. No doubt many Jews felt that Elijah in the flesh would appear among the people, or perhaps be reincarnated. Matt 16:14. The words of Gabriel angel to Zachariah indicate that his son John was to be filled with the spirit of Elijah, and that he would be the one to proceed to reconcile parents and children in Israel. Luke 1:16-17. John's ministry is also described in the song of Zachariah, Luke 1:68-79. He is also called a prophet of God. Luke 1:76. He personally denied that he was Elijah and the fulfillment of the words of Malachi, John 1:21, and in his humility preferred to be identified with Isaiah's lone voice in the desert. Is 40:3. Jesus nevertheless clearly stated that he was Elijah. Matt 11:14.

John as a prophet of God had the ability to see distant into the future, to see the result or culmination of the path that the people of Israel were taking. What he saw was the great and terrible day of *Yahweh* God, His judgment upon Israel for their sins. If the older generation and younger generation were not reconciled, then for sure war would erupt and the nation would be devastated by the Romans. If he did not prepare the people for their acceptance of Jesus of Nazareth, for sure *Yahweh* would smite the land with a curse. Mal 4:6. This is of what the ministry of John the Baptizer consisted: the reconciliation of the generations, for them to abide in harmony with a common goal, and the preparation of the people through the baptism by water for the remission of sins, so they could accept the gospel of the spiritual kingdom as taught by Jesus and his disciples.

When Pharisees and Sadducees came to him to be baptized, he said to them.

Who warned you to flee from the wrath to come. Matt 3:7.

The wrath to come was the devastation John saw in the distant future, defeat and devastation by the Romans, if the people would not repent. In these words John chided the Pharisees and Sadducees, informing them that their self-righteousness served as a hindrance to their repentance. He preached to them in Matt 3:7-10, wanting them to desist in their self-righteous and haughty attitude and to show conduct in their life characteristic of repentant individuals. No doubt John hoped that his message would turn Israel away from its course of eventual defeat and devastation.

## THE MINISTRY OF PAUL APOSTLE

The missionary effort of Paul apostle was to preach the gospel of the spiritual kingdom to all the gentiles, as was commanded him by Jesus in the vision along the road to Damascus, Acts 9:15. Paul accepted this commission and so proceeded to fulfill it with the strength given him, making it his life's purpose. The assignment of the original apostles was to Israel, while Paul, or Saul, was selected specifically to go to the non-Jews or gentiles. This he states in the following words:

> I have fully preached the gospel of the Anointed, thus making it my ambition to preach the gospel. Rom 15:19-20.

Having completed his work in the areas of the Middle East and Asia Minor, he wanted to expand his ministry in Rome and areas further west, even to Spain. Acts 15:24.

Just as with Jesus and the disciples in Judea, whose purpose in preaching the gospel was to turn the people from their crimes and to the spiritual kingdom to deliver them from the impending devastation of the Jewish Wars, so it was with Paul apostle, except that that his ministry primarily pertained to the moral disintegration of Roman society under Nero Caesar and the upheaval of politics and civil war of the near future. This was the period beginning with the burning of the city of Rome in July, 64 AD, to the death of Nero Caesar in June, 68 AD, and concluding with the ascension of Vespacian as Roman emperor in December, 69 AD. Paul apostle was to turn the people to the good news of the spiritual kingdom, for them to enter the new covenant of Jesus, so not to perish both morally and physically during these years of moral and political chaos. This period especially includes the burning of the Temple of Jupiter in Rome by political insurgents against Vespacian on December 19, 69 AD, just days before his ascension as emperor.

Paul apostle received his commission for evangelism about 3 years after the ascension of Jesus, based on the premise that the first half of Daniel's $70^{th}$ week was the ministry of Jesus and the second half was an interim until the termination of the old covenant with the nation of Israel.

Dan 9:27. The year was about 34 AD. The actual evangelization to the nations by Paul apostle did not begin until about 38 AD, allowing time for him first in Damascus, then Arabia and then 3 more years in Damascus. Gal 1:17-21. Acts 13:2-3. The primary portion of his ministry lasted about 20 years, through year 57 AD, when he was imprisoned at Caesarea for 2 years. Acts 23:33, 25:1. Nero Caesar was emperor 54-68 AD.

I contend that the 4 letters known as the prison epistles were written during the 2 year confinement of Paul apostle at Herod's praetorian in Caesarea, about 57-59 AD. Acts 23:35. These letters are Philippians, Colossians, Ephesians, and Philemon. While at Caesarea his brethren could have visited him on a regular basis and transmitted his concerns and messages to them. This period of Paul's imprisonment is still close enough to the time of his travels for him to continue communication with the Messianic congregations he founded. By the time of his imprisonment at Rome, about 60 AD, Paul was already distant from the Messianic assemblies of Turkey and Greece. The 1st letter to Timothy and the letter to Titus Paul wrote from Rome before his first trial. His 2nd letter to Timothy he wrote before his second and final trial before Nero Caesar about 64 AD, before the outbreak of war in Judea and after the burning of Rome.

## PAUL APOSTLE AND THE END OF THE AGE

Paul apostle wrote regarding his era, the Roman Empire of the 1st century. That was his world. His concern was to deliver both the Jewish population, his countrymen, and the non-Jewish population from devastation through their acceptance of the moral code and divine instruction of *Yahweh* God, and the formation of Messianic communities. Paul apostle's concern was not the distant future and especially not 2,000 years into the distant future. He was concerned with the events of his own era, his arena and his generation. The following are a few selections from Paul apostle's letters to indicate his teaching regarding the end of the age of the old covenant and kingdom.

> Rom 1:18. Roman society was to decay and collapse as a result of its own moral and political decadence. The corruption of Roman society is described in Rom 1:21-32.

Rom 2:5. The day of the wrath of *Yahweh* God upon Roman society was the final years of the reign of Nero Caesar, beginning with the burning of the city of Rome in July, 64 AD, and to the ascension of Vespacian in December, 69 AD.

Rom 13:11. The deliverance of the people from the distress of that era, the great tribulation, was very near, with the culmination of the spiritual kingdom in their communities.

1 Cor 2:13-15. Much like the parables of Jesus, those who adhere to the moral code and reside in the Messianic communities will easily survive the upheavals of 64-69 AD. The balance of the population of Roman society will suffer intensely incurring the loss of property, possessions, health, and perhaps even life.

1 Cor 7:1-2, 26-29. This chapter deals with the topic: To marry now or to wait until later to marry. It does not deal with marriage in general. When Paul apostle penned these words about 55 AD, it was good advice. Nero Caesar had just ascended the throne after the infamous death of Claudius Caesar. Marriage at that time would cause great sorrow for the spouses and their family because of the "impending distress." He felt the time of wrath upon the Roman empire to begin very soon and feared that the difficulties of this period would exert unbearable stress on the marriage. To marry is good. 1 Cor 7:36. But the person who postpones his marriage until after this era of upheaval will be better off. 1 Cor 7:38.

Phil 2:16. The day of the Anointed is the day initiating the Marriage Feast of the King's Son. Paul apostle hoped that all those for whom he labored would be attending and participating in this glorious era. He hoped he would not be disappointed in those whom he taught, he wanted to feel a sense of accomplishment at the initiation of the kingdom.

Phil 4:5. Col 3:6. I Thess 1:10. In these short passages in Paul's letters to his Messianic communities, he mentions that the advent of *Yahweh* God to fulfill his judgment on the Roman Empire is very near. The 2 letters to Philippians and Colossians were written in the period 57-59 AD at Caesarea, and the upheavals in the Roman Empire were to begin in just a few years. The theme of the impending distress and immense execution of the wrath of *Yahweh* God is recurring, all of which point to the same years, from about 64 to 70 AD, in both Judea and the Roman Empire in general.

1 Thess 2:16. This passage beginning at verse 13 is similar to the reprimand of the Sadducees by Jesus and his statement of their guilt for persecution and the impending judgment on them. Because the contemporary haughty and aristocratic Jews persecuted the members of the new Messianic communities, they likewise are pronounced guilty by Paul apostle and must now face the judgment upon them.

1 Thess 5:9. The salvation of the Messianic community at Thessalonica is its safe survival of the turmoil and upheaval of those few years ahead in the Roman Empire.

2 Thess 1:5-10. The persecution of the Messianic community at Thessalonica increased since Paul composed and sent his first letter. He repeats the verdict of guilty of persecution of innocent people on them and sentences them to death. This execution of the sentence was to occur in the near future.

2 Thess 2:1-11. The gathering of the Messianic communities to greet Jesus is a reference to the migration out of the areas of the Roman Empire to be affected by the Jewish War and Roman Civil Wars, to areas unaffected. The specific areas for the residents of Turkey and Greece to migrate to are not mentioned, but under the political and military conditions of the era I would surmise that they would migrate to the mountainous interior of their countries. The migration of the residents of Judea was to the ancient areas previously known as Moab, Ammon and Edom, based on the prophecy of Dan 11:41. In these areas a spiritual arrival of Jesus through the descent and immersion of the holy Spirit would occur and inaugurate the Marriage of the king's Son.

This letter was composed by Paul apostle about 50-52 AD, prior to the ascension of Nero Caesar in 54 AD. He is the man of lawlessness and son of perdition who is to die a shameful death at the hands of his own countrymen. The reign of Nero Caesar is the greatest tragedy in the history of the Roman Empire, and no emperor ever died in such loathsome and heinous circumstances as he did. No emperor caused as much damage during such a ruthless and despotic reign as did Nero during his 12 years. Paul apostle prophesied of his taking a seat in the temple proclaiming himself divine. Nero expected the subjects of his realm to worship his as a living deity. 2 Thess 2:4. Those who denied the gospel of the kingdom taught by Paul apostle and preferred to support Nero Caesar were led to delusion during his reign in order to perish. 2 Thess 2:11. A study of the career of Nero Caesar will prove the correlation between him and the words of Paul apostle in this passage. Paul apostle most likely died under Nero Caesar during the persecution of Christians in the capital during the final months of 64 AD, after the burning of the city by Nero's subjects. The Christians were blamed for the conflagration and many were executed, including those who were crucified and set afire. The cruelty and savagery of such a despicable sub-human is well chronicled in history along with the ignoble demise of himself and his subjects and family.

> 2 Tim 1:16-18. Paul apostle desired that Onesiphorus be delivered from the turmoil of the era because of the sincere concern he had for Paul and the efforts on Paul's behalf during his imprisonment in Rome.
> 
> 2 Tim 3:1-8. The final days of old Israel is vividly portrayed in this passage. These verses are a description of the total moral, cultural, religious and political decadence and corruption of the population and leadership of Israel during the years of the Jewish Wars. Paul wanted Timothy to know what to expect during these last days of old Israel, so that he and other members of the Messianic communities would not fail in their faith and likewise join the masses in a loss of morality and observance to the divine law. This parallels the words of Jesus in Matt 24:5-13.

With the evidence provided above in the interpretation of the passages dealing with the subject of the last days in the writings of Paul apostle, it is apparent that his focus was on the events to occur in the near future, within a few years of his prophetic message. I wonder whether Paul apostle knew that history was still to progress after the upheavals subdued, that his prophetic words would be fulfilled in a spiritual manner and not in a strictly literal one.

That Paul apostle included the resurrection of the dead and translation of the living into the same letters describing the events of the termination of the age of Moses with the initiation of the age of Jesus and his spiritual kingdom, such as 1 Thess 4-5, causes a person to wonder if Paul apostle believed that the one would actually follow after the other, that is, that the restoration of the earth and resurrection of the dead were to occur during his era and not in the distant future. This was the same attitude of other disciples as noted in Acts 1:6. Paul apostle seems to follow in the same vein, prophesying events to occur but himself not aware of their sequence, or that some have an immediate application, while the restoration is distant.

## APOSTLES JAMES AND PETER AND THE END OF THE AGE

I contend that this letter was composed by the apostle James son of Alphaeus, and not by any half-brother of Jesus. Matt 10:5. James apostle deals primary with practical Christian teaching, and only one passage deals with the end of the age.

Jam 5:7-8. No doubt many were anxious in regard to the end of the age and the initiation of the new. Here James admonishes them to be patient, that it will arrive in due time.

It is the $2^{nd}$ letter of Peter that primarily deals with the end of the age and this is chapter 3. No doubt there were individuals similar to those in Acts 1:6, who felt that the time had arrived for the kingdom to materialize and that there was no reason for any delay. Others were critical and made joke of their expectations. They were more than critical, trying to upset the faith of the Messianic community, by telling them that if it hadn't occurred by now, it will never occur. The reply of Peter apostle is that God's calendar is not measured in time duration as is Earth's calendar. God transcends time, and He will accomplish His work based on His own calculation of the progress of events on earth, and has no intentions of delaying. The members, however, should take advantage of the interval up to the end of the age and utilize it for the benefit of themselves and the community.

I contend that Peter apostle did write the book bearing his name at Babylon. 1 Pet 5:13. When Jesus told Peter, "Feed my sheep," John 21:15-17, this was a repeat of the command that was given to him a few years earlier, when Jesus told all of the 12, "Go to the lost sheep of the house of Israel." Matt 10:6. The majority of Jews during this era lived in Babylon, remaining there since the exile, and so Peter apostle would have followed the command and traveled to the region of the highest concentration of Jews. Rome was not the city of large Jewish population, because Claudius Caesar expelled the Jews from Rome. Acts 18:2. The few that remained there knew little of the gospel, such as those who met with Paul apostle.

Acts 28:21-22. Peter was an apostle to the circumcised. Gal 2:7. It was only right for him to travel to preach the gospel of the kingdom in that area that had the greatest population of Jews in the entire world. This was Babylon, and so he wrote his letter there and sent it to other Jewish Messianic communities in the world.

## THE ANTICHRIST

The word antichrist is only found in the first 2 letters of John apostle: 4 times in the singular and 1 time in the plural. 1 John 2:18, 22; 4:3, 2 John 7. As with the balance of such texts, the proper interpretation is to apply the word in its historical context, and this is clearly the intent of John apostle. He mentions the fact that "many antichrists have arrived," and that the antichrist is the person who denies the Father and the Son. There is no equivalent term in the OT, and because there was no need for it. Because the apostles' native language was Aramaic, the equivalent term would have been "the one against the Anointed."

I contend that the Jews who refused to accept Jesus as the Anointed are the antichrists of John's letter; and that the specific or most prominent antichrist would be the high priest of the temple of Jerusalem. Because the Jewish religion continued services in the temple for many decades after the ministry of Jesus, the religious hierarchy of the Sadducees were those that were against Jesus as the Anointed, and especially the installed high priest, of which several were the sons, a son-in-law, and one grandson, of the infamous Annas of the gospels. Perhaps Annas was the antichrist to which John apostle was referring. The spirit of antichrist, or against-the Anointed, pervaded the hierarchy of religious leadership in Jerusalem. John apostle warns of this, so that the Jewish Messianic groups would not fall victims to their propaganda and denounce Jesus as high priest of the new covenant. John did not even want the members of the Messianic communities to associate with anybody who did not accept Jesus as the Anointed. 2 John 10-11.

## THE APOCALYPSE OF JESUS

The title of the final book of the NT, meaning unveiling or disclosure, or the popular Revelation, deals with the manner Jesus will reveal himself in judgment and consummate his assignment as the Anointed, king, and high-priest over Israel. A better title for the book would be, "The manner of the imminent appearance of Jesus as described by visions received by John apostle in allegorical terms." I contend that John apostle received his visions on the island of Patmos at the beginning of the reign of Nero Caesar, about 54 AD, since his purpose was to warn and inform the Jewish population of events to occur at the conclusion of that age, and describe the upheaval of both the worlds of Rome and Judea from that time and through 135 AD, the end of the $2^{nd}$ Jewish war. John apostle was not referring to events reiterative every generation, or events distant into the future, but to events the reader of the book would see with their own eyes and be part of themselves. This is so noted.

> The revelation of Jesus the Anointed, which God gave [John] to show his servants what must soon take place. Rev 1:1.
> Because the time is near. Rev 1:3.
> The Lord, the God of the spirits of the prophets, sent his messenger to show his servants what must soon occur. Rev 22:6.
> "Behold, I am coming soon." Rev 22:12, 20.

I will not comment on every passage in the entire book of his revelation, but only on a few specific that deal will the conclusion of the age and major events of Judea and Rome.

> Rev 6:1-2. The initial seal describes the pseudo-messiahs to appear in Israel for its deliverance. These were the freedom fighters and revolutionaries from Galilee. They will gain a victory in Judea among their countrymen.
> Rev 6:3-8. The $2^{nd}$ through the $4^{th}$ seals. These are the turmoil of war, famine, and subsequent disease in the land with the invasion of Vespacian in 66 AD.
> Rev 6:9-11. The $5^{th}$ seal. These are the Messianic saints who were killed during the war by Jewish revolutionaries.
> Rev 6:12-17. The $6^{th}$ seal. With the invasion of Judea by Roman troops, many will try to escape by hiding in the hills and mountains of Judea, but they will be unable to escape.
> Rev 7:7:1-8. These are the elect of the community mentioned in Matt 24:22. They will not suffer the subsequent turmoil. They are also

those symbolized by the 5 wise virgins who had oil in their lamps. Matt 25:10.

Rev 7:9-17. These are the members of the Messianic community who will suffer in the turmoil, but eventually survive. They are mentioned in 1 Cor 3:15, who build their foundation on the Anointed using consumable materials; they are also the 5 foolish virgin who did not have sufficient oil. Matt 25:11-12.

Rev 8 and 9. This is a description of the invasion by Roman troops into Judea.

Rev 11. The 2 witnesses are the word and spirit, discussed above, which symbolize the continuation of the evangelism during this era. Even though Rome may feel it has defeated the Christians, they will only again reappear after the conclusion of the upheaval.

Rev 12. This is the wife of the Anointed in her glory. She flees into the wilderness of Judea in Rev 12:6, that is, the Messianic community migrates out of Judea to area east of the Jordan River and Dead Sea to a place of refuge for these 3-1/2 years, and escapes the turmoil of war.

Rev 13. The beast with 7 heads and 10 horns is Nero Caesar. His name is symbolized by 666. This is well attested to by scholars researching the history of this era.

Every Jewish reader, of course, saw that the beast was a symbol for Nero. The Jewish Christians could not have hesitated for a moment in the conclusion that in the Hebrew name of Nero the solution of the riddle stood revealed.[17]

That no one could buy or sell without the identity of Nero Caesar, meaning the mark of the beast of Rev 13:16-17, could well apply to the necessity of being a citizen of Rome during his reign in order to be part of the economy of the Roman Empire.

Rev 17-18. The Jewish temple worship is symbolized by a prostitute, having committed spiritual infidelity with paganism; and she is sitting upon the beast, which is its support by the Roman government. Rome turning against Jerusalem and burning the temple is described in Rev 17:16-18.

---

[17] *The Early Days of Christianity*, F.W. Farrar, pages 471-472.

Rev 19:1-10. This describes the termination of old Israel, symbolized as the destruction of the prostitute wife, and the exaltation of the new spiritual Israel, which is the bride of the Anointed.

Rev 19:11-21. These are the upheaval of the Roman Empire in the period 68-69 AD, culminating in the burning of the temple of Jupiter in Rome.

Rev 20:1-3. This is the defeat of Jerusalem by Titus, and its occupation by Rome.

Rev 20: 4-6 This is the triumph of the saints, the members of the Messianic communities, who survive the turmoil and upheaval of this era.

Rev 20:7-15. The release of satan is the $2^{nd}$ Jewish War of 132-135 AD, when a second attempt is made for Jewish nationalism. It too is suppressed by Rome, and the Jews forbidden to enter Jerusalem. The name of the city was changed at this time to Aelia Capitolina, and a new Roman city was built on its ruins.

Rev 21-22. The new holy city Jerusalem is the spiritual kingdom of Jesus.

Although not every passage of Revelation is commented on, this should suffice for the reader to understand that this book of Bible was written to describe the means that Jesus would consummate his work as the Anointed. I contend that this book was included in the canon of the NT, because the early Christians felt it to be prophecy fulfilled.

## JESUS THE ANOINTED AND JEWISH TRADITION

The surmise of many that Jesus purpose in his ministry was to destroy the religion as established by Moses and other in earlier times is without credibility. His was the fulfillment of those facets that had a culmination in him as the Anointed.

> Do not think that I have come to abolish the law and prophets. I have come not to abolish them, but to fulfill (consummate) them. Whoever relaxes one of the least of these commandments and teaches people so, he will be called least in the kingdom of heaven. But he who does them and teaches them, will be called great in the kingdom of heaven. Matt 5:17, 19.

The point of contention between Jesus and the scribes and Pharisees and Sadducees was that of the additions to the divine instruction in the form of the oral law.

> Matt 11:28-30. This passage is understood when compared to the denunciation of the Pharisees and Sadducees of Matt 23. These Jewish elders loaded their traditions on the shoulders of the common people, a heavy burden for them to carry. Matt 23:4. Jesus knew how difficult life was for the common person and did not want to make it any more difficult. By turning toward the spiritual understanding of the priesthood, temple and sacrifices, life was made easier for the population. In contrast to the scribes and Pharisees, the yoke of Jesus was light and his burden was easy. And it was especially their hypocrisy that he rebuked. Matt 23:13-36.
>
> Matt 15:17, Mark 7:19. Rules regarding the manner of washing hands prior to dining was one of the traditions placed upon the shoulders of common people to make religious observance unbearable. The passage does not deal with the food laws. (See Peter apostle's statement in Acts 10:14.) Jesus states in his reply that washing of the hands is not as important as the Pharisees dictated to the people, since any minute particles of dirt only passed through the body, and do not affect the moral state of the individual. It is more important to concentrate on the conduct of a person than on traditions or superficial cleanliness.[18]
>
> Matt 12:1-8. The observance of the Sabbath rest day is not abrogated anywhere in the gospels. The reprimand of Jesus was due to the manner that scribes and Pharisees demanded a cessation from labor on this day. This attitude is also dealt with in John 9, when Jesus healed a man of his blindness on the Sabbath day. John 9:14.

Jesus provided the disciples a means of understanding properly the OT law, covenants, and dictates of *Yahweh* God.

---

[18] Modern translations of this verse have converted Jesus statement of food exiting (purging) the body, into a parenthetical statement of Jesus abrogating the food laws. A perusal of the original KJV with modern translation will prove this.

## WHEN DID JESUS RESURRECT?

With a close investigation into the time of the resurrection of Jesus from death, it can easily be proven to have occurred about Saturday late afternoon, prior to sunset, our time, which is the Bible equivalent to very early on the $1^{st}$ day. Bible chronology follows the pattern established in Gen 1, that the old day ends and the new day begins at sunset, and so the $1^{st}$ day of the week begins sundown Saturday our time. A comparison of descriptions follow with the author's rendering.

> Matt 28:1. After the Sabbaths toward the onset of the $1^{st}$ day of the week. (The Gk. *epiphosko*, translated as dawn, actually means onset.)
> Mark 16:2. Very early on the first day of the week, when the sun was still up, they were on their way to the tomb.
> Luke 24:1. Very early on the first day of the week.
> John 20:1. Early on the first day of the week when it was already dark.

The Passover was celebrated on the $14^{th}$ Nisan; this would have been a Tuesday. The day of Jesus' crucifixion was Wednesday. Three days and 3 nights later would Thursday-Friday-Saturday, with the resurrection Saturday evening sunset. This can also be explained in these terms.

The dawn of the $1^{st}$ day in Hebrew terms is not Sunday morning our time, but is twilight Saturday night our time. Following the sequence of events in the NT, 3 women, Mary Magdalene, Mary mother of James, and Salome, wanted to travel to the tomb on the $1^{st}$ day of the Feast of Unleavened Bread, but they were unable to do so, because this day was considered a Sabbath or rest. The next day was the $7^{th}$ day Sabbath, equivalent to our Saturday. This is why the Sabbath is plural in Matt 28:1. Since the women could not travel on these days, they remained and rested in Jerusalem according to the commandment. Luke 23:56. Once the sun set, or was setting, indicating the conclusion of the Sabbath on Saturday sunset, the restrictions were terminated and they were able to travel the distance to the tomb outside Jerusalem. Mark states that the sun was still up, or above the horizon when the women left Jerusalem, and then by the time they reached the tomb, the sun had set, as John apostle relates that it was dark; although the light of the full moon would have lit up the area.

We must remember that Mark translated into Greek the account in Aramaic from Peter apostle, and so the Gk. *anatelantos toi hilias*, indicates that the sun was still above the horizon. This is the reason for the use of the term: very early on the 1st day. The word morning used in the KJV and early translations is the Gk. *orthros*, which has been replaced by the correct word early in modern versions. Based on this study, since Jesus had already resurrected by the time the women arrived at the tomb, his resurrection must have occurred about the time of our Saturday late afternoon.

The next appearance of Jesus was on the evening of the 1st day of the week. John 20:19. In Hebrew terms, this would be the equivalent of Sunday late afternoon our time.

# 3. THE ISRAEL OF GOD

## THE CHURCH

The basic use of the Greek word *ecclesia* in the vernacular is that of assembly. This Greek word in general use throughout the Hellenic and Roman Empires refers to a assembled gathering of people for some specific purpose. The assembly could be for business, political, judicial or civic functions, as also for religious reasons, and can also refer to an established assembly of individuals for religious purposes. The non-religious uses of *ecclesia* in the NT are found in Acts 19:32, 39, 41, and are not translated as church, but are rendered into English correctly as assembly.

In the Greek translation of the OT known as the Septuagint, the word *ecclesia* is found about 100 times. Of the 123 occurrences of the Hebrew word *qahal*, the Greek *ecclesia* is used as its equivalent in these 100 places. The Hebrew *qahal* is used in general for various types of assemblies: Gen 49:6, Num 22:4, 2 Sam 20:14, I King 12:23, etc. But is equally used translated as the English word congregation and assembly when referring to Israel. Deut 9:10, 10:4, 23:2, and others. Of the balance of the 23 uses of *qahal*, 21 places translate this as the Greek synagogue; the Greek *ochlos* in 1 place as crowd; and the Greek *plethos* in 1 place as multitude. This should evidence that the general use of *ecclesia* in the Greek OT was the equivalent of the assembly and congregation of old Israel, as well as an organized assembly of any sort. When Stephen martyr called Israel the *ecclesia* in the desert, Acts 7:38, he was definitely using *ecclesia* in its proper context.

Although the Greek *synagogue* is also used regularly in the Greek Septuagint OT to refer to the congregation of Israel, its use was not adapted by the early Messianic community, but avoided, in order not to identify themselves with the existing established synagogue system in Judea and the Jewish world. The Messianic or Christian communities of the 1st century accepted the concept of the *qahal* and expressed it using the term *ecclesia*. In essence, the new Messianic or Christian community is a continuation of the OT congregation of Israel, but now they are the Israel of God, the fulfillment of the promises and hopes given to OT Israel. Gal 6:16. Rom 15:16.

The age of the *ecclesia* began at Sinai, and not on the holiday of Pentecost. The translation of the word *ecclesia* posed a problem for Bible translators who are aligned with the interpretation that the intent of the Anointed and the apostles was to create a new entity distinct and separate from Israel. They could not translate it as assembly or congregation, because the identity was too obvious. A new word was then created by early Bible translators to serve as the identity of the new body of gentile Christians, but the word *church* is a misnomer. The concept of what is called the church as existing during the centuries after the ministry of Jesus and to our present era is in reality distant from His and the apostles' original intent.

The words of Jesus referring to the *ecclesia* with key words in Hebrew were most likely:

"And on this *sela* I will erect my *qahal*, and the gates of *sheol* will not prevail over it." Matt 16:18

The use of the word *sela* is most likely for rock, since this is the word used in such famous passages as Ps 18:2, 31:3, and Is 51:1. This word refers to a rocky cliff or crag, upon which fortresses were erected in OT eras. 1 Sam 14:4, Num 20:8, Is 31:9. Jesus would have also utilized Hebrew *sheol* in lieu of Greek *hades*, as a paraphrase of the verse Job 38:17, referring to the gates of death and darkness.

The English word *church* is a transliteration of *ecclesia* and was created by Bible translators to distinguish and separate the new Christian community from the community of Israel. Even though the initial adherents were primarily those Jews who accepted Jesus of Nazareth as the Anointed, but as the gentile membership grew, and anti-Semitism also, and since the gospels as published in Greek did use the word *ecclesia* and not the Hebrew *qahal*, and since the Greek term *Christianos* was used referring to this new entity instead of the equivalent of Messianic, the tendency was in favor of the gentile assemblies in the early centuries.

The better literal translations of the NT do render *ecclesia* correctly as either assembly or community (Young's *Literal Bible*, David Stern's

*Jewish NT*, Rotherham's *Emphasized Bible*). One translation, Adolf Knoch's *Concordant NT*, renders the word exactly as *ecclesia*.

The proper rendering of *ecclesia* in the English should be its equivalent in the OT, which is *qahal*, referring to the congregation or assembly of Israel. The correct or original rendering of the phrase church of Christ should be assembly of the Anointed or Messiah, or Messianic assembly. Gal 1:22, Rom 16:16.

## THE NEW ISRAEL NOT A DENOMINATION

The genuine assembly of new Israel is not a church or denomination or its membership. Such institutions are secular for the most part with little religious nature, and any individual can become a member of one or another denomination, regardless of moral character, conduct, belief in Bible doctrines, or even belief in *Yahweh* God. Conventional churches are more concerned with recognition, size, social activities, and acceptance by civil authorities, than adherence to Scripture. The members of the church or assembly founded on the rock, or the *sela* of Matt 16:18, have their names recorded on the roster or membership list in heaven. This is the book of life. Because these are the people to inherit eternal life and enter the holy city Jerusalem, then the gates of *sheol* will not prevail over them. This is an allegory. The enrollment or membership of the Messianic assembly of the spiritual Israel, whose members are not under the authority of the second death, is in heaven. The gates of *sheol* symbolize permanent death. But death has no permanent grip on those whose names are recorded in this book of life, since they resurrect unto eternal life. So the members of the true spiritual assembly that Jesus spoke of have their name recorded in heaven and are members of the assembly of the first-born. Heb 12:23.

I feel that when a person is born from above, and subsequently is born of the word and spirit, this enrolls that person in the membership of the assembly in heaven, which is called the book of life. To become a member of the assembly of the first-born in heaven *Yahweh* God looks at the heart of the individual, repentance, conversion, sanctification, and the baptism by word and spirit. This person is now admitted unto the membership of the assembly in heaven and his name is recorded in *Yahweh* God's annals.

The doctrine that is called ecclesiology, the doctrine of the church, is non-Scriptural. This doctrine recently formulated generates a separate set of rules for life than that of Israel and separate areas for their deceased and separate rewards, which have no basis if the NT ecclesia is a continuation of the OT *qahal*.

## MEMBERSHIP IN THE NEW ISRAEL

Conduct in accord with the moral code of Sacred Scripture is primary in determining whether an individual has repented, converted, and is now sanctified. If a person conducts themselves inappropriately or unacceptably, meaning, activities as specified in the above passages for example, this is indicative of an unrepentant heart, a lack of conversion, and no sanctification. 2 Pet 1:9. The entire passage of 2 Pet 2:1-22, deals with this theme. Such individuals use religion as a superficial front to cover their sins, which they do not want to abandon in favor of a genuine pious life. Their involvement in religion is like the hog who is washed superficially, but once in private, or back in business, or when out of town, or in the company of strangers, they practice the same immoral, dishonest and inappropriate activities, and so the hog is again wallowing in the mire. 2 Pet 2:22.

Because the kingdom is spiritual entrance is obvious, because adherence to the moral code is obvious. Rev 7:14, 22:14. Gal 5:22-23. Col 3:12.

James apostle wrote about the complement of works and faith. Jam 2:18. The point to be brought out by James apostle was that true faith or true religion is evidenced by conduct. A repentant, converted and sanctified individual is identified by corresponding conduct, and testifies whether a person is a member of the spiritual kingdom. It may be possible to fool other people with membership in a church or some related type of religious organization, a religious order, or officer or cleric in a religious community, but it is impossible to fool *Yahweh* God. The enrollment is in heaven, and only you and *Yahweh* God know if your name is on that membership roll.

This follows the same rule dictated by Moses to the old covenant Israel. The community of Israel was a closed community, and was not open to everybody. The conditions for membership had 2 prerequisites. First was to be of the genealogy of one of the 12 sons of Jacob. This was upheld stringently, and only a few exceptions are noted. Any woman outside the genealogical posterity of Jacob was unwanted. The best example is Cozbi. Num 25. She was executed by Phineas for leading a male member of Israel into immorality. Other unwanted women were the wives of Solomon. 1 King 11:1-2,4. The wives of many Israelites during the era of Nehemiah as governor. Neh 13:23-27. Likewise under Ezra priest, many of the gentile women who married Jewish men were to be divorced and banished from the community. Ezra 9:1-2.

The example of Ruth is a rare exception. She gained entrance due to her sincerity and love for *Yahweh* God. Ruth 1:16-17. Her words, "Your people shall be my people, and your God shall be my God," attested to her faith in *Yahweh* God, her repentance, conversion and sanctification. The balance of non-Israelite women who were severed from the community of Israel no doubt did not have the love or sincerity as Ruth did for *Yahweh* God and His true religion. Gentiles did have the opportunity to enter the membership of Israel, but this was on rare occasion.

## THE BODY OF JESUS

Even though Jesus may be in heaven, yet he is spiritually on earth via his body, the assembly of the new covenant, the *ecclesia*. For this reason the assembly is identified as the body of the Anointed, since it continues his ministry, work, and presence on earth, in proclaiming the gospel of the kingdom.

It was never the intent of Jesus to create a new religious institution called the church. The existing assembly was to progress and develop unto perfection through the Anointed. This was the intention of Jesus, *which* he was able to accomplish through his apostles beginning Pentecost. The assembly was now renewed from above through the activity of the holy Spirit. This renovation or perfection pertained to the ceremony, the worship services, which are the religious aspects of the divine instruction. This can be confirmed by focusing on the following verse, "For the Anointed is the goal of Torah, so that every one who has faith may be justified." Rom 10:3. This rendering conveys the meaning of the text in the manner to be understood by the listener of the era, but it is opposite to the meaning conveyed in most translations. The KJV, RSV, and modern versions read, "the Anointed is the end of the law." But the Anointed is and never was any end or termination of the divine instruction. Isaiah wrote,

"*Yahweh* was pleased for His righteousness' sake to magnify His law and make it glorious." Is 42:21.

The spiritual kingdom and Messianic community today is the new spiritual Israel. Gal 6:15. It follows the pattern established by Jesus and apostles and early elders of the apostolic community, and establishes the moral code and divine instruction and true religion provided Israel by Moses and as perfected and supplemented by Jesus. John apostle said,

"The law came through Moses, grace and truth through Jesus." John 1:17.

The word law is *Torah* in Hebrew, the divine instruction that *Yahweh* God provided to Israel. There is an Anointed who was to come to perfect the *Torah*. The grace and truth referred to the perfection of the priesthood, the tabernacle/temple and its services, and the animal sacrifices. These facets of the *Torah* were to have their consummation in the Anointed. The perfection applied to that area of the *Torah* that needed completion, that area that was imperfect.

I contend that certain points of divine instruction delivered to Israel in earlier eras were never abrogated by Jesus, because they were inherent characteristics of the life of the people of *Yahweh* God. These were part of their divine religion which intent was to direct their mind toward the purposes *Yahweh* God intended for His people, to separate them from other religions and deities, to make them a divine example of true religion for the other nations, and for reasons of general health, wealth and welfare. The areas that did not require a fulfillment in the Anointed continued on: the civil code, business ethics, morality, holidays, seventh day Sabbath, food laws and slaughter of animals, punishment of crime, and prohibitions against harmful and injurious conduct. All of this was to continue on and be transferred to the new covenant community. The grace and truth brought by the Anointed Jesus was the consummation or complement of the sections of the *Torah* dealing with sin, sanctification, and conciliation with *Yahweh* God.

The contemporary Messianic community continues to observe the holidays, food laws, morality and ethics and all the areas that can be applied and pertain to the prosperity of the spiritual Israel, and which also continues to marry within itself, that is, within the culture and ethic group of which it is composed. The spiritual Israel does not intermarry with any other culture, ethic group, race, color, nationality. This provides a strong inherent culture and heritage for its own community. It also provides compatibility in marriage for successive generations. This community is invisibly located within secular societies, in them but not of them. But just as with the OT congregation of *Yahweh* God, their access to the blessings is only to the extent that the new spiritual nation adheres to the new covenant of the Anointed, Jesus of Nazareth.

## THE BRIDE AND WIFE OF THE ANOINTED

The Messianic community in the NT is referred to as both the bride of the Anointed as well as its wife. This allegory is basically the same and varies only in its application and comparison to earthly situations. In the OT Israel was referred to as both a bride and wife of *Yahweh* God.

> I remember the devotion of your youth, how as a bride you loved me. Jer 2:2.
> For your maker is your husband, *Yahweh* almighty is His name. Is 54:5.
> I will betroth you to me forever. I will betroth you in virtue and justice, and love and compassion. Hos 2:19.

This allegory is transferred over to the NT by both Paul and John apostles in their letters. The most popular passage is that of Eph 5:22-33, where the mutual devotion of the Messianic community and the Anointed was to be similar to that of a husband and wife. Eph 5:33. A second passage dealing with the devotion between the spiritual community and the Anointed is 2 Cor 10:2-3, where Paul apostle warns the community that a deviation from adherence and observance of the gospel is comparable to spiritual infidelity; the spiritual seduction of the progenitress Eve in Eden by the serpent is used as a symbolic example. The community will only lose its spiritual paradise by abandoning the Anointed and adhering to instruction and precepts that are not part of the gospel. This continued departure will eventually result in a prostitute church, and subsequent divorce from the Anointed as a result of spiritual infidelity. Jer 3:8. Mal 2:11. Only with a sincere repentance and return to the faithful husband will the marriage be reinstated.

John apostle received a vision of the wife of the Anointed, the community of new Israel, in her glory and beauty as the wife of the king, who is the true queen of heaven.

> A magnificent and wondrous sign appeared in the sky, a woman clothed with the sun, standing on the moon and wearing a crown of 12 stars. Rev 12:1.

This is the wife of the Anointed in allegorical description. The crown of 12 stars assigns her the capacity of the true queen of heaven, because she is wife of the king, Jesus. The child to whom she gives birth symbolizes children of salvation attaining the victory over sin, since they ascend to God and His throne. Rev 12:5. Other children of hers will suffer for their faith in the Anointed. Rev 12:17. The concept of Israel as a wife producing children of salvation is based on Is 66:9-11. This same woman is mentioned again in Rev 19:7, where the wedding garment of the bride is described as the righteousness of the saints. This woman is further interpreted in Rev 21:9-10, where a divine messenger explains in a vision to John apostle that the new holy city Jerusalem is the wife of the Anointed. This is in contradistinction to the city Babylon of Rev 17-18: the denominations of pseudo-christianity that have compromised with paganism, mythology, and philosophy which symbolize the prostitute church.

## THE NEW TEMPLE

With a new covenant a new temple or tabernacle was also erected and in place of the old. This new temple replaced the material and fabricated temple. The new spiritual temple is the holy Spirit-filled body of the member of the covenant community and is mentioned several times by Paul apostle.

> Do you not know that you are God's temple and that God's spirit resides in you. 1 Cor 3:16, 6:19-20, 2 Cor 6:16.
> In [Jesus] the entire structure is joined together and grows into a holy temple in the Lord; in whom you also are built into it for a residence of God in the spirit. Eph 2:22.

This association is made 3 times in his letters to the community at Corinth, no doubt because of the many pagan temples that filled the city. Likewise Ephesus boasted of its famous temple of Artemis. Acts 19:27. Instead of promoting and maintaining the pagan temple dedicated to Artemis, the Messianic community was to promote and maintain their bodies as a residence for the holy Spirit.

Jesus' conflict with Jews in the temple narrated in John 2:18-22 focused attention on the destruction of that same temple, and also indirectly indicated to the disciples that the real temple is the human body. This especially pertains to the body of Jesus, which would resurrect in 3 days after its death.

The new temple of *Yahweh* God is that human body that the holy Spirit resides in. Not every body is a temple of *Yahweh* God, but only that body which the holy Spirit has made its residence. The parallel here is first, the tabernacle, which only became sanctified for service when the glory of *Yahweh* God filled it. Ex 40:34-35. Then it was suitable and dedicated for worship services. The same pertains to the temple built by Solomon. This magnificent edifice was likewise filled with the holy Spirit or glory of *Yahweh* God on the day of its dedication, in order to sanctify it. 1 King 8:10-11. Peter apostle writing to the Jewish dispersion calls the individual members of the Messianic community living stones. He informed them that each one of them is part of the spiritual house, which is the real ecclesia. 1 Pet 2:5. The Messianic assembly of the new spiritual Israel is a living temple that continued in existence long after the magnificent edifices of by-gone ages were destroyed or fell into ruins.

## THE NEW PRIESTHOOD

The priesthood of the new covenant is the order of Melchizedek, while that of the old covenant was the order of Aaron. Upon his ascension into heaven Jesus has become our high priest forever. Heb 3:14. The membership of the new spiritual Israel are also priests, each in his own right. No longer is it one special anointed person having only the privilege to pray on behalf of another. Every member can pray on behalf of another person.

"A holy priesthood," is how Peter apostle refers to the new spiritual Israel. 1 Pet 2:5. The members who "offer spiritual sacrifices acceptable to God through Jesus." They are a royal priesthood, a holy nation." 1 Pet 2:9.

The spiritual sacrifice is our praise unto His name, the spoken or sung words that proceed from our lips to acknowledge the holy name of our living deity *Yahweh* God and His son Jesus. Heb 1:15.

The Messianic community does have offices or capacities of responsibility for the care of the organized body. The offices are primarily 2 ranks: a major and a minor. The major is the overseer, which is also translated as presbyter or elder. The credentials and prerequisites of this capacity are described in 1 Tim 3:1-7 and Titus 1:5-9. The word *bishop* used in some Bibles is derived from this position in many churches, which found its way into the Bible by the translators (such as the Church of England as the translators of the King James-Authorized Version Bible.). The terms elder and *presbyteros* and overseer are essentially synonymous. The minor capacity is that of deacon, referring to assistants. The prerequisites and credentials are noted in 1 Tim 3:8-13. The offices that Paul apostle notes here are the Hebrew equivalents of offices in the Jewish synagogue. The ruler of the synagogue was the overseer who conducted the services. Luke 8:41.

Lists of other offices are located at 1 Cor 12:27-28 and Eph 4:11. These offices are not independent of the presbyter-elder or deacon. Within these ranks are those to whom *Yahweh* God has bestowed gifts of the holy Spirit for the edification of his body, the assembly of the Anointed. For the new spiritual Israel community to be stable and productive a system of elders had to be provided similar to the Levitical priesthood of old Israel. The original spiritual priesthood consisted of ordained elders who were anointed by the holy Spirit through the laying-on of the hands of other elders. These elders in the early centuries were those of the apostolic era, such as Paul apostle or Apollos apostle. 2 Tim 1:6. Acts 6:6, 13:3. In later eras the Messianic assemblies would nominate and elect their own elders.

The presbyter-elders and deacons are selected by the congregation and affirmed by the prophetic word through the senior elders. The same senior elders would then ordain them by laying their hands on their heads and reciting a blessing. This rite of ordination symbolizes authority now bestowed upon that person from *Yahweh* God. The hands of the senior elders are the vehicle by which the authority of *Yahweh* God is bestowed on the ordained member for him or her to fulfill their office effectively and successfully. There is no evidence in Scripture that indicates these offices and capacities were only for the apostolic era. These are part of the new spiritual priesthood after the order of Melchizedek. Heb 7:15-16. Just as the Levitical priesthood and those of the lineage of Aaron were to fulfill the capacities of priest, teacher, counselor, and etc., under the old covenant, so with the new spiritual Israel. The elders with the responsibilities assigned them by *Yahweh* God as apostles, teachers, prophets, administrators, evangelists, and etc., are to continue within the assembly and community as long as the covenant was in effect. The covenant was to be permanent, but the gifts and spiritual capacities would prosper to the extent the spiritual Israel would adhere to the new covenant.

## GIFTS OF THE HOLY SPIRIT

The gifts of the holy Spirit are a very important facet of the worship of God in the new apostolic or Messianic community. The manifestation of the gifts of the holy Spirit into the future of the new spiritual Israel separated it from the balance of the religions of the era. Much like the words of *Yahweh* God to Moses, and the words to Isaiah, and the words of John apostle.

> Is it not in Your travel with us, that we are distinct, I and Your people, from all other people that are upon the face of the earth? Ex 33:16.
> As for Me, this is My covenant with them, says *Yahweh*: My spirit which is upon you and My words which I have put in your mouth shall not depart out of our mouth, or out of the mouth of your children, or out of the mouth of your children's children, says *Yahweh*, from this time and for ever. Is 59:21.
> For the spirit of prophecy is the testimony of Jesus the Anointed. Rev 19:10.

The holy Spirit would always rest upon the new spiritual Israel and manifest itself as evidence and justification that it was the true religion on Earth. It was by way of this manifestation of gifts that the apostles evidenced the resurrection of Jesus from the dead. Acts 4:33. Knowledge as perennial is categorized along with prophecy and speech in languages. 1 Cor 13:8. I do not recognize evidence in the above passage to justify that the gifts of the holy Spirit was solely for the apostolic era and terminated with the demise of the apostles and their successors. No more than the termination of knowledge. The point to be made by Paul apostle is that gifts and prophecy and scholarship are perennial, not absolutes. Occasions will arise that will increase the gifts of the holy Spirit, and occasions will arise with a decrease in the gifts of the holy Spirit, occasions that will de-emphasize or reduce their magnitude. Love, however, is not perennial, not transitory, but absolute in every era.

To reason a bit further, the gifts were not to attest the superiority of the individual members who possessed them, in contradistinction to those who did not. These gifts were the manner Jesus in heaven would manifest his presence on earth. Every member of the spiritual Israel possessed a manifestation of the presence of the holy Spirit residing in them. 1 Cor 11:6. Rom 8:15-16. This manifestation possessed by every member was the raising of hands. 1 Tim 2:8. Ps 134:2. I contend that this manner of praising *Yahweh* God was equally applicable under the old covenant. Ps 28:2. This is the proper and acceptable manner of public worship in the congregation.

## IMMERSION INTO THE HOLY SPIRIT

When a person makes the commitment to enter the new covenant and promises to *Yahweh* God obedience, that person is immersed into the holy Spirit. This immersion into the living essence of *Yahweh* God sent to us upon Earth is for that new believer and member the testimony of the resurrection of Jesus of Nazareth from death and his ascension to heaven. It is also their comfort and consolation for all the trials and difficulties that may incur on earth. It is the Spirit of truth that will inspire the person to properly conduct themselves on earth, and warn them of evil. This Spirit of truth opens the inner or spiritual eyes to recognize the activity of *Yahweh* God in their life. Ps 119:18. And opens their spiritual ears to hear and recognize the truths and understanding of the secrets of the kingdom of God. Matt 13:9, 16-17.

Not every spiritual Israelite receives the immersion in the holy Spirit to the extent that the community at Ephesus did in Acts 19:5. Not every spiritual Israelite receives verification of the resurrected Jesus in the same manner as Paul apostle or to the extent of Thomas apostle. But every one does receive sufficient Spirit and testimony to convince them of this fact, the resurrection from death of Jesus, and for this conviction to reside in them their entire life. This is the reason many believers in Jesus died as believers, without renouncing their faith even under the most excruciating of circumstances, and to old age. They looked forward beyond the grave while enduring the worst of tortures and temptations.

With the birth from above every spiritual Israelite is immersed into the holy Spirit. Better described, *Yahweh* God sends His divine life-giving essence from heaven to the material world and this spirit envelopes and saturates the new child of *Yahweh* God. Much like a new born child that takes its first breath seconds after its birth, so does the new born child of *Yahweh* God breathe the breath of *Yahweh* God with a spiritual enlivening. The same occurred with Adam with his enlivening from the figure of earth into a living soul. Gen 2:7. *Yahweh* God breathed into him a spirit for the earthly career. Today every child of *Yahweh* God is a new Adam, since *Yahweh* God breathes into him his eternal spirit for his spiritual career.

This is the same Spirit that will resurrect this child of *Yahweh* God from death. As the Father sent His Spirit to resurrect His son Jesus, so will He again at the restoration send the same Spirit to resurrect from death every child of His. Rom 8:11. The new child of *Yahweh* God now immersed in the living essence of the eternal and true supreme deity receives all verification he or she would need to accept as fact the realm of the spirit, heaven and the residence of *Yahweh* God, and accept as fact the resurrection from death and ascension into heaven of Jesus of Nazareth. This immersion into the holy Spirit also presents to the new member the fact of their own resurrection from death.

## SABBATH

The original reason for the institution of the $7^{th}$ day rest in noted in Gen 2:2-3. Even though *Yahweh* God is an infinite and omnipotent spirit who is incapable of fatigue and exhaustion, this passage was explained in this manner by Moses by divine inspiration as an example for created humanity. The precept of the $7^{th}$ day Sabbath did not originate with Moses at Sinai, but was from the beginning, an original precept. The reason to observe this command was for every family to cease from the daily drudgery of work and business and earning a living, and to spend an entire day in rest and in family social involvement. Ex 20:8-11. One day every week parents would spend time with their children and the children with their parents. This was the social aspect and a benefit and blessing to every family who would observe it.

The 2$^{nd}$ reason for the 7$^{th}$ day Sabbath is noted in Ex 31:17. Every person was commanded to work for 6 days and rest on the 7$^{th}$. By following this ordained pattern the observer was acknowledging that *Yahweh* God created the sky and land in 6 days as noted in Gen 1. This was an outward sign that the observer believed in supernatural divine creation by *Yahweh* God, and not evolution or creation by some pseudo-deity. In Deut 5:12-15, the Sabbath reminded them of their emancipation from slavery in Egypt and their new rest in the promised land.

The word Sabbath itself means rest. This Hebrew word is generally translated as Sabbath referring to the 7$^{th}$ day of the week, but it is also translated plainly as rest in certain other passages. The first and final day of the Feast of Unleavened Bread and Tabernacles were to be Sabbaths, that is, rest days. Lev 23:7-8, 35-36. Labor was prohibited on these days, and so the nation would observe these days in the same manner as the 7$^{th}$ day Sabbath. The Day of Atonement is also a Sabbath or rest day. Lev 23:32. This day especially was to be a day of meditation along with fasting, the "affliction of the soul." Lev 23:27. The verb form of Sabbath or rest in Hebrew is regularly rendered as rest. Gen 2:3. Ex 16:30, 23:12. Lev 26:34. Often translated as cease. Gen 8:22: the seasons will not cease or rest, meaning that they will continue. In Josh 5:12, the manna ceased, or rested. When *Yahweh* God commanded Israel to observe His Sabbaths, this was a general phrase referring to the observance of all the feast and memorial days established by *Yahweh* God. Lev 19:3, 30. Lam 2:6. Ex 44:24.

Jesus also observed this day on a regular basis as noted in several passages in the NT. Luke 4:16, 13:1-17. Matt 12:9-13. Luke 14:1. The conflict that surfaced during the ministry of Jesus was the manner that Sabbath should be observed, not whether the day itself is valid for observance. The promise of *Yahweh* God was that Sabbath observance would be a benefit and blessing. Is 58:13-14. It was the oral law of the Jewish sages that made Sabbath observance a chore and defeated its purpose.

The continued observance of Sabbath for the new covenant community is noted in Heb 4:9. The Greek word *sabbatismos* means Sabbath observance. The point to be made in this verse is that the new covenant community observes the 7$^{th}$ day Sabbath in honor of the awaited future rest to be bestowed on creation at the restoration. It still serves as a memorial of the 6 days of creation labor. An additional meaning is now applied, in lieu of the rest in place of the 430 years of slavery in Egypt. Deut 5:15. Now it is the awaited rest to appear in the eternal kingdom, as a release from the bondage and decay of the present age.

There is no indication of any abrogation of Sabbath observance in the NT or allocation to another day. Paul apostle regularly preached on Sabbaths. Acts 13:14, 16:13. Even though occasional mention is made of the 1$^{st}$ day of the week this is not divine instruction for Sunday observance. Acts 20:7. 1 Cor 16:2. If these passages are closely studied, neither approaches any type of directive regarding the validity of 1$^{st}$ day sanctification. The preaching of Paul apostle occurred Saturday night according to our table of time keeping, and not Sunday. Because the 7$^{th}$ day Sabbath ended at sundown, Paul preached on the 1$^{st}$ day of the week, which according to timekeeping as dictated in Scripture began Saturday night sunset our time. Likewise money to be set aside on the 1$^{st}$ day of the week for the Corinthians was a convenience. In Rev 1:10, John apostle received his divine revelation on the Lord's Day. I contend that the reference is to the Sabbath, and John practiced his inherited tradition of resting on this day and sanctifying it.

## FESTIVALS

Much like the Sabbath, the festivals or feasts of *Yahweh* are still effective for the assembly of the new spiritual Israel. Lev 23:2. In contemporary terms they are often referred to as holidays, a short form of holy day, but the Hebrew term actually means festival or feast. Only twice in the KJV Bible is the term holiday or holy day used. In Ex 35:2, the proper rendering is holy Sabbath; and in Col 2:16, the proper rendering is holy feast or festival. These feasts of *Yahweh* of Lev 23 were to be periods of meditation and periods of festivity and celebration. The 3 festivals toward the beginning of the year are termed those of the early rain, while the later festivals are those of the latter rain. The lunar calendar is utilized to establish the correct dates for these festivals. According to Scripture, the first day of the new year is the New Moon after the Vernal Equinox; Passover occurring on the 14$^{th}$ day of the 1$^{st}$ month. (In later centuries Jews changed their new year to the Memorial of Trumpets.)

All governments and religions have days set aside for commemoration and celebration. *Yahweh* God likewise instituted for His nation Israel their appointed religious days to be observed on a regular basis. Each one of these festivals has a strong spiritual meaning along with historical association. The observance likewise has a secondary purpose of building a strong moral community. To put away sin in a person's life and to adhere to the divine instructions was the underlying purpose of the festivals appointed by *Yahweh* God. Lev 23:4.

Every festival and memorial day established by *Yahweh* God for His people is effective throughout all history. Lev 23:14, 21,31,41, Ex 12:14. The nation of old Israel had an interpretation for each of these days. The new spiritual Israel also provides for these same days an interpretation in the light of the ministry of Jesus and the future plan and intention of *Yahweh* God for His people and the world we live in. Because the cares and obligations of our life can creep up on us like weeds and choke us, Matt 13:22, *Yahweh* God supplied these days throughout the calendar year for the benefit of His people Israel, both the old and new. If his people observe these festivals and memorials on a regular basis, they will be a blessing upon every participant. The blessing consists in the impression the meaning these festivals has upon every person who observes them.

> Therefore let no one pass judgment on you in regard to food and drink or with regard to a festival or a new moon or a Sabbath. These are only a shadow of what is to come, but the substance belongs to the Anointed. Col 2:16-17

The passage does not abrogate celebration of these holidays any more than invalidate the food laws. I contend that the Colossians accepted observance of these holidays and the food laws, and then the congregation was criticized for doing so by members of Greek mystery religions and their secret rites and acetic practices. Paul apostle wrote to strengthen the faith of the people to resist this censure from others for accepting their observance. They were also to remember that the Anointed was the intent of these holidays, that they are a shadow of the future, meaning, they possessed a significance for the future.

## PASSOVER AND THE FEAST OF UNLEAVENED BREAD

Passover originally commemorated the release of the Hebrews from slavery in Egypt, their emancipation. Deut 6:20-21. It allegorically represents emancipation from slavery to sin. Rom 6:17-18. The observance of this festival was to impress upon the people the necessity to be freed from bondage to carnal impulse and become liberated individuals, now without constraint and able to fulfill the divine instruction of *Yahweh* God without the weight of sin. Just as the Passover lamb died at their own hands so each was to die unto sin. Eating the lamb was to gain strength to overcome temptation. The divine instruction for the new covenant community to continue observation of this Passover and the subsequent Feast of Unleavened Bread is noted as follows.

> For the Anointed – our lamb of the Passover – has been sacrificed. So let us therefore celebrate the festival: not with the old leaven, the leaven of malice and evil, but with the unleavened bread of sincerity and truth. 1 Cor 5:7-8.

Jesus is the lamb which takes away the sin of the world. John 1:29. The leaven of the OT symbolized those areas and facets of a person's life that corrupted them or lead them astray from living a Scripture-based life.

The new spiritual Israel continues to celebrate the Passover and Feast of Unleavened Bread as commanded by Jesus,

> "Do this in remembrance of me." 1 Cor 11:24.

Now however the lamb and its sacrifice and consumption is replaced with Jesus. The apostle repeats this command in 1 Cor 11:26, and indicates in 1 Cor 10:6 and 11:27-32, that the early new covenant community continued to gather on an annual basis to commemorate the agony and death of Jesus. This gathering would have occurred on the same day Passover as Paul apostle commanded in 1 Cor 5:8, along with the week-long Feast of Unleavened Bread. The new purpose of this festival is to remind the participants of the removal of sin from our life, no longer with animal sacrifices and unleavened bread, or the wave of the sheaf. Lev 23:9-14. The unleavened bread finds its spiritual fulfillment in the sanctified life of the members of the new spiritual Israel. Today the new leaven is the spiritual kingdom. Matt 13:33. Once placed into the hearts and souls of the participants it grows and develops within the covenant community. The festival is also the annual commemoration of the institution of the new covenant.

One item to note is that Peter apostle's trial was to occur after the Passover, Acts 12:4. (Although mistranslated as Easter in the KJV version.) This passage of Acts 12:1-4, indicating that Peter apostle continued to observe both Passover and the Feast of Unleavened Bread.

## PENTECOST

This term Pentecost is derived from the Greek *pentekoste*, meaning fiftieth-day, and is used only in the NT in Acts 2:1, 20:16. In the OT the festival is designated the Feast of Weeks or the Feast of Harvest. Ex 23:16. Deut 16:9-10. The point made of putting the sickle to the wheat is no doubt a reference to the wave of the sheaf, which occurred during Passover week, or during the Feast of Unleavened Bread. Lev 23:10. Pentecost was one of the 3 festivals during which every male in Israel was commanded to bring his offering to the tabernacle.

According to the Jewish sages, 50 days after the departure of Israel from Egypt Moses received the torah from *Yahweh* God on Mount Sinai. This is the divine instruction consisting of the 10 commandments and the supplement noted in Ex 21-23.

For the new spiritual Israel this feast commemorates the descend of the holy Spirit upon the 120 gathered in the upstairs hall in Jerusalem and upon the thousands of Israelites who accepted the promise of *Yahweh* God. Acts 2:39. Paul apostle acknowledges the celebration of this feast. 1 Cor 16:8.

## MEMORIAL OF TRUMPETS

The 3 festivals of the latter rain are mid-year in the divine calendar. They likewise have many parallels with the new covenant and direct the attention of the participant to events yet to occur. The Memorial of Trumpets was originally instituted to commemorate assembly of the Hebrews at Sinai by way of the sound of a trumpet. Ex 19:13,19. The 2 silver trumpets of Num 10:1-10, used to proclaim important messages and alarms to the people of Israel likewise were involved in this festival.

For the new spiritual Israel the celebration of this festival, the Memorial of Trumpets, annually reminds us of the return of Jesus to initiate the restoration. This event is parallel to that which occurred at Sinai. The trumpet blast was to inform the people of the descent of *Yahweh*

God to them. Likewise at the conclusion of the ages at the consummation, *Yahweh* God will likewise appear in some spiritual manner to execute the resurrection of the saints and the restoration of the earth to its original state of perfection.

The parallels in the NT Scripture are the following:

He will send His messengers with a loud trumpet call and they will gather His elect from the four winds, from one end of heaven to the other. Matt 24:31.
For the trumpet will sound and the dead will be raised. 1 Cor 15:52.

This is the $7^{th}$ trumpet mentioned in Rev 11:15, which will herald the close of the imperfect age and introduce the eternal and perfect age.

This festival applies to the new Israel more than any other festival of *Yahweh* God in His calendar and so should be observed with this new application in mind. During the $1^{st}$ century the new covenant community gathered once a year to celebrate the Memorial of Trumpets awaiting that great day of the spiritual summons of the archangel with the descent of the powers of heaven for the restoration of the earth.

## DAY OF ATONEMENT

The Day of Atonement is the highest and most holy day of the entire divine calendar of festivals for Israel. It was the day that the priest first among his brethren acquired propitiation from *Yahweh* God from Israel. Described in detail in Lev 16, the anointed intercessor and mediator unto *Yahweh* God on behalf of His people 3 times entered the most holy space, that hidden and secured enclave known at the holy of holies. The ark of covenant or ark of testimony was located here, the hidden residence of *Yahweh* God on earth and in the midst of His nation Israel.

In regard to the original rites of this day in Lev 16, 2 goats and a bull had special significance in the removal of sin from the nation of Israel corporately and from the members individually. The burning of 1 goat and bull outside the camp symbolized the destruction of sin. As the smoke of these 2 animals ascended unto the sky, visible to the entire assembly of Israel, the people were to realize how the last enemy is now put to death. "The sting of death is sin." 1 Cor 15:55. With sin destroyed the people could inherit the promise of *Yahweh* God and live long in the land that *Yahweh* God gave to them.

The high priest this day transferred all the sins of the nation of Israel to this 2$^{nd}$ goat by laying his hands on its head and reciting a confession. Lev 16:21. The live goat is identified by being appropriated to *Azazel* or *Azazael*. The actual meaning of this Hebrew word is long lost in history. The KJV and colloquial translations render this term as scapegoat, while the more literal directly transliterated the word as *Azazel*. Some commentators claim this as indication that sin returns back to the originator of sin, the devil. I do not accept this interpretation. The use of Azazel indicated the sin-laden animal was to be released to its own fate. The goat was to be released alive into the desert area by some assigned individual at a distance from any residence or population, and in some area accessible or inhabited by wild or carnivorous animals, this goat would not survive long, and within a day or so would be attacked by some wild animal that roamed the Judean desert. Judg 14:5. 1 Sam 17:34-35. The people were to recognize this goat as banishment or exile of social sin from Israel, that is, that enmity or animosity that could surface between individuals and families, creating an unpleasant or hostile social environment or general distrust. Once completed the community was to be reconciled among each other, now in a concordant state to celebrate the final great festival of Israel's divine calendar.

The fulfillment of the purpose and symbolism of the Day of Atonement is clearly described in Heb 9. This entire chapter details how Jesus as high priest brought his own blood into the new tabernacle, the most holy place in heaven unto *Yahweh* God his father. Now there is a genuine cleansing of the participants with the holy Spirit, with the result of a clean conscience and reconciliation with *Yahweh* God and brethren. The sacrifice or death of the animals was a type of the mortification of the sinful body and all of its lust and temptation and impulses to sin. Rom 6:7. The atonement of the earth is an event that should be reflected upon on the Day of Atonement. The sins of the earth must be likewise expunged, but not by sacrifice or propitiation, but by the sentence and penalty of the judge who sits on the great white throne. As discussed earlier, the early world was repossessed by *Yahweh* God after evicting its residents using a flood of water. The present world will be atoned for by the just penalty upon its residents with their eviction from the earth and its cleansing by fire. Rev 11:18. *Yahweh* God will destroy those who destroy the earth.

Peter apostle described the removal of the evil and wickedness upon the earth in these terms likewise. 2 Pet 3:7,11.

## FEAST OF TABERNACLES

This festival was designed to be a vacation at home for the one week along with a visit to the location of the tabernacle or temple. It is called Tabernacles in Lev 23:34, the Feast of Ingathering in Ex 23:16. The residents of Israel were to build huts out of branches from trees near their home, and spend the week living in this hut at home. The feast was designed to occur coincident with the conclusion of harvest, usually early or mid-October. It was a celebration of thanksgiving unto *Yahweh* God, with the tithe of the produce and harvest brought to the location of the tabernacle or temple as an offering to *Yahweh* God. The entire family would have attended some time during the week.

When the participant brought his gift and tithe to the priest he would recite the passage of Deut 26:5-10. This was a reflection of the attitude of every worshipper and pilgrim attending the celebration. The overall attitude is described in Deut 26:11, and the prayer on the heart of every worshipper and pilgrim is Deut 26:15. Every year the family expressed gratitude to the Supreme Deity who blessed them with their wealth and abundance, and which also reminds themselves of their transience.

During the journey of 40 years from Egypt to Palestine the Israelites lived in tents as a type of nomadic or transient ethnic and religious community. They were migrants to a better place. Every year during this celebration they were to be reminded that they were transient, that our existence on earth is transient. But at the same time we are migrants to a better world. Our preparation for this better world occurs during this transitional phase of our life, our earthly career. Residing a few days each year in a hut impressed on the family their transience, and that during this temporary sojourn they should enjoy the blessings of *Yahweh* God to the fullest extent that he should bless them on earth. The patriarchs Abraham, Isaac, Jacob, lived in tents during the years of their residence in Canaan. Heb 11:9. They were temporary residents of the area seeking a homeland, a better country, a heavenly one. So the Israelites would every year identify with the transience of their patriarchs and forefathers, and impress upon themselves the wait of a future and better world.

The Feast of Tabernacles officially is a 7 day festival. Lev 23:34. The 8th day is added as a conclusion to the annual cycle of divine festivals. Lev 23:36. This day is also designated as a Sabbath or rest day, with work prohibited. This day also has its own significance as that eternal kingdom to evolve after the restoration. Paul apostle mentions this in 1 Cor 15:24-28. At some distant time in the future a consummation will occur, and *Yahweh* God will become all in all. This is the universal reconciliation.

For the new spiritual Israel the parallel is applied and understood. Every year the new covenant community utilizes this week in worship, thanksgiving and fraternization with the brethren of the community. The new spiritual Israel no longer gathers in huts or booths, the fulfillment is spiritual. Our daily life should indicate that we are transient in this material world and are in the process of migrating to the better world, modern pilgrims and exiles. 1 Pet 2:11. The new spiritual Israel displays gratitude to *Yahweh* God with charity and benefits to the underprivileged, and reside in peace and concord with all others. During this life we prepare for the future, the eternal kingdom, when we will inherit the new and transformed Earth. Matt 5:5. 2 Pet 3:13.

## LATER JEWISH FESTIVALS

New holidays in later years of Bible history were instituted by Israel apart from those in Lev 23. There was no divine injunction to do this, but they were instituted to have a certain importance and significance in the social and religious life of the people. These festivals are purely Jewish and pertain to the Jews as an ethnic and cultural entity. Such festivals are Purim and Hanukkah.

The festival Purim has its basis in the book of Esther. It generally lasts 2 days. The heroine of the story is a Jewish young lady who became the Persian king's favorite concubine and subsequently his wife. This king is Ahasuerus, identified as Xerxes, king of Persia, 486-465 BC. The event that promoted an annual celebration was the vengeance of the Jews against the Persians and other non-Jews living in the area. Following the context of the narrative the massacre was an annihilation without purpose. I contend that this festival has no place in the Messianic community. It may pertain to the Jews as part of their later history as an ethnic group or nationality, but does not apply to the people of the new covenant.

The Festival of Lights, Hanukkah, was introduced by the Hasmonaens, the family of Mattathias in 164 BC. 1 Macc 4:52-59. Its basis for commemoration was the dedication of the altar in the newly consecrated temple after its recapture from the Greeks. In 169 BC the city was captured by the Greeks under Antiochus Epiphanes. 1 Macc 1:20. For about 5 years the temple was utilized for sacrifices to the deities of Greek mythology. A Jewish army under Judas Maccabees recaptured the city in 164 BC. He then cleansed the temple of the remnants of their paganism and restored the worship as in prior years. An 8-day festival initiated the restoration of the temple and reintroduction of worship services. This 8-day festival became know as the Feast of Lights, Hanukkah, and is normally celebrated early or mid December. It is called the Feast of Dedication in John 10:22

Much like Purim, there is no divine injunction for the observance of this festival. The purpose of its initiation was to bind scattered Jewry into a solid political bulwark against the influence of Hellenism. It definitely had its advantages and still does as a means of uniting ethnic Jews for social and political purposes. Although this may appear to be a good reason, but it was not *Yahweh* God who instituted this religious festival. The new covenant community does not recognize or accept this festival as part of the divine calendar.

## DIET

Prior to the fall and metamorphosis of creation only plants were the diet for the initial family. Fruits, vegetables, and related herbs were sufficient nutrition for the initial residents of Eden. The lesser reason for abstention of meat was that of not killing an animal. No doubt the thought of killing an animal for any reason was totally repulsive to the first family, and especially with all life eternal in this Eden of theirs. With the change of the nature of the human after the fall due to the sin of Adam and Eve, meat became a required and staple diet of created humanity. For the human to continue life on earth in a physically healthy manner, meat on a regular basis became a necessity. But not all meat, that is, not the flesh of every and any animal, but only the flesh of those animals which *Yahweh* God dictated as fit and satisfactory for human consumption, and only if butchered in the proper manner, were to be consumed as food.

Since *Yahweh* God is the creator of the bodies and organs and minute constituents of the human, the creator would also know well what is fit and proper for consumption, for our health and mental and physical benefit. The use of the word clean for animals should not be interpreted in terms of ritual cleanliness; but that these animals were created in such a manner that when butchered and cooked properly they are fit for human consumption. The animals called unclean are not ritually unclean, but that their creation is for reasons other than human consumption. *Kosher* is a word utilized to indicate that the meat meets the criteria of the food laws and is properly butchered and so fit for human consumption.

The fact that food laws, or divine instruction regarding what is fit and proper for human consumption, were in existence long before Moses can be evidenced by the fact that Noah knew the difference between clean and unclean animals. Noah, at his age of 500 years, when he brought his sacrifice of thanksgiving, brought a sacrifice of clean animals. I contend that this law regarding food was transmitted from Adam through the generations to Noah and subsequently to the later patriarchs. Moses then codified it.

Cutting the primary veins and arteries in the neck of the animal while on the altar of stones caused the heart to pump out a majority of the blood from the body. The heart would continue to pump until no more blood remained. The prohibition of blood as food was clearly stated to Noah after his descent from the ark at Ararat. Gen 9:4. All of this was later codified in the divine instruction given by *Yahweh* God to Moses at Sinai. Lev 7:26. This prohibition of the consumption of blood was also repeated as an apostolic edict. Act 15:20, 29. The use of the term, "and what is strangled," in the above passages in Acts, refers to the necessity of bleeding the animal in the manner established, and not killing the animal in any other manner. All of this still pertains equally to our present era.

The diet of the young Jewish men in Dan 1:12-16, was because they did not want to defile themselves with the unclean meat served by the Babylonian servants. Since they could be guaranteed *kosher* food, they preferred a vegetarian diet, which they also knew was healthier for them than the fat of the unclean animals served to the rest of the palace personnel.

## FOOD AND THE NEW TESTAMENT

The NT contains passages regarding the divine instruction for food. One is the vision of Peter. Acts 10:9-16. In this vision Peter replies to the test of

*Yahweh* God, "I have never eaten anything unclean or common." This is apostolic witness. Peter continued to adhere to these food laws during his ministry. The words of *Yahweh* God, "What God has cleansed do not call unclean." is an analogy between animals and humans. Certain animals *Yahweh* God was cleansed or created to be fit for consumption and so should not be rejected. Likewise those individuals whose heart and soul *Yahweh* God has cleansed from sin and dead matters should not be rejected nor considered unclean. Acts 10:34-35. Heb 9:14.

A conflict between the Jesus and Pharisees also has been utilized over the centuries as justification to abrogate the food laws. In Matt 15:1-20 the discussion arises in regard to traditions upheld by Jews during that era and its legitimacy. Notice that the topic to be debated in this section of Scripture is not a point pertaining to the law of *Yahweh* God, what is explicitly contained in Scripture. The topic is tradition: the legitimacy of the specific manner that hands should be washed as dictated by the Pharisees and previous Jewish sages. This section is concluded by Jesus with the following words, "but to eat with unwashed hands does not defile a person." Matt 15:20. This statement indicates that this passage does not at all deal with food, but specifically with this particular tradition, and to apply it to food is incorrect application. The parallel section in Mark's gospel account has a verse that has been mistranslated in order to apply it as a repeal and rescission of the food laws. Mark 7:19. But such is not the intent in the passage. (Peter apostle who had never eaten anything unclean or common in his life would hardly have dictated to Mark that Jesus declared all foods clean.)

The intent of Jesus' statement is that food does not affect the morals of a person; food does not drive an individual to be evil or wicked or commit a crime. The food laws should be adhered to for the sake of our health, since *Yahweh* God did create our bodies and demands that we care for it unto old age. This is the point of Mark 7:15 and Matt 15:18-20, that food passes through the alimentary canal and eventually is evacuated. Whatever is consumed is eventually cleansed from the alimentary canal once it is ejected. That food cannot have an effect on the character traits of an individual is apparent, except in the situations when food causes illness or some other physical malady. Then there is an effect on personality and character. This is why food laws exist: for our health, and so should be complied with.

The passage in Heb 13:9, refers to a more stringent set of dietary laws than those instituted by *Yahweh* God as discussed above. This is also referred to in 1 Tim 4:3. Many of the mystery religions of the era promoted vegetarianism, and this may have had some influence on the Messianic communities. There is no divine injunction not to eat meat, and vegetarianism is derived from the eastern religions of India who believed in the reincarnation of human souls in animals.

The point made by Paul apostle in Rom 14:1-23, regarding food must be understood in the light of 1 Cor 8:1 and 10:14-28. This pertains to meat that was dedicated to some pagan deity when it was sacrificed. Even though clean meat is clean regardless whether it was killed as a sacrifice to *Yahweh* God or as a sacrifice to some pseudo-deity of mythology, the Messianic community was to distance themselves from the worshippers of such pseudo-deities. The meat sold in the market place was acceptable as long as it met the criteria in the OT, but the members of the Messianic community were not to attend dinners to eat the same food if it was killed in a sacrifice to some pagan deity.

## POLITICS AND THE NEW ISRAEL

The members of the new Israel are not involved with military conscription or the armed forces of any nation. In accord with the gospel teaching of Jesus the covenant members live in peaceful coexistence with any and all people, where ever they reside. They are not a separate political entity, since it is not their intent to become involved in federal politics. They do not pledge allegiance to a nation and its secular government, because allegiance belongs only to *Yahweh* God. Is 42:8. To pledge allegiance to a secular government, or to ally oneself with a political party, is to be part of the secular kingdom and to be disloyal to the spiritual kingdom. Covenant members are citizens of the kingdom of God, and so cannot ally ourselves with any secular government. Because the new Israel is found in every race, color, nation and culture, it is unrealistic for them to participate in organized warfare and wage combat against another nation.

In general the members of new Israel comply with and observe the laws established by the government of whatever country they reside in. Rom 13:1-2. 1 Pet 2:13-14. They give unto the secular authority what is legitimately due them, and give to *Yahweh* God what is due Him. Matt 22:21. They do not fulfill what is not permitted by Scripture to be granted the secular government. Only when the laws of the nation they reside in conflict with Scripture is civil disobedience required, and even then always non-violently and without giving the Messianic community a bad reputation.

Just because the government states that certain conduct or practices are legal does not mean then can be practiced by members of the Messianic community, because we have a higher law. Although gambling, alcohol, marijuana, homosexual and lesbian conduct and marriage, idolatry, pornography and other such obscene conduct, is permissible and legal in the USA does not mean it is acceptable in the Messianic community. None of these are because they violate God's moral code:

> Do not get drunk with wine, as that is debauchery, but be filled with the Spirit. Eph 5:16
> But immorality and all impurity or covetousness must not even be mentioned among you, as is fitting among saints. Let there be no filthiness, nor profanity, nor obscenity, which are not fitting... Eph 4:3-4.

The are just a few examples to note.

## EXCOMMUNICATION FROM THE NEW ISRAEL

The reasons for excommunication are 2, and contain a beneficial purpose for the community as well as for the excommunicated. The elders have the responsibility of implementing a high moral standard for the community, and an unrepentant person serves as a stumbling block, as a bad example. If a person violates the moral code, that person can still repent and remain in the community. To allow a person who violates the moral code and refuses to repent to remain in the Messianic community lowers the moral standard of that community. Gal 5:9. In reality then, Jesus becomes the license to sin. Excommunication of an individual persisting in unacceptable or inappropriate conduct is necessary to keep the moral standard of the Messianic community high. This serves as an example to the balance of the community, that theirs is a closed community, open only to those adhering to the moral code, and that any attempt to lower the standards is not tolerated.

But rather I wrote to you not to associate with any one who bears the name of brother if he is guilty of immorality or greed, or is an idolater, reviler, alcoholic, or thief, not even to dine with such a person. 1 Cor 5:11.

Elders who fail to uphold the edit of excommunication will only invite more crises and more violation of the moral code into their community. If this compromise continues then eventually the intent of creating a spiritual community has lost purpose and is defeated. The Messianic community now evolves into a social club or fraternity, a congregation of holy losers. The once Messianic assembly, losing its moral basis, defeats its original purpose and so succumbs to the level of a secular and political and social organization. Now the salt has lost its savor. Matt 5:13. It is no more of a moral benefit than any other civic or social association of the secular world.

A strong criteria for continued membership is essential for a spiritual community of high moral character. Those that did uphold the law of *Yahweh* God were blessed for their efforts. Phineas grandson of Aaron was blessed for executing an Israelite man and Midianite female involved in an illicit affair. Num 25:12-13. Gideon was likewise blessed for destroying the alter of Baal that belonged to his father. Judg 8:22,29-32. Both Ezra and Nehemiah were blessed for implementing the laws against intermarriage with foreign women. Ezra 10:10-11. Neh 13:23-25.

The failure of old covenant Israel was due to lack of implementation of such rules, for example, prohibitions against idolatry, intermarriage, necromancy and sorcery, immorality, and recognition of foreign deities. Eventually both the southern and northern kingdoms of Israel and Judah collapsed. They became no different than their pagan neighbors in terms of moral strength. Eli priest was reprimanded by *Yahweh* God because he did not restrain the crimes and corruption of his sons. 1 Sam 3:13. Samuel likewise had sons who were very corrupt and took bribes. 1 Sam 8:3. This is one of the reasons the people wanted a king, rather than priests and judges. The priests had failed in their obligation to their office and became morally corrupt. The people could no longer tolerate it and so wanted a strong leadership.

These are all examples of what occurred in the past for failure of the elders to implement a high moral standard and be willing to excommunicate any person that lowered such standards. The benefits to be gained for the community in terms of blessing from *Yahweh* God is far greater than any persecution or threats or harassment an elder will have to endure in implementing a high moral standard. John the Baptizer was beheaded for reprimanding Herod Antipas, who was involved in an incestuous relationship with his niece Herodias. Matt 14:1-11. Yet in Rev 20:4, those beheaded are specifically mentioned as resurrecting from death in the 1$^{st}$ resurrection. For this reason Paul apostle wrote to Timothy:

> Preach the word, at every occasion teach, admonish, rebuke, and exhort, be unfailing in patience and instruction. Because the time is coming when people will not endure sound teaching, but having itching ears they will accumulate for themselves teacher to flatter their ears. 2 Tim 4:1-4.

It takes elders strong in the faith to reprimand sin in the community. Without dedicated and brave elders willing to implement the moral code and face criticism and persecution, the spiritual community can easily loose its moral strength.

## DEALING WITH VIOLATION

The rule of excommunication should always impress upon the membership the seriousness of offense, whether someone is hurt or injured, physically or psychologically. The rule of excommunication should impose a feeling of rejection and guilt, informing violators of the code of conduct that they are unwanted. If they persist in this sin, they can continue in it elsewhere, outside the spiritual community. Exile must impose a sense of guilt on the individual. Any pride in the person will prevent acknowledgement of wrong conduct and repentance and submission to community rule under elders. To "deliver this man to the accuser (satan)," refers to exile from the spiritual community and to the corruption of the secular society. "That his spirit be saved on the day of Adonai Jesus," refers to an overwhelming sense of guilt that will produce repentance. 1 Cor 5:5.

Capital punishment for capital crime is permitted. Gen 9:5-6, Rom 13:4.

The members of the spiritual Israel do not. The criminal is only to be excommunicated from the spiritual community as noted in 1 Cor 5:9. The passage mentioning, "deliver to satan for the destruction of his flesh," would pertain to the civil judicial system taking charge of the matter.

## APOSTASY

Apostasy is a serious matter in Scripture. Heb 6:4-6, 10:26-27. It can also be compared to a husband or wife who is unfaithful during their marriage and is apprehended.

> A person who is heretic, after the first and second admonition, reject. Titus 3:10.
> Make my joy complete by thinking the same way, having the same love, united in spirit, intent on one purpose. Phil 2:2

For a successful community, there cannot be dissention. Any person who causes dissent is a detriment, and so must be admonished or else excommunicated. Each member must realize that it was their choice to become part of something larger and greater than themselves, and so to do this they need to give up certain personal rights or individual preferences. They cannot just conduct themselves how they want and expect the community to modify their ideology to match their conduct. They need to conform to the community, not for the community to change for them.

However, the backslider or apostate may repent and return to the community.

# 4. HISTORIC CHRISTIANITY'S DEVIATION FROM SCRIPTURAL CONCEPTS

## INTRODUCTION

This section deals with the deviation from concepts covered in the initial sections of this volume. I contend that the previous sections are accurate, reliable and in total accord with the truth of *Yahweh* God as revealed in Sacred Scripture. I have no doubt that the reader has noticed a variation between the concepts of this volume with that of historical and contemporary Christianity.

This section is a historical analysis regarding the deviation of doctrinal concepts from Scripture to that of historical Christianity. I contend that shortly after the $2^{nd}$ Jewish War of 132-135 AD, the newly formed churches gradually departed from a Scriptural basis of doctrines and concepts which existed in the original Messianic communities. These churches that deviated from the original state of the spiritual Israel were primarily gentile, or non-Jewish, in membership. The deviation from Scripturally correct concepts were due to 2 influences and attitudes that prevailed in the gentile membership and especially in the new generation of non-Jewish church leaders and apologists.

1. Anti-Semitism.
2. Greek philosophy.

These 2 influences and attitudes which resided in the gentile membership of Churches operated coincidentally in the following manner: The attitude of anti-Semitism caused a reduction of respect for the authority of the OT, which subsequently caused a void in its use and application for deriving Scriptural truth. This caused an incorrect or incomplete interpretation of the NT. The void was then filled by Greek philosophy. The anti-Semitism equally affected the Jewish Messianic communities, who were branded as Judaizers, Ebionites, Nazoraens or Nazarenes, and heretics.

The use of the Greek Septuagint OT likewise contributed because the new generation of gentile Christians did not speak Hebrew and so depended on the Greek translation.

The defeat of Israel as a nation and their exile from the domain of Jerusalem shortly after the failed 2$^{nd}$ revolt, that under Semeon bar Kochba in 132-135 BC, inflated the ego of many a gentile preacher of the gospel. Their attitude was a haughty display of spite against the defeated Israel, that they finally reaped as they had sown. This likewise gave the non-Jewish membership justification to promote themselves as the rightful heirs to the kingdom and promises. But this haughty attitude of gentile church leaders only alienated them from OT Scripture and all else that comprised the Jewish religion.

This section will not deal with the historical or psychological reasons for racial or religious prejudice. These aspects of racism and bigotry is well covered by many authors, especially that dealing with the phenomenon of anti-Semitism. This section will deal with its historical progress beginning with the Roman victory over the Jews in both wars of 66-70 AD, and 132-135 AD. As a comparison, to the extent anti-Semitism exists today in contemporary Christianity, to the same extent it existed in the latter decades of the First and succeeding centuries.

## ROOTS OF ANTI-SEMITISM

The gentile church was easily able to identify the several defeats of the Jewish nation as a fulfillment of the prophetic words of Matt 27:25, "His blood be upon us and our children." For the typical non-Jew sitting in the pew in church year after year hearing the same words recited outside of their historical content the impression would be deep and grave. The parishioner would easily conclude that the term "us" referred to world-wide Jewry of the era, and that the term "and our children," referred to the unending descendents of these same Jews. The Jews of previous generations were likewise equally guilty, since they persecuted the earlier prophets. Matt 23:31.

The following passage referring to Judaism applies, as indicating the end of any ideological or practical benefit they may provide in the future.

And when he saw a fig tree in the way, he came to it, and found nothing thereon, but leaves only, and said unto it, Let no fruit grow on thee henceforward for ever. And presently the fig tree withered away. Matt 21:19-20.

This attitude has been inculcated into the minds of parishioners now for 19 centuries and still continues.

## CLEMENT

The earliest of the letters of the post-apostolic period does not reflect the anti-Semitic tendency so prevalent beginning with the $2^{nd}$ century apologists. The letter of Clement of Rome, composed about 96 AD, still includes some vestiges of the attitude of the original Messianic communities toward Jews.

> These things therefore being manifest to us, and since we look into the depths of the divine knowledge, it behooves us to be all things in their proper order, which the Lord has commanded us to perform at stated times. He has enjoined offerings to be presented and service to be performed to Him, and that not thoughtlessly or irregularly but at the appointed times and hours.[19]

The early Messianic communities continued to abide by those obligations still in effect, those services not abrogated by Jesus, but now in the light of the new covenant.

## THE BIRTH OF THE SON OF YAHWEH GOD

The earliest extant documents of the post-apostolic age indicate a belief in the divine birth of the son from the Father, similar to the concepts stated in earlier sections of this volume. The following excerpts from Clement of Rome and Ignatius letter to the Magnesians will indicate this.

> But concerning His Son the Lord spoke thus, "Thou art my Son, today have I begotten Thee. Ask of Me and I will give Thee the heathen for Thine inheritance, and the uttermost parts of the earth for Thy possession."[20]

---

[19] Ante-Nicene Fathers, vol. 1, page 16. First Epistle of Clement, chap. 40.
[20] Ibid, vol 1. Pg. 15.

Do ye therefore all run together as into one temple of God, as to one altar, as to one Jesus the Anointed, who came forth from one Father, and is with and has gone to God.[21]

The author of the 2nd Letter of Clement acknowledges the existence of Jesus as a Spirit prior to his incarnation.[22]

## LETTER OF DIOGNETUS

Beginning with the conclusion of the 2nd Jewish War, writings surfaced with evidence of anti-Semitism. The anonymous letter to Diognetus excellently summarizes the anti-Semitic sentiments of the 2nd century AD.

> But as to their scrupulosity concerning meats, and their superstition as respects the Sabbaths, and their boasting about circumcision, and their fancies about fasting and the new moons, which are utterly ridiculous and unworthy of notice.[23]

This letter was composed shortly after the conclusion of the 2nd Jewish War. It reflects the attitude of gentiles towards Jews prevalent at the time. The famous philosopher Bertrand Russell also notes the same attitude:

> After the first century, Christianity also crystallized, and the relations of Judaism and Christianity were wholly hostile and external; as we shall see, Christianity powerfully stimulated anti-Semitism.[24]
> As soon as the state became Christian, anti-Semitism, in its medieval form, began, nominally as a manifestation of Christian zeal.[25]

This attitude of superiority and bigotry of non-Jewish members of the Christian churches toward Jews is well documented, and which was created by the new generation of Christian leaders themselves.

---

[21] Ibid, pg. 62.
[22] Ibid, vol 9.pg. 253.
[23] *Ante-Nicene Fathers*, vol. 1, page 26. *Letter to Diognetus*.
[24] *A History of Western Philosophy*, Bertrand Russell, pg. 322.
25 Ibid, page 326.

## JUSTIN OF CAESAREA

The apologists of the early church reflected the attitude of the era. These "Christian" writers were very influential in the Roman world, and so defined the attitude of the gentile Christian church toward Jews for future generations. Justin martyr at the early date of 150-165 AD, wrote his Dialogue with Trypho, a Jew. This massive treatise was intended to convey to the reader the superiority of this new "Christ" and the new Christian church over the Jew and his religion. The dialogue is actually manufactured and Trypho was no doubt a fictitious character, a creation of Justin in order to devise comments and rhetoric to the disadvantage of the Jew of the era and inclined toward Justin's definition of the new gentile Christian faith. Interwoven in the treatise is discredit and criticism of Jews and their religion.

> For the law promulgated on Horeb is now old, and belongs to yourselves (Jews) alone; but this (gospel) is for all universally.[26]
> For the circumcision according to the flesh, which is from Abraham, was given for a sign; that you may be separated from other nations and from us; and that you alone may suffer that which you now justly suffer; and that your land may be desolate and you cities burned with fire; and that strangers may eat your fruit in your presence, and not one of you may go up to Jerusalem.[27]
> Moreover you were commanded to abstain from certain kinds of food, in order that you might keep God before your eyes while you ate and drank, seeing that you were prone and very ready to depart from his knowledge.[28]
> Moreover that God enjoined you to keep the Sabbath, and impose on you other precepts for a sign, as I have already said, on account of your unrighteousness, and that of your fathers.[29]

The attitude of Justin toward Jews is so clear in these passages: God deliberately placed Jews in the shackles and chains of the law of Moses to restrain their inherent rebellious nature. Jews, according to Justin, had a

---

[26] *Ante-Nicene Fathers*, vol. 1, page 200. *Dialogue with Trypho*, chap. XI.
[27] Ibid, page 202, chap. XVI.
[28] ibid, page 204, chap. XX.
[29] Ibid. page 204, chap. XXI.

natural tendency to disobedience to God and inclination to resistance to authority and insubordination. They were this way from their very beginning, and so God legislated laws to counteract their nature. These laws were intended to put Jews in religious slavery to restrain them from sin and subdue their rebellion. None of this applied to gentiles. According to Justin, this natural drive toward sin and disobedience did not exist in the nature of gentiles.

People of the era and later actually believed his conclusions, that if God did not legislate these laws then the Jews would have long ago destroyed themselves as a result of their rebellious nature. This made more reason for the gentiles to develop a racism against Jews and place less authority on the OT.

## TERTULLIAN AND JOHN CHRYSOSTOM

Tertullian writing about 200 AD, was also vehemently anti-Semitic. The following a description of Tertullian's conclusion about Jews.

> Tertullian argues that all the commandments of the *Torah* were given to the Jews to curb their tendency to idolatry, sensuality, and greed – a tendency unique to them and not shared with the rest of the human race, an attitude similar to that of Justin mentioned above. Their trail of crimes had culminated in the killing of the Anointed. The Jews had always conducted themselves unworthily of their election, and finally lost it. God's choice was transferred to another people, gentiles, capable of living by higher standards than those that had been imposed on the Jews.[30]
>
> This anti-Semitic attitude was also prevalent among other popular Christian figures of the early centuries, such as John Chrysostom, Cyril of Alexandria, and Augustine. John Chrysostom, presbyter at Antioch and later bishop of Constantinople, delivered a series of sermons against Jews. Two years after Chrysostom delivered these sermons, a Christian mob, led by the local bishop, destroyed a Jewish synagogue.[31]

---

[30] Nicholls, Wm. *Christian Antisemitism*, pg.182.
[31] Shanks, Hershel, *Christianity and Rabbinic Judaism*, pg. 246

This anti-Semitic attitude was also prevalent among other popular Christian figures of the early centuries, such as John Chrysostom, Cyril of Alexandria, and Augustine. John Chrysostom, presbyter at Antioch and later bishop of Constantinople, delivered a series of sermons against Jews. Two years after Chrysostom delivered these sermons, a Christian mob, led by the local bishop, destroyed a Jewish synagogue.

> Cyril's virulent anti-Semitism, and the anti-Judaism of Christian theologians of his day, seems to have been inflamed by fears of Judaism's legitimate claim to be the continuation of the biblical Israel.[32]

The anti-Jewish rhetoric of the apologists of these initial centuries during the rise of the gentile churches has been repeated by later Catholic and Protestant theologians and is still echoed in the modern age.

## THE ENIGMA OF THE APOLOGISTS

Of course this perplexes me, why the balance of treatises and discourses of the apologists are venerated by students and teachers of the Bible. With the attitude of anti-Semitism so obvious and vocal, the entire vein of conclusions and doctrines of these apologists is inclined in a direction away from any interpretation or application of OT that was held by the nation of Israel in earlier ages. In essence the entire OT now has a stigma attached to it.

The typical parishioner, after listening to anti-Jewish rhetoric and manipulation of prophetic passages, develops a preconception of the nation of Israel: they persecuted the ancient saints and prophets and were the ancestors of those who killed the son of God, these are the predecessors of the Christ-killers. They had a natural inclination toward sin and rebellion, which God had to restrain with ceremonial laws. This same parishioner continued this prejudice outside the church in social, business and civic areas. No association with Jews, no business with Jews, and instituting laws precluding and restraining the involvement of Jews in civic affairs.

The new gentile attitude was that *Yahweh* God deliberately enslaved the nation of Israel from Moses to the Anointed in a type of ceremonial

---

[32] Ibid. pg. 297.

and religious slavery. Only with the advent of the Anointed was this yoke of slavery removed. Irenaeus in his treatise *Against Heresies* mentions this.

> For in that which He says, "I will not now call you servants," He indicates in the most marked manner that it was Himself who did originally appoint for men that bondage with respect to God through the law, and then afterwards conferred upon them freedom. And in that He says, "The servant knows not what his lord doeth," He points out, by means of His own advent, the ignorance of a people in a servile condition.[33]
>
> The laws of bondage, however, were one by one promulgated to the people by Moses, suited for their instruction or for their punishment, as Moses himself declared, "And the Lord commanded me at that time to teach you statutes and judgments." These things, therefore, which were given for bondage, and for a sign to them, he cancelled by the new covenant of liberty.[34]

The attitude of the gentile Christians towards Jews in the years after the 2nd Jewish War is well described by the apologist: typical of their ancestors, they persisted in sin and rebellion by refusing their Anointed as Savior.

## GNOSTICISM

The next step in the deviation from Scriptural accuracy was to divide the sole God of the Bible into a god of the OT and a god of the NT. Thus the OT god or Supreme Deity was different from the god or Supreme Deity of the NT. This led to the organized denial of the authority of the Old Testament god and subsequently depriving the OT of any authority, except for those passages interpreted as Messianic. This theory advanced beginning in the 2nd century from the influence of gnosticism.

This religious philosophy taught the creation of the world by an inferior god, while salvation and freedom was attained through the superior god. The god of the OT was an inferior and evil god known as the Demiurge. The superior God was the God of the NT, who brought grace and truth and forgiveness to the world. Tillich describes it best as follows:

---

[33] *Ante-Nicene Fathers*, vol. 1, page 478.
[34] Ibid, pg. 482.

For the gnostics the created world is evil; it was created by an evil god whom they equated with the god of the Old Testament. Therefore salvation is liberation from the world, and had to be accomplished through ascetic means.[35]

This inferior god was the *Demiurge*. Gnosticism was very prevalent in the Roman Empire and especially in the area of North Africa and middle east. It much influenced the apologists and adherents of the post-apostolic communities. Gnosticism deprived the OT of its authority by equating *Yahweh* God of the OT with the inferior and evil god *Demiurge*. The god of the OT was full of vengeance and required blood sacrifices to appease his wrath. He seemed to be intent on punishing people for their sins with stoning and exile. The god of the NT was full of forgiveness and taught an entrance into a heavenly kingdom. The god of the NT sent his son into the world to save it, not to condemn it. This was the manner of separation between the OT and NT that was promoted by gnosticism. The gradual influence of this facet of gnosticism on Christianity is well documented by scholars.

> This subordinate god, called the *Demiurge*, is identified with the God of the Old Testament and is described as an inferior, limited, passionate and vengeful being. He is contrasted with the supreme god, the source of goodness, virtue and truth, who revealed Himself in the Anointed.[36]
> In any event its massive rejection of the God of the Old Testament appealed to Gentile Christians radically disaffected from Jewish traditions or stung by Jewish repudiation of their message.[37]

The influence of gnosticism caused a greater breach with the OT, and caused the OT to be inferior in doctrine and instruction as compared to the NT. It also caused a distortion of the person of *Yahweh*, thinking that He was a "bad deity" who had to be appeased with sacrifices and who imposed ruthless penalty for disobedience. This created a misunderstanding of the purpose for the OT religious system and so further distanced the gentile Christians from OT validity or annulled it.

---

[35] *A History of Christian Thought*, Paul Tillich. Pg. 34.

[36] *History of Christian Doctrine*, Louis Berkhof. Pg. 48.

[37] *Christianity and Rabinic Judaism*, Harold Attridge, pg. 176.

## MARCION

Subsequent to the influence of gnosticism was the popular teacher Marcion. His primary objective was the abrogation of OT Sacred Scripture. He was heavily influenced by gnosticism. Marcion taught that the God of the OT *Yahweh* was intent on enslaving people, taking out His vengeance on them, and could only be appeased by blood sacrifice. The God of the NT was loving and forgiving, sending His son to die on the stake for His people. It was the people loyal to the *Demiurge*, the God of the OT, who were motivated to kill Jesus, the son of the good God of the NT. The God and Father of Jesus was not the same God the creator and giver of the law to Moses in the OT. In essence, Marcion taught that the Jews worshipped a different God than the one Christians worshipped. The god of the OT was different from the god of the NT. This made the Jewish religion and its OT Scripture a different religion than Christianity. Only faith was required in the new God and His son.

Marcion abandoned the entirety of OT Scripture. He even condensed his NT to solely a condensed version of the gospel of Luke and the writings of Paul apostle. The rest of the books of the NT he rejected, feeling they were tainted by the influences of the OT god *Yahweh*.

Although Marcion was condemned by the primary apologists as a heretic his influence pervaded the gentile Christian sphere. It caused a separation: the God of the OT for Jews, the God of the NT and His son Jesus for Christians. This same attitude prevails today. The theology of Marcion is actually the Christian gospel of the present era.

This platform of Marcion implemented a new definition for Bible understanding and which also served as the pattern of belief for later and present Christianity. The result of Marcion's teaching is that Jews worshipped a different and inferior god than did Christians, and that Judaism and the Mosaic OT religion was a completely different and separate religion from the Christian church. Since now the OT God was recognized as the inferior God of a different religion the void of a NT God had to be filled by a superior God. This superior God then surfaced as the god of Plato, the One of Aristotle, in Christian garb.

Marcion's influence was considerable during the 3$^{rd}$ and 4$^{th}$ centuries.

## USE OF OLD TESTAMENT

The church could not however reject or denounce the body of writings known as the OT, as much as they would have liked to. Then the gentile church would jeopardize its position as the New Israel, the heir of the status as the new people of God.

In response to this the OT was utilized for its prophesies pertaining to Jesus, and the balance was allegorized as a shadow of the coming of the Anointed. In this manner anything the new generation of Christian leaders and coverts did not agree with or did not want to accept or implement could be allegorized. All of it now only pertained to Jews and its observance in every respect was abrogated for Christians, and all of it now to be understood as a massive allegory. The additional benefit of keeping the Bible intact allowed gentile Christians to use the OT as a weapon against Jews. The sections of reprimand and denouncement of Jews came in handy on a regular basis whenever Christians sought a scapegoat for some evil or crime. Resurrecting such passages keep alive among Christians the tradition of Jews as persistently disobedient and rebellious.

The effect of this anti-Jewish rhetoric is noticeable especially in the attitude towards the use of the word "law" (*nomos*) in the NT. Now whenever the word *nomos* was heard it referred to the entire body of the divine instruction from Exodus to Deuteronomy. Unless there existed a specific injunction for observance in the NT, and especially by Paul apostle, that instruction was either allegorized out of observance or just discarded.

No longer was the Anointed the goal of the *Torah*. Rom 10:2. Instead the Anointed was the termination of the law. The Anointed freed gentiles from bondage to the law. Gal 4:9, 5:11. This applied to the entirety of the OT divine instruction, even though the topic in this treatise of Paul apostle is circumcision. Gal 5:6, 6:12.

## THE HEBREW LANGUAGE

The Hebrew language also came under discredit and attack in the same vein. Few of the apologists spoke or read Hebrew. They were mainly Greek or Latin fluent. The Greek Septuagint translation of the OT became the divinely inspired OT for the Greek speaking gentile Christians. This likewise included the books known as Apocrypha. All the apologists and including Augustine quoted equally from these books as from the balance of the Hebrew Scripture. Augustine accepted the story of the miraculous agreement of the 70 independent translators and accepted this as proof of the divine inspiration of the Septuagint.[38]

> Tertullian utilized only the Septuagint, as Dr. Holmes comments in the introduction to his translation. "Be this as it may, it is manifest that Tertullian's Scripture passages never resemble the Hebrew, but in nearly every instance the Septuagint."[39]

Irenaeus in his treatise Against Heresies mentions apostolic recognition of the Septuagint as divinely inspired, which was especially to be utilized by the gentile Church.[40]

This attitude became a justification for the apologists and preachers not to utilize the original Hebrew texts in formulating their doctrines, and so not to even learn Hebrew. The same stigma of anti-Semitism was applied to the Hebrew language and original Hebrew texts of the OT.

The apologists applied an attitude of inspiration to the Latin Vulgate, translated by Jerome.

## THE NAME OF GOD

This lack of study of the OT in its original Hebrew and Aramaic counterparts caused the readers to distance themselves from the original divine concept of the Supreme Deity. This was due to the flaw in the Septuagint translation regarding the translation of the name of the supreme deity *Yahweh* God. In the Greek the name YHWH was replaced by *kyrios*, lord, the equivalent of the Hebrew *adonai*. The name *Yahweh* or the tetragrameton is not to be found in the Greek Septuagint. The reader of the Greek OT would conclude much the same as a reader of a contemporary English Bible, that the Supreme Deity either has no name, or His name is unknown, or His name is Lord. Therefore He is simply God or Lord God. In English Bibles there is an absence of YHWH or *Yahweh*. The OT Supreme Deity is simply God or Lord God.

---

[38] *A History of Western Philosophy*, B. Russell. Pg.361.

[39] *Ante-Nicene Fathers*, vol. 3, page 7.

[40] Ibid, vol. 1, page 452.

With the name of the Supreme Deity deleted from Scripture, combined with the anti-Semitism of the apologists, the attitude toward *Yahweh* turned for the worse. Justin Martyr in both his First and Second Apology states his attitude.

> For no one can utter the name of the ineffable God; and if any one dare to say that there is a name, he raves with a hopeless madness.[41]
>
> For God cannot be called by any proper name... On this account then, as I before said, God did not, when He sent Moses to the Hebrews, mention any name, but by a participle he mystically teaches them that He is the one and only God.[42]
>
> But to the Father of all, who is unbegotten, there is no name given.[43]
>
> And we have been taught, and are convinced, and do believe, that He accepts those only who imitate the excellencies which reside in Him, temperance, and justice, and philanthropy, and as many virtues as are peculiar to a God who is called by no proper name.[44]

Once the name *Yahweh* God, the Supreme Deity, was deleted from Scripture, He lost His position as supreme deity. *Yahweh* God now lost His personal identity and so was deposed from His capacity as sole deity by the apologists. The person of *Yahweh* was no longer recognized as the Supreme Deity of the OT and Father of Jesus, and as creator. As a result of His name expunged from Scripture, His authority in divine instruction was also reduced. (The OT Scripture contains the name *Yahweh* about 7,800 times.) He was subsequently replaced by a nebulous and distant entity without personal identity; a deity undefinable, known only as God. *Yahweh* became the Jewish God, while the triune Lord God became the Christian God. *Yahweh* was now replaced by the Holy Trinity of Christianity.

Translators of the Bible in this respect have not been faithful to their vocation. The attitude of Bible translators can be summarized in the following words, part of the preface to the RSV translation.

---

[41] Ibid, vol. 1, page 183.

[42] Ibid, vol 1, page 281.

[43] Ibid, vol 1, page 190.

[44] Ibid, vol 1, page 165.

The use of any proper name for the one and only God, as though there were other gods from whom He had to be distinguished, was discontinued in Judaism before the Christian era and is entirely inappropriate for the universal faith of the Christian Church.[45]

Quite the contrary I contend. It is very appropriate to use the name *Yahweh* or even Jehovah. This statement by the translators is included as a pretext to cover up anti-Semitism. Translations are available that are far more accurate than contemporary versions, but these are either little utilized or branded as heretic or cultic. The name of God is rendered as Jehovah in *Young's Literal*, the *American Standard* of 1901, and the *New World*. The name is rendered Yahweh is *Rotherham's Emphasized Bible*; and as *Ieue* in Adolf Knoch's *Concordant Version*. Few translators have been faithful to their vocation and have not allowed the attitude of anti-Semitism to influence them in correct Bible translation.

## CHRIST OR MESSIAH OR ANOINTED

Next in importance to depriving the Supreme Deity of His name is depriving Jesus of his title of Messiah, or the Anointed. The general attitude of Christianity is, "But isn't Christ the same as Messiah?" No, it is not. Messiah is a Hebrew term with certain connotations that are not conveyed when using the moniker Christ. The Hebrew word for Anointed is *Meshiah*, which is transliterated as Messiah. Anointed is correct in every respect as the proper translation of Christ or Messiah to convey the proper meaning of Jesus being anointed of God for a special purpose in the perfection of the Jewish religion.

The term Messiah was coined by Jewish sages subsequent to the Roman conquest of Judea about 65 BC under Pompey. The word has its origin in several passages of OT prophecy, and is expanded by the sages as documented in the *Mishna*. The word Messiah is derived from the Hebrew *masah*, to anoint. The term Messiah definitely has Jewish roots. The Messiah identifies Jesus as the awaited deliverer of the Jewish nation, a deliverance from the enemy, the occupation forces of Roman soldiers. He was to initiate the new age of his spiritual kingdom. As discussed earlier, the Anointed would conclude the age of Moses and initiate the new

---

[45] Preface to the *Revised Standard Version*, 1952 edition.

covenant. This covenant under the Anointed would spread to all the world, to fulfill the blessing of Abraham upon all nations.

The moniker Christ does not convey the same meaning. For most Christians the word Christ has no actual meaning or application. It is almost his surname or a mystic title. The moniker Christ is distant and alien from the intended meaning of Messiah as defined by the OT prophets and Jewish sages. By replacing Messiah with Christ, Jesus was deprived of his Jewishness, deprived of his purpose of teaching the gospel of the spiritual kingdom to his countrymen to deliver them from devastation.

> It was no longer understood that Christ was a translation of the Anointed, and meant that Jesus was the Lord of the age of redemption; the title simply became a proper name.[46]

The first and early second century Greek speaking Jewish and gentile population were able to understand the intended meaning in the translation of Messiah or the Anointed into Christ. By the middle of the $2^{nd}$ century, after the $2^{nd}$ Jewish War, this identity was lost and especially among the new generation of non-Jewish apologists with their attitude of anti-Semitism. This new generation of apologists and preachers created a new purpose and new intention for a new Christ, one deprived of his Jewishness, one alien and opposite to the original Jewish hope in the Anointed. A new Christ was introduced, a Christ now appearing to initiate a new religion to replace the religion of the OT. This new Christ was a person Greeks and Romans could identify with. This new interpretation of Jesus the Christ was based on the teachings of gnosticism and Marcion, and was likewise more easily adaptable into neo-Platonism than the Jewish Messiah or Anointed. A Greek Christ could be defined in terms of neo-Platonism while a Jewish one could not.

---

[46] Primitive Christianity, Rudolph Bultmann, pg. 176.

# 5. CHRISTIANITY: A NEW RELIGION

An important note to consider is that the apologists were originally students of the philosophy of Plato under the development of neo-Platonism as formulated by Plotinus; many were also disciples of Mani. With the rejection of the concept of *Yahweh* as Supreme Deity and Jesus as His born son – this in a real sense and not in a mystic or gnostic – these same apologists utilized their previous education in Greek philosophy and influence of gnosticism to redefine the concept of God, Jesus, Holy Spirit, the human, and etc. Their anti-Semitism was a mental block, hindering them using the OT Scripture and wisdom of Jewish sages to understand the value and correct application of *Torah* to the Messianic community and new spiritual Israel. These new concepts of the apologists were propagated to the masses of gentile Christian parishioners and so became the basis and definition of a new religion: Christianity, distinct and separate from Judaism. This new religion surfaced toward the conclusion of the 2nd century AD and was in full development by the middle of the 3rd century AD. The new religion no longer retained any of its Jewish roots.

The typical non-Jewish parishioner who would approach Jesus as the Christ, beginning the 3rd century AD, could not identify Jesus as Jewish. The apologists deprived Jesus of his Jewishness. The typical non-Jewish parishioner could not relate to Jesus of Nazareth as having an upbringing as a Jewish child, having a adult life of a devout Jew, and conducting himself as a respected Jewish Rabbi, itinerant preacher, prophet and healer among his countrymen. This new Christ appeared to establish a new religion and to abolish the old religion and Israel. The same can be applied to Paul apostle. He was no longer a Jewish rabbi who accepted Jesus of Nazareth as the Anointed, the fulfillment of the hope of Israel. Paul apostle was no longer the teacher to bring the gospel of the spiritual kingdom of *Yahweh* God to the gentiles, for them to accept Jesus of Nazareth as the Anointed and join Messianic community as their salvation from the sins of society. Paul apostle under the apologists became the founder of a new religion: Christianity, distinct and separate from Judaism.

Ignatius mentions this in a brief passage, composed about 105 AD, in his *Letter to the Magnesians*.

Lay aside therefore the evil, the old, the corrupt leaven, and be ye changed into the new leaven of grace. Abide in Christ, that the stranger may not have dominion over you. It is absurd to speak of Jesus Christ with the tongue and to cherish in the mind a Judaism that has now come to an end. For where there is Christianity there cannot be Judaism.[47]

It is apparent that the efforts of the apologists were to create a new religion without any ties to Judaism and with a Jesus uprooted from his Jewish background. Christianity as the movement that developed into the Catholic church of history was definitely not founded by Jesus, since it contains too many anti-Jewish ideas almost inseparable from it. This redefined movement is largely the creation of the second century apologists. It even has little in common theologically with the work of Paul.[48]

This basis of creating a new religion based on a non-Jewish Jesus with a severance from the OT Scripture and the writings of Jewish sages caused a lack of true understanding of the mission and purpose of the Anointed. Uprooting Jesus from his Jewish environment and the historic background of the era caused likewise new meanings to be attached to his parables. All of this was reinterpreted anew by the apologists, now in the light of their gnostic and philosophic inheritance. With the new gentile church now deprived of Jewish culture, tradition, expectations and history, there was no way to correctly interpret the teachings and prophesies of Jesus except to redefine them in the light of their own gentile culture, tradition and philosophy.

## GREEK PHILOSOPHY

From early childhood I attended Sunday School where he learned all the stories of the Bible, from the OT and NT. I likewise had my children attend the same until their mid-teenage years. The apologists however did not advocate the study of OT Bible stories for their students. Rather the study of Greek philosophy was promoted. Because the population was entrenched in the various philosophies, including Socrates, Plato, Aristotle, Pythagoras, Plotinus, Epicurus, and Zeno, they felt a knowledge of this was more applicable to the understanding of the NT and "Christian

---

[47] *Ante-Nicene Fathers*, vol. 1, page 63.
[48] *Christian Anti-Semitism*, William Nicholls, pg. 43.

doctrine" rather than a fluency in the OT. Perhaps they feared being branded as Judaizers if they were to emphasize the OT Jewish history, law and hymns, rather than their own non-Jewish philosophic sages. Clement of Alexandria felt that Greek philosophy had its origin and derivation from God. He even went to the extreme of stating that Plato was a Greek Moses.

> The Greek preparatory culture, therefore, with philosophy itself, is shown to have come down from God to men.[49]
>
> And in general terms, we shall not err in alleging that all things necessary and profitable for life came to us from God, and that philosophy more especially was given to the Greeks, as a covenant peculiar to them – being, as it is, a stepping-stone to the philosophy which is according to Christ.[50]
>
> It is He who also gave philosophy to the Greeks by means of the inferior angels. For by an ancient and divine order the angels are distributed among the nations.[51]
>
> For what is Plato, but Moses speaking in Attic Greek?[52]

Origin in his Letter to Gregory, to whom he referred as a son, likewise promoted the study of philosophy as a means of better understanding and interpreting the Bible.

> But I am anxious that you should devote all the strength of your natural good parts to Christianity for your end; and in order to this, I wish to ask you to extract from the philosophy of the Greeks what may serve as a course of study or a preparation for Christianity, and from geometry and astronomy what will serve to explain the sacred Scriptures.[53]

As a result of this emphasis on study of non-Biblical literature, the theories and concepts of Plato were transferred to Christianity, rather than the concepts found in the OT Scripture. Eventually the god of Plato and

---

[49] Ibid, vol. 2, pg. 308.
[50] Ibid, vol. 2, pg. 495.
[51] Ibid, vol. 2, pg. 524.
[52] Ibid, vol. 2, pg. 334.
[53] Ibid, vol. 4, pg. 393.

Aristotle became the Christian god. Paul Tillich, the noted theologian, states this.

> Clement's thought is a great example of a synthesis of Christian thinking and Greek philosophy. Christianity had to cope with Neo-Platonism as a universal and extremely impressive system.... Clement and Origen were both Greek philosophers, and at the same time faithful and obedient members of the Christian church. They had no doubt that it is possible to combine these two things.[54]
> Later the Aristotelian God, as the highest form, entered into Christian theology and exerted a tremendous influence upon it.[55]
> When Clement speaks of philosophy, he does not have in mind a particular philosophy, but that which is true in all philosophies. In this thought many elements from Greek philosophy are mixed with biblical materials. He quoted whole sections from Stoic sources.[56]

Justin of Caesarea likewise taught that the Christians were followers of Plato.[57]

To state the attitude of the apologists more correctly, it was they who used Greek philosophy instead of the OT and NT to define the new religion of Christianity, by selecting those facets of philosophy that could be used to justify their new religion. This is the essence of Justin's Heathen Analogies to Christian Doctrine, chapter 20 of his First Apology, to show that the new Christianity is a conglomeration of points and doctrines already prevailing in paganism, mythology and philosophy.[58]

## THE GOD OF PLATO THE NEW GOD OF CHRISTIANITY

Although the claim by the apologists is that Plato received his teaching from Moses, the concepts provided by Plato regarding theology are all antithesis to what was provided by Moses and the other authors of Sacred Scripture. Plotinus with his philosophy labeled neo-Platonism was the primary contributor for the theology of the new religion called

---

[54] *A History of Christian Thought*, Paul Tillich, pgg. 56-57.

[55] Ibid. pg. 7.

[56] Ibid. pg. 55.

[57] *A History of God*, Karen Armstrong. Pg. 94.

58 *Ante-Nicene Fathers*, vol. 1, pg. 169.

Christianity. The apologists, having rejected what Scripture provides in its original and Hebrew form for theology, but not wanting to discard it, now utilized bits and pieces from it to justify the theology of the new religion. This new religion was dependent on Plato and gnosticism and not the Bible.

> Dean Inge, in his invaluable book on Plotinus, rightly emphasizes what Christianity owes to him. "Platonism, he says, "is part of the vital structure of Christian theology, with which no other philosophy, I venture to say, can work without friction," There is, he says, an "utter impossibility of excising Platonism from Christianity without tearing Christianity to pieces.[59]

The new definition of God was not *Yahweh* God of the Bible as expounded in previous sections of this volume, but derived from Plato. This was the source for the apologists in their treatises regarding the Deity. Irenaeus for example, as a theologian was still a man of his time. For him, God the Father was a simple being, without parts, without passions – in other words, the One of Later neo-Platonism in Christian dress – and God the Son, the *Logos*, is his revelation.

> Clement, and the whole Alexandrian school, have no hesitation at all in using Platonism and Stoicism to explain and interpret the Christian tradition. He actually refers to God the Father as the One, adding that he is beyond form, beyond limit, beyond conception, beyond description. In his writings there are many passages where it would be very difficult (unless one knew the author) to decide of one were reading the work of a Christian or a hard-line Platonist. The Son he refers to as Mind – the Divine Mind of Later Platonism – and this Mind became man in order to provide the human race with the most complete and perfect revelation possible, and enable humankind to progress slowly but steadily in the knowledge of God.[60]

The new Christian God was essentially a central power, distant and vague. He was no longer an entity with whom a believer could identity.

---

[59] *A History of Western Philosophy*, B. Russell, pg. 284-285.
[60] *A History of Christian Doctrines*, Louis Berkof, pg. 46.

## NEO-PLATONISM, THE PREDECESSOR OF CHRISTIANITY

Origen lived about 185-254 AD, and Plotinus lived about 204-270 AD. Both were disciples of Ammonius Saccas the founder of neo-Platonism, a further development of the doctrines provided by Plato. Both men were reared in Alexandria, Egypt, and spent their years teaching there. Plotinus continued in the area of neo-Platonism and developed it more fully. This philosophy became very prevalent and accepted by many in the Roman Empire. Origen adhered to the newly formed Christianity, and then utilized his education in neo-Platonism to define various concepts dealing with the new religion.

> To all of them, Christians and pagans alike, the world of practical affairs seemed to offer no hope, and only the Other World seemed worthy of allegiance. To the Christian, the Other World was the Kingdom of Heaven, to be enjoyed after death; to the Platonist, it was the eternal world of ideas, the real world as opposed to that of illusory appearance. Christian theologians combined these points of view, and embodied much of the philosophy of Plotinus.[61]

With their lack of OT and Hebrew scholarship and this prevalence of anti-Semitism, the apologists were better able to adopt Platonic ideas into the new Christian theology.

## MITHRA BECOMES JESUS
## AND MITHRAISM BECOMES CHRISTIANITY

The new group of these who accepted Jesus as the Anointed were gentiles, whose congregations were established by the Apostle Paul, except his message was interwoven with Greek neo-Platonic philosophy and the paganism of Mithraism – the most prominent religion of the Roman Empire at the time – and obedience to Roman authority. The original message of Jesus was erased from existence and replaced with a new Jesus, meaning Mithra.

I will not go into detail regarding the similarities between Mithra as the replacement Jesus of historic Christianity, but yes, he was born on

---

[61] *A History of Western Philosophy*, B. Russell, pg. 284.

December 25; he had a sacred meal called the Last Supper; he was crucified on Good Friday and he did resurrect on Easter Sunday morning.

Items to realize here is that the Last Supper was invented by Mithraism to replace the Passover and supposed the crucifixion occurring on Good Friday, when none of this is in the NT. The date of Easter, a festivity based on the pagan goddess *Astarte*, was not set until the First Ecumenical Council in 325 AD. The sequence of days of this holy week is defined in the OT, the Passover on the 14$^{th}$ day of the new month or new moon, and which could occur on any day of the week, as it is a lunar calculation, so the day of the crucifixion would be the following day and Jesus' resurrection would have occurred 3 days later, based on his words. So only one chance in 7 that Jesus' resurrection would have occurred on a Sunday, otherwise the holy day of Passover would dictate the day of Jesus' crucifixion and his resurrection.

It was during the reign of Emperor Marcus Aurelius, the philosopher king, 161-180 AD, that Messianic Christianity was usurped by Mithraism, meaning that Mithraism was now labeled Christianity. The Messiah Jesus was replaced by Mithra, who now became the new Jesus. All of which Mithraism consisted now became the new Christian religion, and freedom of religion was established in the Roman Empire, provided that the population accept and recognize Christianity. This was formally accomplished by Emperor Constantine the Great at the First Ecumenical Council, 325 AD, at Nicea, Turkey. Of course to acquire freedom of religion the members capitulated to Imperial Rome, including military service. The Roman Empire now became "Christian," although it was actually Mithraism with a new face of Jesus instead of Mithra and new appellation of Christianity, but the same religion for all practical purposes.

The original members of the Messianic community were now either absorbed into the Greek-Roman style Christianity, or dispersed.

## THE HOLY TRINITY

The Christian concept of the holy trinity, or Triune Godhead, has an important advocate in Plotinus. His discourses provided reasoning that could be adapted easily into the concept of the triune godhead. This volume will not discuss in detail the neo-Platonism of Plotinus, but only will briefly note its concepts to provide the reader the evidence that the doctrine of the holy trinity has its roots and derivation from him.

The First person is the One. The 2$^{nd}$, which is spirit, Plotinus identified with the mind. The mind was then equated with the *logos*. The lowest member is the soul. The synopsis of neo-Platonism was subsequently modified by the apologists of following generations until it evolved in the Christian Holy Trinity: God the Father, God the Son, and God the Holy Spirit.

> Plotinus regarded the first two emanations to radiate from the One as divine, since they enabled us to know and to participate in the life of God. Together with the One, they formed a Triad of divinity which was in some ways close to the final Christian solution of the Trinity.[62]

Since the *logos* was identified as the 2$^{nd}$ person of Plotinus' triad the emanation or generation was eternal into the past and eternal into the future. The emanation or generation of the *logos* or mind was always in process. It never had a beginning but was occurring from the time infinitely into the past or continuous. The concept of the emanation of the *logos* from the One was transferred from neo-Platonism into the new Christian theology. Beginning with Tertullian, the void for a definition of deity for the new Christian religion was filled by this neo-Platonic concept of the One and the eternal emanation of the *logos* from the One, now identified as the Father, and the *logos* now identified as the Son. Tertullian then took the next step in designating this emanation of the *logos* as another person. Tertullian explains this process in his treatise *Against Praxeas*, first as a comparison of a person's own speech in relation to himself, and then the same application to the One.

> Thus in a certain sense, the word is a second person within you, through which in thinking you utter speech, and through which also (by reciprocity of process,) in uttering speech you generate thought. The word is itself a different thing from yourself.... I may therefore without rashness first lay this down (as a fixed principle) that even then before the creation of the universe God was not alone, since He had within Himself both Reason, and, inherent in Reason, His Word, which he made send to Himself by agitating it within Himself.[63]

---

[62] *A History of God*, Karen Armstrong, pg. 103.
[63] *Ante-Nicene Fathers*, vol. 3, pg. 601.

> This will be the prolation [appendage], taught by the truth, the guardian of the Unity, wherein we declare that the Son is a prolation from the Father, without being separated from Him.[64]

The error made by Tertullian in this chapter is his designation of the mind or expression of the Father, which he designates as the son, as a separate person from the Father. This is not sola-Scriptura, it is neo-Platonism. The *logos* of *Yahweh* God is His mind or expression or word, but when emanated from the Father it does not constitute a separate person. *Yahweh* God does have a mind, but the expression or word that results from the mind of *Yahweh* God is the same. It is a command or disclosure of the mind of *Yahweh* God, not a separate entity or person. This concept can be compared with ourselves. The ideas of our mind when brought into public are our expression or word. It is the public disclosure of what a person has on their mind. It is not another entity within us and yet distinct from us. Our word is the expression of ourselves.

The error of Tertullian and other apologists in applying Plotinus to definition of Deity is due to a disregard and lack of knowledge of OT and especially in Hebrew and the purpose of the Anointed. The explanation of John 1:1-18 was dealt with in a previous section in detail. With the baptism of the Holy Spirit *Yahweh* God delivered His message, the message which existed from the beginning in His dealings with Israel, to Jesus to disclose to the nation Israel. This is also repeated in Heb 1:1-2. Nothing spoken in the OT regarding *Yahweh* God was applied in this new doctrine.

With Tertullian and subsequent apologists into the future this eternal generation of the word-son became orthodox truth for the new Christian religion. The immediate problem was to still somehow profess 1 God when now 2 emanations are professed which are likewise designated persons. The solution was more philosophic rhetoric.

## ARIUS

Arius, who was the primary developer of the controversy that bears his name, was actually closer to the truth in regards to Deity than the Cappadocian Fathers or any of his opponents. He was also a student of Origin and voraciously consumed all his writings. I do not claim

---

[64] Ibid, pg. 603.

orthodoxy for either Arius or the Cappadocian Fathers. The error of each can be summarized as follows. Arius was correct is concluding that Jesus was a distinct entity born of *Yahweh* God at some point in the infinite past. The flaw of his concept lies in that he could not attribute to this new entity the nature or substance of *Yahweh* God. This deprived Jesus of being of the hypostasis of God and *homo-ousian* (the same) as *Yahweh* God. Arius did however assign true deity to Jesus, but as an inheritance and not as a matter of generation from the Father.

> Arius was not denying the divinity of Christ; indeed, he called Jesus "strong God" and "Full God." But he argued that it was blasphemous to think that he was divine by nature: Jesus had specifically said that the Father was greater than he.[65]

According to Arius, the *logos* took the place of the soul in Jesus.[66] Arius has been discredited far too much by the apologists and Nicene Fathers, and with no sensible reason except to their unwillingness to acknowledge Scripture in its correct sense. The theology of Arius was easily understood by the masses, while the apologists promoted a deity that could not be grasped by human intellect. With Arius the parishioners could identify with God and He having a son Jesus, which tendency was curtailed by the apologists with their nebulous and impersonal Triune emanating Deity.

The Cappadocian fathers focused on the Trinity as primarily defined by Tertullian. It was their conclusion that gained the victory at the First Ecumenical Council. But this did not settle the question of the state of Jesus the incarnate word during his earthly ministry.

## THE NEW GODS OF CHRISTIANITY

I contend that the trinity of Tertullian and subsequent apologists and theologians is absurd and ludicrous. The efforts exerted toward the theology of a Christian deity diverted the people from the understanding of *Yahweh* God as clearly defined in the OT and the relationship of Jesus to his Father and his role in Israel as the Anointed as defined in the NT.

In subsequent generations *Yahweh* God completely lost his identity as Supreme Deity. There is no place for *Yahweh* God in the new theology of

---

[65] Armstrong, Karen, *A History of God*. Pg. 107.

[66] O'Collins, Gerald, *Christology*, pg. 177.

Christian deity. He was replaced by the One, or First Principal, a distant and nebulous entity, who at the same time had a emanation continually in process: the Word/Son. A second emanation was likewise in process, the Holy Spirit. These emanations being persons of equal state and condition as the One/Father but indivisible from Him. Jesus was likewise no longer viewed as a son born of *Yahweh* God, but as the 2nd person of this Holy Triune Deity, a separate person with his own identity from the Father but indivisible from Him. This theology of the emanation of the Word/Son replaced the identity of Emmanuel.

It was impossible for the apologists to accept the concept of a birth in the realm of the spirit, because the ideas of neo-Platonism were vague and nebulous; God was indefinable, distant, with no real substance or essence, an impersonal central power. How could something of intangible and ethereal substance produce another entity like itself? This was the dilemma of the apologists with their philosophic background. Eternal emanation can only generate an impersonal emanation of intangible substance like itself, but not a separate entity of real spirit-substance.

Even though Tertullian quoted texts regarding Jesus as the only-begotten in his treatise *Against Praxeas*, he immediately denies this by advocating eternal generation. This is not birth!

Origen admits to the existence of the son as a tangible entity in heaven, a servant of the Father in the creation of the universe. Origen likewise confirms the *kenosis*, Jesus abandoning his heavenly glory and majesty to become human and subsequently die. But then the flaw arises later in *De Principiis* where the son is identified eternally into the past as the wisdom or word of the Father.

> For we must of a necessity hold that there is something exceptional and worthy of God which does not admit of any comparison at all not merely in things, but which cannot even be conceived by thought or discovered by perception, so that a human mind should be able to apprehend how the unbegotten God is made the Father of the only-begotten Son. Because His generation is as eternal and everlasting as the brilliancy which is produced from the sun. For it is not by receiving the breath of life that he is made a Son, by any outward act, but by his own nature.[67]

---

[67] Ibid. vol. 4, pg. 247.

Although several times Origen states correct conclusions in the evolution of Jesus from his Father, but then he descends into the same neo-Platonic and gnostic trap of eternal generation.

## KENOSIS OF THE SECOND PERSON OF THE TRIUNE DEITY

The *kenosis* or deprivation of glory of Jesus does not comply with the theories of emanation. If Jesus is eternally the Word/Son, $2^{nd}$ person of a Triune indivisible Deity, then he has no capability to empty himself of such a glory because it is his inherent state. Jesus cannot be both eternally emanating from the Father and vacating his deity to become human. The same apologists denied the passage of Phil 2:6-12, indicating that it was impossible. In order for this *kenosis* to be executed, Jesus could not be an eternal and continuous emanation of Word/Son from the Father. He would have to be separate and distinct. It was easier for the apologists to interpret away the *kenosis* passage, than to admit a flaw in their theology. The eminent theologian Louis Berkhof, comments on the *kenosis* in its true sense.

> It means a virtual destruction of the Trinity, and therefore takes away our very God. The humanized Son, self-emptied of His divine attributes, could no longer be a divine subsistence in the Trinitarian life.[68]

Both concepts cannot prevail simultaneously. Either the *kenosis* occurred or it did not. Paul apostle was correct in this passage regarding the self-humiliation of Jesus. He did deny himself and deprive himself of all his glory and majesty in heaven and became human just as any other person on earth. This was earlier discussed. To do this Jesus had to be a separate and distinct entity from the Father. He could not be a continuous emanation and at the same time become human.

## THE PARADOX

If the conclusion of the apologists is correct there was no Jesus in heaven prior to the incarnation of the *logos*. There was no personal entity Jesus alongside Father. Rather, there was a nebulous mind or expression that

---

[68] Berkhof, Louis, *Systematic Theology* , pg.329.

emanated from the One, but not a Jesus. In heaven there was the One Father and an impersonal *logos* non-entity and a spirit. Clement of Alexandria attempts to philosophize away the paradox in the following, in Book 7 of his *Stromata*

> He is the true Only-begotten, the express image of the glory of the universal King and Almighty Father, who impresses on the Gnostic the seal of the perfect contemplation, according to his own image; so that there is now a third divine image, made as far as possible like the Second Cause, the Essential Life, through which we live the true life.[69] And among intellectual ideas, what is oldest in origin, the timeless and unoriginated First Principal, and Beginning of existences – the Son – from whom we are to learn the remoter Cause, the Father, of the universe, the most ancient and the most beneficent of all.[70]

This is solely gnostic jargon of absurd elucidation. The Christian philosopher Athenagoras in his *Plea For The Christians* describes the paradox in this manner.

> But if in your surpassing intelligence, it occurs to you to inquire what is meant by the Son, I will state briefly that he is the first product of the Father, not as having been brought into existence, for from the beginning, God, who is the eternal mind, had the *logos* in Himself, being from eternity instinct with *Logos*; but inasmuch as he came forth to be the idea and energizing power of all material things, which lay like a nature without attributes, and an inactive earth, the grosser particles being mixed up with the lighter.[71]

No matter how the paradox of the non-existence of Jesus in heaven coincident with the existence of the emanating *logos* is viewed or attempted to be explained, it is still gnostic, not Biblical. The apologists realized their inability to rationalize or reason the paradox of an emanating Word/Son without the existence of a Jesus. Rather than admit possible misunderstanding in their theology, to cover up the paradox was easier. So

---

[69] *Ante Nicene Fathers*, vol. 2, pg. 527.
[70] Ibid, pg. 523.
[71] Ibid. pg. 133.

they labeled it the mystery of the trinity. Tertullian admits the paradox and labels it a mystery in his treatise *Against Praxaes*.

> As if in this way also One were not All, in that All are of One, by unity (that is) of substance; while the mystery of the dispensation is still guarded, which distributed the Unity into a Trinity, placing in their order the three Persons – the Father, the Son, and the Holy Ghost.[72]

In the final chapter of *Against Praxeas*, Tertullian states that the doctrine of the trinity constitutes the primary difference between Judaism and Christianity.[73] He is only so true in this statement, the Supreme Deity of the Bible now replaced by gnostic rhetoric.

## CONSTANTINE THE GREAT

The controversy within the Christian church was viewed by Constantine the Great as a threat to the stability of his empire. He knew that a nation fragmented and feuding over religion would not contribute to the cohesion and harmony of his reign. What would help he felt was a council of these elders to conclude this controversy in some amiable manner and acquire a unified church to the benefit of his empire.

Constantine realized the value of having religious harmony in his empire. His reason for issuing an edict of religious toleration was to cease persecution of minority religious groups, and thereby decrease strife within the empire. Christianity valued this as a blessing of God, especially after the persecution under Constantine's predecessor Diocletian. Constantine realized the importance of such an advanced religion and its benefit for his empire, and especially the facets of the teaching that required them to be good citizens and submissive subjects of the emperor. But in time the freedom caused the ecumenical Christian church to evolve into the state-sanctioned religion and intolerance toward those who did not conform to the dictates of the First Ecumenical Council of 325 AD began. As early as 326 AD, Christian denominations that were now labeled heretic or schismatic were excluded from the privileges that Constantine conferred on the ecumenical church. Open persecution by the bishops of the

---

[72] Ibid. vol. 3, pg. 598.

[73] Ibid, pg. 627.

ecumenical church followed after, and this especially applied to Christian pacifist denominations. Historian Schaff described it as follows:

> But the elevation of Christianity as the religion of the state presents also an opposite aspect to our contemplation. It involved great risk of degeneracy to the church. The Roman state, with its laws, institutions, and usages, was still deeply rooted in heathenism, and could not be transformed by a magical stroke. The Christianizing of the state amounted therefore in great measure to a paganizing and secularizing of the church. The world overcame the church, as much as the church overcame the world, and the temporal gain of Christianity was in many respects cancelled by spiritual loss. The mass of the Roman empire was baptized only with water, not with the Spirit and fire of the gospel, and it smuggled heathen manners and practices into the sanctuary under a new name.[74]

The religion that Constantine promoted for the empire was not the religion of the Bible. Constantine's concept of a state religion was that of *sol invictus*, the unconquerable sun, not Jesus the Anointed. The resultant religion under the Ecumenical Councils was a Christianity redefined in terms of neo-Platonism. The attempt of the Nicene Fathers working together with the secular authority of the Roman state to create a Christian nation was in reality the materialization of Plato's envisioned *Republic*.

Constantine to install one religion in his Roman Empire continued what Emperor Marcus Aurelius implemented. The old Mithraism was now the new religion of Christianity, meaning that Mithraism was now labeled Christianity. The Messiah Jesus was replaced by Mithra, who now became the new Jesus. All of which Mithraism consisted now became the new Christian religion, and freedom of religion was established in the Roman Empire, provided that the population accept and recognize Christianity.

## THE CHRISTOLOGICAL CONTROVERSY

Further discussions on the incarnation of the *Logos*/Son emanation lead to what is known as the Christological controversy. These were a series of confrontations among Christian theologians of the 4$^{th}$ and 5$^{th}$ centuries to try to accurately explain the incarnation of a facet of the new triune deity

---

[74] Schaff, Philip, *History of the Christian Church*, vol. 3, chap. 13.

into a distinct human with his own mind and will. Who Jesus was in his incarnation could not be easily defined since the *logos* was not an entity but the mind of the Father. Since a human is a soul which is his identity, where did Jesus acquire a soul or identity if he was mind or *logos*? According to Origin the Father assigned to the *Logos*/Son a soul at the incarnation.

> And so we must believe that there existed in the Christ a human and rational soul, without supposing that it had any feeling or possibility of sin.[75]

Now that the *Logos*/Son merged with a soul to allow his existence as a human, this made him a distinct identity separate from the Father, and he is now assigned the name Jesus. Prior to the incarnation there was no actual Jesus according to the theology of the apologists, because the neo-Platonic system could not recognize a distinct entity such as Jesus in heaven. With the appearance of this man-god-logos-2$^{nd}$ person of trinity, confusion erupted in the Christological controversies. This surrounded the topics of Jesus' wills and natures.

The flaw in the theology of the Nicene and ante-Nicene Fathers consisted in not accepting the Supreme Deity as a personal entity named *Yahweh*, who generated another distinct entity identical to Himself consisting of the same substance whom He designated His son, and to whom he assigned His nature and deity. The fact that this derivation of the doctrine of the Holy Trinity as defined by the early ecumenical councils is not to be located in the NT and was developed over the years heavily dependant on neo-Platonism is clearly admitted by every major scholar studying the history of the development of Christian theology, including the apologists themselves.

> The Church had to wait for more than three hundred years for a final synthesis, for not until the council of Constantinople (381 AD) was the formula of one God existing in three co-equal Persons formally ratified.[76]

---

[75] Ibid. Vol 4, pgg. 282, 283.
[76] Kelly, J.N.D, *Early Christian Doctrine*., pgg. 87-88.

The statement of Constantinople was a take it or leave it conclusion by the attending membership: The indivisible triune deity of 3 separate persons, which was a mystery to the human mind, was to be accepted for the future without further debate. Those that accepted it would be considered orthodox and consistent with historical Christianity; those who would not would be branded as heretic or unorthodox. No further discussions were permitted on the subject. But this did not resolve the original conflict. The conclusion is stated best in the following.

> In this way the Trinitarian dogma became a sacred mystery. The sacred mystery was placed on the altar, so to speak, and adored. It was introduced into the icons, the pictures which are so important for the cult in the Eastern church, into liturgical formulae and hymns, and there the mystery has liver ever since. However, it lost its power to interpret the meaning of the living God.[77]

In later years, other theologians, such as Augustine, would compose volumes on the doctrine of the Holy Trinity, but never trying to prove it. It was accepted as a fact by blind faith. No further discussion was necessary. The Trinitarian Creed of Constantinople became the bedrock of future generations of Christian theology.

## THE COUNCIL OF CHALCEDON

The Christological controversy in the hierarchy of the ecumenical church continued on until its superficial resolution at the Council of Chalcedon in 451 AD. The question focused on Jesus as human. To what extent was he divine and human? While in the flesh how could be still be the $2^{nd}$ person of an indivisible deity? The Nicene fathers proceeded on the basis that the man Jesus was just a temporary entity: from birth to death to ascension. All his statements of subjection and weakness and need of strength and comfort only pertained to the man Jesus, not to the $2^{nd}$ person of the Trinity. The person of Jesus was generated with the conception and dissolved with the ascension. This was the doctrine of the 2 natures and the 2 wills, one human and one divine: both living together in the body of this person, separate and unmixed but united together in one body. The *logos*

---

[77] Tillich, Paul, *A History of Christian Thought*, pg. 79.

became the soul of the person Jesus on earth. In essence Jesus the Anointed was just a body by which the *Logos*/Son was incarnated.

The Council of Chalcedon was considered the triumph of Christology. But it did not explain or resolve the controversy. Like the Trinitarian Creed of Constantinople, the decision of Chalcedon was a "take it or leave it." It was to be accepted as a statement of fact without further discussion, and the basis of orthodox and historical Christianity for future generations. If the conclusion of Chalcedon is to be taken seriously, there is still no real person Jesus in heaven. The $2^{nd}$ person of the Trinity, the *Logos*/Son, now has a name assigned to it, but he is still not an entity, because Jesus dissolved with the ascension!

For the serious Bible student, the triumph of Chalcedon only caused more questions to surface. Did Jesus really die? Not if he was the indivisible $2^{nd}$ person of the Holy Trinity. Since God cannot die, and no part of God can actually terminate existence, then Jesus did not die. In the theory of Chalcedon, only his body died, but he as the *Logos*/Son continued to live and so preached to the spirits in *hades* during this interval. The *Logos*/Son then returned back to the body of Jesus after about 3 days, Jesus being just a body in which the *Logos*/Son resided. If the doctrines of Chalcedon be true, there was no Jesus son of *Yahweh* God who died for our sins!

The great obstacle to the feasibility of the Holy Trinity and the Nature of Jesus as defined at Chalcedon is the role of *Yahweh* God. He has no more role! He cannot have a role! There is no place for the entity of *Yahweh* or for Emmanuel/Jesus in the Chalcedon doctrine of the Holy Trinity or in the Nature of Jesus. Once a Supreme Deity who is a personal entity is introduced, the entire foundation of sand washes away and the edifice constructed by the Apologists and Nicene Fathers collapses. As long as the philosophy of neo-Platonism ruled in the intellect of the apologists and Nicene-Fathers, the controversy could be concluded with their rhetoric. But nowhere was any mention of the *Yahweh* of the Bible, but always God defined in their neo-Platonic terms. They fought against any concept that would collide or disagree with their preconceived theology of the emanations and would label it Jewish. There was no room for a Jewish God or a real Son in the new theology of the Christian church.

## THE NEW HUMAN SOUL

It was not only in regard to theology that Greek philosophy and anti-Semitism had its influence and impact, but also in regard to anthropology, the constitution of the human. No longer did the human consist of body and soul (identity) and spirit. This was replaced by the 2-fold constitution of spirit and body, the soul now identified as the spirit. It was Tertullian who equated the soul with the spirit. This he explains in his Treatise on the Soul.

> Therefore this entire process, both of breathing and living, belongs to that to which living belongs, that is, to the soul. How much firmer ground have you for believing that the soul and the spirit are one, since you assign to them no difference; so that the soul is itself the spirit, respiration being the function of that of which life also is?... But the nature of my present inquiry obliges me to call the soul spirit or breath.[78]

Tertullian could not grasp the concept of a human being as a living soul in accord with Gen 2:7, the soul being the identity of that human. The person in their entirety now became spirit and body. This new concept for the Christian realm became the pivot point for the immortality of the soul. Tertullian preferred to agree with Plato in regard to the composition of the human, rather than the Bible.[79]

## THE SOUL FROM MORTAL TO IMMORTAL

The earliest of the apologists, not completely enveloped by neo-Platonism and anti-Semitism, still acknowledged the temporality of the soul. Such was Tatian, which he mentions in his Address to the Greeks.

> The soul is not in itself immortal, O Greeks, but mortal. Yet it is possible for it not to die.[80]

---

[78] Ante-Nicene Fathers, vol.3, pg. 190.
[79] Ibid. pg. 189.
[80] Ibid. vol. 2, pg. 70.

Tatian lived about 110-172 AD; he was an Assyrian, and not Greek. The concept of the immortality of the soul enters into Christian doctrine after this time. It was easy to make the spirit-soul facet of a human immortal by indicating that spirit cannot die. Since soul is really spirit, and spirit cannot die, therefore the soul is immortal, so was their argument. This spirit/soul just returns to God. Eccl 12:7. Tertullian subsequently promoted the immortality of the soul based on his own arguments, the same arguments as neo-Platonism.

> Whereas the soul is immortal; and being immortal, it is therefore indissoluble; and being indissoluble, it is figureless: for it, on the contrary, if had figure, it would be of a composite and structural formation.[81]

Following the logic of Tertullian, other apologists likewise taught the same. Hyppolytus in Book 3 of his *Refutation of all Heresies* mentions the correlation between the new Christian view of the immoral soul and Plato's.[82] It is no secret to historians that this entire concept of the immortality of the soul in Christian doctrine had its derivation from Plato. Bible texts dealing with the demise of the soul were all eventually allegorized or were interpreted such that they only pertained to the earthly life. As Paul Tilich states:

> First of all it shows that the apostolic fathers did not believe in the immortality of the soul. There is no natural immortality, otherwise it would be meaningless for them to speak about immortal life that Christ offers. They believed that man is naturally mortal.... In light of this we can conclude that our traditional way of speaking of the immortality of the soul is not classically Christian doctrine, but a distortion of it, not in a genuine, but in a pseudo-Platonic sense.[83]

This concept of Plato adopted by the apologists eventually became part of orthodox Christian doctrine. Eternal consciousness became the new state of every human born into this world.

---

[81] Ibid. pg. 188.
[82] Ibid. vol. 5, pg. 18.
[83] *A History of Christian Thought*, Pgg. 23-24.

## THE NEW DEATH

Once the apologists published their interpretation of the human having eternal consciousness, the state of death had to be redefined. No longer could death be the termination of life. Death was defined in Platonic terms as separation. Death now became the separation of the body from the spirit, which is also soul. The body would decay into the earth from which it was taken, while the spirit-soul would live on in some distant undefined place. Tertullian defined this clearly in his *Treatise on the Soul*.

> But the operation of death is plain and obvious: it is the separation of body and soul.... The truth is the soul is indivisible, because it is immortal; [and this fact] compels us to believe that death itself is an indivisible process, accruing indivisibly to the soul, not indeed because it is immortal, but because it is indivisible.[84]
>
> Such then is the work of death – the separation of the soul from the body.[85]

The above is aligned with earlier philosophy:

> Death, says Socrates, is the separation of soul and body.[86]

The mention of indivisibility in Tertullian's above account refers to the separation of soul from spirit. Since the two are equated in his previous statements, death likewise cannot sever the two, since spirit is immortal. Therefore the soul attached to spirit continues in consciousness after separation from the body. Excellent Platonic rhetoric, but not Scripture.

## AFTER DEATH

Once the apologists established the eternal consciousness of an individual after death, or better said, the continued consciousness after the departure of the soul-spirit from the body, they had to define their new environment. Instead of the grave as the residence until the resurrection, the apologist adapted from paganism the various states and recesses of heaven and hell

---

[84] *Ante-Nicene Fathers*. Vol 3, pg. 228.
[85] Ibid. pg. 229.
[86] Bertrand, Russell, *A History of Western Philosophy*, pg. 134.

for the departed soul-spirits. To justify their existence they were given names found in Scripture. The departed spirit-souls descended to *hades*, which was divided into 2 regions: a place of torment and Paradise. In his pseudo-*Dialogue with Trypho* Justin of Caesarea states:

> The souls of the pious remain in a better place, while those of the unjust and wicked are in a worse, waiting for the time of judgment. Thus some which have appeared worthy of God never die; but others are punished so long as God will them to exist and to be punished.[87]

Justin felt that the soul was not immortal by nature, but made such if willed by God. Yet he was convinced along with Plato of a punishment and reward in the environment after death. That the spirit-soul did experience consciousness is stated by Tertullian along with advocating a punishment or discipline for its sins in this environment of hades, in his *Treatise on the Soul*.

> Full well then, does the soul even in *Hades* know how to joy and to sorrow even without the body; since when in the flesh it feels pain when it likes, though the body is unhurt; and when it likes it feels joy though the body is in pain. Now if such sensations occur at its will during life, how much rather may they not happen after death by the judicial appointment of God.... Therefore, even for this cause it is most fitting that the soul, without at all waiting for the flesh, should be punished for what it has done without the partnership of the flesh....No one will hesitate to believe that the soul undergoes in Hades some compensatory discipline.[88]

Plato felt that true perfection could only be gained in the after-world. The cares and difficulties of the present life hindered the advancement of the soul, the material world served as an obstacle to attain true wisdom. The after-life ascension of Plato is comparable to the Christian's heaven. This he learned from his mentor Socrates.

> The soul of the true philosopher, which has, in life, been liberated from thralldom to the flesh, will, after death, depart to the invisible

---

[87] Ante-Nicene Fathers. vol. 1, pg. 197.
[88] Ibid. vol. 3, pg. 235.

> world, to live in bliss in the company of the gods.... Only the true philosopher goes to heaven when he dies.[89]
>
> At last he (Socrates) describes the fate of souls after death: the good to heaven, the bad to hell, the intermediate to purgatory... His (Socrates') courage in the face of death would have been more remarkable if he had not believed that he was going to enjoy eternal bliss in the company of gods.[90]

The Christian philosopher Hyppolytus likewise states the similarities between the existing concept of Plato and the new doctrine of the Christians in his *Refutation Against all Heresies*.

> Those however who assert the immortality of the soul are especially strengthened in their opinion by those passages (in Plato's writings). Where he says, that both there are judgments after death, and tribunals of justice in *Hades*, and that the virtuous (souls) receive a good reward, while the wicked (ones) suitable punishment.[91]

Historians likewise concluded the apologists' derivation of the environment of a heaven for reward from the concepts provided by Plato. The Alexandrian tradition tended to think of heaven as the realm of the Platonic Ideas, of the perfect archetypes of the imperfect realities here below.

> The Idea of hell as a place of torment was still foreign to the Old Testament, and was adopted only much later from Iranian sources. It is called Gehenna, after the Valley of Hinnom, where children were sacrificed to Moloch in olden times.[92]

The concept of "going to heaven" when a person dies still leaves many questions unresolved: Where is this heaven? Why go to heaven if there is a resurrection?

---

[89] *A History of Western Philosophy*, pg. 141
[90] ibid. pg. 142.
[91] *Ante-Nicene Fathers*. vol. 5, pg. 18.
[92] Bultmann, Rudolph, *Primitive Christianity*, pg. 86.

## THE NEW HUMAN NATURE

The Jewish sages taught that a human had both a good impulse and evil impulse. The evil impulse was actually a survival or defense mechanism. The person progressed with his life based on which impulse they allowed control over their body. Essentially the human was good from the start, even though the capability to do evil was inherent in their nature. A person had a choice to do good or evil, turn to God or deny him. Many early students of Scripture accepted this concept, but it conflicted with the new doctrines of the apologists. In later years the ante-Nicene Fathers labeled this concept of human nature as Pelagianism, named after its promoter in the $4^{th}$ century, Pelagius. They branded Pelagianism as heresy later in the $5^{th}$ century.

Tertullian in his early years adhered to the teaching of Montanus, a very conservative group, though considered to be non-Orthodox. He taught that man was originally created good, and fell to sin due to his own freedom. Sin was spiritual, as well as carnal, he taught. Tertullian however was affected by the impact of Montanus in regard to a regimented life. Montanus taught celibacy and extreme deprivation of worldly pleasures.

Although himself married, Tertullian views marriage as good, but that celibacy is preferred.[93]

The attitude towards the body or human nature in general changed with the apologists. As with a new concept of the human soul, a new concept of human nature surfaced in the writings of the apologists, likewise a result of gnostic and Platonic ideas. The human body was now inherently and congenitally evil or naturally inclined toward evil. There was no hope for the human on their own volition. As mentioned earlier, the gnostics taught that the body was a creation of the inferior god, the *Demiurge*, along with the earth.

The views of Marcion, mentioned earlier, was influential on a popular teacher from Persia, Mani, who synthesized the various concepts of gnosticism into an organized religion. Mani called himself an apostle of Jesus and his religion became known as Manichaeism. He taught against marriage, against eating meat, and advocated living a ascetic life, one of austerity. Since he felt that the human body was evil, and that the original nature of created humanity was inclined toward sin, salvation was by

---

[93] *Ante-Nicene Fathers*, vol. 4, pg. 14.

asceticism: deprivation of the flesh of the joys of life and subjection of the flesh to a austere and regimented rule of life.

> Much Puritanism in Catholic, Protestant and Orthodox history has been founded on the belief that matter, the physical, the body and its appetites, are fundamentally evil. Such a belief is gnostic, contrary to the faith which is a basic tenet of both Judaism and Christianity, that when God created his physical universe, he looked upon his word and saw it was very good.[94]
> The same was true, later of Manichaeism, through which Saint Augustine come to the Catholic faith. Manichaeism combined Christian and Zoroastrian elements, teaching that evil is a positive principle, embodied in matter, while the good principle is embodied in spirit. It condemned meat-eating, and all sex, even in marriage.[95]

This began trends in the new Christianity of asceticism, such as the desert hermits of Egypt, and celibacy. No longer was the human body a means of enjoying the blessings of God, and especially marriage. The human body became the cause of sin and salvation was attained by deprivation.

## AUGUSTINE OF HIPPO

As the religion of Mani spread throughout the world it influenced many teachers of the new Christian church. One of these, Augustine of Hippo, was a Manichean for 12 years, prior to his conversion to the Catholic faith. Augustine brought into the Christian church many of the teachings of Mani and gnosticism. These concepts later flourished in the writings of Augustine in his doctrine of original sin.

> Augustine believed that God had condemned humanity to an eternal damnation, simply because of Adam's one sin. The inherited guilt was passed on to all his descendants through the sexual act, which was polluted by what Augustine called "concupiscence."[96]

---

[94] David, Christie-Murray, *A History of Heresy.* pg. 61.
[95] *A History of Western Philosophy*, pg. 325.
[96] *A History of God,* , pg. 123.

Augustine's obsession with sex as the source of lust and spiritual defilement is so rampant that he taught the reason of the necessity for a virgin birth was to keep Jesus' conception undefiled from the sexual pleasure that normal parents enjoy during procreation.[97]

The conclusion of Augustine in regard to his doctrine of original sin was also due to his own personal failure in a relationship with a female. He had a concubine for most of his early life, and bore a son through her. This was primarily during his years as a disciple of Mani. His son died sometime in his late-teenage years. After converting to the Catholic church, Augustine's mother Monica arranged a legitimate marriage for him to an Italian lady from a respectable family. He had to release his concubine, who then later died. His mother Monica died about this time also. Augustine's relationship with his new and legitimate wife was short lived. They eventually separated and Augustine retreated to a monastery and became a monk. These sour and psychologically devastating experiences with women contributed to his formulation of the doctrine of original sin. Since Augustine could not develop a stable home and relationship with another woman, he concluded that the human body was inherently evil and women were the great temptation leading humanity to sin. Augustine's conclusion is summarized as follows:

> Woman's only function was the childbearing, which passed the contagion of Original Sin to the next generation, like a venereal disease.[98]

Augustine gained the victory in Rome in his controversy with Pelagius, a monk from Britain. Pelagius' doctrine, labeled Pelagianism, was declared heresy. This impressed the Christian church with its doctrines of the natural moral corruption of every born individual. It also made celibacy mandatory for priests and all clergy in the Catholic church. The Eastern church also imposes celibacy on all its higher clergy. Personal austerity was popularized by the Catholic church.

A second though important effect of the teaching of Augustine was the demotion of women to that of the temptress. Woman became the temptation to man, leading man away from God and into sin and the world. The female became the source of lust in the male gender. Lust was

---

[97] *Early Christian Doctrines*, J.N.D. Kelly, pg. 365.
[98] *A History of God*, Karen Armstrong, pg. 124.

carnal, inherited from Adam as a result of the temptation by Eve. As with Tertullian, marriage was only acceptable to Augustine provided sexual intercourse was performed solely for procreation and not for reasons of marital pleasure. Virtue or holiness could only be attained with a mortification of the sexual drive, according to Augustine.

## DEVILS AND DEMONS AND ANGELS

The devil and demons entered into Christian theology as a result of the ignorance and superstition of the people. The people of the era attributed illness, congenital deformities, and other malignancies, to unseen evil spirits. They at that time had no understanding of biology or medicine, that disease was organic in nature. Mental disorder was considered possession of a demon or evil spirit instead of a chemical imbalance. These superstitions of invisible demons and devils carried over into Christian theology.

The devil was a product of Zoroastrian influence, which slowly permeated Christianity from the east. Mani, who combined elements of both Jesus and Zoroaster, promoted a devil having tremendous power. Augustine continued the thinking of Mani in regard to a personal devil. He taught that a Christian was in a continual struggle with the devil and his demons and so has to be defeated. Augustine taught that God was restraining the power of this superhuman creature, and if the devil was fully unleashed he would morally destroy the entire Christian church.[99]

Demonology was not without its effect by Plato. Originally demons were a type of angelic entity in Plato's philosophy. They were intermediaries between humans and the gods. Later he taught that the demons were the living spirits of men who died valiantly in war, or attained some special virtue or triumph. Contemporary angelology is actually Plato's demons redefined using the language of the Bible pertaining to spirit messengers.

Demons and the devil as the instigator of sin or temptation was the result of a combination of these influences on the early Christian church.

---

[99] Brown, Peter, *Augustine of Hippo*, pgg. 244, 395.

## A NEW RETURN OF JESUS

The attitude of Christianity failing to recognize this effort of Jesus the Anointed in the rescue of Israel from annihilation by the Romans is noticeable first in the writings of the apostolic fathers and apologists beginning about the middle of the $2^{nd}$ century, shortly after the conclusion of the $2^{nd}$ Jewish War of 132-135 AD. A new interpretation of the gospels surfaced at this time deviating from the above explained purpose of the ministry of Jesus divided into 2 advents: first, the suffering servant of Isaiah; second, the image of King David to install the millennial kingdom. Now we have 2 advents: the first advent being his ministry, death and resurrection; the second advent to occur at some indefinite date into the distant future.

They could not grasp the installation of a spiritual kingdom that began the Holiday of Pentecost as the spiritual return of Jesus, now his body – the church – becoming his physical presence. The apologists were still in a historical mode of thinking as those in Acts 1:6: a Kingdom of God on Earth comparable to the Roman Empire, except with Jesus on the throne. They viewed the events of Rev 19 and 2 Thess 1, very literally.

As a result the return of Jesus was redefined and a new school of doctrine developed. This was eschatology: the study of the final era. A non-Jewish doctrine or definition of the return of Jesus was now developed, since its application to the Jews of Israel could not ideally be applied to the non-Jewish parishioner. All that pertained to the immediate crises in Israel spoken of by the Anointed Jesus and apostles – fulfilled within a century after prophesied – were now projected into the indefinite and distant future by the new generation of apologists. In this manner the return of Jesus was redefined so it could pertain to the non-Jews of all the world. In order to make the NT applicable or palatable to the non-Jew, its historical setting was ignored and all the prophetic indications of a return of Jesus was redefined in a distant future context.

The Messianic Jews who fled Jerusalem believing in the words of Jesus were not consulted or considered in this new approach. These people were labeled Ebionites or Judaizers or Nazarenes because of their Jewish roots. It is apparent that the apostolic fathers' and apologists' distance and alienation from the Messianic Jews in Judea blurred their perception of the return of Jesus for judgment. The gentile Christian scholars could not grasp the return of Jesus in terms of OT Scripture and its historical setting.

The new approach of the apologists is initially described by Justin of Caesarea in the pseudo-dialogue with his fictitious Trypho the Jew about 150 AD.

> But if so great a power is shown to have followed and to be still following the covenant era of His suffering, how great shall that be which shall follow His glorious advent! For He shall come on the clouds as the Son of man, so Daniel foretold, and His angels shall come with Him.[100]
> 
> And it was prophesied by Jacob the patriarch that there would be two advents of Christ, and that in the first He would suffer, and that after He came there would be neither prophet nor king in your nation, and that the nations who believed in the suffering Christ would look for His future appearance.[101]
> 
> Justin likewise felt the man of sin of 2 Thess 2 must reign at least 350 years before the next advent of Christ.[102]

As far as gentiles were concerned, the promise of Jesus advent was not yet fulfilled and was still to occur. It was difficult for the apologists to project all of Jesus prophetic words into the distant future because portions of these passages were clearly interwoven with the destruction of the temple and devastation of Jerusalem. Matt 24. Luke 21. To separate the verses pertaining to one event from the other proved an impossible and exhaustive strategy. Even to this date the separation of passages is still vague. The fulfillment of his return and its immediate events became then very literal. This included a literal descent from the sky onto Mt. Olives, which would then split in half; the destruction of the man of sin; and all the events mentioned in the Book of Revelation.

Those terms and passages in the NT that indicated impending or immediate occurrence were spiritualized or allegorized, projected into the future, or ignored in their entirety. The passage of Matt 23:36, 24:34, and so alluded in Matt 10:23, were projected to some future generation. It was no longer that generation, but some generation in the indefinite future.

---

[100] *Ante-Nicene Fathers*, vol. 1, page 209.

[101] Ibid, page 210.

[102] Ibid, page.210.

## THE KINGDOM OF GOD

Subsequently the apologists concluded and taught that the kingdom of God also did not arrive as preached by John the Baptizer and Jesus and Paul apostle. For many the new interpretation was the postponement of the kingdom by 2000 years because of the Jews rejection of their Anointed or Messiah. Others felt that the church, and primarily the Catholic Church, was the kingdom. With the rise of a "Christian state" under Constantine the Great and an ecumenical church, many felt this unification of church and state was the kingdom of God.

The concept of a spiritual kingdom for the covenant members could not be grasped by the apologists. Their gnostic and philosophic background served as a veil over their eyes, a mental block.

## BOOK OF REVELATION

The most perplexing postponement made by the apologists pertains to the fulfillment of the words of the Book of Revelation. Even the name of the book was altered to modify its meaning. The new title became Revelation to John. The 4 passages that indicate an impending and immediate occurrence of the events described in allegory in the book, Rev 1:1, 3, 22:10, 29, were allegorized or postponed into the distant future by the apologists.

Tertullian, in an entire chapter in his treatise *Against Marcion*, juggles passages in both OT and NT to project the return of Jesus to the distant future.[103] Likewise Origen in his treatise *Against Celsus* advocates a future return of Jesus.[104] Hyppolytus in his *Treatise on Christ and Antichrist*, composed at the beginning of the 3rd century AD, provides readers with basically the type of interpretation that is taught at the present in regards to the antichrist, the 2 witnesses and return of Jesus. He interpreted the week of Daniel as "the last week which is to be at the end of the whole world."[105] The apologist Lactantius likewise interpreted a very literal Book of Revelation in Book 7 of his *Divine Institutes*, beginning with chapter 14 and to the end.[106]

---

[103] Ibid, vol. 3, pgg. 414-417.

[104] Ibid, vol 4. Page 421.

[105] Ibid, vol. 5, pg. 213.

106 Ibid, vol. 7, pgg. 211-223.

This concept of a future return of Jesus has created an avalanche of controversy and conflict over the ages and even today stirs up the imagination and fear of the population. The characters of the man of sin, 2 Thess 2, antichrist, 1 John 2, and every allegorical figure in Revelation have been regularly applied to every political and religious figure of influence and corruption. Popes, kings, dictators, presidents, financial giants, and religious leaders, have all been labeled the fulfillment of the dragon and beast and false prophet. Rev 16:13. Churches and religious institutions not having met the expectations of adherents or critics, or having deviated from Scriptural truth as defined by the censurer, have been identified as the immoral woman riding on the beast. Rev 17-18. The main expected event, the return of the Anointed, has been repeatedly incorrectly ascertained by every generation beginning with the 2$^{nd}$ generation after the apostles.

## OTHER-WORLDLINESS

Another attitude introduced into Christian doctrine by the apologists was that of other-worldliness. This was acquired from gnostic sources and based on the premise that the present world is evil and created by the inferior deity. The goal of a believer in God and the Bible was no longer acquiring the blessings of God for a prosperous and beneficial earthly life, but attaining heaven. There is a complexity of issues that arise from this fixation on other-worldliness by Christianity.

> Otherworldliness is a conception which Jews and Christians, in a sense, share with later Platonism, but it takes, with them, a much more concrete form than with Greek philosophers.[107]

This concept was a natural development from the immortality of the soul combined with the attainment of heaven at the time of a true believer's death, or separation from the body. Since the present world was evil, all the efforts of the believer was not to be directed toward success in or enjoyment of the present life. The goal was now heaven.

---

[107] *A History of Western Philosophy*, Bertrand Russell, pg. 309.

## SALVATION OF THE SOUL

The second facet of other-worldliness combined the attitude of austerity with the concept that the human essence was his soul-spirit. The virtuous life was no longer one in accord with the divine instruction and moral code of *Yahweh* God. The Bible-based life was redefined as effort directed toward the "salvation of the soul". It was only by incurring a life pattern of deprivation of the joys and pleasures of the earthly sojourn, a regimented austerity, that a person will gain the salvation of his soul at their death, or when their spirit-soul leaves the corrupt body.

This attitude of control over other individuals by preachers striking fear into the hearts of parishioners has prevailed for centuries. This threat of losing your salvation by religion charlatans has been effective. Psychologically weak and unstable people have been caught by this snare, and which has only distorted the view of God as loving and benevolent.

The new attitude of salvation of the soul varied in its meaning for Christians. To one Christian the soul was not a part of or related to the body. It is the body that sins and not the soul, in the opinion of many. The body can continue to sin as long as the person retains a clean heart and good conscience. The soul is kept undefiled or prepared for heaven through religious observance. This would consist in sacraments and rites, and veneration of saints, and a superficial subjection to the established church through its agents the priests and ministers. They now taught that because the body dies and decays into dust, it is the soul that stands before judgment. I feel a personal regret and empathy for those individuals having such an attitude. To think that salvation of the soul is not salvation of all that life consists of is self-defeating.

To another Christian austerity is salvation of the soul. A person cannot enter heaven if he enjoys life on earth, is successful or wealthy, prosperous, respected, receiving reward and gratitude for beneficial accomplishments on behalf of society. This is all considered worldly, while deprivation and austerity is holiness. This attitude is the basis of monasticism and reclusion. Some even go to the extent of deprivation of medical help, education and financial solvency to try to attain this holiness, the salvation of the soul. But this is all superficial, and much like the words of Paul Apostle.

Why do you still submit to regulation? "Do not handle. Do not taste. Do not touch." Referring to things which all perish as they are used, according to human precepts and doctrines. These have indeed an appearance of wisdom in promoting rigor of devotion and self-abasement and severity to the body, but they are of no value in restraining the indulgence of the flesh. Col 2:21-23

Paul apostle may well have been referring to an attitude prevailing in the city Colossae that was inherited from the philosopher Socrates.

In like manner, the philosopher must not care for the pleasures of love, or costly raiment, or sandals, or other adornments of the person. He must be entirely concerned with the soul, and not with the body: "He would like, as far as he can, to get away from the body and to turn to the soul."[108]

The apologists of early centuries were so enveloped in their quest for a superficial holiness that they lost sight of the God-given joys of the earthly life, and deprived themselves of a salvation on earth. Likewise the idea of heaven as the residence of the saved caused a mental block to attaining community, domestic and personal success and prosperity during the earthly life.

## OLD FESTIVALS AND NEW FESTIVALS

Observance of the Feasts of *Yahweh*, those mentioned in Lev 23, did continue among the original Messianic communities, the group called Ebionites. They eventually vanished into history. The group labeled as Nazarenes or Nazoraens likewise.

The Passover was labeled as Jewish and replaced by Easter, a spring fertility festival held in honor of the female deity Astarte, a fertility goddess.[109] The general population of the Roman Empire held to these pagan festivals and so the transfer from observance to one to observance of the other was easy. The anti-Semitism of the populace led them to want to reject the Jewish holidays and celebrate their new Christian ones.

---

[108] *A History of Western Philosophy*, Bertrand Russell, pg. 135.
[109] Hislop, Alexander, *The Two Babylons*, pg. 103.

The date for the observance of Easter created a controversy in the new Christian church. Many were celebrating it on the same day as the Jewish Passover. But this was not to be tolerated by the leaders of the new religion. After considerable controversy the Easter date was fixed by Pope Victor, 189-198 AD. Even then there was difference in opinion. The dispute was finally settled at the 1st Ecumenical Council of Nicea in 325 AD. Easter since then is celebrated on the Sunday following the full moon after the vernal equinox. An excerpt from the letter of Constantine the Great, Emperor and overseer of the affairs at the Council of Nicea, will evidence his anti-Semitism in legislating the observance of Easter on the new date.

> It was declared to be particularly unworthy for this, the holiest of all festivals, to follow the custom [the calculation] of the Jews, who had soiled their hands with the most fearful of crimes, and whose minds were blinded. We ought not, therefore, to have anything in common with the Jews;... and consequently, in unanimously adopting this mode, we desire, dearest brethren, to separate ourselves from the detestable company of the Jews,...[110]

Now that the calendar was expunged of Bible-stipulated festivals, new holidays were introduced. These were Christmas, Epiphany, Ascension, Lent, Good Friday, Ash Wednesday, Palm Sunday, and Lent, all of a religious nature. There may be good reason and good intentions in instituting and observing these holidays, but it is the word of *Yahweh* God that must be observed. 1 Sam 15:22-23. The pattern of replacement of the original festivals of *Yahweh* God with those of later origin follows the precedent of Jeroboam. 1 King 13:32-33. The new holidays of Jeroboam were instituted to keep the residents of the northern kingdom Israel from going to Jerusalem located in the southern kingdom Judah. So it is with the later holidays of Christianity that were installed to replace the original divinely instituted festivals of *Yahweh* God.

## THE LAST SUPPER OR PASSOVER?

The term *Last Supper* is not to be found in Scripture. By using the term last supper, anti-Semitic Christian leaders hoped to direct the attention of

---

[110] *The Nicene and Post-Nicene Fathers*, Second Series, Vol. 14. Pg. 54.

their parishioners away from the observance of Passover by Jesus and his disciples.

The fact that Jesus and his disciples observed Passover remains, even though the event has been expunged of its Bible-based label and replaced by the designation of Last Supper. This was accomplished by the early church fathers to distance further the festivals of *Yahweh* God from the new religion. The bread and wine were no longer interpreted in the context of the standard Passover *Seder*, the family festive meal on Passover evening. The apologists were not interested in what they considered as Jewish traditions and rites. The new interpretation of the apologists was based on Greek mystery religions, very familiar to the population. The Passover *Seder* was replaced by a rite consisting solely of bread and wine and with a new name attached to it, the Eucharist. The transition is first mentioned by Ignatius about 100-110 AD, first in his letter to the Philadelphians, and then in his letter to the Smyrnaeans.

> Take heed then to have but one Eucharist. For there is one flesh of our Lord Jesus Christ, and one cup to the unity of his blood;...[111]

At this early date, the development of the rite was still in its embryonic stage. This concept of the bread and wine as the actual flesh and blood of Jesus is further developed by Justin, as noted in his First Apology.

> And this food is called among us the Eucharist, of which no one is allowed to partake but the man who believes that the things which we teach are true,... so likewise we have been taught that the food which is blessed by the prayer of His word, and from which our blood and flesh by transmutation are nourished, is the flesh and blood of that Jesus who was made flesh.[112]

Already by the middle of the 2nd century the Passover *Seder* was replaced by a rite adopted from the mystery religions, which only the "believers" could partake it. The doctrine of substantiation was now in progress of development. The apologist Irenaeus furthers develops it, in Book 5 of his *Treatise Against Heresies*.

---

[111] *Ante-Nicene Fathers*, vol. 1, pg. 80.
[112] Ibid. pg. 185.

He has acknowledged the cup as His own blood, from which He strengthens our blood; and the bread He has established as His own body, from which he gives increase to our bodies.[113]

The interpretation of the Last Supper has varied over the centuries, anywhere by a purely symbolic understanding of the bread and wine, to believing that the wafer is the actual body and the wine the actual blood of Jesus. This latter conclusion is totally absurd, and only exemplifies to what extent the words of Jesus can be manipulated to mean without a knowledge of their historical context, and when combined with pagan mystery religion concepts.

## FOOD LAWS

The attitude of the apologists toward the food laws of *Yahweh* God is the same as for the festivals. The original Messianic community upheld the food laws, in accord with the words of Peter apostle.

> No, Lord, I have never eaten anything that is common or unclean. Acts 10:14.

The approach of the gentiles was opposite. Clement of Alexandria, in Book 2 of his Instructor, when dealing with the vision of Peter apostle stated.

> The use of them is accordingly indifferent with us. "For not what entereth into the mouth defileth the man," but the vain opinion respecting uncleanness. For God when He created man, said, "All things shall be to you as meat."[114]

Clement felt that the food laws were an injunction for the Jews; but they were also intended to have allegorical meanings. The words of Jesus in Luke 10:18 to his disciples are taken out of context by Clement in this same chapter. He felt these words meant that everything should be eaten any place a person should visit. This is not the understanding of Jesus words in their intended context. The homes that the disciples were to visit

---

[113] Ibid. pg. 528.
[114] Ibid. vol. 2, pg. 241.

were Jewish homes, their own countrymen. The disciples were not to insult the host of the homes they visit by refusing hospitality.

It was especially Irenaeus who wrote that God instituted food laws for the Jews to curb their excess and gluttony.[115] Barnabas attributed a totally spiritual significance to the food laws allegorizing them.[116] A later treatise titled The Constitutions of the Holy Apostles, composed about the 2nd half of the 3rd century, deals with the subject of food. Its approach is much the same as Clement's. The Christian was to eat whatever is served him, with the exception of food offered to idols.[117]

The apologists missed entirely the point regarding God's institution of food laws. It is only in recent years that medical investigation into the dietary laws have discovered their value for the health and longevity of the human.

## PICTURES IN WORSHIP

The earliest of the apologists condemned the use of images in the paganism and mythology of their era. Any image was equated with the pseudo-gods of false-religion and considered idolatry. This is mentioned by Justin in chapters 9 and 10 of his *First Apology*.[118] Justin defines the true worship of God in this section as conduct in accord with the established divine instruction. However true this statement be, like the other prohibitions of the OT divine instruction, it was soon overwhelmed by the future generation of church leaders. In time art was allowed into the worship service and subsequently images. Then followed the veneration of such images.

The point made by the later apologists to justify their use was that the images of the saints and divine entities were Christian, and so are permitted; while the images of the pseudo-deities were pagan, and so prohibited. A lesser reason for the entrance of images and portrayals of Biblical scenes follows the adage that, A picture is worth a thousand words. The later church leaders felt that events of the OT and NT, the lives of contemporary martyrs, and feats of Christian heroes, would be better conveyed to the audience through the use of pictures, rather than reading text from a book.

---

[115] Ibid. vol. 1, pg. 204.
[116] Ibid. vol. 1, pg. 143.
[117] Ibid. vol. 7, pg. 469.
[118] Ibid. vol. 1, pg. 165.

Tertullian, and no doubt because of his Montanist influence, equated the manufacture and veneration of an image for worship a violation of the 2nd commandment. His entire treatise *On Idolatry* is written to prove this.[119] The historical basis of the early worship of *Yahweh* God in spirit and truth is well documented.

> The primitive church, had no images of Christ, since most Christians at that time still adhered to the commandment of Moses. Ex 20:4; this pertained as well to the gentile Christians as to the Jewish and forbade all use of images. To the latter the exhibition and veneration of images would, of course, be an abomination, and to the newly converted heathen it might be a temptation to relapse into idolatry. In addition, the church was obliged, for her own honor, to abstain from images, particularly from any representation of the Lord, lest she should be regarded by unbelievers as merely a new king and special sort of heathenism and creature-worship…. The first representations of Christ are of heretical and pagan origin.[120]

This use of the portraits of Jesus and saints and other Bible figures caused conflict and controversy or the next 5 centuries. Those who fought against their inclusion in worship were labeled iconoclast. It was not until the 7th Ecumenical Council that a final verdict was decreed for the universal Christian religion.

> The Pope was represented and the gathering is generally regarded as the Seventh Ecumenical Council. The council approved the use of icons, but regulated the manner in which they should be honored…. The decisions of the council did not immediately win universal acceptance.[121]

The inclusion of images and figures within Christianity has varied from one extreme to the other. Some denominations prohibit them entirely, including the sign of the cross. The opposite extreme is the religion possessing an array of statutes of every ecclesiastical figure available, their veneration, and locating them wherever possible.

---

[119] Ibid. vol. 3, pgg. 61-76.
[120] *History of the Christian Church*, Phillip Schaff, Vol. 2, Section 110.
[121] *A History of Christianity*, K.S. Latourette, pg. 296.

# THE FALL OF ROME

The so-called Christian Empire began under Constantine the Great about 322 AD, but did not even last a hundred years. In 410 AD, Rome was sacked by the Goths, barbarian tribes under their leader Alaric. During the 3$^{rd}$ and 4$^{th}$ centuries Christian Rome regressed and tended toward ruin, both moral and material. While the Jewish communities of the middle east and north Africa prospered. The enigma is provided here not to justify the Jewish sages whose grandparents earlier rejected Jesus of Nazareth as the Anointed and led their country to devastation in a war against Rome, but to show that the basic concepts of the morality of the OT was still adhered to by Jewish communities, which promoted their success and prosperity. The gentile Christian apologists gravely lacked this revelation and enlightenment.

While scholars debated over theology, defined heresy, and discredited Jews and dissidents, Rome as a empire morally disintegrated. Instead of implementing rules for proper conduct and initiating organizations for the welfare of the people, they implemented rules demanding proper belief and profession of their new religion, and anathematized those who confronted and disagreed with them.

Rome was next in the sequence of devastation after Jerusalem for apostasy. The real heretic was Rome and the real heresy was the new religion of the apologists and Nicene fathers. Just as Rome executed and excommunicated those they judged as heretic and apostate, so did *Yahweh* God do to Rome in 409-410 AD. Next after Rome was Constantinople in 1452; and then Moscow, the 3$^{rd}$ Rome, in 1917. Each was summarily judged, sentenced and excommunicated and executed for apostasy and heresy: not by man, but by *Yahweh* God. As they did to others, so did *Yahweh* God unto them.

# COMPETITION OF THE APOLOGISTS WITH THE JEWISH SAGES

I sometimes wonder whether a type of competition may have surfaced in the Roman Empire of the 3$^{rd}$ century between the new generation of "Christian" apologists and the Jewish redactors of the *Mishna*. This book was completed about 220 AD, and was a compilation of Jewish wisdom, instruction, laws and traditions. It was distributed throughout the Jewish communities of the Roman Empire and Middle East with great success. The wisdom and debates of the foremost of Jewish scholars of the era were reflected in the *Mishna*, the new Jewish Scripture. These were Rabbis Hillel, Shammai, and Gamaliel I, of the First century, and Rabbis Johannan ben Zakkai, Akiva, Meir, Gamaliel II, of the $2^{nd}$ century. Rabban Judah ha Nazi (the Prince) was the primary redactor of the *Mishna*. His contemporaries were the learned Rabbis Eleazar ben Simeon, Simeon ben Eleazar, and Rabbi Nathan. The contemporaries of Rabbi Judah ha Nazi continued Jewish education and scholarship after the publication of the *Mishna*. These scholars are known in Jewish history as the *Tannaim*, teachers of the *Mishna*.

The $4^{th}$ century likewise produced many talented and scholarly Jewish educators. These became known as the *Amoraim*, teachers of the *Gemara*, the commentary on the *Mishna*.

Jews enjoyed some rest and harmony in their communities during the years after the $2^{nd}$ Jewish War of 132-135 AD, and until about 235 AD, with the death of Alexander Severus. The next 50 years were political chaos in the Roman Empire, but which had little effect on Jews. Peace was again established about 284 AD, with the reign of Diocletian. Although anti-Semitism did prevail in the Roman Empire, it was without the type of violence as occurred in the period of 66 AD to 135 AD. Any persecution or oppression was sporadic but not major. This harmony, or gentile tolerance of Jews, ended about 425 AD, with the abolishment of the Jewish Patriarchate.

The greatest of Jewish sages during this era was Rabbi Johannan bar Napha, who died about 279 AD. He was considered the supreme Palestinian sage of the *Talmudic* era. He was head of the Jewish academy at Tiberius, and was very influential in the later *Talmud*.

It is no wonder that the apologists of the same eras had to work overtime on their refutation of heresies and their apologies, and composing fictitious dialogues with Jews, to prove their new religion as superior and the successor to Judaism. Such apologists as Tertullian, Origin, Clement, Irenaeus and Cyprian had for competition the *Tannaim* and *Amoraim*, a new and advanced generation of scholars of the Jewish academy. The apologists had to provide evidence that the new Jewish religion, now known as Rabbinic Judaism, was inferior to their Christianity. As noted in above passages regarding anti-Semitism, the apologists and church fathers did not shy from any type of libel or distortion of the Jewish religion and their beliefs to discredit the remnants of Old Covenant Israel.

I sometimes wonder whether the new generation of gentile apologists, educated in Greek philosophy but not in OT Hebrew and Scripture, were perhaps envious of their contemporary Jewish sages and Rabbis. Envious to the point of using blood-libel as an attack, and pressing the Roman government to legislate laws against Jews. Since the apologists with their new religion and new churches had difficulty in attaining the community and domestic success of the disciples of Jewish sages, they had to resort to denunciation and persecution to prove themselves right.

## CONCLUSION

A greater success would have been achieved if the attitude of anti-Semitism was set aside and the study of Greek philosophy abandoned. A theology of Sacred Scripture in accord with the concepts outlined in the initial sections of this volume would then develop among them. The spiritual kingdom would arise and last forever with the grace and blessing of *Yahweh* God abounding in the life and community of us all.

Based on the conclusions drawn in this volume, it was not the intention of Jesus or his apostles to create a new theology or a new religion separate from Israel. The theology proposed by the writers of the NT continues that already established in the OT with the inclusion of Emmanuel, Jesus the Anointed. The apostles and Paul especially explained the capacity and role of the son of *Yahweh* God in the realm of spirit to both Jews and gentiles. It is especially the Book to the Hebrews that expounded the Deity and position of Jesus in divine theology to Messianic Jews.

That a new religion should arise separate and distinct from Israel, the faith of the Scriptures, was totally alien in the mind of Jesus and his apostles, including Paul apostle. The term Christianity is a paradox, because never did Jesus organize or direct anybody toward establishing a new religion having that designation. I contend that sufficient evidence was provided to prove that historical and orthodox Christian theology since the era of the apologists is the materialization of the philosophy of neo-Platonism along with some pagan inclusions. The new religion of the apologists culminating in the dictates of the First Ecumenical Council of Nicea in 325 AD, is a church rooted in anti-Semitism and neo-Platonism, it is Mithraism to the core.

The renovation of the religion under the new covenant and the establishment of the spiritual kingdom continued under the apostles and their later successors and adherents to their original message. It has always resided in individuals and groups throughout the ages who have discarded the inroads of philosophy and adhered to the original theology of the Scripture of the Old and New Testaments, and likewise also resides in the present era.

# 6. JESUS THE ESSENE OR THE NAZORAEN

( Another Perspective of his Life and Ministry )

The intent of this chapter is to present Jesus and his ministry from a perspective different than the one above, based on the premise that he was a regular human being and only God's son by adoption, and that Jesus was a Nazoraen of the Essene community. This was standard belief by the group calling itself Ebionite, convened by the apostles in Jerusalem after the Holy Day of Pentecost, who viewed Jesus as a regular person, but being a prophet of God who installed the Spiritual Kingdom. He fulfilled his embassy as Messiah or Anointed of God in spiritualizing the Israelite religion. Based on the ideology of the Essenes Jesus became son of God upon his baptism by the Holy Spirit. Because the Ebionites consisted of the original apostles of Jesus and his other disciples and adherents (the 120 on Pentecost for example), some scholars feel their community and ideology is closest to the original that was taught by Jesus, rather than Apostle Paul's of later decades to his gentile audience.

## THE GOSPEL OF MARK

The Gospel of Mark is the shortest and the earliest of all the Gospels. The scholars I have read date his composition to a few years prior to the start of the Jewish War in 66 AD. It is the most Jewish of all the 4 Gospels, if this is the proper term to use. It contains little of anything that might be inclined toward the Greek or Roman influences of the era. This Gospel includes solely those narratives of Jesus' life that pertain to the issue at hand: The preaching of the Kingdom of God and miracles he performed to verify the veracity of his message.

None of the embellishments of his early life up to the point of his appearance at the Jordan River to John the Baptizer are included, and they do not add or even pertain to the Gospel of the Kingdom and their inclusion adds nothing to the essential parts of Jesus' message. The same would apply to all the appearances of Jesus after his resurrection from death to women and the disciples, to Thomas, to those who went fishing in Galilee, and to the 500 that Paul mentions, or his ascension to heaven. (This is all good information but incidental to the message of the Gospel, and neither adds or subtracts.) So Mark's Gospel as the earliest contains only the bare essentials and which are, as far as I am concerned, sufficient for the purpose at hand.

As with scholars who have researched the oldest extant copies of the Gospel of Mark, I likewise recognize the final passage of Mark 16:8 to the end, as an emendation by some scribe or copyist who felt the abrupt ending of Mark's narration to be insufficient, and so had to add stuff from the other Gospels to provide the reader a better conclusion as well as additional testimony. Likewise the first verse of Mark in Tischendorf's New Testament, and also Robert Price, does not included the statement, "Son of God;" meaning that it was added by a later redactor. The most original reading being:

The beginning of the gospel of Jesus the Anointed. Mark 1:1

From the information I acquired from scholars who researched the chronology of the composition of the 4 Gospels, the Gospel of Mark was originally composed about 60 AD, 30 years after Jesus death, just before the Jewish War; the next Gospel of Matthew about 80 to 90 AD, and shortly thereafter the Gospel of Luke about 90 to 100 AD, both after the conclusion of the Jewish War. Later the Gospel of John was composed, about 120-130 AD, just before the Bar Kochba Rebellion of 132-135 AD.

Mark only has a ministry of Jesus about 1-1/2 years, and which I feel is the most accurate. The others add supplementary information to further embellish Jesus' ministry with more events. All of the additional testimony provided by Matthew and Luke and John I feel extraneous and in many respects deviating from, and distracting the reader from, the essence of Jesus' message. Of course, it is all good intentions, and added to increase the volume of his ministry with more trips to Jerusalem and more miracles and more discourses – all of which may or may not have happened. This is why I prefer the Gospel of Mark, as being the least possible adulterated by later scribes who had this inclination to expand the volume and for the most part turning Jesus into something he was not or including non-essentials.

In reality, the final versions of the gospels of Matthew, Luke and John were compiled by later gentile Christians whose purpose was to use this biographical and ministerial study of Jesus' life as a means to attract new converts to the new religion now formed of gentile Christians, as opposed to the earlier Messianic Christianity of the Ebionites. These writers took existing Ebionite or Messianic records and compiled them into a form that could be utilized as a method of teaching or converting Greeks and Romans to the new religion and this would have occurred more than likely 200 years after the ministry of Jesus, or about 230 AD, or 100 years after the compilation of the original gospels.

According to Eusebius, the ecclesiastical historian, Matthew composed his gospel originally in Hebrew and then it was translated into Greek. That the apostles were Hebrew and Aramaic speaking persons testifies to the validity of this statements, they the original gospel manuscripts were in either Hebrew or Aramaic and were subsequently translated into Greek and then modified or embellished for their new purpose of attracting converts to the new religion. This would apply to the earlier gospel Mark and subsequently to Matthew. Luke however, as most of the evidence testifies, used the Greek versions of the above as the basis of his narrative and so it was composed in Greek, and John was originally composed by a Greek-speaking Jew using sources independent of the other three.

## THE ESSENES

It is not my intent to repeat all the information regarding the Jewish sect of the Essenes as other scholars have already accomplished this and to a far greater extent and intensity than I can.[122] However I will mention a few essential items for the reader that will apply to the issue at hand.

The following is part of the account of Josephus, *Jewish War*, book 2, chapter 8.

> 119. For three forms of philosophy are pursued among the Judeans: the members of one are Pharisees, of another Sadducees, and the third [school], who certainly are reputed to cultivate seriousness, are called

---

[122] I especially recommend *Jesus of Nazareth*, Joseph Klausner. Also any good translation of the Dead Sea Scrolls, and mainly The Rules of the Community and the Damascus Document. I use the following two translations: Theodor Gasters and Garcia Martinez.

Essenes; although Judeans by ancestry, they are even more mutually affectionate than the others.

120 Whereas these men shun the pleasures as vice, they consider self-control and not succumbing to the passions virtue. And although there is among them a disdain for marriage, adopting the children of outsiders while they are still malleable enough for the lessons they regard them as family and instill in them their principles of character:

121 without doing away with marriage or the succession resulting from it, they nevertheless protect themselves from the wanton ways of women, having been persuaded that none of them preserves her faithfulness to one man.

122 Since [they are] despisers of wealth—their communal stock is astonishing—, one cannot find a person among them who has more in terms of possessions. For by a law, those coming into the school must yield up their funds to the order, with the result that in all [their ranks] neither the humiliation of poverty nor the superiority of wealth is detectable, but the assets of each one have been mixed in together, as if they were brothers, to create one fund for all.

When they send gifts to the Temple they do not offer sacrifices because of the different degrees of purity and holiness they claim; therefore they keep themselves away from the common court of the Temple and bring offerings [vegetable sacrifices] of their own. They excel all men in conduct, and devote themselves altogether to agriculture. Especially admirable is their practice of righteousness, which, while the like may have existed among Greeks or barbarians for a little while, has been kept up by them from ancient days; for they, like the Spartans of old and others, have still all things in common, and a rich man has no more enjoyment of his property than he who never possessed anything. There are about 4,000 men who live in such manner. They neither marry, nor do they desire to keep slaves, as they think the latter practice leads to injustice

The following is part of the account of Philo:

A number of men living in Syria and Palestine, over 4,000 according to my judgment, called Essæi (ὅσιοι) from their saintliness (though not exactly after the meaning of the Greek language), they being eminently worshipers of God — not in the sense that they sacrifice living animals (like the priests in the Temple), but that they are anxious to keep their minds in a priestly state of holiness. They prefer to live in villages and avoid cities on account of the habitual wickedness of those who inhabit them, knowing, as they do, that just as foul air breeds disease, so there is danger of contracting an incurable disease of the soul from such bad associations.

Thus they are taught piety, holiness, righteousness, the mode of governing private and social affairs, and the knowledge of what is conducive or harmful or indifferent to truth, so that they may choose the one and shun the other, their main rule and maxim being a threefold one: love of God, love of manhood (self-control), and love of man. Of the love of God they exhibit myriads of examples, inasmuch as they strive for a continued, uninterrupted life of purity and holiness; they avoid swearing and falsehood, and they declare that God causes only good and no evil whatsoever.

Their love of virtue is proved by their freedom from love of money, of high station, and of pleasure, by their temperance and endurance, by their having few wants, by their simplicity and mild temper, by their lack of pride, by their obedience to the Law, by their equanimity, and the like. Of their love for man they give proof by their good will and pleasant conduct toward all alike, and by their fellowship, which is beautiful beyond description.[123]

The high moral standard that exists among the Essenes, as well as the integrity of its members, is apparent from the above accounts of both Josephus and Philo. It definitely surpasses that of most of humanity and especially what is noticeable from Jesus' reprimands of the hypocrisy of the Pharisees and the conduct of the Sadducees.

The following are a few selections that I want to quote from the Dead Sea scrolls that pertain to the conduct of its members and to joining its covenant community. The high moral standards to which the community adheres is also noticeable, and that it is a covenant, meaning, that all the members enter into this special covenant with God.

---

[123] Philo, *Every good man is free*, parts of 75-80

## COMMUNITY RULE OR MANUAL OF DISCIPLINE

Of the Commitment:
Everyone who wishes to join the community must pledge himself to respect God and man; to live according to the communal rule: to seek God; to do what is good and upright in His sight, in accordance with what He has commanded through Moses and through His servants the prophets; to love all that He has chosen and hate all that He has rejected; to keep far from evil and to cling to all good works; to act truthfully and righteously and justly on earth and to walk no more in the stubbornness of a guilty heart and of lustful eyes, doing all manner of evil; to bring into a bond of mutual love all who have declared their willingness to carry out the statutes of God; to join the formal community of God; to walk blamelessly before Him in conformity with all that has been revealed as relevant to the several periods during which they are to bear witness (to Him); to love all the children of light, each according to the measure of his guilt, which God will ultimately requite.

All who declare their willingness to serve God's truth must bring all of their mind, all of their strength, and all of their wealth into the community of God, so that their minds may be purified by the truth of His precepts, their strength controlled by His perfect ways, and their wealth disposed in accordance with His just design. They must not deviate by a single step from carrying out the orders of God at the times appointed for them; they must neither advance the statutory times nor postpone the prescribed seasons. They must not turn aside from the ordinances of God's truth either to the right or to the left.

The Master shall teach the saints to live according to the Book of the Community Rule that they may seek God with a whole heart and soul, and do what is good and right before Him as He commanded by the hand of Moses and all His servants the Prophets; that they may love all that He has chosen and hate all that He has rejected that they may abstain from all evil and hold fast to all good; that they may practice truth, righteousness, and justice upon earth and no longer stubbornly follow a sinful heart and lustful eyes committing all manner of evil.

He shall admit into the Covenant of Grace all those who have freely devoted themselves to the observance of God's precepts at they may be joined to the counsel of Go and may live a perfectly before Him in accordance with al that has been revealed concerning their appointed times, and that they may love all the sons of light, each according to his lot in God's design, and hate all the sons of darkness, each according to his guilt in God's vengeance.

All those who freely devote themselves to His truth shall bring all their knowledge, powers, and possessions into the Community of God, that they may purify their knowledge in the truth of God's precepts and order their powers according to His ways of perfection and all their possessions according to His righteous counsel.

They shall not depart from any command of God concerning their times; they shall be neither early nor late for any of their appointed times, they shall stray neither to right nor to left of any of His true precepts. All those who embrace the Community Rule shall enter into the Covenant before God to obey all His commandments and not to abandon Him during the dominion of Satan because of fear or terror or affliction.

Whoever approaches the Council of the Community shall enter the Covenant of God in the presence of all who have freely pledged themselves. He shall undertake by a binding oath to return with all his heart and soul to every commandment of the Law of Moses in accordance with all that has been revealed of it to the sons of Zadok, the Keepers of the Covenant and Seekers of His will, and to the multitude of the men of their Covenant who together have freely pledged themselves to His truth and to walking in the way of His delight. And he shall undertake by the Covenant to separate from all the men of falsehood who walk in the way of wickedness.

But when a man enters the Covenant to walk according to all these precepts that he may join the holy congregation, they shall examine his spirit in community with respect to his understanding and practice of the Law, under the authority of the sons of Aaron who have freely pledged themselves in the Community to restore His Covenant and to heed all the precepts commanded by Him, and of the multitude of Israel who have freely pledged themselves in the Community to return to His Covenant.

They shall practice truth and humility in common, and justice and uprightness and charity and modesty in all their ways. No man shall walk in the stubbornness of his heart so that he strays after his heart and eyes and evil inclination, but he shall circumcise in the Community the foreskin of evil inclination and of stiffness of neck that they may lay a foundation of truth for Israel, for the Community of the everlasting Covenant.

The number of parallels between the above description and the moral instruction of Jesus and the Apostolic Letters is innumerable. As mentioned above, there were about 4,000 in the various cities and villages of Palestine. Jesus would have been one of their members. The fact that he was not married also falls into one of their criteria.

The Essenes who lived in Alexandria, Egypt, were also known as Therapudae, meaning healers, as they worked hard to keep the members of their community healthy.

Hopefully the above should be sufficient to provide the reader the moral standard of the Essene community.

## JESUS' PREACHING ESSENE IDEOLOGY

According to Mark:

> Now after John was put in prison, Jesus came to Galilee, preaching the gospel of the kingdom of God, and saying, "The time is fulfilled, and the kingdom of God is at hand. Repent, and believe in the gospel." Mark 1:14-15
> But He said to them, "Let us go into the next towns, that I may preach there also, because for this purpose I have come forth." And He was preaching in their synagogues throughout all Galilee, and casting out demons. Mark 1:38-39
> And he went about all Galilee teaching in their synagogues and preaching the gospel of the kingdom. Matt 4:23.

So this is what Jesus did over the 1-1/2 years or so of his ministry: he traveled in Galilee and what is today known as Lebanon and Jordan, teaching the Essene ideology, healing the sick, organizing their individual communities to be a spiritual kingdom of God, to live in peaceful coexistence with the Roman occupation; that there was no need to present animal sacrifices in Jerusalem, and perhaps even that there was no need to even patronize the city or attend the Jerusalem temple (as their body was the temple of God).

From another perspective, the so-called 40 days of Jesus in the wilderness may have been his life with the Essenes of the Dead Sea community. The use of 40 days was obviously selected by the author to correlate with the 40 years of Israel in the desert wilderness of Sinai Peninsula, but it reality the time could have been much more, perhaps years as we really have no accurate timeline of Jesus ministry. Luke claims that Jesus was about 30 years of age at the time of his baptism. This age agrees with the age that Levites could begin their ministry, as noted for example in Num 4:3, 23, 30 and others, and so the selection in Luke's Gospel. Pharisees however felt that Jesus was much older, pushing 50 years of age. John 8:57. So maybe a couple of decades passed between the baptism and the beginning of Jesus' ministry, with the time spent among the Essenes rising to the rank of a Nazoraen.

So after the water baptism or Essene cleansing rite performed by John at the Jordan River, Jesus departed to reside with the Essenes for some indefinite period of time to study under them and learn their teachings, in order to fulfill his ministry as Messiah, the Anointed, or perhaps as the subsequent Teacher of Righteousness.

This being another reason as to why Jesus die not marry, as many of the Essenes felt that marriage was not conducive to a saintly person, the sexual act being one of total carnal performance, and not one of a spirit nature. Marriage as mentioned above would also have interfered with the tedious and overwhelming responsibility of Jesus' ministry as the Anointed.

Jesus making the statement about the new covenant during the Passover meal fits in well with the Essenes communities being a covenant community, a fulfillment of the prophecy of Jer 31:31-34. These were the new communities that Jesus established. There was no reason for Jesus to travel to Jerusalem.

A secondary reason for the concentration of Jesus' ministry in Galilee and Jordan is that this area was also a fomenting ground for rebellion against Roman occupation. With Jesus' teaching of pacifism and coexistence with the Roman occupation he hoped to quell or subdue the attitude of the residents toward rebellion against Roman authority, as he knew that these Jewish revolutionaries would have little chance against the powerful Roman army.

Jesus' conflict with Pharisees was obviously due to a conflict in ideology: the Pharisees emphasizing custom and tradition and ceremony and attire, while Jesus promoting morality and ethic.

With Jesus entrance into Jerusalem at the conclusion of his ministry, and according to Mark the only occasion of his visit to Jerusalem, the Sadducees viewed Jesus as a threat, due to his preaching that sacrifices were no longer needed, the priesthood was no longer needed, the temple was no longer needed, and their collusion with the Romans was a betrayal of their obedience to God.

The Sadducees sentenced Jesus to death as a heretic, but could not execute him themselves, and so delivered him to Pontius Pilate as a usurper, a fraudulent king. Pilate, being a cruel tyrant, immediately sentenced Jesus to execution and which was quickly accomplished.

Jesus however resurrected from death 3 days later.

## THE EXECUTION OF JESUS

Jesus did not specifically die for our sins. This is a misnomer and mistranslation. Jesus died as a result of sins, meaning the sins of the Pharisees and the Sadducees and the Roman government of Judea. This premise that Jesus died for sins was a modification of the gospel message by later emendators of the New Testament to shift the message of Jesus away from him being an Essene Messiah or Anointed preaching the Kingdom of God. Jesus died because he was executed by Roman soldiers under orders of Pontius Pilate for being a usurper king. Plain and simple. He was determined to be a political criminal, not having anything to do with religion.

Jesus died 2,000 years ago and he did not know that any of us even existed.

Jesus knew that he would eventually be arrested and accused falsely and be innocently sentenced by the Jewish sacerdotal hierarchy, and then be executed. But he did not do this as a propitiation for the sins of the people; this was not his intent. The writer of Hebrews later created this premise to portray Jesus as the fulfillment of the Passover sacrifice, but this was done in later decades. This premise does not coincide with the original reason for Jesus' ministry as noted above in the first chapter of Mark, it was all added later. The writer of Hebrews distracted the attention of his audience from Jesus being an Essene Messiah with the goal of establishing covenant communities – the spiritual kingdom of God – while in coexistence with Roman occupation.

The so-called church in Jerusalem was an Essene Messianic community with James and John and Peter at the head. Nothing more. They incorporated Jesus' tenets into their ideology and slowly grew. As a result God placed upon them His seal of the Holy Spirit, that they attained the correct understand of Jesus as Essene Messiah, and they were now the New Israel, the new covenant people of God, the spiritual kingdom of God on Earth.

The groups that subsequently formed were known as Ebionites or Nazarenes. They held the true percepts and tenets of the Essene Messiah Jesus.

## LATER CHRISTIANITY

The new group was established by the Apostle Paul, except his message was interwoven with Greek neo-Platonic philosophy and the paganism of Mithraism – the most prominent religion of the Roman Empire at the time – and obedience to Roman authority. The original message of the Essene Jesus was erased from existence and replaced with a new Jesus, meaning Mithra.

I will not go into detail regarding the similarities between Mithra and the replacement Jesus of historic Christianity, but yes, he was born on December 25; he had a sacred meal, he was crucified and he did resurrect. Items to realize here is that the Last Supper was invented by Mithraism to replace the Passover and supposed occurring on Good Friday, when none of this is in the NT. The date of Easter, a festivity based on the pagan Goddess Astarte, was not set until the beginning of the $4^{th}$ century.

It was during the reign of Emperor Marcus Aurelius, the philosopher king, 161-180 AD, that Messianic Christianity was usurped by Mithraism, meaning that Mithraism was now labeled Christianity. The Essene Messiah Jesus was replaced by Mithra, who now became the new Jesus. All of which Mithraism consisted now became the new Christian religion, and freedom of religion was established in the Roman Empire, provided that the population accept and recognize Christianity. This was formally accomplished by Emperor Constantine the Great at the First Ecumenical Council, 325 AD, at Nicea, Turkey.

The original members of the Essene Messianic community were now either absorbed into the Greek-Roman style Christianity, or dispersed.

Some of the above is further detailed in other chapters of this volume dealing with the departures of historical Christianity from the original concepts taught by the Essene Messiah Jesus.

Jesus created spiritual communities out of the synagogue congregations that were based on Essene ideology. They had various appellations, such as: Ebionites and Nazoraens or Nazarenes. They continued their previous life now in spiritual understanding of the Jewish religion, without need for temple, animal sacrifices, priesthood, Pharisees or Sadducees or Zealots, or participation in the Jewish military or war against the Roman occupation. How wonderful.

## THE HUMAN GENEALOGY OF JESUS

The majority of those who called themselves Christians or Messianic prior to the First Ecumenical Council believed that Jesus was a regular human being and only God's son by adoption, and that Jesus was a Nazoraen of the Essene community. They did not feel Jesus to be a deity or divine entity, or the materialization or incarnation of a third part of a triune supreme deity, until Greek philosophy was merged into the new Christian church and developed it as its new theology. The Scriptural basis for this conclusion are the following points.

> ... the gospel concerning His son who was descended from the seed of David and designated son of God in power according to the spirit of holiness by his resurrection from the dead, Jesus the anointed our lord. Rom 1:3-4 (KJV)
> ... descended from David according to the flesh... (RSV)
> ... born of the posterity of David according to the flesh... (Emphatic Diaglott)

Based on the above passage, and remember that Romans was written to Jews living in Rome who knew somewhat of Jesus, Paul stipulates that Jesus was from the seed or flesh of David. This indicates the male line of genealogy directly from David to Jesus. In addition the apostle Paul states that Jesus became son of God after and as a result of his resurrection from death. In explaining this to Jews in Rome it was something they could understand as something that was already inherent in their traditional understanding of the coming Messiah or Anointed, as being a corporeal descendant of their King David.

One item to also note is the statement of Mary to Jesus when they found him in the temple at the age of 12, having a discussion with the elders:

> Behold, your father and I have been looking for you anxiously.
> Luke 2:48

Mary definitely states that Joseph is Jesus' father in this passage.

Note that there is no genealogy of Jesus anywhere mentioned in any of Paul's letters. Not one word is mentioned regarding his mother or father or relatives or what tribe of Israel or city of birth or city of early residence or education or visit to Jerusalem as an adolescent. To the apostle Paul none of this was important or relevant to his case. What he does mention is that Jesus was born as a corporeal entity of his mother at the proper time in the ecumenical scope of history. Gal 4:4.

The apostle Peter mentions something similar to this in his address to the residents of Jerusalem as recorded by Luke, that Jesus was descended from David according to the flesh:

> Brethren I may say to you confidently of the patriarch David that he both died and was buried and his tomb is with us to this day. Being therefore a prophet and knowing that God had sworn with an oath to him that he would set one of his descendents upon his throne... Acts 2:29-39

The gospel of Mark does not include anything regarding Jesus' genealogy, not one word of his parentage, as Mark begins his history with John the Baptizer. The Gospel writer John begins his gospel with the revelation of the Word to humanity and then migrates to John the Baptizer, also ignoring any genealogy.

The Gospel of John does contain a couple of passages that state that Jesus is the son of Joseph. The first is one comment made by Philipp to Nathanael, the second is the statement of Pharisees to Jesus:

> We have found him of whom Moses in the law and also the prophets wrote, Jesus from Nazareth, the son of Joseph. John 1:45
> And they said, "Isn't this Jesus the son of Joseph, whose father and mother we know? How can he say he descended from heaven?" John 6:42

There was no doubt about Jesus being the natural son of Joseph among his listeners and disciples.

The writer of the Letter to the Hebrews follows the same vein as Paul to the Romans at the beginning of his treatise.

> For it is evident that our Lord was descended from Judah. Heb 7:14.

Again, the genealogy is through the father and Judah is mentioned in both the genealogies of Matt 1:3 and Luke 3:33. Nowhere is the genealogy of the mother Mary mentioned.

The Gospels several times mention that Jesus had brothers and sisters:

> Is not this the carpenter's son? Is not his mother called Mary? And are not his brothers James and Joseph and Simon and Judas? And not all his sisters with us? Matt 13:55-56, Mark 6:3.

They were not called his half-brothers or half-sisters. These people were definitely Jesus' full brothers and sisters as the obvious intent of the passage reads. Jesus is also called the carpenter's son to establish him as a son. That Jesus would incur the dislike of his brothers noted in John 7:5, was due to that they did could not accept him as being Messiah or Anointed of God as a member of the Essenes.

## NAZARETH, NAZARENE, NAZARITE AND NAZORAEN?

First, Jesus was not a Nazarite as mentioned in the OT. He drank wine, touched dead bodies, and there is no indication in the Gospels to identify Jesus as a Nazarite. Num 6:1-8.

Many recent researchers claim there was no city Nazareth at the time of Jesus lifetime or any city Bethlehem, although there was a city Bethlehem near Sephorris in Galilee. The present city Nazareth did not develop until much later in history. The earlier mention of a city with that name in secular history occurs about 200 AD, nothing more than a hamlet with an estimated population of about 400.

A Nazarene was not a resident of Nazareth. The redactor of the Gospel of Matthew in Greek includes a verse that states this, but it is without any Biblical authenticity:

> He went and resided in a city called Nazareth, that was spoken by the prophets might be fulfilled, He shall be called a Nazarene. Matt 2:23

Except there is no passage of this sort in the OT. The Greek redactor of the Gospel of Matthew created this in order to have people think Jesus as a Nazarene meant he was from the city Nazareth. Not the case. The original Greek uses the term Nazoraen in this verse.

Nazarene is primarily used by Mark, while Nazorean is used in the other Gospels, and have the same meaning to pertain to Jesus. A Nazarene or Nazorean is an Essene of the higher dedicated or ascetic order. This is the term that is used regarding Jesus, but removed from the NT by modern English translators to remove the possibility of Jesus' identification with the Essenes. A few places where these appellations are found in the Greek NT are the following:

Jesus the Nazarene: Mark 1:24, 10:47, 14:67, 16:6, Luke 4:34, 24:19.
Jesus the Nazoraen: Matt 2:23, 26:71, Luke 18:37, John 18:5, 7, Acts 2:22, 3:6, 24:5.

Bible translators have attempted to erase Jesus' identification with the Essenes by mistranslating Nazoraen or Nazarene as Nazareth in several passages: Matt 26:71, 10:47, 14:67, 16:6, Luke 18:37, 24:19, for example.

The reader can use Strong's Concordance to view the various passages where Nazoraen is used but mistranslated by using Nazareth.

## THE EBIONITE PERSPECTIVE OF JESUS

The original source of the appellation of Ebionites appears to be the Hebrew word *Ebyon*, meaning poor. This was utilized to correlate with Jesus' statements

> Blessed are the poor in spirit for theirs is the kingdom of heaven. Matt 5:3
> Blessed are the poor for yours is the kingdom of God. Luke 6:20

When Apostle Paul mentions gathering charity or donations for the poor in Jerusalem, what he was actually talking about was the Ebionite community.

> For Macedonia and Achaia have been pleased to make some contribution for the poor among the saints in Jerusalem. Rom 15:26
> Only they would have us remember the poor, which very thing I was eager to do. Gal 2:10

The Greek word *ptochos* is used here, which is the equivalent of the Hebrew *ebyon*.

## THE GOSPEL OF THE EBIONITES

The Ebionites possessed their own gospel record of the ministry of Jesus, and which was very similar to the gospel record of Matthew, except that it began with the beginning of the ministry of John the Baptizer, instead of at the genealogy of Jesus and the virgin conception of Mary. It does not contain anything of Jesus' birth or early life.

The little available of the gospel of the Ebionites is preserved by Epiphanius of Salamis (310-403 AD) who composed his Panarion, a treatise consisting of his expose of 80 groups of Christians that he considered to be heretic. The Ebionites are included with them, because they considered Jesus to be a regular person by birth, meaning, not through a virgin conception of his mother and who became God's son through his baptism by the Holy Spirit.

The following is one passage from Epiphanius' account of the Ebionites:

> 13:6 But the beginning of their Gospel is, 'It came to pass in the days of Herod, king of Judea, in the high-priesthood of Caiaphas, that a certain man, John by name, came baptizing with the baptism of repentance in the river Jordan, and he was said to be of the lineage of Aaron the priest, the son of Zachariah and Elizabeth, and all went out unto him.'
> 13:7 And after saying a good deal it adds, 'When the people had been baptized Jesus came also and was baptized of John. And as he came up out of the water the heavens were opened, and he saw the Holy Spirit in the form of a dove which descended and entered into him. And (there came) a voice from heaven saying, Thou art my beloved Son, in thee I am well pleased, and again, This day have I begotten thee. And straightway a great light shone round about the place. Seeing this,' it says, 'John said unto him, Who art thou, Lord? And again (there came) a voice to him from heaven, This is my beloved Son, in whom I am well pleased.
> 13:8 And then,' it says, 'John fell down before him and said, I pray thee, Lord, do thou baptize me. But he forbade him saying, Let it alone, for thus it is meet that all be fulfilled.'
> 14:1 See how their utterly false teaching is all lame, crooked, and not right anywhere!
> 14:2 For by supposedly using their same so-called Gospel according to Matthew Cerinthus and Carpocrates want to prove from the beginning of Matthew, by the genealogy, that Christ is the product of Joseph's seed and Mary.
> 14:3 But these people have something else in mind. They falsify the genealogical tables in *Matthew's Gospel* and make its opening, as I said, 'It came to pass in the days of Herod, king of Judea, in the high-priesthood of Caiaphas, that a certain man, John by name, came baptizing with the baptism of repentance in the river Jordan' and so on.
> 14:4 This is because they maintain that Jesus is really a man, as I said, but that Christ, who descended in the form of a dove, has entered him—as we have found already in other sects—and been united with

him. Christ himself is from God on high, but Jesus is the offspring of a man's seed and a woman.[124]

The 2 items to be noticed in Epiphanius' account is: First, that Jesus was a regular person born of Joseph and Mary; second, that Jesus became God's son upon his baptism.

The validity of the claims of the Ebionites is based on the fact that they were closest to Jesus, they were his original disciples and no doubt those 120 who were gathered on the Holy Day of Pentecost, and so were able to record their ideology and history of Jesus in this manner.

## THE GENEALOGIES

Over the years of my study of the gospels I found the inclusion of the genealogy of Jesus in Matthew and Luke in 2 different forms to be an anomaly and it took me a long while to finally decipher them. The original and most accurate is that of Matthew as it was compiled much earlier than the genealogy of Luke and most likely in the Aramaic language. I consider Matthew to be the most accurate as it follows the list of I Chron 1-3 very closely. Luke deviates from this. One grave error in Luke's list is the name of Neri as the father of Shealtiel, who is not mentioned in the genealogy of 1 Chronicles or anywhere else in the Bible, but Jeconiah instead. Luke seems to have done some guessing and not intense individual research in the matter in the compilation of his list. As a result Luke's is not dependable. Matthew misses a few names and contracts the list, but with the intent of having a package of 3 each 14 name genealogies makes sense.

What I notice is that the genealogies are only included in the 2 Gospels that include the narrative of Mary's virgin conception. However, both cannot be true: both Jesus' genealogy and Mary's virgin conception cannot be true at the same time. It is either one or the other. To have both of them is inconsistent. One of them is redundant and the other is the right one. But which one?

If Jesus is God's son directly via the virgin conception of his mother Mary by means of the Holy Spirit, then why do the Gospel writers include a genealogy? It is useless as it serves no purpose. All that is important is Mary's conception by the Holy Spirit and her birth as a virgin. Nothing

---

[124] Epiphanius, *Panarion*, Part 30, *Against the Ebionites*

else matters. Any corporeal derivation of Jesus does not matter, but only deviates from the purpose intended.

The same vis-à-vis. If Jesus is Joseph's son directly via the normal conception of his mother Mary, then why do the Gospel writers include the story of a virgin conception through the Holy Spirit? It is useless as it serves no purpose. All that is important is Mary's conception by her husband Joseph. Nothing else matters. Any Holy Spirit derivation of Jesus does not matter, but only deviates from the purpose intended. So which one is the correct scenario?

The Hebrew text of the OT verse, Is 7:14, uses the word *almah*, which refers to a young girl, regardless if she is married. This is also the contextual use of the word in the content and subject matter of Isaiah 7; just read the entire passage. It just refers to a young girl recently married who will have a son and he will be named Immanuel. Easy as that.

The Greek redactors of the Gospels of Matthew and Luke used the Greek Septuagint version of the OT, where the same word is translated as *parthenos*, and it actually means a virgin girl. As a result, to justify the use of the word *parthenos*, they created the narrative of the visit of Angel Gabriel to Mary and her conception by the Holy Spirit.

No where else in the NT, except Matt 2 and Luke 1, is this event of a virgin conception mentioned. Nothing of sort can be found anywhere in the Apostle Paul's letters or the letters of the others apostles James, Peter, John and Jude or Hebrews. And obviously because it just did not happen. If this was so important, as is emphasized by contemporary Christianity, it would have been definitely repeated as an important tenet of Christian belief by one of the other 2 Gospel writers or by one of the other apostles, including Paul with his 14 letters and Hebrews, which seems to be specific on Jesus' materialization in the corporeal world in Heb 1.

The reason it is so convenient for the gospel writers to include this is because it aligns with other *avatars* of history, meaning, the materialization or incarnations of gods in human form. And so the reason for its inclusion by the redactors of the Gospels. They wanted Jesus to be a deity incarnated and just as good as any other deity found in Greek, Roman or Egyptian mythology who acquired human form. So the goal was to attract converts from paganism by providing another God – Jesus – who was the incarnation of a third part of a triune supreme deity, by creating this scenario.

## THE MINISTRY OF JESUS THE ANOINTED

So what did Jesus do during the couple years of his ministry? According to the Gospel accounts he taught in their synagogues, as well as along the roads, in the streets, on the shores of Lake of Galilee, and in their homes. As the Anointed his goal was the perfection of the original religion of Israel that God provided through Moses. Apostle Paul mentions this:

> That the Anointed is the end of the law, that every one who has faith may be justified. Rom 10:4 (RSV)
> The Anointed is the consummation of the *Torah*... (translation based on Hebrew comparison)

Jesus spiritualized the religion to bring it to its consummation or its perfection. All the types of the OT were now to be understood or interpreted spiritually or allegorically in the light of himself as the Anointed or Messiah.

There was no more need to offer animal sacrifices at the temple in Jerusalem, as Jesus was the final sacrifice. Now the individuals themselves were to be living sacrifices unto God, as the Apostle Paul described:

> Present your bodies as a living sacrifice unto God, holy and acceptable to God, which is your spiritual worship (Rom 12:1).

There was no need to travel to Jerusalem to specifically worship at the temple, because now their bodies were the new temple of God. Now they could worship God at any place and at any time.

> Do you not know that you are God's temple and that God's spirit resides in you? (1 Cor 3:16)
> The time shall come when neither on this mountain or in Jerusalem will you worship the Father... But the time is coming and now is when the true worshippers will worship the Father in spirit and truth. (John 4:21, 23)

So it did not matter anymore where the people will worship God; they could now in their homes or outdoors should they want, or a local building constructed for this purpose.

The priesthood was also not necessary, as now Jesus was the new high priest of the new covenant, and each of them were priests in the order of Melchizedek, and were kings and priests themselves. So no need to offer their gifts to the priests as intercessors or intermediaries on their behalf. Now the people did not need Jerusalem or the temple at all or the priesthood or the animal sacrifices. It was all now spiritual; all was now allegorically understood.

The final item he taught was that the land of Israel was no longer sacred, and no need to have to fight over it. Since returning from Babylon some 400 years earlier, the Jews were in a constant and never-ending warfare against either enemies from the outside, such as the Romans or Persians or Greeks, or it was an internal power struggle, as with the Hasmonaens. Now they were to accept the Kingdom of God or Heaven, and not the kingdom of this world, meaning the land.

> Our residence is in heaven… (Phil 3:20)
> An inheritance which is imperishable, undefiled and unfading, kept in heaven for you (1 Peter 1:4)

So the new land or residence, their eternal legacy, was now in heaven, no longer on Earth. If this be the case, then there was no reason to have to fight enemies over possession of this land of Israel, Palestine. It was not important anymore since they would just reside on it for the few years of their corporeal existence and then die and that was the end of it on Earth. What was important was a residence in heaven.

Now a Jewish person could live anywhere on Earth, worship God in spirit and truth, offer spiritual sacrifices on their own through the high priest in heaven Jesus, and look forward to the eternal inheritance. The result of this concept was that there was no need to have to fight or war for occupation of this land that in earlier generations they felt to be sacred because God gave it to the patriarchs.

This is also mentioned by the apostle in the Letter to the Hebrews in regard to Abraham:

> For he looked forward to the city whose foundation, builder and maker was God. (Heb 11:10)

Regardless of the travels and settlements of Abraham in the new promised land, into Egypt and back again, it was not the property itself that was important as a legacy, but what the entire scenario represented: Ur of the Chaldees was sin; leaving Ur was leaving sin; Palestine represented heaven. But the subsequent generations could not grasp this concept and viewed the land as sacred: as long as they possessed the land of the promise they had God's favor on them. The two concepts were inextricable connected to each other: God and property.

Now Jesus disclosed to them that property, or the land of Israel, was insignificant in terms of salvation or God's favor. Earth is a temporary residence through which we must pass to inherit eternal life in the heavens. The ideological result is that, if this be the case, there is no reason to fight over the land, this property. No reason to risk your life or the life of others to possess it. If you are threatened with invasion, either reconcile or leave. Somehow just keep peace to reduce casualties.

As a result the spiritual communities founded by Jesus refused to join the Jewish military, refusing to fight the Roman occupation or in the Jewish War of 66-70 AD. They preferred to leave to a city Pella on the east side of the Jordan River in present day Jordan.

This teaching did not bring Jesus into any favor with the Pharisees with their meticulous adherence to the oral law of tradition. The Sadducees likewise would have liked to see Jesus' dead with his teaching of the obsolescence of the temple, animal sacrifices, priesthood and land of Israel as theirs. The Sadducees could not grasp the concept of a spiritual residence in heaven, but only that piece of property where they resided. Jesus' became public enemy Number One, as his ideology would deprive the Pharisees of their position of teachers and promoters of the oral law. His ideology would deprive the Sadducees of their immense income from temple sacrifices, their high positions in the ecclesiastical hierarchy, and control of the Jewish religion and the temple facilities. Jesus' ideology conflicted with the Zealots, who wanted to use force and insurrection and violence and war to rid Israel of its occupation by the Roman government.

As mentioned above, the only manner they could all achieve their goal was to have Jesus permanently removed, but now to stain their own hands with his blood, and knowing that the majority of common people, the residents of the land, acknowledge him as a prophet and new king and the Anointed of Israel. So they falsely presented Jesus as a political agitator to Pontius Pilate, and in order to keep peace in Judea and in favor with Rome, immediately ordered Jesus to execution by crucifixion.

# PART FIVE

# HEAVENLY RELATIONSHIPS

A COLLECTION OF ESSAYS ON BIBLE TOPICS

### 1. COVENANT LIGHTS

The role of Jesus as the light of the world evolves from the earliest of God's dealings with His elect nation Israel and His body the church. The light of the world is understood as the light for all those in the world who desire it.

> Then Jesus spoke to them again, saying, "I am the light of the world. He who follows me shall not walk in darkness, but have the light of life." John 8:12.
> But he who does the truth comes to the light, that his deeds may be clearly seen, that they have been done in God. John 3:21.

The darkness hides truth and reality and obscures understanding. The light reveals and discloses to all receivers of this light the reality and truth of the world and state we live in. The light in Old Covenant days quite accurately parallels and harmonizes with the words given to us in the New Covenant. *Yahweh* manifested Himself as a flaming pillar of fire and cloud of brightness for over forty years in the wildernesses of Zin, Paran and Sinai. First appearing at Etham, on the western edge of the wilderness, it's primary purpose was to give the estimated 2 to 3 million Hebrews light during the night to assist their escape from Egypt on the night following the Passover. This night was the 15$^{th}$ of Nisan.

> And *Yahweh* went before them by day in a pillar of cloud to lead the way, and by night in a pillar of fire to give them light, so as to go by

day and night. He did not take away the pillar of cloud by day or the pillar of fire by night from before the people. Ex 13:21-22.

Now that the entire area was well illuminated, the darkness and fear of night did not hinder the people in their flight from the slavery of Egypt. Now they were able to travel both day and night to deliverance. *Yahweh* the Deliverer of His people did not want any misfortune to occur to the people, but that all reach their destination safety. So it is also for us today who flee from this slavery to sin and transgression. The darkness of this wicked and sinister world encompasses us daily, and makes difficult our lives with the efforts and armies of satan continually pursuing after us. After partaking of our Passover, Jesus, we flee from slavery to sin and are led by this light through the darkness of this age. The Hebrews ran willingly and took great advantage of the night-light. They did not slack behind in this race, but hastened quickly, covering a great distance in a short time.

In harmony with the activities earlier, Jesus spoke to the masses, saying:

> I have come as a light into the world, that whoever believes in me should not abide in darkness. John 12:46.

But why not remain in darkness?

How can one journey anywhere or even take as step it he cannot see what is in front of himself? So with this light of the Hebrews, they were able to travel to Sinai the mountain of God, to receive there the words of life from *Yahweh* God. If it were not for this light they surely would have perished at they hands of Pharaoh's army. In like manner for us today, we journey also to Zion the house of God receive there words of life. This daily cloud and pillar of light stayed with he Israelites until their arrival at the borders of the Promised Land. Then cloud and pillar ceased to shine over the people. Much also will be put aside after we complete out journey to the millennial Kingdom. But at that time all the area will be illumined: not just our hearts and souls as during our stay in the darkness of this age.

> And the city had no need of the sun or of the moon to shine in it, for the glory of God illuminated it, and the Lamb is its light. Its gates shall not be shut at all by day: there shall be no night there. Rev 21:23, 25.

The guiding light the Hebrews followed beginning at the initial Passover until their arrival to the promised land is a great allegory for our own era, with the light in our hearts and souls leading us, protecting us from faltering in darkness and harming ourselves. and giving us a clear and lighted path to walk by until our entrance into the millennial Kingdom.

Along with the pillar of immense magnitude was another light of comparatively small construction. In the tabernacle, within the curtain or veil, was the seven-branched candlestick or lamp. This is detailed in Ex 25:31-40 and 37:17-24. It stood on the ground and weighed about 75 pounds, constructed of pure gold. Seven branches ascended out of a common trunk. These seven lights symbolized light perfected.

In Revelations we read of the representation of these seven lights:

> And from the throne proceeded lightning, thunder, and voices. And there were seven lamps of fire burning before the throne, which are the seven Spirits of God. Rev 4:5.
> And in the midst of the elders, stood a Lamb as though it had been slain, having seven horns and seven eyes, which are the seven Spirits of God sent out into all the earth. Rev 5:6.

These are the seven Spirits of God sent out from the sacrificed Lamb unto all the earth. The seven flames, or torches, of God that burn before the throne are also designated as the seven Spirits of God. The torches of fire signified the perfection of this light which stood in the vicinity of the throne. Likewise the seven-branched lamp stand also symbolized the perfection of light that stood within the curtain of the tabernacle. The one trunk symbolized the fact that all true enlightenment derives from one source. Jesus among the disciples and among us is the source of all true enlightenment of heart and souls, as He said:

> Then Jesus said to them, "A little while longer the light is with you. Walk while you have the light, lest darkness overtake you; he who walks in darkness does not know where he is going. John 12:35.

And so was this same light among the Hebrews, signified by the lampstand, which *Yahweh* commanded Moses to have in the tabernacle as a continual reminder of His presence. The source of light, the oil of the lamp, was not just any oil. This was only to be pure olive oil, which was to be obtained by heavy labor.

> And you shall command the children of Israel that they bring you pure oil of pressed olives for the light, to cause the lamp to burn continually. In the tabernacle of meeting, outside the veil which is before the Testimony, Aaron and his sons shall tend it from evening until morning before *Yahweh*. It shall be a statute forever to their generations on behalf of the children of Israel. Ex 27:20-21.

The trees were shaken to loosen the olives; then they were crushed and beaten to extract the precious drops from them. This parallels the martyrdom of our Savior, who was also abused, beaten and whipped, and finally cruelly crucified. The true and pure oil was not easily obtained, but with much effort. The entire nation of Israel was to be a lamp for the nations, having the perfected lights. They were to have been molded of pure and precious gold; also not obtained easily, but only through laborious mining and crucible refining, valuable in the eyes of God. They were to be the instrument through which the oil would flow and burn as a light unto the gentiles.

> Gentiles shall come to your light, and kings to the brightness of your rising. Is 60:3.
> You are the light of the world. A city that is set on a hill cannot be hidden. Matt 5:14.

Even so did Jesus mention the candle or lamp set on a hill and on a lamp stand in a home, in order to shine. Here He refers back to His own commands given to Israel. Now it is to his believers: they are to endeavor to become this lamp stand of pure gold having the seven branches, that through them oil would flow and the perfected light of truth would shine to all the gentiles. This lamp stand was to burn without ceasing day and night for all the generation of the olden Israel, and today it should continue to burn in the church, the body of Jesus, impressed on our minds and memories for the great purpose the Israel of God of the new covenant would play in time to come. The continual shining light also emphasized the perpetuity and availability of God's light for seekers of truth. Our Savior disclosed himself to His people ages ago in activities of power and in allegories, as a light to bring them out of darkness and onto the journey unto the Kingdom. It has always been his desire for all people to acknowledge him as wisdom and knowledge. This is reflected in the magnitude of the pillar, light enough to lead and enlighten all the world. He continues this today among His elect, eager to bring them to salvation with no misfortune along the well-lighted path.

## 2. THE SAGA OF JOHN THE BAPTIZER

### 1

The decision of whether to rebuke sin or reprimand an individual for conduct and behavior in violation of the law of God and the gospel of the Kingdom is very difficult to make and even harder to accomplish. If you were to find somebody on the street and reprimand him for conduct in violation of the ethics and morals as indicated in the Scriptures, no doubt that he would indicate to you very quickly that you should do something else with your time, and indicate this to you perhaps even violently. Or perhaps he will question your authority or right to do so. If his conduct was a violation of the law or a crime, and your exposure of him publicly would lead to some penalty or fine or worse sentence, you might even jeopardize your own safety and well-being, or even be risking your life. Especially if the violation was a capital crime you would be putting yourself in a very delicate situation, with life and more at risk. In most situations a minor infraction or violation is ignored and overlooked. A large infraction may also be overlooked if it did not concern us directly. Only if it concerns us directly, that is, a crime attacking us directly and effecting our own personal health and welfare, property and possessions, would we then intervene and expose the violation and demand justice. Nonetheless the apostle Paul commanded it in the following:

> Do not receive an accusation against an elder except from two or three witnesses. Those who are sinning rebuke in the presence of all, that the rest also may fear. 1 Tim 5:19-20.
> Preach the word! Be ready in season and out of season. Convince, rebuke, exhort, with all longsuffering and teaching. 2 Tim 4:2.
> But exhort one another daily, while it is called today, lest any of you be hardened through the deceitfulness of sin. Heb 3:13.

It is a requirement of the Scriptures that any individual who is conducting himself improperly and in violation of the conduct established by the law of God and gospel of the Kingdom be reprimanded by other elders and responsible people. The purpose of course is to curb sin, that the person would turn away from his misconduct, repent, and then return to be in the favor of God and his congregation. If the sin is not reprimanded and exposed and bridled at this early time, then it will continue to infect the others in the congregation like a virus, and it will also appear as if the balance of elders in the church and the congregation approve of conduct that is unchristian and non-Biblical. This silent acquiescence will only tend to slowly corrode the moral fiber of the congregation. Similar sins or worse conduct will eventually be likewise condoned by the congregation since a precedent is already established. But it is not a popular posture to be the individual who should reprimand another for misconduct. The ancient prophet Amos indicated this:

> They hate the one who rebukes in the gate, and they abhor the one who speaks uprightly. Amos 5:10.

Sometimes we even wonder whether it is worth it to reprimand sin and rebuke the hypocrisy of individuals. Easily ostracized from the community are the few of this class who would risk reputation and life and family to be willing to stand up for what is right. Such a person likewise places himself at the forefront of censure. No doubt this is not the choice of any average individual because of the risks involved. God the Father of glory selects and raises such a person, and with careful scrutiny observes his life, for it to be impeccable, lest the prophet himself fall under self-condemnation by those to be reprimanded. To reprimand is not a choice to be arbitrarily taken.

2

John the son of Zechariah and Elizabeth had a special mission in Israel. He was to proceed among the people in the power and spirit of Elijah the prophet. He was the one whom the prophet Malachi prophesied about, some 400 years earlier, and whom an angel of *Yahweh* spoke to Zachariah about while he was in the temple offering incense.

> Behold, I will send you Elijah the prophet before the coming of the great and dreadful day of *Yahweh*. And he will turn the hearts of the fathers to the children, and the hearts of the children to their fathers, lest I come and strike the earth with a curse. Mal 4:5-6.
> But the angel said to him, "Do not be afraid, Zachariah, for your prayer is heard; and your wife Elizabeth will bear you a son, and you shall call his name John. And you will have joy and gladness, and

many will rejoice at his birth. For he will be great in the sight of *Yahweh*, and shall drink neither wine nor strong drink. He will also be filled with the Holy Spirit, even from his mother's womb. And he will turn many of the children of Israel to *Yahweh* their God. He will also go before Him in the spirit and power of Elijah, to turn the hearts of the fathers to the children, and the disobedient to the wisdom of the just, to make ready a people prepared for the Lord. Luke 1:13-17.

The age of John the Baptizer when he began his ministry is not exactly known, but knowing that he was imprisoned about the second year of the ministry of Jesus, and allowing him 7 or 8 years for a ministry, this would place him at about 25 years old. This age was in accord with the age established by God through Moses, as to when a priest would begin his ministry in the tabernacle services. Num 8:24. Elizabeth was probably a sister to one of Mary's grandparents, since the age difference between them was great. Because Mary herself was of the tribe of Judah, while Zachariah and Elizabeth were of the tribe of Levi, a tribal intermarriage apparently occurred with the grandmothers. The Scriptures do not mention his education in the law of God during his early years, except that he lived in the desert areas. But as the son of a priest, following the tradition of the era, father Zachariah would have provided son John a thorough knowledge of the law and the prophets, to read and be fluent in them in order to follow the family tradition. No doubt Zechariah hoped that John would in later years also serve in Jerusalem, just as his father had done.

> John came baptizing in the wilderness and preaching a baptism of repentance for the remission of sins. And all the land of Judea, and those from Jerusalem, went out to him and were all baptized by him in the Jordan River, confessing their sins. Mark 1:4-5.
> There was a man sent from God, whose name was John. This man came for a witness, to bear witness of the Light, that all through him might believe. He was not that Light, but was sent to bear witness of that Light. John 1:6-8.

At about this age he proceeded from the deserts of Israel and into the populated and dense cities and preached repentance. The goal and purpose of his ministry was directed towards family reconciliation and domestic success: to turn the hearts of the children to the fathers, and the hearts of the fathers to the children, and for individuals to abandon their poor lives in order to lead a better life: to turn the disobedient to the wisdom of the righteous. He accomplished this by inviting the people out to the river Jordan, there to review their lives and all that they did wrong in their lives, and to recite these specific wrongs, misconduct, bad behavior, bad habits and vices, offenses and crimes and violations, to him directly in confession. John would then immerse them in water as a symbolic cleansing. This was allegorically removing the defilement from them, to allow them to start all over again with a new life. The people were now also prepared, in a condition to receive the Anointed of Israel and the immersion in the Holy Spirit which he was to bring to them.

Because John the Baptizer was a direct descendent of the first highpriest Aaron, the brother of Moses, Luke 1:5, he exercised this privilege and acted in the role of a priest for the common people. The blessing of John on the people at the time of confession and immersion would have been similar to that recited by his ancestors upon Israel:

*Yahweh* bless you and keep you;
*Yahweh* make His face shine upon you, and be gracious to you;
*Yahweh* lift up His countenance upon you, and give you peace. Num 6:23-26.

The words of John the Baptizer to make the paths of God straight, with the leveling of the earth, was a prophecy of Isaiah prophet, for the people to remedy and restore their life in accord with the law of God. John's father was a priest, and on a regular basis had his turn and responsibility at the Temple in Jerusalem. John would have learned about the law, history and prophesy of Israel from his father, along with the purpose, demands and operation of the priests and temple services. John would have been well aware of all that went on in the upper levels of the religious hierarchy in Israel, including the corruption, shortcomings, and competition of the scribes, Pharisees, Sadducees, and other schools of thought in the religious domain and arena of Israel. This may have been the reason why John withdrew into the wilderness areas to live, as it was difficult for him to contend with and understand and accept the wide variation between what his forefather Aaron instituted in Israel, and what actually went on before his very eyes. Somehow the sincerity and benevolence of the original priesthood, the compassion and empathy of the ancients, was inherited by

John, and which did not exist in those that assumed the religious leadership in Israel.

Could John have been an Essene? Yes, possibly. Sufficient information was provided above on the possibility of Jesus being an Essene that can also be equally applied to John to determine this.

### 3

To understand the ministry of John the Baptizer a review of the ministry of Elisha prophet is required. The ministry of Elijah prophet essentially lasted during the reigns of the kings of Israel Ahab and Ahaziah, from about 875 BC to about 850 BC. Elijah was from the city of Tishbi. At the conclusion of his ministry he was transported into the heavens on a fiery chariot. 2 Kings 2:11. In brief the mission of the prophet was centered on witnessing to the living God in the presence of a corrupt and idolatrous Israelite nation. 1 King 18:36. The miracles of the prophet were the testimony and proof of the existence of the living God, as opposed to the vain idolatry of the pagan superstition.

About three and-a-half years after Elijah made the statement that it would only be through his word that there would be rain upon the earth, he gathered the prophets of Baal and Asherah for a contest. After his supplication to *Yahweh* to reveal His existence in fire, with the fiery consumption of the sacrifices soaked in water, Elijah then personally executed 450 prophets of Baal and 400 prophets of Asherah in his effort to exterminate idolatry and to administer the judgment of God upon them for their religious corruption. 1 King 18:40. Soon after this event, and at the word of Elijah to Ahab the king of Israel, rain fell on the land, concluding a drought of three and-a-half years. 1 Kings 18:41-45. Elijah also brought back to life the deceased son of a widow, whom he also provided with food through a miracle of God. 1 King 17.

Apparently there must also have been considerately more accomplished by the prophet during his 25 years or so of ministry in the land of Israel, for the prophet Malachi to mention that he would turn the hearts of the children to the fathers, and the hearts of the fathers to the children. This indicates the initiation of family reconciliation and harmony. Malachi must have known of efforts of Elijah in developing family stability and unity, items not recorded in the Scriptures, in order to use him as the figurehead or exemplified as the individual who would promote and institute strong family ties and domestic stability by having parents and children drawn closer together.

The pagan religions were not family oriented, as was the religion of the Hebrews. A personal ministry of family counseling and domestic success based on the law of God as given to the people of Israel would have been much the effort of Elijah among the smaller communities of the area, not documented in the Scriptures but known and revealed to Malachi, as opposed to the major events of his life on a national scale, which appears to be the intentions of the author of the Books of the Kings to be worth recording.

### 4

As far as his cousin Jesus was concerned, John was the embodiment of the spirit and power of Elijah the prophet. Unlike the religious hierarchy of Israel, John dressed like the common people of his day, and had no special garb as did the other priests to distinguish them from the common people, as though they were imitating Aaron with his special high-priests' robes and attire.

> As they departed, Jesus began to say to the multitudes concerning John: What did you go out into the wilderness to see? A reed shaken by the wind? But what did you go out to see? A man clothed in soft garments? Indeed, those who wear soft clothing are in kings' houses. Matt 11:7-8.

John was no reed shaken by the wind. He was firm in his convictions, unswayed by anybody's opinion or by the feelings of the people. He knew exactly the dictates of God as revealed in the law and prophets and Psalms, and was willing to stand up for them. He never bent in the direction of the motives of others or inclined towards popular sentiments. Although John did not create any miracle, the people still regarded him as a prophet, and Jesus considered him a prophet and more than a prophet.

> But what did you go out to see? A prophet? Yes, I say to you, and more than a prophet. For this is he of whom it is written: Behold, I send My messenger before Your face, who will prepare Your way before You. Assuredly, I say to you, among those born of women there has not risen one greater than John the Baptizer; but he who is least in

the kingdom of heaven is greater than he. And from the days of John the Baptizer until now the kingdom of heaven suffers violence, and the violent take it by force. For all the prophets and the law prophesied until John. And if you are willing to receive it, he is Elijah who is to come. Matt 11:9-14.

The violence of the Kingdom of God is the recent history of Israel, with the attempt of Jewish revolutionaries in the northern cities of Sephorris and Girshala, who had turned violently against the Roman occupation army. The city of Sephorris was burnt to the ground about 4 AD, while Jesus was in Egypt, due to the revolt of Jewish revolutionaries, while those who were to incite the people to rebellion leading to the Jewish War of 66-70 AD, were from Girshala. But the time now begins for the violence of the Kingdom of God to cease with the ministry of the prophet John the Baptizer. With his ministry the Kingdom of God of the New Covenant is revealed and installed with the Anointed of Israel at it head, the Prince of Peace. The fulfillment of all the words of the law and prophets regarding the advent of the Anointed now begins. The actual means of the preparation of the way of *Yahweh* was obviously not known to the people at this time. The very words of Jesus also confirm the ministry of John the Baptizer as the fulfillment of the words of Malachi:

> But I say to you that Elijah has come already, and they did not know him but did to him whatever they wished. Likewise this Person is also about to suffer at their hands. Then the disciples understood that He spoke to them of John the Baptizer. Matt 11:17, 17:12-13.
> Then many came to him and said, "John performed no sign, but all the things that John spoke about this Man were true." John 10:41.

Although John may have had the power and spirit of Elijah, no miracles are recorded of him during his ministry. Apparently John's ministry was concentrated on preparing the people for the advent of Jesus, as the Angel indicated to Zechariah. Through the baptism of repentance, the people were now prepared to receive the Anointed of Israel, whom they all awaited, in the person of Jesus of Nazareth, the Son of the living God.

> He confessed, and did not deny, but confessed, "I am not the Anointed." And they asked him, "What then? Are you Elijah?" He

said, "I am not." "Are you the Prophet?" And he answered, "No." John 1:20.

John clearly denied that he was Elijah. The only rational reason for this would be to preclude the people from thinking that the ascended Elijah had now returned to earth under the name of John the son of Zechariah, as a re-incarnation. Of course this would cause much havoc: he would be worshipped as a deity by many, while others would discredit him as a charlatan. John's purpose was not to exalt himself, but the One who was to follow him. For this reason he diminished his own role so as not to cause the people to detract from his introduction of Jesus. In this regard, John preferred to identify himself with the prophesy of Isaiah 40:3.

5

What was exactly the corruption of the religious realm and hierarchy that John the Baptizer recognized, and which annoyed him, and which *Yahweh* called him to rebuke and admonish? What Jesus saw so did his cousin John. The following are examples extracted from various portions of the gospels dealing with the corruption of the existing priesthood.

John saw the money changers and bankers at the temple, along with the vendors of animals for sacrifice. All done with a motive of profit, and a portion of which profit was paid as a commission to the family of the high-priest. Matt 21:12-13.

John saw people afraid of voicing their opinions against hypocrisy if it conflicted with that of the synagogue authorities, because they would excommunicate them. John 9:22.

John saw that the people in authority loved to be commended for their work in the community, John 12:42-43; and then dressed themselves to be distinguished from the rest of the populace, and demanded the foremost seats during synagogue services. Matt 23:5-6. They expected to be called "Teacher" whenever in public. Matt 23:7-8. Their piety was very superficial, while their hypocrisy was quite obvious. Matt 23:27-28. Their tendency was to say one thing to the people, while their conduct was quite the opposite. Matt 23:3. John saw the Pharisees boasting of their charitable donations, Matt 6:2; saw them praying in public to gain recognition from the public, Matt 6:5; and saw them disfigure themselves as a indication of fasting Matt 6:16.

John noticed that the religious leaders acted as if they were designated to sit in the seat of Moses, Matt 23:2; and then he saw them circumvent the law of God, while establishing their own designed traditions which were to their own selfish advantage, Matt 15:1-6. John saw them deprive the people of the knowledge of the law of God, while burdening the people with traditions with which they themselves would not assist them. Matt 23:4,13. And then they considered the people cursed, because they did not know the law. John 7:49. John saw sincere and dedicated people turned into haughty and sanctimonious hypocrites once they became involved with the religious hierarchy. Matt 23:15.

John saw them boast of their genealogical purity, directly to Abraham, as if this was sufficient for their identification with him, and ignored conduct comparable to Abraham's, John 8:39, and which only inflated their egos above the non-Jews. Matt 3:9. The religious hierarchy was willing to kill to protect their own interests. John 12:10, 8:37. And they did pay money for the betrayal of an innocent man to put him to death. Matt 26:15. All of this was the same which Jesus himself also recognized and had to deal with among the religious hierarchy.

## 6

When John the Baptizer was at work in his divine ministry bringing people to repentance at the river Jordan, and immersing them in water for the allegorical cleansing of their souls from sin, the Pharisees and Sadducees came to him.

> But when he saw many of the Pharisees and Sadducees coming to his baptism, he said to them, "Brood of vipers! Who has warned you to flee from the wrath to come? Therefore bear fruits worthy of repentance, and do not think to say to yourselves, We have Abraham as our father. For I say to you that God is able to raise up children to Abraham from these stones. And even now the ax is laid to the root of the trees. Therefore every tree which does not bear good fruit is cut down and thrown into the fire." Matt 3:7-10.

The reprimand and admonishment was straight and to the point. They were to curb their hypocrisy and have their lives conform to the morals and ethics as defined in the Scriptures; and deflate their egos because of identification with the patriarchs. Otherwise, because of their many years of corruption they and their organization would be cut down like a tree that produces bitter or wild fruit, or a rotten and decayed tree, and burned to ashes. (All of this came true in the Jewish War of 66-70 AD, and in the Bar Kochba Rebellion of 132-135 AD.) John the Baptizer was not intimidated or frightened by any of the religious hierarchy, and the authority they felt they possessed. He took the sword of the Spirit, which is the Word of God, and penetrated right to their hearts and souls with it, and exposed the hypocrisy and corruption that filled their inner self.

> For the word of God is living and powerful, and sharper than any two-edged sword, piercing even to the division of soul and spirit, and of joints and marrow, and is a discerner of the thoughts and intents of the heart. And there is no creature hidden from His sight, but all things are naked and open to the eyes of Him to whom we must give account. Heb 4:12-13.

The priest and prophet of God, John the Baptizer, skillfully used the word of God to expose and render an effective rebuke and reprimand against the corruption of individuals who attempted to whitewash themselves with a guise of superficial religious piety.

Many other sincere and troubled people came to John the Baptizer at the river Jordan seeking advice as what to do with their lives. They realized that they had fallen short of the glory of God, and so they came and recited their faults and offenses and vices to John the Baptizer and were immersed in the water representative of a beginning of a new life.

> And the multitudes asked him: What then shall we do? Luke 3:10-14.

To the general public the gospel of John the Baptizer was to have a concern for the welfare of others, not just yourself. This consisted in honesty and integrity, without personal advancement at the expense of others; to be just and correct in decisions made; and earn a living at a honest and worthy occupation, and without corruption. All of this would reflect and incorporate in their life the immersion they had received, and continue to preserve them and their souls unstained and further unsoiled from the evil and wickedness of the world around them. This would also be a preparation for them to be able to accept the real and heavenly immersion, that of the Holy Spirit. The water was solely applied to the surface of the body, and its cleansing of the inner man was strictly allegorical, much like the sacrifices and ablutions of the Old Covenant. Heb 9:9-10. John the Baptizer patterned his immersion into water after the rite of the ablution of the priests in the basin installed in the Tabernacle. Ex 30:17-21, and after the sea installed in the Temple of Solomon for the priests to wash in. 2 Chron 4:6. The Essenes also practiced this rite. The fulfillment of the rite of ablutions, or immersions, is the baptism of the Holy Spirit and described in the following:

> That He might sanctify and cleanse it with the washing of water by the word. Eph 5:26.
> Not by works of righteousness that we have done, but according to His mercy He saved us, through the washing of regeneration and renewing of the Holy Spirit. Titus 3:5.

John the Baptizer cleansed the people superficially in order to prepare them for the genuine cleansing and immersion – the Holy Spirit. By accepting the allegory contained in the immersion of John, the people would accept the immersion into the power and essence of God, to be sent by their Anointed, Jesus of Nazareth, upon his glorification.

> John answered, saying to them all, I indeed baptize you with water; but One mightier than I is coming, whose sandal strap I am not worthy to loose. He will baptize you with the Holy Spirit and with fire. Luke 3:16. John 1:32-34.

John paved the way, blazed the trail, for the transition of the people of Israel from the Old Covenant to the New Covenant, out from Moses and unto Jesus of Nazareth. John 1:31. First by providing to Israel repentance and a renewal of life; and secondly by introducing and witnessing to Jesus of Nazareth as the Son of God and the Lamb of God who removes the sins of the world.

## 7

It was not unusual for immorality to be dominating in the ruling class families of governments of this age; and especially among the family of Herod the Great, who himself had 9 wives. Because of the massive incest as well as duplication of names within the family, describing the family in a text is very difficult. But a few of the important characters will be noted.

Herod the Great had 2 sons named Philip. One of these was Philip who was tetrarch of the northern region of his father's domain. Luke 3:3. He was the daughter of Cleopatra of Jerusalem, the 5th wife of Herod the Great. This Philip married his niece Salome, the daughter of Herodias through her first husband. They had no children.

Another son was known as Herod Philip, whose mother was Mariamme II, the 3rd wife of Herod the Great. He was the first husband of Herodias. Their daughter was Salome.

The son who is mentioned as tetrarch as Galilee, Luke 3:1, 23:6-7, is Herod Antipas, whose mother was Malthake, the 5th wife of Herod the Great. After he divorced his first wife, the daughter of Aretas king of Arabia, he became the 2nd husband of Herodias. It was this Herod Antipas, the tetrarch of Galilee whom John the Baptizer reprimanded for his marriage to his niece, after her divorce from her first husband, who was also an uncle. John the Baptizer did not hesitate (or maybe he did) to rebuke and reprimand the immorality and incest that was so prevalent in the family of the King of the Jews, as Herod the Great was titled by the Roman senate.

Herodias was the daughter of Aristobulus, son of Herod the Great, and whose mother was Mariamme I, part of the Maccabean succession. This would make Herodias the half-niece of both her husbands.

> For Herod [Antipas] had laid hold of John and bound him, and put him in prison for the sake of Herodias, his brother [Herod] Philip's wife. For John had said to him, It is not lawful for you to have her. And although he wanted to put him to death, he feared the multitude, because they counted him as a prophet. Matt 14:3-5.

The most vile and malicious female in the entirety of the New Testament is Herodias. As noted above, she was first the wife of one uncle, and divorcing him, became the wife of another uncle, who was also a divorcee. She was not about to let anybody tell her that her personal conduct and behavior was wrong and unacceptable, and beware of anybody who tried, and this included John the Baptizer. But this prophet was not about to let a female intimidate him or control him, and especially a gentile involved in incestuous and illegitimate relationships.

> Therefore Herodias held it against him and wanted to kill him, but she could not; for Herod [Antipas] feared John, knowing that he was a just and holy man, and he protected him. And when he heard him, he did many things, and heard him gladly. Mark 6:19-20.

At first Herod thought only to imprison John to isolate him from the common people and in order to protect him from further harm. Herod on occasion actually enjoyed the sermons of John the Baptizer, and probably learned much from him. But all in all, Herod despised him for his austerity and integrity, but also feared him because of his virtuous qualities.

8

No doubt we can see here a parallel between Herodias and John the Baptizer with Jezebel of the Old Testament, the wife of Ahab, and Elijah the prophet of God. Jezebel was a gentile, a daughter of Ethbaal king of the Sidonians. She was a great advocate of the pagan erotic-cult religions of her era, was able to sway her husband away from *Yahweh* God and to the worship of the false deities.

> Then Jezebel sent a messenger to Elijah, saying, "So let the gods do to me, and more also, if I do not make your life as the life of one of them by tomorrow about this time." 1 King 19:2.

To cleanse the land of Judah from the influence of the erotic-cult religions, Elijah put to death 400 prophets of Baal and 450 prophets of Asherah, advocates and promoters of the chief male and female deities of the corrupt and pagan religion of the Canaanites. 1 King 18. As a result of this, Jezebel wanted Elijah dead. Nobody was going to tell Jezebel that her personal conduct and religion was wrong; nobody was going to reprimand her and get away with it. But as the story goes, Elijah fled to Sinai to escape his execution, where he was reprimanded by *Yahweh*, and shortly after he ascended into heaven on a chariot in a whirlwind. 1 King 2:11.

About 8 years later, Jezebel was thrown out of a window and into the street by some eunuchs at the command of Jehu King of Israel, where she was trampled by horses. When the servants came around to finally bury her, all they found were her skull and feet and palms of her hands: Jezebel was eaten by dogs. 1 King 9:30-36. This same Jehu was anointed to be king by Elisha, the successor of Elijah. But the one who later succeeded Elijah in his power and spirit, John the Baptizer, was not as fortunate.

### 9

Herod Antipas' birthday party came along. It is the second birthday festivity that is mentioned in the Bible. The only other one was the birthday of Pharaoh of Egypt. At this earlier festivity, the chief butler was restored to his former position, as head; while the chief baker was hung and lost his. Gen 40:20-22. So with the parallel with the birthday festivity of Herod Antipas.

> But when Herod's birthday was celebrated, the daughter of Herodias danced before them and pleased Herod. Therefore he promised with an oath to give her whatever she might ask. Matt 14:6-7.

The dance of Salome, the daughter of Herodias, would follow the tradition of entertainment for the dignitaries of the era. Salome would be in her late teens and blossoming with an enticing figure. It was her type that was allowed to dance before the invited male guests: she who had the best to offer in visual erotic stimulation. As Salome promenaded and frolicked in the presence of several dozen men the age of her great-uncle Herod, who himself was in his 60's at this time, she removed bits of clothing with motions having sexual undertones until nothing remained for the imagination. Herodias her mother stood off to the side and watched. Salome's finale at close proximity to the guests of honor was a real climax for the birthday boy and he promised her anything she wanted.

> So she, having been prompted by her mother, said, "Give me John the Baptizer's head here on a platter." And the king was sorry; nevertheless, because of the oaths and because of those who sat with him at the table, he commanded it to be given to her. So he sent and had John beheaded in prison. And his head was brought on a platter and given to the girl, and she brought it to her mother. Matt 14:8-11.

Herodias finally got her way. There was no lower level to stoop for Herodias in order to take vengeance on someone who was willing to stand against her and rebuke her dissolute conduct and reprimand her decadent behavior. Of course this was more than just sad for the other disciples, who took the body of John the Baptizer and gave it an honorable funeral. It was hard and tearful for Jesus also.

> Then his disciples came and took away the body and buried it, and went and told Jesus. When Jesus heard it, He departed from there by boat to a deserted place by Himself. Matt 14:12-13.

Jesus and John the Baptizer were cousins, close relatives, and how sorrowful this must have been for him, seeing how corrupt and unprincipled, and arbitrary, the ruling class acted in regard to this prophet of God. Sorrowful not only because this was the man who baptized Jesus at the Jordan River and witnessed the descent of the Holy Spirit upon him as though it was a dove, but also that this was also a blood relative of Jesus. Part of Jesus may also have died when his cousin died at the demands of injustice, and so he had to remain alone to mourn over his death.

And what about the soldiers who kept John the Baptizer under arrest? and the one that tied up and knelt John down on the block? and the executioner who swung the sword with all his might to make a single clean cut right between the bottom of the head and top of the shoulders of the greatest prophet to be born of a women. Did they feel any remorse or regret? Or were they just doing their job? What did the messenger who arrived with the order think? Or the one who delivered the righteous man's head to Herodias? While Herodias no doubt looked at his head upon that platter with supporters and friends and laughed her heart out. No doubt she felt she had the last laugh, and with her seared and insensitive conscience probably thought nothing of it. As the granddaughter of Herod the Great, it went with the territory. But in later years her life was not as good for her; she and her husband lost everything when involved in a conspiracy against another brother Agrippa I. This occurred about 39/40 AD. The two were banished to the city of Lyons in Gaul (ancient France) by the emperor.

The event surrounding Herodias is only one of the incestuous relationships apparent in the family of Herod the Great. Another is noted in the case of King Herod Agrippa II and his sister/concubine Bernice. Acts 25:13. The 2 of them were niece and nephew to Herodias. Bernice went to live together with him after the death of her first husband, Herod of Chalcis, who was also her uncle. Neither relationship produced any offspring. Now it was the apostle Paul who to give testimony on behalf of his own defense before this incestuous brother-sister relationship. Acts 26.

## 10

To reprimand sin and rebuke hypocrisy is not a matter to be taken lightly. It is serious because of the possible results. The extent of decadence of the era in the high levels of authority in the government, along with the insolence and domineering attitude of the women, even back to the era of Ahab and Jezebel, is well made obvious in the above situation. The malice and vile of Herodias was through to the bone in her personal conduct, as well as her up-bringing of her daughter to be just like her or possibly worse, if a female could be worse. But it was a necessity for John the Baptizer to follow in the path beaten by his predecessor Elijah, who confronted and withstood Jezebel. Although the latter was not as fortunate as his predecessor. But was he really?

> And when [Elijah] saw that, he arose and ran for his life, and went to Beersheba, which belongs to Judah, and left his servant there. 1 King 19:3.

Elijah fled for his life. John the Baptizer did not. Later when Elijah reached Mount Sinai, God had to rebuke him for fleeing, and he ended up having to hide his face and repent before God, 1 King 19:13, and subsequently had to give up his ministry in favor of Elisha the son of Shaphat. 1 King 19:16,19. God's removal of Elijah from office, a forced retirement, by his ascension into heaven in a chariot by a whirlwind, may have been a maneuver to protect the face and reputation of Elijah before the other prophets and the people of Israel rather than disgracing him because he fled for his life instead of confronting and being willing to withstand Jezebel right to her face.

Now question of the ages remains to be resolved. Was it really worth it for John the Baptizer to rebuke and reprimand sin and hypocrisy? Hopefully the following passage can answer this question.

> And I saw thrones, and they sat on them, and judgment was committed to them. And I saw the souls of those who had been beheaded for their witness to Jesus and for the word of God, who had not worshiped the beast or his image, and had not received his mark on their foreheads or

on their hands. And they lived and reigned with Jesus for a thousand years. Rev 20:4.

The beheaded are part of the first resurrection, to inherit eternal life. Over them the second death has no authority. No doubt John the Baptizer will also be part of this as a martyr for *Yahweh*.

## 4. LUKE: EVANGELIST AND PHYSICIAN

### 1

Throughout history a conflict has always existed between medical science and faith healing, between the natural and supernatural changes that occur in the human body in regard to healing and recovery from disease and injury. The medical industry - and it is an industry, just like the auto industry or the construction industry - including doctors, hospitals and medicine manufacturers, view with contempt and distrust any individual claiming the power of curing an individual's sickness or impairment by the use of faith in God, and including faith in Jesus of Nazareth, the Anointed of Israel. The medical industry has generally discredited the power of healing by faith, and the reasons for this are quite understandable. No money is to be made by the medical industry if faith did heal.

Any individual claiming healing in a situation where no help could be offered by medical treatment, is investigated thoroughly to ascertain the credibility of the healing. Such investigations include determining if the patient was actually sick (if the patient wasn't really sick or diseased or impaired then there was no healing); and whether medical attention was being applied at the time or earlier (the industry can easily discredit a healing if the patient was under medical care or taking prescription drugs); and is followed by an examination to determine that the patient was cured in all respects (not to die a month later of the same or indirect cause). For some, the faith healing did cause the person to superficially feel better, but did not actually cure the ailment or impairment.

There is no doubt that many frauds and scams have existed and so exist in religion regarding those calling themselves "faith healers", as well as those who claim to have been "healed". Many these are exposed as time goes along - that there never really was a true healing. But on the other hand, many are true and genuine. Many throughout the ages were terminally ill, permanently deformed, congenitally handicapped, without medical attention or beyond the help of medical science, and by faith in Jesus the Son of God were cured whole and well. These few survive the scrutiny of the medical industry and the skeptics.

God the Father of Glory in His wisdom chose an individual who would investigate and verify the miracles of the gospels and subsequently document them, this was Luke the beloved physician, the author of the gospel that bears his name and the Acts of the Apostles.

Luke the beloved physician and Demas greet you. Col 4:14.

Traditional and historical information indicates that Luke was a Greek, not a Jew. Such being the case, Like was the only professional author of any book of the Bible (all the others were mainly of the labor or trade classes), as also the only gentile (the others all Israelite or Jewish). This can be noticed in the details that Luke delves into in both his gospel and the Acts, in describing miracles, and documenting the parables and the sermons of the apostles and recording the prophesies of Mary, Zachariah, Peter, Paul and others. Luke as a physician also investigated the miracles and healing recorded in his gospels and in the Acts. He ascertained their credibility, and left us with this record, that he, as a physician, found no fraud or scam in any of them. That all of these miracles occurred just as he, a physician, documented them.

Luke would have also been a disinterested third party. Whether or not Jesus was the fulfillment of that prophet like unto Moses, Deut 18, or Isaiah's prophecy of the virgin to give birth to a child named Emmanuel, Is 9, or the relationship between Elijah and John the Baptizer, Mal 4, was irrelevant to Luke. There was no reason for him, as a Greek, to want or try to prove that there was a fulfillment of prophecy. His was strictly an investigation and research into the life and ministry of Jesus and the apostles. Although the gospel Luke is the longest of the gospels, not once does he use the phrase "this was done as a fulfillment of that spoken by the prophets." This was used by the other gospel writers, but not Luke. Matt 12:17. Whether Jesus of Nazareth was the Anointed of the Jews would have been just as irrelevant to the Greek Luke.

There are several areas and passages in Luke that are not to be located in any of the other gospels. This is indicative of his thorough research. Some of these sections are: John the Baptizer's annunciation and birth, the visit by Mary to Elizabeth, Mary's song, Zechariah's song; the visit of Gabriel to Mary, the shepherds in the field, the birth in the stable; His presentation in the temple; Jesus' visit to Jerusalem at age of 12; the raising of the son of the widow of Nain; the women who followed and ministered to Jesus; the parables of the Good Samaritan, the friend at midnight, the rich fool, the Prodigal Son, the rich man and Lazarus; the visit with Zacchaeus; the healing of the ten lepers, and the man with dropsy; Jesus before Herod at His trial; the conversation with the thieves on the stake; the walk to Emmaus; and the detail of the ascension. All of this evidences the massive research and efforts of Luke to compile an accurate and thorough history for the benefit of a close and admired friend of his.

Luke as a Greek physician would have been under the obligations of the Hippocratic Oath, which bound him to certain morals and ethics in his profession. Luke's gospel and the Acts were addressed to his friend Theophilus.

> Inasmuch as many have taken in hand to set in order a narrative of those things which are most surely believed among us, just as those who from the beginning were eyewitnesses and ministers of the word delivered them to us, it seemed good to me also, having had perfect understanding of all things from the very first, to write to you an orderly account, most excellent Theophilus, that you may know the certainty of those things in which you were instructed. Luke 1:1-4.

For Luke to have a perfect understanding of the ministry of Jesus and the ministry of the apostles, and especially Peter and Paul, he would have investigated every facet of it to determine its accuracy and reliability, in order for Theophilus to know the certainty of those things in which he was instructed. Under the Hippocratic Oath, Luke was obligated to certain morals and ethics in his profession.

A few examples of recorded miracles in the Gospel of Luke and the Acts will be surveyed here, and the involvement of Luke from a medical and physician's standpoint. All of these would have included his own personal investigation into the miracle, and Luke's own conclusion to the conformation of the miracle would be his own record.

## 2

One lady suffered for 12 years from uterine bleeding, and spent all her livelihood on physicians and could not be healed by any.

> She came from behind and touched the border of His garment. And immediately her flow of blood stopped. And Jesus said, "Who touched Me?" When all denied it, Peter and those with him said, "Master, the

multitudes surround You and press You, and You say, Who touched Me?" But Jesus said, "Somebody touched Me, for I perceived power going out from Me." Now when the woman saw that she was not hidden, she came trembling; and falling down before Him, she declared to Him in the presence of all the people the reason she had touched Him and how she was healed immediately. And He said to her, "Daughter, be of good cheer; your faith has made you well. Go in peace." Luke 8:44-48.

Suffering this long from uterine bleeding she was probably in dire need of a hysterectomy. Along with the other physicians she went to and spent all her money on and suffered with, she may have gone also to Luke, who just like the others, could not help her. But Jesus did help her. Luke the physician investigated her condition before and after and left us with the record of his medical conclusion: her immediate cure from uterine bleeding by faith in Jesus.

### 3

One particular incident only documented by Luke in his Gospel, is the pregnancy of a woman well beyond child-bearing age. This was Zechariah and his wife Elizabeth.

> But they had no child, because Elizabeth was barren, and they were both well advanced in years. Luke 1:7.

Elizabeth was past the stage of menopause according to the above passage. For some reason Elizabeth was unable to conceive her entire life and so the couple was childless, and now she was beyond child-bearing age. Apart from the condition of the wife in her early years, we cannot discount the possibility of Zechariah being impotent. Luke the physician investigated their situation and concluded this. But by the miracle of God, she did become pregnant and gave birth to a healthy baby boy, whom they named John. Co-incident with this is Zechariah developing aphonia, a loss of speech.

> But when he came out, he could not speak to them; and they perceived that he had seen a vision in the temple, for he beckoned to them and remained speechless. Luke 1:22.

This occurred immediately, without previous indication of any speech difficulty or impediment, and without direct or obvious damage to the vocal cords. And just as unexpectedly as Zachariah had developed aphonia, he regained normal speech co-incidentally with the time of the naming of his son, about a week after his birth.

> And he asked for a writing tablet, and wrote, saying, "His name is John." And they all marveled. Immediately his mouth was opened and his tongue loosed, and he spoke, praising God. Luke 1:63-64.

Luke also investigated this and concluded that it was no fluke of nature and beyond any possible co-incidence, but was consistent with the miracle of his son's birth.

4

It is also Luke the physician that documents in detail the single most astonishing of any miracle that is recorded in the Bible: the asexual conception of a child.

> Then the angel said to her, "Do not be afraid, Mary, for you have found favor with God. And behold, you will conceive in your womb and bring forth a Son, and shall call His name Jesus. Luke 1:30-31.

In this scenario, Luke details the visit of the angel Gabriel to the home of a young lady, Mary, probably in her late teens and who is engaged to be married to a local carpenter Joseph. According to Jewish tradition of the era, the normal marriage age for women early, usually in their late teens. Here Gabriel informs Mary that she is to become pregnant with a son, whose name will be Jesus. Mary replies to the heavenly messenger that this is impossible, because she has never had relations with a male, herself familiar with the process of reproduction.

> Then Mary said to the angel, "How can this be, since I do not know a man?" And the angel answered and said to her, "The Holy Spirit will come upon you, and the power of the Highest will overshadow you; therefore, also, that Holy One who is to be born will be called the Son of God. Luke 1:34-35.

Gabriel then informs Mary that it will be God the Father through His Holy Spirit who will impregnate Mary invisibly and miraculously. Mary apparently still knows better, how impossible this is and only condescendingly replies:

> Then Mary said, "Behold the maidservant of *Yahweh*! Let it be to me according to your word." And the angel departed from her. Luke 1:38.

It was not Mary's intention to have a relation until marriage, or else she would be subject to severe penalties in Israel, even death, as well as for the male involved. And if this did come about, it was not due to promiscuity of Mary, but it would be in accord with the words of Gabriel, that all things were possible with God. Luke 1:37. Joseph at first wanted to quietly annul the engagement to Mary when he found about her pregnancy; he did not want to have an immoral girl for a wife. But it was only because of a warning from God in a dream that he kept his engagement to Mary. Matt 1:18-25. They were probably married in a small and private ceremony to avoid turmoil and family criticism.

> And did not know her till she had brought forth her firstborn Son. And he called His name Jesus. Matt 1:25.

About 9 months later, Mary, still in her virginity (not yet having consummated her marriage with Joseph, and without having an affair with anybody else), gave birth to a baby boy in a barn in Bethlehem. This could have been a reason why there was no room for them at the inn, since they did not want an woman of ill repute giving birth to an illegitimate child in their hotel. Regardless of the claims of the Pharisees, who indirectly hinted to Jesus his questionable birth by emphasizing their own legitimacy, Jesus knew His beginnings. John 8:41-42. And so did Luke. Prior to documenting as accurate and credible the miracle of miracles, this marvel, for his friend Theophilus, the physician investigated. No doubt he interrogated both Mary and Joseph to determine the truth. Luke's conclusion is evidenced by his own narrative, that Mary did conceive and was still in her virginity when she delivered her child. Mary and Joseph proceeded to have additional children between themselves after the birth of their firstborn Jesus.

5

Luke recording the death and resurrection of Jesus leads us to more of his medical investigation. That Luke was the other individual along with Cleopas on the way to Emmaus is likely, as this was the typical manner for the Biblical writers to refer to themselves indirectly. Luke 24:13-35. Luke is also the only gospel writer to record this particular incident, except for Mark who only mentions it in passing. Mark 16:12. Luke's thorough description of the crucifixion, more than the other gospel writers reflects his more thorough investigation and could make him a witness to it and to the death and resurrection of Jesus.

In the prologue to the Book of Acts, Luke inscribes:

> To whom He also presented Himself alive after His suffering by many infallible proofs, being seen by them during 40 days and speaking of the things pertaining to the kingdom of God. Acts 1:3.

Luke's own record bears the witness of a doctor's scrutiny of the death and return to life of Jesus of Nazareth. When Jesus commissioned his apostles to preach the gospel of the Kingdom throughout the world, he told them that certain signs would accompany them as the evidence of the truth and credibility of their teaching.

> And these signs will follow those who believe: In My name they will cast out demons; they will speak with new tongues; they will take up serpents; and if they drink anything deadly, it will by no means hurt them; they will lay hands on the sick, and they will recover. Mark 16:17-18

Much like the selection of Luke by the wise God to investigate the miracles of Jesus and all that is recorded in his gospel, so did Luke investigate and document and even accompany the apostles on their ministry, as verification of Jesus' words. A few selections from the Acts will likewise be discussed.

Luke's own presence with the apostle Paul during his travels and ministry is apparent as he uses the pronoun "we" in several sections of the Book of Acts. Combining the detail of description of the words and activities of the apostle Paul with the indication of Luke's personal presence, it appears that Luke joined Paul while in Ephesus, about 57/58 AD, in western Turkey on his third missionary journey, Acts 19, stayed with him there, and went on to Macedonia and Greece in Acts 20:1-4. Luke and Paul celebrated the Feast of Unleavened Bread at Philippi, and then traveled to Troas, on the western coast of Turkey to rejoin Paul's other companions.

Luke records the death of a young man and how Paul brought him back to life in Acts 20:7-12. Leaving Troas, the two traveled to Assos, and continued together to Mitylene, Samos and Miletus, to Rhodes and finally Tyre, and Caesarea. Luke then accompanied Paul all the way to Jerusalem concluding his third journey and remained there with him. The explicit details of the meeting of Paul with the other apostles in Jerusalem, his vow, the uproar of the crowds and the arrest of Paul by the Roman cohort and his defense before them indicates a personal presence. Luke, as a professional level person, a physician, would have had access to the proceedings between Paul and the Pharisees and Sadducees, as well as his defense before Felix and Drusilla; and before Festus, king Agrippa and Bernice. Luke then accompanied Paul to Rome, and stayed with him some time. Acts 27:1. On the journey to Rome from Caesarea, the ship was wrecked on the island of Malta. The natives there showed them unusual kindness. They together gathered sticks and built a fire to warm themselves in the rain and hopefully and dry themselves from the swim through the ocean to land.

> But when Paul had gathered a bundle of sticks and laid them on the fire, a viper came out because of the heat, and fastened on his hand. So when the natives saw the creature hanging from his hand, they said to one another, "No doubt this man is a murderer, whom, though he has escaped the sea, yet justice does not allow to live." But he shook off the creature into the fire and suffered no harm. However, they were expecting that he would swell up or suddenly fall down dead; but after they had looked for a long time and saw no harm come to him, they changed their minds and said that he was a god. Acts 28:3-6.

Paul had apparently included a poisonous snake along with the bundle of sticks he gathered. The heat bothered the snake when Paul placed the bundle on the fire; defending itself the snake bit and envenomed Paul. The natives were aware that nothing could be done for Paul, and waited for him to suffer the effects of the venom and die. Paul shook off the snake back into the fire. The natives verified to Luke that this was a venomous snake, and had in the past caused death within a matter of minutes. But Luke investigated the incident there in his presence and documents it as true fact: that the apostle Paul was bitten by a poisonous snake and suffered no effects at all. Later on the island the local governor Publius invited Paul apostle and Luke physician to stay for a few days at his home. They would have been distinguished guests for the local governor, knowing of their popularity.

> And it happened that the father of Publius lay sick of a fever and dysentery. Paul went in to him and prayed, and he laid his hands on him and healed him. Acts 28:8.

Luke diagnosed his condition. An individual does not recover from dysentery quickly, but over time even with medication; and so without the proper medical treatment there was nothing that Luke could do for the man as he lay suffering. Paul however laid his hands upon the man and prayed for him, and in the name of Jesus of Nazareth, he recovered immediately. Luke verified the healing, and documented it. The local residents, hearing of this, also wanted their sick to be healed.

> So when this was done, the rest of those on the island who had diseases also came and were healed. They also honored us in many ways; and when we departed, they provided such things as were necessary. Luke 28:9-10.

They proceeded to flock around apostle Paul to also be healed of their own illnesses. Luke the physician was also there with apostle Paul, as Luke diagnosed and verified that they were definitely in need of serious medical attention. And then the apostle would lay his hands upon them and they would recover. The residents were so appreciative of Paul's visit and his efforts on their behalf, that they loaded him up with gifts as he left the island to continue to Rome.

## 6

Luke continued with Paul to Rome, where Paul stood before Caesar to testify to the Kingdom of God. Acts 28:16. All of the other companions and fellow-workers in the gospel had abandoned Paul or else were off somewhere else. And so Paul writes to Timothy:

> Be diligent to come to me quickly; for Demas has forsaken me, having loved this present world, and has departed for Thessalonica—Crescens for Galatia, Titus for Dalmatia. Only Luke is with me. Get Mark and bring him with you, for he is useful to me for ministry. 2 Tim 4:9-11.

Luke was not considered to be a fellow worker in the ministry of evangelism. He was there to record and document the activities and ministry of Paul the apostle. Since Luke did not join the apostle Paul until in Ephesus on Paul's third missionary journey, Luke may well have been a practicing Greek physician in this city, and who heard the preaching of the apostle and accepted the gospel of the Kingdom along with many other gentiles. Acts 19:8-10. From this point on he documented the continuing ministry of Paul, as well as acquiring the information on the beginnings of Paul, or Saul as he first appears in the narrative at the stoning of Stephen. Acts 7:58. Luke accompanied Paul to Jerusalem and who introduced him to the other brethren, including the apostle James and all the other elders.

> And when we had come to Jerusalem, the brethren received us gladly. On the following day Paul went in with us to James, and all the elders were present. When he had greeted them, he told in detail those things which God had done among the Gentiles through his ministry. Acts 21:17-19.

Here the apostle also related to Luke and the others the entirety of his ministry throughout Asia Minor, the Mediterranean area, Greece and Syria. This period would have been an opportune time for Luke to research the life of Jesus and His ministry and all that surrounded it, including the early ministry of the other apostles. Luke would have been in Judea at least 2 years, during the period that Paul spent in prison locally in Caesarea. Acts 24:27. Since Luke did leave with Paul to Rome to appear before Caesar. The gospel that bears the authorship of Luke would have been written during his two year stay in Judea with the apostles, as a confirmed record for his friend Theophilus, and no doubt for many other Greeks. The Acts of the Apostles would have been written in Rome at the time mentioned in 2 Tim 4:11, about 64 AD. Since two years passed in Rome after Paul's and Luke's arrival there when the book of Acts closes, Acts 28:30, this may have been the time that Paul was finally summoned to appear before Caesar to testify to the Kingdom of God and the resurrection of Jesus. Luke saw him no more after this time.

## 4. CAN YOU LET YOUR CONSCIENCE BE YOUR GUIDE ?

Among those living creatures in the world today it is only the human that has the capability to distinguish between proper and improper conduct, acceptable and unacceptable behavior, within the society and culture he is part of. There is no morality or ethic among animals. Within the physical portion of instinct which is inherent in all animals is all the education they will ever need to survive. Animals can hunt and find food without farming or cooking; they are born with all the clothing they will ever need; they mate and reproduce, and defend themselves and attack others according to their instinct. But the animal still has no real concept of right or wrong; no moral concept or ethical standard. Morality and ethic as they exist among humans do not exist among animals.

Likewise, animals have no conscience as inherent in a human being. Animals act based on their God-given instinct and there is no evidence of guilt or remorse as one would find in a human. Also, without a concept of morals, conscience cannot exist; but it does exist in humans. The pit bull that mauls a child, or the tiger that attacks an adult feels no regret for their action. But God has instilled in His human creation a type of inner invisible warning system regarding moral conduct and behavior: conscience. The conscience will work and react if our behavior or intentions conflict with the law of God. For individuals who do not know the law of God, it serves as some type of guidance. The psychoanalyst Freud defined the conscience as one of the 2 subsystems that comprise the super-ego. The other being the super-ideal. His attitude was that the super-ego developed the person's moral code. As a person grew, and especially during childhood and adolescence, his parents and other influential individuals molded the super-ego and the person's concept of morals. The super-ideal corresponded to the morally good side, directing the person to moral perfection; while the conscience would have a negative effect by informing the person of violation of this inner moral code formed during childhood.

The psychoanalyst is not without disciples in believing that the conscience is developed by parental and other authority figures during adolescence, rather than part of the inherent nature of the human as designed by God. In several places the apostle makes mentioned of how the conscience worked within certain individuals in warning them about partaking in food offered to idols:

> If any of those who do not believe invites you to dinner, and you desire to go, eat whatever is set before you, asking no question for conscience' sake. But if anyone says to you, This was offered to idols. Do not eat it for the sake of the one who told you, and for conscience' sake; for the earth is the Lord's, and all its fullness. 1 Cor 10:27-28.

But on the other hand, the apostle described some individuals who had no conscience:

> Now the Spirit expressly says that in latter times some will depart from the faith, giving heed to deceiving spirits and doctrines of demons, speaking lies in hypocrisy, having their own conscience seared with a hot iron. 1 Tim 2:1-2.

Apparently due to the effect of external forces imposed an individual can extinguish and mortify the conscience so it has no effect on an individual when his intentions are to harm or damage. Although the above passage pertains to people who abandon the gospel teaching and turn to deception, and use this deception without any feelings of guilt or regret, throughout the ages we can readily see individuals whose conscience has been seared, those without feeling, pity or sensation, or without cognizance that their actions are brutal and cause havoc. A person will cause this to himself through mental and physical conditioning, competition, pride, and conceit. The organized military also trains individuals to obedience to their officer's command without regard to their conscience. Without a feeling of regret, remorse or guilt for one's wrongdoing, an individual is on the same level as an animal.

The purpose of the conscience is specifically defined by the apostle in the following passage:

> For not the hearers of the law are justified in the sight of God, but the doers of the law will be justified; for when gentiles, who do not have the law, by nature do the things contained in the law, these, although not having the law, are a law to themselves, who show the work of the law written in their hearts, their conscience also bearing witness, and

between themselves their thoughts accusing or else excusing them. Rom 2:13-15.

The apostle specifically refers to people who have never heard the law of God or the gospel of the Kingdom. Due to a lack of this knowledge the judgment upon them at the Great White Throne, Rev 20:11-15, will be based on their conscience, their adherence and obedience to inner guilt feelings on matters pertaining to morals, conduct and social behavior. The evidence of God to such persons living in areas or eras where the law of God or gospel of the Kingdom was not available is the creation and the nature of God within His own creation. Ps 19:1-4 and Rom 1:19-20 are two passages where the Bible authors indicate the proof of God evidenced in His own creation, and that this is sufficient to evolve a faith in God in individuals. Conscience combined with the evidence of God's existence inherent in His own creation would lend to develop a sufficient code of ethics and social conduct for such people who have never heard the actual law of God as codified in the Bible. This would be the basis for the judgment of God upon them at the general resurrection as they stand before the Great White Throne. Not knowing specifics of God's standards, their own inner guilt feelings that stems from conscience becomes the basis for judgment.

However for those that know the law of God and gospel of the Kingdom the conscience is not the basis for judgment, but the same law and gospel. If you know God's standards you will be judged accordingly. If you know God's law conscience is not an adequate substitute to conduct oneself in violation of the codified word, and neither is the inner voice or inner enlightenment or personal inspiration. If these inner feelings do not lay guilt on us does not mean what we are doing or intend to do is acceptable conduct. The psychoanalyst in his teachings and therapy wanted people to do away with guilt and these imposed repressions (as he termed them), and that an individual conduct himself as he wanted without inner guilt (repressions). This concept is not Biblical: the moral and ethical code for acceptable conduct and behavior is the law of God and gospel of the Kingdom. The psychoanalyst errs gravely in this matter.

Letting your conscience be your guide may be fine for people and situations where the specific requirements of God are unknown, but if you are disobedient to these feelings of guilt in these situations you will also answer for it, as the apostle wrote:

> For whatever is not from faith is sin. Rom 14:15.

Even then the apostle was convinced of himself and wrote that this pertained also to those true spiritual Christians of his own era, that:

> For we are confident that we have a good conscience, in all things desiring to live honorably. Heb 13:18.

Brothers and sisters, let us have in all respects a clean and good conscience that will not violate us in any situation as we fulfill every facet of our life in conduct acceptable to Him at every occasion.

## 5. THE GREAT CONCESSION

The extent to which the Christian must obey the laws of the land in which he lives has always been a provocative and volatile question. Some or most of Christianity in whatever nation they live in tend to feel the necessity of obedience of all laws and all demands of them by the government. In order to give unto Caesar what is Caesar's, the vast majority of Christians, as well as those of any other religion, including the agnostic or atheistic, their leaders and adherents, accommodate and oblige themselves to the fulfillment of all requirements and demands of the government. Even if such demands may be against the personal conscience of the individual, or against his/her prior moral or ethical training, all this is often conceded in favor of the requirements of the government of the nation. To a great extent this is the requirement of the Bible upon Christians: to give to Caesar what is Caesar's. Matt 22:21. We can define this as the concession that Christians must concede to the government for the benefit of living in this or any country until the establishment of the Kingdom of God at the advent of Jesus, the King of Glory.

The apostle Paul realized the situation of the Christians in Rome, the capital of the Roman Empire, ruled over by the Caesars who were also deified by the Roman senate and worshiped as gods by the Roman populace. Rome was very superstitious in its religion and retained reverence to many household gods and deities, as well as ancestor worship. The time Paul wrote the letter to the Romans is estimated at about 56 AD. During this period it was Nero as the emperor, 54-68 AD, one of the most brutal and unconscionable figures in the history of the rulers of Rome, yet the Christians were in every respect role models for the denizens of Rome in regards to morals, ethics, and concession to the requirements of the government. Their attitude is explained in the Apostle's words:

> Let every soul be subject to the governing authorities. For there is no authority except from God, and the authorities that exist are appointed by God. Therefore whoever resists the authority resists the ordinance of God, and those who resist will bring judgment on themselves. For rulers are not a terror to good works, but to evil. Do you want to be unafraid of the authority? Do what is good, and you will have praise

from the same. For he is God's minister to you for good. But if you do evil, be afraid; for he does not bear the sword in vain; for he is God's minister, an avenger to execute wrath on him who practices evil. Therefore you must be subject, not only because of wrath but also for conscience' sake. For because of this you also pay taxes, for they are God's ministers attending continually to this very thing. Render therefore to all their due: taxes to whom taxes are due, customs to whom customs, fear to whom fear, honor to whom honor. Rom 13:1-7.

The apostle Paul in these verses commends the more noble traits and aspects of an individual: that of establishing and governing a society and people in peace and with a welfare towards all its denizens. The Christians in these verses are commanded to comply with all the laws, regulations, and obligations of the country they live in, and also to concede to the government their right to rule the temporal kingdom of this world. This is our concession as true Christians, to concede to the present government our obedience in civil matters in exchange for allowing us the opportunity to live here until the Kingdom. The Christians were told by the apostle to render the judges, police, the county, state and federal officials, whether elected or appointed, any and all honor they felt they were due; and to pay all such taxes and fines that would be imposed upon them by the same people. This is our concession to them to allow us to live here in the United States, and in return for this the government provides for the safety and welfare of its denizens, until the arrival of the Kingdom of God.

Our lives today as Christians must be impeccable, without any possible accusation by anybody of crime, delinquency, violations of the law, or failure to adhere to the civil laws as established by the United States. Otherwise we become stumbling blocks and a poor example to those individuals, especially the gentiles, in regards to Bible-based people of high morals and ethics. Our off-spring should follow likewise in school and work: blameless of any possible accusation.

> Moreover he (elder candidate) must be well thought of by outsiders. 1 Tim 3:7.
> But let none of you suffer as a murderer, a thief, an evildoer, or mischief-maker. 1 Pet 4:15.

But along with the concession of adherence to local laws, the Bible also requires we make the concession to subjection to the penalties that arise from the deliberate infraction and violation of these laws. Even though God may forgive us, we are still liable to answer to the local judicial system and comply with their verdict if we should commit a crime, and so pay our debt to society, even if it be a minor violation. Our entitlement to be punished is no different than that of any other individual in the American society who violates the law, and so we must accept whatever judgment is rendered. The penalty applies whether it is a few dollars for a traffic violation, or imprisonment or capital punishment for a major crime. This is part of the concession that the scriptures require of us.

However a great divide exists between divine law and secular law, as noted in the words of the Apostles to the members of the Jewish court,

"We must obey God rather than men." Acts 5:29.

This stems from the prohibition demanded by the Jewish leaders that the apostles cease from teaching in the name of Jesus the Son of God, the Anointed of Israel. Once the requirement was dictated that the apostles cease their testimony of the resurrection and the preaching of the gospel, those items that they had the obligation to God to fulfill, here the line was drawn. A decision had to be made in favor of God's dictates. The line is drawn when the requirement demands from us more than the Bible allows us to concede. No longer is there a concession when items are demanded of us that directly conflict with the requirements of the Bible.

The reputation of a community also increases with law-abiding adherents. In this manner no person can have reason to malign our faith, and say that our faith is a detriment to society, that it produces individuals of poor conscience; or that we preach one thing and practice another, as pious hypocrites. But that everyone would only be able to say that our community is a good one, a blessing to the world we live in.

## 6. THE PRIVILEGE TO LIFE

If we were to just stop and think about our life, and ask ourselves whether life is a right or a privilege, how would we answer? To give a very earthly example, in the state we live in, California, the Department of Motor Vehicles makes it very clear to every individual seeking a driver's license that it is a privilege to drive. It is not a right to have a driver's license and to be able to operate a motor vehicle on the highways and streets of California, it is to be considered a privilege. There is no obligation on their part to have to give you this privilege, and especially if an individual violates some part of the Motor Vehicle Code. If there is a violation, and the violator refuses to subject to the penalty involved, whether it be a fine or punishment, your license can be revoked. Driving is a privilege, not a right.

Life is a privilege; it is not a right. No where and at no time was God under any obligation or coercion to benefit you with this particular grace of His and to gift you with life. Life is conscious existence: the ability to realize your existence and have an independent capability to advance and prosper and achieve some measure of happiness and success and comfort for the few years of our stay on earth. And this encompasses not only our own personal life, but also all else that the creator God has created to supplement our life: the earth and sun and moon and stars; the plants and forests, oceans and rivers, animals and wild life. All of this the creator God has given to His creation the human being. The author of Genesis described it in this manner as God presented it to the progenitors Adam and Eve:

> Then God blessed them, and God said to them, Be fruitful and multiply; fill the earth and subdue it; have dominion over the fish of the sea, over the birds of the air, and over every living thing that moves on the earth. Gen 1:28.

The wise king Solomon saw this among his own subjects, and described it in the following:

> I know that there is nothing better for them than to rejoice, and to do good in their lives, and also that every man should eat and drink and enjoy the good of all his labor, it is the gift of God. Eccl 3:12-13,
> Behold that which I have seen: it is good and comely for one to eat and to drink, and to enjoy the good of all his labor that he takes under the sun all the days of his life, which God gives him: for it is his portion. Every man also to whom God hath given riches and wealth, and hath given him power to eat thereof, and to take his portion, and to rejoice in his labor; this is the gift of God. For he shall not much remember the days of his life; because God answers him in the joy of his heart. Eccl 5:18-20.

This is no doubt the greatest gift that anyone can ever receive, the gift of life. But yet we must still realize that the creator God is never and was never under obligation to bestow such a valuable benefit upon us. Now what will we do in return? Do not we now have a gratitude that we must repay somehow? It is only apparent that every individual of the human race is totally indebted to the creator God for His love towards us, in our creation. How to repay God for the immeasurable grace poured out upon us will no doubt take volumes to detail, however only a few passages from the Holy Scriptures are quoted regarding this:

> He has shown you, O man, what is good; and what does *Yahweh* require of you but to do justly, to love mercy, and to walk humbly with your God? Micah 6:8.
> So he said to him, Why do you call me good? No one is good but One, that is, God. But if you want to enter into life, observe the commandments. Matt 19:17.

By way of obedience to the instruction and order of our Creator God does an individual repay the debt we are under. This is how an individual indicates his gratitude to the creator God for the gift of life: obedience to His word. Returning to the earthly example of the privilege, if there is a violation of the law, the privilege can be revoked. This item was clearly indicated to the initial creation in the garden of Eden, to Adam and Eve.

> But of the tree of the knowledge of good and evil you shall not eat, for in the day that you eat of it you shall surely die. Gen 2:17.

Capital punishment as the due penalty for disobedience to the word of the Creator is indicated in several sections of the Scriptures:

> Behold, all souls are Mine; the soul of the father as well as the soul of the son is Mine; the soul who sins shall die. Eze 18:4.

Is this too harsh of a penalty? Not from the perspective of God it isn't. The Scriptures make clear that capital punishment is the due recompense and penalty for a number of violations of the law of God. These violations include murder, Ex 21:12, rape, kidnapping, Ex 21:16, sacrifice to or worship of false-gods and idols, Ex 22:20, violence against parents, Ex 22:15, using God's name in profanity, and others. The penalty of capital punishment for a capital crime must be viewed in several contexts to fully realize the deeper impact it has on the heavenly relationships, along with the relationships within the development of a stable and safe society. Crime is not only an attack against God in the defiance of His authority, it is also against other people, against the society and community, and often against the criminal himself. The violation of God's law in the damage or harm against another is a crime against the people and community. One circumstance to review is that of capital punishment applied to the use of profanity of violence against parents.

There is only today left for us to abide in the grace of God, to continue in the gospel of the Kingdom and the law of God. To overcome sin by way of the salvation of Jesus.

> To him that overcomes I will give to eat from the tree of life that stands in the midst of the paradise of God. Rev 2:7.

Gaining the victory over sin, the victory over disobedience to the law of God and the gospel of the Kingdom, will gain us the access back to the paradise and access to the tree of life; to again have the immortality that our progenitors once had. The privilege to live is just as revocable in the judgment at the end of time as much as it was in the beginning. Capital crime is punished by death not only in the secular courts of justice in the temporal governments of this age, but is also to be punished by the great Judge Jesus the Son of God, where all shall stand before His judgment seat. 2 Cor 5:10. Since all judgment is given to the Son by the Father, John 5:22, and that God has appointed a day when He will judge the world in righteousness by the Man whom He has ordained. Acts 17:31. The capital crimes deserving of capital punishment are specified in the following:

> But the cowardly, unbelieving, sacrilegious, murderers, sexually immoral, sorcerers, idolaters, and all liars shall have their part in the lake which burns with fire and brimstone, which is the second death. Rev 21:8.

No doubt the above crimes are very encompassing, and include many related and various violations. The same argument and requirement for capital punishment can be applied here as was applied above. The violation indicates a disregard for the creator God and His authority, not to mention a crime against people, society and against his own person. There is no obligation on the part of the creator God to have to gift someone eternal life, but because of the sacrifice of the Savior Jesus, the Son of God, corrupt man can gain the victory over sin and disobedience through the grace of God. By faith in Jesus and an accompanied obedience to the word of God, eternal life will be gifted to us, and just as the creator God gifted us with life at our conception to live for the few years or the many upon the earth, so will He gift us with eternal life. Not out of obligation or coercion, because there is none, but out of His love for us.

## 7. ABOUT THE HUMAN

### 1

We, the topic that would seem to be the most basic and simple of all to deal with in explanation, has on occasion become a topic of much debate. However by focusing directly on the words of the Holy Scriptures and accepting the understanding as provided the Word of God, the study is interesting and informative, as also simple. A consistency of translation of terms from the original Hebrew and Greek for its uses in the Bible passages to be studied will also add to clarity in understanding.

What is a human being? First, a human being is not just another animal. Although in terms of certain physical attributes it can be compared in contradistinction to an animal. Physically the human is the highest form of animal in terms of design and capability, and is the most complex organism of them all with its assortment of organs, limbs, and physical attributes, beyond that of any animal. The human is combined with emotions, temperaments, characteristics, conscience, and with such attitudes as love, hate, spite, pride, lust, and kindness and gentleness, which do not exist in the balance of the animal kingdom. Also marital relations as it exists in humans is not the same as in animals. Within animals this is solely for procreation, and based on instinct, while among human the marital facet of life is based on love, a life-long cherished relationship.

One area of translation where conformance is required to develop a systematic and accurate study of man and animals according to the Holy Bible, is that of the Hebrew word *nephesh*, which is the Greek *psyche*, the equivalent of the English word soul. Although in the KJV for example the word *nephesh* is correctly translated as soul 428 times, it is also variously translated as 26 other words, including creature, desire, heart, life, lust, mind, person, pleasure, self and thing. This makes it very difficult for the Bible student focusing on a study of the Word of God. The word *psyche* also translated properly 58 times, but also having various readings such as heart, life and mind, much like *nephesh*. In the following contexts of verses quoted from the Holy Bible, the use of the above words will be correctly rendered as soul in any place where the translation of the Bible have translated it otherwise, so the reader can follow the word study part of this treatise.

The equivalence of the Hebrew *nephesh* and the Greek *psyche* can be found in the quote of Gen 2:7 (Hebrew) which is repeated in 1 Cor 14:45 (Greek), and other direct quotes from the Hebrew Old Testament in the New Testament. The word soul refers to both animals and humans in various contexts, as well as to a living soul as well as a dead soul. A person is a soul, who dwells in a body and is kept alive by the spirit. All of this will be investigated as we continue our study.

## 2

The original creation of animals begins to occur on the $5^{th}$ day of creation week and continues on to the $6^{th}$ day. One item noticeable is that God is the creator of the species. God is the designer and creator and initiator of all the species. God created original species of every animal, based on some original design. Out of this he also then created the sub-species within the species group of every animal. This standardization within the species is very noticeable within the animal kingdom. If evolution had some credibility to it, we would have vestiges at the present time of continued evolution of species. But this does not exist; there are no species that are still in the process of evolution, and no new species to be yet evolved. Because God the great creator has created all the species that will ever be created on these 2 days and will create no more.

The adaptation of animal species to environmental condition is no different that ability which exists in humans. The human being exists in every possible climate and environment in the world. From the cold arctics of Siberia, Alaska and Scandinavia, to the tropics of the Amazon and central Africa. From the dry deserts of the Sahara to the humid rain forests of Malaysia. But God has designed the human being such that he has the capability to adapt to such variations in environment: heat and cold; dry and wet. This is the adaptation of species to environment: as in humans so in the other animals.

The creation of the human is described by the author of Genesis in the following:

> Then God said, "Let Us make man in Our image, according to Our likeness; let them have dominion over the fish of the sea, over the birds of the air, and over the cattle, over all the earth and over every

creeping thing that creeps on the earth." So God created man in His own image; in the image of God He created him; male and female He created them. Gen 1:26-27.

This is the book of the genealogy of Adam. In the day that God created man, He made him in the likeness of God. He created them male and female, and blessed them and called them Man in the day they were created. Gen 5:1-2.

Unlike the animals of the 5th and 6th day that were each created after an original species of their own design, God the creator designed the human being after Himself. The human being was created after the God species, so to say. But this is an attribute that is not physical, but of the soul. We cannot have a physical likeness after the image and likeness of God because God is an invisible spirit that dwells in a spirit realm. Also the above verses indicate that both male and female have the image of God. So does God have the male image or the female? God has neither, because He is an invisible spirit without form or shape.

How does the human have the image and likeness of God and his superiority over animals? The following list is an assortment of various facets of design and construction where the human is superior to the animal, where the image and likeness of God in the human is evident, while not in the animal, as well as indicating a complete distinction between the human and animal.

1. The ability to stand upright and have the hands free for invention and construction. No animal has this.
2. The love relationship that humans are bestowed with; "love" does not exist between the mates of animals.
3. The procreation of children and family as a result of the love between a male and female. Such does not exist in animals.
4. The human is the only creature that must wear clothes to beautify his body. Animals are beautiful with the covering that God has created each of them with.
5. The human is the only creature that must wear clothes to protect his body, from heat, from cold, from rain, etc. Animals have sufficient external growth as a protection from the elements.

6. Human must live indoors in a sheltered area and are incapable of living exposed to the elements. Animals can live in direct exposure to the environment, underground, or in water.
7. Humans alone can appreciate beauty in the opposite sex. This does not exist in animals. Although many animals have special features of inherent beauty, it is the human that appreciates this beauty, which is not evident with animals. These features may be a distinction between sexes among the animals, but the beauty itself is not realized.
8. Humans alone have a written language.
9. Humans alone need an education for survival. Animals all have an inherent instinct which God gifted them, gifted the first of the species.
10. Humans alone have the ability to advance in terms of original design and invention. The beaver and bird still build their burrow and nest in the identical manner that the first of the species did when God created them on the $5^{th}$ and $6^{th}$ days of creation.
11. Humans alone farm and have organized agriculture. Animals live off nature in the wild.
12. Emotions due to tragedy, such as sorrow, sadness, misery, and weeping and crying, does not exist among animals.
13. Emotions due to good-fortune, such as happiness, joy, gladness, and glee, does not exist among animals.
14. Hate, spite, desire for vengeance, animosity, malice, resentment, in attitudes towards others is only prevalent among humans.
15. Only humans can discredit, malign and slander one another; this type of defamation does not exist among animals.
16. Development of a military and subsequent use of the military in organized war is only prevalent among humans.
17. Development of charity and welfare organizations to assist and benefit the underprivileged only exists among humans.
18. Development of hospitals, medical clinics, and related medical research and medicines, to cure disease and especially to lengthen the human life, only exists among humans.
19. Only humans need to eat cooked food.
20. Only humans have redundant organs that serve no real purpose and need to be removed, i.e., tonsils, adenoids, appendix, foreskin.

21. Only humans have two sets of teeth, tooth decay and need to brush their teeth.
22. Only humans need to bathe regular; otherwise the stench of their own bodies would be unbearable.
23. Only the female human needs assistance during childbirth, and a severance of the umbilical cord. Only the female human has a monthly cycle.
24. Only humans shave or cut the hair on their bodies (not that they have to, but they do it anyway).
25. Only humans need a written code of morals and ethics in order to live in peace, and have laws and treaties, and initiate a government. Most animals can live together without laws, and they kill only for food or else to defend themselves from attack to be used as food.
26. Only humans have a fear of the unknown beyond death. Although animals do defend themselves against death; it is a survival motive, and not one tied to the state of the unknown at death.
27. Only humans revere their dead (cemeteries, funeral processions, funeral services, memorial services).
28. Only humans have a comprehension of the existence of God, and as a result of this built edifices to magnify and honor the god of their choice, and develop routines for the worship of their god.
29. Only humans have a sense of regret or guilt for an action done wrong, an offence or crime.
30. Crime and violations of the law exist only among humans.
31. Only humans have a sense of identification.
32. Humans alone have a sense of shame, requiring toilet facilities in private, and a sense of repulsion towards lewdness, pornography and voyeurism.

No doubt there may be some vestiges of some human qualities in animals, such as a dogs' affection for its master, or training monkeys to do simple acts, God the creator placed these abilities in the animals for them to be of better use for the human. These qualities are very shallow and limited in the animal and does not nullify or disqualify any of the points of distinction of the above list. The list can go on and on indefinitely on the variations between the human and the animal, both physical and mental, and an entire treatise with numerous and detailed examples can be written.

However, the above few specific points will suffice in detailing the superiority of man over animal, the difference between them.

The identification of the areas that indicate the human in the image of God is primarily those dealing with our mental faculties. This would include independent thinking and problem solving, invention and creation, education, cognizance of God, and appreciation for beauty; and also those associated with the emotions, such as love, hate, sorrow, conscience, regret and guilt. These are invisible faculties that are not connected directly the body itself. Animals do not have such qualities. Although there are areas that are tied to the operation and function of the body, such as hunger and thirst, these evolve from the nervous system due to the deprivation of nutrients to the body.

3

What is the human composed of? This is answered by a verse in the Bible as follows:

> Now may the God of peace Himself sanctify you completely; and may your whole spirit, soul, and body be preserved blameless at the coming of our Jesus the Anointed. 1 Thess 5:23.

This is the very simple composition of the human person: body, soul and spirit. Each one of these three items will be dealt with and its part in the importance and function of the human. Although the initial creation account was quoted above in regard to the human, the author of Genesis, Moses, continues on in more detail:

> And *Yahweh* God formed man of the dust of the ground, and breathed into his nostrils the breath of life; and man became a living soul. Gen 2:7.

Just as it says in the above verse, God blew spirit out of His lips that filled the earthen figure that He made, and this earthen figure became a living soul. God is the great artisan, the skilled artisan, the great sculptor. Although God is an invisible spirit, if we could just imagine the artist at work, taking clay out of the ground and molding it with His hands into a figure of His own design and imagination, and then taking this figure and blowing into it, and watching it gain conscious existence, watching it come to life. And this is what life is, conscious existence.

> Remember, I pray, that You have made me from clay. And will You turn me into dust again? Job 10:9.
> And so it is written, The first man Adam became a living soul. The first man was of the earth, made of dust. 1 Cor 15:45a, 47a.
> In the sweat of your face you shall eat bread till you return to the ground, for out of it you were taken; for dust you are, and to dust you shall return. Gen 3:19.
> But now, *Yahweh*, You are our Father; we are the clay, and You our potter; and all we are the work of Your hand. Is 94:8.

The above verses should suffice to explain that the basic composition of the man is soil. When an individual passes away, dies, his body returns back to the original composition, soil. In order for a person to have conscious existence, he must have a body. For the spirit to continually dwell in the body, the body must be healthy. If the bodily mechanism begins to fail, this forces the spirit out. If the bodily mechanism totally fails, due to serious illness, failure of some organism, or loss of blood or oxygen, this forces the spirit to vacate the body. For man to continually have conscious existence, there must be a healthy relation between the spirit and the body.

It is only obvious that we really don't know what Adam looked like, or his wife Eve. We don't have any idea of their actual physical features, other than that they had the basic characteristics of male and female. Beginning the next generation, Cain and Abel inherited the physical traits of their parents. Cain the firstborn probably looked just like his father, while Abel may have looked like his mother. Due to the genes passing on the traits of our parents and the traits of previous generations, most individuals have a physical similarity to a parent. The similarity may be so intense that a person can be identified if his parents are known by just looking at him. Other traits are also passed on which are not necessarily physical, such as talents, inclinations and prejudices, habits and even obsessions. Both the physical as well as the non-material characteristics are inherited by the off-spring, and if not in the next generation even to the following and the one after.

This also has a spiritual application to it. As the children of God our Father, born again through the Word of Truth, born of the water and the Spirit, we also have an inheritance of certain of God's traits. Not physical, but spiritual, or non-material. These characteristics that we inherit from God our Father, in the same way that we inherit non-material characteristics from our earthly parents, are described in the following:

> The Spirit of *Yahweh* shall rest upon Him, the Spirit of wisdom and understanding, the Spirit of counsel and might, the Spirit of knowledge and of the fear of *Yahweh*. Is 11:2.

Although these are traits that exist in the Father of glory which were inherited by His Son, Jesus, true sons and daughters of God likewise would inherit these traits, but not in the full degree as Jesus His Son. In another place similar characteristics are also described:

> And that you put on the new man which was created according to God, in righteousness and true holiness. Eph 4:24.
> And have put on the new man who is renewed in knowledge according to the image of Him who created him. Col 3:10.

A Christian can be identified with his parent, because he possesses the image and likeness of God his Father, which he inherited when he was born again in the Spirit. But the formation of man did not end with the original creation. Even today God continues to work as an artist with the souls and bodies of His children. God the great artist wants to form all of us into the image of Himself. Much like a painter painting a portrait of himself, or a sculptor in the process of chipping away a large block of limestone with a heavy hammer, sharp chisel and the craftsman's hands to produce a beautiful image, and the artisan with his clay, God likewise is working hard today taking us into His hands and digging deep His fingers into us, and molding us into a image of Himself.

> For we are His workmanship, created in the Anointed Jesus for good works, which God prepared beforehand that we should walk in them. Eph 2:10.
> But indeed, O man, who are you to reply against God? Will the thing formed say to him who formed it, Why have you made me like this?

Does not the potter have power over the clay, from the same lump to make one vessel for honor and another for dishonor? Rom 9:20-21.

We should always pray and allow *Yahweh* to take us in His hands and mold us into the type of person that He wants us to be, to be vessels for an honorable use. If we are stubborn and proud, we are like clay that is hard and dry, and the artist is unable to mold us easily; and we can easily fracture or break into fragments. If we are weak in faith and timid, we are like clay that is too soft, and fall out of proportion whenever the artist tries to mold us; we collapse quickly. Nothing but dishonorable vessels. Somewhere there is a consistency that is acceptable, a submission of ourselves to the divine will, a subjection of ourselves to the law of God and the gospel of the Kingdom, where we are pliable enough for God the great artist to mold us into exactly the type of character and person He wants us to be. But to do this we must give ourselves into His hands and trust Him in all respects.

4

A person is a soul. The soul is the identity of the person: you are a soul. You live in a body and the spirit that comes from God makes the both alive. All of the features that make up you are your soul. And God has given you a body that will allow you to have conscious existence; and allow you to perform, function, and enjoy the life that God has given you. These are the constituents of the human, body, soul, and spirit, beginning with the original Adam and Eve and to our day. Your emotions, feelings and sentiments; your habits and whims; your intelligence, mentality, and aptitude; your temperament, disposition and nature; your preferences, what you are attracted to and what you are repulsed by; all about you that makes you a distinct and unique human being and a separate identity from all other upon the earth is your soul. You as a distinct entity and identity are your soul. Why you are attracted to a certain female with millions of them around and not another (or a female attracted to a certain male) is because your soul feels and sees a similarity and compatibility in another soul, and so causes a natural attraction for it and subsequently an affection. This why marriages most often last a lifetime, because the soul of each sees a similarity and compatibility in the soul of the other. (Yes, marriages are made in heaven).

A few passages from the Scriptures will be noted where the term soul (*nephesh* or *psyche*) is used to describe the person:

> Return to your rest, my soul, For *Yahweh* has dealt bountifully with you. For You have delivered my soul from death, my eyes from tears, and my feet from falling. Ps 116:7-8, also Ps 56:13.
>
> Therefore I say to you, do not worry about your soul, what you will eat or what you will drink; nor about your body, what you will put on. Is not the soul more than food and the body more than clothing? Matt 6:25.
>
> He who finds his soul will lose it, and he who loses his soul for My sake will find it. Matt 10:39.
>
> For whoever desires to save his soul will lose it, and whoever loses his soul for My sake will find it. For what is a man profited if he gains the whole world, and loses his own soul? Or what will a man give in exchange for his soul? Matt 16:25-26.

In all the above passages, which are just a representative few, the person is the soul. God created this non-material and invisible soul and made it self-conscious when He blew His spirit into the figure of soil that He made. You are essentially a non-material and invisible entity, but which cannot have conscious existence unless assigned a complete and functional human body that is made alive by the spirit from God. You did not exist prior to your birth, because you were in the process of development. And then at your birth when the breath of life entered into you, you became a unique and distinct entity and living soul. You became yourself. God created the living soul, which is you when He blew into you with His lips and you began to breath at birth. What a miracle of God.

### 5

God is a spirit, meaning that God is non-material or not composed of matter, but composed of a substance that is not part of the material realm we are part of. God is also the author of life, just as the apostle Peter told the Jewish elders and leaders about His Son:

> But the author of life you killed. Acts 3:15.
>
> Thus says God *Yahweh*, Who created the heavens and stretched them out, Who spread forth the earth and that which comes from it, Who

gives breath to the people on it, and spirit to those who walk on it. Is 42:5.

It is the spirit that emanates from God that makes life, since God is life-giving. Life cannot exist without the direct involvement of God the Father of glory, because God is the author and inaugurator of reproduction. Reproduction was created as part of the physique and design of all of the plant and animal creation on the $4^{th}$, $5^{th}$ and $6^{th}$ days of creation week. Reproduction cannot evolve. Somewhere in time it must begin at a certain point, with all the faculties and capabilities in efficient operating order, and then reproduction of the same creation occurs. This is what God did. When the plants and trees were created, they had seeds with the complete capability of continuing the reproduction of the same species. Every species of every plant and animal that exists in the world today is a descendent from that original plant and animal which God created and put in the garden of Eden.

Science cannot create a means for the reproduction of life, and the evolutionary theory does not allow for a specific point when reproduction begins. Reproduction cannot have evolved, and which is impossible because reproduction cannot be artificially generated. It is the spirit that emanates from God that makes alive. Likewise in regard to humans, the entirety of the human race evolved from Adam and Eve about 6000 years ago. There were no other human creations on earth: no cavemen, or any other human or type of evolutionary Neanderthal that would be a bridge or "link" between the primate and the human. They arrived later. This is stated in the following:

And Adam named his wife Eve, and she became the mother of all the living. Gen 3:20.

The word Eve in Hebrew means life. The entirety of the human race has evolved from the children to whom Eve gave birth and from her husband Adam. The so-called cavemen were no doubt humans that lived during the difficult periods in the early years prior to the flood: deprived of education and exposed to the elements, much like the native aborigines of Australia, and the ancestors of the jungle dwellers of Borneo, Malaysia, central Africa or the Amazon.

If these types of societies and cultures of ignorance and superstition still exist in isolated areas in the concluding years of the 20$^{th}$ century, how much more uncivilized and savage would the ancestors be some 3000 to 6000 years ago? These would be the so-called cavemen. And in regard to bone structure, the human has an entire range of height from the 4 foot Pygmies of Africa to many throughout the world of 7 foot height; along with every size and shape in between; and not to mention the many possibilities of bone and posture deformities that do occur. Any selection of the bones of these people assembled can easily introduce some new caveman. Bones themselves exist for only a few years in a moist or wet environment and perhaps a hundred years in a dry climate before disintegrating. If embedded in tar or frozen solid in ice or petrified, no doubt they will last longer. But thousands of years is ludicrous, much less millions.

### 6

When does life begin? Does it begin at conception? When the fetus is capable of living on its own outside of the mother? Or not until birth and breathing on its own? These questions haunt us all, and especially at the present with the many debates and demonstrations regarding the legality of abortion, which has its basis in regard to the beginning of rights for a person. When is a person a person? Several areas in the Bible touch upon this topic.

> Your hands have made me and fashioned me, an intricate unity; yet You would destroy me. Remember, I pray, that You have made me from clay. And will You turn me into dust again? Did you not pour me out like milk, and curdle me like cheese, clothe me with skin and flesh, and knit me together with bones and sinews? You have granted me life and favor, and Your care has preserved my spirit. Job 10:8-12.
> Your hands have made me and fashioned me; give me understanding, that I may learn Your commandments. Ps 119:73.
> For You have formed my inward parts; You have covered me in my mother's womb. I will praise You, for I am fearfully and wonderfully made. Marvelous are Your works, And that my soul knows very well. My frame was not hidden from You, When I was made in secret, and skillfully wrought in the lowest parts of the earth. Your eyes saw my substance, being yet unformed. And in Your book they all were

written, the days fashioned for me, when as yet there were none of them. Ps 139:13-16.

As you do not know what is the way of the wind, or how the bones grow in the womb of her who is with child, so you do not know the works of God who makes all things. Eccl 11:5.

Thus says *Yahweh* who made you, who formed you from the womb and will help you. Is 44:2

In these passages the authors Moses (Job), David (Psalms) and Solomon (Ecclesiastes), and the prophet Isaiah, indicate the direct involvement of God in the creation process. It is as if the hands of God are busy at work in the uterus designing and assembling and forming a child. The work is done in secret, but the work is God's. An independent entity begins at conception. God is busy with the total development of the human from the point of conception to its birth. At birth the child is developed enough to the point where it can independently exist, apart from the mother and can breathe. So comes the childbirth. When a child is born it is as if God Himself blows with His own lips into the child and then the child begins to breathe on its own. Not only is the child independent from its mother, but now has its own personal identity. But the development still continues: through childhood, puberty, adolescence, and finally into adulthood. God continues the development, but now external to the body of the mother.

Sometimes for reasons unknown to us, the embryo or fetus may be naturally aborted (instantaneous abortion). No doubt due to the fact that the spirit cannot dwell in a body that is incapable of retaining it (as discussed above), and this is apparent early in pregnancy. Many also die at childbirth, and for the same reason: the body must be in a condition of being to retain the spirit of life that God blows into it when it takes its first breath. Otherwise the spirit will not enter into it. Although the unborn child, or fetus, can be considered similar to an organ in the body of the mother, since it cannot exist independent of the mother, and has no personal identity, this does not deprive it of status. It is not just another piece of tissue. It is a creation of God in process and development. It is a unique and distinct entity, a human being in the early process of development.

## 7

The deliberate termination of pregnancy is not directly discussed in the Bible, and primarily because they would never have thought of such a thing. Children were always considered to be a blessing. And if an individual was expecting, there was joy and gladness. It was a very sad occasion if the parents lost a child or were unable to have children.

> Blessed shall be the fruit of your body (womb), the produce of your ground and the increase of your herds, the increase of your cattle and the offspring of your flocks. Deut 28:4.
> Your wife shall be like a fruitful vine within your house, Your children like olive shoots all around your table. Behold, thus shall the man be blessed who fears *Yahweh*. Ps 128:3-4.
> Now Elizabeth's full time came for her to be delivered, and she brought forth a son. When her neighbors and relatives heard how *Yahweh* had shown great mercy to her, they rejoiced with her. Luke 1:57-58.

The people of God in the Old Testament, the nation of Israel, cherished children as blessings from God; they would never have thought to deliberately cause the termination of a pregnancy. There is however one direct example in the Bible regarding the loss of an unborn child:

> If men fight, and hurt a woman with child, so that she gives birth prematurely, yet no lasting harm follows, he shall surely be punished accordingly as the woman's husband imposes on him; and he shall pay as the judges determine. Ex 21:22.

The loss is not considered as serious as a matter of murder, because the unborn child did not yet attain independence and an identity, which occurs at birth. But because this was not an accident, it was not without penalty and depended on the father and judges, and any other harm or damage that the woman sustained would be required directly from him. The intent of this law was to protect any woman who was expecting from either deliberate or accidental harm. For the people to realize that pregnancy was a serious issue, penalties were involved if any harm should occur to an expectant mother. Exactly how large of a penalty the father and judges would impose for the loss of a child and harm to the mother is not mentioned, but could be substantial depending on the time of period of pregnancy and the amount of any other harm the woman would incur. Probably not the death penalty, but a compensation very high no doubt.

In Bible times also, a woman getting pregnant outside of marriage constituted a heinous crime. She was required to answer for her crime of prostitution, not just immorality. This in noted in the situation with Judah and Tamar, with the capital punishment specified in Gen 38:24. Deliberate termination of pregnancy existed among the non-believing pagans and gentiles, along with exposure and other heinous and abhorrent practices.

## 8

Because we are human we have inherited both the bad traits of our progenitors Adam and Eve along with the good ones. We have also inherited faults, shortcomings, deficiencies, and weaknesses. All of this as a result of the sin of Adam and Eve in their disobedience to God. This also becomes apparent in childbirth with the birth of children that are not necessarily completely normal. The ancient wise men described it in the following:

> Who can bring a clean thing out of an unclean? No one! Job 14:4.
> What is man, that he could be pure? And he who is born of a woman, that he could be righteous? Job 15:14.
> Behold, I was brought forth in iniquity, and in sin my mother conceived me. Ps 51:5.

No doubt both Moses the author of Job, along with David who had many wives and concubines and scores of off-spring, saw many stillborns, and children born with various handicaps and impairments. Some lived longer than others, especially with the lack of medical care. The child born to David out of his affair with Bathsheba the wife of Uriah may have had a birth defect, which caused its death 7 days after its birth. 2 Sam 12:12-18.

Some of these are mentioned in other Scriptures, such as the man born blind mentioned in John 9, whom Jesus then healed; or the crippled man, born in this condition, whom the apostles Peter and John met at the Beautiful Gate of the Temple and then healed in Acts 3. Also we must mention the man in the city of Lystra who was crippled from his birth, and who was healed of this through the healing of the apostle Paul. Acts 14:8-10. Moses himself had a speech impediment, apparently from birth, since

God Himself indicates that He is the source of all such congenital impairments:

> Then Moses said to *Yahweh*, "O my Lord, I am not eloquent, neither before nor since You have spoken to Your servant; but I am slow of speech and slow of tongue." So *Yahweh* said to him, "Who has made man's mouth? Or who makes the mute, the deaf, the seeing, or the blind? Have not I, *Yahweh*? Ex 4:10-11.

Congenital birth defects, along with other faults, shortcomings, and weaknesses which we inherit from our parents, is God's way of showing us how human we really are, and how god we are really not. On occasion the great God finds it necessary to make it clear to His creation that we are imperfect. That we are imperfect and defective in many respects, thereby having even more the need for a Savior, and especially one that is perfect, that by faith in Jesus, we will one day became perfect, without physical deformities and flaws in our nature, both physical and mental. We only deceive ourselves when we fail to realize and face up to this fact; and quite often God finds it necessary to make this known to us, how frail and imperfect we really are, and right from our birth, and how much we really need God.

9

The human body is designed to be the dwelling place of the spirit of God. As a result of this many of the admonitions in the Bible concern every person, whether just a son of Adam or a child of God, and apply to the sanctification of his body. 1 Thess 4:4. This spirit of God that dwells in every son of Adam is that spirit which is blown into us by God when we are born, and causes us to breathe on our own and exist and function independently of our mother. The apostle mentions this in the following, and which applies to all the descendent of Adam and Eve:

> Do you not know that you are the temple of God and that the Spirit of God dwells in you? If anyone defiles the temple of God, God will destroy him. For the temple of God is holy, which temple you are. 1 Cor 3:16-17.

The living human body is no joke or fluke of nature or accident of the evolutionary or biological process. It is a serious matter and is the handiwork of the living God. For this reason does the apostle dictate the stringent and forceful command in the above verse. God will definitely take vengeance on that individual who will abuse or desecrate his body. This type of abuse or desecration can be in the various forms of damage or harm that an individual imposes on his body. Any action that will jeopardize the health of the body is included, such as drug abuse, smoking, and consumption of alcoholic beverages. Poor dietary habits such as obesity and bulimia, or modern obsessions such as anorexia nervosa, also cause harm to the human body. In addition to the above the apostle also includes the following:

> Flee immorality. Every sin that a man does is outside the body, but he who commits immorality sins against his own body. 1 Cor 6:18.

The inclusion of sexual involvement with another person outside the sacred institution of marriage is included not only because of its violation of the marriage vow, but also because of the rampage and devastation that is caused by venereal disease. The only method of not ever contracting a venereal disease is by two people only having sex with one another during their lifetime (or with the widow or widower of such a person). The sin against your own body that the apostle speaks of is the various infections and diseases that an individual can contract with multiple sexual partners. This includes several sexually transmitted diseases as well as the HIV. The apostle was well familiar with these as prevalent as was immorality in the moral corruption of the Roman Empire. So prevalent was perversion and infidelity in the empire that the apostle continually mentions abstaining from it in his writings, such as Rom 1:27, 1 Cor 6:9, and especially 1 Thess 4:3-4. Almost every letter of the apostle Paul makes mention of the necessity of abstention from the immorality of the era. An important facet of this a method of precluding infections or diseases of sexual transmission. The disease itself the method of God for vengeance against the person for the violation of his own body; and quickly the body itself suffers through pain and misery through death. The ultimate desecration of the human body is suicide, or any activity that we participate in that will result in an ignominious death.

For the born again Christian the obligation is more critical. Within the Christian dwells the Holy Spirit of God, which he receives with the birth of the water (Word) and the Spirit. John 3:5. With the human body as the dwelling place of the Holy Spirit it becomes the Temple of God, just as was the Temple of Solomon when the *shekinah*, the glory of *Yahweh* filled it. 1 King 8:10-11. In a parallel understanding wrote the apostle Paul:

> Or do you not know that your body is the temple of the Holy Spirit who is in you, whom you have from God, and you are not your own? For you were bought at a price; therefore glorify God in your body and in your spirit, which are God's. 1 Cor 6:19-20.
> For no one ever hated his own flesh, but nourishes and cherishes it, just as the Lord does the church. Eph 5:29.

Our body, the dwelling place of the Holy Spirit of God should be used in all respects and activities to honor the God that created us and gave us life. To hate our body would be to desecrate it as in the examples given above. But if we love God then we will keep the temple of our body without defilement and desecration in order that God may continue to dwell in us and use us for His good purpose.

### 10

The law of God concerning food is also of exceptional benefit and value, and no doubt God did intend this when He decreed such laws to the people of Israel. He definitely had their best interests and health in mind; especially people who had no knowledge or education in regards to diet or effects of certain foods on the body. There is much debate as to the enforcement of this in the New Testament based on sections such as Matt 15:17 and 1 Cor 6:13 (both of which sections are subject to interpretation). Nonetheless, if we consider the body as the temple of God and also realize that the Word of God given to the ancient nation of God, the people of Israel, was given so that they would continue in body, soul, and spirit, unto the coming of the Anointed, Jesus the Son of God, we would recognize much benefit that can evolve from the admonitions given in the food laws. These sections are Lev 11 and Deut 14, and codify what was permissible among the animals for the people of Israel for human consumption. In addition are the following commands:

> This shall be a perpetual statute throughout your generations in all your dwellings: you shall eat neither fat nor blood. Lev 3:17, also Lev 7:22-27.

The use of blood and fat for human consumption must be recognized not as a ceremonial defilement in these verses, but as a detriment to a person's health. Modern medical research has indicated that blood does transmit the diseases of an animal into a human. For meat to be consumed as food it should be properly cooked. This consists of having it cooked through, that is, all the blood and bacteria must be destroy by raising it to or above the boiling point of water.

Fat likewise is a health problem. The removal of fat from meat before cooking or eating is beneficial for human health. Decreasing overall fat consumption from other foods such as butter, is also to our benefit. For us to seriously consider the advantage and even validity of the law that God issued in regard to food proper for human consumption would definitely benefit our overall health.

## 11

There is a continuing struggle within each and every human body. The spirit of God within it wants the body to live, while the forces outside the body tend to lead it to self-destruction. Although most of us do not view it as a self-destruction, but the Bible speaks of it as the temptation to sin, the motivation to do harm and damage to ourselves and to others in disobedience to the Word of God. The apostle Paul himself had to deal with this difficult problem as he mentions:

> For what I am doing, I do not understand. For what I will to do, that I do not practice; but what I hate, that I do. If, then, I do what I will not to do, I agree with the law that it is good. But now, it is no longer I who do it, but sin that dwells in me. For I know that in me (that is, in my flesh) nothing good dwells; for to will is present with me, but how to perform what is good I do not find. For the good that I will to do, I do not do; but the evil I will not to do, that I practice. Rom 7:15-19.

The apostle knew what the right thing to do was; but now he had to overcome the forces of temptation part of the inherent nature of the human in order to do it. This inherent part of our nature to disobey God we inherit from our progenitors Adam and Eve, who also disobeyed God. Apparently, the apostle many times ended up doing what he did not want to do because the forces of temptation were so strong. But what he really intended to do he failed. He no doubt talks about his earlier life before he received the grace of Jesus. Now with the grace of God he can walk in the Spirit and not in the flesh, and the Spirit of life delivered and freed him from this struggle. Rom 8:2. Earlier he had no spiritual strength to resist temptation, but now with the grace of God, he has the capability to withstand temptation, and further discussed in Rom 8, the entire chapter on how he is now led by the Spirit of God, rather than by the dominion of his flesh.

But the apostle Paul was not the first to realize this struggle within himself and this bondage to the influence and motivation of submission to temptation and sin, this struggle of the spirit of God and the flesh of man. Back several thousand years earlier the author of Genesis recorded the following:

> And *Yahweh* said, For my spirit shall not any longer struggle with man because he is flesh; for his lifespan shall now be a hundred and twenty years. Gen 6:3.
> Then *Yahweh* saw that the wickedness of man was great in the earth, and that every intent of the thoughts of his heart was only evil continually. Gen 6:5.

The evil and wickedness of the era prior to the flood caused a massive struggle in the soul and body of every individual. God through His spirit, which was in each person, struggled to keep the soul alive, while the people succumbed to temptation and sin which resulted in their desecration and premature death. Once the person succumbed to the temptation of the era, the body was no longer any more capable of retaining the spirit to keep the soul alive. God was exhausted with working so hard to keep His spirit inside of every body to keep the person alive, when the person did nothing all day long and all night long except to desecrate his body with every manner of abuse and violation possible. Prior to the flood the lifespan among the saints of God, the patriarchs, was 800 to 900 years and upwards. Among the sinful generation it started out the same, and then decreased and decreased as time progressed from the creation to the time of the flood. Due to the transgression of God's law by the people, God was no longer willing for His spirit to try to keep the people alive when their own intent was to only destroy it by means of self-inflicted harm and abuse in their activities and conduct. The body was only able to endure so much to a point, and God likewise, and then God removed His spirit from the body, and the soul became lifeless, the person was no longer a living soul.

This same topic is dealt with in the following passages where God can and will no longer endure the corruption and perversion of man, and releases man to his own inevitable end.

> And even as they did not like to retain God in their knowledge, God gave them over to a debased mind, to do those inappropriate things; filled with all injustice, immorality, wickedness, covetousness, maliciousness; full of envy, murder, strife, deceit, evil-mindedness; they are whisperers, backbiters, haters of God, violent, proud, boasters, inventors of evil things, disobedient to parents, undiscerning, untrustworthy, unloving, unforgiving, unmerciful; who, knowing the righteous judgment of God, that those who practice such things are worthy of death, not only do the same but also approve of those who practice them. Rom 1:28-32.
>
> And for this reason God will send them strong delusion, that they should believe the lie, that they all may be condemned who did not believe the truth but had pleasure in evil. 2 Thess 2:11-12.

In both these passages, the people struggle against the spirit of God and choose the way of death. God will only deal with them to a certain point, and when the people reject the efforts of the living God and reach a point of hopelessness, incorrigible, then God begins the withdrawal of His spirit from them and they all receive the due compensation and penalty for their conduct and behavior.

This short treatise on understanding the human and his constituents is a necessity to understand the need and purpose of the resurrection, and the state of an individual in death. There is no more serious creation on earth than that of the living human, the creation of God in His image and likeness.

# PART SIX

# THE GOSPEL OF THE PRINCE OF PEACE

## 1. Historical Background

This chapter will provide an insight into the message preached by Jesus of Nazareth, the Son of God, that one important facet of the gospel is the deliverance of humanity from its perpetual self-destructive trend of warfare. This chapter will also unveil how his message of peaceful coexistence and toleration was transformed into a message of militarism, and how the Apostolic community was transformed into an ecclesiastical political institution. Evidence will also be provided to the reader to testify that the only proper manner for a Christian to conduct himself in the matter of war and military service is to refuse.

Jonathan Dymond wrote in 1847 regarding the purpose of Christianity, and which is just as applicable, if not the more so, today.

> It was the will of God that war be eventually abolished, and Christianity was the means by which this was to occur. Christianity with its present principles and obligations is to produce universal peace. It is because we violate the principles of our religion, because we are not what they require us to be, that wars continue.[125]

These words describe the primary topic of this chapter: the manner that the gospel message will curb war and military aggression.

At the same time, this chapter is a history of the development of militarist Christendom and especially the development of the misconception of the militarist Messiah. This includes the manner events and persons of Biblical and ecclesiastical history were interwoven to create an institution that possesses the façade of Jesus, but denies the primary message of the gospel, and which has subjected itself to secular authority for some 1,700 years. As a result, war has progressed generation after

---

[125] Dymond, Jonathan, *An Inquiry into the Accordancy of War*, pg. 55.

generation in Christian countries because the Christian Church as an institution has failed in its obligation to its founder Jesus. All of the information that I provide in this book is readily available, and to which every student and scholar of Biblical and ecclesiastical history and philosophy has easy access.

## PLATO

The inclusion of militarism in Christendom has its roots in the political philosophy of the Greek philosopher Plato. In his *Republic*, Plato states that the creation of the state as a means of providing for the best interests of its residents is the greatest good.[126] The creation of a class to fight the enemies of the state, and for the sate to expand its borders and enlarge its realm – should the guardians deem it necessary – is treated as an axiom. Residents become the subjects of the state, and are not treated as having individual rights, but are utilized as necessary for the benefit of the state, even if they need to be treated as expendable or as a commodity. The life of an individual belongs to the state, and not to the individual, because the greatest good is the use of the individual to the benefit of the state as dictated by the philosopher-king.

At the same time Plato taught the god or gods of the state – the supernatural deity – are to be represented such that they are aligned with the good that the state wants to provide its residents. Such a god had the obligation to impress on the warrior it is better to "choose death in battle, rather than defeat and slavery."[127] Plato believed that a nation cannot be strong unless it believes in God; he realized the value of a uniform religion to the stability and success of the military. According to Plato, a mere cosmic force or first cause that was not a person could hardly inspire hope or loyalty or sacrifice, and could not offer comfort to the hearts of the distressed, nor courage to embattled souls. Plato taught that a living God could do all this, and advised that the state promote a living God whose doctrines and demands parallel those of the state; religious belief would be used to gain control over the citizens. Plato also taught that control would be more effective if a belief in personal immortality was promoted along with belief in God. This conviction of immortality, the hope of another life, would give the soldiers courage to meet their own death on the

---

[126] Plato, *Republic*, book 4, 420 b-c, book 5, 471 d-e.
[127] ibid, book 3, 386 b.

battlefield and be able to bear the death of other soldiers and innocent victims.[128]

The propagandists, also known as narrators or poets, had the obligation to provide the residents a god aligned with the interests of the state, which was also to the best good of the residents. According to the text of the *Republic*, no subject or resident would question or doubt that their best interests were at all times maintained in the dictates of the state.

One interesting comment of Plato is the importance that military service plays in the reputation of the state.

> Well, I said, everyone who calls any state courageous or cowardly will be thinking of the part that fights and goes out to war on the state's behalf. No one, he replied, would ever think of any other.[129]

The reason is obvious: the military preserves and expands the civilization as developed by the state. Since this is in the best interest of the state, then the supreme deity likewise approves of the effort of the military in this area. Residents are to be taught to depend on the military as their source of security. Any warrior who abandons the military or resigns due to cowardice is considered a traitor to the state and demoted to a lower rank of service and outside of the armed forces.[130] Those who die in battle are presented the highest honors, as if there was no greater manner for them to serve their country. It is not in areas of virtue, morality, peace or those areas that develop civilization, such as science or engineering, that are magnified by Plato as significant in the reputation of the state in the world-scene, but the strength and success of the military. The pathetic part is that greater honor is bestowed on soldiers than on reconcilers, and this keeps the tradition of military service at the forefront of civil service.

This allurement or attraction of war and the military profession as described by Plato is repeated by Jonathan Dymond in his book on the causes of war:

> But I believe the greatest cause of the popularity of war,... consists in this: that an idea of glory is attached to military exploits, and of honor to the military profession. Something of elevation is supposed

---

[128] ibid, book 3, 387 d-e.
[129] ibid, book 4, 429 b.
[130] ibid, book 5, 468 a-c.

to belong to the character of the soldier; whether it be that we involuntarily presume his personal courage, or that he who makes it his business to defend the rest of the community, acquires the superiority of a protector; on that the profession implies an exemption form the laborious and meaner occupation of life. There is something in war, whether phantom or reality, which glitters and allures; and the allurement is powerful, since we seen that it induces us to endure hardships and injuries, and expose life to a continual danger. The glories of battle, and of those who perish in it, or who return in triumph to their country, are favorite topics of declamation with the historian.[131]

One topic regularly debated is whether Emperor Constantine I may have considered himself the philosopher-king as the pinnacle of sovereign principle, now having defeated his enemies, and uniting the entirety of the Roman Empire under a religion superior to that of his predecessors and aligned with the interests of the state, conforming to Plato's *Republic*.

## SADDUCEES

This section is written in order to present background information on the period that Jesus lived and taught, and also to explain why the Sadducee group of Jews made the statement that Caesar was their king, rather than accepting Jesus as the Anointed. From about 6 AD on, the high-priest's office was retained by a small quantity of aristocratic and wealthy Sadducean families. Once having attained this most influential and important plateau in the sacerdotal realm of Judaism, Sadducees were careful not to do anything, or permit anything, which might be to their detriment. They exerted all effort to make sure everything accomplished was in their best interests without incurring any wrath or displeasure of the Roman occupation.

The date of 6 AD is selected because that year Annas son of Seth was appointed high-priest in place of Joazar son of Boethus, and because he became the most powerful of any high-priest of the history of the second temple period, and was the progenitor of the greatest posterity of future high-priests. Anna maintained the position 6 to 15 AD, and was the real

---

[131] Dymond, Jonathan, *An Inquiry into the Accordancy of War with the Principles of Christianity*, 1870.

power behind the position until his death. Subsequent to Annas and until the beginning of the Jewish War in 66 AD, 5 sons, one son-in-law – the infamous Joseph Caiaphas of the New Testament – and one grandson, all held the office. The family of Boethus also provided at least 3 high-priests, and the family of Kanthera at least 2.

The reference in the NT to high-priests in the plural referred to the senior members of the Saducean families that held the high-priest office at the time. Because of their sacerdotal zeal to resurrect the ancient Levitical and Zadokite priesthood under their own names, Saducees were the majority of the Sanhedrin on a regular basis, and especially during the ministry of Jesus of Nazareth.

To protect their hard-earned sacerdotal supremacy the Saducees opposed any popular movement that appeared threatening or that had political overtones. Especially formidable to the Saducean stance was Jesus of Nazareth as the Anointed or King, since a claim of this type would cause the suspicion of, and increased oppression by, the Roman occupation, and so undermine the freedoms and power of the Saducees. This opposition to Jesus' claims of his Messianic office was certainly political, not sacerdotal. The attitude of the Saducees easily led to the statement of Caiaphas that it would be in the best interests of the Saducees for Jesus to somehow be eliminated.

> So the chief-priests and the Pharisees gathered a council (Sanhedrin), and said, "What are we to do" For this man performs many signs. If we let him go on in this manner, every one will believe in him, and the Romans will come and destroy both our place and our nation." But one of them named Caiaphas, who was high-priest that year, said to them, "You know nothing at all; you do not understand that it is expedient for you that one man should die for the people, and that the whole nation should not perish." John 11:49-50

The statement of the Saducees to Pilate culminates their relationship to the Roman occupation.

> They cried out, "Away with him, away with him, crucify him."
> Pilate said to them, "Shall I crucify your king?"
> The chief priests answered, "We have no king but Caesar." John 19:125

Sadducees accepted the Romans as the greater power, and the benefactor of sacerdotal freedom and temple authority. If Sadducees were to recognize Jesus as the Anointed, the Roman occupation would deprive them of their freedoms and authority. The Saducean political institution and social fraternity had no choice except to voice their loyalty, patriotism and acceptance of Roman occupation. To protect themselves, they sacrificed Jesus. As far as the covenant of God was concerned, they had now betrayed *Yahweh* God in favor of a gentile and pagan king who allotted them superficial earthly gain and the prestige of sacramental ceremonialism.

Jesus was sacrificed in order for the Sadducees to remain in good terms and approval of the Roman occupation, and their fear that the Romans would increase authority and defeat entirely what little of the nation of Israel remained. Jesus became the victim of political expediency, the sacrifice necessary to keep the social order in Judea balanced.

## WAR AND LOVE IN THE OLD TESTAMENT

The student of the Bible must realize that God dealt with His nation Israel and the other nations of the Middle East in the manner of their culture and era. Their education was meager, science and mathematics and engineering were shallow, and communication was slow. People lived in fear; might was right. Few rules were imposed by God for the success of His people and any others who would take advantage of them, and few rules were provided for their interaction with other nations. God designed the course of history of the 4,000 years from Adam to Jesus taking into serious consideration the barbarism of the people and lack of civilization. God's perfect law included many accommodations due to the uncivilized nature of their society.

The first documented war in the Old Testament is in Gen 14, when the patriarch Abraham armed his servant warriors to defeat 4 alien kings and their armies. Abraham's primarily purpose was to rescue his nephew Lot from these invaders. Abraham and his small force was the method God accomplished his vengeance on these 4 alien kings for their invasion and pillage of the 5 communities of southern Canaan.

The use of the descendents of Abraham for the execution of God's wrath on the sinful and wicked nations of Canaan is mentioned in a statement of God to Abraham.

For the iniquity of the Amorites is not yet complete. Gen 15:16.

God was to utilize the arrival of the new nation of Israel to the land promised by God to execute His judgment and penalty upon the indigenous nations of Canaan for their crimes. This is essentially capital punishment on a large scale. The crimes of the residents of Jericho and other areas on both sides of the Jordan River were so serious that God from heaven pronounced them guilty and sentenced them to death. Their execution occurred in their defeat by the armies of Israel, and none was to be spared. Deut 7:1-2. The history of the wars against the Canaanites is documented in the book of Joshua.

God did utilize the nation of Israel to impose penalty on local nations whenever their individual and national crimes increased to some intolerable extent. God pronounced his judgment and sentenced them from heaven, some to slavery, some to death, whatever the proper penalty was that they deserved, and sent His army of Israel to fulfill His command. I Sam 15:1-3. The reverse would also occur when Israel would sin against God. He would summon a local pagan nation to invade Israel and execute the penalty on them. Judg 2:14. This is the history of Israel and the nations of the Middle East as noted in the historical books of the Old Testament.

The devastation of the northern kingdom Israel and their deportation to Assyria and Media by the army of Assyria over the course of several years was the judgment of God upon them for their crimes against Him. 2 Kings 17. Likewise God utilized the army of Babylon as His method of executing His penalty on the southern kingdom Judah for their crimes. 2 Kings 24-25. The defeat of Israel and Judah is viewed as penalty on a massive scale for their crimes against one another and against God, and they rightfully deserved such retribution. Such use of the army of Israel in establishing the kingdom and imposing the judgment of God upon the nations was the typical course of national life during the years of the kings of both Israel and Judah, and continued until the war of independence under the forces of the Maccabees.

An indication that a military was not the perfect will of God, but only a temporary accommodation, is evidenced in the reprimand of Samuel prophet when the people of Israel requested a king. I Sam 8. They people wanted a military leader to rule over them and be militarized like the balance of the nations. Although it was not the perfect will of God, he accommodated them and granted their request.

Another incident to be noted is the words of God to King David, that the temple could not be constructed by him because he was a soldier during his career. 1 Chron 28:3. Only a person not contaminated by bloodshed could build the temple and this was Solomon.

The $6^{th}$ Commandment is, Do not murder, although translated as, Do not kill. Ex 20:13. No person had the right to arbitrarily deprive another person of their life, and if he did he would have to face the penalty. Subsequent commandments were instituted to curb violence.

The use of a military to fulfill the objectives of God in imposing His penalty on disobedient nations was only temporary. It had a definite purpose during the ages from the army of Abraham to the army of the Maccabees. The achievement of Jewish independence from the Greeks by the military force under the sons of Mattathias was the final military struggle of the nation Israel. As it began with Abraham their national progenitor, so it ended with the final military king and priest of Israel, Simon son of Mattathias. 1 Macc 15.

## THE OLD TESTAMENT WAY OF LOVE

The Old Testament also contains many examples and admonitions of the way of love and non-violence. When there was strife between the herdsmen of Abraham and Lot, Abraham peacefully divided the land between the 2 of them. Gen 13:7-12. When the envious Philistines plugged Isaac's wells, Isaac did not take vengeance, but in a Christ-like spirit he moved to other grounds. Gen 26:12-33. When Joseph was sold into Egypt by his brothers, and after he rose to a position of second ruler in the land, he did not deal with them in the spirit of vengeance, but had an attitude of forgiveness. Gen 43-45. In certain portions of the Old Testament, God's people were commanded to show love to their enemies, for example the command, If you find your enemy's ox or donkey astray, you will surely bring it back to him. Ex 23:4. On one occasion Elisha the prophet took a Syrian army captive, and then fed the men and sent them home. 2 Kings 6:8-23. These examples prove that God's perfect law was that of harmony and reconciliation between enemies.

## BIBLICAL JUSTICE

During the Old Testament era capital punishment for a capital crime was legislated by God. To a great extent, these same criteria for determining if a crime deserves capital punishment were transferred over to ecclesiastical law in the middle ages and subsequently into legislated law of western Europe and the Americas.

The purpose of capital punishment was to provide justice to the offended party and those affected by the seriousness of the crime, and also to deter future criminal infraction. Deut 13:5, 10-11. With a speedy trial and conviction by responsible members of the community and their execution of the criminal, crime was to decrease and people would be able to live in greater security.

The initial statute legislating capital punishment is noted in Gen 9:6, for murder, which is defined as a capital crime. Ex 21:12. This was a violation of the fifth commandment, Ex 20:13. Other capital crimes noted in the Old Testament are kidnapping, Ex 21:16. Sorcery, Ex 22:18. False-prophesy, Deut 13:6-11. Premarital sex, Deut 22:20-21. Rape, Deut 22:25. Adultery, Deut 22:24. Necromancy, Lev 20:27. Incest, Lev 20:11-14. Prostitution, Lev 21:9. False-witness in a capital case, Deut 19:15-20. Homosexuality, Lev 20:3. Accidental homicide was not considered murder.

Capital punishment for a capital crime is justice and is classified separately from military combat. To deprive a person of their life was a serious matter and was regulated by the law of God.

## THE FUTURE MESSIAH OR ANOINTED OF GOD

The following passages are prophesies of Isaiah, Micah and Zechariah. Each of them prophesied during the later eras of the kingdoms of Judah and Israel. The prophecies quoted here pertain to the Redeemer of Israel, the future Anointed, and deal with the termination of the military of Israel and the transition into a pacifist society at the time of the installation of his reign.

> He will judge between the nations, and will decide for many peoples; and they will beat their swords into plows and their spears into pruning

hooks; nation shall not lift up sword against nation, neither shall they learn war any more. Is 2:4. Micah 4:1-3.

For every boot of the trampling warrior in battle tumult and every garment rolled in blood will be burned as fuel for the fire. For unto us a child is born, to us a son is given; and the government will be upon his shoulders, and his name will be called: Wonderful, counselor, mighty God, everlasting father, prince of peace. Is 9:5-6.

Rejoice greatly, O daughter of Zion. Shout, daughter of Jerusalem. Behold, your king comes to you righteous and having salvation, gentle and riding a donkey, on a colt the foal of a donkey. I will take away the chariots from Ephraim and the war-horses from Jerusalem, and the battle bow will be broken. He will proclaim peace to the nations. His rule will extend from sea to sea and from the [Euphrates] River to the ends of the earth. Zech 9:9-10

The new redeemer of Israel, the Anointed, was to install a new type of kingdom or government that would not utilize or have need of a military. Is 2:4 refers to the conversion of the production of factories from weapons and artillery to that of agricultural implements. Military preparation, training and enlistment will terminate in this new kingdom. Is 9:5 refers to the destruction of weapons and armaments.

The Anointed possessing the title of Sovereign of Peace refers to his reign over a kingdom that is not engaged in military service, preparation or conflict. Under the Anointed, the military would desist and the citizens of his kingdom will be adherents of peaceful coexistence with all other nations and nationalities. War will cease to exist in the kingdom of the Anointed.

## 2. THE GOSPEL OF THE PRINCE OF PEACE

There are many incidents that occurred in the 100 years before the ministry of Jesus that serve as preliminary events molding the character of discontents in the Jewish nation, that would lead to 2 wars of unprecedented proportions. In the summer of 63 BC, Pompey's entrance into Jerusalem was essentially bloodless and without resistance – the city just surrendered itself to him. It was not as easy to gain control over the temple area. No less than 12,000 Jews died as Pompey's troops captured the temple area and secured it under their control. Thus began the odious Roman military occupation of Judea. Rebellions were regular: in 56 BC under Aristobulus; in 53-51 BC a revolt was led by Pitholaus, where 30,000 Jews were captured and sold as slaves;[132] in 47 BC, a rebellion was led by the robber chief Hezekiah; Herod the Great's siege and storm of Jerusalem in 37 BC, where as many that his soldiers could lay their hands on were murdered; 45 elders executed by Herod in 36 BC; the rebellion against Archelaus in 4 BC shortly after the death of Herod the Great; the burning of Sepphoris by King Aretus; and the crucifixion of 2,000 Jews of Jerusalem by Varus, governor of Syria.[133] The Zealots formed their group during this era, an extremely fanatical patriotic group who organized the resistance against Roman occupation.

The leaders selected to govern Judea only increased the odium of the populace, such as the rule of Archelaus, who was tyrannical. He is mentioned in the NT, in the account where Joseph decided to travel directly to Nazareth instead of Jerusalem because of fear. Archelaus had the worst reputation of any of Herod's posterity, and he was so violent that Augustus Caesar deposed him in 6 AD.

Pontius Pilate was governor of Judea during the ministry of Jesus, 26-36 AD, but the contemporary historical account of his rule does not give him any credit. One gospel account mentions that he sent his soldiers to kill some devotees as they were offering sacrifice in the temple. Luke 13:1.

---

[132] Schurer, Emil, *A History of the Jewish People at the Time of Christ*, 1st Div. Vol 1, pgg 374-375.
[133] ibid, 1st Div. Vol 2, pgg 4-5.

As Philo recorded his opinion of Pilate:

> His corruption, his acts of violence, and his rapine, and his habit of insulting people, and his cruelty, and his continual murders of people untried and uncondemned, and his never ending, and gratuitous, and most grievous inhumanity.[134]

As far as the people of Judea were concerned, and their civic and religious leaders, they all agreed on one primary point during the rule of Pontius Pilate, and that was by any means to somehow be freed from the authority of Roman occupation.[135] As a result, the people sought a militarist Anointed or Messiah to deliver them from Roman military occupation, one who would arrive as a genuine son of King David, and would rid the country of Romans in the same manner that David rid the country of the Philistines. The women sang about King David, how he killed his tens of thousands, and this is the type of Messiah that Judea of that era sought for. They did not want an Anointed who was to tell them to reconcile themselves with the occupation, or to turn the other cheek and suffer offenses, or to put down their weapons, or not get angry with anyone. The Zealots and discontent residents wanted a militarist Anointed, who would gather an army and go to war against the Romans, which they did to their own devastation in the Jewish War of 66-70 AD. Eventually they found him in Simon Bar Kosiba, who was renamed Bar Kochba, Son of the Star, an allusion to Num 24:17, and actually thought he was the militarist Anointed. He was confirmed as their deliverer from Roman occupation by Rabbi Akiva. Bar Kosiba led Judea to their final devastation in the war of 132-135 AD, which was suppressed by Emperor Hadrian.

This leads us to the following conclusion: The primary purpose of the gospel taught by Jesus to his Jewish countrymen was to curb the rebellion and civil war that Jesus realized was going to occur in the future if the Jews continued their enmity against the Roman occupation that they had at present. When the angel appeared to Joseph in a dream and told him to name the future child of Mary Jesus, it was because the child was going to "Save his people from their sins." The sins referred to were the sins of violence against the Roman occupation: vendetta and reprisal for the

---

[134] Philo, *On the Embassy to Gaius*, (tr. by C.D. Yonge) XXVIII (par. 302)
[135] Schurer, Emil, *A History of the Jewish People at the Time of Christ*, 1st Div. Vol 2, pg 4.

oppression, execution and enslavement of their residing in Judea. The gospel of the Kingdom was taught in order to turn the discontent populace away from executing vengeance and preparing further revolt and rebellion against the Roman military occupation. As Prince of Peace, Jesus attempted to reconcile the 2 groups: Jewish native subjects and Roman foreign occupiers. The gospel of the Kingdom would then expand to terminate all war, reprisal and aggression on earth for those that would accept Jesus as the Prince of Peace.

In summary, the purpose of the preaching of the gospel of the Kingdom of God and the principles of Christian tenets as taught by Jesus during his ministry was the abolition or elimination of war through either reconciliation between parties, or refusal to participate in violence, reprisal or aggression.

## THE MESSAGE OF JOHN THE BAPTIZER

John the Baptizer was the last of the OT prophets, so his injunction to the soldiers who came to him for divine counsel was in the light of the OT precepts for members of the military: for the soldier not be dishonest or unnecessarily violent, or discontent with their wages. His words, "Do violence to no person," applied to unjust use of force that was so prevalent in occupation armies, who would tend to take advantage of their foreign subjects.

John as a prophet of God had the ability to see distant into the future, to see the result or culmination of the path that the people of Israel were taking. What he saw was the great and terrible day of *Yahweh* God, His judgment upon Israel for their sins. If the older generation and younger generation were not reconciled, then for sure war would erupt and the nation would be devastated by the Romans. If he did not prepare the people for their acceptance of the Anointed, Jesus of Nazareth, for sure *Yahweh* would smite the land with a curse. Mal 4:6. This is what the ministry of John the Baptizer consisted of: the reconciliation of the generations, for them to abide in harmony with a common goal, and the preparation of the people through the baptism by water for the remission of sins, so they could accept the gospel of the divine kingdom as taught by Jesus and his disciples.

When Pharisees and Sadducees came to him to be baptized, John said to them, "Who warned you to flee from the wrath to come." Matt 3:7. The wrath to come was the devastation John saw in the distant future, defeat and devastation by the Romans, if the people would not repent. In these words John chided the Pharisees and Sadducees, informing them that their self-righteousness served as a hindrance to their repentance. He preached to them in Matt 3:7-10, wanting them to desist in their self-righteous and haughty attitude and to show in their life conduct characteristic of repentant individuals. No doubt John hoped that his message would turn Israel away from the vein of thinking that the population had now been inculcated with for several decades and so alter its course of eventual defeat and devastation.

## JESUS THE ANOINTED OF GOD

Violence in previous generations only decimated the population of Israel, devastated the land and brought more tragedy to the nation. The Jews were ill-equipped to defeat a powerful and formidable enemy such as Rome. The manner proposed by Jesus to deliver the nation from devastation was by reconciling the people as individuals with the Roman occupation. Peaceful coexistence was the sole means of the survival of Israel under Roman occupation.

When Jesus said, "Resist not evil," he was not speaking of the general law of retribution for a crime committed. Matt 5:39. Crime must be resisted and dealt with judicially. In this context the words of not resisting evil are followed by the attitude that the soldiers of Roman occupation had toward the Jews: abusing them in public; illegal appropriation of their property; demands of the Jews for transport, food and other services. Jesus was requiring his fellow Jews to be tolerant of this mistreatment by the Roman soldiers, and not seek retribution or vengeance. Eventually the divine kingdom will gain the victory if the Jews place their hope in *Yahweh* God and not their revolutionary leaders.

When Jesus said, "You have heard that it was said in olden times, Love you neighbor and hate your enemy. But I say unto you, Love your enemies and pray for those who persecute you," (Matt 5:44) he was not referring to any enemy in general, because nowhere in Scripture does it say to hate your enemy. Even when Moses dictates to the people of Israel to annihilate the nations of Canaan he does not utilize the word hate. There was a difference between the necessity of executing the judgment of *Yahweh* God upon the identified enemy in organized warfare in OT times and the judgment upon a criminal, and the attitude of hate. In reality there is no reason to hate anybody. Hate is an emotion; execution of a criminal is judgment. Regularly David, king and psalm-writer, relates vengeance and retribution on enemies. Ps 41:10. But the explicit statement to hate an enemy is not to be found.

This concept of hating an enemy evolved during the era of the Hasmonaens and their struggle for independence from Greek occupation and Hellenic philosophical invasion. 1 Macc 4:18. This attitude again surfaced with the Roman occupation beginning in 65 BC, and which climaxed under the rule of Herod the Great during the final decade of his life. The freedom fighters and many of the Jewish hierarchy taught the people to hate the Romans, and which only caused a greater rift between the residents and the occupation forces. This resulted in the massacre of tens of thousands of Jews during the reign of Herod the Great. Jewish children were inculcated with the attitude from childhood that the Roman occupation forces were the enemy and should be hated. Jesus wanted them to change their vein of thinking from that which was prevalent during his era, and so curb further conflict.

When Jesus told his disciples, "Bless those that curse you and do good to those who hate you," he referring to a change of attitude the Jews must undergo toward the Roman occupation force, if they wanted to avoid total annihilation in the future. Matt 5:44. The victory over the enemy was to be gained by reconciliation. This change of attitude by the Jewish population of Palestine towards the Roman occupation forces would deliver them from their enemies. Luke 1:68-71. The divine kingdom would then flourish in the new divine Israel coincidental with peaceful coexistence. His would materialize as a divine community flourishing within a secular government.

Growing up in Nazareth only 3 miles from the political center of Galilee, the city Sepphoris, and traveling with his father in the carpentry business throughout most of Galilee, Jesus was well familiar with the political unrest of the area. It was in Galilee that violent overthrow was conceived by disenchanted and oppressed Jews seeking independence, and all of this Jesus saw during those years living in Nazareth. He also saw the regiments of Roman troops in rank and file marching down the main roads and highways with their banners, and the armed disciplined soldiers making their presence known to all the residents.

As a prophet Jesus saw in the distant future the annihilation of his people if this course of adverse political action against Roman authority persisted. Even as a young man he heard rumors and no doubt was propositioned with invitations to join such groups, but he early realized that the Romans were no match for the unorganized Jews. The regimented military force of Rome could easily quell any disturbance or even war. These unorganized Jewish splinter groups with their own unstable leadership and lack of cohesion were no match for the well-trained and disciplined ranks of Roman soldiers, who were instilled by their leadership to savage and ruthless war. Cowardice or desertion by a Roman soldier was treason and grounds for immediate and public execution and disgrace of office. The Jews who advocated independence through violent overthrow had no such discipline or organization on such a large scale. Jesus wanted his people to show Romans that there was no intention of violent overthrown, and that the 2 uncommon nationalities could reside in a peaceful coexistence. Jesus wanted Jews to go out of their way to cooperate with Romans to show them they meant them no harm. The few revolutionaries who sought independence from Rome were to cease and desist with a cognizance that the divine kingdom was not to be gained by war and military struggle.

The relative status or relation of the 2 factions was later summarized in the parable noted in Luke 14:31-32. Here Jesus spoke of a king having an army of 10,000 who should first consider whether his military force is enough to defeat another king whose army was 20,000. The wise and intelligent king would send a delegation to conclude a peace treaty rather than risk defeat. With such a peace treaty agreed to by both parties, neither will suffer casualties and property losses. This is to the greatest benefit of the king with the smaller army, who has now secured deliverance of his entire population instead of massive and shameful defeat. This was the intent of this parable to the multitudes. Luke 14:25. Their leaders in Galilee promoting violent overthrow of Roman occupation were the king with the army of 10,000; and the Romans were the army of 20,000. If their countrymen and themselves had any wisdom at all they would seek peaceful coexistence with the Romans. In this manner they would deliver themselves from military defeat and massive devastation.

The purpose of the ministry of Jesus is disclosed in this parable. It was not armed revolt against the Romans to gain independence, but the effort on behalf of the people to them to conclude a peace treaty, peaceful coexistence with the Romans. This seems to be the most difficult point for Christianity to accept, that the primary reason for the ministry of Jesus as the Anointed was to rescue the contemporary and successive generations of Jews from annihilation and the land from devastation by the Roman military. In this manner Jesus was to rescue his people from their crimes.

This is what Jesus sensed in Judea and foresaw in the near future, 40 years in the distance. The consistent animosity of Jews towards Roman occupation embittered their lives and caused them to develop attitudes of vengeance toward their occupiers. The Roman occupation, to protect itself, increased their suspicion of Jews and executed those they suspected of treason or revolt. Barabbas is an example, who was sentenced to execution for murder, probably killing a Roman soldier during an insurrection. Armed defense and reprisal increased the savagery of the invader and occupation army, and this develops into a vicious cycle, one that Jesus hoped to terminate in Judea by telling his fellow Jews to live in love: peaceful coexistence with the Roman occupation. Although life will be difficult, less lives will be lost. But it was Jewish nationalism that defeated the gospel of the Prince of Peace, and the result was the defeat of the Jewish nation: a million dead, a million taken into captivity, and the devastation of the country in the years 66-70 AD, and total annihilation in 132-135 AD. By refusing the message taught by their Anointed, the Jews crucified Jesus and won the battle – but they lost the war.

## THE GOSPEL OF THE DIVINE KINGDOM

John the Baptizer first taught the people the good news of the divine kingdom of God. Matt 3:1. After John was committed to prison, shortly after the 40 day fast of Jesus in the desert, Jesus began the proclamation saying, "The time is fulfilled, and the kingdom of heaven is arriving. Repent and believe in the good news." Mark 1:15. The gospel of the divine kingdom was the primary topic of the ministry of Jesus during his 3-1/2 year career. The 12 disciples and later the 70 disciples were sent to preach the good news of the divine kingdom to all the Jews. Matt 10:7. Jesus continued to teach his apostles about the divine kingdom after his resurrection and to the time of his ascension to heaven. Acts 1:3. Apostle Paul taught this gospel throughout his ministry. Acts 28:31. The members of the Messianic assembly at Colossae entered into this divine kingdom. Col 1:13.

This kingdom taught by Jesus is not a material or corporeal government as it existed in Israel in earlier ages, or like the Roman Empire of the era or any other nation. The people accepting the gospel as proclaimed were to repent – turn their life around – and allow God to rule over their life. This would be accompanied by the people being obedient to the code of conduct and morality of the Bible. Jesus said to Nicodemus, that those born of the word (water) and of the Spirit would enter this kingdom. John 3:6.

The divine kingdom materialized on Pentecost among the 120 gathered in the upper room when the holy Spirit descended upon them. With the baptism of the Spirit they spiritually entered the divine kingdom and became its citizens. Although they were in this world, they were members of a realm which had its capital in heaven. Although the disciples of Jesus reside in the world, they are not part of the world. John 17:16. This is a difficult facet of the divine kingdom to be able to grasp: To be in the world, but not of the world.

The establishment of the divine kingdom on this day also meant the fulfillment of the prophesies of Isaiah, Micah and Zechariah among the members of the new kingdom of Jesus. (Evidence of this is provided in the section on the Apostolic Fathers.)

The Kingdom of Heaven – or, of God, as in some of the Gospels – transcends the secular states of this world. If a person is a member of this divine Kingdom then he cannot identify himself with the defense or patriotism of the secular states of this world. The present world is temporal and will soon pass away like the change of scenes on a stage, but the Kingdom of Heaven is eternal. This inheritance is presently reserved for us in heaven, and will be revealed at the proper time, at the descent of the holy, heavenly city Jerusalem, our residence for eternity. Why defend a polity or state, then, if it is temporal and if we ourselves are alien from it? The genuine Christian defends the Kingdom of Heaven by testifying to it and refuses to deny it, even if it leads to his own death. The divine kingdom cannot be defended by physical means because it is in heaven, and such a kingdom is unassailable, and so has no need of physical defense. Only the kingdoms of this world require a physical defense.

This is the reason why Jesus reprimanded disciple Peter, who told him not to suffer in Jerusalem. Matt 16:22-23. Peter could not grasp the fact that no matter what should occur to Jesus – even his death – the divine Kingdom is not harmed, because it is unassailable. Even if all the

Christians in the world would die as a result of persecution, and all Christian establishments were closed, the Kingdom of Heaven would endure and continue unaffected, because it is unassailable.

The Gospel of the Kingdom of Heaven was preached to the Jews for them to realize that the Anointed came to introduce a kingdom that transcended the secular kingdom that they awaited. To grasp the Kingdom of Heaven, the Jews had to detach themselves from the physical kingdom and transcend it. To place this concept into its historical context, Jesus wanted the Jews to understand the divine concept of the Kingdom of Heaven, that is was not earthly, but heavenly; not secular, but divine. And if they were citizens of a kingdom that was in heaven, no longer would they have a citizenship in their earthly kingdom of Israel or retain patriotism or the need for its defense. This being the cause, there would then be no reason to defend their physical state from Roman occupation and seek a militarist Anointed. Their drive for independence would vanish because something greater would take its place. By accepting the concept of the divine kingdom, reprisal against the Romans would end, and so would the possibility of a civil war, thus fulfilling the words of the angel to Joseph, saving the people from the consequences of their sins. They would no longer consider the Roman occupation their enemy, because only the physical states have enemies, while the enemy of the divine Kingdom is spiritual, it is sin. This is why Jesus said, in reference to the Roman occupation, "Love your enemy," meaning, do not consider the Roman occupation your enemy, because you are citizens of the divine kingdom in heaven.

The same concept applies to the present for genuine Christians who are citizens of the Kingdom of Heaven. They transcend the present secular governments with no obligation to defend the country of their residency from enemies, because these other countries are not their enemy. Other countries are the enemy of the residents who consider themselves citizens and patriots of the physical country, but they are not the enemy of the genuine Christian.

## THE TESTIMONY OF JESUS CHRIST

When Jesus stood before Pontius Pilate, he was asked if he was a king. Jesus answered in these words, "My kingdom is not of this world." John 18:36. Pilate could not grasp the concept of a person being a ruler over some intangible or incorporeal government or realm. He was perplexed, but then concluded that Jesus was of no threat to his rule as governor over Judea or to the Roman Empire, and so wanted to free him.

The Jews persecuting Jesus likewise could not grasp his message and preferred a militant king who would gather an army and lead Israel to overthrow the Romans and institute a material kingdom similar to those of Old Testament eras. They could not fathom the concept that the Messianic Kingdom of the New Testament is the spiritual Kingdom of God.

That violence is not a solution to a conflict of ideas or physical altercation was exemplified by Jesus when he was arrested by the Roman soldiers.

> And behold one of those [Peter] who were with Jesus stretched out his hand and drew his sword and struck the slave of the high priest, and cut off his ear. Then Jesus said to him, "Put your sword back into its place; for all who take the sword will perish by the sword." Matt 26:51-52.

Jesus followed this reprimand of Peter by healing the wound on the soldier, and then stating that if it was the will of God that he should defend himself from the arresting officers, he could summon Angels from heaven to rescue him. Matt 26:53.

In the Sermon on the Mount, the most studied and applicable passage of the New Testament for disciples of Jesus, he makes 3 profound statements.

> "You have heard it said of old, Do not kill, and whoever kills will be liable to judgment. But I say to you, that every one who is angry with his brother will be liable to judgment." Matt 5:21-22
> "You have heard it said, And eye for an eye and a tooth for a tooth. But I say to you, Do not resist one who is evil. But if any one strikes you on the right cheek, turn to him the other also." Matt 5:38-39.
> "You have heard it was said, You will love your neighbor and hate your enemy. But I say to you, Love your enemies and pray for those who persecute you." Matt 5:43-44.

In these passages Jesus forbid his disciples to kill and be violent, or even to become angry. As the Anointed of Israel, Jesus perfected the law of

God, and taught that no longer was violence, hate, anger, malice, or vengeance to exist among the members of his new church.

Armed combat and military service now terminates with the establishment of the divine kingdom: they are the Church of the Anointed, the adherents of the New Covenant, the disciples of Jesus. The fulfillment of the prophesies of Isaiah, Micah and Zechariah materialize in the divine kingdom under the Redeemer of Israel, the Anointed, Jesus of Nazareth. The concept of Christian pacifism and non-resistance to aggression and violence under the Prince of Peace replaces the military struggle against enemies under the ancient kingdom of Israel, now obsolete. No more are the members of God's people to become involved in the manufacture of weapons and military equipment; this vocation is replaced by those that promote the society and are aimed toward peace and harmony. They are non-violent in every situation and refuse retaliation for offenses or aggression, realizing that there is no justification to violence in any situation, even if means a person's own injury or death.

Jesus said to his disciples, "The disciple is not above his teacher and a servant is not above his master." Matt 10:24. Jesus conducted himself in a non-violent manner when persecuted, and so should his disciples and servants. 1 Pet 2:22-23.

## THE REAL WAR

For the true Christian, the real war is a spiritual war. It is the war against sin, against the lust of the flesh, and the victory is gained in defeating temptation. Apostle Paul defined it in the following terms:

> Put on the entire armor of God that you may be able to stand against the wiles of the devil. For we do not contend against flesh and blood, but against the principalities, against the power, against the world rulers of this present darkness, against the spiritual hosts of wickedness in the heavenly places. Eph 6:11-12.

Apostle Paul wrote the letter to the Ephesians during his 2 year imprisonment at Caesarea. Roman soldiers stationed in the prison as sentries, and no doubt an entire regiment or battalion always in training for combat. This led Apostle Paul to utilize the vocation and gear of the secular soldier as an analogy to apply to the real war of the spiritual soldier. The enemy according to Apostle Paul is not flesh and blood, it is not the person on the battlefield. The real enemy is the impulse inside a person that causes him and her to inflict damage and act violently. Sin and lust is the real enemy, and the real victory is gained when temptation is defeated. Apostle James also realized this.

> What causes wars, and what causes fighting among you? It is not your passions that are at war in your members? You desire and do not have; so you kill. And you covet and cannot obtain, so you fight and wage war. Jam 4:1-2.

The apostle Paul described it in the following terms:

> For though we walk in the flesh, we are not waging war according to the flesh. For the weapons of our warfare are not of the flesh but have divine power to destroy strongholds. We destroy arguments and every lofty opinion raised against the knowledge of God, and take every thought captive to obey the Anointed... 2 Cor 10:3-5

The real war is against the flawed nature of humanity which contains this impulse of aggression and retaliation. The real war is won with faith, the gospel of peace, which is reconciliation, and with a knowledge of the word of God, knowing how a person should conduct himself. Using these spiritual weapons a person can defend themselves from temptation and gain the spiritual victory.

## ATTEMPT OF A GOSPEL JUSTIFICATION OF WAR

NT evidence for the justification of war will is abundant in the many volumes on the topic in historical Christianity. I will defuse these arguments with a comparison with statements in the NT that they utilize.

In the Sermon on the Mount, Jesus taught his disciples to love their enemies, and this referred to the Roman occupation. The incident of Matt 8:5-13, is a good example of how Jesus put his words into action: Jesus acted charitably to the person who held his people in contempt as political subjects and occupied their territory. The concern of the soldier was his servant, paralyzed and seriously ill, perhaps even near death, and so he, a Roman, was desperate to find someone who would heal him. The Roman soldier was willing to subject himself to a Jewish faith healer – this is probably the manner that the soldier approached Jesus – whom he had heard of: this was the faith that Jesus commended. Jesus as a prophet knew that by commending this faith – or perhaps desperation – of a Roman willing to condescend to a Jew, and by healing the servant, he could display compassion to the soldier and indicate to him that the Jews were not his enemies.

> When Jesus heard him, he marveled, and said to those who followed him, "Truly, I say to you, not even in Israel have I found such faith." Matt 8:11.

Viewing this statement from the perspective of Jesus' precept to love their enemies, by commending his faith and healing the servant, Jesus displayed love to the enemy of the Jews – the Roman occupation. Jesus overcame evil with good. Rom 12:21. It is obvious that Jesus intended that an act of charity of this type toward the soldier would convince him that the Jews were really not his enemies, and then the soldier would no longer see the need to continue being a soldier and so resign. One of the most quoted passages to defend the military vocation is this comment of Jesus to the Roman centurion, yet its intent is entirely opposite. There is no evidence in this passage that because Jesus complemented his faith, and did not directly reprimand him for his vocation, that Jesus was indirectly approving of, if not at least condoning, his vocation as a soldier in Rome's army.

    The same logic can be applied to the visit of Apostle Peter to the home of Cornelius the Roman centurion in Act 10. Peter going to the home of Cornelius and preaching the gospel to him, and them receiving the gift of the Holy Spirit, was the manner that Peter showed love to his enemy: the Roman occupation. Through this act of charity Peter impressed on Cornelius that he was not their enemy, but now, having received the new birth from above, Cornelius and his household were now Peter's brothers and sisters in Jesus. From this point on, Cornelius was to no longer consider either Jews or the members of the new Messianic community his enemy, and he would eventually cease his vocation as a soldier.

    That Jesus or Apostle Peter approved of such a vocation as a soldier in commending the faith of the soldier and Cornelius has no more validity than Apostle James approving the vocation of a prostitute by commending the faith of Rahab in James 2:25. I doubt very much that Rahab continued her business among the people of Israel after her and her family's deliverance from the divine demolition of Jericho.

Herding animals out of the temple area can hardly be utilized as a comparable event to the vocation of a soldier and the practice and atrocities of warfare. John 2:14, Matt 21:12. The whip used by Jesus was made of the ropes that tied to cattle together. Apparently, Jesus first untied the cattle, then used the ropes to herd them out of the temple premises. As the Anointed, Jesus had the right to reprimand those who corrupted the true worship of God in his Father's house. Jesus impressed on the Sadducees their corruption of temple worship by upsetting the tables of the money changes and driving out the sacrificial animals for sale. In each case they ignored him and shortly after continued their business practices. The point of discussion applicable is whether Jesus would have defended himself if attacked by these religious criminals. He would not have, just as he did not defend himself when arrested.

The final passage to be discussed is the statement of Jesus to his disciples just prior to leaving the Passover for the garden of Gethsemane.

> And they said, "Look Lord, here are two swords." And he said to them, "It is enough." Luke 22:38.

If Jesus really thought that 2 swords were enough to defend him, he was far from right. Viewing the incident objectively, what good would only 2 swords serve among 12 of them against a crowd of soldiers and temple servants who had swords and clubs. To think that Jesus felt 2 swords were enough to defend him against his arrest is ludicrous. The passage of Luke 22:35-38 requires interpretation as an allegory, interpreted in the light of the use of swords in similar passages, such as Matt 10:34-35, Luke 2:35, Eph 6:17, and Heb 4:12. As Jean Lassere interpreted the incident:

> By solemnly commanding them to take a purse, a scrip, and a sword, He wanted to make them understand through striking imagery that the hour had come for them to prepare themselves for a tragic spiritual battle. They would need a supply of moral forces and a spiritual pugnacity to help them overcome the ordeal of their dispersion and the despair in which He would leave them by His

death. For then each of them could count on his own resources alone.[136]

Jean Calvin likewise provided a similar conclusion:

> It was truly shameful and stupid ignorance that the disciples, after having been so often informed about bearing the cross, imagine that they must fight with *swords* of iron. When they say that they have *two swords,* it is uncertain whether they mean that they are well prepared against their enemies, or complain that they are ill provided with arms. It is evident, at least, that they were so stupid as not to think of a spiritual enemy.[137]

That the disciples misinterpreted Jesus statement to sell their mantle and purchase a sword is evidenced when one of the disciples, Peter, actually used the sword to defend Jesus when the soldiers attempted to arrest him.

> And behold one of those [Peter] who were with Jesus stretched out his hand and drew his sword and struck the slave of the high priest, and cut off his ear. Then Jesus said to him, "Put your sword back into its place; for all who take the sword will perish by the sword." Matt 26:51-52.

Jesus followed this reprimand of Peter by healing the wound on the soldier, and then stating that if it was the will of God that he should defend himself from the arresting officers, he could summon Angels from heaven to rescue him. Matt 26:53

The law was superceded by the gospel, however, because of necessity, militarist Christendom grasps one of the tenets that were made obsolete by the death and resurrection of Jesus and utilizes every passage in the NT to prove that it has not been abolished. The several statements of Jesus in the Sermon on the Mount, where the old law was replaced by a new mode of conduct that contain the phrase, "You have heard it said of old,… but I say unto you,…" likewise pertain to war, reprisal and violent aggression. Christendom dismisses Moses and the laws of his dispensation to justify Christian freedom, except in the case of Christian freedom from war. Then

---

[136] Lassere, Jean, *War and the Gospel*, pg. 42.
[137] Calvin, Jean, *Commentaries*, Luke 22:38

Christendom applies the OT with full force as its justification, even though the general trend of the gospel is that of peace and reconciliation and endurance of offense and abuse without reprisal.

To use human weakness as an excuse to not observe the command to not be angry with your brother, or not to turn the other cheek, is no different than using the same excuse to violate any other command of God, which ever one it might be. If we are unable to observe the command then it is our attitude we should change, not the gospel. We should pray for the strength to follow in the footsteps of Jesus and not revile in return when we are reviled, not threaten in return when we are threatened, and die to sin and live to righteousness. If we are unable to turn the other cheek, put down that weapon, not become angry with someone, love our enemy, and suffer even unto death, the problem is not with the commands of Jesus, but with us, and we must change our attitude through prayer and fasting and penance to conform to his example.

## 3. THE FIRST THREE CENTURIES

During the initial 150 years after the ministry of Jesus the members of the newly-formed Christian churches, or Messianic communities as they rightly should be called, abstained from combat and military service. The earliest of these were the Messianic Jews of the apostolic period: the Ebionities and Nazoraens. These Jews fled Judea to Pella, on the east side of the Jordan River by prophecy to escape the invasion of Judea by the Roman army, the Jewish War and the devastation of the country, which occurred in the years 66-70 AD. Their migration fulfilled the prophecy of Dan 11:41. The Jewish Christians of Judea were delivered from catastrophe on the east side of the Jordan River and Dead Sea, according to Eusebius, the church historian. None of the Messianic Jews joined the Jewish revolutionaries or took up arms to defend their country from invasion by the Roman army or in the defense of Jerusalem during the siege.[138]

Although the Ebionites and Nazarenes were accused of being legalistic, nonetheless, they were pacifist, having accepted the gospel directly from Jesus and his immediate listeners and disciples. After the final defeat of Jerusalem under Hadrian in the war of 132-135 AD, and the conversion of the city into the Roman Aelia Capitolina, some of the Nazarenes were able to return to the city as Christians and not as Jews and resettled there. Edward Gibbon noted the following regarding these earliest of Christians:

> Their simplicity was offended by the use of oaths, by the pomp of magistracy, and by the active contention of public life; nor could their humane ignorance be convinced that it was lawful on any occasion to shed the blood of our fellow-creatures, either by the sword of justice, or by that of war; even though their criminal or hostile attempts should threaten the peace and safety of the whole community. It was acknowledged, that, under a less perfect law, the powers of the Jewish constitution had been exercised, with the approbation of Heaven, by inspired prophets and by anointed kings.

---

[138] Eusebius, *Ecclesiastical History*, book 3, chapter 5.

The Christians felt and confessed that such institutions might be necessary for the present system of the world, and they cheerfully submitted to the authority of their Pagan governors.

But while they inculcated the maxims of passive obedience, they refused to take any active part in the civil administration or the military defense of the empire. Some indulgence might, perhaps, be allowed to those persons who, before their conversion, were already engaged in such violent and sanguinary occupations; but it was impossible that the Christians, without renouncing a more sacred duty, could assume the character of soldiers, of magistrates, or of princes. This indolent, or even criminal disregard to the public welfare, exposed them to the contempt and reproaches of the Pagans who very frequently asked, what must be the fate of the empire, attacked on every side by the barbarians, if all mankind should adopt the pusillanimous sentiments of the new sect. To this insulting question the Christian apologists returned obscure and ambiguous answers, as they were unwilling to reveal the secret cause of their security; the expectation that, before the conversion of mankind was accomplished, war, government, the Roman empire, and the world itself, would be no more.

It may be observed, that, in this instance likewise, the situation of the first Christians coincided very happily with their religious scruples, and that their aversion to an active life contributed rather to excuse them from the service, than to exclude them from the honors, of the state and army.[139]

If we seriously consider the purity of the Christian religion, the sanctity of its moral precepts, and the innocent as well as austere lives of the greater number of those who during the first ages embraced the faith of the gospel, we should naturally suppose, that so benevolent a doctrine would have been received with due reverence, even by the unbelieving world; that the learned and the polite, however they may deride the miracles, would have esteemed the virtues, of the new sect; and that the magistrates, instead of persecuting, would have protected an order of men who yielded the

---

[139] Gibbon, Edward *Decline and Fall of the Roman Empire*, vol 1, chapter 15, part 5.

most passive obedience to the laws, though they declined the active cares of war and government.[140]

Other historians note the following:

> For the first three centuries, no Christian writing that has survived to our time condoned Christian participation in war.[141]
> But as a matter of fact, there is no trace of the existence of any Christian soldiers between these cases mentioned in Acts and say, 170 AD.[142]
> It is thus not surprising that there was no military question in the congregations until roughly the time of Marcus Aurelius.[143] The baptized Christians did not become a soldier, and those who were converted to the Christian faith in the camp had to determine how they might come to terms with their soldier's life.[144]

All available testimony regarding the earliest of Christians – both Jewish and gentile – prevails in indicating that the members of the original Messianic communities refused to be part of the Roman military, as well as government in general. The reasons for the vocation of a soldier being offensive to a Christian are very apparent when comparing the Christian teaching to the expected responsibilities of a soldier: Christianity on principle rejected war and bloodshed; the soldiers would have to execute criminals; the unconditional oath of the soldier that the supreme authority was the Emperor was in conflict with sole allegiance to the God and Father of Jesus; the cult of the emperor was strong in the armed forces and no soldier could avoid it; sacrifices to pagan gods were regularly offered by officers, and soldiers were required to participate; the military standards were identified with pagan deities and the emperor; the general conduct of soldiers conflicted with the high moral standards of the NT; the soldiers participated in various festivals, parades and amusements that deviated from the NT teaching.[145]

---

[140] Gibbon, vol 1, chapter 16, part 1.
[141] Latourette, K.C., *A History of Christianity*, Vol. 1, pg. 242-243.
[142] Cadoux, C. John, *The Early Christian Attitude toward War*, pg. 229.
[143] Roman Emperor, 161-180 AD.
[144] Harnack, Adolf, *Militia Christi*, pg. 69.
[145] Harnack, pg. 65.

The first notice of a person professing to be Christian that was in the service of the Roman military was about 150 years after Jesus concluded his ministry, and they were vehemently censured for it, and it was another 150 years before any writer or apologist who was a professing Christian condoned the profession of a soldier in the Roman army. These men who were in the military in about 170 AD, based on the evidence that is available, were baptized into the religion while still soldiers, but were not required to leave their military vocation by the local bishop or congregation. The most probable reason was that no war was in progress at the time, and the bishop was morally too weak to require the novitiate's resignation or the novitiate felt no reason to resign.

However it was during this same period that Tertullian wrote his several treatises against Roman military service, and so did Irenaus, Clement of Alexandria, Origin and Cyprian. No doubt they had heard of professing Christian novitiates who were soldiers and who saw no need to resign from their vocation as a professional soldier, and especially in time of peace. The compromise with the state began at the local parish level, which motivated the apologists to refute the compromise immediately with their treatises, lest the practice further spread to other parishes and other morally weak bishops.

The evidence provided by the apologists of the ante-Nicene era, from the beginning of the $2^{nd}$ century to the early $4^{th}$ century, indicates that the Christian religion was different than the balance of religions and philosophies in the Roman Empire in its attitude towards war and military service. They identified the insignias, flags, oaths, and practices of the military with pagan and idolatrous rites. The conduct of military personal in peacetime was corrupt, amoral and obscene, while in war it was the most inhumane and barbaric, no different than our present era.

The gospel the apologists received from the apostles and their direct spiritual descendents was that the cessation of war and its preparation was fulfilled in Jesus, and that a renouncement of military service was required for the members of the Christian church. This attitude was not retained easily by the Christian of early centuries and especially due to persecution. Some Christians succumbed to the pressure of the military and accepted service, and their history is also noted in the annals of the apologists. Persecution against Christians occurred regularly in the Roman Empire and many who refused military service were executed. The worst of the persecutions was under Diocletian, beginning 303 AD, and until 312 AD.

The following are excerpts from the apologists of the 2nd and 3rd century. They reflect the attitudes and practices of Christians during the early centuries prior to the Council of Nicea. Not every writer of the period will be mentioned, and not every passage dealing with this topic from the writers selected, but only the more influential and popular. The authors are also from various segments of the Roman Empire, including North Africa, Europe and Middle East. This will provide sufficient evidence of the conscientious objection nature and attitude of the Christian churches of the first three centuries.

## TERTULLIAN

The primary witness to the exclusion of early followers and disciples of the teachings of Jesus to military conscription is Tertullian. He was also a Montanist during part of his life, and would have inherited his conviction from them regarding Christian pacifism. He was the first of the great Latin apologists, writing 160-220 AD, having his center of ministry in northern Africa. The following passage is from Tertullian's treatise *On Idolatry*.

Chapter XIX. - Concerning Military Service.
In that last section, decision may seem to have been given likewise concerning military service, which is between dignity and power. But now inquiry is made about this point, whether a believer may turn himself unto military service, and whether the military may be admitted unto the faith, even the rank and file, or each inferior grade, to whom there is no necessity for taking part in sacrifices or capital punishments. There is no agreement between the divine and the human sacrament, the standard of Christ and the standard of the devil, the camp of light and the camp of darkness. One soul cannot be due to two masters-God and Caesar. And yet Moses carried a rod, and Aaron wore a buckle, and John (the Baptizer) is girt with leather and Joshua the son of Nun leads a line of march; and the People warred: if it pleases you to sport with the subject. But how will a Christian man war, nay, how will he serve even in peace, without a sword, which the Lord has taken away? For albeit soldiers had come unto John, and had received the formula of their rule; albeit, likewise, a centurion had believed; still the Lord afterward, in disarming Peter,

disarmed every soldier. No uniform is lawful among us, if assigned to any unlawful action.[146]

The introductory paragraph to the *De Chaplet or Corona* (*Treatise on the Crown*) is a narrative of a soldier who can no longer be a member of the Roman military. More than likely, and in the tradition of the Roman military, he was executed for desertion.

> Chapter I.
> Very lately it happened thus: while the bounty of our most excellent emperors was dispensed in the camp, the soldiers, laurel-crowned, were approaching. One of them, more a soldier of God, more steadfast than the rest of his brethren, who had imagined that they could serve two masters, his head alone uncovered, the useless crown in his hand-already even by that peculiarity known to every one as a Christian-was nobly conspicuous. Accordingly, all began to mark him out, jeering him at a distance, gnashing on him near at hand. The murmur is wafted to the tribune, when the person had just left the ranks. The tribune at once puts the question to him, Why are you so different in your attire? He declared that he had no liberty to wear the crown with the rest. Being urgently asked for his reasons, he answered, I am a Christian. O soldier! boasting thyself in God. Then the case was considered and voted on; the matter was remitted to a higher tribunal; the offender was conducted to the prefects. At once he put away the heavy cloak, his disburdening commenced; he loosed from his foot the military shoe, beginning to stand upon holy ground; he gave up the sword, which was not necessary either for the protection of our Lord; from his hand likewise dropped the laurel crown; and now, purple-clad with the hope of his own blood, shod with the preparation of the gospel, girt with the sharper word of God, completely equipped in the apostles' armor, and crowned more worthily with the white crown of martyrdom, he awaits in prison the largess of Christ.[147]

The following is chapter 11 from the *Treatise on the Crown*.

---

[146] Ante-Nicene Fathers, vol. 3, pg. 99-100
[147] Ante-Nicene Fathers, vol. 3, pg. 99-100

Chapter XI.

To begin with the real ground of the military crown, I think we must first inquire whether warfare is proper at all for Christians. What sense is there in discussing the merely accidental, when that on which it rests is to be condemned? Do we believe it lawful for a human oath to be superadded to one divine, for a man to come under promise to another master after Christ, and to abjure father, mother, and all nearest kinsfolk, whom even the law has commanded us to honor and love next to God Himself, to whom the gospel, too, holding them only of less account than Christ, has in like manner rendered honor? Shall it be held lawful to make an occupation of the sword, when the Lord proclaims that he who uses the sword shall perish by the sword? And shall the son of peace take part in the battle when it does not become him even to sue at law? And shall he apply the chain, and the prison, and the torture, and the punishment, who is not the avenger even of his own wrongs? Shall he, forsooth, either keep watch-service for others more than for Christ, or shall he do it on the Lord's day, when he does not even do it for Christ Himself? And shall he keep guard before the temples which he has renounced? And shall he take a meal where the apostle has forbidden him? And shall he diligently protect by night those whom in the day-time he has put to flight by his exorcisms, leaning and resting on the spear the while with which Christ's side was pierced? Shall he carry a flag, too, hostile to Christ? And shall *he* ask a watchword from the emperor who has already received one from God? Shall *he* be disturbed in death by the trumpet of the trumpeter, who expects to be aroused by the angel's trump? And shall the Christian be burned according to camp rule, when he was not permitted to burn incense to an idol, when to him Christ remitted the punishment of fire? Then how many other offences there are involved in the performances of camp offices, which we must hold to involve a transgression of God's law, you may see by a slight survey. The very carrying of the name over from the camp of light to the camp of darkness is a violation of it. Of course, if faith comes later, and finds any preoccupied with military service, their case is different, as in the instance of those whom John used to receive for baptism, and of those most faithful centurions, I mean the centurion whom Christ approves, and the centurion whom Peter instructs; yet, at the same time, when a man has become a believer, and faith has been sealed, there must be either an immediate abandonment of it, which has been the course with many; or all sorts of quibbling will have to be resorted to in order to avoid offending God, and that is not allowed even outside of military service; or, last of all, for God the fate must be endured which a citizen-faith has been no less ready to accept. Neither does military service hold out escape from punishment of sins, or exemption from martyrdom. Nowhere does the Christian change his character. There is one gospel, and the same Jesus, who will one day deny every one who denies, and acknowledge every one who acknowledges God,-who will save, too, the life which has been lost for His sake; but, on the other hand, destroy that which for gain has been saved to His dishonor.[148]

Tertullian felt the allegiance given to the state through the military oath to defend the nation against all enemies as defined by their Senate to be disloyal to the true God. The oath would have included a testimony of obedience to the Roman Emperor, likewise repulsive to Tertullian. The flag or banner carried by the troops was antithesis to the spiritual signs and character traits of true Christians, and in general, all that the military entailed was antithesis to the teachings of Jesus. Tertullian also mentions that soldiers who become Christians while in the military resigned themselves from that vocation.

## CYPRIAN

Cyprian, known to be a disciple of Tertullian likewise wrote in several passages that involvement in war was unacceptable to Christians as well as unjust and hypocrisy. The following is an excerpt from his Epistles.

> The whole world is wet with mutual blood; and murder, which in the case of an individual is admitted to be a crime, is called a virtue when it is committed wholesale.[149]

Cyprian claims that it is hypocrisy to proclaim as a hero and valiant the person who will destroy and devastate the life and property of innocent

---

[148] Ante-Nicene Fathers, vol. 3, pg. 99-100
[149] Ante-Nicene Fathers, vol. 5, pg. 277

people in organized warfare, when it is considered a crime if the same occurs in peacetime.

## JUSTIN OF CAESAREA

One of the earliest apologists was Justin of Caesarea, often titled, Justin Martyr. He wrote about the years 140 to 160 AD, during the era when those who were taught by the apostles transmitted the gospel to his – the next – generation, and which original gospel was still untainted by later Greek philosophy and anti-Semitism.

Justin taught that the prophecy of Is 2:4 was fulfilled in the gospel preached by the 12 apostles, and so they ceased any involvement in war and military service. This he mentions in his *First Apology*, chapter 39:

> And when the Spirit of prophesy speaks as predicting things that are to come to pass, He speaks in this way, "For out of Zion shall go forth the law, and the word of the Lord from Jerusalem. And He shall judge among the nations, and shall rebuke many people; and they shall beat their swords in to ploughshares, and their spears into pruning hooks; nations shall not lift up sword against nation, neither shall they learn war any more.:" And that it did so come to pass, we can convince you. For from Jerusalem there went out into the world, men, twelve in number, and these illiterate, of no ability in speaking; but by the power of God they proclaimed to every race of men that they were sent by Christ to teach to all the word of God; and we who formerly used to murder one another do not only now refrain from making war upon our enemies, but also, that we may not lie nor deceive our examiners, willingly die confessing Christ.[150]

A similar definition of the fulfillment of Isaiah's prophetic words in the Messianic communities is mentioned in his *Dialogue with Trypho*, chapter 50.

> And we who were filled with war, and mutual slaughter, and every wickedness, have each through the whole earth changed our warlike weapons, - our swords into ploughs, and our spears into implements of tillage, - and we cultivate piety, righteousness, philanthropy, faith,

---

[150] Ante-Nicene Fathers, vol. 1, page 175-176

and hope, which we have from the Father Himself through Him who was crucified.[151]

In both these passages Justin indicates that the Christians of his era felt the era of military service to conclude, and the new era of pacifism to inaugurate, with Jesus.

## HYPPOLYTUS

Another early witness to Christian refusal to war and military service is the 16th Canon of the Apostolic Tradition of Hyppolytus (170-236 AD), which was composed about 215 AD in Rome:

> 16. Inquiry shall likewise be made about the professions and trades of those who are brought to be admitted to the faith. If a man is a panderer, he must desist or be rejected. If a man is a sculptor or painter, he must be charged not to make idols; if he does not desist he must be rejected. If a man is an actor or pantomimist, he must desist or be rejected. A teacher of young children had best desist, but if he has no other occupation, he may be permitted to continue. A charioteer, likewise, who races or frequents races, must desist or be rejected. A gladiator or a trainer of gladiators, or a huntsman [in the wild beast shows], or anyone connected with these shows, or a public official in charge of gladiatorial exhibitions must desist or be rejected. A heathen priest or anyone who tends idols must desist or be rejected. A soldier of the civil authority must be taught not to kill men and to refuse to do so if he is commanded, and to refuse to take an oath; if he is unwilling to comply, he must be rejected. A military commander or civic magistrate that wears the purple must resign or be rejected. If a catechumen or a believer seeks to become a soldier they must be rejected, for they have despised God. [152]

This section deals with the professions that are not acceptable practice for Christians, and which a newly-converted Christian must resign from in order to be admitted into the local Church.

---

[151] Ante-Nicene Fathers, Vol. 1, page 254
[152] Hyppolytus, *Apostolic Tradition*, part 2, section 16.

## IRENAEUS

Irenaeus had his home in southern Gaul, modern France, although he also spent much time in Rome. His writings were primarily directed against the prevalent heresy of Gnosticism during the era of 180-190 AD. The following is an except from his treatise *Against Heresies*, 4:34:4.

> But preached by the apostles – who went forth from Jerusalem – throughout all the earth, caused such a change in the state of things, that these [nations] did form the swords and war-lances into plows, and changed them into pruning hooks for reaping the corn, that is, into instruments used for peaceful purposes, and that they are now unaccustomed to fighting, but when smitten, offer the other cheek. [153]

This excerpt follows the same vein of Justin that the words of Isaiah were fulfilled in the gospel taught by Jesus, and which new mode of conduct was accepted by the gentiles of the Roman Empire.

## CLEMENT OF ALEXANDRIA

Clement taught in Alexandria, Egypt, and wrote about 190-210 AD. He inclines toward pacifism as a character trait of the Christian. The following is a passage from Clement's *Instructor*, book 1, chapter 12.

> For it is not in war, but in peace, that we are trained. War needs great preparation, and luxury craves profusion; but peace and love, simple and quiet sisters, require no arms, nor excessive preparation. The Word is their sustenance. [154]

## ORIGEN

Origen in several passages mentions pacifism as a trait of the Christians. These are primarily located in his treatise *Against Celsus*.

> And yet, if a revolt had led to the formation of the Christian commonwealth, so that it derived its existence in this way from that

---

[153] Ante-Nicene Fathers, Vol. 1, page 512
[154] Ante-Nicene Fathers, vol. 2, pg. 234-235

of the Jews, who were permitted to take up arms in defense of the members of their families, and to slay their enemies, the Christian Lawgiver would not have altogether forbidden the putting of men to death; and yet He nowhere teaches that it is right for His own disciples to offer violence to any one, however wicked. For He did not deem it in keeping with such laws as His, which were derived from a divine source, to allow the killing of any individual whatever.[155] (*Against Celsus*, 3:7)

But with regard to the Christians, because they were taught not to avenge themselves upon their enemies (and have thus observed laws of a mild and philanthropic character); and because they would not, although able, have made war even if they had received authority to do so,--they have obtained this reward from God, that He has always warred in their behalf, and on certain occasions has restrained those who rose up against them and desired to destroy them.[156] (*Against Celsus*, 3:8)

And to those who inquire of us whence we come, or who is our founder, we reply that we are come, agreeably to the counsels of Jesus, to cut down our hostile and insolent wordy swords into plows, and to convert into pruning-hooks the spears formerly employed in war. For we no longer take up sword against nation, nor do we learn war any more, having become children of peace, for the sake of Jesus, who is our leader, instead of those who our fathers followed, among whom we were strangers to the covenant.[157] (*Against Celsus*, 5:33)

In the next place, Celsus urges us "to help the king with all our might, and to labor with him in the maintenance of justice, to fight for him; and if he requires it, to fight under him, or lead an army along with him." To this our answer is, that we do, when occasion requires, give help to kings, and that, so to say, a divine help, "putting on the whole armor of God." And this we do in obedience to the injunction of the apostle, "I exhort, therefore, that first of all, supplications, prayers,

---

[155] Ante-Nicene Fathers, vol. 4, pg. 467
[156] Ante-Nicene Fathers, vol. 4, pg. 467-468
[157] Ante-Nicene Fathers, vol. 4, pg. 558

intercessions, and giving of thanks, be made for all men; for kings, and for all that are in authority;" and the more any one excels in piety, the more effective help does he render to kings, even more than is given by soldiers, who go forth to fight and slay as many of the enemy as they can. And to those enemies of our faith who require us to bear arms for the commonwealth, and to slay men, we can reply: "Do not those who are priests at certain shrines, and those who attend on certain gods, as you account them, keep their hands free from blood, that they may with hands unstained and free from human blood offer the appointed sacrifices to your gods; and even when war is upon you, you never enlist the priests in the army. If that, then, is a laudable custom, how much more so, that while others are engaged in battle, these too should engage as the priests and ministers of God, keeping their hands pure, and wrestling in prayers to God on behalf of those who are fighting in a righteous cause, and for the king who reigns righteously, that whatever is opposed to those who act righteously may be destroyed!" And as we by our prayers vanquish all demons who stir up war, and lead to the violation of oaths, and disturb the peace, we in this way are much more helpful to the kings than those who go into the field to fight for them. And we do take our part in public affairs, when along with righteous prayers we join self-denying exercises and meditations, which teach us to despise pleasures, and not to be led away by them. And none fight better for the king than we do. We do not indeed fight under him, although he require it; but we fight on his behalf, forming a special army--an army of piety--by offering our prayers to God.[158] (*Against Celsus*, 8:73)

In every passage dealing with this topic, Origen makes is clear that war and military service was abrogated by Jesus, and that Christians of his era refused to take up arms under any circumstance. Origen acknowledges that war was permitted in OT times, but now under the New Covenant, this is no longer permitted.

---

[158] Ante-Nicene Fathers, vol. 4, pg. 667-668

## ARNOBIUS

The treatise of Arnobius, *The Seven Books against the Heathen*, testifies further to Jesus' fundamental precept of prohibition of violence and bloodshed, and the preference to suffer offense, rather than to take vengeance. Arnobius further states that if all people would grasp this principle, harmony would prevail in the world. The following is a selection from Book 1:

> 6. Although you allege that those wars which you speak of were excited through hatred of our religion, it would not be difficult to prove, that after the name of Christ was heard in the world, not only were they not increased, but they were even in great measure diminished by the restraining of furious passions. For since we, a numerous band of men as we are, have learned from His teaching and His laws that evil ought not to be requited with evil, that it is better to suffer wrong than to inflict it, that we should rather shed our own blood than stain our hands and our conscience with that of another, an ungrateful world is now for a long period enjoying a benefit from Christ, inasmuch as by His means the rage of savage ferocity has been softened, and has begun to withhold hostile hands from the blood of a fellow-creature. But if all without exception, who feel that they are men not in form of body but in power of reason, would lend an ear for a little to His salutary and peaceful rules, and would not, in the pride and arrogance of enlightenment, trust to their own senses rather than to His admonitions, the whole world, having turned the use of steel into more peaceful occupations, would now be living in the most placid tranquility, and would unite in blessed harmony, maintaining inviolate the sanctity of treaties.[159]

## LACTANTIUS

Lactantius was the last of the prominent apologists prior to the era of Constantine and wrote his massive treatise The *Divine Institutes* about 300 AD. He records also the attitude of the earliest Christians toward military conscription in several sections of his apology.

---

[159] Ante-Nicene Fathers, vol. 6, pg. 415

> For when God forbids us to kill, He not only prohibits us from open violence, which is not even allowed by the public laws, but He warns us against the commission of those things which are esteemed lawful among men. Thus it will be neither lawful for a just man to engage in warfare, since his warfare is justice itself, not to accuse any one of a capital charge, because it makes no difference whether you put a man to death by word, or rather by the sword, since it is the act of putting to death itself which is prohibited.[160] (*Divine Institutes*, Bk. IV, Chap. XX)

> Or why should he carry on war, and mix himself with the passions of others, when his mind is engaged in perpetual peace with men? [The Christian] considers it unlawful not only himself to commit slaughter, but to be present with those who do it, and to behold it.[161] (*Divine Institutes*, Bk. V, Chap. XVIII)

In the *Divine Institutes*, Lactantius exposes the errors of pagan religion and the vanity of heather philosophy, and defends the Christian religion and the character of the Christian, which includes conscientious objector to war. Because the Messianic communities were a divine kingdom, enlistment in a military detachment into the service of any nation was alien to their beliefs. The thought of military conscription to wage organized war against another nation labeled as an enemy was repulsive to them.

## THE DIDIACHE

The Didiache, or Teaching of the Twelve Apostles, is also valuable because it repeats several of the commands of the Sermon on the Mount. The following the introductory chapter.

> THERE are two ways, one of life and one of death; but a great difference between the two ways. The way of life, then, is this: First, thou shalt love God who made thee; second, thy neighbor as thyself; and all things whatsoever thou wouldst should not occur to thee, thou also to another do not do. And of these sayings the teaching is this: Bless them that curse you, and pray for your enemies, and fast for

---

[160] Ante-Nicene Fathers, vol. 7. pg. 187
[161] Ante-Nicene Fathers, vol. 7. pg. 153

them that persecute you. For what thank is there, if ye love them that love you? Do not also the Gentiles do the same? But do ye love them that hate you; and ye shall not have an enemy. Abstain thou from fleshly and worldly lusts. If one give thee a blow upon thy right cheek, turn to him the other also; and thou shalt be perfect. If one impress thee for one mile, go with him two. If one take away thy cloak, give him also thy coat. If one take from thee thine own, ask it not back? for indeed thou art not able. Give to every one that asketh thee, and ask it not back; for the Father willeth that to all should be given of our own blessings (free gifts).[162]

## ATHANASIUS

Athanasius, 298-373 AD, is the transitional prelate from the era of the apologists to the Nicean era, and whose doctrines contained elements of both eras. Anathasius was Bishop of Alexandria 45 years (328-373 AD). He was a fervent opponent of the Arian doctrines, but yet was not tainted by Constantine's reformation of Christianity to meet the needs of the empire. The following are excerpts from *On the Incarnation of the Word*, written about 318 AD.

51. The New, Virtue of Continence. Revolution of Society, Purified and Pacified by Christianity:
4. For formerly, while in idolatry, Greeks and Barbarians used to war against each other, and were actually cruel to their own kin. For it was impossible for any one to cross sea or land at all, without arming the hand with swords, because of their implacable fighting among themselves. 5. For the whole course of their life was carried on by arms, and the sword with them took the place of a staff, and was their support in every emergency; and still, as I said before, they were serving idols, and offering sacrifices to demons, while for all their idolatrous superstition they could not be reclaimed from this spirit. 6. But when they have come over to the school of Christ, then, strangely enough, as men truly pricked in conscience, they have laid aside the savagery of their murders and no longer mind the things of war: but all is at peace with them, and from henceforth what makes for friendship is to their liking.

---

[162] Ante-Nicene Fathers, vol. 7, pg. 377

52. Wars, &C., Roused by Demons, Lulled by Christianity.

Who then is He that has done this, or who is He that has united in peace men that hated one another, save the beloved Son of the Father, the common Savior of all, even Jesus Christ, Who by His own love underwent all things for our salvation? For even from of old it was prophesied of the peace He was to usher in, where the Scripture says: "They shall beat their swords into ploughshares, and their pikes into sickles, and nation shall not take the sword against nation, neither shall they learn war any more." 2. And this is at least not incredible, inasmuch as even now those barbarians who have an innate savagery of manners, while they still sacrifice to the idols of their country, are mad against one another, and cannot endure to be a single hour without weapons: 3. but when they hear the teaching of Christ, straightway instead of fighting they turn to husbandry, and instead of arming their hands with weapons they raise them in prayer, and in a word, in place of fighting among themselves, henceforth they arm against the devil and against evil spirits, subduing these by self-restraint and virtue of soul. 4. Now this is at once a proof of the divinity of the Savior, since what men could not learn among idols they have learned from Him; and no small exposure of the weakness and nothingness of demons and idols. For demons, knowing their own weakness, for this reason formerly set men to make war against one another, lest, if they ceased from mutual strife, they should turn to battle against demons. 5. Why, they who become disciples of Christ, instead of warring with each other, stand arrayed against demons by their habits and their virtuous actions: and they rout them, and mock at their captain the devil; so that in youth they are self-restrained, in temptations endure, in labors persevere, when insulted are patient, when robbed make light of it: and, wonderful as it is, they despise even death and become martyrs of Christ.[163]

The testimony of Athanasius is that barbarian and pagan peoples, having heard the gospel of Jesus, change their mode of life, becoming peaceful and pacifist. Athanasius also mentions that the prophecy of Isaiah 2 is fulfilled in Jesus at the present time.

---

[163] Nicene and Post-Nicene Fathers, series 2, vol. 4, pg. 64-65

The following passage is a section of his letter dealing *On Fasting, and Trumpets, and Feasts*, written 329 AD. Athanasius states that the true war is now a spiritual war against sin and temptation, and not a physical war.

> 3. For the law was admirable, and the shadow was excellent, otherwise, it would not have wrought fear, and induced reverence in those who heard; especially in those who at that time not only heard but saw these things. Now these things were typical, and done as in a shadow. But let us pass on to the meaning, and henceforth leaving the figure at a distance, come to the truth, and look upon the priestly trumpets of our Savior, which cry out, and call us, at one time to war, as the blessed Paul saith, We wrestle not with flesh and blood, but with principalities, with powers, with the rulers of this dark world, with wicked spirits in heaven.[164]

This next selection is the letter of Athanasius *To Amun*, written before 354 AD.

> For example, it is not right to kill, yet in war it is lawful and praiseworthy to destroy the enemy; accordingly not only are they who have distinguished themselves in the field held worthy of great honors, but monuments are put up proclaiming their achievements. So that the same act is at one time and under some circumstances unlawful, while under others, and at the right time, it is lawful and permissible.[165]

Athanasius discusses in this passage the hypocrisy of Roman legislature, which prohibits murder on an individual basis, considering it a crime, but approves if it if it is executed on a massive scale by the Roman military.

## EARLY MARTYRS

Of special testimony to the pacifism of early Christians are the accounts of martyrdom for refusing military service in the Roman army. There are 2 prominent accounts that will be mentioned. The first is Maximilian, who

---

[164] Nicene and Post-Nicene Fathers, series 2, vol. 4, pg. 507, *Festal Letters*, Letter 1.
[165] Nicene and Post-Nicene Fathers, series 2, vol. 4, pg. 557

refused service on March 12, 295 AD. In the record of the proceedings, Maximilian, age 21, stated at his induction, "I cannot serve because I am a Christian." He was executed after the hearing.

The second is the martyrdom of Marcellus in 298 AD. He was a centurion in the Roman army and, while in the military, took an oath as a disciple of Jesus and was baptized. Marcellus felt that he could no longer serve in the military and removed the military insignia from himself, along with his sword and belt. Marcellus stated to Agricolanus, a military officer at the trial.

> For it is not proper for a Christian, who fears Christ the Lord, to fight for the troubles of this world.

Marcellus was sentenced to death and was executed by decapitation after the trial.

Other martyrs are also mentioned in early accounts, Dasius and Julius for example, who were already soldiers, but then decided to no longer sacrifice to the emperors, meaning, to burn incense while acknowledging his deity.[166]

---

[166] Musurillo, Herbert, *The Acts of Christian Martyrs*, pg 244-279.

## 4. THE DEVELOPMENT OF MILITARIST CHRISTENDOM

A military is an important facet of the identity and political independence of the nation because, it symbolizes the establishment of a sovereign state and which will defend its existence as a corporate entity. The military is thus designed to serve in the best interests of the state as defined by the ruling party, and to violently defend the ideals that the state represents. War benefits the political and military leadership and the industrial giants and financial institutions, while to the detriment of individuals, society and civilization. The attitude of the state is that military production and recruits are expendable and renewable.

Soldiers are trained to kill, and this is expected of them. The soldier fulfills his obligation when he kills or destroys property belonging to the enemy in a foreign land. Wars are won only by killing more of the enemy and destroying more of their property, than they destroy of you and your property. Wars are fought to be won, not to be lost. A soldier is not in the military to give his life for his country, but to make sure that the enemy gives up his life for his country and as many that he can without losing his own life in the process. Others that are members of the military have the responsibility to assist the soldier in valiantly performing his task, whether giving him the orders to kill and destroy, supplying him with the weapons or equipment necessary to perform this task, tending to his wounds if he is wounded, or by comforting and encouraging him when he loses courage. Non-combatants also support the war effort.

The migration into Christendom of the concepts of Plato regarding his militancy, and the gods of the city-state who justified the edicts of the state, and the concept of the philosopher-king, occurred easily as a result of the study of the works of Plato by the ecclesiastical apologists and theologians. As far as Augustine was concerned, Plato was more highly valued than the study of the OT. Augustine did not know Hebrew, and knew very little Greek, and was dependant solely on Latin versions of the Bible. In the *City of God*, Augustine lauds Plato:

> But among the disciples of Socrates, Plato was the one who shone with a glory which far excelled that of the others, and who not

unjustly eclipsed them all. By birth an Athenian of honorable parentage, he far surpassed his fellow-disciples in natural endowments, of which he was possessed in a wonderful degree.[167]
If then Plato defined the wise man as one who imitates, knows, loves this God, and who is rendered blessed through fellowship with Him in His own blessedness, why discuss with the other philosophers? It is evident that none come near to us than the Platonists.[168]

The further a student investigates Augustine, the more credible the premise that Augustine plagiarized Plato. Substituting Plato's good with Augustine's God, and Plato's forms with Augustine's triune deity, develops Augustine's theology. The promotion of advocacy of the study of Plato by other ecclesiastical apologists acted as a catalyst for the migration of the concepts of the *Republic* into ecumenical Christendom.

Once Constantine assumed power as philosopher-king, Plato was rebaptized as the new Jesus of the Christendom of Constantine's Roman Empire, as opposed to the Jewish Anointed proclaiming the divine kingdom. As a result of early education in the philosophy of Plato, military service was easily channeled into the doctrines of the accepted – and expected – practice of Christians.

## CONSTANTINE THE GREAT

The history of this era and its prime historical figure is of exceptional importance because of the massive metamorphosis in the Christian Church that occurred as a result of the edicts of Emperor Constantine.

Constantine was a soldier, a general of the Roman army. The turning point in the career of Constantine that was to affect Christianity was his vision at the Milvan Bridge near Rome in 312 AD, during his invasion of Italy to capture Rome, as he was preparing to battle his final competitor Maxentius for sole rule of the Roman Empire. With his army Constantine proceeded into combat and gained the victory over the army of Maxentius his opponent, and took possession of Rome. The following passage is quoted from Eusebius' *Life of Constantine*, Book 1, which was composed as a panegyric for Constantine after his death in 337 AD, (Eusebius died in 340 AD).

---

[167] Augustine, *The City of God*, book VIII, chapter 4.
[168] Augustine, book VIII, chapter 5.

CHAPTER XXVIII: How, while he was praying, God sent him a Vision of a Cross of Light in the Heavens at Mid-day, with an Inscription admonishing him to conquer by that.

ACCORDINGLY he called on him with earnest prayer and supplications that he would reveal to him who he was, and stretch forth his right hand to help him in his present difficulties. And while he was thus praying with fervent entreaty, a most marvelous sign appeared to him from heaven, the account of which it might have been hard to believe had it been related by any other person. But since the victorious emperor himself long afterwards declared it to the writer of this history, when he was honored with his acquaintance and society, and confirmed his statement by an oath, who could hesitate to accredit the relation, especially since the testimony of after-time has established its truth? He said that about noon, when the day was already beginning to decline, he saw with his own eyes the trophy of a cross of light in the heavens, above the sun, and bearing the inscription, CONQUER BY THIS. At this sight he himself was struck with amazement, and his whole army also, which followed him on this expedition, and witnessed the miracle.

CHAFFER XXIX: How the Christ of God appeared to him in his Sleep, and commanded him to use in his Wars a Standard made in the Form of the Cross.

He said, moreover, that he doubted within himself what the import of this apparition could be. And while he continued to ponder and reason on its meaning, night suddenly came on; then in his sleep the Christ of God appeared to him with the same sign which he had seen in the heavens, and commanded him to make a likeness of that sign which he had seen in the heavens, and to use it as a safeguard in all engagements with his enemies.

CHAPTER XXX: The Making of the Standard of the Cross.

AT dawn of day he arose, and communicated the marvel to his friends: and then, calling together the workers in gold and precious stones, he sat in the midst of them, and described to them the figure of the sign he had seen, bidding them represent it in gold and precious stones. And this representation I myself have had an opportunity of seeing.

CHAPTER XXXI: A Description of the Standard of the Cross, which the Romans now call the Labarum.

Now it was made in the following manner. A long spear, overlaid with gold, formed the figure of the cross by means of a transverse bar laid over it. On the top of the whole was fixed a wreath of gold and precious stones; and within this, the symbol of the Savior's name, two letters indicating the name of Christ by means of its initial characters, the letter P being intersected by X in its center: and these letters the emperor was in the habit of wearing on his helmet at a later period. From the cross-bar of the spear was suspended a cloth, a royal piece, covered with a profuse embroidery of most brilliant precious stones; and which, being also richly interlaced with gold, presented an indescribable degree of beauty to the beholder. This banner was of a square form, and the upright staff, whose lower section was of great length, bore a golden half-length portrait of the pious emperor and his children on its upper part, beneath the trophy of the cross, and immediately above the embroidered banner.

The emperor constantly made use of this sign of salvation as a safeguard against every adverse and hostile power, and commanded that others similar to it should be carried at the head of all his armies.[169]

But what Constantine actually saw in the sky was not a cross, but the Chi-Rho sign, which he placed at the top of his standard as noted above in Chapter XXXI. This is verified by Lactantius, who also records the same event, although not in the same manner as such a brilliant revelation as the record of Eusebius.

---

[169] Eusebius, *Life of Constantine*, Nicene and Post-Nicene Fathers, series 2, vol. 1. pg. 490-491

The following is the record of Lactantius from his treatise *On the Manner in which the Persecutors Died*, Chap. LXIV.

> Constantine was directed in a dream to cause the heavenly sign to be delineated on the shields of his soldiers, and so to proceed to battle. He did as he had been commanded, and he marked on their shields the letter X, with a perpendicular line drawn through it and turned round thus at the top, being the cipher of CHRIST. Having this sign, his troops stood to arms. The enemies advanced, but without their emperor, and they crossed the bridge. The armies met, and fought with the utmost exertions of valor, and firmly maintained their ground.
>
> The hand of the Lord prevailed, and the forces of Maxentius were routed. He fled towards the broken bridge; but the multitude pressing on him, he was driven headlong into the Tiber.
>
> This destructive war being ended, Constantine was acknowledged as emperor, with great rejoicings, by the senate and people of Rome.[170]

The record of Lactantius is definitely more reliable and accurate than the record of Eusebius for several reasons. Lactantius recorded his within 3 years after the event and as a historical record, while Eusebius' record was part of a panegyric on behalf of Constantine and written 26 years after the fact and after the death of Constantine. What makes Eusebius' account unpalatable is that the command is antithesis to the gospel. At no time did Jesus Christ ever advocate force, much less active armed military force, for any purpose at all. And if the vision would have stated anything at all, it would have repeated the previous commands of the NT in regard to armed struggle: for Constantine to retract and discard his weapon and those of his army, for him to overcome evil with good, to treat his enemy Maxentius with kindness and goodness, to indicate to him that they are not enemies, but could reconcile and live in peaceful accord. I see a massive disconnect between the account of Eusebius regarding Constantine and the Gospel message. Historian Philip Schaff in his history describes the more probable occurrence, and taken in the light of the more reliable account of Lactantius. Schaff provides the following version of the events:

---

[170] Ante-Nicene Fathers, vol. 7, pg. 318.

But even if we waive the purely critical objections to the Eusebian narrative, the assumed connection, in this case, of the gentle Prince of peace with the god of battle, and the subservience of the sacred symbol of redemption to military ambition, is repugnant to the genius of the gospel and to solid Christian feeling, unless we stretch the theory of divine accommodation to the spirit of the age and the passions and interests of individuals beyond ordinary limits. We should suppose, moreover, that Christ, if he had really appeared to Constantine either in person (according to Eusebius) or through angels, would have exhorted him to repent and be baptized, rather than to construct a military ensign for a bloody battle.[171]

The facts, therefore, may have been these. Before the battle Constantine, leaning already towards Christianity as probably the best and most hopeful of the various religions, seriously sought in prayer, as he related to Eusebius, the assistance of the God of the Christians, while his heathen antagonist Maxentius, according to Zosimus, was consulting the sibylline books and offering sacrifice to the idols. Filled with mingled fears and hopes about the issue of the conflict, he fell asleep and saw in a dream the sign of the cross of Christ with a significant inscription and promise of victory. Being already familiar with the general use of this sign among the numerous Christians of the empire, many of whom no doubt were in his own army, he constructed the labarum, or rather he changed the heathen labarum into a standard of the Christian cross with the Greek monogram of Christ, which he had also put upon the shields of the soldiers. To this cross-standard, which now took the place of the Roman eagles, he attributed the decisive victory over the heathen Maxentius.[172]

In reality, Constantine's interpretation of his vision and/or dream was opposite to its intent. Jesus was the Prince of Peace, and the purpose of these revelations was to indicate to Constantine that God wanted him to gain control over the empire through reconciliation with his enemy. But since Constantine was a soldier, he proceeded in the manner that he felt proper, that this sign represented a new religion or new deity that would

---

[171] Schaff, Philip, *History of the Christian Church*, vol. 3, chap. 2.
[172] Schaff, vol. 3, chap. 2

grant him military victory and political control through combat using its emblem. The benefit was mixed: good to Constantine and his concept of Roman government, but detrimental to the original gospel of the spiritual kingdom. As Charles Freeman in his study of the impact of Constantine on philosophy states:

> The adoption of Christianity was not, however to prove entirely straightforward. Constantine knew so little about Christianity that he immediately ran into difficulties. First, Christ was not a God of war. The Old Testament frequently involved God in the slaughter of his enemies, but the New Testament did not. Constantine would have to create a totally new conception of Christianity if he was to sustain the link between the Christian God and the victory in war.[173]

> One of the most important of Constantine's legacies was the creation of a relationship between Christianity and war. Constantine was a brilliant and effective soldier, and he associated his continuing success with the support of the Christian God. Once he had used the victory at the Milvan Bridge as a platform for the granting of toleration to Christians, each new victory strengthened the link.[174]

The benefit of Constantine's effort of giving legal status and freedom to Christianity was mixed: good to Constantine and his concept of Roman government, but detrimental to the original gospel of the Prince of Peace. The bishops of his era traded in their convictions for superficial freedoms, but at the expense of modifying Jesus into a militarist Anointed.

## THE EFFECTS OF CONSTANTINE

The following year, in January 313 AD, Constantine along with emperor Licinius issued an edict of toleration granting freedom of religion to all residents of the Roman Empire, and which also extended to those calling themselves Christians. This was the famous edict of Milan, and with its issue, persecution against the Christians finally ceased in the Roman Empire. Constantine then proceeded to raise the ecumenical Christian religion, now Christendom, to have the supremacy among all the religions

---

[173] Freeman, Charles, *The Closing of the Western Mind*, pg. 158.
[174] Freeman, pg. 176.

in the Roman Empire. Eusebius mentions this in *The Life of Constantine*, Book 1

> CHAPTER XLII: The Honors conferred upon Bishops, and the Building of Churches.
> The emperor, also personally inviting the society of God's ministers, distinguished them with the highest possible respect and honor, showing them favor in deed and word as persons consecrated to the service of his God. Accordingly, they were admitted to his table, though mean in their attire and outward appearance; yet not so in his estimation, since he thought he saw not the man as seen by the vulgar eye, but the God in him. He made them also his companions in travel, believing that He whose servants they were would thus help him. Besides this, he gave from his own private resources costly benefactions to the churches of God, both enlarging and heightening the sacred edifices, and embellishing the august sanctuaries of the church with abundant offerings.[175]

Christian bishops took advantage of the freedoms that were now extended towards them, and especially after having endured severe persecution just a couple of decades earlier under Diocletian.

Constantine realized the value of having religious harmony in his empire. His reason for issuing an edict of religious toleration was to cease persecution of minority religious groups, and thereby decrease strife within the empire. Christianity valued this as a blessing of God, especially after the persecution under Constantine's predecessor Diocletian. Constantine realized the importance of such an advanced religion and its benefit for his empire, and especially the facets of the teaching that required them to be good citizens and submissive subjects of the emperor. But in time the freedom caused the ecumenical Christian church to evolve into the state-sanctioned religion and intolerance toward those who did not conform to the dictates of the First Ecumenical Council of 325 AD began. As early as 326 AD, Christian denominations that were now labeled heretic or schismatic were excluded from the privileges that Constantine conferred on the ecumenical church. Open persecution by the bishops of the ecumenical church followed after, and this especially applied to Christian pacifism denominations. Historian Schaff described it as follows:

---

[175] Eusebius, *Life of Constantine*, Nicene and Post-Nicene Fathers, series 2, vol. 1, pg. 494.

But the elevation of Christianity as the religion of the state presents also an opposite aspect to our contemplation. It involved great risk of degeneracy to the church. The Roman state, with its laws, institutions, and usages, was still deeply rooted in heathenism, and could not be transformed by a magical stroke. The Christianizing of the state amounted therefore in great measure to a paganizing and secularizing of the church. The world overcame the church, as much as the church overcame the world, and the temporal gain of Christianity was in many respects cancelled by spiritual loss. The mass of the Roman empire was baptized only with water, not with the Spirit and fire of the gospel, and it smuggled heathen manners and practices into the sanctuary under a new name.[176]

The religion that Constantine promoted for the empire was not the religion of the Bible. Constantine's concept of a state religion was that of Plato, not Jesus. The resultant religion under the Ecumenical Councils was a Christianity redefined in terms of neo-Platonism. The attempt of the Nicene Fathers working together with the secular authority of the Roman state to create a Christian nation was in reality the materialization of Plato's envisioned *Republic*.

The Christian leaders under Constantine then took the fatal leap of approving this new concept of the gospel. It now became part of Christian service to serve in the Roman military, since the emperor was "Christian" and the empire was "Christian." There was no longer a distinction between the divine and secular kingdoms. This identification of the kingdom of God with the contemporary secular government created in the mind of the population the attitude that service to the government was service to God. To join the military and fight the emperor's battles was to give service to both God and Caesar. The military now under the authority of a "Christian" ruler then promoted the enlistment of Christians and accepted the conversion of soldiers to Christianity. As historian Latourette states:

> Moreover, after the Emperors had espoused Christianity and they and Christian officials were charged with the responsibility for the body politic and for making decisions for the government, the attitude of

---

[176] Schaff, Philip, *History of the Christian Church*, vol. 3, chap. 13.

the majority of Christian towards war changed. Christians now began to believe that some wars are just.[177]

Constantine is heralded by Catholicism and Protestantism as a champion of the cross of Jesus, although he continued as a military administrator in his rule over the empire, and permitted the Roman senate to classify him as a god in the tradition of the Roman Emperors. Constantine himself had no personal Christian virtues or morality to speak of; he was a soldier and pagan to his dying day. (He used one of the nails from the cross of Jesus that his mother Helena brought from Jerusalem as a bit for his horse.) It was not until Constantine was on his deathbed that he made confession and was baptized, and even then, by a heretic Arian priest. Constantine is called the Great not because of his morality or ethic, but because he increased the size of his military into a formidable and modern power and was able to expand the size of the Roman Empire into the northern European frontiers and secure them, and reunite the eastern and western divisions into one government under himself.

## AUGUSTINE OF HIPPO

Augustine in his early years was part of the membership of the Manichaeans, who were disciples of Mani. They taught dualism, the ethereal struggle between good and evil forces, and they were also objectors to military service. Augustine became a Manichaean in 373 AD, and was a disciple for 9 years. His letters *Against Faustus*, who was a Manichaean, were written about 400 AD, but Augustine's influence by his mentor Ambrose changed his attitude toward war. Augustine's earlier writings that justified the participation of the Christian in a defensive war seem to treat war in the abstract and subjective, and not as the result of personal experience and conviction, but his new convictions were finally molded as a result of the defeat and sack of Rome by the Goths in 409-410 AD. Augustine now viewed the state and church as 2 divine spheres each having the responsibility to save the nation, including the defense against enemies, and to each of which the Christian had equal obligations. Therefore if the state required war to carry out its purpose, the Christian was required to participate. Augustine's new convictions concurred with the political-religious philosophy of his mentor Ambrose.

---

[177] Latourette, K.C., *A History of Christianity*, Vol. 1, pgg. 243-244.

As opposed to popular opinion, Augustine did not formulate or compile a just-war theory, although he penned some lines in the *City of God* and other writings on what he felt were sufficient reasons to justify a defense by the state if it was attacked by an aggressive military force – but Christians were not included in the defense. Such justification was not original, but adopted from the Roman philosopher Cicero as well as the Greek Plato. Later generations seem to have taken the little justification available in Augustine and redefined it, attaching his name to something he did not envision, in order to attribute credibility to it. Nonetheless, it becomes apparent after studying *The City of God* that it is Augustine's attempt to justify a defensive war, although he was unable to do so, realizing it was a compromise of principle Christian ethics. Nonetheless, he felt that Christians had an equal responsibility in regard to the security of the state as did non-Christians, and must also contribute their share. The concept of a just-war theory was not developed for another 900 years, first under Thomas Aquinas (to justify the Crusades), and then during the Reformation by Hugo Grotius (to try to curb the religious Thirty Years War of Europe). The basis for the concept of a just-war is Augustine's *City of God*, chapter 19, except that the inclusion of points related to a justifiable war was incidental to the primary topic. Chapter 19 deals with the failure of various philosophers, and philosophy in general, to impose a true peace on earth, and which true peace can only be installed by Christianity. As far as the Roman Empire was concerned, as noted in chapter 7 of the *City of God*, peace is the absence of war, and Augustine condemns war because of its detrimental effect on the population.

> But, say they, the wise man will wage just wars. As if he would not all the rather lament the necessity of just wars, if he remembers that he is a man; for if they were not just he would not wage them, and would therefore be delivered from all wars. For it is the wrongdoing of the opposing party which compels the wise man to wage just wars; and this wrong-doing, even though it gave rise to no war, would still be matter of grief to man because it is man's wrong-doing. Let every one, then, who thinks with pain on all these great evils, so horrible, so ruthless, acknowledge that this is misery. And if any one either endures or thinks of them without mental pain, this is a more

miserable plight still, for he thinks himself happy because he has lost human feeling.[178]

As Augustine expounds above, the justification of non-believers – the Roman state – to wage war is that only wise men would initiate a defensive war, and the purpose of such a war would only be defense, defeating the invading enemy to again impose peace. This was in summary the Pax Romana. Augustine's preference is for the wise man to grieve over the necessity of a war, and so preclude it from occurring because of its damage on people and property. Defense in this passage become the sole justifiable purpose to war, and because of war being inherently wrong. An offensive army is wrong to initiate an attack, and the defensive army is likewise in the wrong, because in defending itself it will cause more misery. However, what is notable is that this passage gives greater justification to not defending ourselves in defense if attacked, not to use force as a means of defense, thereby avoiding additional misery and devastation. Remember though, that this passage does not deal with Christians or the Christian church, but a secular state and society in general. Chapter 12 of Book 19 of the *City of God* states:

> For even they who make war desire nothing but victory,--desire, that is to say, to attain to peace with glory. For what else is victory than the conquest of those who resist us? and when this is done there is peace. It is therefore with the desire for peace that wars are waged, even by those who take pleasure in exercising their warlike nature in command and battle. And hence it is obvious that peace is the end sought for by war. For every man seeks peace by waging war, but no man seeks war by making peace. For even they who intentionally interrupt the peace in which they are living have no hatred of peace, but only wish it changed into a peace that suits them better. They do not, therefore, wish to have no peace, but only one more to their mind.[179]

So peace, Augustine writes, means different things to different states. For one state, the absence of war is peace; while for another the conquest of a neighboring state and the institution of a totalitarian rule is peace, like the

---

[178] Augustine, *The City of God*, Book 19, chapter 7.
[179] Augustine, *The City of God*, Book 19, chapter 12.

*Pax Romana*. This likewise pertains not to Christians, but to pagan and secular states. Chapter 26 of Book 19 mentions temporal peace, which, when applied to the Roman Empire, would be those periods of the absence of war.

Augustine concludes in chapter 28, that war is executed by the wicked of this world, and so it is confined to the secular or earthly city, and not to the city of God. Based on such passages, there is more reason provided in Book 19 for a genuine Christian not to participate in war, and even a defensive war. By not participating in either an offensive or defensive war, the genuine Christian does not identify himself with the temporal peace of the secular earthly city, but with the city of God, which strives after the true divine peace. Augustine realized that only God can introduce true peace on earth, and that wars will also pervade history, since the earthly city will always exist on earth. Nonetheless, Augustine proceeds to provide justification to soldiery, explaining his imbalanced logic, but not in the *City of God*, but in his letter to Faustus, a Manichaean.

> What is the evil in war? Is it the death of some who will soon die in any case, that others may live in peaceful subjection? This is mere cowardly dislike, not any religious feeling. The real evils in war are love of violence, revengeful cruelty, fierce and implacable enmity, wild resistance, and the lust of power, and such like; and it is generally to punish these things, when force is required to inflict the punishment, that, in obedience to God or some lawful authority, good men undertake wars, when they find themselves in such a position as regards the conduct of human affairs, that right conduct requires them to act, or to make others act in this way.[180]

Augustine's conclusion was that since the enemy is going to die at some time anyway in his life, it would be better for him to die the sooner so he would not continue his evil, and that only cowards – referring to religious pacifists – would consider war wrong. If the postulate of Augustine is correct, then it is best to kill the enemy since this will stop him from further perpetrating his crime of killing. But won't each consider the other the aggressor who should be stopped? Each one is doing exactly what the other is doing. And if the enemy is killing another because of orders from his superior, and because of his own conclusion that the war is just, based

---

[180] Augustine, *Against Faustus*, 22:74

on his own determination of the war corresponding with the concepts of Augustine's justifiable war, then where is the line of demarcation? Who exactly is the aggressor and who is the defender, since each one claims the same criteria for the justification of their aggression and armed attack, each one obeying the orders of their respective states? So where is Christian love in this act to kill the attacker, when his criteria for attack are the same? The following paragraph continues his thinking:

> When war is undertaken in obedience to God, who would rebuke, or humble, or crush the pride of man, it must be allowed to be a righteous war; for even the wars which arise from human passion cannot harm the eternal well-being of God, nor even hurt His saints; for in the trial of their patience, and the chastening of their spirit, and in bearing fatherly correction, they are rather benefited than injured. No one can have any power against them but what is given him from above. For there is no power but of God, who either orders or permits. Since, therefore, a righteous man, serving it may be under an ungodly king, may do the duty belonging to his position in the State in fighting by the order of his sovereign,--for in some cases it is plainly the will of God that he should fight, and in others, where this is not so plain, it may be an unrighteous command on the part of the king, while the soldier is innocent, because his position makes obedience a duty,--how much more must the man be blameless who carries on war on the authority of God, of whom every one who serves Him knows that He can never require what is wrong?[181]

In this passage Augustine clearly states that the Christian should fight in a war even if ordered by an ungodly king because of the necessity of obedience to the state, and that he would be innocent of any crime committed, because God requires this obedience to the order of the king.

In the same vein it was very easy for Augustine to rationalize away the statements of Jesus in the Sermon on the Mount:

> If it is supposed that God could not enjoin warfare, because in after times it was said by the Lord Jesus Christ, "I say unto you, That ye resist not evil: but if any one strike thee on the right cheek, turn to

---

[181] Augustine, *Against Faustus*, 22:75

him the left also," the answer is, that what is here required is not a bodily action, but an inward disposition.[182]

Based on the above expositions, a Christian soldier should never feel guilty or sense wrong in his actions when killing the enemy on the battlefield when ordered to do so by his commanding officer as long as the soldier has inner inclinations of peace. Therefore, if this conclusion of Augustine is correctly interpreted, external actions must be isolated from personal conviction, and a person could continue to retain Christian humility, but it should not interfere with executing orders. This section also lists a few points that would later become the criteria for a just-war theory:

1. The monarch is to issue the edict for war.
2. The purpose is the peace of the region.
3. Cruelty is not to be utilized, but war is to be waged in love.

The primary flaw in the statements of Augustine regarding justifying war is that both sides can claim the same justification. Each side claims that peaceful means of resolution have been exhausted to no success; the war is declared by their sovereign; each nation is defending itself from aggravated assault; each nation is attempting to bring peace by punishing the other for their injustice and atrocity. But war is not war without the death of civilians and the massive destruction of private property. Augustine's criteria have given Christian denominations greater justification to promoting war, rather than ceasing war.

A contemporary Episcopal priest had the following conclusion in regard to Augustine and the topic of justifiable war:

> I can find no passage in the *City of God* wherein Augustine describes, even theoretically, Christian participation in war, let alone a Christian *obligation* to wage war. To the contrary, he presents the logic of so-called "just-war thinking" as an *inferior and unworthy* logic, a failure on the part of his pagan contemporaries to think through the true nature of human striving for the good. Of the supreme good, which Christians know as the true peace of the City of God, the so-called peace that is

---

[182] Augustine, *Against Faustus*, 22:76

trumpeted as the goal of every war is only a dim approximation.[183]

Another major flaw in the rational of Augustine is his direction of specifically focusing on just-war, rather than seeking justification of the violation of any other commandment of God or the Gospel. There are 10 Commandments, and not just the one prohibiting arbitrary killing, and many rules of life that are provided by Jesus and the apostles in the NT, but Augustine seeks no justification to violate any of them, except this one. But could not the same criteria be used towards, for example, adultery? A just-adultery criteria? Or a just-false-witness criteria? Or a just-violate-the-Sabbath criteria? James indicated in his letter, that if a person violates one commandment, he violates them all. Taking Augustine's premises into consideration, the Christian should then be able to utilize the same criteria into justifiably violating every command in the Bible. But this ludicrous approach will never materialize, yet it serves to unveil the major flaw of any type of Biblical rational to justify war and military aggression.

---

[183] Elliott, Rev Niel, *Revisiting Augustine & Just-War Theory*

## 5. BRIEF HISTORY OF CHRISTIAN PACIFISM

### THE MONTANISTS

The extant history of small Christian denominations and sects that separated from the doctrine of the ecumenical church during the early centuries is very brief and meager. However there is sufficient evidence to establish a continuous vein of thinking from the ante-Nicene era to the present pertaining to conscientious objection as part of the gospel of the divine kingdom.

The Montanists of central Turkey of the $2^{nd}$ to the $5^{th}$ centuries were most likely pacifist. The group at its initiation would have had close ties to the original disciples of the apostles, and their refusal to be part of the Roman military coincided with their eschatological convictions. This conclusion is also based on the available information of Tertullian who was a Montanist for several years.

### MANI AND MANICHAEISM

Mani is included in this history as a result of his incorporation of some unadulterated teachings of Jesus Christ into his eclectic religion. Mani was born with the Persian name Shuriak about 216 AD. At the age of about 20 he had a vision and, inspired by divine revelation, he proceeded as a new prophet, called himself an Apostle of Jesus Christ, and proclaimed himself to be Mani, meaning, the Vessel. Mani's teaching is a synthesis of the teachings of Zoroaster, Buddha and Jesus Christ, and had a very high morality and ethic.

> The vast bulk of Mani's adherents -- ninety-nine out of every hundred -- were Hearers. They were only bound by Mani's Ten Commandments, which forbade idolatry, mendacity, avarice, murder (i.e. all killing), fornication, theft, seduction to deceit, magic, hypocrisy, secret infidelity (to Manichaeism).[184]

---

[184] Arendzen, J.P., *Mani and His Message*

Mani taught Christian pacifism, and his religion persevered for several centuries throughout the Mediterranean world. Augustine's letter against the Manicheans includes his section refuting them for refusing to engage in war or military service.

## PAULICIANS

Paul of Samosota is traditionally the founder of the sect that bears his name, the Paulicians, although others claim that the honor belongs to Apostle Paul, whose writings were highly respected and observed. Paul of Samosota was a bishop of Antioch during the 3rd quarter of the 3rd century AD. His disciples were primarily living in central and eastern Turkey and Armenia. The Paulicians absorbed several of the tenets of Marcion (hence their respect for Apostle Paul): they were dualist. Paulicians were iconoclastic and rejected all the rites of the ecumenical church and all material symbols used in ecclesiastical worship. The only rite they observed was baptism at the age of 30, following the example of Jesus Christ. The Paulicians were likewise pacifist, as Steven Runciman mentions in his history regarding them.

> The authorities in that hard bellicose age, with civilization on the defensive against the barbarian invader, could not approve of a faith wherein all killing, even of animals, was forbidden, and whereof a considerable number of believers wandered about, refusing to work, refusing to notice secular regulations, and exercising a vast influence on the whole community...[185]

Under Emperor Justinian in the 6th century, some 100,000 were executed by order of his wife Theodora, and the balance were exiled to the Balkans. There in the following centuries many compromised their tenets and joined the Roman military to escape further persecution. The influence of the Paulicians migrating east into Bulgaria to escape persecution gave impetus to the rise of another sect, the Bogomils.

---

[185] Runciman, Steven, *The Medieval Manichee*, pg. 17

## BOGOMILS

The Bulgarian Bogomils, 'The Friends of God," were also known as Patarines and Messalians. They were earnest and ascetic, having acquired their tenets from the earlier Paulicians that were exiled to the Balkans, and whose influence then spread east into Bulgaria. They primarily lived in Bulgaria, and likewise repudiated the Catholic rites and theology and were pacifist. They flourished during the 8$^{th}$ through the 12$^{th}$ centuries. Runciman likewise states regarding them:

> But the true Bogomils were unwilling to shed blood.[186]

With the beginning of the Crusades, they steadily migrated further east into Russia, and there in later centuries influenced the individuals who formed the sects of the Strigolniki and Judaizers. Bogomils of the 12$^{th}$ century had lost by that time their dualist philosophy and were closer to the contemporary Baptists in doctrine and practice.

## THE CATHARI AND ALBIGENCES

The Cathari were the popular name of the group, which was derived from the Greek *kathros*, meaning pure. In southern France they were known as the Albigences from the city Albi, one of their capitals. This group appeared in historical records about the year 1000 AD, with the appearance of members who rejected the rites and teachings of the Catholic church. They continued the tenets of the Paulicians and assimilated many of the doctrines of the Bogomils. This group re-introduced pacifism into the instruction and practice of those seeking a true teaching of the gospels, as opposed to that of the Catholic church. Historians Philip Schaff and Latourette describes them as follows:

> The condemnation of capital punishment was based on such passages as, Give place unto wrath, vengeance is Mine, I will repay, saith the Lord, Rom 12:19; and the judicial execution of heretics and criminals was pronounced homicide, a survival from the Old Testament and the influence of its evil god. The Cathari quoted Christ's words, You have heard bow it has been said, An eye for an eye and a tooth for a tooth.

---

[186] Runciman, pg. 68

One of the charges made against the established church was that is countenanced war and marshaled armies.[187]

Cathari were not to engage in war.[188]

The Cathari reached the apex of their numbers at the beginning of the 12th century, numbering about 4 million. Eventually, massive persecution by the Catholic church beginning in 1120 AD, broke the sect and caused them to assimilate into the general population. The Inquisition under Pope Innocent III especially affected the Albigences and Waldenses.

## PIERRE WALDES AND THE WALDENSES

He was also known as Peter Waldo, founder of the Christian sect that became known as the Waldenses. Pierre Waldes lived in Lyons, France toward the end of the 12th century, about 100 years before Thomas Aquinas, and during the 2nd and 3rd Crusades. Unlike the Cathari and Bogomils, the Waldenses attempted to work within the Catholic and reform it, much like the earlier disciples of Martin Luther. However, as a result of their preaching, the Waldenses were excommunicated by the pope in 1184 at the Council of Verona, and then they were treated as heretics. They were then included in the inquisition of the 14th century against the Albigenses, and the Piedmont Waldenses suffered the most in the Catholic persecution of the 15th century. One Baptist historian concluded the following:

> The very charges against them, in reference to personal revelations and the community of good, or opposition to war and oaths, to which the apostolic and modern communities are equally liable, only more clearly attest their exalted life, character, and discipline.[189]

The Waldenses were pacifist, and accepted the New Testament literally. The group spread from southern France to Italy and then into Germany. In Italy, they were known as the Lombards. The sect lasted into the era of the

---

[187] Schaff, Philip, *History of the Christian Church*, vol 5, chapter 80.
[188] Latourette, K.C., *A History of Christianity*, Vol. 1, pg. 454.
[189] Everts, W.W., *The Church in the Wilderness, or, the Baptists before the Reformation*

Protestant reformation and then apparently assimilated into other denominations, and primarily the Reformed Faith.

## MENNO SIMONS AND THE MENNONITES

Menno Simons was a ex-Catholic Franciscan priest who lived in the Netherlands, about 1496 to 1561. He became a priest in 1524 but abandoned the Catholic church and priesthood about 1534 after a personal study of the Bible. He joined the Anabaptist movement and later became a leader of a group in Holland and north-west Germany. They became known as the Mennonites.

One of the main precepts of Menno Simons was conscientious objection to military service. His group was persecuted for this in later years. The Mennonite congregations increased in Germany and eastern Europe in subsequent generations, but became a wandering sect for a while, journeying to escape persecution. Many immigrated to Russia, and later many immigrated to America. The Mennonites in America have been a tremendous promoter of the attitude of conscientious objection and have offices available for support and consultation for those who seek assistance in avoiding military service.

> A strong Mennonite belief is nonviolence or pacifism. Mennonites believe that violence is never the best answer to problems or conflict, and that Jesus taught us a better way than the way of fighting and wars. They try to take seriously Jesus' words to love your enemy. For that reason, Mennonites do not take part in war. During World War II, many Mennonites in the United States served in Civilian Public Service rather than participate in fighting. Some Mennonites chose to serve in non-combatant positions. Still others refused to register at all. Some Mennonites today choose not to pay the portion of their taxes that goes to maintaining the military.[190]

The following is a selection from the writings of Menno Simons:

> The regenerated do not go to war, nor engage in strife. They are the children of peace who have beaten their swords into plowshares and their spears into pruning hooks, and know of no war. They render unto

---

[190] Who Are the Mennonites?

Caesar the things that are Caesar's and unto God the things that are God's. Their sword is the sword of the Spirit which they wield with a good conscience through the Holy Ghost.[191]

During World War 1, 138 Mennonites were courts-martialed and sentenced to incarceration for refusing induction into the armed forces. During World War 2, 4,665 Mennonites were COs (conscientious objectors) and assigned to civilian public service, while about 1,200 were absolutists and incarcerated at various prisons, During the Vietnam War, Mennonites provided 8,000 COs in 1968, 8,800 COs in 1969, and 11,000 COs in 1970.

## JACOB HUTTER AND THE HUTTERITES

A group of German Anabaptists who migrated to Moravia in southeast Europe under Jacob Hutter in the 1530's became known as the Hutterites. They were driven into exile similar to their Dutch cousins the Mennonites due to religious persecution. Non-violence was a firm part of their religious persuasion. Additional persecution in later years forced the Hutterites to move to the Ukraine in the 1770's, and then into Russia in 1802, seeking religious freedom and the ability to live as conscientious objectors. Many Hutterites then migrated from Russia to America and Canada after Tsar Alexander II passed the universal military service act of 1874.

The following is a selection from the writings of Jacob Hutter:

We will not do a wrong or an injury to any man, yea, not to our greatest enemy, neither to Ferdinandus,[192] nor any one else, great or small. All our actions and conduct, word and work, life and walk, are open; there is no secret about it all. Rather than knowingly to rob a man of a penny we would willingly give up a hundred guilders. And before we would give our greatest enemy a blow with the hand, to say nothing of spear, sword or halberd as is the manner of the world, we would be willing to lose our lives.[193]

---

[191] Simons, Menno, *Complete Works*, Part II, pg. 170b.
[192] Holy Roman Emperor, 1558-1564.
[193] quoted from John Horsh, *The Principle of Nonresistance as held by the Mennonite Church, 1985.*

Like other Anabaptists, the Hutterites are conscientious objectors opposed to any kind of military service. At the time of World War I some of them received shocking mistreatment from the authorities because of their refusal to be inducted into the army or to wear uniforms.[194]

Few Hutterite communities remain in America at present as a result of the religious persecution they suffered in America during the world wars.

## GEORGE FOX AND THE QUAKERS (SOCIETY OF FRIENDS)

George Fox is rightly called the founder of the Quakers, today known as the Society of Friends. He died about 1691. His group first began to gather about 1650. The Quakers are dedicated to the morals and ethics of Scripture and are also guided by the Inner Light of Christ residing in every person. One common vein in Quaker belief is conscientious objection to military service. Since their inception, the Quakers have been recognized as a peace church. They migrated to America seeking religious freedom in the late 1600's and early 1700's. In America they continued their pacifist convictions.

A sample of the codified convictions of Quakers regarding this topic is the following section quoted from the *Declaration of Faith* issued by the Richmond Conference of 1887, under the heading of Peace:

> We feel bound explicitly to avow our unshaken persuasion that all war is utterly incompatible with the plain precepts of our divine Lord and Law-giver, and the whole spirit of His Gospel, and that no plea of necessity or policy, however urgent or peculiar, can avail to release either individuals or nations from the paramount allegiance which they owe to Him who hath said, "Love your enemies." (Matt 5:44, Luke 6:27) In enjoining this love, and the forgiveness of injuries, He who has brought us to Himself has not prescribed for man precepts which are incapable of being carried into practice, or of which the practice is to be postponed until all shall be persuaded to act upon them. We cannot doubt that they are incumbent now, and that we have in the prophetic Scriptures the distinct intimation of their direct application not only to individuals, but to nations also. (Isa 2:4, Micah 4:1) When

---

[194] Merrill, Peter, C., *German Immigrant Culture in America*

nations conform their laws to this divine teaching, wars must necessarily cease.

We would, in humility, but in faithfulness to our Lord, express our firm persuasion that all the exigencies of civil government and social order may be met under the banner of the Prince of Peace, in strict conformity with His commands.

With the Revolutionary War, the attitude of other American settlers changed toward the peaceful Quakers. For failure to join the regiments against the British, Quaker COs (conscientious objectors) were imprisoned and their property confiscated; some were heavily fined.

The Quakers found themselves in the same dilemma with the outbreak of the Civil War in America. Many young members of the sect not well founded in their persuasion joined the armed forces. The patriotic zeal and anti-slavery sentiment was more compelling for them than the archaic religion of their forefathers. The CO (conscientious objector) Quakers were in a minority. Abraham Lincoln's administration provided for COs, and a person claiming to be a conscientious objector had to pay $300 to circumvent military service, a sizeable amount at that time. Still others were forced into service by ruthless military commanders, or had property confiscated as a type of persecution for refusing inscription.

During both World Wars and all wars since, the Quakers have been firm in their conviction as conscientious objectors. They also have offices available for conscientious objection counseling. During World War 1, 13 Quakers were courts-martialed and sentenced to incarceration for refusing induction into the armed forces. During World War 2, 951 Quakers were COs and assigned to civilian public service. During the Vietnam War, Friends provided 600 COs in 1968, 1,700 COs in 1969, and 2,300 COs in 1970.

## THE DUKHABORS

The concepts held by the Dukhabors of Russia are documented beginning about 1734 during the reign of Empress Anna. The Dukhabors repudiated the rites and theology of the Russian Orthodox Church, were pacifist and refused military service in the army of the Tsar of Russia. Their leader Ilarion Pobirokhin and his followers migrated to the Tambov region about 1760, and from which center the Dukhabor philosophy spread throughout

Russia. The Dukhabors as a religious entity were exiled from central Russian by Tsar Pavel I, in 1802, to the southern Ukraine and Caucasus regions of Russia.

The tenets of the Dukhabors were codified in 1791 in a confession of faith that was presented to Governor Kakhovski of Ekaterinoslav. Tenet XVII pertains to war:

> Dukhabors want to extend this spirit of peacefulness to both those of their community and to enemies; and war is prohibited, affirming the evangelic teaching of love toward enemies. Matt 5:38-39.[195]

An important event in Dukhabor history is the burning of arms on June 29, 1895, advised by their leader at the time, Peter Vasilivich Veregin. Much like the decree of universal military service of his father, Tsar Alexander III required an oath of allegiance from all his subjects in Russia. As a protest to this requirement, which the Dukhabors would not fulfill, they gathered all their weapons, those used for hunting, or personal collections, and destroyed them in large bonfires. Dukhabors again began to refuse orders to take up weapons or participate in military exercises. Needless to say, they were severely persecuted. Eventually the Dukhabors migrated from Russia to Canada seeking religious freedom and the ability to live as conscientious objectors.

## LEO N. TOLSTOY

The famous Russian author Leo Nikolaevich Tolstoy made the concept of Christ's teaching on non-violence and non-resistance to aggression the theme of his book, *The Kingdom of God is Within You*. It was first published in 1893, and immediately became popular among the many sectarian groups in Russia. The book was a result of Tolstoy's personal conversion and study of Christ's teachings. In later years, Tolstoy incorporated his philosophy in his novels.

Tolstoy served in the Russia army, 1855-1856, in the Crimean War against Turkey, and personally experienced the horror of organized warfare and the bloodshed of the battlefield. This experience impressed upon him the futility of the objectives of armed struggle and the

---

[195] Livanov, Feodor Vasilich, *Raskolniki I Ostrozhniki*, vol. 2, chapter IV, (my translation from the Russian.)

senselessness of the many wounded and dead in battle. His study of the gospels and especially the Sermon on the Mount in later years converted him to pacifism. The concept of Tolstoy in this book was that the divine kingdom as taught by Jesus Christ was antithetical and alien to military service. The 2 concepts were of 2 different domains: one of the divine kingdom and the other of the secular government.

> Christianity in its true significance annuls the state. So it was understood from the very beginning, and for this reason Christ was crucified, and people who were not bound by the obligation of justifying the Christian state understood it in this manner. Only from the time of the acceptance of a nominal and superficial Christianity by the heads of states did there begin the contrivance of all of these improbable cunningly-woven theories, which allowed the compatibility of Christianity and the state. But for every sincere and serious person of our era there cannot but exist an apparent incompatibility between true Christianity – the teachings of humility, forgiveness of offenses, love – and the state and its supremacy, violence, executions and wars. The profession of true Christianity does not only exclude the possibility of the acknowledgement of the state, but annuls its foundations.
>
> I know regarding myself that I do not need to attack other nations, killing them, neither do I need to defend myself from them with a weapon in my hands, and so I cannot participate in war or the preparation for it.[196]

His book did influence many, explaining that the only acceptable conduct of a true follower of Christ was that of non-violence and especially not resorting to retaliation or aggression. The person in whom the kingdom of God resided was not to succumb to the politics of national struggle and ideology of military service. To Tolstoy, peaceful coexistence with all other individuals, societies and nationalities was attaining an earthly kingdom of God. Tolstoy's attitude of non-violence and pacifism was influential on many religious and political leaders of the 20th century.

---

[196] Tolstoy, Leo, *The Kingdom of God is within You*, chapter 10.

## SEMEON UKLEIN AND THE MOLOKANS

The primary preceptor of the Russian Molokans was Semeon Matveeich Uklein, who preached from 1760 to 1805 throughout central Russia. Uklein was son-in-law of the Dukhabor leader Ilarion Pobirokhin, and lived with him in the same village. Uklein was evangelical in contrast to the philosophic Pobirokhin, and later separated from his father-in-law and joined the Molokans, who like the Dukhabors, were conscientious objectors.

Uklein, along with Matvei Semeonich Dalmatov, compiled a confession of faith of the Molokan religion. Point 23 of his teaching is the following:

> About oaths and war. Fulfilling the divine commandments, they [Molokans] do not have need for human ones, and must escape the fulfillment of those laws that are contrary to the teaching of the Word of God. So they must, for example, escape servility to landowners, war, military obligation, and oaths, and matters not permitted by the Holy Scriptures.[197]

Historically the Russian Molokans have been conscientious objectors, and over the years have suffered imprisonment and exile for refusing to join the military. As a result of their pacifist convictions, Molokans would not participate in the mandatory conscription imposed by Tsar Alexander III in the years 1887-1889. Rather than opposing any further persecution by the Tsarist government, they migrated out of Russia to America in the years 1904-1911.

## THE CHRISTADELPHIANS

This denomination originated here in America under Dr. John Thomas. He came to America from England about 1833 and joined the Disciples of Christ, studying the Bible under the Cambellites. He discovered the inadequacies of historic Christianity and broke away starting his own congregations in about 1848. He taught a return to primitive Christianity, and conscientious objection to military service was one of their tenets. The Christadelphians were conscientious objectors during the Civil War and

---

[197] Livanov, vol. 2, chapter XII.

have been since that time. Thomas' convictions were continued under the preacher Robert Roberts.

> The Christadelphians do not believe in participating in war. So, when the Civil War broke out, they refused to go. In order to be recognized as a religious group that did not believe in fighting, they needed a name. Dr. Thomas gave them the name "Christadelphian" which, in Greek means "Brethren of Christ."[198]

During World War 1, one Christadelphian was courts-martialed and sentenced to incarceration for refusing induction into the armed forces. During World War 2, 127 Christadelphians were COs and assigned to civilian public service.

## JEHOVAH'S WITNESSES

Properly titled the Watchtower Bible and Tract Society, they are labeled as a cult by historical Christianity because of their refusal to accept several tenets of ecumenical Christendom as Biblically-valid. One of the main criticisms is that the JWs are non-secular. They do not pledge allegiance to the flag or serve in the armed forces, and have been heavily persecuted as a result of this in America and in other countries. The JWs are the largest single absolutist group in America.

> Following the examples set by Jesus and first-century Christians, Jehovah's Witnesses do not share in the politics or wars of any nation. Their stand of Christian neutrality is well documented in history. They firmly believe that they must "beat their swords into plowshares" and not "learn war anymore." (Isaiah 2:4)[199]

During World War 1, 27 JWs were courts-martialed and incarcerated for refusal of induction into the armed forces. During World War 2, of the 6,086 conscientious objectors who were absolutists, or who refused civilian public service as an alternative to military service and were subsequently tried and convicted and sentenced to incarceration, 4,441

---

[198] Christadelphian History (www.carm.org)
[199] Office of Public Information of Jehovah's Witnesses

were JWs. Of the 12,000 COs who accepted civilian public service during WW2, 409 were JWs.[200]

## BERTRAND RUSSELL

A section on Bertrand Russell is included in this treatise because of his life-long dedication to the area of anti-war protest and effort and intervention to curb warfare during the 20th century, while at the same time, able to discredit the entirety of Christendom due to their lack of intervention into this matter. Russell stated emphatically that he did not believe in God, and that he was not Christian.[201] Yet Russell, wrote book after book upholding pacifist principles, intervening between world leaders to reconcile them and to convince them of the futility of deliberate war, and protested regularly against arms proliferation and the use of nuclear weapons.

Much like Tolstoy who, after reading the Gospels, was driven to create a Christian philosophy based on the basic principles of the Sermon on the Mount, Russell was affected in the same manner, but to develop a pacifist philosophy based on humanitarian and political principles. The repulsion of Russell toward Christianity appears to be due to his annoyance over Christians' failure to observe the most basic tenets that were taught by Jesus Christ.

> You will remember that He said: "Resist not evil, but whosoever shall smite thee on thy right cheek, turn to him the other also." That is not a new precept or a new principle. It was used by Lao-Tse and Buddha some 500 or 600 years before Christ, but it is not a principle, which as a matter of fact, Christians accept.[202]
> 
> …religion prevents us from removing the fundamental causes of war;[203]

Bertrand Russell succeeded in doing for Jesus Christ what his disciples of the 20th century would not do, which was to actively protest war and be

---

[200] Keim, Albert N., *The CPS Story*, pgg. 8, 81.
[201] Russell, Bertrand, *Why I am not a Christian*, pg. 5
[202] Russell, Bertrand, *Why I am not a Christian*
[203] Russell, Bertrand, *Has Religion Made Useful Contributions to Civilization?*

willing to suffer the consequences for it. Russell – the non-Christian – was a greater benefit to the cause of Christian pacifism than any Christian leader of his era.

## PACIFISM IN LATER HISTORY

There are many small denominations in America that adhere to pacifist convictions, and many more in history past, but which could not all be mentioned here. The above examples are provided as evidence that throughout Christian history, from the apostolic age and to the present, there have always been those who believed in the concept of the divine kingdom accompanied by the conviction of conscientious objection to military service. Although small in number they retain a place in history for refusing to conform to the demands of the state and pressure from militarist Christian denominations regarding military service.

## 6. THE CONTEMPORARY CHRISTIAN PACIFIST

There is no justification to armed conflict, because violence propagates more violence. There will never be a war to end war. A person proceeding to battle convinced he will institute peace will not terminate war, but will only contribute to and continue the incessant history of warfare and the manufacture of weapons and military equipment. After the conclusion of one conflict another will arise shortly after in another region and between other nations. The only manner of ceasing war is to refuse to be part of it, even if on an individual basis.

The Christian pacifist is a conscientious objector to war in any form, and to military service and training, because he is a disciple of Jesus the Son of God and Prince of Peace and conducts himself based on the precepts he taught.

There is only one manner for the disciple of Jesus to conduct himself in regard to the question of war and military service and that is to refuse. An example of a response to testify to a person's conviction would be the following. "I will not participate in military service to training, armed combat, or any aggression because I am a disciple of Jesus of Nazareth, the son of God, and a member of the spiritual Kingdom of God. Jesus exemplified in his personal life and ministry that I am not to retaliate or take vengeance for any injury committed against me or against another person or society. The gospels further teach that aggression does not resolve conflict. I cannot face the judgment seat of Jesus knowing that I have taken the life of a soldier or an innocent person, or destroyed property in war, or caused people to suffer. Although I am in the world, I am not of the world. As a member of the New Covenant, I would rather die for my convictions, rather than violate my commitment to my Savior Jesus."

The disciple of Jesus considers war organized and premeditated murder on an international scale. It is controlled criminal insanity resulting in violence and devastation, and without justification. They recognize that the purpose of military training is to make men killing machines. There is only one manner for the disciple of Jesus to conduct himself in regard to the question of military service and that is to refuse. The conscience of the true Christian will prohibit them from such participation, and which includes employment manufacturing military equipment and weapons.

A person who claims to be Christian and is faced with the dilemma of whether to enlist in the military should contemplate in the following terms, "Will my service in the military institute peace, or will it promote more war and aggression? Is the military a service unto the living God, or is it service unto the secular god of war? If I die in combat, do I die for a purpose that is worth the value of my life, or do I die as a pawn of the state? Do I acknowledge as supreme the dictates of the secular state, or those of the spiritual kingdom? Should I suffer on the battlefield as a sacrifice to the state, or should I suffer for my faith as a Christian?"

A Christian is a pacifist in these terms. "My convictions will not allow me to participate in military service, armed combat, or any aggression. Jesus of Nazareth, the son of God, taught pacifism as part of his gospel of the Kingdom. He exemplified in his personal life and ministry that I am not to retaliate or take vengeance for any injury committed against me or against another person or society. even if it means my own injury or death. The gospels teach that further aggression does not resolve conflict. I cannot face the judgment seat of Jesus knowing that I have taken the life of a soldier or an innocent person, or destroyed property in war, or caused people to suffer. I will not have a clean conscience if I am employed manufacturing military equipment or weapons. Although I am in the world, I am not of the world."

The Christian pacifist is an enigma in society. He is an enigma as well in the ecclesiastical world. The most popular cliché, "Anything worth having is worth fighting for," does not apply to the Christian pacifist, because the entirety of the material world is temporal as a result of the short life span of the individual. There is nothing so valuable or indispensable that it is necessary for the Christian pacifist to use violence or weapons to defend it or retain it. The philosophy of the Christian pacifist makes him distinct from the balance of other individuals: he refuses to utilize force or violence or weapons to prove his convictions, defend himself or his Christian faith or congregation, or to compel any person to do his will, even if it means the loss of his property, mortal or physical harm, deprivation of freedom, or even the loss of his own life.

Viewing the matter from another aspect, how can a person be converted, led to accept Jesus as their savior, be reborn, if that person is burned at the stake as a heretic or executed in the name of God, or killed on the battlefield, or destroyed or maimed by a bomb dropped on them from a jet bomber flown by a Christian? It is impossible to be both patriotic and nationalistic and spiritual at the same time. A person can only have one supreme master on any matter, or legislator that he will subject himself to as the final authority.

## CHRISTIAN RESPONSIBILITY TO THE STATE

Christian responsibility to the state was discussed in a chapter above titled The Great Concession. I will only repeat a couple of important point here.

> Let every person be subject to the governing authorities. For there is no authority except from God, and those that exist have been instituted by God. Therefore he who resists the authorities resists what God has appointed, and those who resist will incur judgment. For rulers are not a terror to good conduct, but to bad. Would you have no fear of him who is in authority? Then do what is good and you will receive his approval, for he is a servant of God for your good. But if you do wrong, be afraid for he does not bear the sword in vain; he is the servant of God to execute his wrath on the criminal. Therefore one must be subject, not only to avoid God's wrath but also for the sake of conscience. For the same reason you also pay taxes, for the authorities are ministers of God, attending to this very thing. Pay all of them their dues, taxes to whom taxes are due, revenue to whom revenue is due, respect to whom respect is due, honor to whom honor is due. Rom 13:1-7.
> Be subject for the sake of the Lord to every human institution, whether it be to the emperor as supreme, or to governors as sent by him to punish those who do wrong and to praise those who do right. 1 Pet 2:13-14.

Apostle Paul prefaces his passage by stating that the concept of government is divine, meaning that the motivation to establish a ruling body over the population for civil purposes is based on a correct understanding of the intention of God for humanity. But also notice in verse 4, the statement that the state was made for people, and not the opposite. The state exists to serve its subjects, not vice versa, meaning that the state's purpose is to protect its residents. The laws and legislation of the state are the dictates of a corporate body of individuals such as ourselves to whom we have allocated authority. Unconditional obedience to the state cannot be reconciled with the doctrine of the absolute sovereignty of God. The priority must be given to God, as Peter and the apostles stated, "We must obey God rather than men." Acts 5:29.

## CHRISTIAN PACIFISM AND THE STATE

Pacifism does not weaken the defense of a country. The tendency to be attacked is reduced if a country is non-pretentious in the worldview. Countries will be more conducive to peaceful relations if neither has an army. By joining the armed forces of your particular country, the military strength necessarily increases and such an increase contributes to an arms race in neighboring and distant countries. A country noticing arms and military development in its neighbor will sense the necessity of increasing its own military strength suspicious of his neighbor's intents. Increase of armaments increases the suspicions of neighboring countries that would not otherwise come to such conclusions, thereby increasing arms themselves, and perhaps even attacking their neighbor, thinking that their neighbor is preparing to do the same – a pre-emptive attack. A powder-keg is created once both neighbors are saturated with weapons, and only a spark is required to ignite the powder and initiate war. Any preparation for war creates an environment conducive to war, whether this is intended or not, and this will easily precipitate war. Such occurred in Europe in the years prior to World War 1.

In the process, peace movements are stifled and discredited, politicians and patriotic citizens accuse anti-war protestors of being traitors and clandestine supporters of the enemy. Patriots claim that such peace efforts bolster the enemy's strength by psychologically reducing the vigilance of their own national military. In reality, such extreme patriotism creates a windfall of arms supply and interferes with any possible reconciliation efforts to curb or preclude combat, now the inevitable. The best way of avoiding war is not to prepare for it, because preparations for war hasten war.

Even if a nation develops an attitude of militant imperialism and attacks another country, the least amount of defense, reprisal or vengeance will reduce the number of casualties. True that many will suffer and die in the process of the invasion, but the overall amount will be reduced if the residents of the invaded country conduct themselves non-pretentiously; turning the cheek, putting down their weapon, not living by the sword. The difficulty in taking this approach is the prevailing attitude of nationalism, it is the patriotic rhetoric of "Give me liberty or give me death." If a person's attitude is peaceful coexistence between the occupation army and subjected residents, then their existence will be tolerable, and at least no revolt or revolutionary war will cause additional loss of lives or destruction of property.

The extent of civil obedience is defined by Jesus in a conversation with Herodians, residents of Judea who had political affiliation with the family of Herod the Great.

> "Tell us what you think. It is lawful to pay taxes to Caesar or not?" But Jesus, aware of their malice, said, "Why put me to the test, you hypocrites? Show me the money for the tax." And they brought him a coin. Jesus said to them, "Whose likeness and inscription is this?" They said, "Caesar's." Then he said to them, "Render therefore to Caesar what is Caesar's, and to God what is God's." Matt 21:17-21.

This passage can be interpreted in the following manner in the light of the earlier passages by the apostle regarding civil obedience. The reimbursement to the state for the privilege of living in this country is payment of taxes and obedience of civil law. The line of obedience is drawn when the state requires a person to sacrifice their life for the country they reside in. At this point the state is usurping authority over life which only belongs to God the author of life. The state in demanding the life of a person installs itself as deity, and which is a capacity beyond that which the Bible rightfully attributes to and allows the state. This is the right of the Christian, to refuse to yield to the state what belongs to God, their allegiance and life.

The Christian is only a pilgrim and spiritual migrant in this world, a temporal resident, a person traveling through the valley of earthly experience on their journey to the eternal kingdom. The apostles wrote regarding this in the following:

> These all died in faith, not having received what was promised, but having seen it and greeted if from afar, and having acknowledged that they were strangers and exiles on the earth. Heb 11:13.
> Beloved, I beseech you as aliens and exiles to abstain from the passions of the flesh that wage war against you soul. I Pet 2:11.

Because of this the Christian does not become involved in the politics of secular government. These are matters that envelop the personality of a political figure and more than often do not pertain to issues. Christian involvement in government should always pertain to issues of a moral and ethical nature. What is important an individual should accomplish with their own family and associates and their religious community. Involvement in politics tends to direct the sight of the spiritual migrant away from the eternal kingdom and to the temporal issues of the state.

Jesus said, "And when you hear of wars and rumors of wars, do not be alarmed; this must take place, but the end is not near." Mark 13:7. He was absolutely right. Armed military conflict has existed from the initial stages of civilization and news of them travels to other areas rapidly.

The one unanswerable question proposed often to the conscientious objector by advocates of defense and retaliation is the following, "What would you do if somebody attacked your wife or mother or child in your presence?" A concrete answer cannot be offered because nobody actual knows what they will do in such a situation. The sincere Christian will only state that they hope they will react in such a manner to curb the attack, or not cause any more injury, or perhaps sacrifice their own safety to protect the other person.

## WHAT NEEDS TO BE DONE

True and genuine Christians, disciples of Jesus of Nazareth, must refuse participation in war in any form. Priests and ministers must corporately voice to their congregations for their members to not enlist in the military, to refuse conscription and participation in war, and to not have a vocation in the manufacture of weapons and munitions. Only the Christian Church can stop the tide of the devastating results of war and military aggression by taking this stand. Only by returning to its Apostolic roots can the Christian Church fulfill its responsibility to its founder Jesus of Nazareth, who said, "Put down that sword Peter, for whoever takes the sword will perish by the sword." First and foremost priests and ministers must be willing to lay down their life in imitation of Jesus as an example to others, instead of condoning, advocating or further contributing to war and devastation. Peace is the way to terminating the existence of war, even if it entails suffering or martyrdom, as with the example provided by Jesus the Son of God in his earthly career.

Go to your minister and priest and elder and tell them, "It's time for our congregation to return to our Apostolic roots and adhere to the gospel as taught by our founder Jesus of Nazareth, the Anointed of Israel, and to withdraw that weapon from use. It's time to become a peace church, to teach religious objection to the military in our congregation and for all the members to refuse to have a vocation in a military-related industry."

It is difficult to be a conscientious objector because you are in the minority and are liable to be labeled a traitor, a coward, unpatriotic, and not willing to serve your country as others have done in the wars of previous generations. The choice is a difficult one and Jesus knew that it would not be easy, just as he said, "If any person will follow me, let him deny himself and take up his stake and follow me." Matt 16:24. Others have suffered and the contemporary true Christian must realize that he may have to also. The true Christian must have the attitude that he or she would rather die and lose his life rather than contribute to war and military aggression. This can be accomplished due to their belief in their resurrection from death: that if they die for the principles of the Gospel of Jesus, they will resurrect at His second advent. True Christians do not fear death, because it is the transition to eternal life. Others have suffered and the contemporary true Christian must realize that he may have to also. It is this faith that will lead to the termination of war, and likewise enlighten the population, cease aggression, and serve as an example to others, and especially those of future generations to curb war entirely and eventually.

www.ingramcontent.com/pod-product-compliance
Lightning Source LLC
Chambersburg PA
CBHW052039290426
44111CB00011B/1560